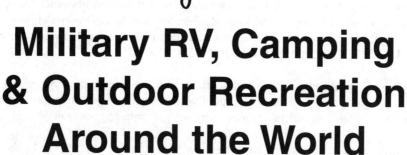

# Military RV, Camping & Outdoor Recreation Around the World
## Including Golf Courses and Marinas

By

**William "Roy" Crawford, Sr., Ph.D.**
**President, Military Marketing Services, Inc.**
**and Military Living Publications**

And

**L. Ann Crawford**
**Vice-President, Military Marketing Services, Inc.**
**and Publisher, Military Living Publications**

**R.J. Crawford - Executive Vice President-Marketing**

**J.J. Caddell - Vice President-Editorial**

Donna Russell - Editor

Elizabeth Cahill, Jason Jacks and Margaret Volpe - Editorial Assistants

OFFICE STAFF - John Camp, Nigel Fellers, Margaux Garbowski, Mohamed Hussan, Irene Kearney, Lourdes Medina, Tin Ngo, Joel Thomas, MSG, USA (Ret), Liliane Williamson.

Military Living Publications
P.O. Box 2347
Falls Church, Virginia 22042-0347
**TEL: 703-237-0203** - FAX: 703-237-2233
E-mail: milliving@aol.com
Homepage: http://www.militaryliving.com

# NOTICE

**Copyright 1998**
**William Roy Crawford and L. Ann Crawford**

**MILITARY LIVING PUBLICATIONS**
**First Printing - November 1998**

**Library of Congress Cataloging-in-Publication Data**

Crawford, William Roy, 1932-
    Military RV, camping, and outdoor recreation around the world :
including golf courses and marinas / by William Roy Crawford and
Lela Ann Crawford ; Donna Russell, editor.
        p.    cm.
    includes index.
    ISBN 0-914862-74-X
    1. United States--Armed Forces--Facilities--Guidebooks.
    2. Recreation areas--United States--Guidebooks. 3. Military bases-
-Guidebooks.  4. Recreation areas--Guidebooks.  5. Golf courses-
-United States--Guidebooks  6. Golf courses----Guidebooks.
    7. Marinas--United States--Guidebooks.  8. Marinas--Guidebooks.
    I. Crawford, Ann Caddell.  II. Russell, Donna L.  III. Title.
    UC403.C7438  1998
    647.947309--dc21                                                          98-31698
                                                                                        CIP

**ISBN: 0-914862-74-X**

# INTRODUCTION

You can have a lot of fun with Military Living's all-new edition of ***Military RV Camping & Outdoor Recreation Around the World Including Golf Courses and Marinas***. If you are a long time user of our books, you will notice that this new edition has a new name. We try to stay in-tune with our readers' requests, and over the past few years, we have had more and more requests for information regarding military golf courses and marinas, outdoor recreation and Ticket and Tours offices. This information is now included in this book, showing you even *more* ways you can have fun!

Many military families, both active and retired, use their recreational vehicles or camp for fun, while others use them to save money while visiting many famous tourist attractions. Many of the most well-know attractions are referenced in the individual listings in this book.

Having just become RV'ers ourselves, we have seen first-hand the information one needs when traveling, and have added additional information in the RV and camping listings. We hope you enjoy this newly-revised, bigger and  better edition.

***Military RV Camping & Outdoor Recreation Around the World Including Golf Courses and Marinas*** is the first commercial book to focus on Military RV, camping and recreation areas, golf courses and marinas of all services. including Army, Navy, Marine Corps, Coast Guard and Air Force. We have provided information in this edition that many military families have requested, and that we believe will be of the most value to you. We have included most of the active locations. You may know of other locations that we did not find. Please tell us of any that we missed so we can research the location to share with you and your fellow military families in the next printing/edition or between editions in our travel newsletter, Military Living's R&R Space-A Report®

The publishers of Military Living want to thank all of the military recreation and public affairs personnel who so diligently serve the military and their families.

Looking for maps and phone numbers for other logistical support facilities? This book focuses on military RV, camping & outdoor recreation. Please take a look at our other books, which give more logistical support information such as phone numbers, locations and maps. An order coupon is located at the end of this book for your convenience.

## HOW TO USE THIS DIRECTORY

**State Maps:** At the top of each state listing is a map that shows you where each installation/facility is located within that state. The location of each installation can be found by matching the camping graphic, with its Location Identifier, to the Name of the Installation/Facility in the text portion of the listing. For example, the sample below shows that an installation has a Location Identifier of (OK06R3). Just match (OK06R3) with OK06R3 in the text of the listing, and you have located the general location of that installation within the state/country.

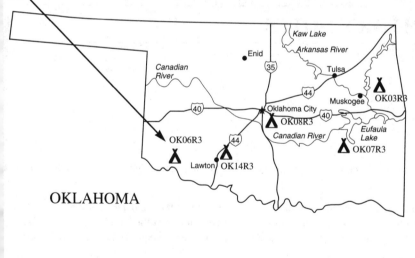

Each individual installation/facility listing begins as follows:

**Name of Installation/Facility (LI)**
**Name of Installation which has Management Control**
**City/Base/APO/FPO, State/AE/AP, ZIP Code**

**Location Identifier (LI):** Example (OK06R3). The first two characters (letters) are Country/State abbreviations used in Military Living's books (contents and listings). The next two-character set is a random number (01-99) assigned to a specific location. The fifth character (letter) is an R indicating region and the sixth character (0-9) is the regional location. The location identifiers for listings in this book are keyed to the state map at the beginning of each state listing. The state maps are designed to provide you with the relative geographic location of each installation/facility in the United States.

**Telephone Number Information:** The telephone numbers given under this heading are usually for the installation's main information and/or assistance operator. **C-:** The commercial telephone service for the installation. Within the U.S. Area Code System, the first three digits are the area code. The next three digits are the area telephone exchange/switch number. The last four digits are the line number. For foreign country locations, 011 (international access) is listed first, then the next one, two or three digits are the Country Code, the next two or three digits are the city code, if used. The exchange number can be either fewer or more digits than in the U.S. system. The last four digits are usually the information or operator assistance number. Again, in foreign countries this number may be fewer or more than four digits. Consult your local directory or operator for specific dialing instructions. **D-:** The Department of Defense worldwide Defense Switched Network (DSN). **DSN-E:** The Defense Switched Network European Telephone System. DSN-E prefixes for military communities are the same as DSN prefixes.

**Location:** The specific driving directions to the installation/facility from local major cities, interstate highways and routes are in this section. **USMRA:** indicates **Military Living's** *United States Military Road Atlas* coordinates for the installation/facility. **NMI:** The nearest military installation if the recreation area is not located on post/base. **NMC:** The nearest major city. The distance in miles and the direction from the installation/facility to the NMI or NMC is given.

**Description of Area:** This section provides a description of the RV, camping or recreation area in the listing. Special geographic and topographic features are listed. Other recreational opportunities and military support facilities are noted. Special facilities are included.

**Season of Operation:** The time frame during which the facility is available for general use is specified in this section.

**Eligibility:** The category/status of uniformed military and civilian employees who may use the facility is stated in this section. In most cases, eligible family members may also use the facilities. Some categories of eligibility are at the discretion of the base/post commander. Therefore, if you have a question about your eligibility, it would be advisable to call the number shown under "Reservations" to determine whether you are authorized to use the facilities.

**Reservations:** The procedure for establishing reservations, the mailing address, commercial and defense contact numbers and special instructions are contained in this section. Please call these numbers for additional information as required. We have also included fax numbers for those installations which accept reservations via fax. When available, E-mail and Homepage addresses have been listed. When known, check in and check out times are given. Some areas have complicated priority systems. If the facilities are very limited, priority for space is often given to personnel/families of the sponsoring installation. When writing, it is advisable to include a self-addressed, stamped envelope.

**Camp Facilities:** This section details any recreational lodging, RV spaces, camping spaces and tent spaces. The number of units is specified along with the hookup facilities available and the fee for each facility used. You should anticipate possible changes in rates/fees and facilities provided.

**Support Facilities:** Installation facilities available to patrons of the camping/recreation area are listed in this section.

**Activities:** General recreational activities available to patrons are listed in this section.

**Credit Cards Accepted**: Lists which credit cards can be used as payment at each facility.

**Restrictions:** Details of any restrictions, limitations and rules for the use of the facility are in this section.

**EDITOR'S NOTE**: Because of budget reductions within the Federal Government, both seasons of operation and hours of operation within seasons may be reduced or otherwise changed after the press date of this book.

# EDITOR'S NOTES

## PHOTO CREDITS

All photos are courtesy of the facility shown or by R.J. Crawford, Military Living Staff.

## BASE CLOSURES

The 1995 Defense Base Closure and Realignment Commission's Report was accepted by Congress and became Public Law on 28 September 1995.

The 1995 law, along with previous directed closures and realignments in the basic law in 1988, 1990, 1991, and 1993, complete the base closure and realignments which have been approved by Congress. These directed closures have been noted at the beginning of each listing affected with the DoD estimated date of final closure. Some bases have already closed and consequently have been deleted from this edition.

It should also be noted that final closure dates will be established for each installation. These dates could change as the DoD completes the final closure plans and as funding becomes available to effect the closures. Support facilities on the affected bases will normally decrease gradually; therefore, it is best to check with each military installation scheduled for closure or realignment before you go. Some bases scheduled for closure or realignment do not have RV Camping/Rec Areas and, consequently, are not listed in this book.

We have noted in the title of each listing scheduled for closure the planned closure date of the RV, camping and rec area.

Lastly, it should be noted that the 1995 Defense Base Closure and Realignment Law along with previous base closure laws only apply to domestic United States Bases and United States Bases located in U.S. possessions. The Secretary of Defense, acting within his authority, announced on 1 July 1993 and 24 February 1994, the further reduction or realignment of United States Military Sites Overseas (in Foreign countries). In early 1997 the Secretary of Defense announced the closing of the Augsburg, GE Community and related realignments.

# CONTENTS

# SECTION II
# Military Golf Courses

## UNITED STATES

## SECTION III
## Military Marinas

### UNITED STATES

## SECTION IV -
## Military Outdoor Recreation

## SECTION V -
## Military ITRs and ITTs

## APPENDICES

# SECTION I - Military RV and Camping Facilities

# UNITED STATES

## ALABAMA

**DAUPHIN ISLAND COAST GUARD
RECREATION FACILITY (AL07R2)**
Mobile Coast Guard Group
Mobile, AL 36615-1390

**TELEPHONE NUMBER INFORMATION:** Main installation numbers: C-334-861-7113. Police for recreation complex, C-334-861-5523.

**LOCATION:** Off base. On Gulf of Mexico approximately 40 miles south of Mobile. I-10 to AL-193 S (exit 17) to a left on Laurendine Road to Dauphin Island. Left on Bienville Blvd, follow signs to Recreation Bldg. Follow signs to complex. *USMRA: page 36 (B-10).* NMI: Mobile Coast Guard Group, 40 miles north. NMC: Mobile, 40 miles north.

**DESCRIPTION OF AREA:** Dauphin Island offers a variety of outdoor and sightseeing activities with a peaceful environment. Explore old Fort Gaines, ancient Indian Shell Mounds, Audubon Bird Sanctuary or just enjoy the great fishing. Limited support facilities available at Mobile Coast Guard Base.

**SEASON OF OPERATION:** Year round.

**ELIGIBILITY:** Active/Reservists/Retired/some DoD civilian employees.

**RESERVATIONS:** Required by phone then followed by reservation request form sent with payment 2 weeks prior to arrival. Payment due before check in. Active duty Coast Guard up to 60 days in advance. Other active branches and reserve up to 45 days in advance. Retired and DoD civilians up to 30 days. Address: Dauphin Island Coast Guard Recreation Facility, P.O. Box 436, Dauphin Island, AL 36528-0436. **C-334-861-7113.** Check in 1600-2000 hours, check out 1200 hours; Fri and Sun.

**Cottages:** Three-bedroom (13-3 handicap accessible), kitchen, microwave, utensils, CATV, linens. Patrons must provide wash cloths and dish cloths. Rates: $100-$120 Fri-Sun; $140-$160 Sun-Fri (five-day week); $240-$280 Fri-Fri or Sun-Sun (seven-day week) (monthly rate of $525 available after Oct 1.).

**Camper Spaces:** Hardstand (5), E (110V/30A)/S/W/CATV hookups. Rates: $10 daily (monthly rate of $185 available after Oct 1).

**Camper/Tent Spaces:** 100. Rates: $5 daily (monthly rate available after Oct 1).

**SUPPORT FACILITIES:**

| | | |
|---|---|---|
| Bath House | Beach/private | Convenience Store |
| Exchange | Fishing Poles/Bait | Grills |
| Laundry | Picnic Area | Playground |
| Rec Equipment | Restrooms* | Sewage Dump |
| Showers* | Snack Vending | Sun Deck |

* Handicap accessible.

**ACTIVITIES:**

| | | |
|---|---|---|
| Bicycling | Boating | Fishing |
| Swimming | | |

**CREDIT CARDS ACCEPTED:** None.

**RESTRICTIONS:** No pets allowed. No firearms allowed. Seven day limit for cottages, fourteen day limit for camper sites.

**LAKE MARTIN MAXWELL/
GUNTER RECREATION AREA (AL05R2)**
Maxwell Air Force Base
Maxwell AFB, AL 36112-5000

**TELEPHONE NUMBER INFORMATION:** Main installation numbers: C-334-953-1110, D-312-493-1110.

**LOCATION:** Off base. Located near Dadeville, southeast of Birmingham, northeast of Montgomery. From I-85 north of Montgomery take exit 32, north on AL-49 to Stillwaters Road (County Road 34) and proceed 2.5 miles to recreation area. *USMRA: page 36 (F-5).* NMI: Maxwell AFB, 60 miles southwest. NMC: Montgomery, 60 miles southwest.

**DESCRIPTION OF AREA:** Located on Lake Martin Reservoir near dam. Excellent fishing; variety of water- and woods-oriented activities. Recreation area includes areas for day picnicking and rough camping. Voted outstanding recreation area of the Air Force. Full range of support facilities available at Maxwell AFB.

**SEASON OF OPERATION:** Year round.

**ALABAMA**
*Lake Martin Maxwell/Gunter Recreation Area, continued*

**ELIGIBILITY:** Active/Reservists/Retired/DoD civilians at Maxwell/Gunter AFB.

**RESERVATIONS:** Required with payment in full, cash or check within ten days of registering. Active up to six months in advance; others up to three months. Address: Outdoor Recreation Reservations Office, 204 West Selfridge Street, Maxwell AFB, AL 36112-5000. **C-334-953-3509/3510, D-312-493-3510.** For information, C-256-825-6251. Check in at marina after 1700 hours (15 Mar-15 Oct); after 1200 hours (16 Oct-14 Mar), check out 1600 hours.

**Mobile Homes:** Three-bedroom (12), handicap accessible ramp, E (110/220V/30A)/W hookups, A/C, heat, linens, blankets. TV and radio rental available. Rates: $35-$50 daily (monthly rates available 16 Oct-14 Mar).

**Camper Spaces:** Gravel (61), E (110/220V/30A)/W hookups. Rates: $13 daily (monthly rates available 16 Oct-14 Mar).

**Tent Spaces:** 15, no hookups. Rates: $7 daily (monthly rates available 16 Oct-14 Mar).

**SUPPORT FACILITIES:**

| | | |
|---|---|---|
| Beach | Boat Launch/fee | Boat Rental |
| Boat Storage | Fishing Pier | Gas |
| Grills | Laundry | Marina |
| Pay Telephone | Picnic Area | Playground |
| Restrooms* | Sewage Dump | Showers* |
| Trail | | |

* Handicap accessible.

**ACTIVITIES:**

| | | |
|---|---|---|
| Boating | Fishing/license | Hiking |
| Jogging | Sailing | Swimming |
| Volleyball | Water Skiing | |

**CREDIT CARDS ACCEPTED:** Visa, MasterCard and AF Services Club Card.

**RESTRICTIONS:** No pets allowed. No firearms allowed. No open fires. Fireworks, BB guns, bows and arrows are prohibited. Minimum of two nights or weekend 15 Mar-15 Oct. As facility is in an isolated area, check your supplies carefully before arriving.

# MAXWELL/GUNTER FAMCAMP (AL11R2)
Maxwell Air Force Base
Maxwell AFB, AL 36112-5000

**TELEPHONE NUMBER INFORMATION:** Main installation numbers: C-334-953-1110, D-312-493-1110.

**LOCATION:** On base. From I-95 N or S to I-65 W, take Day Street exit, exit 171, to main gate. *USMRA: page 36 (E-6).* NMC: Montgomery, 1.5 miles southeast.

**DESCRIPTION OF AREA:** Situated next to a small lake on base. Martin Lake and many other freshwater lakes and reservoirs located within 50 miles. Site of Wright Brothers Flying School and historical airplanes which have been retired. Historical city of Montgomery has much to offer in the way of sightseeing. Full range of support facilities available on base.

**SEASON OF OPERATION:** Year round.

**ELIGIBILITY:** Active/Reservists/Retired.

**RESERVATIONS:** No advance reservations. Address: FAMCAMP, Outdoor Recreation, March Road, Maxwell AFB, AL 36112-5005. **C-334-953-5161, D-312-493-5161.** Check in at FAMCAMP office.

**Camper Spaces:** Paved (31), E (110/220V/30A)/S/W hookups. Rates: $12 daily/$75 weekly/$275 monthly. Overflow, E (110/220V)/W hookups. Rates: $8 daily (overflow).

**Tent Spaces:** Open, no hookups. Rates: $5 daily.

**SUPPORT FACILITIES:**

| | | |
|---|---|---|
| Boat Launch | Chapel | Community Bldg |
| Equipment Rental | Gas | Golf |
| Grills | Laundry | Picnic Area |
| Rec Center | Restrooms* | Sewage Dump |
| Showers | Snack Bar | Sports Fields |
| Stables | Trails | |

* Handicap accessible.

**ACTIVITIES:**

| | | |
|---|---|---|
| Fishing/license | Golfing | Jogging |

**CREDIT CARDS ACCEPTED:** Visa, MasterCard and AF Services Club Card.

**RESTRICTIONS:** Pets allowed. No firearms allowed.

# McCLELLAN RECREATION AREA AND CAMPGROUND (AL09R2)
Fort McClellan
Fort McClellan, AL 36205-5000
*Scheduled to close in September 1999.*

**TELEPHONE NUMBER INFORMATION:** Main installation numbers: C-256-848-4611, D-312-865-1110.

**LOCATION:** On post. From I-20 E or W, take AL-21 N to fort on right. Also located 25 miles southeast of I-59. Take US-431 S to fort. *USMRA: page 36 (F-3).* NMC: Anniston, three miles southeast.

**DESCRIPTION OF AREA:** Located in Alabama hills west of Atlanta, GA, and east of Birmingham. Campgrounds located three miles from main post area above an eight-acre lake. Heated restrooms and shower facilities, full range of support facilities available on post.

**SEASON OF OPERATION:** Year round.

**ELIGIBILITY:** Active/Reservists/Retired/DoD civilians at Fort McClellan/General public when spaces available.

**RESERVATIONS:** Recommended. Address: MWR Central Warehouse/Rental Center, Bldg 305, Fort McClellan, AL 36205-5000. **C-256-848-3158/820-5459, D-312-865-3158.** Discounts available to holders of Golden Age and Golden Access Passports.

**Camper Spaces:** Hardstand (12), E (110V/20/30/50A)/W hookups. Rates: $10 daily. Primitive (4), no hookups. Rates: $5 daily.

**SUPPORT FACILITIES:**

| | | |
|---|---|---|
| Auto Craft Shop | Bowling Center | Fitness Center |
| Go-Karts/Seasonal | Golf/Seasonal | Laundry |
| Picnic Area | Restrooms | Sewage Dump |
| Showers | Sports Fields | |

**ACTIVITIES:**

Fishing/license      Hunting/license

**CREDIT CARDS ACCEPTED:** Visa, MasterCard, American Express and Discover,

**RESTRICTIONS:** No firearms allowed.

## REDSTONE ARSENAL CAMPGROUND (AL12R2)

Redstone Arsenal
Redstone Arsenal, AL 35808-5000

**TELEPHONE NUMBER INFORMATION:** Main installation numbers: C-256-876-2151, D-312-746-0011. Police for campground, C-256-876-2222.

**LOCATION:** On post. From US-231 N or S, go west on Martin Road to main gate with visitor control. For uniformed personnel, Gate 8 is on Drake Avenue. Take US-72 E to Jordan Lane, south to Drake Avenue (becomes Goss Road at arsenal). *USMRA: page 36 (E-1)*. NMC: Huntsville, adjacent north and east sides. Huntsville International Airport, off I-565, is ten miles from Redstone arsenal.

**DESCRIPTION OF AREA:** Situated along Tennessee River in northern Alabama. Alabama Space and Rocket Center nearby. Full range of support facilities available on post.

**SEASON OF OPERATION:** Year round; no water in winter months.

**ELIGIBILITY:** Active/Reservists/Retired/DoD civilians.

**RESERVATIONS:** No advance reservations. Address: Outdoor Recreation, Bldg 5132, Sportsman's Road, P.O. Box 8192, Redstone Arsenal, AL 35898-0192. **C-256-876-4868/6854, D-312-746-4868/6854** 0930-1700 hours. Fax: C-256-842-9134. Check in 0930-1700 hours. If arriving after hours, check in at Outdoor Recreation Center in the morning.

**Camper/Tent Spaces:** Hardstand (23), E (110V/20/30/50A)/W hookups. Rates: $5 daily, $30 weekly. Overflow, no hookups. Rates: $5 daily, $30 weekly. *Note: Campground can accommodate RVs up to 30 feet long; larger vehicles will experience difficulties.*

**SUPPORT FACILITIES:**

| | | |
|---|---|---|
| Auto Craft Shop | Bath House | Boat Launch |
| Chapel | Commissary | Fitness Center |
| Gas | Golf | Grills |
| Ice | Pavilions | Picnic Area |
| Playground | Pool | Rec Center |
| Rec Equipment | Restrooms | Sewage Dump |
| Showers | Shoppette | Showers |
| Snack Bar | Softball Field | Telephones |
| Tennis Courts | Trails | |

**ACTIVITIES:**

| | | |
|---|---|---|
| Boating | Fishing/license | Hunting/license |
| Jogging | Tennis | |

**CREDIT CARDS ACCEPTED:** None.

**RESTRICTIONS:** Pets allowed on leash.

## RUCKER OUTDOOR RECREATION AREA (AL10R2)

Fort Rucker
Fort Rucker, AL 36362-5000

**TELEPHONE NUMBER INFORMATION:** Main installation numbers: C-334-255-6181, D-312-558-1110. Police for the recreation area, C-334-255-2222.

**LOCATION:** On post. From US-231, take AL-249 S to Daleville. After passing through Fort Rucker gates (approximately five miles), turn right at first blinking light onto Christian Road. Continue approximately 2.4 miles to a right on Johnson Road. Campground is about five miles further on right. *USMRA: page 36 (F-8)*. NMC: Dothan, 22 miles southeast.

**DESCRIPTION OF AREA:** Located in the southeast corner of Alabama approximately 85 miles south of Montgomery and 90 miles north of the Florida Gulf Coast, the camping area is on the shores of 660-acre Lake Tholocco. Full range of support facilities available on post.

**SEASON OF OPERATION:** Year round.

**ELIGIBILITY:** Active/Reservists/Retired/DoD civilians.

**RESERVATIONS:** No advance reservations. Address: Community Activities, Outdoor Recreation, Bldg 24236, Camper Shed, Fort Rucker, AL 36362-5000. **C-334-255-4305, D-312-558-4305.** Discounts available to holders of Golden Age, Golden Access or Golden Eagle Passports.

**Camper Spaces:** Hardstand (18), E (110V/20/30/50A)/W hookups. Rates: $10 daily. *Note: No water hookup from Oct 1-Dec 31.*

**SUPPORT FACILITIES:**

| | | |
|---|---|---|
| Archery | Beach | Boat Launch |
| Boat Rental | Camping Equipment | Golf |
| Grills | Ice | Laundry |
| Picnic Area | Pistol Range | Rec Equipment |
| Restrooms* | Sewage Dump | Showers |
| Skeet Range | Snack Bar | Stables |
| Trails | | |

\* Handicap accessible.

**ACTIVITIES:**

Fishing/license      Hunting

**CREDIT CARDS ACCEPTED:** Visa and MasterCard.

**RESTRICTIONS:** No pets allowed. Toll to enter recreation area from May through September.

# ALASKA

*See map on following page.*

## BIRCH LAKE RECREATION AREA (AK01R5)

Eielson Air Force Base
Eielson AFB, AK 99702-1720

**TELEPHONE NUMBER INFORMATION:** Main installation numbers: C-907-377-1110, D-317-377-1110. Police for recreation area, C-907-377-5130.

*ALASKA*

ALASKA

**Camper Spaces:** 40, E (110/220V/30A) hookup. Rates: $12 daily.

**Tent Spaces:** 14 , no hookups. Rates: $6 daily.

**SUPPORT FACILITIES:**

| | |
|---|---|
| Beach | Boat Launch |
| Boat Rental | Country Store |
| Fire Rings | Lodge* |
| Picnic Area | Playground |
| Restrooms* | Showers |

\* Handicap accessible.

**ACTIVITIES:**

| | |
|---|---|
| Berry Picking | Fishing/license |
| Hiking | Wading |
| Water Skiing | |

**CREDIT CARDS ACCEPTED:** Visa and MasterCard.

**RESTRICTIONS:** Pets allowed on leash. No firearms permitted in site; must be secured in vehicle. Check camper pad size when making reservations. Numerous water faucets throughout the camp supply potable water.

# BLACK SPRUCE TRAVEL CAMP (AK16R5)

Fort Richardson
Fort Richardson, AK 99505-6625

**TELEPHONE NUMBER INFORMATION:** Main installation numbers: C-907-384-1110, D-317-384-1110. Police for travel camp, C-907-384-0820.

**LOCATION:** On post. Main gate is on Glenn Highway AK-1, five miles south of Eagle River. Camp is located off Loop Road. Patrons may go directly to camp and report to Outdoor Recreation, Bldg 794, the next day. *USMRA: page 128 (F-5).* NMC: Anchorage, 8 miles southwest.

**DESCRIPTION OF AREA:** Beautiful mountain scenery. Lakes and rivers provide excellent fishing. Varied sightseeing and outdoor recreational opportunities. Full range of support facilities available on post.

**SEASON OF OPERATION:** 1 May-1 Oct.

**ELIGIBILITY:** Active/Reservists/Retired/DoD and NAF civilians.

**RESERVATIONS:** No advance reservations. Address: Community Recreation Division, Attn: APVR-RPA-CRO, 600 Richardson Drive, #6600, Fort Richardson, AK 99505-6600. **C-907-384-1476, C-907-428-0001.**

**Camper Spaces:** Gravel (39), E (110V/30A)/S/W hookups. Rates: $15 daily. Gravel (5), E (110V/30A)/W hookups. Rates: $13 daily.

**Camper/Tent Spaces:** 20, located at Upper Otter Lake Campground, no hookups. Rates: $5 daily.

**SUPPORT FACILITIES:**

| | | |
|---|---|---|
| Archery | Golf | Grills |
| Laundry | Racquetball | Rec Equipment |
| Sewage Dump | Showers | Tennis Courts |

**ACTIVITIES:**

| | |
|---|---|
| Fishing | Hunting |

*Birch Lake Recreation Area, continued*

**LOCATION:** Off base. On southwest side of Richardson Highway (AK-2) at mile post 305, 38 miles south of AFB. Turn at Recreation Area sign; one mile to entrance. Check in at Boat Shop. *USMRA: page 128 (F-4).* NMI: Eielson AFB, 35 miles north. NMC: Fairbanks, 64 miles north.

**DESCRIPTION OF AREA:** Located on Birch Lake which covers 804 acres, is spring-fed, and is stocked with rainbow trout and silver salmon. Harding Lake Recreation Area approximately ten miles north; Denali National Park, 130 miles southwest. Area provides rustic base for enjoying state's unlimited outdoor recreational resources. Spectacular mountain scenery, unsurpassed fishing and hunting in general area. Full range of support facilities at Eielson AFB.

**SEASON OF OPERATION:** Memorial Day-Labor Day. (Over the winter season the Outdoor Adventure Program does weekend cabin rental on selected weekends along with ice fishing and snow mobile trips. Call C-907-377-1232 for more information.)

**ELIGIBILITY:** Active/Reservists/Retired/DoD civilians.

**RESERVATIONS:** Accepted. Address: 354 SVS/SVRO, 3112 Broadway Street, U-6, Eielson AFB, AK 99702-1875. **C-907-488-6161, D-317-377-1232** 0900-1100 hours. Fax: C-907-377-2770. For information off-season, C-907-377-1839.

**CABINS:**

**Deluxe:** One-bedroom (2), sofabed, table, refrigerator, stove, water for dishes and showers only, E (110V) hookup. Rates: $50 daily.

**Family:** One- and two-room cabins (16), beds, sofabed, refrigerator, stove, E (110V) hookup, wood-burning stove. No indoor plumbing facilities. Rates: $40-$45 daily.

**2-man:** One-room (4), two single beds, refrigerator, E (110V) hookup. Patrons must provide utensils and linens. No indoor cooking or plumbing facilities. Rates: $20 daily.

*Black Spruce Travel Camp, continued*

**CREDIT CARDS ACCEPTED:** Visa, MasterCard and Discover.

**RESTRICTIONS:** Pets allowed on leash. Firearms must be registered with the military police. Hunters must check with Fish & Wildlife as there are many regulations. Fourteen day limit, a break of seven days is required between stays.

# EIELSON FAMCAMP (AK02R5)

Eielson Air Force Base
Eielson AFB, AK 99702-1720

**TELEPHONE NUMBER INFORMATION:** Main installation numbers: C-907-377-1110, D-317-377-1110. Police for FAMCAMP, C-907-377-5130.

**LOCATION:** On base. On Richardson Highway AK-2. AFB is east of AK-2, clearly marked. Ask for a map at the main gate. *USMRA: page 128 (F,G-4).* NMC: Fairbanks, 26 miles northwest.

**DESCRIPTION OF AREA:** Located in interior of Alaska. Provides base for enjoying state's unlimited outdoor recreational resources. Spectacular mountain scenery; unsurpassed fishing and hunting in general area. Denali National Park approximately 130 miles southwest. Full range of support facilities available on base.

**SEASON OF OPERATION:** 15 May-7 Sep.

**ELIGIBILITY:** Active/Reservists/Retired/DoD civilians.

**RESERVATIONS:** Accepted. Address: Eielson FAMCAMP, 354 SVS/SVRO, 3112 Broadway Avenue, Unit 6B, Eielson AFB, AK 99702-1885. **C-907-377-1232, D-317-377-1232.** Fax: C-907-377-2770. For information off-season, C-907-377-1232/1839. Check in at Outdoor Recreation, Bldg 6214 0800-1700 hours. Check out 1200 hours.

**Camper Spaces:** Paved (24), E (110V/20A)/S/W hookups. Rates: $14 daily (full hookup), $10 (partial hookup), $5 (overflow).

**SUPPORT FACILITIES:**
Sewage Dump

(All other facilities are on the main part of the base, 1.5 miles away.)

**ACTIVITIES:**

| | | |
|---|---|---|
| Boating | Fishing | Hiking |
| Skeet/Trap Range* | | |

* Hours of operation: 1700-2100 hours Tue-Thu, 1500-2000 hours Sat.

**CREDIT CARDS ACCEPTED:** Visa and MasterCard.

**RESTRICTIONS:** Pets allowed on leash. No firearms permitted in FAMCAMP; must be secured in vehicle. Fourteen day limit.

# ELMENDORF FAMCAMP (AK12R5)

Elmendorf Air Force Base
Elmendorf AFB, AK 99506-2760

**TELEPHONE NUMBER INFORMATION:** Main installation numbers: C-907-552-1110, D-317-552-1110.

**LOCATION:** On base. From Glenn Highway AK-1, take Muldoon Gate, Boniface Gate, Post Road Gate or Government Hill Gate exits. AFB is two miles northeast of Anchorage and next to Fort Richardson. Follow signs. FAMCAMP is adjacent to hospital. *USMRA: page 131 (B,C,D-1).* NMC: Anchorage, adjacent.

**DESCRIPTION OF AREA:** Located on the state's southern coast at the head of Cook Inlet in a low-timbered area surrounded by mountains. The camp provides a good base for enjoying spectacular and varied sightseeing and outdoor recreational opportunities. Full range of support facilities available on base.

**SEASON OF OPERATION:** Mid May-mid Sep.

**ELIGIBILITY:** Active/Reservists/Retired/DoD and NAF civilians.

**RESERVATIONS:** No advance reservations. Address: SVS, RE: Elmendorf FAMCAMP AK 12R5, 3 SVS/SVRO, 6-920 12th Street, Elmendorf AFB, AK 99506-5000. No phone at FAMCAMP listed. **C-907-552-2023.** Fax: C-907-753-2498. For information off season, C-907-552-4838. Check in with Camp Host, Space 2, check out 1300 hours.

**Camper Spaces:** Gravel (39), E (110V/30A)/W hookups. Rates: $12 daily.

**Tent Spaces:** 10, no hookups. Rates: $6 daily.

**SUPPORT FACILITIES:**

| | | |
|---|---|---|
| Auto Craft Shop | Boat Rental | Chapel |
| Commissary | Equipment Rental | Exchange |
| Fire Rings | Fitness Center | Gas |
| Golf | Grills | Laundry |
| Playground | Restrooms | Sewage Dump |
| Shoppette | Showers | Shuttle Bus |
| Snack Bar | Sports Fields | Stables |
| Telephones | Tennis Courts | Trails |

**ACTIVITIES:**

| | | |
|---|---|---|
| Fishing/license | Hiking | Hunting/license |
| Tour Boats | | |

**CREDIT CARDS ACCEPTED:** Visa and MasterCard.

**RESTRICTIONS:** Pets must be leashed. No firearms.

# GLASS PARK (AK14R5)

Fort Wainwright
Fort Wainwright, AK 99703-6600

**TELEPHONE NUMBER INFORMATION:** Main installation numbers: C-907-353-6113/7500, D-317-353-6113/7500.

**LOCATION:** On post. From Fairbanks, take Airport Way East AK-3, which leads to main gate of the post. *USMRA: page 128 (F-4).* NMC: Fairbanks, 3 miles west.

**DESCRIPTION OF AREA:** Alaska's lakes and rivers abound with many species of fish, and forests teem with many kinds of wildlife. There is plenty of sunshine and great fishing. Both the post and the Fairbanks community offer many and varied activities. Full range of support facilities on post.

**SEASON OF OPERATION:** Memorial Day-Labor Day.

**ELIGIBILITY:** Active/Reservists/Retired/DoD civilians.

*ALASKA*
*Glass Park, continued*

**RESERVATIONS:** Accepted for large groups only. Address: Commander, FWA, Attn: APVR-FW-PA-CRD/ODR, 1555 Gaffney Road, Fort Wainwright, AK 99703-5320. **C-907-353-6349/6350, D-317-353-6349/6350.** Write or call for Wilderness Adventure in Alaska information. Check in with Outdoor Recreation Director, Bldg 2062 (Recreation Center), at or soon after arrival.

**RV/Camper/Tent Spaces:** Open area, no hookups, $5 daily.

**SUPPORT FACILITIES:**

| | | |
|---|---|---|
| Arts/Crafts Center | Auto Craft Shop | Boat Launch |
| Boat Rental/Storage | Chapel | Commissary |
| Exchange | Fitness Center | Gas |
| Golf/9 holes | Grills | Marina/North Post |
| Pavilions | Picnic Area | Playground |
| Rec Center | Rec Equipment | Restrooms |
| Sewage Dump | Shoppette | Sports Fields |
| Telephones | Tennis Courts | Trails |

**ACTIVITIES:**

| | | |
|---|---|---|
| Boating | Canoeing | Fishing |
| Hiking | Hunting | Mountain Biking |

**CREDIT CARDS ACCEPTED:** Visa and MasterCard.

**RESTRICTIONS:** Pets allowed on leash. Firearms not allowed on grounds, must be in vehicle at all times. Fourteen day limit.

# RAVENWOOD SKI LODGE (AK13R5)
Eielson Air Force Base
Eielson AFB, AK 99702-1720

**TELEPHONE NUMBER INFORMATION:** Main installation numbers: C-907-377-1110, D-317-377-1110. Police for area, C-907-377-5130.

**LOCATION:** On base. On Richardson Highway AK-2. AFB is east of AK-2, clearly marked. *USMRA: page 128 (F,G-4).* NMC: Fairbanks, 26 miles northwest.

**DESCRIPTION OF AREA:** Located four miles southeast of main base. Spectacular mountain scenery. Full range of support facilities available on base.

**SEASON OF OPERATION:** Depends on snowfall (normally Nov-Mar). Closed Mon-Wed.

**ELIGIBILITY:** Active/Reservists/Retired/DoD civilians.

**RESERVATIONS:** Accepted. Address: 354 SVS/SVRO, 3112 Broadway Avenue, U-6, Eielson AFB, AK 99702-1870. **C-907-377-1232.** Fax: C-907-377-2770.

**Lodge:** 1, two baths, small kitchen, two fireplaces. No overnight accommodations, patron must be out by 0200 hours. Rates: $65 per event.

**SUPPORT FACILITIES:**

| | | |
|---|---|---|
| Skeet/Trap Range** | Ski Rental | Ski Lift |
| Ski Lodge* | Ski Trails | Sled Rides (Hill) |
| Snack Bar | | |

* Handicap accessible.
** 1700-2100 hours Tue-Thu, 1500-2000 hours Sat.

**ACTIVITIES:**

| | |
|---|---|
| Sledding | Snow Skiing |

**CREDIT CARDS ACCEPTED:** Visa and MasterCard.

**RESTRICTIONS:** No pets allowed. No firearms permitted in site, must be secured in vehicle.

# SEWARD RECREATION CAMP (AK05R5)
Elmendorf Air Force Base
Elmendorf AFB, AK 99506-2760

**TELEPHONE NUMBER INFORMATION:** Main installation numbers: C-907-552-1110, D-907-552-1110.

**LOCATION:** Off base. From Anchorage, proceed south on the Seward Highway for approximately 2.5 hours to the city of Seward. Located on the right, at mile post 2.1 of the Seward Highway. Located on Resurrection Bay near Seward off AK-1 on AK-9. Follow signs. *USMRA: page 128 (F-6).* NMI: Elmendorf AFB, 120 miles north. NMC: Anchorage, 110 miles north.

**DESCRIPTION OF AREA:** Located on scenic, heavily wooded, 16-acre site. Within five minute walking distance to the mountains, ocean and town center. Multiple glaciers can be viewed from the campground. A haven for saltwater fishermen. Full range of facilities on Elmendorf AFB.

**SEASON OF OPERATION:** mid May-mid Sep.

**ELIGIBILITY:** Active/Reservists/Retired/DoD/NAF and their families and guests.

**RESERVATIONS:** Reservations accepted beginning 1 Feb for each year. Address: Air Force Seward Recreation Camp, P.O. Box 159, Seward, AK 99664-5000. **C-1-800-501-5643, C-907-552-5526, D-317-552-5526.** Fax: C-907-224-2279. Check out for cabins 1100 hours, for tents 1200 hours.

**Duplex Cabins:** One-bedroom (12-1 handicap accessible), sleeps six, sofabed, shower, furnished, kitchen, linens. Rates: $99 daily.

**RV/Trailer Spaces:** Gravel (35), central W, E (110V/30A) hookup. Rates: Electric $20 daily; water only $15 daily.

**Tent/Camper Spaces:** 47, no hookups. Rates: $10 daily.

**SUPPORT FACILITIES:**

| | | |
|---|---|---|
| Auto Craft Shop | Boat Rental/Storage | Chapel |
| Commissary | Convenience Store | Equipment Rental |
| Exchange | Fish Cleaning | Fish Freezer |
| Fitness Center | Gas | Golf |
| Grills | Ice | Laundry |
| Pavilion | Picnic Area | Playground |
| Pool | Rec Center | Restrooms |
| Sewage Dump | Shoppette | Showers |
| Shuttle Bus | Snack Bar | Sports Fields |
| Stables | Telephones | Tennis Courts |
| Trails | | |

**ACTIVITIES:**

| | | |
|---|---|---|
| Bicycle Rental* | Charter Fishing** | Fishing/License |
| Hiking | Wildlife Tour*** | |

* Rental $10 daily.
** Deep Sea Fishing Charters have a fee.
*** Tour $39 daily.

**CREDIT CARDS ACCEPTED:** Visa and MasterCard.

Seward Recreation Camp, continued

**RESTRICTIONS:** Pets are not allowed on boats, in cabins or common buildings. Pets must be kept on a short leash (six feet and under) and are not to be left unattended. Owner must clean up after pets. No fish cleaning or smoking in rooms.

# SEWARD RESORT (AK06R5)

Fort Richardson
Fort Richardson, AK 99505-6625

**TELEPHONE NUMBER INFORMATION:** Main installation numbers: C-907-384-1110, D-317-384-1110.

**LOCATION:** Off post. Located on Resurrection Bay near Seward, off AK-1 on AK-9. Follow signs. *USMRA: page 128 (F-6)*. NMI: Fort Richardson, 126 miles north. NMC: Anchorage, 126 miles north.

**DESCRIPTION OF AREA:** Pine trees throughout picturesque 12-acre site surrounded by mountains on three sides. Superb fishing for salmon, halibut, snapper, ling cod, black bass and flounder. Nearby streams and lakes also offer outstanding trout fishing. Area is a photographer's dream. Travelers in late July to mid-August see active salmon spawning areas on drive to Seward. Full range of support facilities at Fort Richardson.

**SEASON OF OPERATION:** 1 May-15 Sep, 0600-2300 hours. 16 Sep-30 Apr, 1100-1900 hours.

**ELIGIBILITY:** Active/Reservists/Retired/DoD, NAF and Contract civilians.

**RESERVATIONS:** Call for specific information 0600-2300 hours local time, seven days a week. No reservations may be made by mail. Address: Seward Resort, P.O. Box 329, Seward, AK 99664-5000. **C-1-800-770-1858, C-907-224-2659, D-317-384-FISH (3474)/LINE (5463).** Fax: C-907-224-5573, D-317-384-0248. HP: http://143.213.12.254/mwr/seward. htm. Check in 1500-2300 hours, check out 1100 hours.

**Premier Townhouse:** One-bedroom (2), sleeps six, double bed, loft with two twin beds, sofabed, full bath, furnished, living room, full kitchen, fireplace, linens, six person boat w/ driver. Rates: $660 (E1-E5), $680 (E6-E9, W1-CW3, O1-O3), $700 (CW4-CW5, O4-O10, DoD/NAF, other Federal Government employees). Winter Rates: $150 for all.

**Deluxe Townhouse:** One-bedroom (2), sleeps six, double bed, sofabed, loft with two twin beds, full bath, furnished, living room, full kitchen, coffee maker, fireplace, phone, CATV/VCR, linens. Rates: $159 (E1-E5), $179 (E6-E9, W1-CW3, O1-O3), $199 (CW4-CW5, O4-O10, DoD/NAF, other Federal Government employees). Winter Rates: $100 for all.

**Standard Townhouse:** One-bedroom (10), double bed, loft with two twin beds, full bath, furnished, living room, kitchen, coffee maker, fireplace, CATV/VCR, phone, linens. Rates: $129 (E1-E5), $149 (E6-E9, W1-CW3, O1-O3), $169 (CW4-CW5, O4-O10, DoD/NAF, other Federal Government employees). Winter Rates: $100 for all.

**Log Cabin:** One-bedroom (10-1 handicap accessible), sleeps six, queen size bed, full bath, furnished, kitchen, linens, hot tub, BBQ. Rates: $120 (E1-E5), $140 (E6-E9, W1-CW3, O1-O3), $160 (CW4-CW5, O4-O10, DoD/NAF, other Federal Government employees). Winter Rates: $100 for all.

**Motel:** Rooms (56-3 handicap accessible), sleeps four, two double beds, full bath, small refrigerator, microwave, coffee maker, CATV/VCR, phone, linens. Rates: $79 (E1-E5), $99 (E6-E9, W1-CW3, O1-O3), $119 (CW4-CW5, O4-O10, DoD/NAF, other Federal Government employees). Winter Rates: $50 for all.

**RV/Trailer Spaces:** Gravel (40), E (110V/30A)/S/W hookups. Rates: $17 (E1-E5), $19 (E6-E9, W1-CW3, O1-O3), $21 (CW4-CW5, O4-O10, DoD/NAF, other Federal Government employees).

**Tent Spaces:** 15, no hookups, picnic table, grill. Rates: $7 (E1-E5), $10 (E6-E9, W1-CW3, O1-O3), $12 (CW4-CW5, O4-O10, DoD/NAF, other Federal Government employees).

**SUPPORT FACILITIES:**

| | | |
|---|---|---|
| Boat Rental* | Commissary | Equipment Rental |
| Fire Rings | Fish Cleaning Facility | Fish Freezer |
| Fishing Rods | Grills | Ice |
| Laundry Facility | Playground | Picnic Area |
| Rec Center | Restrooms | Sewage Dump |
| Showers | Shoppette | Showers |
| Ski Rental | Snack Bar | Vending Machines |

* Deep-sea fishing, by drawing/free. Deep-sea fishing charters/fee.

**ACTIVITIES:**

| | | |
|---|---|---|
| Basketball | Fishing/license | Hiking |
| Hunting/license | Volleyball | Wildlife Tour/fee |

**CREDIT CARDS ACCEPTED:** Visa, MasterCard, American Express and Discover.

**RESTRICTIONS:** Pets are not permitted in Cabins, Motel units or Common buildings. Pets must be kept on a short leash (six feet and under); are not to be left unattended; are not allowed on boats; owner must clean up after pets. No open fires; grills and fire rings may be used. No smoking in cabins, motel units, or common buildings. No fish cleaning in motels or cabins. Seven day limit; manager approval for up to 14.

# ARIZONA

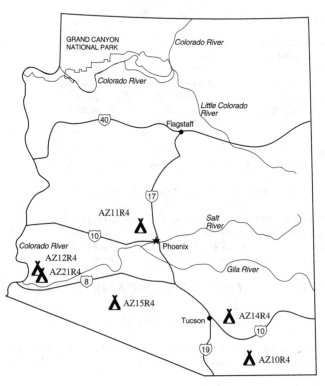

*ARIZONA*

# APACHE RV PARK (AZ10R4)

Fort Huachuca
Fort Huachuca, AZ 85613-6000

**TELEPHONE NUMBER INFORMATION:** Main installation numbers: C-520-538-7111, D-312-879-0111.

**LOCATION:** On post. From I-10 E or W, take AZ-90 S to Sierra Vista and main gate of fort. *USMRA: page 108 (F,G-9,10).* NMC: Tucson, 75 miles northwest.

**DESCRIPTION OF AREA:** Fort Huachuca, located at an altitude of 5,000 feet, is at the base of the Huachuca Mountains. Old mining towns of Bisbee and Tombstone are within short driving distance. Full range of support facilities available on post.

**SEASON OF OPERATION:** Year round.

**ELIGIBILITY:** Active/Reservists/Retired/DoD and NAF civilians and up to two guests.

**RESERVATIONS:** Accepted by phone 60 days in advance. Address: Apache RV Park: P.O. Box 12100, Fort Huachuca, AZ 85670-2100. **C-520-533-1335, D-312-879-1335** 0800-1700 Mon-Fri. Fax: C-520-533-1349 (Equipment Check-out Center). Check in at RV park 1100 hours, check out 1000 hours.

**Camper Spaces:** Hardstand, extra wide, pull through (50), E (110/120V/30/50A)/S/W/CATV hookups. Rates: $13 daily/$75 weekly/$275 monthly.

**Camper Spaces:** Overflow, dirt (24), E (110V/30A)/W hookups. Rates: $8 daily.

**Tent Spaces:** 4, no hookups. Rates: $5 daily.

**SUPPORT FACILITIES:**

| | | |
|---|---|---|
| Boat Rental | Chapel | Gas |
| Golf | Laundry | Picnic Area |
| Playground | Propane Sales | Rec Center |
| Rec Equipment | Sewage Dump | Showers |
| Skeet/Trap Range | Sports Fields | Stables |
| Tennis Courts | Walking Trails | |

**ACTIVITIES:**

| | |
|---|---|
| Fishing/license | Hunting/license |

**CREDIT CARDS ACCEPTED:** Visa and MasterCard.

**RESTRICTIONS:** No zoo animals. Pets must be kept indoors or on leash and controlled, two pet limit. Pets also must be registered at Animal Disease Prevention and Control Facility, Bldg 30022. Animals must have valid rabies certificates. Firearms must be registered. Ninety day limit.

# DAVIS-MONTHAN FAMCAMP (AZ14R4)

Davis-Monthan Air Force Base
Davis-Monthan AFB, AZ 85707-0001

**TELEPHONE NUMBER INFORMATION:** Main installation numbers: C-520-750-3900/4717, D-312-361-1110. Police for FAMCAMP, C-520-228-4444.

**LOCATION:** On base. From the east, take I-10 to exit 270, Kolb Road N. Turn left on Golf Links Road, then left on Craycroft Road through the main gate. From the west, take I-10 to exit 265, Alvernon Road N. Turn right on Golf Links Road, then right on Craycroft Road through the main gate. At first traffic light, turn left on Quijota Blvd to FAMCAMP on right. *USMRA: page 108 (F-9).* NMC: Tucson, 4 miles northwest.

**DESCRIPTION OF AREA:** Located in a wide desert valley which has beautiful weather year round. Colorado Rockies Spring Training Site. Nearby attractions include Arizona-Sonora Desert Museum, Pima Air Museum, Saguaro National Monument, Old Tucson and Reid Park and Zoo. Full range of support facilities available on base.

**SEASON OF OPERATION:** Year round.

**ELIGIBILITY:** Active/Reservists/Retired/DoD civilians/TDY personnel.

**RESERVATIONS:** No advance reservations. Address: FAMCAMP, 355 SVS/SVRO, 5465 E Nuggat Street, Davis-Monthan AFB, AZ 85707-5000. **C-520-747-9144, D-312-361-1110** (ask for FAMCAMP). Check in at Bldg 6015, check out 1000 hours.

**Camper Spaces:** Hardstand (106), E (110V/30A)/S/W hookups. Hardstand (12), E (220V/50A)/S/W hookups. Rates: $12 daily.

**Overflow:** 80, no hookups. Rates: $3 daily.

**SUPPORT FACILITIES:**

| | | |
|---|---|---|
| Auto Craft Shop | Bath House | Chapel |
| Commissary | Convenience Store | Equipment Rental |
| Exchange | Fitness Center | Gas |
| Golf | Ice | Laundry |
| Picnic Area | Playground | Pool (seasonal) |
| Rec Center | Restrooms* | Sewage Dump |
| Shoppette | Showers* | Snack Bar |
| Sports Fields | Stables | Telephones |
| Tennis Courts | | |

* Handicap accessible.

**ACTIVITIES:**

| | | |
|---|---|---|
| Golf | Horseback Riding | Swimming |
| Tennis | Tours Available (May-Sep) | Water Aerobics |

**CREDIT CARDS ACCEPTED:** Visa and MasterCard.

**RESTRICTIONS:** Pets allowed, except in buildings. Owners must keep pets on leash at all times and dispose of pet droppings. Firearms must be declared at Visitor Control upon entry. Fourteen day limit Jan-May.

# DESERT BREEZE TRAVEL CAMP (AZ21R4)

Yuma Army Proving Ground
Yuma, AZ 85365-9111

**TELEPHONE NUMBER INFORMATION:** Main installation numbers: C-520-329-8710, D-312-899-2151. Fax: C-520-328-3580.

**LOCATION:** On post. From I-8 N or S, take US-95 N and watch for gates. Also, from I-10 turn left on US-95 S. Exit US-95 at Yuma Proving Ground (YPG) sign and go five miles to main gate. FAMCAMP can also be entered from the road outside main gate. *USMRA: page 108 (A,B-7).* NMC: Yuma, 27 miles south.

*Desert Breeze Travel Camp, continued*

**DESCRIPTION OF AREA:** Located near the Colorado River in a desert area near California and Mexico. The Colorado River has numerous irrigation canals and hundreds of small lakes with excellent boating, fishing, swimming and water skiing opportunities. Various support facilities available on post.

**SEASON OF OPERATION:** Year round.

**ELIGIBILITY:** Active/Reservists/Retired.

**RESERVATIONS:** No advance reservations. First come, first serve basis. Address: STEYP-CS-MWR-TC, USAYPG, Yuma, AZ 85365-9111. **C-520-329-8710.** Fax: C-520-328-3580. Check in at Travel Camp Host, 0800-1700 hours.

**Camper Spaces:** 42, E (110V/20/30/50A)/S/W/CATV hookups. Rates: $10 daily/$55 weekly/$195 monthly. 12, E (110V/30A/50A)/S/W. Rates: $8 daily/$48 weekly/$165 monthly.

**SUPPORT FACILITIES:**

| | | |
|---|---|---|
| Bowling Center | Chapel | Commissary |
| Exchange | Gym | Laundry |

**ACTIVITIES:**

| | | |
|---|---|---|
| Arts/Crafts | Boating | Fishing |
| Hunting | | |

**CREDIT CARDS ACCEPTED:** None.

**RESTRICTIONS:** Pets allowed on leash, owner must clean up after pet. Firearms must be registered.

# FORT TUTHILL
# RECREATION AREA (AZ11R4)

Luke Air Force Base
Luke AFB, AZ 85309-1520

**TELEPHONE NUMBER INFORMATION:** Main installation numbers: C-602-856-0111, D-312-896-0111. Police for recreation area, call 911 (Coconino County Sheriff).

**LOCATION:** Off base. Located four miles south of Flagstaff. Take I-17 to exit 337 (Airport/Sedona). Enter park area at Fort Tuthill (adjoins Coconino County fairgrounds). Take first road to left. *USMRA: page 108 (E-4).* NMI: Luke AFB, 140 miles southwest. NMC: Flagstaff, 4 miles north.

**DESCRIPTION OF AREA:** Located at an elevation of 7,000 feet at the base of the San Francisco Peaks. Fort Tuthill Recreation Area was created in 1928 as a National Guard summer camp and it is the closest military lodging near the Grand Canyon, 80 miles away. Tall pines, mild summer temperatures, and skiing in the winter make this an ideal vacation spot. Many opportunities for both sportsperson and tourist within a 30-mile radius. Full range of support facilities at Luke AFB.

**SEASON OF OPERATION:** Hotel, Chalets, cabins and yurts: year round. Camping area: May-Oct.

**ELIGIBILITY:** Active/Reservists/Retired/DoD civilians.

**RESERVATIONS:** Required, confirm with credit card or mail deposit. Reservations are accepted at Fort Tuthill. Active duty military may make reservations for any 12 month period beginning with the month in which the reservation is made. All other authorized personnel may make reservations for any six month period beginning with the month in which the reservation is made. Reservations should be confirmed with a credit card. Check guarantees are due within ten days after the date the reservation is made. Cancellations must be received at least 48 hours in advance of arrival to avoid penalty fees. Address: Luke Recreation Area, HC 30, Box 5, Flagstaff, AZ 86001-8701. **C-1-800-552-6268, C-602-856-7990.** Fax: C-602-856-7990, D-312-896-3401, 24 daily. Check in after 1500 hours, check out 1100 hours.

**Multi Family Chalet:** Three-bedroom (1), furnished, E/S/W hookups. Rates: $150 daily.

**Chalets:** Two-bedroom (11), furnished, E/S/W hookups. Rates: $75 daily.

**Cabin:** 1, furnished, E/S/W hookups. Rates: $50 daily.

**Hotel:** Double (8), sleeps four. Rates: $40 daily. Queen (10-2 handicap accessible), sleeps two. Rates: $35 daily. Queen (2), sleeps two, kitchenette. Rates: $40 daily.

**Yurts:** 9, E (110V/30A) hookup. Rates: $25 daily. *Note: A yurt is a cabin/tent structure, 24 feet in diameter with wooden floor, deck and door, two windows, and stretched-canvas covering with skylight. It is furnished, but has no bathroom or kitchen.*

**Camper Spaces:** Gravel (21), E (110V/30A)/W hookups. Rates: $14 daily.

**Camper/Tent Spaces:** Gravel (13), no hookups. Rates: $9 daily.

*ARIZONA*
*Fort Tuthill Recreation Area, continued*

**SUPPORT FACILITIES:**

| | | |
|---|---|---|
| Arcade | Bicycle Rental | Canoe Rental |
| Conference Facility | Country Store | Golf |
| Grills | Handball | Laundry |
| Lodge | Picnic Area | Playground |
| Rec Equipment | Restrooms | RV Storage |
| Sewage Dump | Showers | Ski Equipment |
| Sports Fields | Tennis Courts | Theaters |

**ACTIVITIES:**

| | | |
|---|---|---|
| Boating | Day Trips | Fishing |
| Hiking | Horseback Riding | Hunting |
| Mountain Biking | Nature Trails | Outdoor Adventure |
| Trips | Sledding/Tubing | Snow Skiing |

**CREDIT CARDS ACCEPTED:** Visa, MasterCard and American Express.

**RESTRICTIONS:** No pets allowed in any rental unit. Pets allowed on leash in RV Area only. Firearms are permitted but must remain unloaded and secured in vehicle at all times.

## GILA BEND FAMCAMP (AZ15R4)

Gila Bend Air Force Auxiliary Field
Gila Bend AFAF, AZ 85337-5000

**TELEPHONE NUMBER INFORMATION:** Main installation numbers: C-520-683-6200, D-312-896-5200.

**LOCATION:** On base. From Phoenix, take I-10 W to AZ-85 S to Gila Bend. The Field is four miles out of town. Also, off I-8 between Yuma and Casa Grande. *USMRA: page 108 (C-8).* NMC: Phoenix, 80 miles northeast.

**DESCRIPTION OF AREA:** Located between Yuma and Phoenix in area that enjoys pleasant winter weather. Mountain areas and Mexico within easy driving distance. Limited support facilities available on base, full range of facilities available at Luke AFB.

**SEASON OF OPERATION:** Year round.

**ELIGIBILITY:** Active/Reservists/Retired/DoD and NAF civilians.

**RESERVATIONS:** No advance reservations. First come, first serve. Address: Lodging Office, HCO1 Box 22, Gila Bend AFAF, AZ 85337-5000. **C-520-683-6238/6211, D-312-896-5238/5211.** Host and hostess are present for check in and information (Nov-Mar); contact Lodging Office, Bldg 4300 during remainder of the year.

**Camper Spaces:** Gravel (42), E (110V/30A)/S/W/CATV hookups. Rates: $7 daily/flat fee.

**Dry Camp Area:** No hookups. Rates: $3 daily.

**SUPPORT FACILITIES:**

| | | |
|---|---|---|
| Basketball Court | Laundry Room | Lobby (with TV and |
| Mini Fitness Center | Picnic Area | card tables) |
| Sewage Dump | Tennis Courts | |

**ACTIVITIES:**

| | | |
|---|---|---|
| Basketball | Jogging | Tennis |

**CREDIT CARDS ACCEPTED:** Visa, MasterCard and American Express.

**RESTRICTIONS:** Pets allowed on leash. Animals must have rabies shots. Firearms must be registered in Arizona. Thirty day limit.

## LAKE MARTINEZ RECREATION FACILITY (AZ12R4)

Yuma Marine Corps Air Station
Yuma MCAS, AZ 85369-9131

**TELEPHONE NUMBER INFORMATION:** Main installation numbers: C-520-341-2278, D-312-951-2011.

**LOCATION:** Off base. Located on Colorado River 38 miles north of Yuma. North on US-95, left on Imperial Wildlife Refuge access road for approximately ten miles. Turn right at sign for USMC Recreation Area, follow road approximately two miles. *USMRA: page 108 (A-7).* NMI: Yuma Army Proving Ground, 15 miles north. NMC: Yuma, 38 miles south.

**DESCRIPTION OF AREA:** Located on land administered by the Bureau of Land Management. Area provides rustic semi-private fishing camp. Campground is barren desert peninsula extending into lake. Full range of support facilities available at Yuma US Army Proving Ground.

**SEASON OF OPERATION:** Year round.

**ELIGIBILITY:** Active/Reservists/Retired.

**RESERVATIONS:** Accepted. Address: MWR Ticket & Tours, Bldg 693, P.O. Box 99119, Yuma, AZ 85369-9119. **C-520-341-2278, D-312-951-2278** 0900-1800 hours Mon-Fri. Recreation Area: Martinez Lake Recreation Area, P.O. Box 72202, Martinez Lake, AZ 85365-5000. **C-520-783-3422.** Check in and out 1200 hours.

*Lake Martinez Recreation Facility, continued*

**Cabins:** 4, sleeps eight, furnished, kitchen, A/C. Patrons must provide dishes and linens. Rates: $40 daily (DoD add $1 daily).

**Mobile Homes:** 8, sleeps four, kitchen, A/C. Patrons must provide dishes and linens. Rates: $ 30 daily (DoD add $1 daily).

**Camper Spaces:** Hardstand (17), E (110V/20A)/W hookups. Rates: $7 daily/$180 monthly (DoD add $1 daily).

**Camper/Tent Spaces:** Primitive (3), no hookups. Rates: $5 daily (DoD add $1 daily).

**SUPPORT FACILITIES:**

| | | |
|---|---|---|
| Boat Rental | Grills | Picnic Area |
| Playground | Restrooms | Showers |
| Swimming Area | | |

**ACTIVITIES:**

| | | |
|---|---|---|
| Boating | Fishing | Horseshoes |
| Hunting | Swimming | Trails |

**CREDIT CARDS ACCEPTED:** None.

**RESTRICTIONS:** No pets allowed in mobile homes. Pets allowed on leash in other areas. No weapons allowed. No smoking allowed in mobile homes. Fourteen day limit for cabins and some campsites.

# ARKANSAS

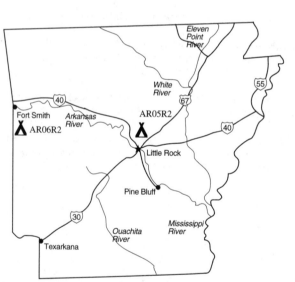

# CHAFFEE TRAILER PARK (AR06R2)

Fort Chaffee Maneuver Training Center
Fort Chaffee, AR 72905-5000

**TELEPHONE NUMBER INFORMATION:** Main installation numbers: C-501-484-2141, D-312-962-2141.

**LOCATION:** On post. From I-40 E or W, take the I-540 spur south to Fort Smith. From I-540, exit at Fort Chaffee exit 3 sign. Take Highway 59 S across Arkansas River to Highway 22, which goes past Fort Chaffee main gate. Five to six miles total. *USMRA: page 76 (A,B-4,5).* NMC: Fort Smith, 6 miles northwest.

**DESCRIPTION OF AREA:** Situated in a flat, wooded area near the Arkansas/Oklahoma state line. Limited support facilities available on post.

**SEASON OF OPERATION:** Year round.

**ELIGIBILITY:** Active/Reservists/Retired/Federal employees.

**RESERVATIONS:** Accepted up to two weeks in advance. Address: Bldg 1370, Fort Chaffee, AR 72905-5000. **C-501-484-2252/2917, D-312-962-2252/2917** 0730-1530 hours Mon-Thu, 0700-2000 hours Fri, 0700-1600 hours Sat-Sun. Check in at Golf Course, Bldg 3910, 0700-dark Sun-Sat.

**Camper Spaces:** Gravel (39), E (110/220V/20/30A)/S/W hookups. Rates: $6 daily/$150 monthly.

**SUPPORT FACILITIES:**

| | | |
|---|---|---|
| Bath House | Pool | Showers |

**ACTIVITIES:**

| | | |
|---|---|---|
| Golf | Fishing | Swimming |

**CREDIT CARDS ACCEPTED:** Visa, MasterCard, American Express and Discover.

**RESTRICTIONS:** Pets allowed on leash. No firearms allowed. Space is extremely limited during annual training in May through August. Camper spaces cannot accommodate mobile homes.

# LITTLE ROCK FAMCAMP (AR05R2)

Little Rock Air Force Base
Little Rock AFB, AR 72099-5288

**TELEPHONE NUMBER INFORMATION:** Main installation numbers: C-501-987-3131, D-312-731-1110. Police for FAMCAMP, C-501-987-3221.

**LOCATION:** On base. From US-67/167 southwest towards Jacksonville, follow signs to main gate. *USMRA: page 76 (D-5).* NMC: Little Rock, 10 miles southwest.

**DESCRIPTION OF AREA:** Located in central region of state in open terrain near lakes and wooded area. Full range of support facilities available on base.

**SEASON OF OPERATION:** Year round.

**ELIGIBILITY:** Active/Reservists/Retired/DoD civilians.

**RESERVATIONS:** No reservations accepted. Address: Recreation Services, 314 SVS/SVRO, 1255 Vandenberg, Little Rock AFB, AR 72099-5013. **C-501-987-3365, D-312-731-3365.** Fax: C-501-987-6164, D-312-731-6164. Check in at FAMCAMP, check out 1400 hours.

**Camper Spaces:** Hardstand (18), E (110V/30A)/W hookups. Rates: $10 daily. A $5 refundable deposit is required for key to enter bath house/laundry room.

**Camper Spaces:** Gravel (6), E (110V/30A)/W hookups. Rates: $10 daily. A $5 refundable deposit is required for key to enter bath house/laundry room.

**Tent Spaces:** 6, no hookups. Rates: $5 daily. A $5 refundable deposit is required for key to enter bath house/laundry room.

*ARKANSAS/CALIFORNIA*
*Little Rock FAMCAMP, continued*

**SUPPORT FACILITIES:**

| | | |
|---|---|---|
| Boat Rental | Camping Equipment | Chapel |
| Gas | Golf | Grills |
| Laundry | Picnic Area | Playground |
| Racquetball | Rec Center | Rec Equipment |
| Restrooms | Sewage Dump | Shoppette |
| Sports Fields | Tennis Courts | Trailer Rental |

**ACTIVITIES:**

| | | |
|---|---|---|
| Fishing/license | Hunting/license | Jogging |
| Racquetball | Tennis | |

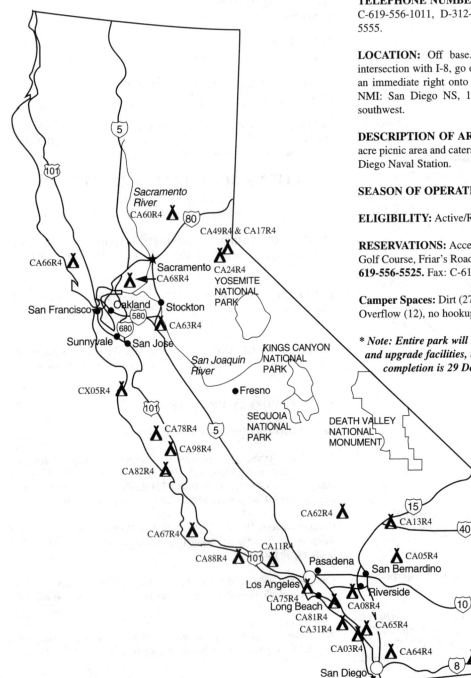

**CREDIT CARDS ACCEPTED:** Visa and MasterCard.

**RESTRICTIONS:** Pets allowed on leash. No firearms allowed. Seven day limit.

# CALIFORNIA

*See map below and to left.*

## ADMIRAL BAKER FIELD CAMPGROUND (CA64R4)

San Diego Naval Station
San Diego, CA 92136-5000

**TELEPHONE NUMBER INFORMATION:** Main installation numbers: C-619-556-1011, D-312-526-1011. Police for campground, C-619-556-5555.

**LOCATION:** Off base. From I-15 approximately .5 miles north of intersection with I-8, go east on Friar's Road, then left on Santo Road and an immediate right onto Admiral Baker Road. *USMRA: page 118 (D-4).* NMI: San Diego NS, 11 miles southwest. NMC: San Diego, 4 miles southwest.

**DESCRIPTION OF AREA:** Campground is located in the midst of 44-acre picnic area and caters to families. Full range of support facilities at San Diego Naval Station.

**SEASON OF OPERATION:** Year round.

**ELIGIBILITY:** Active/Reservists/Retired/DoD civilians.

**RESERVATIONS:** Accepted. Address: Mission Gorge RV Park, c/o Navy Golf Course, Friar's Road and Santo Road, San Diego, CA 92120-5000. **C-619-556-5525.** Fax: C-619-556-5501.

**Camper Spaces:** Dirt (27), E (110V/20/30A)/W hookups. Rates: $12 daily. Overflow (12), no hookups. Rates: $10 daily.

*** Note: Entire park will be undergoing renovations to add more spaces and upgrade facilities, including electricity. Estimated date of completion is 29 December 1998.**

# California's Central Coast

## One Stop Leisure Travel and Outdoor Recreation Center

### Outdoor Recreation
### Bldg. 228, Lewis Hall
### Presidio of Monterey, California
### (831) 242-5506/6133

**SKI OR SNOWBOARDING VACATIONS**
Specializing in the Lake Tahoe Area
Customized Ski Tours to all California Ski Areas
Lake Tahoe Accommodations
Motel - Condo - Cabins - A-Frame
Full Equipment Rental Center
Charter Bus Service
Airline Connections

**RENTAL EQUIPMENT CENTER**
Camping
Boating
Skiing
SCUBA
Fishing
Water Sports
Mountain Bikes
Rollerblades

**LEISURE TICKETS - TOURS - LODGING**
Tickets to all California Attractions
Discount Lodging
Customized Tour Program
Rental Cars
Charter Bus Service

**SCUBA DIVING**
Dive Monterey Bay National Marine Sanctuary
Dive Boats on the Water
Full Dive Equipment Rental Center
NAUI & PADI Certification & Instruction
Snorkel Packages
Intro to Scuba Experience
Lodging Facilities
Connections to all California Diving Destinations

(831) 242-5506/6133　♦　FAX: (831) 242-6310

*CALIFORNIA*
*Admiral Baker Field Campground, continued*

**SUPPORT FACILITIES:**

| | | |
|---|---|---|
| Golf | Grills | Picnic Area |
| Playground | Pool | Rec Equipment |
| Sewage Dump | Showers/at pool | Sports Fields |
| Tennis Courts | | |

**ACTIVITIES:**

| | |
|---|---|
| Basketball | Swimming |

**CREDIT CARDS ACCEPTED:** Visa and MasterCard.

**RESTRICTIONS:** Pets allowed on leash in campground area only. Must keep noise down and clean up after pet. No tent camping.

## BARSTOW RV CAMP (CA13R4)

Barstow Marine Corps Logistics Base
Barstow MCLB, CA 92311-5001

**TELEPHONE NUMBER INFORMATION:** Main installation numbers: C-760-577-6211, D-312-282-611/2.

**LOCATION:** Located on Barstow MCLB. On I-40, 1.5 miles east of Barstow. Take I-15 NE from San Bernardino, or west from Las Vegas, NV. Signs mark direction to MCLB. NMC: San Bernardino, 60 miles southwest.

**DESCRIPTION OF AREA:** Located near the Mojave Desert. Calico Ghost Town, Solar One and Lake Dolores are nearby.

**SEASON OF OPERATION:** Year round.

**ELIGIBILITY:** Active/Reservists/Retired.

**RESERVATIONS:** Address: Food & Hospitality Branch, Bldg 44, Barstow MCLB, CA 92311-5047. **C-760-577-6418.** Fax: 760-577-6542.

**RV/Camper Spaces:** 11, E (110V/20A)/S/W hookups. 9, E (110V/20A)/W hookups. Rates: $5 daily.

**SUPPORT FACILITIES:**
Sewage Dump

**ACTIVITIES:**

| | |
|---|---|
| Hiking | Golf |

**CREDIT CARDS ACCEPTED:** Visa, MasterCard and American Express.

**RESTRICTIONS:** Pets allowed in camping area.

## BEALE AFB FAMCAMP (CA60R4)

Beale Air Force Base
Beale AFB, CA 95903-1525

**TELEPHONE NUMBER INFORMATION:** Main installation numbers: C-530-634-3000, D-312-368-3000. Police for FAMCAMP, C-530-634-2131.

**LOCATION:** On base. Take US-70 S from Marysville for approximately one mile to Beale AFB exit. Follow signs to main gate, approximately ten miles. Clearly marked. *USMRA: page 110 (D-6).* NMC: Sacramento, 40 miles southwest.

**DESCRIPTION OF AREA:** Located in northern California in the midst of a variety of interesting recreational opportunities. Two hour drive to Reno. Full range of support facilities on base.

**SEASON OF OPERATION:** Year round.

**ELIGIBILITY:** Active/Reservists/Retired/DoD civilians.

**RESERVATIONS:** No advance reservations. First come, first serve. Address: Beale AFB FAMCAMP, 9 SVS/SVRO, 6000 C Street, Room 111, Beale AFB, CA 95903-5000. **C-530-634-3382/2054, D-312-368-3382/2054** 1000-1730 hours Sun-Mon, Thu-Sat.

**Camper Spaces:** Hardstand (44), handicap accessible, E (110V/30A and 220/50A)/S/W hookups, self-contained vehicles only. Rates: $8-$11 daily. Check out 1200 hours.

**Tent Spaces:** Grass (6), no hookups. Rates: $5 daily.

**SUPPORT FACILITIES:**

| | | |
|---|---|---|
| Auto Craft Shop | Boat Rental | Camping Equipment |
| Chapel | Commissary | Exchange |
| Fitness Center | Gas | Golf |
| Grills | Ice | Laundry |
| Pavilion | Picnic Area | Pool |
| Rec Center | Restrooms* | Sewage Dump |
| Shoppette | Showers* | Skeet Range |
| Snack Bar | Sports Fields | Telephones |
| Tennis Courts | Trails | |

**ACTIVITIES:**

| | | |
|---|---|---|
| Fishing/license | Hunting/license | Snow Skiing |
| Whitewater Rafting | | |

**CREDIT CARDS ACCEPTED:** Visa, MasterCard and Air Force Club Card.

**RESTRICTIONS:** Pets allowed on leash. Policy on firearms is in accordance with Air Force Regulations and California state laws. Tents allowed with port-a-potty (self-contained).

## BIG BEAR RECREATION FACILITY (CA05R4)

Miramar Marine Corps Air Station
San Diego, CA 92145-2008

**TELEPHONE NUMBER INFORMATION:** Main installation numbers: C-619-537-4141, D-312-577-4141.

**LOCATION:** Off base. Located at Big Bear Lake. From I-10 at Redlands, take CA-30 N a short distance to CA-38. East on CA-38; left on Big Bear Blvd (CA-18); left on Moon Ridge Blvd, then right on Elm. (If you look carefully, you'll see a small sign for Big Bear Recreation Area.) Right on Switzerland and then an immediate left. *Note: Don't be tempted to take a shortcut through Snow Summit Ski Area as many people have been stuck in snow and mud on the forestry service road over which you must travel. USMRA: page 111 (G-13).* NMI: March ARB, approximately 30 miles southwest. NMC: San Bernardino, 50 miles southwest.

**DESCRIPTION OF AREA:** Centrally located 7,000 feet above sea level between Snow Summit and Bear Mountain ski resorts in the San Bernardino National Forest. Area offers excellent fishing, boating, hiking and skiing. Full range of support facilities available at March ARB.

**SEASON OF OPERATION:** Cabins: Year round; RV campsites: May-Oct.

**ELIGIBILITY:** Active/Reservists/Retired/DoD civilians.

**RESERVATIONS:** Required. Address for cabin reservation: MWR Department, ITT-Big Bear, MCAS Miramar, P.O. Box 452008, San Diego, CA 92145-2008. **C-619-537-4141, D-312-577-4141.** For Recreation Facility general information and campsite reservations: Big Bear Recreation Facility, P.O. Box 1664, Big Bear Lake, CA 92315-1664. **C-909-866-3965.** Fax: C-909-866-4069.

**Cabins:** One-bedroom (8), some handicap accessible, sleeps six, queen size bed, two double beds in loft, refrigerator, microwave, gas range, utensils, fireplace, TV/VCR, picnic table, grill. Patrons must provide toiletries, kitchen linens, radio. Active duty at MCAS Miramar have priority. Rates: $45-$65 daily (Depending on season, day of week, length of stay and status of sponsor).

**Camper/Tent Spaces:** Paved (5), E (110V/30A)/W hookups. Rates: $12 daily.

**SUPPORT FACILITIES:**

| | | |
|---|---|---|
| Bicycle Rental | Boat Rental | Grills |
| Group Fire Pit w/BBQ | Picnic Area | Playground |
| Rec Equipment | Restrooms | Showers |
| Snow Play Area | | |

**ACTIVITIES:**

| | | |
|---|---|---|
| Boating | Fishing | Hiking |
| Horseshoes | Snow Skiing | Volleyball |
| Water Skiing | | |

**CREDIT CARDS ACCEPTED:** Visa and MasterCard.

**RESTRICTIONS:** No pets allowed. No firearms (including air-powered and bow weapons) allowed. No campfires. Quiet hours 2200-0800 hours. No fireworks. No wood may be burned in cabin fireplace, use pressed logs only. Maximum of eight occupants per site.

## CAMP ROBERTS (CA98R4)

Camp Roberts
Camp Roberts, CA 93451-5000

**TELEPHONE NUMBER INFORMATION:** Main installation number: C-805-238-8390.

**LOCATION:** On post. Eleven miles north of Paso Robels on Highway 101 on the left hand side. Two miles north of the historic mission San Miguel. *USMRA: page 111 (C-10).* NMC: San Miguel, in city limits.

**DESCRIPTION OF AREA:** RV area in process of being landscaped.

**SEASON OF OPERATION:** Year round.

**ELIGIBILITY:** Active/Reservists/Retired.

**RESERVATIONS:** Accepted. Address: Billeting, Bldg 6038, Camp Roberts, CA 93451-5000. **C-805-238-8312, D-312-949-8312** 0800-1630 Mon-Fri. Fax: C-805-238-8384. Check in at Billeting, Bldg 6038.

**Camper Spaces:** Hardstand (12), E (110V/30A)/S/W hookups. Rates: $10 daily.

**ACTIVITIES:**

| | |
|---|---|
| Fishing | Hunting |

**CREDIT CARDS ACCEPTED:** Visa, MasterCard, American Express and Discover.

**RESTRICTIONS:** Pets allowed on leash.

## CAMP SAN LUIS OBISPO RV PARK (CA82R4)

Camp San Luis Obispo
San Luis Obispo, CA 93403-4360

**TELEPHONE NUMBER INFORMATION:** Main installation numbers: C-805-594-6500.

**LOCATION:** On post. Take CA-1 for five miles northwest to the city of San Luis Obispo. *USMRA: page 111 (C-11).* NMC: San Luis Obispo, 5 miles southeast.

**DESCRIPTION OF AREA:** Located on California Central Coast in an area offering a variety of entertainment, sports, sightseeing and tourist activities, including Mission San Luis Obispo, Hearst Castle and Morro Rock. Limited support facilities available on post; full range of facilities available at Vandenberg AFB, 60 miles south.

**SEASON OF OPERATION:** Year round.

**ELIGIBILITY:** Active/Reservists/Retired/Federal and State employees.

**RESERVATIONS:** Accepted. Address: Billeting Office, Camp San Luis Obispo, P.O. Box 4360, San Luis Obispo, CA 93403-4360. **C-805-594-6500.**

**Camper Spaces:** Hardstand (4), E (110V/30A)/S/W hookups. Rates: $10 daily. Hardstand (8), E (110V/30A)/W hookups. $8 daily.

**Tent Spaces:** Primitive; no hookups. Rates: $5 daily.

**SUPPORT FACILITIES:**

| | | |
|---|---|---|
| Chapel/summer | Exchange | Grills |
| Laundry | Picnic Area | Playground |
| Restrooms | Sewage Dump | Showers |

**ACTIVITIES:**

| | | |
|---|---|---|
| Fishing | Jogging | Sightseeing |

**CREDIT CARDS ACCEPTED:** Visa, MasterCard and American Express.

**RESTRICTIONS:** No pets. No firearms allowed.

## CHANNEL ISLANDS HARBOR FAMILY RECREATIONAL FACILITY (CA88R4)

Channel Islands Coast Guard Station
Oxnard, CA 93035-5000

**TELEPHONE NUMBER INFORMATION:** Main installation numbers: C-805-985-9822.

**LOCATION:** On base. West of Los Angeles. From US-101 at Oxnard take Victoria Avenue exit south past Channel Islands Blvd to Coast Guard Station on right. *USMRA: page 111 (D-13).* NMI: Port Hueneme Naval Construction Battalion Center, adjacent. NMC: Los Angeles, 60 miles southeast.

**DESCRIPTION OF AREA:** Located near the southern coast of California at Channel Islands Harbor. Minutes away from water sports, charter boat fishing, shopping and bicycle touring and within easy driving distance of world-famous tourist attractions in the Los Angeles area. Full range of support facilities available at Port Hueneme Naval Construction Battalion Center.

*CALIFORNIA*
*Channel Islands Harbor Family Recreational Facility, continued*

**SEASON OF OPERATION:** Year round.

**ELIGIBILITY:** Active/Reservists/Retired.

**RESERVATIONS:** Required, by application only. Reservations should be made no more than 50 days in advance. Address: Commanding Officer, US Coast Guard Station, Channel Islands Harbor, 4201 Victoria Avenue, Oxnard, CA 93035-8399. **C-805-985-9822.** Fax: C-805-984-1842. Check in with OOD, 0800-1630 hours.

**Camper Spaces:** Gravel (6), E (110V/30A)/W hookups. Rates: $6 daily.

**SUPPORT FACILITIES:**

| | | |
|---|---|---|
| Grills | Pavilion | Picnic Area |
| Playground | Sewage Dump | Tennis |

**ACTIVITIES:**

| | | |
|---|---|---|
| Bicycling | Boating | Fishing |
| Hiking | Horseshoes | Surfing |
| Swimming | Touring | Volleyball |

**CREDIT CARDS ACCEPTED:** None.

**RESTRICTIONS:** Pets allowed on leash, owner must clean up after pet daily. Firearms must be secured in trunk. No open fires. No restrooms. No tents allowed. Fourteen day limit that can be extended at command discretion.

## DEL MAR BEACH COTTAGES/ CAMPSITES (CA03R4)

Camp Pendleton Marine Corps Base
Camp Pendleton MCB, CA 92055-5019

**TELEPHONE NUMBER INFORMATION:** Main installation numbers: C-760-725-4111, D-312-365-4111.

**LOCATION:** On base. From San Diego, I-5 N to Camp Pendleton main gate. From I-15, take Fallbrook exit, follow signs to Fallbrook and go through Fallbrook Naval Weapons Station gate to mainside Camp Pendleton. *USMRA: page 111 (F-15).* NMC: Oceanside, 1 mile south.

**DESCRIPTION OF AREA:** Located in southern California approximately 90 miles south of Los Angeles. Exit Camp Pendleton from I-5. Campsites situated on 26 miles of Pacific Ocean shoreline. Full range of support facilities available on base.

**SEASON OF OPERATION:** Year round (some restrictions).

**ELIGIBILITY:** Active/Reservists/Retired/DoD civilians/MWR.

**RESERVATIONS:** Accepted by phone or in person, with payment in full due four weeks in advance of reservation; up to 12 weeks in advance for active duty at Camp Pendleton; up to ten weeks in advance for other active duty; up to ten weeks in advance for retirees and reserve. Address: AC/S MWR, Attn: Financial Management Division, Box 555020, Camp Pendleton, CA 92055-5020. **C-760-725-2134** 0800-1600 hours. Check in 1400-1630 hours, late arrivals (until 2300 hours only) should pick up the key at security. *Note: Other camping facilities for Camp Pendleton include Lake O'Neill and San Onofre Beach.*

**Cottages:** One-bedroom (48), full kitchen. Patrons must provide bed linens, blankets, pillows, towels, detergent, radio, and firewood for use in designated fire rings on the beach. Rates: $35 daily (winter rates available; security deposit required).

**Mobile Home:** Double wide, four bedroom (1), sleeps 12, two baths. Rates: $65 daily (winter rates available; security deposit required). Two-bedroom (7), sleeps six, double bed, two sets of bunk beds, microwave, TV. Rates: $40 daily (winter rates available; security deposit required).

**Camper Spaces:** Paved (17), E (110V/30A)/W hookups. Hardpack (39), E (110V/30A)/W hookups. Beach (28), E (110V/30A)/W hookups. Rates: $15 daily (winter rates available; security deposit required).

**SUPPORT FACILITIES:**

| | | |
|---|---|---|
| Bicycle Route | Boat Rental/Supply | Cabanas |
| Chapel | Charter Fishing | Fire Rings |
| Golf | Marina | Picnic Area |
| Racquetball | Rec Equipment | Sewage Dump |
| Snow Ski/nearby | Tennis Courts | |

**ACTIVITIES:**

| | | |
|---|---|---|
| Fishing | Jogging | Swimming |

**CREDIT CARDS ACCEPTED:** Visa, MasterCard, American Express and Discover.

**RESTRICTIONS:** No pets. No firearms allowed. No bottles or glass containers on beach.

## EDWARDS FAMCAMP (CA62R4)

Edwards Air Force Base
Edwards AFB, CA 93524-1860

**TELEPHONE NUMBER INFORMATION:** Main installation numbers: C-805-277-1110, D-312-527-0111. Police for FAMCAMP, C-805-277-3340.

**LOCATION:** On base. Off CA-14, 18 miles east of Rosamond and 30 miles northeast of Lancaster. Also, off CA-58 ten miles southwest of Boron. Check in at FAMCAMP space #26. Follow *USMRA: page 111 (F-12).* NMC: Los Angeles, 90 miles southwest.

**DESCRIPTION OF AREA:** Located in Mojave-Lancaster-Barstow section of California's hilly desert region northeast of Los Angeles metropolitan area. Convenient base for visiting Lake Arrowhead and other points of interest in the San Bernardino-Pasadena-Los Angeles complex. Full range of support facilities available on base.

**SEASON OF OPERATION:** Year round.

**ELIGIBILITY:** Active/Reservists/Retired/DoD civilians.

**RESERVATIONS:** No advance reservations. Address: FAMCAMP, 36 N Wolfe Avenue, Bldg 7211, Edwards AFB, CA 93524-1510. **C-805-277-3546, D-312-527-3546** 0800-2000 hours. Unattended check in. *Note: Renovations planned for the summer of 1998 include a 50 Amp Electrical Service and a new building with showers, restrooms, telephones and a laundromat.*

**Camper Spaces:** Hardstand (26), handicap accessible, E (110V/30A)/S/W hookups. Rates: $11 daily.

**Camper Spaces:** Overflow, hardstand (10), handicap accessible no hookups. Rates: $5 daily.

**Tent Spaces:** Grass (10), no hookups. Rates: $5 daily.

**SUPPORT FACILITIES:**

| | | |
|---|---|---|
| Auto Craft Shop | Bath House | Boat Rental/Storage |
| Bowling Alley | Chapel | Commissary |
| Convenience Store | Exchange | Fishing Pier |

*Edwards FAMCAMP, continued*

| | | |
|---|---|---|
| Fitness Center | Gas | Golf |
| Grills | Ice | Laundry |
| Museums | Picnic Area | Playground |
| Pools/indoor, outdoor | Racquetball | Rec Center |
| Rec Equipment | Restrooms | Sewage Dump |
| Shoppette | Showers | Shuttle Bus |
| Skeet/Trap Range | Snack Bar | Sports Fields |
| Stables | Telephones | Tennis Courts |
| Trails | | |

**ACTIVITIES:**

| | | |
|---|---|---|
| Bowling | Fishing | NASA tours/gift shop |
| Racquetball | Rod and Gun Club | Swimming |

**CREDIT CARDS ACCEPTED:** Visa and MasterCard.

**RESTRICTIONS:** Pets allowed in designated areas. No firearms allowed. No open fires. No feeding of wild animals. Fifteen day limit.

## EL CENTRO NAF CAMPGROUND (CA76R4)

El Centro Naval Air Facility
El Centro NAF, CA 92243-5001

**TELEPHONE NUMBER INFORMATION:** Main installation numbers: C-760-339-2524, D-312-958-2524.

**LOCATION:** On base. From I-8 E or W, two miles west of El Centro, to Forrester Road exit, 1.5 miles to left on Evan Hewes Highway west for four miles. Turn right on Bennet Road to main gate. Clearly marked. *USMRA: page 111 (H-15,16)*. NMC: Yuma AZ, 60 miles east.

**DESCRIPTION OF AREA:** Located in the Imperial Valley of southern California. Climate is warm and dry with more sunshine recorded in the area than in any other in the United States. Temperatures can reach 120° Jun through Aug. Full range of support facilities available on base.

**SEASON OF OPERATION:** Year round.

**ELIGIBILITY:** Active/Reservists/Retired/DoD civilians.

**RESERVATIONS:** No advance reservations. Address: MWR, Bldg 318, Naval Air Facility, El Centro, CA 92243-5001. **C-760-339-2486, D-312-958-8481** 0800-1630 Mon-Fri. Fax: C-760-339-2326. Camp Host is located at Space 43. Check in at Recreation Equipment Rental, Bldg 318, check out 1200 hours.

**Camper Spaces:** Hardstand (82), up to 35', E (110/120V/30/50A)/S/W hookups. Phone and CATV in old park at site expense. Rates: $8-$9 daily (varies with season).

**Dry Camp:** Unlimited, no hookups. Rates: $3 daily.

**SUPPORT FACILITIES:**

| | | |
|---|---|---|
| Auto Craft Shop | Boat Rental | Chapel |
| Commissary | Driving Range | Exchange |
| Fitness Center | Gas/LP | Golf* |
| Grills | Hobby Shop | Ice |
| Laundry | Movies | Picnic Area |
| Pool | Racquet Sports | Rec Equipment |
| Restrooms | Sewage Dump | Showers |
| Snack Bar | Sports Fields | Telephones |
| Trailer Rental | | |

* Three nearby golf courses.

**ACTIVITIES:**

| | | |
|---|---|---|
| Fishing | Hunting (Dove) | Off Roading |
| Swimming | Water Skiing | |

**CREDIT CARDS ACCEPTED:** None.

**RESTRICTIONS:** Pets allowed, must be confined at all times (leash, cage, inside RV, etc). Pets are not allowed on the running track or football field. Firearms must be checked at Security.

## EL TORO CAMPGROUNDS (CA81R4)

El Toro Marine Corps Air Station
Santa Ana, CA 92709-5000
*Scheduled to close June 1999.*

**TELEPHONE NUMBER INFORMATION:** Main installation numbers: C-714-726-3011, D-312-997-3100. Police for campgrounds, C-714-726-6767/3525.

**LOCATION:** On base. Take I-5 N or S, take the Sand Canyon Road exit east, and follow signs to MCAS. *USMRA: page 117 (H-7,8)*. NMC: Anaheim, 15 miles northwest.

**DESCRIPTION OF AREA:** The campsites are located near the picnic grounds. The Lodge offers a limited number of transient rooms. However, when they are filled, the staff will be happy to contact local commercial facilities and obtain accommodations at greatly discounted rates. The area surrounding the MCAS offers many attractions for residents and visitors alike, among them are Disneyland, Anaheim Stadium, Marineland, Crystal Cathedral, mountains, beaches and boating. All are easy to reach. Full range of support facilities available on base.

**SEASON OF OPERATION:** Year round.

**ELIGIBILITY:** Active/Reservists/Retired/DoD civilians.

**RESERVATIONS:** Preferred, up to 30 days in advance. Address: ITT Office, MWR/MCAS, El Toro, P.O. Box 94008, Santa Ana, CA 92709-4008. **C-714-726-2572/2626, D-312-997-2572/2626.**

**Camper Spaces:** 4, E (110V/20A)/S/W hookups. Rates: $12 daily. 21, E/W hookups. Rates: $9 daily. 2, E (110V/20A) hookup. Rates: $7. 6, no hookups. Rates: $4.

**Tents:** 4, no hookups. Rates: $5.

**SUPPORT FACILITIES:**

| | | |
|---|---|---|
| Golf | Grills | Playground |
| Restroom | Roller Hockey Rink | Showers/gym |
| Sports Field | Tennis Courts | Track |

**ACTIVITIES:**

| | | |
|---|---|---|
| Jogging | Sightseeing | Softball |

**CREDIT CARDS ACCEPTED:** Visa, MasterCard and American Express.

**RESTRICTIONS:** Pets allowed on leash. No firearms allowed; all firearms on base must be stored at the armory. Seven day limit.

## FIDDLER'S COVE RV PARK (CA87R4)

Coronado Naval Amphibious Base
San Diego, CA 92155-5000

**TELEPHONE NUMBER INFORMATION:** Main installation numbers: C-619-437-2011, D-312-577-2011. Police for RV park, C-619-437-3432.

*CALIFORNIA*
*Fiddler's Cove RV Park, continued*

**LOCATION:** Off base. From the north, on I-5 in San Diego, take Coronado Bridge exit; cross bridge and go south (left) on CA-75 (Orange Avenue). From the south on I-5, exit to Palm Avenue W, which later becomes CA-75. RV Park is next to Naval Amphibious Base Marina (Navy Yacht Club) and Aquatic Sports Center. *USMRA: page 118 (D-8).* NMI: Coronado Naval Amphibious Base, 1.5 miles north. NMC: San Diego, 6.5 miles northeast.

**DESCRIPTION OF AREA:** Situated on east side of Silver Strand facing San Diego Bay and within .5 miles of the Pacific Ocean and state beach. Popular activities include tours of historic sites, shopping in Tijuana, and attractions in San Diego. Full range of support facilities available on base.

**SEASON OF OPERATION:** Year round.

**ELIGIBILITY:** Active/Reservists/Retired/DoD civilians.

**RESERVATIONS:** Accepted up to 90 days in advance. Address: Fiddler's Cove RV Park, c/o NAS NI MWR, Dept Code 92, Box 357081, San Diego, CA 92135-7081. **C-619-435-8788/4700** 1000-1830 hours Mon-Fri, 0830-1830 hours Sat-Sun. Fax: C-619-437-1389. Check in at RV Office/ Shoppette, Bldg 1203; check out 1100 hours.

**Camper Spaces:** Hardstand (50), E (110V/30A)/W hookups. Rates: $17 daily/$105 weekly (special rates for groups of seven or more RVs).

**SUPPORT FACILITIES:**

| | | |
|---|---|---|
| Beach | Boat Landing | Boat Rental |
| Boat Slip Rental | Fire Rings | Laundry |
| Marina | Patio/covered | Picnic Area |
| Restrooms* | Sewage Dump | Shoppette |
| Showers | Snack Bar | |

* Restrooms undergoing renovation.

**ACTIVITIES:**

| | | |
|---|---|---|
| Bicycling | Boating | Fishing |
| Jogging | Sailing | |

**CREDIT CARDS ACCEPTED:** Visa and MasterCard.

**RESTRICTIONS:** Pets allowed on leash in campground, owner must keep noise down and clean up after pet. No open fires except in designated areas. Towed cars can be parked outside of gate, local bus is available.

## FORT HUNTER LIGGETT PRIMITIVE CAMPGROUND (CA78R4)

Fort Hunter Liggett
Fort Hunter Liggett, CA 93928-5000

**TELEPHONE NUMBER INFORMATION:** Main installation numbers: C-831-386-3310, D-312-6862677. Police for campground, C-831-386-2513/2526.

**LOCATION:** On post. From US-101 S, exit at King City to CA-G-14, south to main gate. Immediately after Military Police booth, left on Alamo Road .5 miles to a right at the fork. Register at Outdoor Rec, Bldg T-630 on left. *USMRA: page 111 (C-10).* NMC: San Luis Obispo, 75 miles south.

**DESCRIPTION OF AREA:** Located approximately five miles from post headquarters in a primitive area abounding in wildlife, including protected species. Observe tule elk, bald eagles, kit fox, pumas, bobcats, and more. Excellent opportunities for hunting and fishing. Visit Mission San Antonio. Limited support facilities available on post.

**SEASON OF OPERATION:** Year round; self serve system-24 hours daily.

**ELIGIBILITY:** Open to public.

**RESERVATIONS:** No advance reservations. Address: Outdoor Recreation, Fort Hunter Liggett, P.O. Box 7130, Jolon, CA 93928-7130. **C-831-386-2550.** Check out 1200 hours.

**Camper/Tent Spaces:** Graded (20), central W hookup. Rates: $5 daily.

**Overflow:** Open during peak seasons, no hookups. Rates: $3 daily.

**SUPPORT FACILITIES:**

| | | |
|---|---|---|
| Archery | Equipment Rental | Fire Rings |
| Grills | Restrooms | Tables |

**ACTIVITIES:**

| | |
|---|---|
| Fishing/license | Hunting/license |

**CREDIT CARDS ACCEPTED:** Visa and MasterCard.

**RESTRICTIONS:** Pets allowed on leash, $1 fee daily. No discharging of firearms allowed in or around camp area. No sidearms with less than a six inch barrel. All rifles must be center fire. Open fires prohibited except in containers or site grills. Quiet hours 2200-0600 hours. Horses not allowed for hunting. Call C-831-386-3310 for specific information on hunting and fishing.

## LAKE O'NEILL RECREATION PARK (CA65R4)

Camp Pendleton Marine Corps Base
Camp Pendleton MCB, CA 92055-5019

**TELEPHONE NUMBER INFORMATION:** Main installation numbers: C-760-725-4111, D-312-365-4111. Police for recreation park, C-760-725-3888/911.

**LOCATION:** On base. From San Diego, I-5 N to Camp Pendleton main gate. Also, from I-15 take Fallbrook exit, follow signs to Fallbrook and go through Fallbrook Naval Weapons Station gate to mainside Camp Pendleton. *USMRA: page 111 (F-15).* NMC: Oceanside, 10 miles southwest.

**DESCRIPTION OF AREA:** Twelve square-mile facility on northern side of Lake O'Neill. Southern side offers a large variety of recreational activities. Full range of support facilities available on base.

**SEASON OF OPERATION:** Year round.

**ELIGIBILITY:** Active/Reservists/Retired.

**RESERVATIONS:** Accepted in person or by telephone, up to 12 weeks in advance for active duty stationed on Marine Corps installations; up to ten weeks in advance for other active duty and retirees; up to nine weeks in advance for all other authorized patrons. Reservations by mail not accepted. Payment required two weeks in advance. Address: AC/S MWR, Attn: Recreation Division, Lake O'Neill, Box 555020, Camp Pendleton, CA 92055-5020. **C-760-725-4241, D-312-365-4241.** *Note: Other camping facilities for Camp Pendleton include Del Mar Beach and San Onofre Beach.*

**Camper Spaces:** Paved (5), E (110V/30A)/S/W hookups. Rates: $15 daily. Paved (40), E (110V/220)/W hookups. Rates: $12 daily. Gravel (20), W hookup. Rates: $10 daily.

**Camper/Tent Spaces:** Dirt (52), no hookups. Rates: $6-$8 daily.

*Lake O'Neill Recreation Park, continued*

**SUPPORT FACILITIES:**

| | | |
|---|---|---|
| Boat Rental | Grills | LP Gas |
| Mini Golf | Playground | Picnic Area |
| Restrooms | Sewage Dump | Showers |
| Sports Fields | | |

**ACTIVITIES:**

| | | |
|---|---|---|
| Basketball | Fishing | Horseshoes |
| Softball | Volleyball | |

**CREDIT CARDS ACCEPTED:** Visa, MasterCard, American Express and Discover.

**RESTRICTIONS:** Pets allowed on leash. Swimming in lake is prohibited.

## LAKE TAHOE COAST GUARD RECREATION FACILITIES (CA24R4)

Lake Tahoe Coast Guard Group
Tahoe City, CA 96145-5000

**TELEPHONE NUMBER INFORMATION:** Main installation numbers: C-530-583-7438 (0700-1500 hours Mon-Fri). Police for recreation facilities, C-911.

**LOCATION:** On base. Take I-80 to CA-89 (N Lake Blvd), south through Tahoe City, north on CA-28 to Lake Forest Blvd, right to USCG Station Lake Tahoe (marked). *USMRA: page 110 (E-6).* NMI: McClellan AFB, Sacramento CA, 80 miles southwest. NMC: Reno NV, 45 miles northeast.

**DESCRIPTION OF AREA:** Located at Coast Guard Station Lake Tahoe on northwest shore of the beautiful lake which is on the California/Nevada border in the heart of the Sierra Nevada Mountains at 6,225 feet above sea level. Much to do and see in nearby cities of Reno and Carson City. Many recreational activities available on Lake Tahoe and surrounding Sierra Nevada mountains. Full range of support facilities available at McClellan AFB.

**SEASON OF OPERATION:** Year round.

**ELIGIBILITY:** Active/Reservists/Retired/CG NAF and other Federal Civilians.

**RESERVATIONS:** Required, by written application only, with payment in full, 45-60 days in advance. Address: A-Frame Coordinator, Coast Guard Station Lake Tahoe, 2500 Lake Forest Road, P.O. Box 882, Tahoe City, CA 96145-0882. **C-530-583-7438** (Leave name, phone, and address). Check in 1600-2000 hours with caretaker check out 1100 hours.

**A-Frame Cottages:** Two-bedroom apartment (2), sleeps nine, private bath, furnished, kitchen, microwave, heat, CATV. Only one apartment will be rented to any applicant. Rates: $30-$45 daily (minimum rates, depending on rank of sponsor and number of persons). One-bedroom (2), sleeps seven, private bath, furnished, kitchen, microwave, heat, CATV. Rates: $15-$30 (minimum rates, depending on rank of sponsor and number of persons).

**SUPPORT FACILITIES:** Boat launch. There are no other military support facilities available but nearby businesses offer marina, boat rental and boat launch facilities.

**ACTIVITIES:**

| | | |
|---|---|---|
| Boating | Fishing | Hiking |
| Picnicking | Playground | Sailing |
| Skiing | Swimming | Water Skiing |

**CREDIT CARDS ACCEPTED:** None.

**RESTRICTIONS:** No pets allowed. Twelve day limit, to include only one weekend. This unit is an operational Search and Rescue and Law Enforcement Unit. Check in is handled by duty personnel on a not-to-interfere basis. Persons residing in the cabins are not allowed to loiter in the area of the main station building.

## LAKE TAHOE OAKLAND CONDOMINIUMS (CA49R4)

Oakland Army Base
Oakland Army Base, CA 94626-5000
*Scheduled to close September 1999.*

**TELEPHONE NUMBER INFORMATION:** Main installation numbers: C-510-466-9111, D-312-859-9111.

**LOCATION:** Off post. Located at Lake Tahoe. Specific directions may be obtained from Jacobs Hall Guest House at the address shown below. *USMRA: page 110 (E-6).* NMI: McClellan AFB, Sacramento CA, 110 miles southwest. NMC: Carson City NV, 30 miles southeast.

**DESCRIPTION OF AREA:** The Oakland Army Base has leased one condominium on both the south and north shore of Lake Tahoe for year-round enjoyment. They are conveniently located for taking advantage of a wide range of mountain and water-oriented recreational activities. Casinos are located within a few miles. Full range of support facilities available at McClellan AFB.

**SEASON OF OPERATION:** Year round.

**ELIGIBILITY:** Active/Reservists/Retired/US Government civilian employees.

**RESERVATIONS:** Accepted up to six months in advance with payment/deposit. Address: Jacobs Hall Guest Facility, Bldg 650, Oakland Army Base, CA 94626-5000. **C-510-444-8107, D-312-859-3113.** Fax: C-510-466-2997.

**CONDOS:**

**Keys Waterfront Condo:** 1, sleeps ten, two baths, full kitchen, fireplace, two sun decks. Also, indoor and outdoor pool, tennis courts, private beach, sauna and nearby playground. Rates: $70 daily (two to five night stay, Sun-Thu), $80 daily (Sun-Thu), $95 daily (Fri-Sat, holidays), $500 seven-day package, $50 refundable key/cleaning deposit.

**Tahoe City Condo:** 1, 2.5 baths, full kitchen, fireplace, jacuzzi/sauna, patio deck, boat launch. Also, two outdoor pools, golf course, tennis courts, volleyball courts and nearby playground. Rates: $70 daily (two to five night stay, Sun-Thu), $80 daily (Sun-Thu), $95 daily (Fri-Sat, holidays), $500 seven-day package, $50 refundable key/cleaning deposit.

**SUPPORT FACILITIES:**

| | | |
|---|---|---|
| Beach | Boat Launch | Playground |
| Pool | Telephones | |

**ACTIVITIES:**

Swimming

**CREDIT CARDS ACCEPTED:** Visa, MasterCard, American Express, Discover and Diners'.

**RESTRICTIONS:** No pets allowed.

*CALIFORNIA*

# LOS ANGELES AFB FAMCAMP (CA75R4)
Los Angeles Air Force Base
Los Angeles AFB, CA 90245-4687

**TELEPHONE NUMBER INFORMATION:** Main installation numbers: C-310-363-2081. Security for FAMCAMP C-310-363-2123.

**LOCATION:** On base, located approximately two miles south of the main base. From San Diego Freeway I-405, take the El Segundo Blvd exit and go west approximately two miles to Douglas Street. Turn right to the Area B main gate to check in at Recreation Services, Bldg 220. Check in at the Area B location is imperative as the FAMCAMP has a gate with a combination lock. Recreation Services will provide the combination to you. *USMRA: page 117 (B-5).* NMC: Los Angeles, 30 miles north.

**DESCRIPTION OF AREA:** Located in southern California; suburban El Segundo city in South Bay Area (Santa Monica Bay). New Green Line Metro Rail system within walking distance from FAMCAMP. Beaches located within 20 minute drive, Los Angeles is approximately 40 minute drive by freeway. San Diego Freeway entrance is located close to base.

**SEASON OF OPERATION:** Year round.

**ELIGIBILITY:** Active/Reservists/Retired/DoD civilians.

**RESERVATIONS:** Accepted 30 days in advance. Address: 61st ABG/SVRE, 340 Challenger Way, Los Angeles AFB, Equipment Rental, Bldg 220, El Segundo, CA 90245-4678. **C-310-363-2081, D-312-833-2081.** Check in Bldg 220 0900-1500 hours Mon-Fri, check out 1200 hours.

**Camper Spaces:** Hardstand (15), E (110V/20A)/W hookups. Rates: $8 daily/$50 weekly.

**SUPPORT FACILITIES:**

| | | |
|---|---|---|
| Equipment Rental | Fitness Centers | Picnic Area |
| Sewage Dump | Sports Fields | Tennis Courts |

**ACTIVITIES:**

| | | |
|---|---|---|
| Beaches | Cycling | Hiking |
| Mountain Climbing | Racquetball | Surf Fishing |

Discount tickets for amusement parks sold on premises.

**CREDIT CARDS ACCEPTED:** Visa and MasterCard.

**RESTRICTIONS:** Pets allowed on leash, must comply with local license laws.

# MARCH ARB FAMCAMP (CA08R4)
March Air Reserve Base
March ARB, CA 92518-1671

**TELEPHONE NUMBER INFORMATION:** Main installation numbers: C-909-655-1110, D-312-947-1110.

**LOCATION:** On base. From CA-60 S, to I-215 which bisects ARB. Second light is main gate. *USMRA: page 111 (G-14).* NMC: Riverside, 9 miles northwest.

**RESERVATIONS:** No advance reservations. First come, first serve basis. Address: Outdoor Recreation Department, 452 SVS/SVRO, Bldg 434, March ARB, CA 92518-5000. **C-909-655-2816, D-312-9472816.** Fax: C-909-655-5221.

**DESCRIPTION OF AREA:** Located in a semi-desert area close to Palm Springs and local casinos. Full range of support facilities on base.

**SEASON OF OPERATION:** Year round.

**ELIGIBILITY:** Active/Reservists/Retired/DoD civilians/ ID Card holders and family members.

**Camper Spaces:** Grass 10, some handicap accessible, E (120/220V/ 30/50A)/W hookups, concrete patio, picnic table, BBQ grill. Rates: $11 daily. Overflow (10), no hookups. Rates: $5 daily.

**SUPPORT FACILITIES:**

| | | |
|---|---|---|
| Beach | Boat Launch | Boat Rental/Storage. |
| Commissary | Convenience Store | Equipment Rental |
| Exchange | Fishing Pier | Gym |
| Ice | Laundry | Marina |
| Pavilion | Picnic Area | Pool |
| Sewage Dump | Shoppette | Showers |
| Snack Bar | Sports Fields | Telephones |
| Tennis Courts | | |

**ACTIVITIES:**

| | |
|---|---|
| Golf | Tennis |

**CREDIT CARDS ACCEPTED:** Visa and MasterCard.

**RESTRICTIONS:** Pets must be on leash. No firearms.

# MONTEREY PINES RV CAMPGROUND (CX05R4)
Monterey Bay Naval Support Activity
Monterey, CA 93943-5001

**TELEPHONE NUMBER INFORMATION:** Main installation numbers: C-831-656-4029, D-312-878-4029.

**LOCATION:** Off base. From Highway 1 S, in Monterey, exit at Casa Verde Way and turn left at the stop sign. Proceed straight through the traffic light (Fremont Blvd) to the stop sign and turn right on Fairgrounds Road. At the next light, turn left on Garden Road, make an immediate left at the entrance to the Monterey Fairgrounds/Navy Golf Course. From Highway 1 N, in Monterey, exit at Mark Thomas Drive/Aguajito Road and follow to third stop light. Turn right on Garden Road, make an immediate left at the entrance to the Monterey Fairgrounds/Navy Golf Course. From Highway 68 W, in Monterey, exit at Olmstead Road. Turn left on Garden Road, then right just before the traffic light at the entrance to the Monterey Fairgrounds/Navy Golf Course.

**DESCRIPTION OF AREA:** Located in a nature sanctuary which is situated between the 13th hole of the golf course and picnic grounds amongst Monterey pine trees on the historic grounds of the old premier coast resort, the Del Monte Hotel.

**SEASON OF OPERATION:** Year round.

**ELIGIBILITY:** Active/Reservists/Retired/immediate family members and bona fide guests. Monterey Bay NSA and Naval Postgraduate School DoD civilians. Guest must be accompanied by sponsor/member. Active/ Reservists have priority.

**RESERVATIONS:** Accepted with fee depending on length of stay. Active duty may make reservations up to 180 days in advance, retirees 160 days, DoD civilians 60 days. Address: Monterey Pines RV Campground/Golf Course, MWR Department NSAMB, 1 University Circle, P.O. Box 8688, Monterey, CA 93943-5000. **C-831-656-4029, D-312-878-4029.** Check in 1300 hours, check out 1200 hours.

*Monterey Pines RV Campground, continued*

**Camper Spaces:** 30-1 is handicap accessible, E (220V/50A)/S/W hookups, picnic table, grill. Rates: $12-$14 daily (the higher rate indicates cost for DoD civilians). 8, E (220V/50A)/W hookups. Rates: $10-$12 daily.

**SUPPORT FACILITIES:**

| | | |
|---|---|---|
| Club/Bar* | Fitness Center* | Laundromat |
| Marina** | Picnic Area | Playground |
| Pool* | Restrooms | Sewage Dump |
| Showers | Snack Bar | Tennis Courts* |
| Ticket Office* | | |

\* Indicates facilities at the Naval Postgraduate School.
\*\* Indicates facility located at the Coast Guard Pier in Monterey.

**ACTIVITIES:**

| | | |
|---|---|---|
| Bicycling | Golfing | Hiking |
| Jogging | Kayaking | Sailing |
| Shopping | Tourist Attractions | |

**CREDIT CARDS ACCEPTED:** Visa and MasterCard.

**RESTRICTIONS:** Two pets are permitted at each campsite and must be leashed at all times. Firearms are prohibited. One extra vehicle per RV is authorized to park in designated areas. Fourteen day limit.

## PETALUMA LAKE AREA CAMPSITES (CA66R4)

Petaluma Coast Guard Training Center
Petaluma, CA 94952-5000

**TELEPHONE NUMBER INFORMATION:** Main installation numbers: C-707-765-7211/7215.

**LOCATION:** On base. From US-101 N or S in Petaluma to East Washington Avenue. Follow nine miles west to CGTC. *USMRA: page 110 (B-6,7).* NMC: San Francisco, 50 miles south.

**DESCRIPTION OF AREA:** Located in beautiful Sonoma County. Campsites are near a small lake in a quiet, rustic atmosphere. Full range of support facilities on base.

**SEASON OF OPERATION:** Year round.

**ELIGIBILITY:** Active/Reservists/Retired/DoD civilians.

**RESERVATIONS:** Required, by application only, at least 30 days in advance. Address: Athletic Department, 599 Tomales Road, Coast Guard Training Center, Petaluma, CA 94952-5000. **C-707-765-7348.** Fax: C-707-765-7657. Check in at gymnasium, 0830-2100 hours.

**Camper Space:** Dirt (6), no hookups. Rates: $7-$14 daily.

**Tent Space:** Grass (25), no hookups. Rates: $3-$6 daily.

**SUPPORT FACILITIES:**

| | | |
|---|---|---|
| Auto Craft Shop | Camping Equipment | Chapel |
| Convenience Store | Equipment Rental | Exchange |
| Fitness Center | Gas | Golf |
| Grills | Ice | Pavilion |
| Picnic Area | Playground | Pool |
| Rec Center | Restrooms | Volleyball (sand) |
| Sewage Dump | Showers | Snack Bar |
| Sports Fields | Telephones | Tennis Courts |

**ACTIVITIES:**

| | | |
|---|---|---|
| Basketball | Fishing | Hiking |
| Horseshoes | Jogging | Racquetball |
| Softball | Tennis | Volleyball |

**CREDIT CARDS ACCEPTED:** Visa.

**RESTRICTIONS:** Pets allowed on leash, owner must clean up after pets daily. No open fires. No restrooms, showers are at the gymnasium. Water hookups are available on a temporary basis. Two week limit.

## POINT MUGU RECREATION FACILITIES (CA11R4)

Point Mugu Naval Air Station
Point Mugu, CA 93042-5001

**TELEPHONE NUMBER INFORMATION:** Main installation numbers: C-805-989-1110, D-312-351-1110. Police for recreation area, C-805-989-7907.

**LOCATION:** On base. Eight miles south of Oxnard and 40 miles north of Santa Monica on Pacific Coastal Highway (PCH), CA-1. Enter Main Gate on Mugu Road, turn left on Laguna Road. *USMRA: page 111 (D,E-13).* NMC: Los Angeles, 50 miles southeast.

**DESCRIPTION OF AREA:** Located along Pacific Ocean north of picturesque Point Mugu State Park and within easy driving distance of world-famous tourist attractions such as Magic Mountain Amusement Park, Disneyland and Knott's Berry Farm. Full range of support facilities available on base.

**SEASON OF OPERATION:** Year round.

**ELIGIBILITY:** Active/Reservists/Retired/DoD civilians/Dependents/Base Contractors.

**RESERVATIONS:** Accepted for motel only, with payment in full, up to 30 days in advance (Point Mugu active duty: up to 90 days). Address: Bldg 774, MWR Department (Code 836300E), Naval Air Station, 521 9th Street, Point Mugu, CA 93042-5001. **C-805-989-8407, D-312-351-8407.** Fax: C-805-989-5413. Check in at Beach Motel.

**Motel Rooms:** Suites (2), handicap accessible, full kitchen, CATV. Rates: $57-$65 daily ($4 each additional person for each motel room regardless of status). 12, handicap accessible, full kitchen, CATV. 10, handicap accessible, full kitchen, refrigerator, microwave, CATV. Rates: $40-$45 daily ($4 each additional person for each motel room regardless of status).

**Camper Spaces:** Paved (49), E (120V/30A)/S/W/CATV hookups, phone hookups available. Rates: $15 daily.

**Tent Spaces:** On Beach (10). Rates: $6 daily.

**SUPPORT FACILITIES:**

| | | |
|---|---|---|
| Auto Craft Shop | Beach | Camping Equipment |
| Chapel | Commissary | Convenience Store |
| Exchange | Fire rings | Fitness Center |
| Gas | Golf | Grills |
| Ice | Laundry | Pavilion |
| Picnic Area | Playground | Pool |
| Rec Equipment | Restrooms* | Sewage Dump |
| Showers* | Skeet Range | Snack Bar |
| Sports Fields | Telephones | Tennis Courts |
| VCR Rental | | |

\* Handicap accessible

**CALIFORNIA**
*Point Mugu Recreation Facilities, continued*

**ACTIVITIES:**

| | | |
|---|---|---|
| Bicycling | Duck Hunting/license | Fishing/license |
| Jogging | Swimming | |

**CREDIT CARDS ACCEPTED:** Visa, MasterCard and American Express.

**RESTRICTIONS:** Pets on leash allowed in camping area. No pets allowed in motel. No firearms allowed unless approved by NAWS Security Department. Fires allowed in fire rings only; all others must be approved by NAWS fire department. Seven day limit for motel during summer, 14 day limit during off-season; one month for campsites.

# SAN ONOFRE RECREATION BEACH (CA31R4)

Camp Pendleton Marine Corps Base
Camp Pendleton MCB, CA 92055-5019

**TELEPHONE NUMBER INFORMATION:** Main installation numbers: C-760-725-4111, D-312-365-4111. Police, C-911.

**LOCATION:** On base. Exit I-5 on Basilone Road three miles south of San Clemente. East to San Onofre Military Gate. Approximately two miles from gate turn right, road will take you to beach. *USMRA: page 111 (F-15).* NMC: Oceanside, 15 miles southeast.

**DESCRIPTION OF AREA:** Located on the oceanfront along one of California's most beautiful beaches. Large variety of recreational activities. Full range of support facilities on base.

**SEASON OF OPERATION:** Year round.

**ELIGIBILITY:** Active/Reservists/Retired/DoD civilians/MWR employees.

**RESERVATIONS:** May-Sep: Accepted by telephone up to 12 weeks in advance for active duty Marines; up to ten weeks in advance for all other active duty and retirees; nine weeks for Reserve, DoD civilians and MWR employees. Oct-Apr: Accepted by telephone up to 12 weeks in advance for all categories. Reservations by mail not accepted. Payment required one month in advance. Address: Morale, Welfare & Recreation (Attn: Finance Division), Box 555020, Marine Corps Base, Camp Pendleton, CA 92055-5020. **C-760-725-7935, D-312-365-7935** (Campsites); **C-760-725-7629** (Cottages). *Note: Renovations are planned for 1999 to include full hookups. Other camping facilities for Camp Pendleton include Del Mar Beach and Lake O'Neill.*

**Mobile Homes/Cottages:** One-, two- and three-bedroom (37-2 allow pets). Rates: $35 daily (one-bedroom), $40 daily (two-bedroom), $50 daily (three-bedroom).

**Camper Spaces:** Dirt/Gravel (80), E (110V/20/30A)/W hookups. Rates: $15 daily.

**Camper/Tent Spaces:** Sand (43),W hookup. Rates: $12 daily.

**Camper Spaces:** Paved/Sand (22), no hookups. Rates: $10 daily.

**Overflow:** Primitive, unlimited, no hookups. Rates: $10 daily

**SUPPORT FACILITIES:**

| | | |
|---|---|---|
| Beach | Beach Club | Bicycle Route** |
| Convenience Store | Gas | Golf |
| Laundry | Mini Exchange | Picnic Area |
| Playground | Rec Equipment | Restrooms |
| Sewage Dump | Showers* | Snack Bar |
| Sports Fields | | |

* Handicap accessible.
** Along coastline. Groups of ten or more must get written permission to use route. Write JPA0, MCB, Camp Pendleton, CA 92055-5018 at least 45 days in advance.

**ACTIVITIES:**

| | | |
|---|---|---|
| Fishing | Hiking | Surfing |
| Swimming | | |

**CREDIT CARDS ACCEPTED:** Visa, MasterCard, American Express and Discover.

**RESTRICTIONS:** No pets in cottages.

# SHARPE TRAVEL CAMP (CA63R4)

Defense Distribution Depot
Stockton, CA 95296-0010

**TELEPHONE NUMBER INFORMATION:** Main installation numbers: C-209-982-2000, D-312-462-2000. Security Police for Travel Camp, C-209-982-2560.

**LOCATION:** On post. Located in Lathrop. From I-5 at Roth Road; or from CA-99 N, left on CA-120, north on Airport Way, left on Roth Road to Depot. *USMRA: Page 110 (C,D-7).* NMC: Stockton, 6 miles north.

**DESCRIPTION OF AREA:** Located in the Delta Country (known for its 1000 miles of waterways). Oakwood Lake Resort within minutes. Easy drive to San Francisco, Lake Tahoe, Yosemite National Park, Great American Park and Sacramento. Limited support facilities available on site.

**SEASON OF OPERATION:** Year round.

**ELIGIBILITY:** Active/Reservists/Retired/DoD civilians/Sponsored guests.

**RESERVATIONS:** No advance reservations. Address: Community Recreation Office, 700 E Roth Road, Bldg 205, DDJC, P.O. Box 960001, Lathrop, CA 95331-5000. **C-209-982-2237, D-312-462-2237.** Check in with camp host at site 1. Discount available to holders of Golden Age and Golden Access Passports.

**Camper Spaces:** Gravel (12), E (110V/30A)/S/W hookups. Rates: $10 daily.

**SUPPORT FACILITIES:**

| | | |
|---|---|---|
| Consolidated Club | Exchange | Fitness Center |
| Grills | Laundry | Picnic Area |
| Playground | Pool | Racquetball |
| Rec Equipment | Restrooms* | Showers* |
| Sports Fields | Tennis Courts | |

* Handicap accessible.

**ACTIVITIES:**

| | |
|---|---|
| Jogging | Swimming |

**CREDIT CARDS ACCEPTED:** None.

**RESTRICTIONS:** Pets allowed on leash. Firearms must be checked in to Security. No open fires.

# SOUTH LAKE TAHOE RECREATION HOUSING (CA17R4)

Presidio of Monterey
Presidio of Monterey, CA 93944-5006

**TELEPHONE NUMBER INFORMATION:** Main installation numbers: C-831-242-5000, D-312-878-5000.

**LOCATION:** Off post. From US-101 100 miles south of San Francisco, take CA-156 W ten miles follow signs to Presidio of Monterey. Located at Lake Tahoe; specific directions will be furnished when reservation is made. Obtain keys in Lake Tahoe by making arrangements with Equipment Center, Bldg 228, Presidio of Monterey. *USMRA: page 110 (E-6).* NMI: McClellan AFB, Sacramento CA, 110 miles southwest. NMC: Carson City NV, 30 miles southeast.

**DESCRIPTION OF AREA:** Leased lodging facilities on the south shore of Lake Tahoe for year-round enjoyment. Located in Heavenly Resort Valley. Conveniently located for taking advantage of a wide range of mountain and water-oriented recreational activities. Casinos located within a few miles. Full range of support facilities available at McClellan AFB.

**SEASON OF OPERATION:** Year round.

**ELIGIBILITY:** Active/Reservists/Retired/US Government civilian employees.

**RESERVATIONS:** Required, with $50 non-refundable deposit, up to six months in advance. Full payment required 30 days before departure. Reservations for holidays accepted only for a complete holiday period-exact days/dates set by Outdoor Recreation based on an annual calendar. Payment in full required for holiday reservations. Checks, Visa, MasterCard accepted. Address: Outdoor Recreation Equipment Center, Bldg 228, Lewis Hall, Presidio of Monterey, CA 93944-5000. **C-831-242-5506/6132, D-312-878-5506/6132** 1030-1400 hours and 1500-1800 hours, Mon-Fri. Check in 1400 hours, check out 1100 hours ($15 check out fee).

**A-Frame Chalet:** Three-bedroom (1), sleeps ten, two private baths, full kitchen, microwave, dishwasher, CATV, entertainment system, washer/dryer. Modern unit located in middle of city off Pioneer Trail in a rural subdivision. Patrons must provide sheets, towels, toiletries, paper towels, bathroom tissue and firewood. Ski vacation packages available. Rates: $100-$110 daily/$600 weekly (depending on day of week, length of stay and holidays, minimum stay two nights, weekly rates apply for seven consecutive days).

**Gardner Cabin:** Three-bedroom (1), sleeps eight, private bath, dining room, full kitchen, microwave, fireplace, CATV, washer/dryer. Rustic cabin located at edge of town off CA-89 in rural subdivision. Patrons must provide sheets, towels, toiletries, paper towels, bathroom tissue and firewood. Rates: $45-$100 daily/$575 weekly (depending on day of week, length of stay and holidays, minimum stay two nights, weekly rates apply for seven consecutive days).

**Ski Run Condos:** Two-bedroom (2), sleeps two to six, two private baths, living room, full kitchen, microwave, dishwasher, fireplace, CATV, washer/dryer. Modern units located next to Heavenly Valley Ski Resort. Patrons must provide sheets, towels, toiletries, paper towels, bathroom tissue and firewood. Rates: $90-$95 (depending on day of week, length of stay and holidays, minimum stay two nights, weekly rates apply for seven consecutive days).

**Motel Lodgings:** (subcontracted units in local motels) two double beds, private bath, CATV, two blocks from casinos. Rates: $45-$70 daily (double occupancy).

**CREDIT CARDS ACCEPTED:** Visa and MasterCard.

**RESTRICTIONS:** No pets allowed. No parties may be held on the premises. No car washing.

# TRAVIS FAMCAMP (CA68R4)

Travis Air Force Base
Travis AFB, CA 94535-2045

**TELEPHONE NUMBER INFORMATION:** Main installation numbers: C-707-424-1110/5000, D-312-837-1110.

**LOCATION:** On base. Off I-80 N, take Airbase Parkway exit. Clearly marked. Camp is adjacent to main gate. *USMRA: page 110 (C-7).* NMC: San Francisco, 45 miles southwest.

**DESCRIPTION OF AREA:** Located in state's famed valley region near Sacramento. Major water sports centers of San Pablo Bay and Lake Berryessa are nearby. Full range of support facilities available on base.

**SEASON OF OPERATION:** Year round.

**ELIGIBILITY:** Active/Reservists/Retired/DoD civilians.

**RESERVATIONS:** Accepted 30 days in advance, less than 30 days first come, first serve. Address: 60 SVS/SVRO, Attn: FAMCAMP Manager, 273 Ellis Street, Travis AFB, CA 94535-5000. **C-707-424-3583, D-312-837-3583.** Fax: C-707-424-3583, D-312-837-3583. Check in at FAMCAMP office 0830-1030 hours or 1530-1700 hours (1630-1800 hours DST) Mon-Sat. On Sun and holidays follow instructions for entering camp posted on office window, check out 1000 hours.

**Camper Spaces:** Gravel (70), E (110V/20/30/50A)/S/W/CATV hookups. Rates: $10 daily.

**Camper/Tent Spaces:** Dirt (8), no hookups. Rates: $3 daily.

**SUPPORT FACILITIES:**

| | | |
|---|---|---|
| Auto Craft Shop | Commissary | Convenience Store |
| Exchange | Fitness Center | Golf |
| Grills | Pavilion | Picnic Area |
| Playground | Rec Equipment | Restrooms |
| Sewage Dump | Showers | Sports Fields |
| Stables | Tennis Courts | Telephones |

**ACTIVITIES:**

| | | |
|---|---|---|
| Biking | Bowling | Fishing/license |
| Golf | Sightseeing | |

**CREDIT CARDS ACCEPTED:** None.

**RESTRICTIONS:** Pets allowed on leash, must not annoy others, owner must clean up after pet immediately. No firearms allowed. No campfires. Quiet hours 2300-0800 hours.

# VANDENBERG FAMCAMP (CA67R4)

Vandenberg Air Force Base
Vandenberg, CA 93437-6223

**TELEPHONE NUMBER INFORMATION:** Main installation numbers: C-805-734-8232, D-312-276-1110. Police for FAMCAMP, C-805-734-8232 ext 6-3911.

CALIFORNIA/COLORADO
*Vandenberg FAMCAMP, continued*

**LOCATION:** On base. Located between Lompoc and Santa Maria. From US-101, west on CA-1 to AFB. *USMRA: page 111 (C-12).* NMC: Lompoc, 6 miles south.

**DESCRIPTION OF AREA:** Space and missile center. Installation covers over 98,000 acres. FAMCAMP is situated on main base and provides unlimited sightseeing and recreational opportunities. Full range of support facilities on base.

**SEASON OF OPERATION:** Year round.

**ELIGIBILITY:** Active/Reservists/Retired/DoD civilians.

**RESERVATIONS:** No advance reservations. Address: FAMCAMP, 30 SVS/SVRO, 1036 California Blvd., Vandenberg AFB, CA 93437-5000. **C-805-734-8232 ext 6-8579, D-312-276-8579.** Fax: C-805-276-0410. Check in at FAMCAMP office, Bldg 5002, during duty hours. To check in after duty hours, use the fee collection box located in front of FAMCAMP office and see office personnel the following day.

**Camper Spaces:** Hardstand (49), E (110V/50A)/S/W hookups. Rates: $12 daily. Gravel (19), no hookups. Rates: $5 daily.

**Tent Spaces:** Grass (15), fenced area, no hookups. Rates: $5 daily.

**SUPPORT FACILITIES:**

| | | |
|---|---|---|
| Camping Equipment | Game Room | Gas |
| Golf | Grills | Laundry |
| Lounge* | Picnic Area | Playground |
| Racquetball | Rec Equipment | Restrooms* |
| RV Parts Store | Sewage Dump | Showers* |
| Skeet Range | Snack Bar | Sports Fields |
| Tennis Courts | Trails | Vending Machines |

* Handicap accessible.

**ACTIVITIES:**

| | | |
|---|---|---|
| Hunting/license | Lake Fishing | Surf Fishing |

**CREDIT CARDS ACCEPTED:** Visa and MasterCard.

**RESTRICTIONS:** Pets allowed, must comply with local license and leash laws. Firearms permitted during hunting season.

# COLORADO

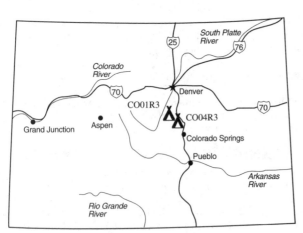

## FARISH RECREATION AREA (CO01R3)

United States Air Force Academy
USAF Academy, CO 80840-9999

**TELEPHONE NUMBER INFORMATION:** Main installation numbers: C-719-333-1818, D-312-333-1818. Police for recreation area C-719-333-2000.

**LOCATION:** Off base. From I-25 at Colorado Springs, take exit 141 W for 17 miles to Woodland Park. At second stoplight (near McDonald's) turn right onto Baldwin (street name changes to Rampart Range Road). Follow road through four stop signs. Road forks just past water-treatment facility, stay left and follow the Farish signs. Approximately 200 yards after the paved road ends, turn right onto Forest Service Road 312 which will dead-end into Farish. Facility is 5.9 miles past stoplight at McDonald's. *USMRA: page 109 (F-4).* NMI: US Air Force Academy, 30 miles southeast. NMC: Colorado Springs, 30 miles southeast.

**DESCRIPTION OF AREA:** Located on 655 acres of magnificent mountain woodlands within the Pike National Forest at an altitude of 9,000+ feet on Colorado's Front Range just northwest of Colorado Springs. Abundant wildlife and three fishing lakes. Enjoy a mountain getaway with a real backwoods feeling yet within driving distance of area attractions. A wide range of support facilities is available at the US Air Force Academy, Peterson AFB and Fort Carson.

**SEASON OF OPERATION:** Year round for lodging and day use; campsites closed November through March.

**ELIGIBILITY:** Active/Reservists/Retired/DoD civilians/Dependent ID card holders.

**RESERVATIONS:** Highly recommended. Accepted up to one year in advance. Cancellations/changes must be made no later than 30 days prior to reservation date to avoid charges. Address: Farish Recreation Area, P.O. Box 146, Woodland Park, CO 80866-0146. **C-719-687-9098** 0800-1700 hours Mon-Fri. Fax: C-719-686-1437. HP: http://www.usafa.af.mil/svk/farish.htm. Check in 1400 hours, check out 1100 hours for lodge, cottage and cabins; check in 1500 hours, check out 1200 hours for duplexes; check in 1200 hours, check out 1100 hours for camping area. Resident caretaker on site for after hours check in and emergencies.

**Duplexes:** One-bedroom with loft or two-bedroom (6-3 handicap accessible), sleeps five, private bath, living room, kitchenette, microwave, range, utensils, TV, basic linens, towels. Rates: $70 daily.

**Cottage:** Two-bedroom (1), sleeps eight, private bath, living room, kitchen, utensils, gas-log fireplace, TV/VCR, basic linens, towels. Rates: $85 daily.

**Lodge:** Bedroom, private bath (1), sleeps five, utensils, TV, basic linens, towels. Bedroom, shared bath (3), sleeps four, utensils, TV, basic linens, towels. Kitchen and dining room located in separate building. No housekeeping service. Rates: $36-$50 daily.

**Camper Cabins:** 4, sleeps four, port-a-potties. Patrons must provide own bedding. Rates: $25 daily with electricity, $20 without electricity.

**Yurt:** 1, guests should provide own bedding. Rates: $20 daily. *Note: A yurt is a cabin/tent structure, 24 feet in diameter with wooden floor, deck and door, two windows, and stretched-canvas covering with skylight. It is furnished, but has no bathroom or kitchen.*

**Camper Spaces:** Gravel (9), E (110/220V/30A) hookup. Rates: $9 daily.

**Camper Space Pavilion:** Gravel (2), covered, E (110/220V/30A) hookup. Rates: $15 daily.

*Farish Recreation Area, continued*

**Tent Spaces:** Gravel (15), primitive, no hookups. Rates: $7.50 daily.

**SUPPORT FACILITIES:**

| | | |
|---|---|---|
| Bath House | Convenience | Fire Rings |
| Grills | Ice | Pavilions/fee |
| Picnic Areas | Playground | Rec Equipment |
| Trails | | |

**ACTIVITIES:**

| | | |
|---|---|---|
| Fishing | Hiking | Horseshoes |
| Ice Fishing | Ice Skating | Paddle Boats |
| Sledding | Skiing/XC | Snow Shoeing |
| Snow Tubing | Volleyball | |

Customized group trips such as downhill skiing or hot springs by advance arrangement.

**CREDIT CARDS ACCEPTED:** Visa and MasterCard.

**RESTRICTIONS:** No pets allowed in lodge, cabins or cottage, allowed on leash with day-use patrons and overnight in tent or RV only, owner must clean up after pet. No firearms allowed. Potable water available from spigot near office and from water buffaloes located throughout campground. Colorado State fishing license and USAF Academy fishing permit are required for anyone 16 years and older, available at office. Patrons with campers more than 26 feet long should contact the Farish staff for directions to an alternate entrance. All visitors are advised to call for road and weather conditions before making the trip especially in winter, fall and spring. Gate fee $4 for day-use patrons. Lakes closed from 2300-0500 hours.

# PEREGRINE PINES FAMCAMP (CO04R3)

United States Air Force Academy
USAF Academy, CO 80840-9999

**TELEPHONE NUMBER INFORMATION:** Main installation numbers: C-719-333-1818, D-312-333-3110.

**LOCATION:** On base. From I-25 north of Colorado Springs, take exit 150 and enter through the south gate. FAMCAMP is just off Stadium Blvd approximately one block north of Falcon Stadium. From Denver, take I-25 S and take exit 156, enter through the north gate. Turn left at B-52 and go approximately .25 miles on Stadium Blvd. Follow FAMCAMP signs to entrance. *USMRA: page 115 (A,B-1,2)*. NMC: Colorado Springs, 5 miles south.

**DESCRIPTION OF AREA:** FAMCAMP is at an elevation of 7,000 feet, nestled in a peaceful, wooded area where wildlife roams free. Enjoy the feeling of seclusion, the varied attractions in the Colorado Springs area, and many activities available through the Outdoor Recreation Center. The Academy has a visitors center (with cafeteria) on Academy Drive. Full range of support facilities available on base.

**SEASON OF OPERATION:** Year round, host on site 1 May-1 Nov.

**ELIGIBILITY:** Active/Reservists/Retired/Cadets.

**RESERVATIONS:** Recommended. Accepted up to 90 days in advance; Academy active duty and their family members and guests have first priority. Address: Outdoor Recreation Center, P.O. Box 217, USAF Academy, CO 80840-0217. **C-719-333-4356** (1 Nov-1 May) **C-719-333-4980** (1 May-1 Nov)**, D-312-333-4356.** Check in at FAMCAMP office during peak season (1 May-1 Nov), check bulletin board off season (1 Nov-1 May). Check in 1200 hours, check out 1100 hours. *Note: Renovations begin October 1998 to include shower and laundry facilities. There are plans for 14 new camper spaces and full hookup upgrades.*

**Yurt:** 1, E/W hookups. Rates: $17 daily. *Note: A yurt is a cabin/tent structure, 24 feet in diameter with wooden floor, deck and door, two windows, and stretched-canvas covering with skylight. It is furnished, but has no bathroom or kitchen.*

**Camper Spaces:** Gravel (60), range from 15'-71', some pull-through, E (110/220V/30/50A)/S/W hookups. Rates: $14 daily. Gravel (27), no hookups. Rates: $7 daily.

**Tent Spaces:** 10, no hookups. Rates: $7 daily.

**SUPPORT FACILITIES:**

| | | |
|---|---|---|
| Camping Equipment | Chapel/base | Falcon Trail |
| Fitness Center | Golf/base | Grills |
| Pavilions/fee | Picnic Area | Port-a-Potties |
| Rec Equipment | Restrooms/nearby | Sewage Dump |
| Snack Bar | Trailer Rental | Trails |

**ACTIVITIES:**

| | | |
|---|---|---|
| Bowling | Fishing | Horseback Riding |
| Jogging | Swimming | Skiing |

**CREDIT CARDS ACCEPTED:** Visa and MasterCard.

**RESTRICTIONS:** Pets allowed on leash, owner must clean up after pet. Limit of two pets per site, must have current immunizations. No open fires permitted. Quiet hours 2200-0800 hours. 14 day limit. No laundry facilities on base. *Note: Do not feed the wild animals. Trees, flowers, plants and nature's debris must remain undisturbed.*

# DELAWARE

## BETHANY BEACH TRAINING SITE (DE03R1)

Delaware Army National Guard
Bethany Beach, DE 19930-5000

**TELEPHONE NUMBER INFORMATION:** Main installation numbers: C-302-854-7902, D-312-440-7902.

**LOCATION:** On Base. Located on west side of DE-1, .5 miles north of DE-26 and DE-1 intersection Bethany Beach. *USMRA: page 42 (J,6)*. NMI: Dover AFB, 50 miles northwest. NMC: Bethany Beach, .5 miles northeast.

**DESCRIPTION OF AREA:** Located approximately ten miles north of Ocean City, MD and 14 miles south of Rehoboth Beach, DE. Ocean City and Rehoboth provide a variety of amusement parks, dining and day or evening entertainment options. Bethany Beach hosts a family oriented atmosphere both day and night.

**SEASON OF OPERATION:** Year round.

**ELIGIBILITY:** Active/Reservists/Retired/DNG civilian employees.

**RESERVATIONS:** Required with payment in full 14 days prior to arrival. Address: Bethany Beach Training Site, Attn: Billeting Office Bldg 114, 163 Scannell Blvd, Bethany Beach, DE 19930-0985. **C-302-854-7900/2, D-312-440-7900/2.** Fax: C-302-854-7999, D-312-440-7999. E-mail: bbts@ de-ngnet.ngb.army.mil. Check in 1500 hours, check out 1000 hours.

*DELAWARE-DISTRICT OF COLUMBIA*
*Bethany Beach Training Site, continued*

**Apartment/Suites:** Three-bedroom (3), full kitchen, A/C, heat, CATV/VCR. Rates: $27 nightly.

**Camper/RV Spaces:** 12, E (110/220V/30A)/S/W/CATV hookups. Rates: $9 nightly.

**Hotel:** Rooms (3). Rates: $18 nightly.

**Mobile Home:** Three-bedroom (23), 14'X70', furnished kitchen, A/C, heat, CATV/VCR. Rates: $27 nightly.

**SUPPORT FACILITIES:**

| | | |
|---|---|---|
| Fishing Pier | Fitness Center | Laundry |
| Ocean/Bay Beaches | Pay Telephones | Picnic Area |
| Playground | Rec Center | Restrooms |
| Sewage Dump | Showers | |

**ACTIVITIES:**

| | | |
|---|---|---|
| Amusement Rides | Basketball | Bicycling |
| Boardwalk | Canoeing | Crabbing/Clamming |
| Fishing | Fitness Center | Golf |
| Horseshoes | Jogging | Outlet Shopping |
| Pedal Boats | Rollerblading | Surfing |
| Swimming | Volleyball | |

**CREDIT CARDS ACCEPTED:** Military issue credit cards only.

**RESTRICTIONS: No pets allowed.** No firearms. Limit seven nights, two night minimum. Posted speed limit 15 mph. One reservation per family at a time. Sponsor must be present during stay.

## DOVER AFB FAMCAMP (DE01R1)

Dover Air Force Base
Dover AFB, DE 19902-7209

**TELEPHONE NUMBER INFORMATION:** Main installation numbers: C-302-677-3000, D-312-445-3000.

**LOCATION:** On base. East of US-113 in Dover. Clearly marked. Located on the south end of the base along Perimeter Road, just to the north of Archery Range. *USMRA: Page 42 (I-3).* NMC: Dover, 5 miles northwest.

**DESCRIPTION OF AREA:** Several historic sites are located within the Dover area, including The John Dickinson Plantation. Rehoboth and Dewey beaches are just 45 minutes way.

**SEASON OF OPERATION:** Year round.

**ELIGIBILITY:** Active/Reservists/Retired/DoD civilians.

**RESERVATIONS:** Accepted up to 14 days in advance. Fees are due in advance and must be paid in full. Address: Equipment Rental, 436 SVS/SVRO, 262 Chad Street Room 331, Dover AFB, DE 19902-7262. **C-302-677-3959, D-312-445-3959.** Check in at Equipment Check Out Bldg 124 after 1100 hours, check out 1200 hours.

**Camper/RV Sites:** 7, E (110/220V/30A-three have 50A)/S/W hookups. 9, E/W hookups. Rates: $9 daily.

**SUPPORT FACILITIES**

| | | |
|---|---|---|
| BBQ Grill | Beaches* | Horseshoes |
| Picnic Area | Playground | Rec Equipment |
| Sewage Dump | | |

* Rehoboth and Dewey Beaches are located 45 minutes away.

**ACTIVITIES:**

| | | |
|---|---|---|
| Dover Downs* | Museum** | Swimming |
| Tourist Attractions | | |

* NASCAR and Indy races from Jun-Sep, harness racing Nov-Mar.
** Air Mobility Command Museum houses a collection of vintage aircraft that reflects the history of Dover AFB and the USAF.

**CREDIT CARDS ACCEPTED:** Visa and MasterCard.

**RESTRICTIONS:** Pets allowed but must be attended at all times and on a leash no longer than six feet when outdoors. Open fires not permitted on camp. Grills are provided along with a receptacle for hot coals. Quiet hours 2200-0700 hours. Guests are required to dispose of trash and debris at their site. Posted speed limit is five miles per hour.

# DISTRICT OF COLUMBIA

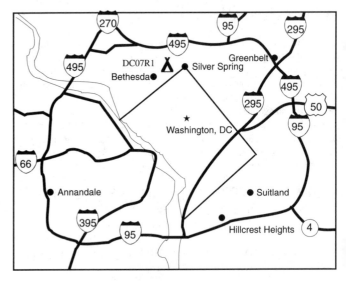

## WALTER REED ARMY MEDICAL CENTER DCA, CRD OUTDOOR RECREATION CENTER (DC07R1)

Walter Reed Army Medical Center
Washington, DC 20307-5001

**TELEPHONE NUMBER INFORMATION:** Main installation numbers: C-202-782-4946/4947. Police for recreation area, C-301-295-7554.

**LOCATION:** On post. From VA to MD or Baltimore to VA, take I-495 to exit Silver Spring, Georgia Avenue. Turn right at second stop light, Seminary Road. Keep going straight to Linden Lane, turn right. Turn left on Stephen Sitter Avenue to Outdoor Rec, Bldg 156. *USMRA: page 54 (E-1).* NMC: Washington, DC, 7 miles south.

**DESCRIPTION OF AREA:** Walter Reed Army Medical Center is one of the largest hospitals in the area. Full range of outdoor activities available.

**SEASON OF OPERATION:** Year round.

**ELIGIBILITY:** Active/Reservists/Retired/DoD civilians/Dependents.

**RESERVATIONS:** Required for RV sites. Walter Reed Army Medical Center DCA, CRD Outdoor Recreation Center, 6825 16th Street, NW, Bldg 11, Suite 1-123, Washington, DC 20307-5001. **C-301-295-8010/8008, 312-295-8010/8008** 0830-1700 hours Mon-Fri. Fax: C-301-295-7635, D-312-295-7635.

# Military RV, Camping & Outdoor Recreation

*Walter Reed Army Medical Center DCA,*
*CRD Outdoor Recreation Center, continued*

**RV Spaces:** 4, handicap accessible, E (110V/20/30A) hookup. Rates: $5 daily/$25 weekly.

**SUPPORT FACILITIES:**

| | | |
|---|---|---|
| Auto Craft Shop | Basketball Court | Boat/RV Storage |
| Boat Rental | Bowling Alley | Camping Equipment |
| Chapel | Commissary | Exchange |
| Fitness Center | Gas | Grills |
| Pavilion | Picnic Area* | Playground |
| Restrooms | Shuttle Bus | Ski Equip Rental |
| Sports Fields | Telephones | Trails |

* Reservation required. Fee: $50 weekday, $75 weekend.

**ACTIVITIES:**

| | | |
|---|---|---|
| Camping | Fishing (Deep Sea) | Skiing |
| Tours | | |

**CREDIT CARDS ACCEPTED:** Visa, MasterCard and American Express.

**RESTRICTIONS:** Pets allowed on leash.

# FLORIDA

*See map below.*

## BLUE ANGEL NAVAL RECREATION AREA (FL36R1)

Corry Station Naval Technical Training Center
Pensacola, FL 32511-5138

**TELEPHONE NUMBER INFORMATION:** Main installation numbers: C-850-452-2000, D-312-922-0111. Police for recreation park, C-850-453-2030/4530.

**LOCATION:** Off base. From I-10 west of Pensacola, take exit 2 (FL-297/Pine Forest Road) south approximately .5 miles to Blue Angel Parkway south for eight miles, then west on US-98 for three miles. Watch for signs to Blue Angel Naval Recreation Area on left. *USMRA: page 39 (A-13).* NMI: Corry Station, 8 miles northeast. NMC: Pensacola, 8 miles east.

**DESCRIPTION OF AREA:** Situated on Perdido Bay amid oak trees and Spanish moss, the park offers spectacular camping, boating, swimming and picnic areas. As there are no currents or drop-offs in this part of the bay, its

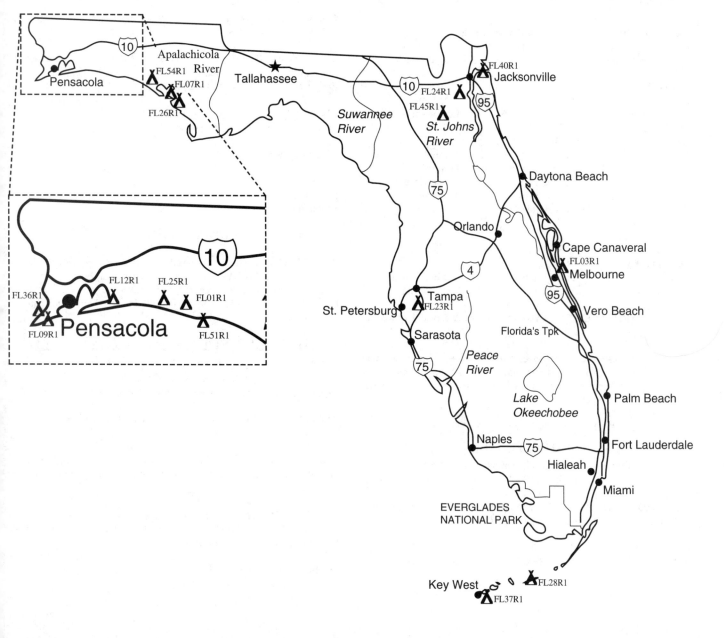

*FLORIDA*
*Blue Angel Naval Recreation Area, continued*

sandy bottom creates an ideal swimming area for children. Fifty acres of the complex have been reserved for youth activities. Organized activities and annual events. Full range of support facilities at Corry Station including Navy shopping mall and Navy hospital.

**SEASON OF OPERATION:** Year round.

**ELIGIBILITY:** Active/Reservists/Retired/DoD civilians and guests.

**RESERVATIONS:** Recommended for rental campers. Address: Blue Angel Naval Recreation Area, 2100 Bronson Road, Pensacola, FL 32506-5000. **C-850-453-9435.** Fax: C-850-453-1147. E-mail: nttc-pen.mwr-0720@nttc-pen.navy.mil. Check in 1400 hours, check out 0800-1100 hours. *Note: Renovations are planned to begin in Fall 1998 to include eight two-bedroom cabins. Estimated date of completion is Spring 1999.*

**Campers:** 17, E (110V/30A)/W hookups. Rates: $15 daily.

**Camper/RV Spaces:** Dirt/Gravel (138), E (110V/30A)/W hookups. Rates: $7 daily.

**Camper/Cabins:** 7, no cooking or bathroom facilities.

**Tent Spaces:** Primitive, unlimited, no hookups. Rates: $3 daily.

**SUPPORT FACILITIES:**

| | | |
|---|---|---|
| Bath House | Beach | Boat Launch |
| Boat Rental/Storage | Convenience Store | Equipment Rental |
| Fire Rings | Fishing Pier* | Gas |
| Golf | Grills | Ice |
| Kayaks | Laundry | Marina |
| Pavilions* | Picnic Areas | Playground |
| Restrooms* | Sailboats | Sewage Dump |
| Showers* | Sports Fields | Telephones |
| Trails | Vending Machine | |

* Handicap accessible.

**ACTIVITIES:**

| | | |
|---|---|---|
| Boating | Fishing/license | Rec Equipment |
| Swimming | Volleyball | Water Skiing |

**CREDIT CARDS ACCEPTED:** Visa, MasterCard, American Express and Discover.

**RESTRICTIONS:** Pets allowed on leash in park, no pets allowed in rental campers. Absolutely No firearms, bows and arrows, BB guns, or other items which could be considered to be weapons. No fireworks. Nominal admission charge for park.

# CAMP BLANDING RV PARK AND CAMPSITES (FL45R1)
Camp Blanding/Florida National Guard Post
Starke, FL 32091-9703

**TELEPHONE NUMBER INFORMATION:** Main installation numbers: C-904-533-3104/3517. Police for campsites: C-904-533-3462.

**LOCATION:** On post. From US-301 N or S, exit in Starke to FL-16 E for two miles. *USMRA: page 38 (F-4).* NMC: Jacksonville, 35 miles north.

**DESCRIPTION OF AREA:** Located on Kingsley Lake in Starke, Camp Blanding is 70,380-acre wildlife management area leased to the army as a training center in 1939. Additional 140,000 surrounding acres acquired for training purposes during World War II. There are two camping areas adjacent to each other. Basic campground (for trailers and tents) is wooded site on shores of Kingsley Lake, located on Avenue A south of NCO Lodge. Improvements have been made to campsite areas within last two years. Limited support facilities on post; full range available at Cecil Field NAS, 30 miles northeast.

**SEASON OF OPERATION:** Year round.

**ELIGIBILITY:** Active/Reservists/Retired/DoD civilians. Florida National Guard has preference.

**RESERVATIONS:** Required for RVs, with $12 deposit. Address: Camp Blanding Recreational Department, Route 1, Box 465, Camp Blanding, Starke, FL 32091-9703. **C-904-533-3104, D-312-533-3104.** Fax: C-904-533-6123. Check in at Recreation Office, Bldg 2540, 0800-1630 hours, Mon-Sat, check out 1100 hours.

**RV Spaces:** Hardstand (16), E (110/220V/30A)/S/W/CATV hookups. Rates: $12 daily (does not include tax).

**Camper/Tent Spaces:** Primitive (52), W hookup. Rates: $6 daily (does not include tax).

**SUPPORT FACILITIES:**

| | | |
|---|---|---|
| Bath House | Beach | Boat Launch |
| Exchange | Fishing Pier | Grills |
| Ice | Laundry | Rec Equipment |
| Restrooms* | Sewage Dump | Snack Bar |
| Sports Fields | Telephones | |

* Handicap accessible.

**ACTIVITIES:**

| | | |
|---|---|---|
| Boating | Hunting | Jogging |
| Swimming | | |

**CREDIT CARDS ACCEPTED:** None.

**RESTRICTIONS:** No pets allowed. Firearms must be registered with Range Control and at main gate. Twenty-one day limit. Boaters should stay clear of swimming areas, fishermen and private residences. Daily boat launch fee to Kingsley Lake $5 for non-Florida NG; Florida NG can buy yearly sticker.

# CHOCTAW RECREATION AREA (FL54R1)
Eglin Air Force base
Eglin AFB, FL 32542-6823
*Project opening date has been delayed. Date uncertain at press time.*

**TELEPHONE NUMBER INFORMATION:** Main installation numbers: C-850-882-1110.

**LOCATION:** Off base. From I-10 at Crestview take FL-85 S to Niceville, turn left on Highway 20. Proceed about ten miles to campground located on right.

**DESCRIPTION OF AREA:** Camping area is situated under an array of oak trees at the beautiful Choctawhatchee Bay, which offers boating, pier fishing in a peaceful, relaxing setting.

**SEASON OF OPERATION:** Year round.

**Tent Spaces:** Dirt (34), W hookup. Rates: $6 daily.

**ELIGIBILITY:** Active/Reservists/Retired/DoD civilians.

**RESERVATIONS:** Reservation policy still under consideration. **C-850-882-6581.**

**Camper Spaces:** Gravel (30), E (110V/20/30A)/W hookups. Rates: $10 daily/$65 weekly/$250 monthly.

**Tent Spaces:** 20. Rates: $5 daily/$30 weekly/$155 monthly.

**SUPPORT FACILITIES:**

| | | |
|---|---|---|
| Beach | Boat Launch | Grills |
| Laundry | Picnic Area | Restrooms* |
| Sewage Dump | Shoppette | Showers* |
| Trails | | |

* Handicap accessible.

**ACTIVITIES:**
Fishing/Beach Activities

**CREDIT CARDS ACCEPTED:** Visa and MasterCard.

**RESTRICTIONS:** Pets allowed on leash, owner must clean up after pet. No open fires on ground.

## COON'S CREEK RECREATION AREA (FL23R1)

MacDill Air Force Base
MacDill AFB, FL 33621-5313

**TELEPHONE NUMBER INFORMATION:** Main installation numbers: C-813-828-1110, D-312-968-1110. Police for recreation area, C-813-828-3322.

**LOCATION:** On base. From I-75 N or S, take FL-618 exit west to FL-573 exit to main gate. *USMRA: page 38 (F-8) and page 56 (E,F-3,4).* NMC: Tampa, 5 miles north.

**DESCRIPTION OF AREA:** Located on south end of installation in coastal peninsula area approximately two miles from main base area. Recreation area consists of FAMCAMP, marina, beach, snack bar and pavilions. Fresh water lakes nearby, nature trail and an abundance of natural flora and fauna. Full range of support facilities on base.

**SEASON OF OPERATION:** Year round.

**ELIGIBILITY:** Active/Reservists/Retired/DoD civilians.

**RESERVATIONS:** Recommended, up to one year in advance; active duty military have priority. $100 deposit (includes $10 processing fee) required to confirm reservation of ten or more days; $10 service fee for reservation of less than ten days. Transient sites available for two weeks (first come, first serve). Address: Coon's Creek Recreation Area, P.O. Box 6825, MacDill AFB, FL 33608-5000. Include self-addressed envelope. **C-1-800-821-4982, C-813-840-6919, D-312-968-4982/2162.** Fax: C-813-828-7507. Check in at marina adjacent to FAMCAMP after 1200 hours, check out 1100 hours.

**Camper Spaces:** Paved/Dirt (256-2 handicap accessible), E (110V/30/50A)/S/W hookups, CATV at some locations. Rates: $13 daily.

**Dry Camp:** Dirt (36), W hookup. Rates: $6 daily.

**SUPPORT FACILITIES:**

| | | |
|---|---|---|
| Activity Room | Bait | Beach |
| Boat Launch | Boat Rental | Boat Slips |
| Equipment Rental | Golf | Grills |
| Ice | Laundry | LP Gas |
| Marina | Nature Trail | Pavilions |
| Picnic Area | Playground | Pools |
| Restrooms | Sewage Dump | Showers |
| Snack Bar | Sports Fields | TV/Game Room |

**ACTIVITIES:**

| | | |
|---|---|---|
| Exercise Room | Fishing/license | Jogging |
| Sailing | Swimming | Walking |
| Windsurfing | | |

**CREDIT CARDS ACCEPTED:** Visa and MasterCard.

**RESTRICTIONS:** Pets allowed on short leash or in RV, owner must clean up after pet even in dog walk area. Pets without complete and current immunizations are not allowed on MacDill AFB and recreation area. Firearms must be registered at FAMCAMP office. No open campfires.

## DESTIN ARMY INFANTRY CENTER RECREATION AREA (FL01R1)

Fort Benning
Fort Benning, GA 31905-5000

**TELEPHONE NUMBER INFORMATION:** Main installation numbers: C-706-544/545-2011, D-312-784/835-2011. Police (Okaloosa County Sheriff) for recreation area, C-850-651-7400/911.

**LOCATION:** Off post. In Destin FL. US-231 S to I-10 W, to US-331 S to US-98 W to Benning Drive, right to area. Also, I-10 to FL-85 S to Fort Walton Beach, US-98 E to Destin, left at Benning Drive to area. *USMRA: page 39 (C-13).* NMI: Eglin AFB FL, 17 miles north. NMC: Pensacola FL, 45 miles west.

**DESCRIPTION OF AREA:** Located on 15-acre site on Choctawhatchee Bay in Destin FL. Enjoy sparkling sugar-white quartz sands of Emerald Coast. Gulf of Mexico fishing and swimming areas approximately two miles from recreation area. Area also offers golf at six public courses, two greyhound race tracks within 45 miles, Deep Sea Fishing Cruise, Destin Fishing Museum, Gulfariam, Zoo, and Indian Temple Mound Museum. Full range of support facilities available at Eglin AFB.

**SEASON OF OPERATION:** Year round.

**ELIGIBILITY:** Active/Reservists/Retired/DoD civilians.

**RESERVATIONS:** Required for cabins, motel and charter boat; not accepted for camper spaces; up to six months in advance for active duty at Fort Benning, four months in advance for others. Address: Destin Recreation Area, 557 Calhoun Avenue, Destin, FL 32541-5000. **C-1-800-642-0466, C-850-837-2725.** Reservations may also be made at Fort Benning, **C-706-545-5600.** Information only, C-850-837-6423, Fax: C-850-837-5706. Check in at office 1600-2000 hours, check out 1100 hours. *Note: Construction of 48 full hookup, 40'-50' concrete pads, patio/parking space, bath house and pavilion is scheduled to be completed in Jan-Feb 1999. Until then, there will be no RV or camping facilities at Destin Recreation Area.*

**Duplex:** Three-bedroom (5), private bath, kitchen, microwave, CATV, phone (free local calls), pots/pans, linens. Rates: $50-$65 daily (includes immediate family only. Additional fee for guests. Off-season rates available

*FLORIDA*
*Destin Army Infantry Center Recreation Area, continued*

15 Oct.-16 Mar.). Two-bedroom (17-5 handicap accessible), private bath, kitchen, microwave, CATV, phone (free local calls), pots/pans, linens. Rates: $44-$58 daily.

**Motel:** Rooms (54). Rates: $39-$52 daily.

**SUPPORT FACILITIES:**

| | | |
|---|---|---|
| AAFES Shoppette | Beach | Boat Launch |
| Boat Rental | Boat Slip Rental | Deep-Sea Charter |
| Class VI | Fishing Pier | Game Room |
| Grills | Laundry | Marina |
| Party Boat | Picnic Area | Playground |
| Pool | Rec Equipment | Restrooms |
| Sewage Dump | Showers | TV Room |
| Vending Machine | Water Sports | |

**ACTIVITIES:**

| | | |
|---|---|---|
| Boating | Deep-Sea Fishing | Jet Skis |
| Pontoon Boats | Swimming | |

**CREDIT CARDS ACCEPTED:** Visa, MasterCard and American Express.

**RESTRICTIONS:** No pets allowed. No firearms allowed. Additional fee for non-family member guests. Posted speed limit ten miles per hour.

## EGLIN FAMCAMP (FL25R1)
Eglin Air Force Base
Eglin AFB, FL 32542-6823

**TELEPHONE NUMBER INFORMATION:** Main installation numbers: C-850-882-1110, D-312-872-1110. Police for FAMCAMP, C-850-882-2502.

**LOCATION:** On base. From I-10 E or W, take FL-85 S to Niceville, turn right on Highway 20 (John Sims Parkway) to east gate at Eglin. *USMRA: page 39 (C,D-13).* NMC: Pensacola, 40 miles west.

**DESCRIPTION OF AREA:** Located on a peninsula on the northern coast of the Gulf of Mexico in Fort Walton area off Choctawhatchee Bay. The FAMCAMP is part of the Post Recreation Area and is situated adjacent to the beach. Beautiful forested areas and fresh-water lakes also nearby. The boat rental marina is within walking distance of the beach. Full range of support facilities available at Eglin AFB.

**SEASON OF OPERATION:** Year round.

**ELIGIBILITY:** Active/Reservists/Retired/DoD civilians.

**RESERVATIONS:** No advance reservations. Address: 96 SVS/SVRO, Outdoor Recreation, 404 N. 7th St. Suite 3, Eglin AFB, FL 32542-5000. **C-850-882-6581.**

**Camper Spaces:** Gravel (22), E (110V/20/30A)/W hookups. Rates: $10 daily/$65 weekly/$250 monthly.

**Tent Spaces:** Grass (20), no hookups. Rates: $5 daily/$30 weekly/$155 monthly.

**SUPPORT FACILITIES:**

| | | |
|---|---|---|
| Beach | Boat Launch | Boat Rental |
| Chapel | Deep-Sea Fishing | Fishing Boats |

| | | |
|---|---|---|
| Golf | Grills | Laundry |
| Marina | Picnic Area | Propane Sales |
| Rec Equipment | Restrooms* | Sewage Dump |
| Shoppette | Showers* | Sports Fields |
| Trails | | |

* Handicap accessible.

**ACTIVITIES:**

| | | |
|---|---|---|
| Fishing/license | Hunting | Jogging |
| Outdoor Adventure Program | | |

**CREDIT CARDS ACCEPTED:** Visa and MasterCard.

**RESTRICTIONS:** Pets allowed, owner must clean up after pet.

## HURLBURT FAMCAMP (FL51R1)
Hurlburt Field
Hurlburt Field, FL 32544-5272

**TELEPHONE NUMBER INFORMATION:** Main installation numbers: C-850-884-6939, D-312-579-6939.

**LOCATION:** Off base. US-98 east of main gate to Hurlburt Air Force Base, 100 yards on left. *USMRA: page 39 (C-13).* NMC: Pensacola, 40 miles west.

**DESCRIPTION OF AREA:** Located on the Gulf of Mexico with the Gulf on south side and US-98 on the other. New sites with large area shaded by oak tree, excellent bird-watching location. All-ranks club located west at Soundside, large picnic area to east.

**SEASON OF OPERATION:** Year round.

**ELIGIBILITY:** Active/Reservists/Retired/DoD civilians.

**RESERVATIONS:** Accepted only for active duty on PCS and TDY orders; others, first come, first serve. Address: 16 SVS/SVRO, Hurlburt Field, FL 32544-5000. **C-850-884-6939, D-312-579-6939.** Check in Bldg 92473. After hours, park and register next day. Check out 1200 hours.

**Camper Spaces:** Concrete (25), E (110V/30A)/S/W hookups, BBQ grill, sitting bench. $10 daily.

**Tent Spaces:** 10, no hookups. Rates: $5 daily.

**SUPPORT FACILITIES:**

| | | |
|---|---|---|
| Beaches | Boat Rental | Camping Equipment |
| Chapel | Club/Bar | Convenience Store |
| Golf | Laundry | Nature Trail |
| Overflow Parking | Picnic Area | Rec Equipment |
| Sewage Dump | Showers | Snack Bar |
| Sports Fields | Tennis Courts | Water Sports Equipment |

**ACTIVITIES:**

| | | |
|---|---|---|
| Boating | Volleyball | Water Sports |

**CREDIT CARDS ACCEPTED:** Visa and MasterCard.

**RESTRICTIONS:** Pets allowed on leash. No firearms.

# JACKSONVILLE RV PARK (FL40R1)

Jacksonville Naval Air Station
Jacksonville, FL 32212-5000

**TELEPHONE NUMBER INFORMATION:** Main installation numbers: C-904-542-2345/2346, D-312-942-2345. Police for RV park, C-904-542-4539. D-312-942-4529.

**LOCATION:** On base. Access from US-17 (Roosevelt Blvd) south of Jacksonville, near intersection with I-295. *USMRA: page 50 (B-6,7).* NMC: Jacksonville, 4 miles north.

**DESCRIPTION OF AREA:** The RV park is located on Manatee Point on the St. Johns River. There are many opportunities for water-related activities. Full range of support facilities available on base, many within walking distance.

**SEASON OF OPERATION:** Year round.

**ELIGIBILITY:** Active/Reservists/Retired/DoD civilians at Jacksonville NAS.

**RESERVATIONS:** Accepted. Address: MWR, 584 Enterprise Avenue, Box 14, Attn: RV Park, Naval Air Station, Jacksonville, FL 32212-5000. **C-904-542-3227, D-312-942-3227.** Fax: C-904-542-3742. E-mail: dahearn@nasjax.org. Check in at Auto Hobby Shop, Bldg 622, on Birmingham Avenue, 0800 hours Mon-Fri, 0900-1700 hours Sat-Sun, holidays. After hours, go directly to RV park (located at Birmingham and Mustang). check in the following morning. Discounts available to holders of Golden Age and Golden Access Passports.

**Camper Spaces:** 8, E (110/220V/30A)/S/W hookups. Rates: $13 daily. 4, E (110/220V/30A)/W hookups. Rates: $10 daily.

**Camper/Tent Spaces:** 14, no hookups. Rates: $5 daily.

**SUPPORT FACILITIES:**

| | | |
|---|---|---|
| Auto Craft Shop | Bath House | Boat Launch |
| Boat Rental/Storage | Chapel | Clubs/nearby |
| Commissary | Convenience Store | Equipment Rental |
| Exchange | Fishing Pier | Fitness Center |
| Gas | Golf/base | Ice |
| Laundry | Marina | Pavilion |
| Picnic Area | Playground | Pool |
| Restrooms | Sewage Dump | Shoppette |
| Showers | Shuttle Bus | Snack Bar |
| Sports Fields | Telephones | Tennis Courts |
| Trails | | |

**ACTIVITIES:**

| | | |
|---|---|---|
| Boating | Fishing/license | Golf |
| Hiking | Manatee Watching | Swimming |
| Tennis | | |

**CREDIT CARDS ACCEPTED:** None.

**RESTRICTIONS:** Pets allowed on leash. No firearms allowed, must be checked at main entrance. Two-week limit.

# LAKE FRETWELL RECREATION AREA (FL24R1)

Cecil Field Naval Air Station
Cecil Filed NAS, FL 32215-0184
*Scheduled to close August 1999.*

**TELEPHONE NUMBER INFORMATION:** Main installation numbers: C-904-778-5626, D-312-860-5626. Police for recreation area, C-904-778-5626.

**LOCATION:** On base. From I-10 E or W, take FL-228 exit east and follow Normandy to main gate. Recreation area approximately two miles from gate. *USMRA: page 38 (G-3).* NMC: Jacksonville, 13 miles northeast.

**DESCRIPTION OF AREA:** Located at Lake Fretwell. Full range of support facilities available on base.

**SEASON OF OPERATION:** Year round.

**ELIGIBILITY:** Active/Reservists/Retired.

**RESERVATIONS:** Accepted up to 30 days in advance. Address: MWR Department, Box 109, Bldg 200, C Avenue, NAS Cecil Field, FL 32215-0109. **C-904-778-6112, D-312-860-6112.** Fax: C-904-778-6636, D-312-860-6636.

**Camper Spaces:** Hardstand (4), E (110/220V/30A)/W hookups. Rates: $5 daily/$25 weekly.

**Tent Spaces:** Only on or adjacent to camper spaces.

**SUPPORT FACILITIES:**

| | | |
|---|---|---|
| Gas | Golf | Grills |
| Nature Trail | Picnic Area | Playground |
| Rec Equipment | Restrooms | Sewage Dump |
| Showers | Sports Fields | Tennis Courts |

**ACTIVITIES:**

| | |
|---|---|
| Hiking | Racquetball |

**CREDIT CARDS ACCEPTED:** None.

**RESTRICTIONS:** Pets allowed on leash. No firearms allowed. No open fires in camping area.

# LAKE PIPPIN, MAXWELL/ GUNTER RECREATION AREA (FL12R1)

Maxwell Air Force Base
Maxwell AFB, AL 36112-5000

**TELEPHONE NUMBER INFORMATION:** Main installation numbers: C-334-953-1110, D-312-493-1110. Police (Eglin AFB) for recreation area, C-850-882-2502.

**LOCATION:** Off base. Near Niceville FL. From I-10 at Crestview take FL-85 S to Niceville. Take FL-20 E approximately 6.5 miles to sign for Maxwell/Gunter Recreation Area. Mid-Bay Bridge (toll) makes area easily accessible from both FL-20 and US-98. *USMRA: page 39 (C,D-13).* NMI: Eglin AFB FL, 15 miles west. NMC: Pensacola FL, 25 miles west.

**DESCRIPTION OF AREA:** Located on Choctawhatchee Bay on northern coast of Gulf of Mexico. Lovely wooded site on beach. Within driving distance of Pensacola, Panama City, Fort Walton Beach and fishing attractions. Easy access to full range of support facilities available at Eglin Air Force Base.

*FLORIDA*
*Lake Pippin, Maxwell/Gunter Recreation Area, continued*

**SEASON OF OPERATION:** Year round.

**ELIGIBILITY:** Active/Reservists/Retired/DoD civilians at Maxwell/Gunter AFB.

**RESERVATIONS:** Required with payment in full. Active up to six months in advance; others up to three months. Patrons must have receipt. Address: Outdoor Recreation Reservations Office, 204 West Selfridge Street, Maxwell AFB, AL 36112-5000. **C-334-953-3509/3510, D-312-493-3509.** Recreation Area, information only, C-850-897-2411. Check in at gate house after 1700 hours (15 Mar-15 Oct); after 1200 hours (16 Oct-14 Mar), check out 1500 hours.

**Mobile Homes:** Two- and three-bedroom (10), heat, A/C, one or 1.5 private baths, blankets, pillows. Rates: $35 daily (monthly and lower daily rates available 16 Oct-14 Mar).

**Camper Spaces:** Gravel (15), E (110V/30/50A)/S/W hookups. Rates: $15 daily/$80 weekly/$255 monthly. Gravel (23), E (110V/50A)/W hookups. Rates: $13 daily/$75 weekly/$230 monthly.

**Tent Spaces:** Gravel (10). Rates: $7 daily.

**SUPPORT FACILITIES:**

| | | |
|---|---|---|
| Beach | Boat Launch | Boat Rental |
| Boat/RV Storage | Grills | Laundry |
| Picnic Area | Playground | Restrooms* |
| Sewage Dump | Showers* | TV Rental |

* Handicap accessible.

**ACTIVITIES:**

| | | |
|---|---|---|
| Boating | Fishing | Hiking |
| Jogging | Sailing | Swimming |

**CREDIT CARDS ACCEPTED:** Visa and MasterCard.

**RESTRICTIONS:** No pets allowed. No firearms allowed. No open fires. Quiet hours after 2200 hours. As facility is in an isolated area, check your supplies carefully before arriving.

## MANATEE COVE CAMPGROUND & RECREATIONAL LODGING (FL03R1)
Patrick Air Force Base
Patrick AFB, FL 32925-3341

**TELEPHONE NUMBER INFORMATION**: Main installation numbers: C-407-494-1110, D-312-854-1110.

**LOCATION:** On base. Take I-95 N or S to exit 73 (Wickam Road) east, three miles to State Road 404 (Pineda Causeway), six miles, left on A-1A, three miles to AFB. *USMRA: page 38 (I-8)*. NMC: Melbourne, 10 miles south.

**DESCRIPTION OF AREA:** Located adjacent to Cape Canaveral Air Force Station and along the Banana River which is host to the remaining population of manatees. Conveniently located for visiting Disney World, Universal Studios, John F. Kennedy Space Center, and many other popular attractions. Full range of support facilities available on base.

**SEASON OF OPERATION:** Year round.

**ELIGIBILITY:** Active/Reservists/Retired/DoD civilians.

**RESERVATIONS:** Accepted up to one year in advance for beach house only via credit card. No advance reservations for others. Address: FAMCAMP, P.O. Box 254740, Patrick AFB, FL 32925-4740. **C-407-494-4787, D-312-854-4787.** Check in 0800-1600 hours Sun-Sat (closed federal holidays); on-site host at other times, check out 1200 hours.

**Beach House:** Three-bedroom (3), sleeps eight, three full baths, furnished, kitchen, CATV/VCR, washer/dryer, linens, garage, Florida room overlooking beach. Rates: $125 daily/$800 weekly Jun-Oct, $150 daily/$1000 weekly Nov-May.

**Camper Spaces:** 55, handicap accessible, E (110V/20/30A)/W hookups. Rates: $11 daily. Overflow (36), handicap accessible, no hookups. Rates: $7 daily. Primitive (5), handicap accessible, no hookups. Rates: $7 daily.

**Tent Spaces:** 8, no hookups. Rates: $7 daily.

**SUPPORT FACILITIES:**

| | | |
|---|---|---|
| Bath House | Bicycle/Helmet Rental | Boat Rental |
| Camping Equipment | Fishing Equipment | Fishing Pier |
| Golf/on base | Laundry | Pavilions |
| Playground | Range (Skeet/Trap) | Restrooms |
| Sewage Dump | Showers | Telephones |

**ACTIVITIES:**

| | | |
|---|---|---|
| Boating | Fishing/license | Jogging |
| Sightseeing | Swimming | Water Skiing |
| Trips | | |

**CREDIT CARDS ACCEPTED:** Visa and MasterCard.

**RESTRICTIONS:** No pets allowed in beach house, pets allowed on leash in other locations. Maximum stay 30 days.

## MARATHON RECREATION COTTAGES (FL28R1)
Marathon Coast Guard Station
Marathon, FL 33050-2199

**TELEPHONE NUMBER INFORMATION:** Main installation numbers: C-305-535-4565.

**LOCATION:** On base. In the Florida Keys on US-1 (Overseas Highway) at mile marker 48 at Marathon. Enter recreation area from US-1. *USMRA: page 39 (H-15)*. NMC: Miami, 111 miles northeast.

**DESCRIPTION OF AREA:** Situated on Vaca Key in the heart of the Florida Keys. Topography is similar to that of islands in the Eastern Caribbean. Beaches on Atlantic side and excellent fishing in both the Gulf and Atlantic. Limited support facilities available on base; full range at Key West Naval Air Station on Boca Chica Key, 40 miles south.

**SEASON OF OPERATION:** Year round.

**ELIGIBILITY:** Active/Reservists/Retired.

**RESERVATIONS:** Required for cottages with full payment in advance, by application only, at least eight weeks in advance. Accepted for RV with full payment which includes a $24 non-refundable deposit. Application may be obtained by phone, but reservations cannot be made by phone. Address: USCG Commanding Officer (PM), 100 MacArthur Causeway, Miami Beach, FL 33139-5101. **C-305-535-4565.** Fax: C-305-535-4566. For information, 1800 Overseas Highway, Marathon, FL 33050-2199. C-305-743-3549. Check in with caretaker 1200-1800 hours, after 1600 hours with OOD, check out 1200 hours.

*Marathon Recreation Cottages, continued*

**Cottages:** One-bedroom (4), sleeps five, one double bed, two single sofabeds, rollaway, furnished, kitchen, A/C, CATV, linens, screened in patio. Rates: $20-$35 daily, depending on rank.

**RV Spaces:** Paved (4), E (110/220V/20/30/50A)/S/W hookups, picnic table, BBQ grill. Rates: $12 daily.

**SUPPORT FACILITIES:**

| | | |
|---|---|---|
| Bicycles | Boat Rental | Boat Dock |
| Grills | Picnic Areas | |

**ACTIVITIES:**

| | | |
|---|---|---|
| Basketball | Bicycling | Boating |
| Fishing/license | Hiking | SCUBA Diving |
| Snorkeling | Swimming | |

**CREDIT CARDS ACCEPTED:** None.

**RESTRICTIONS:** No pets allowed in cottages. No firearms allowed. No waste dumping allowed. Twelve day limit to include only one weekend for cottages, 14 day limit for RV spaces. No cribs provided. Swimming not allowed on CG Station; diving and fishing areas accessible by boat.

# OAK GROVE PARK FAMCAMP (FL09R1)

Pensacola Naval Air Station
Pensacola, FL 32508-5217

**TELEPHONE NUMBER INFORMATION:** Main installation numbers: C-850-452-0111, D-312-922-0111. Police for trailer park, C-850-452-2453.

**LOCATION:** On base. I-10 to exit 2. South on Pine Forest Road. Turn right on highway 173 (Blue Angel Parkway) which will lead south 12 miles and enter back entrance to NAS. *USMRA: page 53 (B-4,5).* NMC: Pensacola, 8 miles east.

**DESCRIPTION OF AREA:** Located in wooded area across from Naval Aviation Museum along a 1.5 miles Gulf of Mexico beachfront with historic lighthouse in center. Old Fort Pickens can be viewed from along beach. Full range of support facilities available on base.

**SEASON OF OPERATION:** Year round.

**ELIGIBILITY:** Active/Reservists/Retired.

**RESERVATIONS:** Accepted up to three months in advance for active duty, up to two months in advance for Retirees with two day's non-refundable deposit. First come, first serve in campground. Address: Oak Grove Park Recreation Department, Pensacola NAS, FL 32508-5000. **C-850-452-2535, D-312-922-2535.** *Note: Renovations of the campground begin Fall 1998 to include eight two-bedroom cabins, ten new camping pads and nine new RV sites. There are also plans to update the water and electrical hookups and to add sewage hookups to each RV site. Estimated date of completion is Spring 1999.*

**Cabins:** One-bedroom (12-1 handicap accessible), private bath, furnished, kitchen, pots/pans, dishes, linens. Rates: $35 daily.

**Camper Spaces:** Dirt (42), E (110V/30A)/W hookups. Rates: $9 daily.

**Tent Spaces:** Dirt (14), no hookups. Rates: $4 daily.

**SUPPORT FACILITIES:**

| | | |
|---|---|---|
| Boat Launch | Boat Rental | Camping Equipment |
| Marina | Picnic Area | Rec Equipment |
| Restrooms | Sailing Facility | Sewage Dump |
| Showers | | |

**ACTIVITIES:**

| | | |
|---|---|---|
| Boating | Fishing/license | Swimming |

National Museum of Naval Aviation is a short walk from on-base accommodations.

**CREDIT CARDS ACCEPTED:** Visa, MasterCard and American Express.

**RESTRICTIONS:** No pets allowed in cabins, allowed on leash in camping area. No firearms allowed.

# PANAMA CITY CSS OUTDOOR RECREATION/MARINA (FL07R1)

Panama City Coastal Systems Station Naval Surface Warfare Center
Panama City, FL 32407-7001

**TELEPHONE NUMBER INFORMATION:** Main installation numbers: C-850-234-4100, D-312-436-4100. Police for recreation area, C-850-234-4373.

**LOCATION:** On base. Located on US-98 at the foot of the Hathaway Bridge in Panama City Beach. *USMRA: page 39 (D-14).* NMC: Panama City, 5 miles west.

**DESCRIPTION OF AREA:** Panama City Beach is considered one of the world's most beautiful beaches because of the brilliant white sand and emerald waters of the Gulf of Mexico. Water sports (jet skiing, sailing, boating, swimming, etc) attract tourists to the area. Limited support facilities available on base.

**SEASON OF OPERATION:** Year round.

**ELIGIBILITY:** Active/Reservists/Retired/DoD civilians at Coastal Systems Station. Active/Retired/DoD civilians at Park Model mobile homes and campground.

**RESERVATIONS:** Accepted six months in advance (three months for DoD), a deposit of 50% is required. Address: CSS/MWR Condos, 349 Soloman Drive, Panama City, FL 32407-7001. **C-850-234-4556, D-312-436-4556.** Fax: C-850-234-4991, D-312-436-4991. For mobile homes or campground, contact MWR Marina and Campground, **C-850-234-4402, D-312-436-4402.** HP: http://www.ncsc.navy.mil. Check in at marina, check out 1100 hours. *Note: A $0.590 million new R/V campground facility has been approved in the Fiscal Year 1998 Major and Minor Construction Program.*

**Condos on the Beach:** Three-bedroom (3), sleeps eight, two baths. Rates: $86-$133 daily (depending on season); $495-$821 weekly (depending on season). Monthly rates available off-season.

**Mobile Homes:** One-bedroom (3-1 handicap accessible), park models, sleeps six, linens. Patrons must provide towels. Rates: $35 daily (E1-E5); $40 daily (E6+); $50 daily (DoD Civilian).

**Camper Spaces:** Concrete pad (22), E (110V/30A)/S/W hookups. Concrete pad (4), E (110V/30A)/W hookups. Rates: $10 daily (E1-E6); $11 daily (E6+); $16 daily (DoD Civilian). Monthly rates available.

*FLORIDA*
*Panama City CSS Outdoor Recreation/Marina, continued*

**Campers, Coachman:** Sleeps five. Rates: $15 off base, $20 on base (E1-E5); $20 off base, $25 on base (E6+); $30 off base, $35 on base (DoD Civilian). Available through MWR Marina and Campground.

**Campers, Casita:** Sleeps three. Rates: $12 off base, $17 on base (E1-E5); $17 off base, $22 on base (E6+); $27 off base, $32 on base (DoD Civilian). Available through MWR Marina and Campground.

**SUPPORT FACILITIES:**

| | | |
|---|---|---|
| Archery Range | Auto Craft Shop | Bath House |
| Beach | Boat Launch | Boat Rental/Storage |
| Camping Equipment | Exchange | Fitness Center |
| Gas | Grills | Ice |
| Marina | Pavilions | Picnic Area |
| Playground | Pool | Rec Equipment |
| Restrooms | Sewage Dump | Showers |
| Sports Fields | Telephones | Tennis Courts |

**ACTIVITIES:**

| | | |
|---|---|---|
| Bicycling | Boating | Fishing/license |
| Horseshoes | Hunting/license | Picnicking |
| Sailing | Scuba Diving | Snorkeling |
| Swimming | Tours | Water Skiing |

**CREDIT CARDS ACCEPTED:** Visa, MasterCard, American Express and Discover.

**RESTRICTIONS:** No pets except in campground, must be on leash. No firearms allowed. Campfires are not permitted on sites.

## SIGSBEE RV PARK (FL37R1)
Key West Naval Air Station
Key West NAS, FL 33040-9037

**TELEPHONE NUMBER INFORMATION:** Main installation numbers: C-305-293-3700, D-312-483-3700. Police for RV park, C-305-293-2114.

**LOCATION:** On base. From US-1 in Key West, turn right on North Roosevelt Blvd. Take first right after Searstown Plaza (Kennedy Drive) to Sigsbee Housing Area. *USMRA: page 39 (G-16).* NMI: Key West NAS, 7 miles north. NMC: Key West, in city limits.

**DESCRIPTION OF AREA:** RV park and tent spaces are located across from the Commissary and Navy Exchange. There are tent spaces on the waterfront, next to the bath house, and across the street adjacent to the new ball field for overflow tenters only. Overflow camper spaces are on Trumbo Point in northwest Key West. It has never been necessary to turn anyone away due to the fact that overflow is open during the busy season. Excellent fishing, diving and snorkeling year round (best in Apr-Sep). Historical sites include Fort Zachary Taylor and Ernest Hemingway House. Limited support facilities at Trumbo Point; full range of facilities available at Sigsbee Park.

**SEASON OF OPERATION:** Year round.

**ELIGIBILITY:** Active/Reservists/Retired/DoD civilians.

**RESERVATIONS:** No advance reservations. First come, first serve basis. Address: Sigsbee RV Park, MWR Department, P.O. Box 9027, Naval Air Station, Key West, FL 33040-9001. **C-1-888-539-7697, C-305-293-4432/4433.** Fax: C-305-293-4413. Check in at Sigsbee Community Center, check out 1200 hours.

**Camper Spaces:** Concrete (70), E (110V/30A)/S/W hookups. Rates: $14 daily. Overflow (200), at Trumbo Point (Dec-Apr), central W hookup. Rates: $7 daily.

**Tent Spaces:** 10, central W hookup. Rates: $7 daily.

**SUPPORT FACILITIES:**

| | | |
|---|---|---|
| Bath House | Beach | Boat Launch |
| Boat Rental | Commissary | Exchange |
| Fishing Tackle | Gas | Grills |
| Ice | Laundry | Lounge/Cafe |
| Marina | Pay Telephones | Picnic Area |
| Playground | Restrooms | Sewage Dump |
| Showers | Snorkel Gear | Sports Fields |
| Wave Runner Rental | | |

**ACTIVITIES:**

| | | |
|---|---|---|
| Boating | Fishing | Snorkeling |
| Swimming | | |

**CREDIT CARDS ACCEPTED:** Visa, MasterCard, American Express and Discover.

**RESTRICTIONS:** Pets allowed on leash, limit two, must have complete and current immunizations, owner must clean up after pet. No open campfires. Quiet hours 2300-0700 hours. Fourteen day limit on spaces with hookups. Only one parking space is available per site.

## TYNDALL FAMCAMP (FL26R1)

Tyndall Air Force Base
Tyndall AFB, FL 32403-5428

**TELEPHONE NUMBER INFORMATION:** Main installation numbers: C-850-283-1110, D-312-523-1110. Police for FAMCAMP, C-850-283-2254.

**LOCATION:** On base. US-231 S to Panama City, US-98 E to base. FAMCAMP .25 miles on right after crossing Dupont Bridge. *USMRA: page 39 (E-14).* NMC: Panama City, 11 miles west.

**DESCRIPTION OF AREA:** Located on the coast of the Gulf of Mexico with the Gulf on one side and East Bay on the other. Some sites have water views; all are larger than normal and shaded by oak trees with Spanish Moss. Bird-watching is excellent. Water sports attract many tourists to the area, beaches and swimming areas are approximately two miles from the FAMCAMP. Full range of support facilities available on base.

**SEASON OF OPERATION:** Year round.

**ELIGIBILITY:** Active/Reservists/Retired/DoD civilians.

**RESERVATIONS:** No advance reservations for campsites; reservations for cottages accepted up to 90 days in advance. Address: FAMCAMP, 101 FAMCAMP Road, Tyndall AFB, FL 32403-1045. **C-850-283-2798, D-312-523-2798.**

**Cottages:** Two-bedroom (3), furnished. Rates: $60 daily/$300 weekly. Off season (1 Nov-31 Mar) Rates: $60 daily/$250 weekly/$600 monthly.

**Camper Spaces:** Concrete (59), E (120V/50A)/S/W/CATV hookups. Rates: $13 daily/$285 monthly. Concrete (31), E (110V/30A)/W/CATV hookups. Rates: $12 daily/$265 monthly. Adequate overflow parking available, some with E/W hookups.

**Tent Spaces:** Cleared (8), no hookups. Rates: $7 daily.

**SUPPORT FACILITIES:**

| | | |
|---|---|---|
| Archery | Beach | Boat Rental |
| Camping Equipment | Chapel | Community Center |
| Convenience Store | Gas | Golf |
| Grills | Laundry | LP Gas |
| Marina | Mini Golf | Nature Trail |
| Picnic Area | Racquetball | Restrooms |
| Sewage Dump | Showers | Shuffleboard |
| Skeet Range | Snack Bar | Sports Fields |
| Stables | Tennis Courts | Water Sports Equipment |

*Note: A new campground community center incorporating shower and laundry facilities, and an indoor recreation center with kitchen is complete and accessible to handicapped.*

**ACTIVITIES:**

| | | |
|---|---|---|
| Fishing/license | Hunting/license | Swimming |

**CREDIT CARDS ACCEPTED:** Visa and MasterCard.

**RESTRICTIONS:** Pets allowed on leash, limit two domestic. No pets allowed in rental cottages. No discharge allowed of firearms or fireworks.

# GEORGIA

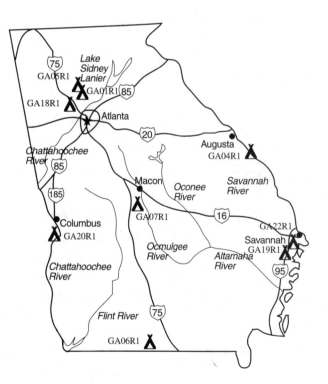

GEORGIA

# DOBBINS LAKESIDE FAMCAMP (GA18R1)

Dobbins Air Reserve Base
Dobbins ARB, GA 30069-5010

**TELEPHONE NUMBER INFORMATION:** Main installation numbers: C-770-919-5000, D-312-925-1110. Police for FAMCAMP, C-770-919-4909.

**LOCATION:** On base. From I-75, south of Marietta, exit to GA-280 W 1.5 miles to AFB. Entrance is on US-41 S. *USMRA: page 49 (A-1)*. NMC: Atlanta, 15 miles south.

**DESCRIPTION OF AREA:** Offers many recreational and leisure activities. Conveniently located for sightseeing in Atlanta and surrounding area. Geese, ducks, beavers and other wildlife frequent the picnic/playground area adjacent to the FAMCAMP. Limited support facilities available on base; wide range available at Atlanta NAS adjacent and to the east of Dobbins ARB.

**SEASON OF OPERATION:** Year round.

**ELIGIBILITY:** Active/Reservists/Retired/DoD civilians.

**RESERVATIONS:** No advance reservations. First come, first serve. Patrons should park RV on available site and report to Bldg 558 to register. Address: Recreational Services, 94 SPTG/MWR, 1335 Dozer Circle, Bldg 558, Dobbins ARB, GA 30069-4510. **C-770-919-4870, D-312-925-4870.**

**Camper Spaces:** Hardstand (18), E (110V/30A)/W hookups. Rates: $8 daily.

**SUPPORT FACILITIES:**

| | | |
|---|---|---|
| Chapel/nearby | Grills | Grocery/nearby |
| Picnic Area | Playground | Rec Center |
| Rec Equipment | Restrooms* | Sewage Dump |
| Showers* | Sports Fields | Tennis Courts |

* Handicap accessible

**ACTIVITIES:**

| | | |
|---|---|---|
| Horseshoes | Jogging | Volleyball |

**CREDIT CARDS ACCEPTED:** Visa and MasterCard.

**RESTRICTIONS:** Pets allowed on leash. No swimming or fishing allowed.

# FORT GORDON RECREATION AREA (GA04R1)

Fort Gordon
Ford Gordon, GA 30905-5000

**TELEPHONE NUMBER INFORMATION:** Main installation numbers: C-706-791-0110, D-312-780-0110. Police for recreation area, C-706-541-1057 ext 131.

**LOCATION:** Off post. From I-20 west of Augusta, take exit 61 Appling to GA-47 N to end (Washington Road). Left on Washington Road to recreation area. *USMRA: page 37 (F-4)*. NMI: Fort Gordon, 25 miles south. NMC: Augusta, 25 miles southeast.

**DESCRIPTION OF AREA:** Located on 904-acre site with a 1200 mile shoreline along Thurmond Lake (formerly Clarks Hill Lake) on Georgia/South Carolina line. Ideal for wide range of outdoor activities in fresh-water lakes and rivers of the area. Savannah about 120 miles southeast. Easy access to full range of support facilities available at Fort Gordon.

**SEASON OF OPERATION:** Year round. Marina closed Oct through Mar.

**ELIGIBILITY:** Active/Reservists/Retired/DoD civilians.

**RESERVATIONS:** Required for mobile homes and cabins for a minimum of two nights; one night's deposit required seven days in advance. May be made up to 45 days in advance for active duty, 30 days in advance for others. Walk-ins accepted when cabins/mobile homes are available. Address: Fort Gordon Recreation Area, P.O. Box 67, Appling, GA 30802-5000. **C-706-541-1057.** Fax: C-706-541-1963. Discounts for campsite rental are available to holders of Golden Age and Golden Access Passports.

**Cabins:** Three-bedroom (9), furnished. Rates: $50-$60 daily.

**Mobile Homes:** Three-bedroom (8), furnished. Rates: $45-$50 daily.

**Bunk House:** 1, double rooms, sleeps 24, kitchen, TV, washer/dryer. Common shower room. Rates: $7 each person daily ($72 minimum).

**Camper Spaces:** Gravel (60), E (110V/30A)/S/W hookups. Rates: $10 daily. Gravel (30), E hookup. Rates: $5 daily.

**Tent Spaces:** Dirt (50), no hookups. Rates: $3 daily.

**Pioneer Camping Area:** Primitive, no hookups. Rates: $1 each person daily; $10 minimum daily for large groups.

**SUPPORT FACILITIES:**

| | | |
|---|---|---|
| Adventure Ropes | Bath House | Beach/summer |
| Boat Launch | Boat Rental | Boat Sheds/Slips |
| Camping Equipment | Country Store | Fish House |
| Marina | Pavilions | Picnic Area |
| Playground | Restrooms | Sewage Dump |
| Showers | Trails | TV Room |

**ACTIVITIES:**

| | | |
|---|---|---|
| Boating | Fishing/license | Hiking |
| Picnicking | Swimming | |

**CREDIT CARDS ACCEPTED:** Visa, MasterCard and American Express.

**RESTRICTIONS:** No pets in cabins, mobile homes or swimming area. Pets allowed on leash in other areas, owners must clean up after pets. Firearms, bows and arrows, explosives, fireworks and all sporting devices capable of causing death or injury are prohibited. Fort Gordon boating safety card required for boat rental.

# GRASSY POND RECREATION AREA (GA06R1)

Moody Air Force Base
Moody AFB, GA 31699-1507

**TELEPHONE NUMBER INFORMATION:** Main installation numbers: C-912-257-4211, D-312-460-1110. Police, C-912-333-5133 (sheriff's office).

**LOCATION:** Off base. From I-75 south of Valdosta, take exit 2, to west on GA-376 (Clyattville Road). Immediately watch for signs and left turn to recreation area. *USMRA: page 37 (D-9)*. NMI: Moody AFB, 25 miles north. NMC: Valdosta, 16 miles north.

**DESCRIPTION OF AREA:** Located along a 275-acre pond surrounded by 500 acres of rolling, wooded terrain near Georgia/Florida line, Grassy Pond is a major fishing area offering a variety of facilities and activities. Full range of support facilities available at Moody AFB.

**SEASON OF OPERATION:** Year round, during daylight hours.

**ELIGIBILITY:** Active/Reservists/Retired/DoD and NAF civilians.

**RESERVATIONS:** Required for cabins. Address: Recreation Services, Grassy Pond, 5360 Grassy Pond Road, Lake Park, GA 31636-5000. **C-912-559-5840, D-312-460-1110 ext 559-5840.** Check in for cabins after 1400 hours, check out 1200 hours.

**Cabins:** 6, sleeps six, private bath, kitchen, pots/pans, dishes, E hookup, linens. Patrons must provide bath and kitchen towels, wash cloths, paper towels, detergent for dishes. Rates: $25 daily. 7, sleeps nine, private bath, kitchen, dishes, pots/pans, E hookup, linens. Patrons must provide bath and kitchen towels, wash cloths, paper towels, detergent for dishes. Rates: $35 daily.

**Camper Spaces:** Gravel (18),E (110V/30A)/S/W $10 daily.

**Tent Spaces:** Many, no hookups. Rates: $5 daily.

**SUPPORT FACILITIES:**

| | | |
|---|---|---|
| Boat Launch | Boat Rental | Fishing Docks |
| Fishing Tackle | Grills | Ice |
| Laundry | Mail Service | Paddle Boats |
| Pay Telephone | Picnic Area | Playground |
| Rec Center | Rec Equipment | Restrooms |
| Sewage Dump | Shelter Rental | Showers |
| Snack Bar | Tackle/Bait | TV Room |
| Wading Pool | | |

Fishing docks and entry doors are handicap accessible.
Wide range of RV maintenance service and parts available in local area.

**ACTIVITIES:**

| | | |
|---|---|---|
| Boating | Fishing/License | Horseshoes |
| Nature Trail | | |

**CREDIT CARDS ACCEPTED:** Visa and MasterCard.

**RESTRICTIONS:** No pets allowed in cabins. Pets allowed on leash at campsite, limit two, owner must clean up after pet. No firearms allowed. Quiet hours 2200-0800 hours.

# HOLBROOK POND RECREATION AREA AND CAMPGROUND (GA19R1)

Fort Stewart
Fort Stewart, GA 31314-5132

**TELEPHONE NUMBER INFORMATION:** Main installation numbers: C-912-767-1110, D-312-870-1110. Police for recreation area and campground, C-912-767-2822.

**LOCATION:** On post. From US-17 or I-95 S of Savannah take exit 15, west on GA-144 approximately 17 miles, left on FS-48 at sign for Outdoor Recreation Service Center Bldg 8325. *USMRA: page 37 (G-7).* NMC: Savannah, 30 miles northeast.

**DESCRIPTION OF AREA:** Located in Holbrook Pond area. Full range of support facilities available on main post, approximately six miles away.

**SEASON OF OPERATION:** Year round.

**ELIGIBILITY:** Active/Reservists/Retired/DoD civilians.

**RESERVATIONS:** Accepted up to 30 days in advance with payment in full. Address: Community Recreation Division (AFZP-PAR), Outdoor Recreation, Bldg 622, Fort Stewart, GA 31313-5000. **C-912-767-2717/2771/5145, D-312-870-2717/2771/5145** 1100-1730 hours Mon, Tue, Thu, Fri, 0700-1500 hours Sat-Sun summer; 1100-1730 hours Mon, Thu, Fri, 0930-1730 hours Sat winter. Check in at Outdoor Recreation, after hours check in with camp host at site 1. Check out 1100 hours. Discounts available to holders of Golden Age and Golden Access Passports.

**Camper Spaces:** Hardstand (20), E (110V/30A)/W hookups. Rates: $8 daily.

**Tent Spaces:** Primitive (20), central W. Rates: $3 daily.

**SUPPORT FACILITIES:**

| | | |
|---|---|---|
| ATV | Bait | Boat Rental |
| Convenience Store | Grills | Ice |
| Laundry | Pavilions | Picnic Area |
| Playground | Restrooms | Sewage Dump |
| Showers | Skeet/Trap Range | Trails |
| Vending Machine | | |

**ACTIVITIES:**

| | | |
|---|---|---|
| Boating | Fishing/license | Hiking |
| Hunting/license | | |

**CREDIT CARDS ACCEPTED:** Visa, MasterCard and Discover.

**RESTRICTIONS:** Pets allowed on leash; must be under owner control at all times. No firearms.

# LAKE ALLATOONA ARMY RECREATION AREA (GA05R1)

Fort McPherson
Fort McPherson, GA 30330-1049

**TELEPHONE NUMBER INFORMATION:** Main installation numbers: C-404-464-3113, D-312-572-1110. Police for recreation area, C-404-464-3712.

**LOCATION:** Off post. From Atlanta, take I-75 N to exit 121. Take a left on Highway 92, go right on top of the bridge, road dead ends into Highway 293, turn left. Follow Highway 293, turn right immediately after crossing the lake onto Sandtown. Clearly marked. *USMRA: page 37 (B-3).* NMI: Dobbins AFB and Atlanta NAS, 15 miles south. NMC: Atlanta, 43 miles south.

**DESCRIPTION OF AREA:** Located on 85 acre site at Lake Allatoona reservoir. Full range of beach and water activities. Conveniently situated for sightseeing in Atlanta and surrounding area, including Stone Mountain Memorial State Park and Six Flags. Full range of support facilities available at Fort McPherson and Dobbins ARB in Atlanta.

**SEASON OF OPERATION:** Year round.

**ELIGIBILITY:** Active/Reservists/Retired/DoD civilians at Fort McPherson and Fort Gillem.

*GEORGIA*
*Lake Allatoona Army Recreation Area, continued*

**RESERVATIONS:** Required for lodging. Active duty at Forts McPherson and Gillem have priority to make reservations during first ten days of any month and three succeeding months; all others may make reservations for same period after 10th day. Address: Army Recreation Area, 40 Old Sandtown Road, Cartersville, GA 30121-5000. **C-770-974-3413/9420.** Fax: C-770-974-1278. Check in 1700 hours to closing.

**Apartment:** Three-bedroom (3), handicap accessible, furnished, microwave, pots/pans, dishes, utensils, A/C, CATV, bed linens. Patrons must provide towels, extra blankets, can opener, soap, detergent, sharpened knives. Rates: $76 daily (off-season rates available 1 Oct-1 Mar). Efficiency (2). Rates: $36.

**Cabins:** Two-bedroom/deluxe (5). Rates: $68 daily (off-season rates available 1 Oct-1 Mar; 25% off cabin rates). Two-bedroom (12). Rates: $60 daily (off-season rates available 1 Oct-1 Mar). One-bedroom (8). Rates: $48 daily (off-season rates available 1 Oct-1 Mar). Furnished, microwave, dishes, pots/pans, utensils, A/C, CATV, bed linens. Patrons must provide towels, extra blankets, can opener, soap, detergent, sharpened knives. *Note: Several two-bedroom cabins are handicap accessible.*

**RV Spaces:** 12, E (110V/30A)/S/W hookups. Rates: $15 daily (off-season rates available 1 Oct-1 Mar).

**Tent Spaces:** 15, E (110V/30A)/W hookups. Rates: $10 daily (off-season rates available 1 Oct-1 Mar).

**SUPPORT FACILITIES:**

| | | |
|---|---|---|
| Basketball Court | Bath Houses* | Beach |
| Boat Launch | Fishing Piers | Game Room |
| Grills | Laundromat | Marina |
| Miniature Golf | Pavilions | Picnic Area |
| Playground | Restrooms | Sewage Dump |
| Showers | Trails | Volleyball (sand) |

* Handicap accessible.

**ACTIVITIES:**

| | | |
|---|---|---|
| Boating | Fishing/license | Horseshoes |
| Swimming | | |

**CREDIT CARDS ACCEPTED:** Visa, MasterCard and American Express.

**RESTRICTIONS:** No pets allowed. No firearms allowed. Open fires within fire rings only. No fireworks. Motorcycles, minibikes, ATVs and motor carts prohibited. Fourteen day limit 1 Apr-31 Oct; cabin rentals-two day minimum on weekends (during peak season 1 Mar-30 Sep). Boat rental from May to Oct. Family members under 18 must be accompanied by authorized adult sponsor to use area. Personal VCRs are prohibited, except with use of TV provided by patron.

# LOTTS ISLAND ARMY AIR FIELD TRAVEL CAMP (GA22R1)
Hunter Army Airfield
Hunter AAF, GA 31409-5014

**TELEPHONE NUMBER INFORMATION:** Main installation numbers: C-912-352-6521, D-312-870-1110. Police for travel camp, C-912-352-5916.

**LOCATION:** On post. From I-95 take Hunter Army Airfield exit. Take GA-204 N approximately four miles to sign on left for Rio Gate, turn left. Go to stop sign make a right. Continue to sign for Outdoor Recreation, then left to Bldg 8454. *USMRA: page 37 (G-7).* NMC: Savannah, 5 miles northeast.

**DESCRIPTION OF AREA:** Located at Lotts Island, the travel camp is convenient to the many water-related activities of the inland harbor. Full range of support facilities available on post.

**SEASON OF OPERATION:** Year round.

**ELIGIBILITY:** Active/Reservists/Retired/Civilians at Fort Stewart and Hunter AAF.

**RESERVATIONS:** Accepted up to 30 days in advance with full payment. Address: Community Recreation Division, Outdoor Recreation, Bldg 8454 Shooting Star Road, Hunter Army Airfield, Savannah, GA 31409-5000. **C-912-352-5916/5722/5274, D-312-870-5722.**

**Camper/Tent Spaces:** 15, W hookup. Rates: $3.50 daily. Tents, sleep four-six. Rates: $10 daily/$25 weekend. Available at Hunter AAF Outdoor Equipment Rental, ext 5722.

**Campers:** Hardshell, sleeps four-six, refrigerator, stove, A/C. Rates: $30 daily/$80 weekend/$200 weekly (with $100 deposit). Available at Hunter AAF Outdoor Equipment Rental, ext 5722.

**SUPPORT FACILITIES:**

| | | |
|---|---|---|
| Archery Range | Boat Docks | Boat Rental |
| Camping Equipment | Camper Rental | Fishing Dock |
| Golf | Grills | Ice |
| Pavilions/fee | Picnic Areas | Restrooms |
| Skeet Range | Vending Machines | |

**ACTIVITIES:**

| | | |
|---|---|---|
| Boating | Fishing | Seasonal Hunting/ license |

**CREDIT CARDS ACCEPTED:** None.

**RESTRICTIONS:** Pets allowed on leash or physically restrained at all times. No firearms allowed.

# ROBINS FAMCAMP (GA07R1)
Robins Air Force Base
Robins AFB, GA 31098-2235

**TELEPHONE NUMBER INFORMATION:** Main installation numbers: C-912-926-1110, D-312-468-1001.

**LOCATION:** On base. From US-129 take GA-247 E at Warner Robins to AFB. *USMRA: page 37 (D-6).* NMC: Macon, 16 miles north.

**DESCRIPTION OF AREA:** FAMCAMP is situated at southeast corner of installation adjacent to Luna Lake. Very rustic setting surrounded by trees. Full range of support facilities available on base.

**SEASON OF OPERATION:** Year round.

**ELIGIBILITY:** Active/Reservists/Retired/DoD civilians.

**RESERVATIONS:** Not required. Address: Outdoor Recreation (SVRO), Bldg 1305, Robins AFB, GA 31098-1469. **C-912-926-4500, D-312-468-4500** 1330-1730 hours Wed-Sat. **C-912-926-3193, D-312-468-3193** Other days. Check in at FAMCAMP.

**Camper Spaces:** 18, E (110V/30A)/W hookups. Rates: $8 daily.

**Tent Spaces:** 12, no hookups. Rates: $6 daily.

**SUPPORT FACILITIES:**

| | | |
|---|---|---|
| Bicycle Path | Chapel/nearby | Gas/nearby |
| Golf/nearby | Picnic Areas | Playground |
| Restrooms | Showers | |

**ACTIVITIES:**

| | | |
|---|---|---|
| Bicycling | Fishing/license | Hiking |

**CREDIT CARDS ACCEPTED:** Visa and MasterCard.

**RESTRICTIONS:** Pets allowed on leash. Firearms are prohibited, for hunting check with Outdoor Recreation, C-912-926-4500.

# UCHEE CREEK ARMY
# CAMPGROUND/MARINA (GA20R1)

Fort Benning
Fort Benning, GA 31905-5000

**TELEPHONE NUMBER INFORMATION:** Main installation numbers: C-706-545-2011/4917, D-312-835-2011. Police for campground/marina, C-706-545-2222.

**LOCATION:** On post. Located on south side of Columbus. Accessible from US-80, I-185, US-27, US-280 and US-165. Clearly marked. *USMRA: page 37 (B-6)*. NMC: Columbus, 18 miles northwest.

**DESCRIPTION OF AREA:** The geography and climate are ideal for most outdoor activities. National Infantry Museum on post. Full range of support facilities available on post.

**SEASON OF OPERATION:** Year round.

**ELIGIBILITY:** Active/Reservists/Retired/DoD civilians stationed at Fort Benning.

**RESERVATIONS:** Accepted for cabins only. Call for availability on camper spaces. Address: Community Recreation Division, Attn: ATZB-PAR-U (Uchee Creek Army Campground/Marina), Bldg 241, Baltzell Street, Fort Benning, GA 31905-5226. **C-706-545-4053/7238/5600, D-312-835-4053/7238.** Check in at facility, check out 1100 hours. Discounts available to holders of Golden Age and Golden Access Passports.

**Log Cabins:** Large (10), one bedroom, sleeps six, private bath, kitchen, refrigerator, microwave, stove, utensils, A/C, heat, TV/VCR. Patrons must provide linens and towels. Rates: $39-$46 daily (depending on rank). Medium (10), one bedroom, sleeps four, private bath, kitchen, refrigerator, microwave, stove, utensils, A/C, heat, TV/VCR. Patrons must provide linens and towels. Rates: $33-$39 daily (depending on rank). Small (10) sleeps four, private bath, kitchen, refrigerator, microwave, stove, utensils, A/C, heat, TV/VCR. Patrons must provide linens and towels. Rates: $29-$35 daily (depending on rank). Primitive (2), sleeps two. Patrons must provide linens and towels. Rates: $21-$23 daily (depending on rank).

**Camper Spaces:** Paved (45), E (110V/20/30/50A)/S/W hookups. Rates: $11.50-$13.50 daily (depending on rank). Paved (40), E (110V/20/30/50A)/W hookups. Rates: $8.50-$11.50 daily (depending on rank).

**Campers: Coachman, 18'** (10), sleeps two adults, two children. Rates: $26-$30 on site (depending on rank), additional $2 road fee for off site.

**Campers: Coachman, 29'** (5), sleeps six. Rates: $38-$40 on site (depending on rank), additional $10 road fee for off site.

**SUPPORT FACILITIES:**

| | | |
|---|---|---|
| Boat Dock | Boat Launch | Boat Rental |
| Boat Slips | Camping Equipment | Country Store |
| Deer Stands | Grills | Ice |
| Laundry* | Lodge | LP Gas |
| Marina | Party Boats | Pavilion |
| Picnic Area | Playground | Pool/summer |
| Rec Equipment | Restrooms* | Sewage Dump |
| Showers* | Snack Bar | Sports Fields |

* Handicap accessible.

**ACTIVITIES:**

| | | |
|---|---|---|
| Fishing/license | Hunting/license | Softball |
| Swimming | Volleyball | |

**CREDIT CARDS ACCEPTED:** Visa, MasterCard and American Express.

**RESTRICTIONS:** Pets allowed on leash in RV area only. No pets in cabins or cabin area. If staying over 72 hours, firearms must be registered at Country Store. Quiet hours 2200-0900 hours.

# WORLD FAMOUS NAVY
# LAKE SITE (GA01R1)

Atlanta Naval Air Station
Marietta, GA 30060-5099

**TELEPHONE NUMBER INFORMATION:** Main installation numbers: C-770-421-6000, D-312-925-5000. Police for recreation site, C-770-919-6394.

**LOCATION:** Off base. From I-75 N of Atlanta, take exit 122, to a right on Sandtown Road going east for approximately three miles to marked entrance on the left. *USMRA: page 37 (B-3)*. NMI: Atlanta NAS, Marietta, 20 miles southeast. NMC: Atlanta, 40 miles southeast.

**DESCRIPTION OF AREA:** Located in a 25 acre park on Lake Allatoona reservoir. Formerly Lake Allatoona Navy Recreation Site. Ideal spot for many outdoor recreational activities. Wide range of support facilities at Atlanta NAS.

**SEASON OF OPERATION:** Year round.

**ELIGIBILITY:** Active/Reservists/Retired/DoD civilians.

**RESERVATIONS:** Required for cabins (with non-refundable deposit for one day's stay). No advance reservations for campers/tents. Address: 166 Sandtown Road, Cartersville, GA 30121. **C-770-974-6309.** Check in 1400-1700 hours, check out 1000 hours.

**Cabins:** Four-bedroom (1), furnished, microwave, pots/pans, dishes, A/C, TV, linens. Rates: $59-$61 daily (depending on season). Three-bedroom (1), furnished, microwave, pots/pans, dishes, A/C, TV, linens. Rates: $52-$54 daily (depending on season). Two-bedroom (6), furnished, microwave, pots/pans, dishes, A/C, TV, linens. Rates: $45-$47 daily (depending on season). One-bedroom (1), furnished, microwave, pots/pans, dishes, A/C, TV, linens. Rates: $38-$40 daily (depending on season). *Note: Cabins 5 and 6 are handicap accessible.*

**Camper/Trailer:** 16' (3). Rates: $15 daily. 5th Wheel (1). Rates: $30 daily.

**RV Camper Spaces:** Paved (10), E (110V/20A)/W hookups. Rates: $8 daily.

**Tent Spaces:** Primitive (13), E (110V/20A)/W hookups. Rates: $5 daily.

**GEORGIA-HAWAII**
*World Famous Navy Lake Site, continued*

**Pavilions:** Lake View Lodge (1), enclosed, kitchen, bathroom. Rates: $125 daily (0900-2000 hours). Pavilions (3), Rates: #1 $25; #2 $50; #3 $35 daily (0900-2000 hours).

**SUPPORT FACILITIES:**

| | | |
|---|---|---|
| Auto Craft Shop | Beach | Boat Dock |
| Boat Rental | Chapel | Equipment Rental |
| Exchange | Fitness Center | Game Room |
| Gas | General Store | Grills |
| Ice | Laundry | Marina |
| Pavilions/fee | Picnic Areas | Playground |
| Pool | Rec Center | Restrooms* |
| Sewage Dump | Shoppette | Showers |
| Snack Bar | Sports Fields | Telephones |
| Tennis Courts | | |

* Handicap accessible.

**ACTIVITIES:**

| | | |
|---|---|---|
| Boating | Fishing | Swimming |

**CREDIT CARDS ACCEPTED:** Visa, MasterCard, American Express and Discover.

**RESTRICTIONS:** No pets allowed. No firearms allowed. Cabin rentals-two day minimum on weekends.

# HAWAII

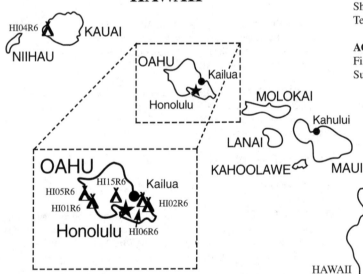

## BARBERS POINT
## RECREATION AREA (HI01R6)

Barbers Point Naval Air Station
Barbers Point NAS, HI 96862-5050
*Scheduled to close July 1999.*

**TELEPHONE NUMBER INFORMATION:** Main installation numbers: C-808-684-6266, D-315-484-6266. Police for recreation area, C-808-684-6222/6223.

**LOCATION:** On base. I-H1 W to Barbers Point exit. Bear left at stop sign and go approximately one mile and through main gate, turn right on Saratoga (traffic light). Reservations office is in Bldg 1924. *USMRA: page 129 (C-7)*. NMC: Pearl Harbor, 10 miles northeast.

**DESCRIPTION OF AREA:** A small, but nice, facility located on southwest coast of Oahu, 13 miles east from Pearl Harbor and 29 miles east from Honolulu. Enlisted cottages are on Nimitz Beach; Officer cottages, and campsites, are on White Plains Beach. Beaches excellent for surfing. Nearby attractions include: Pearl Ridge Phase I and II, Ala Moana Park, Wainae Beach parks, Pearl Harbor Park and Ice Palace (skating). Full range of support facilities available on base.

**SEASON OF OPERATION:** Year round.

**ELIGIBILITY:** Active/Reservists/Retired/DoD civilians on Barbers Point.

**RESERVATIONS:** Written requests required; accepted 60 days in advance. Reservations for campsites must be completed at least five working days in advance of use. Address: MWR Cottage Reservations, NAS Barbers Point, HI 96862-5050. **C-808-682-2019.** Campers check in 1200-1700 hours, check out 1200 hours. Cottage patrons only check in at ITT 1400-1700 hours Mon or Fri only, after hours at Security (on Enterprise), check out 0900 hours.

**Cottages:** Two-bedroom (14 Enlisted; 6 Officer; 2 VIP O6+), furnished. Rates: $35 daily Enlisted; $50 daily Officer; $65 daily VIP. *Note: Some cottages will be closed on a rotating basis for renovations.*

**Camper/Tent Spaces:** 21, W hookup. Rates: $10-$15 daily.

**SUPPORT FACILITIES:**

| | | |
|---|---|---|
| Beach | Bicycle Rental | Cabanas |
| Chapel | Gas | Golf |
| Grills | Laundry | Mini Mart |
| Picnic Area | Playground | Racquetball |
| Rec Equipment | Rec Center | Restrooms |
| Showers | Snack Bar | Sports Fields |
| Tennis Courts | | |

**ACTIVITIES:**

| | | |
|---|---|---|
| Fishing/license | Scuba Diving | Snorkeling |
| Surfing | Swimming | |

**CREDIT CARDS ACCEPTED:** Visa, MasterCard, American Express, Discover and Diners'.

**RESTRICTIONS:** No pets allowed. No firearms allowed. No open fires. Cottages may not be used as a party facility. No glass bottles at beaches. Alcohol: beer only.

## BARKING SANDS
## BEACH COTTAGES (HI04R6)

Barking Sands Pacific Missile Range Facility
Kekaha, Kauai, HI 96752-0128

**TELEPHONE NUMBER INFORMATION:** Main installation numbers: C-808-335-4111, D-315-471-4111. Police for beach cottages, C-808-335-4523.

**LOCATION:** On base. From airport at Lihue take HI-50 W approximately 30 miles. Barking Sands is six miles past the town of Kekaha. *USMRA: page 129 (B-2)*. NMC: Waimea, 8 miles south.

**DESCRIPTION OF AREA:** Located on the picturesque Garden Island of Kauai near Captain Cook's Landing Place. Although the island is small, there are many scenic areas to explore. Waimea Canyon (the Grand Canyon of Hawaii) is 12 miles from the base. Limited support facilities available on base.

**SEASON OF OPERATION:** Year round.

*Barking Sands Beach Cottages, continued*

**ELIGIBILITY:** Active/Reservists/Retired.

**RESERVATIONS:** Required, by written application, 90 days in advance. More requests are received than can be accommodated. For VIP Cottages, reservations by phone up to 90 days in advance. Address: Beach Cottages Reservation, MWR PMRF, P.O. Box 128, Barking Sands, Kekaha, Kauai, HI 96752-0128. **C-808-335-4752, D-315-471-6752** 0730-1600 hours Mon-Fri. Fax: C-808-335-4769, D-315-471-6769. E-mail: sben@pmrf.navy.mil. Check in after 1400 hours at Recreation Center, Bldg 1264, check out by 1000 hours. *Note: It is recommended that you call for operation status prior to camping.*

**Beach Cottages:** 10. Rates: $55 daily for two persons, $5 each additional person. $75 after seventh day.

**SUPPORT FACILITIES:**

| | | |
|---|---|---|
| Beach | Driving Range | Equipment Rental |
| Exchange | Fitness Center | Gas |
| Grills | Rec Center | Shoppette |
| Sports Fields | Telephones | |

**ACTIVITIES:**

| | | |
|---|---|---|
| Golfing | Kayaking | Swimming |
| Tennis | | |

**CREDIT CARDS ACCEPTED:** Visa, MasterCard, American Express and Discover.

**RESTRICTIONS:** No pets allowed. No firearms allowed. Maximum stay of two weeks. No housekeeping service.

# BELLOWS RECREATION CENTER (HI02R6)

Bellows Air Force Station
Waimanalo, HI 96795-5000

**TELEPHONE NUMBER INFORMATION:** Main installation numbers: C-808-259-8080. Police for recreation area, C-808-259-4200.

**LOCATION:** On base. From Honolulu Airport or Hickam AFB, take H-1 E to exit 21A N (Pali Highway), to HI-72 S to Waimanalo Town. AFS is on the left. *USMRA: page 129 (E-7).* NMC: Kailua, 9 miles northwest.

**DESCRIPTION OF AREA:** A seaside recreation facility on the southeast coast of the Island of Oahu, 16.5 miles from the Honolulu business district. One of the oldest places of habitation in the Hawaiian Islands. Three miles of beautiful beachfront. Some support facilities available on base; full range at Kaneohe MCAS, 10 miles northwest.

**SEASON OF OPERATION:** Year round.

**ELIGIBILITY:** Active/Reservists/Retired/DoD and NAF Civilians.

**RESERVATIONS:** Required, may be made 90 days in advance from Memorial Day to Labor Day and Christmas Eve to New Year's Day for active duty, all others 75 days. Up to one year in advance between Sep-May. Deposit (one night's rent) due ten days after reservation is made, cancellations 14 days prior to advance. Address: Bellows Reservation Office, 220 Tinker Road, Waimanalo, HI 96795-1010. **C-808-259-8080** (for Cottage); **C-808-259-4121** (for Camping); **C-1-800-437-2607** (Toll Free from mainland) 24 hours daily. Check in after 1500 hours, check out 1100 hours. *Note: When reservation period includes a Friday, Saturday or Federal holiday-the beginning date of reservation may not be cancelled without cancelling the entire reservation.*

**Beach Cottages:** Oceanview (53), private bath, furnished, kitchenette, TV, linens, towels, pots/pans, dishes, utensils, port-a-cribs. Rates: $54 daily. Backrow (44), private bath, furnished, kitchenette, TV, linens, towels, pots/pans, dishes, utensils, port-a-cribs. Rates: $49 daily.

**Camper/Tent Spaces:** Dirt (44), no hookups. Rates: $6 daily.

**SUPPORT FACILITIES:**

| | | |
|---|---|---|
| Basketball Courts | Bath Houses | Beach |
| Boat Rental | Camping Equipment | Exchange |
| Gas | Golf Driving Range | Laundry |
| Lounge | Mini Golf | Picnic Area |
| Restaurant | Tennis Courts | |

**ACTIVITIES:**

| | | |
|---|---|---|
| Billiards | Fishing | Snorkeling |
| Swimming | | |

**CREDIT CARDS ACCEPTED:** Visa, MasterCard and American Express.

**RESTRICTIONS:** No pets allowed. No firearms allowed. Fourteen day limit. Hiking and hunting are prohibited on Bellows AFS. All overnight guests must be registered with the reservation office. The total number of people permitted to stay overnight in a cottage or campsite is ten. Rental cars are not available on Bellows. Off-island visitors are advised to obtain rental cars for mobility.

# CAMP SMITH STABLES (HI15R6)

Camp H.M. Smith Marine Corps Base
Camp H.M. Smith, HI 96861-5000

**TELEPHONE NUMBER INFORMATION:** C-808-477-6231.

**LOCATION:** On base. Take Halawa Heights exit off Freeway H-2. Camp Smith camping grounds located directly off of Halawa Heights Road. *USMRA: page 129 (D-7).* NMC: Honolulu, 10 miles southeast.

**DESCRIPTION OF AREA:** Camp Hawkins A & B are located in a stand of ironwood trees near a pavilion. There are port-o-lets and running water at the pavilion. Helo pad is a primitive campsite with no running water and one port-o-let.

**SEASON OF OPERATION:** Year round.

**ELIGIBILITY:** Active/Reservists/Retired/DoD and sponsored civilians.

**RESERVATIONS:** Address: Recreation Services, Box 64123, Bldg 366, Camp H.M. Smith USMC, HI 96861-5001. **C-808-484-9417.** Fax: C-808-487-0653. *Note: All camping to have prior reservations with stables; camping reservations then accepted. Release/reservation form signed at stables to include payment.*

**Camp Hawkins A & B tent sites:** 10, up to 15 persons per site, no hookups. Rates: $8 daily.

**Helo Pad tent site:** 1, up to 40 persons, no hookups. Rates: $8 daily.

**SUPPORT FACILITIES:** Most support facilities available on base.

**ACTIVITIES:** Available at the stable are trail rides, lessons, summer camp, boy scout/girl scout merit badges.

**CREDIT CARDS ACCEPTED:** Visa, MasterCard and American Express.

**RESTRICTIONS:** Pets must be on a leash.

*HAWAII*

# KANEOHE BAY BEACH COTTAGES AND CAMPSITES (HI06R6)

Kaneohe Bay Marine Corps Air Station
Kaneohe Bay, HI 96863-3002

**TELEPHONE NUMBER INFORMATION:** Main installation numbers: C-808-471-7110, D-315-430-0110. Police for cottages and campsites, C-808-257-2123.

**LOCATION:** On base. From Honolulu, take H-3 N to the front gate of base. TLF is on your right at 1st stop light. Clearly marked off Mokapu Blvd and Kaneohe Bay Drive. *USMRA: page 129 (E-6).* NMC: Honolulu, 14 miles southwest.

**DESCRIPTION OF AREA:** Located in a secluded area overlooking beautiful Kaneohe Bay. Cottages are across the airstrip along the coastline, near Pyramid Rock. Campsites are near the northern area of the base in a sheltered cove with an excellent view. Full range of support facilities on base.

**SEASON OF OPERATION:** Year round.

**ELIGIBILITY:** Active/Reservists/Retired/DoD civilians.

**RESERVATIONS:** Required for studio units and cottages: up to 60 days in advance for active duty stationed at Kaneohe Bay MCAS; up to 45 days in advance for MCAS MWR employees and Marines stationed elsewhere; up to 30 days in advance for all others. Reservations for campsites accepted up to 6 months in advance for all authorized patrons. Address: MWR, TLF Bldg 3038, P.O. Box 63073, Kaneohe Bay MCBH, HI 96963-3037. **C-808-254-7667** (campsites), **C-808-254-2716** (cottages), **D-315-430-7695.** Fax: C-808-254-7695 (campsites), C-808-254-2716 (cottages). E-mail: morgann@mfp. usmc.mil. Campsites address: Special Services, Bldg 219, MCAS Kaneohe Bay, HI 96863-5000. C-808-254-3230. No check in or out on holidays.

**Studio Units:** 24, handicap accessible, phone. Rates: $55 daily.

**Cottages:** Two-bedroom (11), furnished, phone. Rates: $60 daily.

**Tent Spaces:** Beachfront (17), W hookup. Rates: $8 daily.

**SUPPORT FACILITIES:**

| | | |
|---|---|---|
| Auto Craft Shop | Beach | Boat Launch |
| Boat Rental/Storage | Chapel | Commissary |
| Convenience Store | Equipment Rental | Exchange |
| Fire Rings | Fishing Pier | Fitness Center |
| Gas | Golf | Grills |
| Ice | Laundry | Marina |
| Pavilion/fee | Picnic Area | Playground |
| Pool | Rec Equipment | Shoppette |
| Showers | Snack Bar | Sports Fields |
| Stables | Telephones | Tennis Courts |

**ACTIVITIES:**

| | | |
|---|---|---|
| Boating | Fishing | Golf |
| Horseback Riding | Scuba Diving | Swimming |
| Tennis | | |

**CREDIT CARDS ACCEPTED:** Visa, MasterCard, American Express and Discover.

**RESTRICTIONS:** No pets allowed. Seven day limit for cottages.

# KILAUEA MILITARY CAMP, JOINT SERVICES RECREATION CENTER (HI17R6)

Hawaii Volcanoes National Park, HI 96718-5000

**TELEPHONE NUMBER INFORMATION:** Main installation numbers: C-808-967-7315. Police for rec center, C-808-967-8378.

**LOCATION:** On post. Off HI-11 approximately 1.5 miles inside Hawaii Volcanoes National Park, southwest of Hilo on Island of Hawaii. Honolulu is 216 air miles northwest. Scheduled bus from Hilo airport to Kilauea Military Camp (KMC), reservations required. *USMRA: page 129 (I,J-6,7).* NMC: Hilo, 32 miles northeast.

**DESCRIPTION OF AREA:** Kilauea Military Camp is a Joint Services Recreation Center nestled in cool and relaxed surroundings. This area offers many sights found nowhere else in the world with an active volcano flowing just 40 minutes away.

**SEASON OF OPERATION:** Year round.

**ELIGIBILITY:** Active/Reservists/Retired/DoD civilians and retirees.

**RESERVATIONS:** Accepted, first come, first serve basis. Required: one year in advance during non-peak periods. During peak the following applies: 120 days in advance in writing or 90 days in advance by phone for active duty; 60 days in advance for retirees; 45 days in advance for all others. Address: Kilauea Military Camp, Armed Forces Recreation Center, Attn: Reservations, Hawaii National Park, HI 96718-5000. **C-808-867-8343** (from Oahu only), **C-808-967-8343.**

**Cottages:** Standard rooms to deluxe four-bedroom units (75), some handicap accessible, refrigerator, coffee maker, CATV, phone, housekeeping service, room service. Full kitchen, fireplace and jacuzzi units are also available. Rates: $26-$92 daily. To accommodate large groups, KMC has two dormitories with 100 beds that will be upgraded soon. Rates: $5.25-$10.50 per night.

**SUPPORT FACILITIES:**

| | | |
|---|---|---|
| Cafeteria | Chapel | Conference Rooms |
| Convenience Store | Dispensary | Equipment Rental |
| Fitness Center | Gas | Golf |
| Grills | Ice | Laundry |
| Pavilion | Picnic Area | Playground |
| Recreation Center | Rec Equipment | Restrooms |
| Showers | Shuttle/Bus | Snack Bar |
| Sports Fields | Telephones | Tennis Courts |
| Tour/Charter Service | Trails | |

**ACTIVITIES:**

| | | |
|---|---|---|
| Baseball | Basketball | Bicycling |
| Bowling | Golf | Hiking |
| Miniature Golf | Tennis | Tours |

**CREDIT CARDS ACCEPTED:** Visa, Mastercard and American Express.

**RESTRICTIONS:** No pets allowed. No firearms. Use of dispensary limited to emergency care.

# WAIANAE ARMY RECREATION CENTER (HI05R6)

Fort Shafter
Fort Shafter, HI 96858-5100

**TELEPHONE NUMBER INFORMATION:** Main installation numbers: C-808-471-7110, D-315-430-0111.

*Waianae Army Recreation Center, continued*

**LOCATION:** Off post. On west coast of Oahu. Take H1 W to HI-93 N (Farrington Highway) to Waianae. *USMRA: page 129 (B-6).* NMI: Schofield Barracks, 20 miles northeast. NMC: Honolulu, 35 miles southeast.

**DESCRIPTION OF AREA:** Located along beach of Pokai Bay in once-quiet fishing and plantation village. One of the favorite swimming and fishing spots on Oahu. The facility is one of the finest on the island. Full range of support facilities at Schofield Barracks.

**SEASON OF OPERATION:** Year round.

**ELIGIBILITY:** Active/Reservists/Retired/DoD civilians/Other Federal employees.

**RESERVATIONS:** Required with deposit: up to 90 days in advance for active duty Army; up to 80 days in advance for other active duty and retirees; up to 60 days in advance for reserve and DoD civilians; up to 30 days for other Federal Employees. Address: Waianae Army Recreation Center, 85-010 Army Street, Waianae, HI 96792-5000. **C-808-696-4158, C-1-800-333-4158** (from mainland), **C-1-800-847-6771** (from outer islands), 0900-1600 hours Mon-Fri, Hawaiian time.

| Beach Cabins: | E1-E5 | Rates: E6-W3 | W4-W010 |
|---|---|---|---|
| Deluxe two-bedroom | $65 | $70 | $75 |
| Deluxe two-bedroom (ocean view) | $70 | $75 | $80 |
| Deluxe three-bedroom (ocean view) | $75 | $80 | $85 |
| Standard two-bedroom | $50 | $55 | $60 |
| Standard two-bedroom (ocean view) | $55 | $60 | $65 |
| Studio | $40 | $45 | $50 |

Additional Fees: Cribs-$5, Rollaways-$10
All have kitchen, refrigerator, A/C, TV/VCR, deck, grill. Three cabins handicap accessible.

**SUPPORT FACILITIES:**

| | | |
|---|---|---|
| Beach | Club/all ranks | Convenience/ |
| First Aid Station | Grills |   Package Store |
| Pavilions/fee | Picnic Area | Restrooms |
| Showers | Snack Bar | Water Sports |
| | |   Equipment Rental |

**ACTIVITIES:**

| | | |
|---|---|---|
| Snorkeling | Surfing | Swimming |

Outdoor sports facilities, five minute walk from camp.

**CREDIT CARDS ACCEPTED:** Visa and MasterCard.

**RESTRICTIONS:** No pets allowed. Twenty-one day limit.

# IDAHO

*See map in next column.*

## GOWEN FIELD (ID04R4)

Gowen Field
Boise, ID 83705-5004

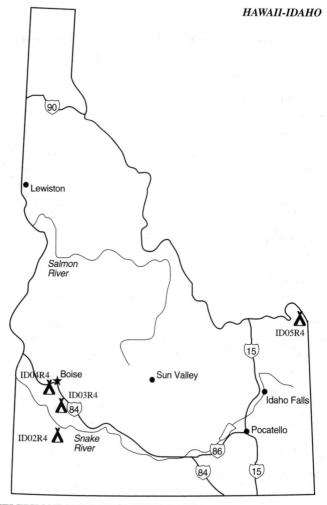

**TELEPHONE NUMBER INFORMATION:** Main installation numbers: C-208-422-5011/5366, D-312-422-5011/5366.

**LOCATION:** On base. From I-84, take Orchard Street exit 52 south, follow road approximately 1.5 miles to gate driveway. *USMRA: page 98 (B-8).* NMC: Boise, 2 miles north.

**DESCRIPTION OF AREA:** Located at the edge of the high desert, near Treasure Valley, within an hour of the Snake River.

**SEASON OF OPERATION:** Year round.

**ELIGIBILITY:** Active/Reservists/Retired.

**REGISTRATION INFORMATION:** Accepted. Address: 4200 West Ellsworth, Boise, ID 83705-8033. **C-208-422-4451, D-312-422-4451** 0730-1630 hours Mon-Fri. Fax: C-208-422-4452, D-312-422-4452. Check in at Billeting Office, Bldg 669, check out 1200 hours.

**Camper Spaces:** Concrete (7), E (110V/20A)/S/W hookups. Rates: $7.50 daily.

**SUPPORT FACILITIES:**

| | |
|---|---|
| Exchange | Fitness Center |

**ACTIVITIES:**

| | | |
|---|---|---|
| Fishing/license | Hunting/license | Skiing/DH, XC |
| Water Sports | | |

**CREDIT CARDS ACCEPTED:** Visa, MasterCard and American Express.

*IDAHO*

# MOUNTAIN HOME FAMCAMP (ID03R4)

Mountain Home Air Force Base
Mountain Home AFB, ID 83648-5237

**TELEPHONE NUMBER INFORMATION:** Main installation numbers: C-208-828-2111, D-312-728-1110. Police for FAMCAMP, C-208-828-2256.

**LOCATION:** On base. From I-84 take ID-67 12 miles southwest to base through main gate. Go right on the first street, go .25 miles, turn right into FAMCAMP. *USMRA: page 98 (C-9)*. NMC: Boise, 50 miles northwest.

**DESCRIPTION OF AREA:** Located in open country surrounded by mountains, close to Snake River. Sun Valley is approximately 100 miles northeast. Excellent access to vast public lands and recreation. Full range of support facilities on base.

**SEASON OF OPERATION:** Year round.

**ELIGIBILITY:** Active/Reservists/Retired/Dependents..

**RESERVATIONS:** No advance reservations. Address: 366 SVS/SVRO, 775 Pine Street, Bldg 2800, Mountain Home AFB, ID 83648-5125. **C-208-828-6333, D-312-728-6333.** Fax: C-208-828-6317. Check in at FAMCAMP, check out 1100 hours.

**Camper Spaces:** Hardstand (22), handicap accessible, E (110V/ 20/30A)/S/W hookups. Rates: $12 daily. *Note: Existing pads were renovated 1993-94 with landscape improvements.*

**Tent Spaces:** Grass (10), no hookups. Rates: $6 daily.

**SUPPORT FACILITIES:**

| | | |
|---|---|---|
| Bath House | Chapel | Golf |
| Grills | Ice | Laundry |
| Picnic Area | Rec Equipment | Restrooms |
| Sewage Dump | Showers | Skeet/Trap Range |
| Telephones | | |

*Note: MWR operates a marina 20 miles south of the base with boat rentals and good fishing. Outdoor Recreation operates a very popular whitewater rafting program.*

**ACTIVITIES:**

| | | |
|---|---|---|
| Fishing (Apr-Sep) | Hunting | Sightseeing |
| Snow Skiing/nearby | | (ghost towns) |

**CREDIT CARDS ACCEPTED:** Visa and MasterCard.

**RESTRICTIONS:** Pets allowed on leash, limit two. Host on site in summer.

# STRIKE DAM MARINA (ID02R4)

Mountain Home Air Force Base
Mountain Home AFB, ID 83648-5237

**TELEPHONE NUMBER INFORMATION:** Main installation numbers: C-208-828-2111, D-312-728-1110. Police for marina area, C-208-828-2256, D-312-728-2256.

**LOCATION:** Off base. From I-84 east of Boise, follow signs to Mountain Home AFB (on ID-67) and on to C.J. Strike Reservoir. *USMRA: page 98 (B-9)*. NMI: Mountain Home AFB, 27 miles northeast. NMC: Boise, 60 miles north.

**DESCRIPTION OF AREA:** Situated along Snake River and surrounded by mountains. Full support for water sports and picnic activities. Full range of support facilities at Mountain Home AFB.

**SEASON OF OPERATION:** 15 Apr-Labor Day.

**ELIGIBILITY:** Active/Reservists/Retired/DoD civilians.

**RESERVATIONS:** Accepted up to two weeks in advance. Address: 366 SVS/SVRM, Attn: Strike Dam Marina, Bldg 2800, Mountain Home AFB, ID 83648-5125. **C-208-828-6333** (Outdoor Adventure Program Info available year round).

**CAMP FACILITIES:** Unlimited, no hookups. Rates: $12 daily. Camper spaces with hookups are available at Mountain Home AFB.

**SUPPORT FACILITIES:**

| | | |
|---|---|---|
| Boat Docks | Boat Launch | Boat Rental |
| Golf/on base | Grills | Marina |
| Picnic Area | Restrooms | Snack Bar |
| Water Sports Equipment Rental | | |

**ACTIVITIES:**

| | | |
|---|---|---|
| Boating | Fishing/license | Jet Skiing |
| Pontoon Boat/26' | Sailing | Water Skiing |
| Wind Surfing | | |

**CREDIT CARDS ACCEPTED:** Visa and MasterCard.

**RESTRICTIONS:** Pets allowed on leash. Day use only.

# YELLOWSTONE COUNTRY TRAILERS (ID05R4)

Mountain Home Air Force Base
Mountain Home AFB, ID 83648-5237

**TELEPHONE NUMBER INFORMATION:** Main installation numbers: C-208-828-2111, D-312-728-1110.

**LOCATION:** Off base. Trailers are placed at commercial RV parks in and around Yellowstone National Park both in Idaho and Wyoming. *USMRA: Page 98 (H-6,7)*. NMI: Malmstrom AFB, 254 miles north. NMC: Idaho Falls, 80 miles south.

**DESCRIPTION OF AREA:** Travel trailers are positioned at four different commercial RV parks in and around Yellowstone National Park. One unit is at Henry's Lake which is nationally known for its trophy cutthroat, rainbow, and brook trout and 15 miles from the west entrance to the park. Two units are located at Mack's Inn Resort-walking distance to the Henry's Fork of the Snake River and its fabled fishing waters and 25 miles from the west entrance to the park. Two units are at Lionshead Resort which is only eight miles from the west entrance and four miles from Hebgen Lake. Six units are at Grant Village-right in the heart of Yellowstone, less than one mile from the western shore of Yellowstone Lake.

**SEASON OF OPERATION:** Memorial Day-1 Oct (depending on occupancy and weather).

**ELIGIBILITY:** Active/Reservists/Retired/DoD civilians.

**RESERVATIONS:** Required. Accepted first business day of the month for two months out (e.g., 1 May for July). Address: Outdoor Recreation, 655 Pine Street, Mountain Home AFB, ID 83648-5125. **C-208-828-6333, D-312-728-6333.** Reservations may not be made by mail.

*Yellowstone Country Trailers, continued*

**Travel Trailers:** 24', fully self-contained (11), sleep six, utensils. Rates: $40 daily. *Grant Village* (6); *Henry's Lake* (1), boat launch, boat rental; *Lionshead Resort* (2), snack bar, restaurant; *Mack's Inn* (2), snack bar, restaurant.

**ACTIVITIES:**

| | | |
|---|---|---|
| Bicycling | Hiking | Nature Trails |

**CREDIT CARDS ACCEPTED:** Visa and MasterCard.

**RESTRICTIONS:** No pets allowed. No smoking. Maximum of six persons per trailer. Minimum two night stay, maximum ten nights.

# ILLINOIS

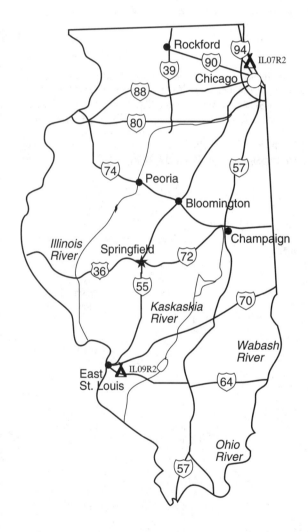

## GREAT LAKES NAVAL TRAINING CENTER (IL07R2)

Great Lakes Naval Training Center
Great Lakes, IL 60088-5000

**TELEPHONE NUMBER INFORMATION:** Main installation numbers: C-847-688-2110, D-312-792-2110.

**LOCATION:** On base. From I-94 N or US-41 N to IL-137 (Buckley Road) to NTC. Clearly marked. RV campsite located on the lakefront near marina. *USMRA: page 64 (G-1)*. NMI: Fort McCoy, WI, 150 miles northwest. NMC: Chicago, 40 miles south.

**DESCRIPTION OF AREA:** Located in an area overlooking Lake Michigan. Full range of support facilities available on base.

**SEASON OF OPERATION:** Year round.

**ELIGIBILITY:** Active/Reservists/Retired/DoD civilians.

**RESERVATIONS:** Advance reservations accepted. Address: MWR, Bldg 160-NTC, Great Lakes, IL 60088-5000. **C-847-688-5417, D-312-792-5417.** Fax: C-847-688-5421, D-312-792-5421.

**Camper Spaces:** 8, no hookups. Rates: $5 daily.

**Tent Spaces:** 8, no hookups. Rates: $5 daily.

**SUPPORT FACILITIES:**

| | | |
|---|---|---|
| Auto Craft Shop | Bath House | Beach |
| Boat Launch | Boat Rental/Storage | Chapel |
| Commissary | Convenience Store | Equipment Rental |
| Exchange | Fire Rings | Fishing Pier |
| Fitness Center | Gas | Golf |
| Grills | Ice | Marina |
| Pavilion | Picnic Area | Playground |
| Pool | Rec Center | Restrooms |
| Sewage Dump | Shoppette | Showers |
| Shuttle Bus | Snack Bar | Sports Fields |
| Telephones | Tennis Courts | Trails |

\* Marina with restroom, showers, and dump station.

**ACTIVITIES:**

| | | |
|---|---|---|
| Beaches | Bowling | Camping* |
| Charter Fishing Trips | Fishing** | Golf |
| Hunting** | Pools | Sailboats* |
| Sea Kayaks* | Skiing* | Theater |

\* Instructional courses are available.
\*\* In compliance with Illinois rules and regulations.

**CREDIT CARDS ACCEPTED:** Visa and MasterCard.

**RESTRICTIONS:** Firearms prohibited.

## SCOTT FAMCAMP (IL09R2)

Scott Air Force Base
Scott AFB, IL 62225-5359

**TELEPHONE NUMBER INFORMATION:** Main installation numbers: C-618-256-1110, D-312-576-1110. Police for FAMCAMP, C-618-256-2223/2224.

**LOCATION:** On base. Off I-64 E or W, exit 19A W to IL-158 S two miles and watch for signs to AFB. Ask gate guard for directions to Outdoor Recreation. *USMRA: page 64 (D-8)*. NMC: St Louis MO, 23 miles west.

**DESCRIPTION OF AREA:** Located east of St. Louis metropolitan area near O'Fallon. Camp is situated in a wooded area on base. Full range of support facilities available on base.

**SEASON OF OPERATION:** Year round.

**ELIGIBILITY:** Active/Reservists/Retired/DoD civilians.

*ILLINOIS/INDIANA*
*Scott FAMCAMP, continued*

**RESERVATIONS:** Advance reservations accepted, $10 deposit required. Address (not location): Outdoor Recreation, 375 SVS/SVRO, Bldg 855, Room 203, Scott AFB, IL 62225-5225. **C-618-256-2067, D-312-576-2067** 0800-1600 hours (1700 hours summer) Mon-Fri, 0800-1200 hours Sat. Check out 1100 hours.

**Camper Spaces:** Gravel (12); Paved (12), E (110V/30A)/W hookups. Rates: $10 daily. Overflow (2), no hookups. Rates: $5 daily.

**SUPPORT FACILITIES:**

| | | |
|---|---|---|
| Chapel | Gas | Golf |
| Grills | Picnic Area | Racquet Sports |
| Rec Equipment | Restrooms | Sewage Dump |
| Shoppette | Skeet/Trap Range | Sports Fields |
| Snack Bar/nearby | Tennis Courts | |

**ACTIVITIES:**
Fishing/base permit

**CREDIT CARDS ACCEPTED:** Visa and MasterCard.

**RESTRICTIONS:** Pets allowed on leash, must have current and complete immunizations. Firearms prohibited. No open campfires. Quiet hours after 2200 hours. Thirty day limit. Water hookups will not be left on continuously when temperatures are below freezing. Fee receipt must be displayed in window of vehicle.

# INDIANA

# CAMP ATTERBURY CAMPGROUNDS (IN07R2)
Camp Atterbury
Edinburgh, IN 46124-1096

**TELEPHONE NUMBER INFORMATION:** Main installation numbers: C-812-526-9711, D-312-786-2499. Police for Campground 812-526-1117/1118.

**LOCATION:** On post. From I-65 N or S, take exit 76 (US-31 N), W on Hospital Road to first flashing yellow light (main gate entrance) at Eggleston Road (Military or dependent ID required). South into post, east on Headquarters Road to south on Durbin Street. Facilities on left. *USMRA: page 65 (E-6,7)*. NMC: Indianapolis, 35 miles north.

**DESCRIPTION OF AREA:** Limited support facilities on post.

**SEASON OF OPERATION:** Year round (limited).

**ELIGIBILITY:** Active/Reservists/Retired/DoD civilians/Camp Atterbury employees.

**RESERVATIONS:** No advance reservations. Address: Bldg 322, MWR, Camp Atterbury, Edinburgh, IN 46124-1096. **C-812-526-1149, D-312-569-2149** 0800-1800 hours 1 May-30 Nov, 0800-1600 hours Mon-Fri 1 Dec-30 Apr. Fax: C-812-526-1445, D-312-569-2445. Check out 1200 hours.

**Camper Spaces:** Gravel/Dirt (16), E (110V/20/30A)/S/W hookups. E hookup only 1 Dec-30 Apr. Rates: $8 daily ($1 non-official users fee per day per vehicle).

**Tent Spaces:** Primitive, grass, unlimited, no hookups. Rates: $5 daily.

**SUPPORT FACILITIES:**

| | | |
|---|---|---|
| Archery Range | Barber Shop | Bath House* |
| Boat Launch | Chapel | Exchange |
| Fire Rings | Fishing Pier | Fitness Center |
| Grills | Ice | Laundry* |
| Library | Mail service | Nature Trail |
| O'/NCO Club | Pavilion | Picnic Area |
| Playground | Pool | Rec Equipment |
| Restrooms* | Shelters | Showers* |
| Snack Bar | Sports Fields | Telephones |
| Tennis Courts | | |

* Handicap accessible.

**ACTIVITIES:**

| | | |
|---|---|---|
| Bicycling | Boating/Canoeing | Fishing/license |
| Hiking | Hunting/license | /permit |
| Swimming | | |

**CREDIT CARDS ACCEPTED:** None.

**RESTRICTIONS:** Pets allowed on leash. No firearms. No ATVs or off-road vehicles allowed. Quiet hours 2200-0600 hours.

# CRANE MWR CAMPGROUNDS (IN06R2)
Crane Division Naval Surface Warfare Center
Crane, IN 47522-5001

**TELEPHONE NUMBER INFORMATION:** Main installation numbers: C-812-854-1225, D-312-482-1225. Police for campgrounds, C-812-854-3300.

*Crane MWR Campgrounds, continued*

# KANSAS

*See map below.*

**LOCATION:** On base. From US-231 N or S exit to IN-645 to enter the center from the west. It is best to use Gate 4 with a camper. *USMRA: page 65 (D-8).* NMC: Bloomington, 32 miles northeast.

**DESCRIPTION OF AREA:** Located on an 800-acre lake in an area offering fishing, hunting, boating and hiking: a sportsman's dream come true. The campgrounds are located adjacent to the marina. Full range of support facilities available on base.*INDIANA*

**SEASON OF OPERATION:** 1 Apr-31 Oct.

**ELIGIBILITY:** Active/Reservists/Retired/DoD civilians/NSWC active and retired civilians.

**RESERVATIONS:** Accepted. A minimum of four campsites will be kept open for daily/weekly rental. Address: MWR Campgrounds, Bldg 1909, 300 Highway 361, Crane, IN 47522-5001. **C-812-854-1368, D-312-482-1368.** Check in at marina 0600-1800 hours, check out 0900 hours.

**Camper Spaces:** Gravel (52), E (110V/20A)/S/W hookups. Rates: $5-$7.50 daily (weekly and monthly rates available).

**Tent Spaces:** Primitive (24), no hookups. Rates: $3-$5 daily (weekly rates available).

**SUPPORT FACILITIES:**

| | | |
|---|---|---|
| Bicycles | Golf | Grills |
| Laundry | Marina | Port-a-Potties |
| Restaurant | Sewage Dump | Showers |
| Stove Rental | Tent Rental | Trails |

**ACTIVITIES:**

| | | |
|---|---|---|
| Boating | Fishing/license | Hiking |

**CREDIT CARDS ACCEPTED:** Visa and MasterCard.

**RESTRICTIONS:** Pets allowed on leash, owner must clean up after pet. No firearms allowed. No open fires. Possession of fireworks is prohibited. Unlicensed motor bikes or mini-bikes are not permitted in campground. All campers without appropriate clearance for other activities must stay in immediate area of campground. Monthly campers allowed a maximum of 30 days on one site, may be rented for another month if there are no other prospective campers. All campers must display current RV plates.

## McCONNELL AFB FAMCAMP (KS03R3)

McConnell Air Force Base
McConnell AFB, KS 67221-3600

**TELEPHONE NUMBER INFORMATION:** Main installation numbers: C-316-652-6100, D-312-743-1110.

**LOCATION:** On base. From the north, take I-35 (Kansas Turnpike toll road) S to Wichita, exit at Kellogg Street W (US-54) to Rock Road S to McConnell AFB. From the south, take I-35 N to Webb Road, west on Rock Road, south to McConnell AFB. NMC: Wichita, 5 miles northwest.

**SEASON OF OPERATION:** Year round.

**ELIGIBILITY:** Active/Reservists/Retired/DoD civilians.

**RESERVATIONS:** 53050 Glen Elder, McConnell AFB, KS 67221-5000. **C-316-652-5999, D-312-743-5999.**

**Camper Spaces:** Concrete (7), E (110V/30A)/S/W hookups. Rates: $10 daily/ $50 weekly.

**SUPPORT FACILITIES:**

| | | |
|---|---|---|
| Auto Craft Shop | Boat Rental/Storage | Chapel |
| Commissary | Convenience Store | Exchange |
| Fitness Center | Gas | Golf |
| Grills | Ice | Pavilion |
| Picnic Area | Playground | Pool |
| Rec Center | Sewage Dump | Shoppette |
| Sports Fields | Telephones | Tennis Courts |

**ACTIVITIES:**

| | |
|---|---|
| Swimming | Tennis |

**CREDIT CARDS ACCEPTED:** Visa, MasterCard and American Express.

**RESTRICTIONS:** Pets on leash. No firearms. No open fires.

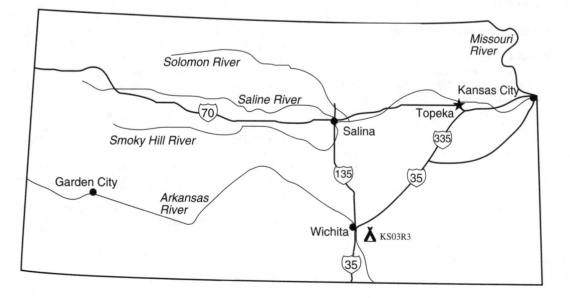

# KENTUCKY

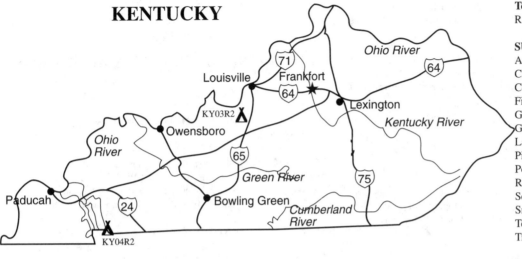

**Tent Spaces:** Unlimited, no hookups. Rates: $4-$7 daily.

**SUPPORT FACILITIES:**

| | |
|---|---|
| Auto Craft Shop | Bath House |
| Chapel | Commissary |
| Convenience Store | Exchange |
| Fire Rings | Fitness Center |
| Gas | Golf |
| Grills | Ice |
| Laundry | Pavilion |
| Picnic Area | Playground |
| Pool | Rec Center |
| Rec Equipment | Restrooms |
| Sewage Dump | Showers |
| Snack Bar | Sports Fields |
| Telephones | Tennis Courts |
| Trails | Vending Machine |

**ACTIVITIES:**

Bicycling          Fishing/license          Hunting/license

**CREDIT CARDS ACCEPTED:** Visa and MasterCard.

**RESTRICTIONS:** Pets allowed on leash. Firearms are not permitted. Tours or visits to the gold vault are not permitted.

## CAMP CARLSON
## ARMY TRAVEL CAMP (KY03R2)
Fort Knox
Fort Knox, KY 40121-5000

**TELEPHONE NUMBER INFORMATION:** Main installation numbers: C-502-624-1000/1181, D-312-464-0111. Police for travel camp, C-502-624-2111 (emergency 624-0911).

**LOCATION:** On post. From I-65 N or S in Louisville, exit Jefferson Freeway, 841 W to 31 W, south to Fort Knox. From I-64, exit I-264 W (Waterson) to I-65 S, to Jefferson Fort Knox to US-31 W, south to Fort Knox. From I-71, exit I-65 S to Jefferson Freeway 841, west to 31 W, south to Fort Knox. Four entrances. Look for main gate. *USMRA: page 41 (I-3,4).* NMC: Louisville, 30 miles north.

**DESCRIPTION OF AREA:** Camp Carlson was formerly the town of Grahamton, site of the longest operational textile mill in Kentucky. Full range of outdoor activities available. Patton Museum on post. Abraham Lincoln birthplace, Mammoth Cave National Park and Rough River State Park are among nearby attractions. Full range of support facilities available five miles from camp.

**SEASON OF OPERATION:** Year round.

**ELIGIBILITY:** Active/Reservists/Retired/DoD civilians.

**RESERVATIONS:** Required for cottages and cabins, accepted for RV sites for summer holiday weekends only. Address: 9186 US Route 60, Muldraugh, KY 40155-5000. **C-502-624-4836, D-312-464-4836.** Fax: C-502-624-8144, D-312-464-8144. Discounts available to holders of Golden Age, Golden Access and Golden Eagle Passports. Check in at Travel Camp, check out 1100 hours.

**Family Cottages:** 4, refrigerator, stove, microwave, TV. Patrons must provide cooking utensils and linens. Rates: $22 daily winter 16 Oct-14 Apr, $25 daily summer 15 Apr-15 Oct.

**Group Cabins:** 4, 18 bunks each with a minimum of ten persons. Rates: $3 per bunk daily.

**RV Spaces:** Gravel (7), E (110V/30/50A)/S/W hookups. Rates: $12 daily/$75 weekly. Gravel (18), E (110V/30/50A)/W hookups. Rates: $9.50 daily/$60 weekly.

## DESTINY PARKS & PAVILIONS
## (ARMY TRAVEL CAMP) (KY04R2)
Fort Campbell
Fort Campbell, KY 42223-5470

**TELEPHONE NUMBER INFORMATION:** Main installation numbers: C-502-798-2151, D-312-635-1110. Police for travel camp, C-502-798-7112.

**LOCATION:** On post. In Southwest part of KY, four miles south of intersection of US-41A and I-24. From I-24 N or S, take exit 86 S to 41A toward Fort Campbell. *USMRA: page 40 (F-7).* NMC: Clarksville TN, 10 miles southeast.

**DESCRIPTION OF AREA:** Located adjacent to Land-between-the-Lakes area, between Clarksville TN and Hopkinsville KY. Tennessee Valley Authority manages an extensive reservoir complex on the Tennessee River along KY/TN line. Unlimited water recreational opportunities. The official name of the recreation area is Wohali which means Eagle in Cherokee. **Eagles' Rest** is the main travel camp area, **Fletchers Fork** (approximately .5 miles away) is an overflow area where all spaces have hookups. Equipment rental center can supply outdoor recreation equipment for a wide variety of activities. Full range of support facilities available on post.

**SEASON OF OPERATION:** Year round.

**ELIGIBILITY:** Active/Reservists/Retired/DoD civilians/Civilian community.

**RESERVATIONS:** Required for log cabins. Campsites are on a first come, first serve basis. Address: Community Recreation Division, Outdoor Recreation Branch, Attn: AFZB-PA-CR-O, Army Travel Camp, Fort Campbell, KY 42223-5000. **C-502-798-3126/5590, D-312-635-3126/5590.** Discounts available to holders of Golden Age Passports.

**EAGLES' REST:**
**Camper Spaces:** Gravel (25), E (120V/20/30A)/W hookups. Rates: $12 daily.

**FLETCHERS FORK:**
**Log Cabins:** 4, single room, beds, sleeps four adults. Patrons must provide all bedding and other supplies. Rates: $27 daily, active duty at Fort Campbell have priority.

**Camper Spaces:** Primitive (37), E (120V/30A)/W hookups. Rates: $12 daily.

**SUPPORT FACILITIES:**

| | | |
|---|---|---|
| Boat Launch | Boat Rental | Fishing Pier |
| Golf | Grills | Laundry |
| Nature Center | Picnic Area | Playground |
| Rec Equipment | Restrooms* | Sewage Dump |
| Showers* | Snack Bar | Sports Fields |
| Stables | Tennis Courts | Vending Machine |

* Handicap accessible.

**ACTIVITIES:**

| | | |
|---|---|---|
| Bicycling | Boating | Fishing/license |
| Hiking | Hunting | |

**CREDIT CARDS ACCEPTED:** Visa, MasterCard, American Express, Discover and Esprit.

**RESTRICTIONS:** Pets allowed on leash. Firearms are permitted for hunting. Thirty day limit with a 72 hour turnaround.

# LOUISIANA

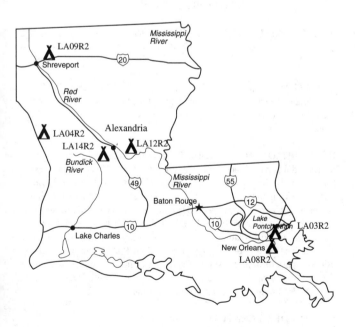

# BARKSDALE FAMCAMP (LA09R2)
Barksdale Air Force Base
Barksdale AFB, LA 71110-2426

**TELEPHONE NUMBER INFORMATION:** Main installation numbers: C-318-456-2679, D-312-781-2679.

**LOCATION:** On base. From I-20 E or W at Airline Drive, go south (right) .24 miles to a left on Old Minden Road for one block. Make a right on North Gate Road, follow one mile to North Gate of AFB. *USMRA: page 79 (B-2).* NMC: Shreveport, 3 miles southwest.

**DESCRIPTION OF AREA:** Camp is situated in alternatingly open and wooded areas shaded by many oaks and hickories. Three lakes and eleven ponds on base offer opportunities for fishing and boating. Also, Toledo Bend, Caddo, Cross and Bistineau Reservoir lakes are conveniently located for a variety of water-oriented recreation. Full range of support facilities available on base.

**SEASON OF OPERATION:** Year round.

**ELIGIBILITY:** Active/Reservists/Retired/DoD civilians.

**RESERVATIONS:** No advance reservations. Address: Barksdale FAMCAMP, Bldg 7262 Red Horse Drive, Barksdale AFB, LA 71110-2164. **C-318-456-2679, D-312-781-2679.** Fax: C-318-742-5236. Check in at FAMCAMP 0800-1700 hours Mon-Sat; after hours, pick site and check in following day, check out 1300 hours.

**Camper Spaces:** Concrete (22), handicap accessible, E (110V/30/40A)/W hookups. Rates: $10 daily/$60 weekly.

**Tent Spaces:** No hookups. Rates: $4 daily.

**SUPPORT FACILITIES:**

| | | |
|---|---|---|
| Auto Craft Shop | Bath House | Boat Launch |
| Boat Rental | Chapel | Commissary |
| Exchange | Fishing Pier | Fitness Center |
| Golf | Grills | Ice |
| Laundry | Pavilions | Picnic Area |
| Playground | Pool | Rec Equipment |
| Restrooms | Sewage Dump | Shoppette |
| Showers* | Sports Fields | Stables |
| Telephones | Tennis Courts | Trails |

* Handicap accessible.

**ACTIVITIES:**

| | | |
|---|---|---|
| ATV Trails | Bicycling | Boating |
| Canoeing | Fishing/license | Hiking |
| Hunting/license | Jogging | Trap/Skeet |

**CREDIT CARDS ACCEPTED:** Visa and MasterCard.

**RESTRICTIONS:** Pets allowed on leash. No firearms allowed. No swimming in lakes or ponds.

# MAGNOLIA SHADE RECREATIONAL VEHICLE PARK (LA03R2)
New Orleans Naval Support Activity
New Orleans, LA 70142-5007

**TELEPHONE NUMBER INFORMATION:** Main installation numbers: C-504-678-2527/2285, D-312-678-2527/2285.

**LOCATION:** On base. On the west bank of the Mississippi River. From I-10 E, follow Business District/Westbank, Gretna signs (90 W) across Mississippi River, take right first exit off of bridge and follow Gen DeGaulle signs to left. Turn left on Shirley Drive. Base is on Gen Meyer Avenue at foot of Shirley Drive. Report to NSA gym, Bldg 752, by RV park. *USMRA: page 90 (E-4).* NMC: New Orleans, 5 miles east.

**LOUISIANA**
*Magnolia Shade Recreational Vehicle Park, continued*

**DESCRIPTION OF AREA:** Attractions along Mississippi River include boat cruises, zoo cruise, bus tours, plantations, museums and historic homes. Famous New Orleans French Quarter and Bourbon Street nearby. Full range of support facilities available on base, many within walking distance.

**SEASON OF OPERATION:** Year round.

**ELIGIBILITY:** Active/Reservists/Retired/DoD civilians.

**RESERVATIONS:** Advance reservations accepted. Address: MWR Department, Bldg 752, New Orleans Naval Support Activity, 2300 General Meyer Avenue, New Orleans, LA 70142-5007. **C-504-678-2527/2285, D-312-678-2527/2285.**

**Camper Spaces:** Hardstand (16), E (110/220V/20A)/W hookups. Rates: $9 daily.

**SUPPORT FACILITIES:**

| | | |
|---|---|---|
| Camping Equipment | Chapel | Gas |
| Mini Mart | Picnic Area | Playground |
| Racquetball Courts | Rec Equipment | Restrooms/gym |
| Sewage Dump | Showers/gym | Sports Fields |
| Tennis Courts | | |

**ACTIVITIES:**

| | | |
|---|---|---|
| Fishing | Sightseeing | Tours |

**CREDIT CARDS ACCEPTED:** None.

**RESTRICTIONS:** Pets allowed on leash. Thirty day limit. As the Naval Support Activity is surrounded by the city of New Orleans, finding your way through the maze requires patience, watch for road signs.

*Note: Discount tickets, tour info and a free gift available at ITT Office. Hours: 1000-1400 hours Mon, 1000-1700 hours Tue-Fri, 0900-1400 hours Sat. Snack Bar at Bowling Center, Bldg 722, open seven days a week.*

# NEW ORLEANS NAS/JRB CAMPGROUND (LA08R2)

New Orleans Naval Air Station/Joint Reserve Base
New Orleans, LA 70143-5012

**TELEPHONE NUMBER INFORMATION:** Main installation numbers: C-504-678-3011, D-312-363-3011. Police for campground, C-504-678-3827.

**LOCATION:** On base. Exit I-10 south of Mississippi River in Gretna. Base is off and west of LA-23 in Belle Chasse. Clearly marked. *USMRA: page 79 (H-7), page 90 (F-6).* NMC: New Orleans, 12 miles north.

**DESCRIPTION OF AREA:** Campground is just minutes from famous French Quarter and downtown New Orleans. Wide range of support facilities on base.

**SEASON OF OPERATION:** Year round.

**ELIGIBILITY:** Active/Reservists/Retired/DoD civilians.

**RESERVATIONS:** Required. Address: MWR Campground, NAS/JRB (Code 132), 400 Russell Avenue, New Orleans, LA 70143-5012. **C-504-678-3142** 0600-1800 hours Mon, 1000-1800 hours Tue, 0800-1200

Wed, 0800-1800 Thu-Fri, 0700-1800 Sat. Fax: C-504-678-3552. Discounts available to holders of Golden Age Passports. Check in at Auto Hobby Shop, Bldg 143, check out 1200 hours.

**Mobile Home:** Two-bedroom (1), handicap accessible, full kitchen, E (110/220V/30A)/W hookups, linens. Rates: $30 daily, $180 weekly.

**Camper Spaces:** Gravel (16), handicap accessible. Rates: $8 daily/$40 weekly.

**Tent Spaces:** Grassy area (10), no hookups. Rates: $2 daily.

**SUPPORT FACILITIES:**

| | | |
|---|---|---|
| Auto Craft Shop | Bath House* | Boat Rental/Storage |
| Chapel | Convenience Store | Exchange |
| Fitness Center | Gas | Golf |
| Grills | Ice | Laundry |
| Pavilion | Picnic Area | Playground |
| Pool | Rec Equipment | Restrooms* |
| Sewage Dump | Shoppette | Showers |
| Skeet Range | Sports Fields | Telephones |
| Tennis Courts | | |

* Handicap accessible.

**ACTIVITIES:**

| | | |
|---|---|---|
| Bicycling | Golfing | Jogging |
| Swimming | Tennis | |

**CREDIT CARDS ACCEPTED:** None.

**RESTRICTIONS:** Pets allowed on leash. No firearms allowed, must be checked with Security at front gate.

# SOUTH FORT RV PARK (LA14R2)

Fort Polk
Fort Polk, LA 71459-5000

**TELEPHONE NUMBER INFORMATION:** Main installation numbers: C-318-531-2911, D-312-863-1110. Police for mobile home park, C-318-531-2227.

**LOCATION:** On post. Off US-171 E, nine miles south Leesville. South to Fort Polk entrance road, east to main gate. One block on Louisiana Avenue, then right on Utah Avenue. *USMRA: page 79 (C-4).* NMC: Alexandria, 45 miles northeast.

**DESCRIPTION OF AREA:** The RV park is located on the main post, not far from the Bayne-Jones Army Community Hospital. The order of priority for use of the RV spaces is as follows: (1) active duty military on PCS orders to/from the post, (2) visiting relatives and guests of patients in Bayne-Jones Army Community Hospital, or military patients in an area hospital, (3) active duty and retired (and other personnel receiving outpatient medical treatment) who must stay near the hospital, (4) friends and relatives visiting military personnel at Fort Polk, (5) military personnel in leave, pass or transient status, (6) retired military in transient status, and (7) other personnel in transient status who are entitled to dependency benefits. Full range of support facilities available on post.

**SEASON OF OPERATION:** Year round.

**ELIGIBILITY:** Active/Reservists/Retired/DoD civilians.

**RESERVATIONS:** Accepted up to 60 days in advance. Address: South Fort RV Park, c/o Magnolia Guest House, P.O. Box 3930, Fort Polk, LA 71459. **C-318-531-9200/9000, D-312-863-9200.** Check in at Magnolia Guest House, Bldg 522, 1300-1800 hours, check out 1100 hours. Patron must arrive prior to 1800 hours on day of reservation or it will be canceled. Exception will be made if Magnolia Guesthouse is informed of late arrival when reservation is made.

**RV Spaces:** Grass (10), E (110/220V/30/50A)/S/W hookups. Vehicle owner is responsible for connection to outlets provided. Sewer connection must be sealed with a joint sealer (PVS or rubber gasket) to insure a leak-free connection. Owner responsible for furnishing materials necessary to accomplish these tasks. Rates: $8 daily.

**CREDIT CARDS ACCEPTED:** Visa, MasterCard and American Express.

**RESTRICTIONS:** Pets must be inoculated and registered in accordance with current regulations and must be controlled so as not to become a public nuisance or menace. No open fires outside of BBQ pits. Children must be supervised at all times. Patrons must take out own trash. Thirty day limit, extensions will be considered on a case-by-case basis.

# TOLEDO BEND
# RECREATION SITE (LA04R2)
Fort Polk
Fort Polk, LA 71459-5227

**TELEPHONE NUMBER INFORMATION:** Main installation numbers: C-318-531-2911, D-312-863-1110. Police for recreation site, C-318-531-6825.

**LOCATION:** Off post. Take US-171 north from Leesville, west on LA-111 at Anacoco, bear right onto LA-392. North on LA-191, left at Army Travel Camp sign. *USMRA: page 79 (B-4).* NMI: Fort Polk, 45 miles southeast. NMC: Alexandria, 60 miles northeast.

**DESCRIPTION OF AREA:** Toledo Bend is the largest man-made lake in the South and fifth largest in the country. Excellent fishing and swimming area. Campsite located on 26 acres of wooded land. Hodges Gardens and Fort Jesup offer sightseeing opportunities. Full range of support facilities available at Fort Polk.

Fort Polk also operates **Alligator Lake Recreation Site** on LA-469 just north of North Fort. It covers approximately 20 acres along a man-made lake. Ample space for picnicking and all sorts of sports. Lake itself offers paddle boating and some good fishing. Community Recreation Division operates a check out center where boats, campers, camping equipment, fishing equipment, scuba gear and water skis can be rented. C-318-531-5332.

**SEASON OF OPERATION:** Year round.

**ELIGIBILITY:** Active/Reservists/Retired/DoD and NAF civilians.

**RESERVATIONS:** Accepted up to 30 days in advance depending on status of sponsor. Address: Toledo Bend Recreation Site, 1310 Army Recreation Road, Florien, LA 71429-5000. **C-1-888-718-9088.** For information only, C-318-565-4235. Discounts to holders of Golden Age Passports (RV only). Check in at Operations Center 1500 hours, check out 1200 hours Mon-Sat, 1400 hours Sun.

**Mobile Homes:** Two-bedroom (12), two baths, sofabed, full kitchen, microwave, pots/pans, utensils, E (110V/50A)/S/W hookups, TV. Patrons must provide bed linens and towels. Rates: $35 daily.

**Camper Spaces:** Gravel (15), up to 33', E (110V/50A)/W hookups. Rates: $8 daily.

**Tent Spaces:** Unlimited, no hookups. Rates: $2 daily.

**SUPPORT FACILITIES:**

| | | |
|---|---|---|
| Beach | Boat Launch | Boat Rental |
| Cabanas | Fishing Equipment | Fishing Pier |
| Grills | Jet Skis | Marina |
| Party Barges | Pavilions | Picnic Areas |
| Playgrounds | Rec Equipment | Restrooms |
| Sewage Dump | Showers | Small Store/summer |
| Vending Machine | | |

**ACTIVITIES:**

| | | |
|---|---|---|
| Boating/safety | Hiking | Horseshoes |
| Swimming | Volleyball | |

**CREDIT CARDS ACCEPTED:** Visa, MasterCard, American Express and Discover.

**RESTRICTIONS:** Pets allowed on leash. No firearms allowed.

# TWIN LAKES RECREATION AREA (LA12R2)
Camp Beauregard
Pineville, LA 71360-3737

**TELEPHONE NUMBER INFORMATION:** Main installation numbers: C-318-640-2080, D-312-485-8222.

**LOCATION:** Off base. Off US-165, via LA-116, four miles. NMC: Alexandria, six miles south.

**DESCRIPTION OF AREA:** Seven miles from Camp Beauregard, State Wildlife Management Area.

**SEASON OF OPERATION:** Year round.

**ELIGIBILITY:** Active/Reservists/Retired.

**RESERVATIONS:** Accepted. Address: 1111 F Street, Camp Beauregard, LA 71360-3737. **C-318-641-8302/8269.** For information on recreation area, C-318-641-3355/65, C-318-640-2080, ext 269.

**Mobile Homes:** 3, E (110V/30A)/S/W hookups. Rates: $10 daily.

**Camper Spaces:** Gravel (4), E/W hookups. Rates: $5 daily.

**Tent Spaces:** Primitive (10), W hookup. Rates: $3 daily.

**SUPPORT FACILITIES:**

| | | |
|---|---|---|
| Bath House | Boat Dock | Pavilion |
| Picnic Areas | BBQ Pits | |

**ACTIVITIES:**

| | | |
|---|---|---|
| ATV Trails | Bicycling | Boating |
| Fishing/license | Hunting/license | |

**CREDIT CARDS ACCEPTED:** None.

**RESTRICTIONS:** Pets allowed on leash. No pets in trailers. No discharging of firearms. Swimming is prohibited. No operation of outboard motors in lakes.

*MAINE*

# MAINE

## SPRAGUE'S NECK (ME02R1)

Cutler Naval Computer and Telecommunications Station
Cutler, ME 04620-9603

**TELEPHONE NUMBER INFORMATION:** Main installation numbers: C-207-259-8229, D-312-476-7229. Police for camp area, C-207-259-8267.

**LOCATION:** On base. Take I-95 N or S to Bangor, take I-395 around Bangor. From Route 1A and Route 1 to East Machias. Route 191 SE to base (seven miles off Route 1). Obtain directions, map and equipment from Cutler NCTS MWR. *USMRA: page 18 (G-7).* NMC: Bangor, 90 miles west.

**DESCRIPTION OF AREA:** Located in a wooded section in the eastern corner of Maine, overlooking rugged Atlantic Coast in Machias Bay area. Very rustic. Wide range of support facilities available at Cutler NCTS.

**SEASON OF OPERATION:** 15 Apr-30 Oct.

**ELIGIBILITY:** Active/Reservists/Retired/DoD civilians.

**RESERVATIONS:** Required: up to three months in advance with 50% deposit. Address: MWR, Cutler Naval Computer and Telecommunications Station, HC 69, Box 1198, Cutler, ME 04626-5000. **C-207-259-8284, D-312-476-7284.**

**Log Cabin:** Rustic, four-bedroom (1), shared bath, shower, gas refrigerator, stove, gas lights, wood heat,front porch. Running water in summer months. Rates: $30 daily, DoD $50 daily.

**Camper Spaces:** Gravel (10), no hookups. Rates: $2 daily.

**SUPPORT FACILITIES:**

| | | |
|---|---|---|
| Auto Craft Shop | Bowling | Fitness Center |
| Grills | Gym | Picnic Area |
| Racquetball | Restaurant | Rec Equipment |
| Sports Field | Trails | |

**ACTIVITIES:**

| | | |
|---|---|---|
| Canoeing | Clamming | Fishing |
| Hiking | Hunting/license | Ice Skating |
| Jogging | Sailing | Sea Kayaking |
| Skiing/XC | Whale Watching | |

**CREDIT CARDS ACCEPTED:** None.

**RESTRICTIONS:** Pets allowed. Firearms must be registered with the Security Department. Fire permits required.

## WINTER HARBOR RECREATION AREA (ME04R1)

Winter Harbor Naval Security Group Activity
Winter Harbor, ME 04693-0900

**TELEPHONE NUMBER INFORMATION:** Main installation numbers: C-207-963-5534, D-312-476-9011.

**LOCATION:** On base. From I-95 at Bangor, take ALT US-1 S to Ellsworth, take US-1 N (traveling east) approximately 20 miles to ME-186, south to Winter Harbor. Installation is six miles from Winter Harbor. Stop at Quarterdeck for directions. *USMRA: page 18 (F-8).* NMC: Bangor, 60 miles northwest.

**DESCRIPTION OF AREA:** Recreation area is located on Schoodic Point in the Winter Harbor section of Acadia National Park along Maine's rugged Atlantic Coast. Many nature and hiking trails, ponds, lakes, and ocean activities are within easy driving distance. Limited support facilities on base within walking distance.

**SEASON OF OPERATION:** 15 Apr-15 Oct campground. Year round others.

**ELIGIBILITY:** Active/Reservists/Retired/DoD civilians.

**RESERVATIONS:** Recommended. Up to 90 days in advance for cabins and trailers. Address: MWR, 20 Department, Winter Harbor Naval Security Group Activity, ME 04693-0138 **C-207-963-5537, C-207-963-5534 ext 287/288, D-312-476-9287/9288.** Fax: C-207-963-5537, D-312-476-9432. Check out 1000 hours.

**Recreation Cabins:** Three-bedroom (3), handicap accessible, full bath, kitchen, microwave, dishes, CATV/VCR, linens. Rates: $50-$65 daily.

**House Trailers:** Three-bedroom (3), full bath, kitchen, microwave, dishes, TV/VCR, washer/dryer, linens. Rates: $50-$65 daily.

**Camper Spaces:** Gravel (8), E (110V/30A)/W hookups. Rates: $10 daily. 1, E hookup. Rates: $ 8 daily.

**Tent Spaces:** 4, no hookups. Rates: $5 daily.

*Winter Harbor Recreation Area, continued*

**Camper Spaces:** Hardstand (14), E (110V/30A)/W hookups. Rates: $15 daily.

**Group Camping Spaces:** Primitive (2), no hookups. Rates: $2 per person daily.

**SUPPORT FACILITIES:**

| | | |
|---|---|---|
| Auto Craft Shop | Boat Rental/Storage | Chapel |
| Commissary | Exchange | Fitness Center |
| Gas | Grill | Laundry |
| Pavilion | Picnic Area | Playground |
| Racquetball Courts | Rec Equipment | Rec Center |
| Restrooms | Sewage Dump | Showers |
| Sports Field | Telephones | Tennis Courts |
| Trails | | |

**ACTIVITIES:**

| | | |
|---|---|---|
| Biking | Boating | Fishing |
| Golf | Hiking | Kayaking |
| Skating | Skiing | Swimming |
| Water Skiing | | |

**CREDIT CARDS ACCEPTED:** Visa, MasterCard, American Express, Discover and Diners'.

**RESTRICTIONS:** Pets allowed in trailers 1 and 2 only, additional fee of $10. Firearms are to be checked in at the Quarter Deck before entering the base.

**SUPPORT FACILITIES:**

| | | |
|---|---|---|
| Boat Rental | Camping Equipment | Chapel |
| Gas | Golf/Academy | Grills |
| Marina | Mini Mart | Picnic Area |
| Playground | Pools | Racquetball |
| Rec Center | Rec Equipment | Restrooms |
| Sewage Dump | Showers | Sports Fields |
| Tennis Courts | | |

**ACTIVITIES:**

| | | |
|---|---|---|
| Crabbing | Fishing | Golf |
| Racquetball | Swimming | Tennis |

**CREDIT CARDS ACCEPTED:** Visa, MasterCard and American Express.

**RESTRICTIONS:** Pets allowed on leash. Firearms are prohibited. No swimming.

# MARYLAND

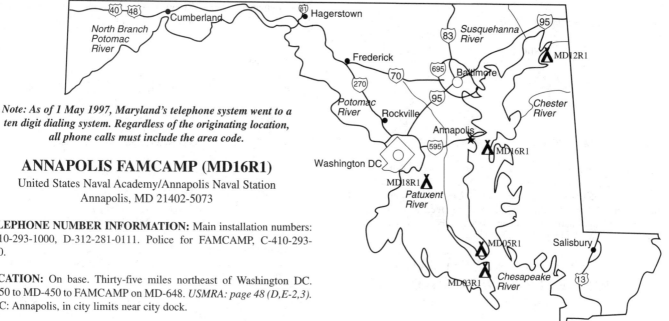

*Note: As of 1 May 1997, Maryland's telephone system went to a ten digit dialing system. Regardless of the originating location, all phone calls must include the area code.*

## ANNAPOLIS FAMCAMP (MD16R1)

United States Naval Academy/Annapolis Naval Station
Annapolis, MD 21402-5073

**TELEPHONE NUMBER INFORMATION:** Main installation numbers: C-410-293-1000, D-312-281-0111. Police for FAMCAMP, C-410-293-9300.

**LOCATION:** On base. Thirty-five miles northeast of Washington DC. US-50 to MD-450 to FAMCAMP on MD-648. *USMRA: page 48 (D,E-2,3).* NMC: Annapolis, in city limits near city dock.

**DESCRIPTION OF AREA:** Scenic and historic Annapolis offers a walking tour of the Naval Academy Museum, city dock area, and much more. Full range of support facilities available at US Naval Academy and Annapolis Naval Station.

**SEASON OF OPERATION:** Year round.

**ELIGIBILITY:** Active/Reservists/Retired/DoD civilians.

**RESERVATIONS:** Advanced reservations accepted. Address: Recreational Services, Bldg 89, Naval Station, Annapolis, MD 21402-5071. **C-410-293-9200, D-312-281-9200.** Discounts available to holders of Golden Age, Golden Access and Golden Eagle Passports.

## CAMP YOCOMICO (MD18R1)

Andrews Air Force Base
Andrews AFB, MD 20762-6421

**TELEPHONE NUMBER INFORMATION:** Main installation numbers: C-301-981-1110, D-312-858-1110. Security Police for FAMCAMP, C-301-981-2001.

**LOCATION:** On base. Southeast of Washington DC. From I-95 (east portion of Capital Beltway, I-495), take exit 9 (Andrews AFB/Allentown Road) to traffic light at end of ramp, left to main gate. *USMRA: page 42 (E-5).* NMC: Washington DC, 10 miles northwest.

*MARYLAND*
*Camp Yocomico, continued*

**DESCRIPTION OF AREA:** Aerial gateway to Washington DC, home of Air Force One, the President's aircraft. There is much to do in the way of entertainment, monuments, parks, museums, restaurants, theaters, zoo, aquariums etc. Three excellent 18 hole golf courses within walking distance of Camp Yocomico. Full range of support facilities available on base.

**SEASON OF OPERATION:** Year round.

**ELIGIBILITY:** Active/Reservists/Retired.

**RESERVATIONS:** Full hookup reservations strongly recommended Apr-Oct with Visa or MasterCard. Not required for electric only, overflow/dry parking, or tenting. Address: Outdoor Recreation, 89 SVS/SVRO, 1235 Menoher Drive, Andrews AFB, MD 20762-7002. Personal mail to be sent to General Delivery, US Post Office, 1668 D Street, Andrews AFB, MD 20762-7002. Make checks payable to Outdoor Recreation. **C-301-981-4109, D-312-981-4109.** Check in after 1100 hours at Camp Yocomico FAMCAMP, Bldg 4520 Wheeling Road, check out 1100 hours.

**Camper Spaces:** Gravel (29), E (110/120V/50A)/S/W hookups. Rates: $16 daily/$100 weekly/$400 monthly. Gravel (10), E (110/120V/50A) hookup. Rates: $13 daily/$80 weekly/$325 monthly. Gravel, overflow (4), no hookups. Rates: $10 daily/$60 weekly/$275 monthly.

**Tent Spaces:** Gravel/dirt (4), no hookups. Rates: $6 daily/$40 weekly/$165 monthly.

**SUPPORT FACILITIES:**

| | | |
|---|---|---|
| Bath House | Grills | Lake |
| Laundry | Picnic Area | Playground |
| Restrooms | Sewage Dump | Showers |
| Telephones | TV Lounge | |

**ACTIVITIES:**

| | |
|---|---|
| Fishing/license | Horseshoes |

**CREDIT CARDS ACCEPTED:** Visa and MasterCard.

**RESTRICTIONS:** Pets allowed on leash. Fenced dog walk area available. All firearms must be registered with security police. No ground fires. Clothes lines not acceptable. Water lines must be disconnected when outside temperature is below 32 degrees. No feeding of wildlife. All personal mail must be received through base U.S. Post Office. Fourteen day limit, 30 day limit for PCS move.

## GOOSE CREEK/WEST BASIN RECREATION AREA (MD03R1)

Patuxent River Naval Air Station
Patuxent River, MD 20670-1132

**TELEPHONE NUMBER INFORMATION:** Main installation numbers: C-301-342-3000, D-312-342-3000. Police for recreation area, C-301-342-3508.

**LOCATION:** On base. From I-95 (east portion of Capital Beltway, I-495) exit 7A to Branch Avenue S (MD-5). Follow MD-5 until it turns into MD-235 near Oraville, on to Lexington Park, and the NAS. Main gate is on MD-235 and MD-246 (Cedar point Road). *USMRA: page 42 (F,G-7)*. NMC: Washington DC, 65 miles northwest.

**DESCRIPTION OF AREA:** There are two campgrounds. One is at Goose Creek, located along the Chesapeake Bay on Cedar Point Road, the other is West Basin, and is on Patrol Road. The Naval Air Station offers a wide range of recreational facilities and a full range of support facilities.

**SEASON OF OPERATION:** Feb-Nov.

**ELIGIBILITY:** Active/Reservists/Retired.

**RESERVATIONS:** Required; accepted 90 days in advance for no more than 30 days in duration. Address: Recreation Office, Bldg 458, 47382 Keane Road, Patuxent River NAS, MD 20670-5423. **C-301-342-3508, D-312-342-3508** 0800-1630 Mon-Fri, other hours at Drill Hall, Building 458. Fax: C-301-342-3232, D-312-342-3232. Ask for a recreation guidebook. Check in 1200 hours at Gymnasium, Bldg 458, check out 1200 hours.

**Camper Spaces:** Gravel (14), E (110V/30A)/W hookups. Rates: $11 daily/$66 weekly/$221 monthly.

**Camper/Tent Spaces:** Dirt (46), no hookups. Rates: $7 daily/$37 weekly/$118 monthly.

**Trailer Rentals:** 17' hardtop, sleeps four, furnished. 15' pop-up, sleeps six, furnished, bath/shower. Rates: $27 daily/$172 weekly/$672 monthly.

**SUPPORT FACILITIES:**

| | | |
|---|---|---|
| Auto Craft Shop | Bath House | Beach |
| Boat Launch | Boat Rental | Camping Equipment |
| Chapel | Commissary | Convenience Store |
| Exchange | Fire Rings | Fishing Pier |
| Fitness Center | Gas | Golf |
| Grills | Ice | Laundry |
| Marina | Pavilion | Picnic Area |
| Playground | Pool | Rec Center |
| Req. Equipment | Restrooms | Sewage Dump |
| Shoppette | Snack Bar | Sports Fields |
| Telephones | Tennis Courts | |

**ACTIVITIES:**

| | | |
|---|---|---|
| Crabbing | Fishing/license | Hunting |
| Jogging | Swimming | Water Skiing |

**CREDIT CARDS ACCEPTED:** Visa and MasterCard.

**RESTRICTIONS:** Pets allowed on leash. No firearms allowed.

## SKIPPER'S POINT RECREATIONAL AREA (MD12R1)

Aberdeen Proving Ground
Aberdeen PG, MD 21005-5001

**TELEPHONE NUMBER INFORMATION:** Main installation numbers: C-410-278-5201, D-312-298-1110. Police for recreation area, C-410-671-2222, D-312-584-2222.

**LOCATION:** On post. Aberdeen Area: From I-95, take exit 85. Go east on MD-22 for three miles to main gate. Also, from US-40 N go east on MD-22 to entrance to main gate. NMC: Baltimore, 30 miles southwest. From Edgewood Area: From I-95 take exit 77. Go east on MD-24, then left on Route 755 E and follow two miles to main gate. Also, From US-40, take Route 755 E to main gate. *USMRA: page 42 (G-2,3)*. NMC: Baltimore, 20 miles southwest.

**DESCRIPTION OF AREA:** This is a primitive camping facility located on a gravel road beside the Bush River approximately ten miles from the Aberdeen Area of the Proving Ground. There are many attractions in nearby Havre de Grace, including Concord Point Lighthouse, Decoy Museum, Stafford Furnace, and the Susquehanna Museum. The Carter Mansion, Jersey Toll House, and Rock Mill Run are all in Susquehanna State Park. Limited support facilities in the Edgewood Area, full range available at Aberdeen Proving Ground.

*Skipper's Point Recreational Area, continued*

**SEASON OF OPERATION:** Year round, staffed on Fri-Sun and holidays from Memorial Day through Labor Day.

**ELIGIBILITY:** Active/Reservists/Retired/Aberdeen PG civilians.

**RESERVATIONS:** Strongly recommended. Address: CRD Outdoor Recreation, 2201 Aberdeen Blvd, Aberdeen Proving Ground, MD 21005-5001. **C-410-278-4124, D-312-298-4124.** Fax: C-410-278-4160. For information Memorial Day weekend-Labor Day weekend, C-410-671-4732. Discounts available to holders of Golden Age, Golden Access and Golden Eagle Passports. Check in before 1900 hours.

**Camper Spaces:** Dirt (6), no hookups. Rates: $5 daily.

**Tent Spaces:** Dirt (15), no hookups. Rates: $3.50 daily.

**SUPPORT FACILITIES:**

| | | |
|---|---|---|
| Boat Launch, 20' | Boat Rental | Chapel* |
| Gas* | Golf* | Grills |
| Gym* | Nature Trail | Pavilion |
| Picnic Area | Playground | Port-a-Potties |

* Located in Edgewood Area, approximately two miles away.

**ACTIVITIES:**

| | | |
|---|---|---|
| Boating | Fishing | Hiking |

**CREDIT CARDS ACCEPTED:** Visa and MasterCard accepted for reservations only.

**RESTRICTIONS:** Pets allowed on a leash. No firearms allowed.

# SOLOMONS NAVY RECREATION CENTER (MD05R1)

Solomons, MD 20688-0147

**TELEPHONE NUMBER INFORMATION:** Main installation numbers: C-410-326-5000.

**LOCATION:** On base. On the Patuxent River. From US-301 N or S, take MD-4 SE to Solomons on right. Also, take MD-5 SE to MD-235, then MD-4 NE to Solomons on left. *USMRA: page 42 (F-6).* NMI: Patuxent River NAWC, 10 miles south. NMC: Washington DC, 65 miles northwest.

**DESCRIPTION OF AREA:** Located in southern Maryland on the delta where the Patuxent River meets the Chesapeake Bay. Rustic and relaxing area that has retained its natural beauty. Campground and facilities encompass approximately 260 acres with extensive frontage on river. Only Navy facility dedicated solely to recreation. Historic waterfront community. Local points of interest include Calvert Marine Museum, Cliffs of Calvert, Oyster Fleet, St Mary's City, Battle Creek Cypress Swamp, Naval Air Test & Evaluation Museum, area festivals, Point Lookout State Park and many other historical sites. Full range of support facilities available at Patuxent River NAWC.

**SEASON OF OPERATION:** Year round.

**ELIGIBILITY:** Active/Reservists/Retired/DoD civilians.

**RESERVATIONS:** Required with payment in full within 60 days from being made. Address: Solomons Navy Recreation Center, P.O. Box 147, Solomons, MD 20688-0147. **C-1-800-NAVY-230 (DC area), C-410-326-1260.** Fax: C-410-326-4280. A refundable cleaning deposit of $50 is payable upon check in.

**Apartments:** One- to four-bedroom, bath, kitchen, utensils, picnic tables, grill. Patrons must provide linens. Rates: Based on rank, see below.

| Bedroom | E1-E5* | E6-E9* | Officers* | DoD* |
|---|---|---|---|---|
| One- | $37-$45 | $45-$50 | $55-$60 | $68-$75 |
| Two- | $41-$55 | $48-$60 | $58-$70 | $73-$85 |
| Three- | $43-$65 | $52-$70 | $62-$80 | $77-$95 |
| Four- | $47-$75 | $55-$80 | $65-$90 | $80-$105 |

* Higher rate includes Leisure Value Package (aquatics facility admission, basketball, crabbing and fishing pier admission, miniature golf, racquetball, sports equipment, and tennis). Maximum three people per bedroom.

**Cottages:** Two- to five-bedroom, bath, kitchen, utensils, A/C, picnic tables, grill. Patrons must provide linens. Waterfront cottages are not heated. Rates: Based on rank, see below.

| Bedroom | E1-E5* | E6-E9* | Officers* | DoD* |
|---|---|---|---|---|
| Two- | $41-$55 | $48-$60 | $58-$70 | $73-$85 |
| Three- | $43-$65 | $52-$70 | $62-$80 | $77-$95 |
| Four- | $47-$75 | $55-$80 | $65-$90 | $80-$105 |
| Five- | $50-$85 | $58-$90 | $67-$100 | $84-$115 |

* Higher rate includes Leisure Value Package (aquatics facility admission, basketball, crabbing and fishing pier admission, miniature golf, racquetball, sports equipment, and tennis). 19 handicap accessible. Maximum three people per bedroom.

**Bungalows:** Three- to four-bedroom, bath, kitchen, utensils, A/C, picnic tables, grill. Patrons must provide linens. Rates: Based on rank, see below.

| Bedroom | E1-E5* | E6-E9* | Officers* | DoD* |
|---|---|---|---|---|
| Three- | $35-$55 | $44-$60 | $54-$70 | $67-$85 |
| Four- | $39-$65 | $46-$70 | $57-$80 | $72-$95 |

* Higher rate includes Leisure Value Package (aquatics facility admission, basketball, crabbing and fishing pier admission, miniature golf, racquetball, sports equipment, and tennis). Maximum three people per bedroom.

**Log Cabins:** One-bedroom, private bath, sleeps six, full bed, bunk beds, sofabed, kitchen, utensils, A/C, picnic tables, grill. Patrons must provide linens. Rates: $46-$70 E1-E5, $52-$75 E6-E9, $58-$85 Officers, $69-$95 DoD. Higher rate includes Leisure Value Package (aquatics facility admission, basketball, crabbing and fishing pier admission, miniature golf, racquetball, sports equipment, and tennis).

**Camper Spaces:** 146, E (110V/30A)/S/W hookups. Rates: $20-$25 daily/$312.50-$365 monthly (Depending on rank. Includes up to four leisure passes per individual campsite. Also available without leisure passes.). E (120V/20A)/S/W hookups. Rates: $20-$35 daily/$289-$315 military, $23-$40 daily/$347-$380 monthly DoD (Includes up to four leisure passes per individual campsite. Also available without leisure passes.). E (120V/20A)/W hookups. Rates: $19-$32 daily/$231-$275 monthly military, $21-$37 daily/$289-$340 monthly DoD (Includes up to four leisure passes per individual campsite. Also available without leisure passes.). E (120V/20A) hookup. Rates: $15-$30 daily/$208-$240 monthly military, $18-$35 daily/$266-$320 monthly DoD (Includes up to four leisure passes per individual campsite. Also available without leisure passes.).

**Camper/Tent Spaces:** 56, no hookups. Rates: $9-$25 daily/$116-$155 monthly military, $12-$30 daily/$174-$220 monthly DoD (Includes up to four leisure passes per individual campsite. Also available without leisure passes.).

**Tent Spaces:** Group Sites (15), no hookups. Rates: $5-$6 per person daily/$25-$60 minimum daily military, $5.50-$6.50 daily/$35-$65 minimum daily DoD. (Includes up to four leisure passes per individual campsite. Also available without leisure passes.)

*MARYLAND/MASSACHUSETTS*
*Solomons Navy Recreation Center, continued*

**SUPPORT FACILITIES:**

| | | |
|---|---|---|
| Bait/Tackle | Ball Fields | Beach |
| Boat Launch | Boat Rental | Boat Slip Rental |
| Camper Rental | Camping Equipment | Fish/Crab Pier |
| Gazebo | Grills | Ice |
| Marina | Miniature Golf | Party Pavilions |
| Picnic Area | Playground | Pools |
| Racquetball Court | Restrooms | RV Storage |
| Sewage Dump | Showers | Softball Field |
| Sports Equipment | Tennis Courts | Video Arcade |

**ACTIVITIES:**

| | | |
|---|---|---|
| Basketball | Bicycling | Boating |
| Crabbing | Duck Hunting | Fishing/license |
| Horseshoes | Special Events | Swimming |
| Volleyball | Windsurfing | |

**CREDIT CARDS ACCEPTED:** Visa, MasterCard and American Express.

**RESTRICTIONS:** Pets are not allowed in lodging units, must have proof of shots and be registered at Reservation and Information Center, must be on leash and under positive control. Open fires prohibited except in group site areas where fire rings are provided. Seven day limit to include only one holiday weekend 1 Apr-15 Oct.

# MASSACHUSETTS

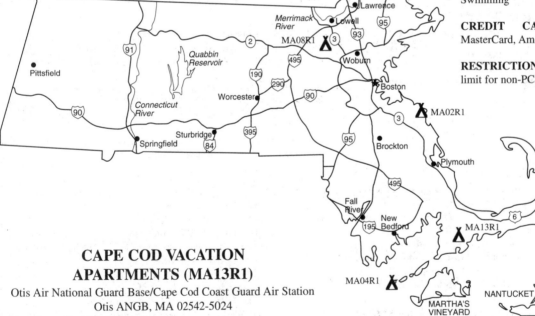

## CAPE COD VACATION APARTMENTS (MA13R1)

Otis Air National Guard Base/Cape Cod Coast Guard Air Station
Otis ANGB, MA 02542-5024

**TELEPHONE NUMBER INFORMATION:** Main installation numbers: C-508-968-6300, D-312-557-6300.

**LOCATION:** On base. South of Plymouth, from MA-28 N or S take Massachusetts Military Reservation exit off MA-28, south on Connley Avenue approximately two miles to Bourne gate. Inquire at gate. *USMRA: page 17 (M-7)*. NMC: Boston, 50 miles northwest.

**DESCRIPTION OF AREA:** Situated on Cape Cod, a famous New England vacation area. Limited support facilities available on base.

**SEASON OF OPERATION:** Year round.

**ELIGIBILITY:** Active/Reservists/Retired.

**RESERVATIONS:** Required with payment: up to 90 days in advance for active duty on PCS, up to 60 days in advance for active duty on TDY or TAD. Vacationers two weeks in advance 1 May-1 Oct, up to 30 days in advance for all others/other times. Address: Coast Guard Air Station, Temporary Quarters, Bldg 5204 Ent Street, Otis ANGB, Cape Cod Coast Guard Air Station, MA 02542-5024. **C-508-968-6461, D-312-557-6461.** Check in at Temporary Quarters, Bldg 5204, 0800-1600 hours Mon-Fri, check in after hours and weekends by prior arrangement and prepayment.

**Townhouse Apartments:** Two-bedroom (12), furnished, sleeps six, one double bed, two twin beds, sofabed, kitchen, TV. Rates: $21-$60 daily (depending on rank).

**Suites:** One-bedroom (18), two double beds, sofabed, sleeps five, refrigerator, microwave. Rates: $40-$50 daily (depending on rank and season).

**Single Quarters:** 2, private bath, furnished. Rates: $35-$40 daily (depending on rank and season).

**SUPPORT FACILITIES:**

| | | |
|---|---|---|
| Boat Rental | Commissary | Dispensary |
| Exchange | Fishing Tackle | Gas |
| Golf/9 holes | Gym | Laundry |
| Picnic Area | Playground | Rec Equipment |
| Stables | Theater | |

**ACTIVITIES:**

| | |
|---|---|
| Boating | Fishing |
| Swimming | |

**CREDIT CARDS ACCEPTED**: Visa, MasterCard, American Express and Discover.

**RESTRICTIONS:** No pets allowed. Two week limit for non-PCS.

# CUTTYHUNK ISLAND RECREATIONAL HOUSING FACILITY (MA04R1)

Boston, MA 02109-5000

**TELEPHONE NUMBER INFORMATION:** Main installation numbers: C-617-223-8047/8375.

**LOCATION:** Off base. On Cuttyhunk Island. From I-195 or MA-6 at New Bedford, south to State Pier (near Elm Street). Transportation to the island is via Cuttyhunk Boat Lines M/V ALERT (C-508-992-1432). *USMRA: page 17 (L-8)*. NMI: Newport Naval Education and Training Center, RI, 35 miles southwest of New Bedford. NMC: Boston, within city limits.

**DESCRIPTION OF AREA:** The dwelling site, a former Coast Guard lifeboat station, is located 14 miles south off the coast of New Bedford and just west of Martha's Vineyard. It is approximately 300 yards from the ferry

*Cuttyhunk Island Recreational Housing Facility, continued*

landing and is within easy walking distance of the local community. As the community is very small and depends on ferry service for delivery of supplies, prices will be understandably higher than on the mainland. A small grocery store is available on the island, but visitors are advised to bring adequate food and laundry supplies to meet most of their needs during their stay. Full range of support facilities at Newport Naval Education and Training Center, RI.

**SEASON OF OPERATION:** Memorial Day-Labor Day

**ELIGIBILITY:** Active/Reservists/Retired/DOT Coast Guard civilian employees/100% DAVs.

**RESERVATIONS:** Required, by application only, with advance payment, based on priority list. During Jun-Aug the facility is usually filled with First Coast Guard District personnel. Address: Commander (APS), ISC, 427 Commercial Street, Boston, MA 02109-5000. **C-617-223-3181.** Fax: C-617-223-3182.

**Apartment:** Three-bedroom (1), sleeps eight, furnished, bath, kitchen, radio. Rates: $350-$500 weekly (depending on rank). Two-bedroom (1), sleeps five, furnished, bath, kitchen, radio TV. Rates: $300-$500 weekly (depending on rank).

**SUPPORT FACILITIES:**

| | | |
|---|---|---|
| Convenience Store | Laundry | Nature Trails |
| Picnic Area | Playground | Rec Room |

**ACTIVITIES:**

| | | |
|---|---|---|
| Bicycling | Boating | Fishing |
| Hiking | Swimming | |

**CREDIT CARDS ACCEPTED:** None.

**RESTRICTIONS:** No pets allowed. Lead paint hazard for children under age of six. One week limit (Sat-Fri) in summer, based on ferry schedule. Preference is given to patrons desiring to stay a full week. Ferry runs daily 15 Jun-1st week of Oct, twice a week other months.

## FOURTH CLIFF FAMILY RECREATION AREA (MA02R1)

Hanscom Air Force Base
Hanscom AFB, MA 01731-5000

**TELEPHONE NUMBER INFORMATION:** Main installation numbers: C-781-377-4441, D-312-478-4441. Police for recreation area, C-781-545-1212 (local police).

**LOCATION:** Off base. I-95 or I-93 to MA-3, approximately ten miles south of Boston, south to exit 12, MA-139 E toward Marshfield. Go straight, through the traffic lights, for 1.5 miles to Furnace Street, turn left. Continue to T intersection, turn left on Ferry Street. Stay on Ferry Street to Sea Street, right over South River Bridge, left on Central Avenue, bear left at fork. (Do not go straight up hill on Cliff Road.) Proceed to gate. *USMRA: page 17 (M-4).* NMI: Hanscom AFB, 55 miles northwest. NMC: Boston, 30 miles north.

**MASSACHUSETTS**
*Fourth Cliff Family Recreation Area, continued*

**DESCRIPTION OF AREA:** Recreation area is 56-acre seaside resort situated high on a cliff on the tip of a small peninsula overlooking the Atlantic Ocean on one side and scenic North River on the other. Easy access to Boston, Cape Cod, Martha's Vineyard, Nantucket Islands and a host of recreational activities. Full support facilities available at Hanscom AFB.

**SEASON OF OPERATION:** May-Oct for cabins and tent spaces. Year round others.

**ELIGIBILITY:** Active/Reservists/Retired/DoD civilians/100% DAVs.

**RESERVATIONS:** Required on credit card or with one night's deposit. (Ask for map, check on refund policy.) Reservation procedure based on status of sponsor. Address: Fourth Cliff Recreation Area, 348 Central Avenue, P.O. Box 479, Humarock, MA 02047-5000. **C-1-800-468-9547, C-781-837-9269** 0900-1630 hours Mon-Fri. HP: http://www.hanscom.af. mil/66abw/sv/fourth.htm. Recreation Hall: C-781-837-6785. Check in at Fourth Cliff Recreation Hall, Bldg 7, 1200 hours, check out 1100 hours. Call desk clerk at C-781-837-6785 (before 1400 hours on weekdays and 1000 hours on Sun and holidays) to make arrangements for other hours to check in or out and for off-season hours. Ask about special discounts.

**Cottage:** Three-bedroom (1), closed porch. Rates: $70-$95 daily (depending on season).

**Townhouse:** Two-bedroom (2). Rates: $50-$70 daily (depending on season).

**Chalets:** Two-bedroom (11), furnished, TV, microwave, crib, highchair, linens, pots/pans, dishes. Patrons must provide toiletries. Rates: $55-$80 daily (depending on season).

**Cabins:** One- and three-bedroom (2), furnished, TV, microwave, pots/pans, dishes, linens, crib, highchair. Patrons must provide toiletries. Available in season only. Rates: $50 daily.

**Camper Spaces:** Concrete (11), E (110V/30A)/S/W hookups. Rates: $12 daily. Other vehicles used as sleeping quarters and parked overnight, $15 daily.

**Tent Spaces:** Primitive, no hookups. Available in season only. Rates: $8 daily.

**SUPPORT FACILITIES:**

| | | |
|---|---|---|
| Beach | Dishwashing Facility | Grills |
| Ice | Laundry | Picnic Area |
| Pay Telephone | Playground | Pavilion* |
| Rec Equipment | Rec Hall | Restrooms |
| Showers | Snack Bar | |

* May be rented for group picnics, reservation required.

**ACTIVITIES:**

| | |
|---|---|
| Fishing | Horseshoes |

Summer and fall programs available.

**CREDIT CARDS ACCEPTED:** Visa and MasterCard.

**RESTRICTIONS:** Pets are not allowed inside any cabins or on the porches. In other areas, they must be leashed or tied at all times and must not annoy others. Firearms and/or hunting equipment are not allowed. No open fires. Children may not be left unattended. Wildlife may not be captured, killed or harassed in any way. Visitor information display for local sights and attractions. Discount passes and season tickets may be available.

# HANSCOM FAMCAMP (MA08R1)

Hanscom Air Force Base
Hanscom AFB, MA 01731-2012

**TELEPHONE NUMBER INFORMATION:** Main installation numbers: C-781-377-4441, D-312-478-4441. Police for FAMCAMP: (Base) C-781-377-2315, (Bedford) C-781-275-1212.

**LOCATION:** Off base. From I-95, exit 31B to MA-4/225, west for .5 miles to west on Hartwell Avenue, right on McGuire Road to end. *USMRA: page 17 (J-3) and page 24 (A-2).* NMI: Hanscom AFB, 2 miles west. NMC: Boston, 20 miles southeast. Check out 1200 hours.

**DESCRIPTION OF AREA:** Located in wooded section adjacent to base six miles from Concord Bridge (site of the shot heard round the world) and other Revolutionary War historical sites. Easy drive to Boston and the cultural and social world of the city known as the Hub of the Universe. Full range of support facilities on base.

**SEASON OF OPERATION:** 1 May-31 Oct.

**ELIGIBILITY:** Active/Reservists/Retired/DoD civilians at Hanscom AFB.

**RESERVATIONS:** No advance reservations, first come, first serve. Address: Recreational Services, 647 MWRS/MWR, Building 1531, 98 Barksdale Street, Attn: FAMCAMP, Hanscom AFB, Bedford, MA 01731-1807. **C-781-377-4670, D-312-478-4670.** Fax: C-781-377-4919, D-312-478-4919. For information off-season, C-781-377-3348. Check in at Campground Office, Bldg T-214, check out 1100 hours.

**Camper Spaces:** Hardstand (16), 60'+, handicap accessible, E (110V/50A)/S/W hookups. Rates: $14 daily. Hardstand (19), 30', handicap accessible, E (110V/30A)/S/W hookups. Rates $14 daily. Gravel (21), handicap accessible, E (110V/30A)/W hookups. Rates: $12 daily.

**Tent Spaces:** 10, no hookups. Rates: $6 daily

**SUPPORT FACILITIES:**

| | | |
|---|---|---|
| Bath House | Bike Path | Convenience Store |
| Grills | Ice | Laundry |
| Pavilion | Picnic Area | Playground |
| Restrooms* | Sewage Dump | Showers* |
| Telephones | Trails | Volleyball Courts |

* Handicap accessible.

**ACTIVITIES:**

| | | |
|---|---|---|
| Bicycling | Horseshoes | Sightseeing |

**CREDIT CARDS ACCEPTED:** Visa and MasterCard.

**RESTRICTIONS:** Pets allowed on leash and in physical control, owner must clean up after pet. Firearms allowed only after Firearms Identification Document has been obtained from local Chief of Police. Quiet hours 2200-0700 hours.

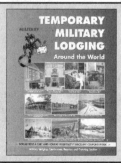

# MICHIGAN

*MICHIGAN*

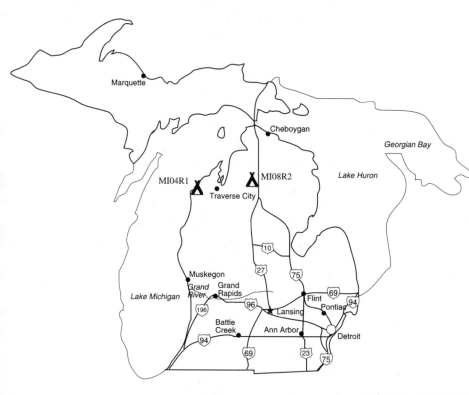

**SUPPORT FACILITIES:**

| | |
|---|---|
| Beach | Boat Launch |
| Boats | Grills |
| Laundry/post | Picnic Area |
| Restrooms | Showers |

**ACTIVITIES:**

| | |
|---|---|
| Boating | Fishing |
| Hiking | Swimming |

**CREDIT CARDS ACCEPTED:** None.

**RESTRICTIONS:** Pets at campsites must be caged or chained, $2 security deposit required. Firearms must be registered and used only with the coordination of Camp Grayling Range Control. Quiet hours after 2300 hours. Motorized two- and three-wheeled vehicles are prohibited in trailer park. Parents will be held responsible for the acts of their children at all times.

## POINT BETSIE RECREATION COTTAGE (MI04R2)

Grand Haven Coast Guard Group
Grand Haven, MI 49417-1762

**TELEPHONE NUMBER INFORMATION:** Main installation numbers: C-616-850-2510.

**LOCATION:** Off base. One hundred fifty miles north of Grand Rapids, take US 131 N to Highway 115 W into Frankfort, go north on M-22 for four miles to Point Betsie Road, cottage is at the end of Point Betsie Road. Recreation cottage is five miles north on MI-22. *USMRA: page 66 (C-5).* NMI: Traverse City Air Station, 45 miles east. NMC: Traverse City, 45 miles east.

**DESCRIPTION OF AREA:** Located in northwest Michigan on eastern shores of Lake Michigan south of Sleeping Bear Dunes National Lakeshore. Crystal Lake and Betsie Bay resorts nearby. Full range of support facilities available at Traverse City Air Station.

**SEASON OF OPERATION:** Year round.

**ELIGIBILITY:** Active/Reservists/Retired/CG civilian employees.

**RESERVATIONS:** Required by phone 90 days in advance for Coast Guard, 60 days for others. Address for information and advance payment: Morale Officer, USCG Group, 650 Harbor Drive, Grand Haven, MI 49417-5000. **C-616-850-2510.** Check in after 1000 hours and get cottage key, check out 1000 hours.

**Cottage:** Two-bedroom (1), sleeps seven, furnished, refrigerator, microwave, utensils, bed linens, blankets, gas grill. Rates: $20-$30 daily.

**SUPPORT FACILITIES:** There are no support facilities at the cottage. The following facilities are nearby or within a short driving distance.

| | | |
|---|---|---|
| Boat Launch | Boat Rental | Bicycle Route |
| Camping | Golf | Rec Equipment |

**ACTIVITIES:**

| | | |
|---|---|---|
| Boating | Fishing | Hunting |
| Skiing | Swimming | Water Skiing |

## CAMP GRAYLING TRAILER PARK (MI08R2)

Camp Grayling Maneuver Training Center
Camp Grayling, MI 49739-0001

**TELEPHONE NUMBER INFORMATION:** Main installation numbers: C-517-348-7621, D-312-722-8621. Police for campground: C-517-348-7621.

**LOCATION:** On post. From I-75 at Grayling, take MI-72 W three miles. Take 93 S two miles. *USMRA: page 66 (D-5).* NMC: Traverse City, 54 miles west.

**DESCRIPTION OF AREA:** Located in the center of northern Michigan's vacationland and easily accessible to major highways and recreational areas that offer excellent in-season hunting and fishing opportunities, as well as camping, boating, golf, trailriding, skiing and snowmobiling. Camp Grayling is the largest National Guard training site in the country. The trailer park is located .1 mile from, and has access to, Lake Margrethe.

**SEASON OF OPERATION:** 15 May-15 Sep.

**ELIGIBILITY:** Active/Reservists/Retired/DoD civilians.

**RESERVATIONS:** Required. Reservations for entire season may be made during Dec for following year, reservations for shorter periods may be made after 1 Jan for current year. Except for weekend rentals, a minimum deposit equal to half of total cost is required. Address: Camp Grayling Trailer Park, c/o Officers' Club, 311 Howe Road, Camp Grayling, MI 49739-0001. **C-517-348-9033.** Fax: C-517-348-9033. Check in with Trailer Park Supervisor, check out 1400 hours.

**Camper Spaces:** Hardstand (70), E (110V/20A)/S/W hookups. Rates: $13 (with air), $12 (without air) daily.

**Tent Spaces:** Gravel (10). Rates: $12 daily.

*MICHIGAN/MISSISSIPPI*
*Point Betsie Recreation Cottage, continued*

**CREDIT CARDS ACCEPTED:** None.

**RESTRICTIONS:** No pets allowed. No smoking. Five day limit in summer, seven day limit in winter, weekly basis preferred. No telephone at cottage.

# MISSISSIPPI

## KEESLER FAMCAMP (MS05R2)
Keesler Air Force Base
Keesler AFB, MS 39534-2554

**TELEPHONE NUMBER INFORMATION:** Main installation numbers: C-228-377-3186, D-312-597-1110. Police for FAMCAMP, C-228-377-3040.

**LOCATION:** Off base. From I-10 take I-110 S to US-90 W approximately 5.5 miles to Beauvoir Road (before Coliseum), right 1.5 miles to Pass Road, right one mile to Jim Money Road, left to Thrower Park Housing, right on Annex Road .25 miles. FAMCAMP is five miles west of gate 7. *USMRA: page 43 (F-10)*. NMC: Biloxi, 2 miles east.

**DESCRIPTION OF AREA:** Mississippi Gulf Coast holds a wealth of history. In Biloxi, tours are available daily at Beauvoir, the home of Jefferson Davis. The marina is located off Ploesti Drive on Back Bay and offers a park, boating and fishing. Numerous large casinos line the beach in Biloxi and Gulfport. Free certificates are available at the FAMCAMP Information Center. Full range of support facilities available on base.

**SEASON OF OPERATION:** Year round.

**ELIGIBILITY:** Active/Reservists/Retired/DoD civilians.

**RESERVATIONS:** No advance reservations. Address: Outdoor Recreation, 81 SVS/SVRO, 625 Marina Drive, Keesler AFB, MS 39534-2623. **C-228-377-3160/3186/0002, D-312-597-3160/3186/0002.** FAMCAMP C-228-594-0543. Check in with Host Camper, slots 1 and 2.

**Camper Spaces:** 40, E (115V/30/50A)/S/W/CATV hookups. Rates: $12 daily. Overflow, E hookup. Rates: $8 daily. Overflow, no hookups. Rates: $6 daily; Active duty on TDY or medical may stay for $250/month.

**SUPPORT FACILITIES:**

| | | |
|---|---|---|
| Archery/marina | Beach | Boat Rental |
| Camping Equipment | Chapel | Fishing Equipment |
| Gas | Golf | Grills |
| Laundry | Marina | Picnic Area |
| Playground | Pool | Quick Shop/nearby |
| Rec Equipment | Showers | Snack Bar |
| Sports Fields | Tennis Courts | |

**ACTIVITIES:**

| | | |
|---|---|---|
| Bicycling | Boating | Casinos |
| Fishing/license | Hiking | Jogging |
| Sailing | Swimming | |

**CREDIT CARDS ACCEPTED:** Visa and MasterCard.

**RESTRICTIONS:** No open fires on beach without city approval.

## LAKE WALKER
## FAMILY CAMPGROUND (MS12R2)
Mississippi Army National Guard
Camp Shelby Training Site
Camp Shelby, MS 39407-5500

**TELEPHONE NUMBER INFORMATION:** Main installation numbers: C-601-558-2000, D-312-921-2000. Police for campground: C-601-558-2477/2448.

**LOCATION:** On post. On US-49 south of Hattiesburg. Exit at South Gate. *USMRA: page 43 (F-8)*. NMC: Hattiesburg, 8 miles north.

**DESCRIPTION OF AREA:** Located on the edge of the DeSoto National Forest, Camp Shelby is one hour away from the Gulf Coast and enjoys a mild climate year round. The campground is beside Lake Walker. Limited support facilities available on post, full range available at Gulfport Naval Construction Battalion Center, 60 miles south.

**SEASON OF OPERATION:** Year round.

**ELIGIBILITY:** Active/Reservists/Retired/Civilian employees.

**RESERVATIONS:** No advance reservations. First come first serve. Address: MSARNG, Special Services Bldg 1300, Forest Avenue, Camp Shelby, MS 39407-5500. **C-601-558-2397, D-312-921-2397** 0600-1630 hours Mon-Fri. Fax: C-601-558-2339.

*Lake Walker Family Campground, continued*

**Camper/Tent Spaces:** Paved (25), E (110V/30A)/S/W hookups. Rates: $7 daily/$40 weekly/$160 monthly.

**SUPPORT FACILITIES:**

| | | |
|---|---|---|
| Grills | Laundry | Picnic Area |
| Rec Equipment | Restrooms | Showers |
| Tennis | | |

A second picnic area is at Dogwood Lake.

**ACTIVITIES:**

| | | |
|---|---|---|
| Boating | Fishing | Swimming |

**CREDIT CARDS ACCEPTED:** None.

**RESTRICTIONS:** Pets allowed on six foot leash. No firearms allowed. Open fires are allowed only in designated areas.

# MISSOURI

## LAKE OF THE OZARKS RECREATION AREA (MO01R2)
Fort Leonard Wood
Fort Leonard Wood, MO 65473-5000

**TELEPHONE NUMBER INFORMATION:** Main installation numbers: C-573-596-0131, D-312-581-0131. Police for recreation area, C-573-346-3693.

**LOCATION:** Off post. From I-70, take Highway 63 to Jefferson City, then take US-54 to Linn Creek area, left at State Road A for six miles to Freedom, left on Lake Road A-33 for approximately five miles to travel camp. From I-44 northeast of Springfield, MO-7 northwest to Richland, right on State Road A and travel approximately 20 miles to Freedom, right on Lake Road A-33 approximately five miles to travel camp. *USMRA: page 81 (D-6)*. NMI: Fort Leonard Wood, 60 miles southeast. NMC: Jefferson City, 40 miles northeast.

**DESCRIPTION OF AREA:** Located on Grand Glaize Arm of the Lake of the Ozarks in the center of a State Wildlife Refuge. Situated on 360-acre reserve with excellent fishing and beautiful scenery. Nearby attractions include Osage Beach, Ozark Caverns, musical shows, theme park, water slides, helicopter rides, etc. Historical and recreational points of interest surround the area. Full range of support facilities available at Fort Leonard Wood.

**SEASON OF OPERATION:** Apr-Oct (full season Memorial Day weekend to Labor Day weekend).

**ELIGIBILITY:** Active/Reservists/Retired/DoD and NAF employees.

**RESERVATIONS:** Required by phone or in person at the Lake of the Ozarks Recreation Area office, Bldg 528 (1 Mar-20 May, 0900-1700 hours Mon-Wed; 21 May-3 Sep, 0900-1700 hours Mon-Fri), with full advance payment. Single night reservations will not be made more than five days in advance for weekends or holidays. No mail reservations. Information address: Fort Leonard Wood LORA, Route 1, Box 380, Linn Creek, MO 65052-5000. **C-573-346-5640.** Discounts to holders of Golden Age Passports for hookup camping only. Check in at Rental Office, Bldg 528, after 1500 hours, check out Fri-Sun 1100 hours.

**Duplex:** Two-bedroom (2), furnished, sofabed, private bath, kitchen, A/C, TV. Patrons must provide cleaning supplies. Rates: $49-$78 daily.

**Cabins:** 3, furnished, sofabed, private bath, kitchen, A/C, TV. Patrons must provide cleaning supplies. Rates: $46-$74 daily.

**Mobile Homes:** Three-bedroom deluxe (17), furnished, sofabed, private bath, kitchen, A/C, TV. Patrons must provide linens, towels and cleaning supplies. Rates: $41-$68 daily.

**Mobile Homes:** Three-bedroom (6), furnished, sofabed, private bath, kitchen, A/C, TV. Patrons must provide cleaning supplies and linens, including towels. Rates: $33-$61 daily.

**Mobile Homes:** Two-bedroom (4), furnished, sofabed, private bath, kitchen, A/C, TV. Patrons must provide linens, towels and cleaning supplies. Rates: $25-$50 daily.

**Camper Spaces:** Hardstand (16), E (110V/30/30A)/W hookups. Rates: $10 daily

**Camper/Tent Spaces:** Hardstand (21), no hookups. Rates: $9 daily.

**SUPPORT FACILITIES:**

| | | |
|---|---|---|
| Beach | Boat Rental | Boat/RV Storage* |
| Country Store | Grills | Laundry |
| Marina | Party Barges | Pavilion/fee |
| Picnic Area | Playground | Restrooms |
| Sewage Dump | Showers | Ski Boats |
| Water Sports Equipment Rental | | |

\* By reservation

**ACTIVITIES:**

| | | |
|---|---|---|
| Boating | Fishing/license | Hiking |
| Jet Skiing | Special Events | Swimming |
| Water Skiing | | |

**CREDIT CARDS ACCEPTED:** Visa, MasterCard and American Express.

**RESTRICTIONS:** Pets are not allowed in cabin or duplex and must be on leash or under voice control and have all shots (tags displayed), owner responsible for damage caused by pet. No open fires. No swimming except in beach area.

*MONTANA/NEBRASKA*

# MONTANA

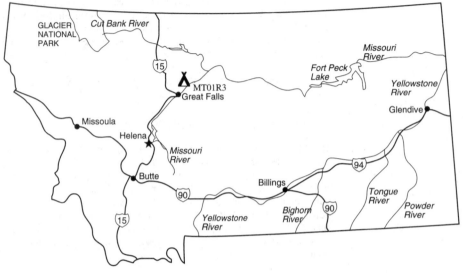

**SUPPORT FACILITIES:**

| | |
|---|---|
| Chapel | Gas/Propane |
| Grills | Pay Telephone |
| Picnic Area | Rec Equipment |
| Restrooms | Sewage Dump |
| Showers | Snack Bar/nearby |

**ACTIVITIES:**

| | |
|---|---|
| Swimming | Tennis |

Programs such as fishing, floating, backpacking, bird hunting, etc.

**CREDIT CARDS ACCEPTED:** Visa and MasterCard.

**RESTRICTIONS:** Pets allowed on leash and in physical control, owner must clean up after pet. Discharging of firearms prohibited on base, must comply with state laws and base regulations. No open fires except in grills. Quiet hours 2300-0700 hours. Fourteen day limit when camp is at full occupancy. On site camp host.

## MALMSTROM FAMCAMP (MT01R3)

Malmstrom Air Force Base
Malmstrom AFB, MT 59402-5000

**TELEPHONE NUMBER INFORMATION:** Main installation numbers: C-406-731-1110, D-312-632-1110. Police for FAMCAMP, C-406-731-3895.

**LOCATION:** On base. From I-15 take 10th Avenue south for approximately four miles, turn north on 57th Street Bypass, watch for signs to AFB. *USMRA: page 99 (E-4)*. NMC: Great Falls, 2 miles west.

**DESCRIPTION OF AREA:** Situated in open terrain surrounded by Highwoods and Little Belt range of the Rockies. Full range of support facilities available on base.

**SEASON OF OPERATION:** Mid May-Oct, depending on weather, for hookups. Year round for limited or no-hookup service.

**ELIGIBILITY:** Active/Reservists/Retired/DoD civilians/Sponsored guests.

**RESERVATIONS:** No advance reservations. Address: Outdoor Recreation, 341 SVS/SVRO, 500 76th Street N, Bldg 1222, Malmstrom AFB, MT 59402-7515. **C-406-731-3263, D-312-632-3263.** Fax: C-406-453-6684. Check in at FAMCAMP, on-site fee station 24 hours daily, check out 1200 hours.

**Camper Spaces:** Gravel (24), E (110V/30A)/S/W hookups. Rates: $11 daily. (Reduced rates off-season. On site fee station, not all fees listed.)

**Camper/Tent Spaces:** Gravel (5), E (110V/30A)/W hookups. Rates: $6 daily. (Reduced rates off-season. On site fee station, not all fees listed.) Overflow, parking lot, no hookups Rates: $7.50 daily.

# NEBRASKA

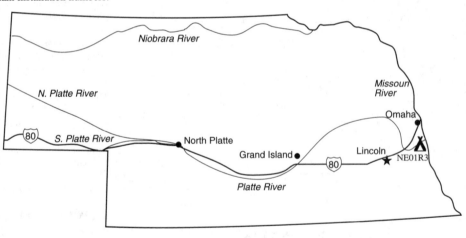

## OFFUTT FAMCAMP (NE01R3)

Offutt Air Force Base
Offutt AFB, NE 68113-5000

**TELEPHONE NUMBER INFORMATION:** Main installation numbers: C-402-294-1110, D-312-271-1110. Police for FAMCAMP, C-402-294-6110.

**LOCATION:** Off base. From I-80 in Omaha, take US-75 S to Bellevue. East on Mission Avenue (NE-370), through town, right on Hancock Street for 1.5 miles, left to base lake and FAMCAMP. *USMRA: page 82 (J-5)*. NMC: Omaha, 8 miles north.

**DESCRIPTION OF AREA:** Located near state's eastern boundary with Iowa. Strategic Command Headquarters. Surrounding area open farm country. Full range of support facilities available on base.

*Offutt FAMCAMP, continued*

**SEASON OF OPERATION:** Year round, electric only 8 Nov-14 Apr.

**ELIGIBILITY:** Active/Reservists/Retired/DoD civilians.

**RESERVATIONS:** Accepted up to 30 days in advance. Address: Outdoor Recreation, FAMCAMP, 55 SVS/SVRO, 109 Grant Circle, Suite 101, Offutt AFB, NE 68113-2084. **C-402-294-2108, D-312-271-2108.** Check in at Outdoor Recreation Office in Castaways (snack bar building) 0800-1700 hours Mon-Fri, after duty hours, check in with FAMCAMP host or call C-402-294-4978, check out 1200 hours. If you do not check in by 1800 hours, you will lose your reservation.

**Camper Spaces:** Gravel (10), E (110V/30A)/S/W hookups. Rates: $10 daily/$7 daily winter season, 8 Nov-14 Apr, E only.

**Tent Spaces:** Wilderness. Rates: $2 daily.

*Note: A new facility is scheduled for completion in mid-summer 1999 consisting of 30 units with E (110V/30/50A)/S/W hookups.*

**SUPPORT FACILITIES:**

| | | |
|---|---|---|
| Archery | Bait | Boat House |
| Boat Launch | Boat Rental | Chapel |
| Gas | Golf | Grills |
| Grocery/nearby | Gym/base | Indoor Track/base |
| Laundry | Marina | Picnic Area |
| Playground | Racquetball | Rec Equipment |
| Restrooms | Showers | Skeet/Trap Range |
| Snack Bar | Sports Fields | Stables |
| Tennis Courts | | |

**ACTIVITIES:**

| | | |
|---|---|---|
| Boating | Fishing/license | Hunting/license |

**CREDIT CARDS ACCEPTED:** Visa and MasterCard.

**RESTRICTIONS:** Pets allowed on leash. No firearms allowed. No campfires allowed. Quiet hours 2200-0600 hours. No swimming or wading in base lake. Fourteen day limit.

# NEVADA

*See map to the right.*

## FALLON RV PARK AND RECREATION AREA (NV05R4)

Fallon Naval Air Station
Fallon NAS, NV 89496-5000

**TELEPHONE NUMBER INFORMATION:** Main installation numbers: C-702-426-5162, D-312-830-2110. *Note: The area code for Fallon NAS is scheduled to change from 702 to 775 in December 1998.*

**LOCATION:** On base. From US-50 at Fallon, take US-95 S for eight miles, left on Union Lane, left on Pasture Road to base, right on Churchill Avenue to main gate. *USMRA: page 113 (C-4).* NMC: Reno, 61 miles west.

**DESCRIPTION OF AREA:** The RV park is on main base. Nearby Carson River and several lakes offer fishing, boating, swimming, and water skiing. Call MWR for special rates to Reno, ghost towns, Virginia City, and other points of interest. Full range of support facilities available on base.

**SEASON OF OPERATION:** Year round.

**ELIGIBILITY:** Active/Reservists/Retired/DoD civilians.

**RESERVATIONS:** Accepted with payment. Address: MWR Department, Pony Express Outfitters, Fallon Naval Air Station, NV 89496-5000. **C-702-426-2598/2279, D-312-830-2598/2279.** Check in Equipment Rental, Bldg 393, 0730-1800 hours Mon-Fri, 0730-1600 hours Sat-Sun.

**Camper Spaces:** Primitive (16), central W, E (120V/15A) hookup. Rates: $5 daily.

**SUPPORT FACILITIES:**

| | | |
|---|---|---|
| Pavilion | Restrooms* | Sewage Dump |

* Closed winter months.

**ACTIVITIES:**

| | | |
|---|---|---|
| Boating | Fishing | Sightseeing |

**CREDIT CARDS ACCEPTED:** Visa and MasterCard.

**RESTRICTIONS:** Pets allowed on leash, owner must clean up after pet. No firearms allowed.

## LUCKY SEVEN FAMCAMP (NV04R4)

Nellis Air Force Base
Nellis AFB, NV 89191-7073

**TELEPHONE NUMBER INFORMATION:** Main installation numbers: C-702-652-1110. Police for FAMCAMP, C-702-652-2311.

**NEVADA/NEW HAMPSHIRE**
*Lucky Seven FAMCAMP, continued*

**LOCATION:** Off base. From I-15 north of Las Vegas, exit east on Craig Road to Las Vegas Blvd N (NV-604), left onto Range Road (directly across from Nellis North Gate). Also, From US-93/95 (Boulder Highway) in Las Vegas, go north on Nellis Blvd approximately eight miles, continue north on Las Vegas Blvd N (NV-604). From both routes, continue to North Gate, turn left onto Range Road directly across from gate. Follow FAMCAMP signs. *USMRA: page 113 (G-9).* NMC: Las Vegas, 8 miles southwest.

**DESCRIPTION OF AREA:** Located in desert Southwest with mountains on one side and Lake Mead National Recreation Area on the other. Easy drive to Grand Canyon. Las Vegas attractions nearby. Full range of support facilities available on base.

**SEASON OF OPERATION:** Year round.

**ELIGIBILITY:** Active/Reservists/Retired/DoD civilians/Guests.

**RESERVATIONS:** Accepted up to 60 days in advance with check for 1st night deposit. Address: 4907 FAMCAMP Drive, Las Vegas, NV 89115-5000. **C-702-643-3060.** E-mail: famcamp@sus99.nellis.af.mil. Discounts available to holders of Golden Age and Golden Access Passports. Check in at FAMCAMP, Bldg 2889, check out by 1000 hours.

**Camper Spaces:** Hardstand (16), E (110V/20/30/50A)/S/W hookups. Rates: $13 daily. Hardstand (32), E (110V/30/50A)/W hookups. Rates: $12 daily.

**Tent Spaces:** 2, no hookups. Overflow, unlimited, no hookups. Rates: $5 daily.

**SUPPORT FACILITIES:**

| | | |
|---|---|---|
| Auto Craft Shop | Boat Rental/Storage** | Chapel |
| Commissary | Convenience Store | Covered Patio* |
| Equipment Rental | Exchange | Fitness Center |
| Gas | Golf | Grills* |
| Laundry* | Pavilion* | Picnic Area* |
| Playground* | Pool | Racquetball |
| Rec Equipment | Rec/Lounge | Restrooms* |
| Sewage Dump* | Shoppette | Showers* |
| Sports Fields* | Telephones* | Tennis Courts |

* Located at Lucky Seven FAMCAMP, others on base.
** Storage available for $1 daily.

**ACTIVITIES:**

| | | |
|---|---|---|
| Boating | Fishing | Snow Skiing |
| Swimming | | |

**CREDIT CARDS ACCEPTED:** None.

**RESTRICTIONS:** Pets allowed on leash, limit two per RV, owner must clean up immediately after pets. No open fires. Fourteen day limit, may be extended if there is no waiting list. Alternate spaces, 90 day stays.

## ROSE CREEK (NV07R4)

Fallon Naval Air Station
Fallon NAS, NV 89496-5000

**TELEPHONE NUMBER INFORMATION:** Main installation numbers: C-702-426-5162, D-312-830-2110. *Note: The area code for Fallon NAS is scheduled to change from 702 to 775 in December 1998.*

**LOCATION:** Off base. Area is located 70 miles south of base off US-95 northwest of Hawthorne at Mount Grant. NMC: Reno, 75 miles northwest.

**SEASON OF OPERATION:** May-Oct, depending on weather.

**ELIGIBILITY:** Active/Reservists/Retired/DoD civilians.

**RESERVATIONS:** Accepted with payment. Address: MWR Department, Pony Express Outfitters, Fallon Naval Air Station, NV 89496-5000. **C-702-426-2598/2279, D-312-830-2598/2279.**

**Cabin:** 1, sleeps six, shared bath, dining table, kitchen, refrigerator, stove, sink, dishes, fireplace. Patrons must provide bed linens and towels. Rates: $30 daily.

**ACTIVITIES:** Fishing. Permit may be purchased in advance ($9.25 daily per person) at Bldg 393 on base, Nevada state fishing license also required.

**CREDIT CARDS ACCEPTED:**

**RESTRICTIONS:** No firearms allowed. No tents or camping allowed. No live bait can be used in reservoir.

# NEW HAMPSHIRE

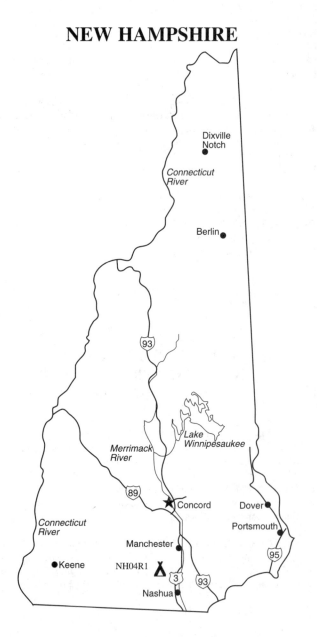

# NEW BOSTON
# RECREATION AREA (NH04R1)

New Boston Air Station
New Boston AS, NH 03071-5125

**TELEPHONE NUMBER INFORMATION:** Main installation numbers: C-603-471-2452/2234, D-312-489-2452/2234. Police for recreation area, C-603-471-2234, D-312-489-2285.

**LOCATION:** On base. From I-293 at Manchester take NH-101 W, straight through a set of traffic lights, road becomes NH-114. Turn left at next set of lights onto New Boston Road for approximately seven miles. AFS is on the right. *USMRA: page 23 (F-9).* NMI: Hanscom AFB MA, 50 miles southeast. NMC: Manchester, 8 miles southeast.

**DESCRIPTION OF AREA:** This 2500-acre recreation area is considered to be the best-kept secret in New England. It has five stocked ponds and a marina with canoes, rowboats and paddleboats for rent. Fishing at Deer Pond is limited to children 15 years of age and under, no license required. Joe English Hill is great for rock climbing, on a clear day one can see the Prudential Center in Boston. Improvements will continue to be made as funds become available. Full range of support facilities available at Hanscom AFB, MA.

**SEASON OF OPERATION:** Memorial Day-Columbus Day.

**ELIGIBILITY:** Active/Reservists/Retired/DoD civilians.

**RESERVATIONS:** Suggested, with 50% of total cost. Address: New Boston Air Station Recreation Area, 317 Chestnut Hill Road, New Boston, NH 03070-5000. **C-603-471-2234, D-312-489-2234.** Check in 1300 hours, check out 1100 hours.

**Mobile Homes:** Two-bedroom (3), furnished, E/S/W hookups. Patrons must provide linens and towels. Rates: $30 daily.

**Pop-up Campers:** 5, E (110V/20A)/S/W hookups. Rates: $15 daily.

**Camper Spaces:** 12, E (110/220V/20/30A)/S/W hookups. Rates: $10 daily.

**Camper/Tent Spaces:** 42, no hookups. Rates: $4 daily.

**SUPPORT FACILITIES:**

| | | |
|---|---|---|
| Boat Rental | Convenience Store | Grills |
| Ice | Marina | Picnic Area |
| Playground | Port-a-Potties | Rec Equipment |
| Sewage Dump | Showers | Sports Fields |
| Trails | Vending Machine | |

**Large picnic area at Deer Pond, accommodating 150-200, has:**

| | | |
|---|---|---|
| Beach/small | Grills | Pavilion |
| Horseshoes | Volleyball | |

**ACTIVITIES:**

| | | |
|---|---|---|
| Basketball | Bicycling | Boating |
| Fishing/license* | Hiking | Jogging |
| Rock Climbing | Skiing/XC | Snowmobiling |
| Soccer | Softball | Swimming |
| Tennis | Volleyball | |

* MWR $5 Guest Fee per person for length of stay.

**CREDIT CARDS ACCEPTED:** Visa and MasterCard.

**RESTRICTIONS:** Pets allowed on leash. No firearms allowed. Quiet hours 2200-0800 hours.

# NEW JERSEY

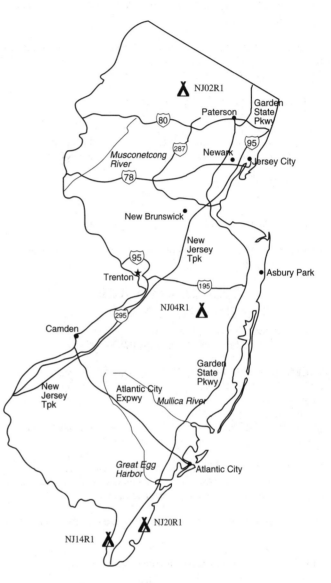

# BRINDLE LAKE TRAVEL CAMP (NJ04R1)

Fort Dix
Fort Dix, NJ 08640-5130

**TELEPHONE NUMBER INFORMATION:** Main installation numbers: C-609-562-1011, D-312-944-1011. Police for travel camp, C-911.

**LOCATION:** On post. Take exit 7 off New Jersey Turnpike, go south on NJ-68 for five miles. Turn left onto County Route 537 and proceed 1.5 miles to the first light, turn right and go one mile to a T intersection with a traffic light ( AFB is directly in front of you). Turn left and go two miles to the first stop sign (this is Cookstown). Go straight (you are now on Hockamick Road) and proceed three miles to Brindle Lake. *USMRA: page 19 (E,F-6).* NMC: Trenton, 20 miles northwest.

**DESCRIPTION OF AREA:** Wooded site located on a 30-acre lake seven miles from main area of post. Full range of support facilities available on post.

**SEASON OF OPERATION:** Year round.

*NEW JERSEY*
*Brindle Lake Travel Camp, continued*

**ELIGIBILITY:** Active/Reservists/Retired/DoD civilians/Members of Fort Dix Rod & Gun Club.

**RESERVATIONS:** Accepted. Address: Outdoor Recreation, Bldg 6045, Doughboy Loop, Fort Dix, NJ 08640-5011. **C-609-562-6667, D-312-944-6667.** Fax: C-609-562-2354.

**Tent Spaces:** Grass (10), no hookups. Rates: $5 daily.

**SUPPORT FACILITIES:**

| | | |
|---|---|---|
| Camping Equipment | Grills | Picnic Areas |
| Port-a-Potties | Rec Equipment | Scout Camp |

**ACTIVITIES:**

| | |
|---|---|
| Firearms Ranges | Fishing/license |

**CREDIT CARDS ACCEPTED:** Visa and MasterCard.

**RESTRICTIONS:** Pets allowed on leash, owner must clean up after pets. No firearms allowed.

## LAKE DENMARK RECREATION AREA (NJ02R1)
Armament Research, Development and Engineering Center
Picatinny Arsenal, NJ 07806-5000

**TELEPHONE NUMBER INFORMATION:** Main installation numbers: C-973-724-4021, D-312-880-4021. Security for recreation area, C-973-724-6666.

**LOCATION:** On post. I-80 to NJ-15, north one mile to post on the right. *USMRA: page 19 (E-2).* NMC: Dover, 2 miles south.

**DESCRIPTION OF AREA:** Situated in picturesque area in northern New Jersey, one hour west of New York City. Limited support facilities available on post, including a Commissary (new) and Exchange.

**SEASON OF OPERATION:** Year round, no water in RV spaces 15 Oct-30 Apr.

**ELIGIBILITY:** Active/Reservists/Retired/DoD civilians.

**RESERVATIONS:** Required. Address for mobile homes: Attn: Trailer Park Office, Bldg 34N, Picatinny Arsenal, NJ 07806-5000. **C-973-724-4014, D-312-880-4014.** For RV and tent spaces, Attn: Outdoor Recreation, Bldg 3050, Picatinny Arsenal, NJ 07806-5000. **C-973-724-4484, D-312-880-4484.** Fax: C-973-724-3263. Check in for mobile homes in Bldg 34N on 4th Avenue; for RV and tent sites, in Bldg 3050 on Main Road.

**Mobile Homes:** Two-bedroom (5), three-bedroom (9), furnished, microwave, pots/pans, dishes, TV, linens. Rates: $35 daily (+ $2/day pet fee).

**RV Spaces:** Gravel (2), E (110V/30A) hookups. Rates: $10 daily. Gravel (15), no hookups. Rates: $7 daily.

**Tent Spaces:** 12, no hookups. Rates: $7 daily.

**SUPPORT FACILITIES:**

| | |
|---|---|
| Laundry | Picnic Area |

**ACTIVITIES:**

| | |
|---|---|
| Fishing* | Hunting* |

* NJ license and Arsenal permit

**CREDIT CARDS ACCEPTED:** Visa and MasterCard.

**RESTRICTIONS:** Pets allowed only in four mobile homes. Two night minimum. Mobile home availability limited, must be left in clean condition. Security ID check required. Hunting and fishing permit eligibility limited. Contact ITT office for information.

## LAKE LAURIE CAMPGROUND (NJ14R1)
Willow Grove Naval Air Station
Willow Grove, PA 19090-5010

**TELEPHONE NUMBER INFORMATION:** Main installation numbers: C-215-443-1000, D-312-991-1000.

**LOCATION:** Off base. In Cape May NJ. Campground entrance is on US-9, two miles north of junction with end of Garden State Parkway. *USMRA: page 19 (D-10).* NMI: Cape May Coast Guard Training Center, 5 miles southeast. NMC: Vineland, approximately 50 miles northwest.

**DESCRIPTION OF AREA:** This well-planned recreation area is located at Lake Laurie in southern New Jersey close to beaches.

**SEASON OF OPERATION:** Mid May-mid Sep.

**ELIGIBILITY:** Active/Reservists/Retired/Civilian employees at Willow Grove NAS only.

**RESERVATIONS:** Reservations must be made in person at Willow Grove NAS ITT Office, Bldg 2, Willow Grove PA, with $50 deposit. No phone or mail reservations taken. Reservations taken beginning mid-April for active duty at Willow Grove NAS, all others after 1 May. Receipt required to check in. For information only: Recreation Services, Bldg 2, Willow Grove Naval Air Station, PA 19090-5010. **C-215-443-6082, D-312-991-6082.**

**Campers:** 2, E (110V/320/30/50A)/S/W hookups. Patrons must provide cookware, dishes, bed linens, utensils, detergent, toiletries. Rates: $120-$130 (Mon-Thu and Fri-Sun), $195-$215 weekly.

**SUPPORT FACILITIES:**

| | | |
|---|---|---|
| Beach | Boat Rental | Camp Store |
| Fire Rings | Firewood/fee | Ice |
| Laundry | Miniature Golf | Picnic Area |
| Playground | Pool | Rec Room |
| Restrooms | Showers/fee | Snack Bar |
| Tennis Courts | | |

**ACTIVITIES:**

| | |
|---|---|
| Boating | Swimming |

**CREDIT CARDS ACCEPTED:** Visa, MasterCard, American Express and Discover.

**RESTRICTIONS:** No pets allowed. Quiet hours 2200-0800 hours. Motorcycles and minibikes are not permitted. No more than one car at each site. All small children must be supervised at all times. No hot water in campers. Insect control fogging at dusk each evening.

## TOWNSENDS INLET RECREATION FACILITY (NJ20R1)

Sea Isle City, NJ 08243-5000

**TELEPHONE NUMBER INFORMATION:** Main installation numbers: C-609-263-3722.

**LOCATION:** Old Coast Guard lifesaving station in Sea Isle City, NJ. Two blocks from beach. *USMRA: page 19 (E-10)*. NMC: Atlantic City 25 miles north.

**DESCRIPTION OF AREA:** Located in southern New Jersey midway between Cape May and Atlantic City, this Victorian house is one block from the ocean and two blocks from the bay. Facility provides all amenities to enjoy a stay here, including beach badges and bicycles.

**SEASON OF OPERATION:** Apr 1-Oct 30.

**ELIGIBILITY:** Active/Reservists/Retired.

**RESERVATIONS:** Accepted. Address: Townsends Inlet Recreation Facility, 8101 Landis Avenue, Sea Isle City, NJ 08243-5000. **C-609-263-3722.**

**Beach House:** Four-apartment, two have private bath, A/C, TV/VCR. Community kitchen and dining room. Rates: $33 nightly E1-E3, $38 nightly E4-E6, $40 E7-E9, $42 O1-O3, $44 O4+, $44 civilians, $260 family.

**SUPPORT FACILITIES:**

| | | |
|---|---|---|
| Beach | Bicycles | Grills |

**ACTIVITIES:**

| | | |
|---|---|---|
| Swimming | Horse Shoes | Shuffle Board |

**CREDIT CARDS ACCEPTED:** None.

**RESTRICTIONS:** No pets allowed.

# NEW MEXICO

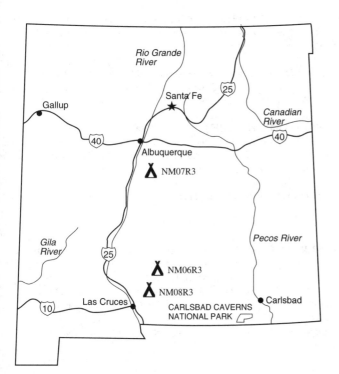

## HOLLOMAN FAMCAMP (NM06R3)

Holloman Air Force Base
Holloman AFB, NM 88330-8035

**TELEPHONE NUMBER INFORMATION:** Main installation numbers: C-505-475-6511, D-312-867-1110. Police for FAMCAMP, C-505-475-3528.

**LOCATION:** On base. Ten miles southwest of Alamogordo off US-70. Turn left immediately inside main gate on Mesquite Road. FAMCAMP is on the left near the entrance. *USMRA: page 114 (D-7)*. NMC: Las Cruces, 50 miles southwest, El Paso TX, 65 miles southeast.

**DESCRIPTION OF AREA:** Situated on open, semi-arid terrain with few trees, but surrounded by shrubs. Nearby attractions include Space Center Hall of Fame, planetarium, zoo, White Sands National Park, horse racing and winter sports. Full range of support facilities available on base.

**SEASON OF OPERATION:** Year round.

**ELIGIBILITY:** Active/Reservists/Retired/DoD and NAF civilians.

**RESERVATIONS:** No advance reservations. Address: Holloman FAMCAMP, 661 Delaware Avenue, Building 234, Holloman AFB, NM 88330-5000. **C-505-475-5369, D-312-867-5369.** E-mail: outdoor.rec@ holloman.af.mil. Check in at Lodging, Bldg 583 24 hours daily, check out 1200 hours.

**Camper Spaces:** Hardstand (24-12 pull through, handicap accessible) E (110V/20/30/50A)/S/W hookups. Rates: $12 daily, $70 weekly, $200 monthly (CATV available for $1 a day).

**SUPPORT FACILITIES:**

| | | |
|---|---|---|
| Auto Craft Shop | Bath House | Chapel |
| Commissary | Exchange | Fitness Center |
| Gas | Golf | Ice |
| Laundry | Picnic Area | Playground |
| Pool | Rec Center | Rec Equipment |
| Restrooms | Shoppette | Showers |
| Snack Bar | Sports Fields | Stables |
| Telephones | Tennis Courts | |

**ACTIVITIES:**

| | | |
|---|---|---|
| Golf | Horseback Riding | Snow Skiing |
| Swimming | Tennis | (29 miles away) |

**CREDIT CARDS ACCEPTED:** Visa and MasterCard.

**RESTRICTIONS:** Pets allowed on leash, must have current immunizations, owner must clean up after pet. No open campfires. $25 fine for camping without a permit. Quiet hours 2000-0800 hours.

## KIRTLAND FAMCAMP (NM07R3)

Kirtland Air Force Base
Kirtland AFB, NM 87117-5521

**TELEPHONE NUMBER INFORMATION:** Main installation numbers: C-505-844/846-0011, D-312-244-0011. Police for FAMCAMP, C-505-846-7926.

**LOCATION:** On base. From I-40 E of Albuquerque take Exit 164, south on Wyoming Blvd to AFB. Go through gate, left on D Street, turn right on Erwin. Registration at office, 24 hour registration box. *USMRA: page 114 (D-4)*. NMC: Albuquerque, adjacent to base.

**DESCRIPTION OF AREA:** Located adjacent to base housing. Sandia and Manzano mountains are east of the base. Sandia Crest Recreation Area and aerial tram nearby. Full range of support facilities available on base.

**SEASON OF OPERATION:** Year round.

**ELIGIBILITY:** Active/Reservists/Retired/DoD civilians.

**RESERVATIONS:** No advance reservations. Address: Outdoor Recreation, 377 SVS, 2000 Wyoming Blvd SE, Bldg 20410, Kirtland AFB, NM 87117-5000. **C-505-846-0337, D-312-246-1275, Outdoor Rec; C-505-846-0337 FAMCAMP** 0900-1130 hours. Check out 1100 hours.

**Camper Spaces:** Hardstand (23-1 handicap accessible), E (110/220V/30/50A)/S/W hookups. Rates: $10 daily. Hardstand (9), S/W hookups. Rates: $7. Hardstand (40), no hookups. Rates: $5 daily.

**SUPPORT FACILITIES:**

| | | |
|---|---|---|
| Auto Craft Shop | Bath House | Boat Rental/Storage |
| Chapel | Commissary | Convenience Store |
| Exchange | Fitness Center | Gas |
| Golf | Grills | Laundry |
| Picnic Area | Playgrounds | Pool |
| Recreation Center | Restrooms | Sewage Dump |
| Shoppette | Showers | Snack Bar |
| Sports Fields | Stables | Telephones |

**ACTIVITIES:**

| | | |
|---|---|---|
| Bicycle | Hiking | Outdoor Sports |
| Swimming | | |

**CREDIT CARDS ACCEPTED:** None.

**RESTRICTIONS:** Pets must be on leash, no exceptions, owner must clean up after pets immediately. No firearms allowed. Quiet hours 2200-0600 hours. No generators 2200-0600 hours. Seven day limit. No vehicle washing. Must sign in before using any facilities.

## VOLUNTEER PARK
## TRAVEL CAMP SITE (NM08R3)
White Sands Missile Range
White Sands Missile Range, NM 88002-5000

**TELEPHONE NUMBER INFORMATION:** Main installation numbers: C-505-678-2121, D-312-258-2211.

**LOCATION:** On post. On US-70 east of Las Cruces. Entry to installation controlled by Military Police, visitor pass required. *USMRA: page 114 (D-6,7,8).* NMC: Las Cruces, 25 miles southwest.

**DESCRIPTION OF AREA:** Many outdoor sports to be found within 100-mile radius. To the east is Cloudcroft ski area, horse racing at Ruidoso Downs, Apache Indian Reservation with Ski Apache, a first-class ski area, and Inn of the Mountain Gods, a resort of international repute. El Paso, where you can cross border into Mexico, is to the south. To the north are Caballo and Elephant Butte Lakes featuring state-operated recreational areas with RV facilities, boating, water skiing, fishing and swimming. Full range of support facilities on post.

**SEASON OF OPERATION:** Year round.

**ELIGIBILITY:** Active/Reservists/Retired/DoD civilians.

**RESERVATIONS:** Accepted. Address: Volunteer Park Travel Camp Site, Attn: STEWS-DP-AR or P.O. Box 400, White Sands Missile Range, NM 88002-5035. **C-505-678-1713, D-312-258-1713.** Fax: C-505-678-5339. Check out 1100 hours.

**Camper Spaces:** Gravel (8), E (110V/30/50A)/S/W hookups. Rates: $8 daily/ $48 weekly.

**SUPPORT FACILITIES:**

| | | |
|---|---|---|
| ACOE Lodge* | Chapel | Fitness Trail |
| Golf/9 holes | Grills | Pavilion |
| Picnic Area | Restrooms | Sewage Dump |
| Showers | | |

* Meeting building available on a reservation basis.

**ACTIVITIES:**

| | | |
|---|---|---|
| Fishing/license | Hiking | Hunting/license* |
| Snow Skiing | | |

* Special hunts only, license available on base.

Tours to Trinity Site, location of world's first nuclear explosion, are conducted on first Sat in Apr and first Sat in Oct. Arrangements may be made through Public Affairs Office, Bldg 122. C-505-678-1134/1135/1700.

**CREDIT CARDS ACCEPTED:** Visa and MasterCard.

**RESTRICTIONS:** Pets allowed on leash.

# NEW YORK

*See map on following page.*

## REMINGTON POND
## RECREATION AREA (NY14R1)
Fort Drum
Fort Drum, NY 13602-5286

**TELEPHONE NUMBER INFORMATION:** Main installation numbers: C-315-772-6900, D-312-341-6011. Police for recreation area, C-315-772-5156.

**LOCATION:** On post. From I-81 at Watertown, take exit 48 NY-342 E, left onto NY-11 to NY-26, NY-3 NE to gates 1, 2 or 3. *USMRA: page 21 (J-3).* NMC: Watertown, 9 miles southwest.

**DESCRIPTION OF AREA:** Beautiful area offering every recreational pursuit. Many tourist attractions such as Sackets Harbor Battleground (from the War of 1812), Thousand Islands, Lake Ontario, Canada, Dry Hill ski area and whitewater rafting. Full range of support facilities on post.

**SEASON OF OPERATION:** 1 Apr-15 Oct.

**ELIGIBILITY:** Active/Reservists/Retired.

**RESERVATIONS:** Accepted. Address: Commander, 10th Mountain Division (LI) and Fort Drum, Attn: AFZS-PA-CRD, Outdoor Recreation Center, Bldg P-11115 N Memorial Drive, Fort Drum, NY 13602-5018. **C-315-772-5169, D-312-341-5169.** Ask for monthly calendar. Discounts to holders of Golden Age, Golden Access and Golden Eagle Passports.

**Camper/Tent Spaces:** Wilderness (6), no hookups. Rates: $6 daily.

*Remington Pond Recreation Area, continued*

*NEW YORK*

## SUPPORT FACILITIES:

| | | |
|---|---|---|
| Arts & Crafts Center | Auto Craft Shop | Bath House |
| Beach | Boat Rental | Bowling Alley |
| Chapel | Commissary | Convenience Store |
| Dock/floating | Exchange | Fitness Center |
| Gas | Grills | Laundry |
| Library | Pavilion | |
| Picnic Area | Pool | |
| Rec Center | | |
| Rec Equipment | | |
| Restrooms | | |
| Shoppette | | |
| Showers | | |
| Shuttle Bus | | |
| Snack Bar | | |
| Sports Fields | | |
| Telephones | | |
| Tennis Courts | | |
| Trails | | |
| Skeet Range | | |

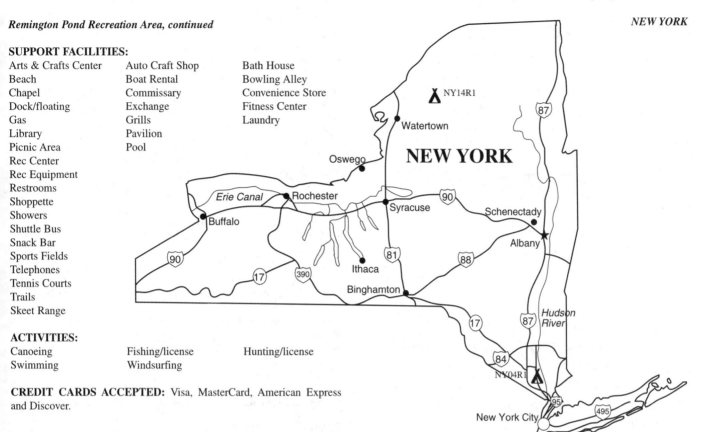

## ACTIVITIES:

| | | |
|---|---|---|
| Canoeing | Fishing/license | Hunting/license |
| Swimming | Windsurfing | |

**CREDIT CARDS ACCEPTED:** Visa, MasterCard, American Express and Discover.

**RESTRICTIONS:** Pets allowed on leash. Fourteen day limit. State hunting and fishing licenses and post fishing and hunting permits available at Outdoor Recreation Center. No motorized boats permitted.

# ROUND POND
# RECREATION AREA (NY04R1)
United States Military Academy, West Point
West Point, NY 10996-5000

**TELEPHONE NUMBER INFORMATION:** Main installation numbers: C-914-938-4011, D-312-688-1110. Police for recreation area, C-914-938-3333.

**LOCATION:** Off post. Three miles west of West Point on NY-293. Exit 16 from I-87, follow US-6 E to NY-293, continue east to recreation area. *USMRA: page 21 (M,N-10) and page 28 (D-3,4).* NMI: US Military Academy, West Point, 3 miles east. NMC: New York City, 50 miles southeast.

**DESCRIPTION OF AREA:** Located on Academy property in rocky, wooded area near old Ramapo mines. Delightful place with natural spring-fed pond. Full range of support facilities available at US Military Academy.

**SEASON OF OPERATION:** 15 Apr-15 Oct.

**ELIGIBILITY:** Active/Reservists/Retired/DoD civilians.

**RESERVATIONS:** Required: up to 180 days in advance for active duty, up to 120 days in advance for retired military, up to 90 days in advance for reserve and DoD civilians working at West Point or Stewart Army Subpost. Address: DCFA-CRD/Round Pond, Bldg 681, West Point, NY 10996-5000. **C-914-938-2503, D-312-688-2503** 0700-1800 hours. Fax: C-914-446-5503. Check in 1200 hours, check out 1100 hours.

**Cabin:** One-bedroom (1), handicap accessible, sleeps four. Rates: $35 daily.

**Camper Spaces:** 26, E (110V/20/30A)/W hookups. Rates: $14 daily. Seasonal camper sites available.

**Tent Spaces:** 26, no hookups. Rates: $8 daily.

**Lake Frederick Area**, six miles from Round Pond: A-Frames (10), sleeps 20, Scout Camping. Rates: $35 daily.

## SUPPORT FACILITIES:

| | | |
|---|---|---|
| Bait Shop | Boat Launch | Boat Rental |
| Fire Rings | Gas/LP | Golf |
| Grills | Hiking Trail | Ice |
| Marina | Pavilions | Playground |
| Picnic Area | Pool | Rental Center |
| Playground | Rec Equipment | Sewage Dump |
| Showers | Telephones | Volleyball Court |

## ACTIVITIES:

| | | |
|---|---|---|
| Bicycling | Fishing/license | Hiking |
| Hunting | Skiing | Swimming |
| Volleyball | | |

**CREDIT CARDS ACCEPTED:** Visa and MasterCard.

**RESTRICTIONS:** Pets allowed on leash. No firearms allowed. Quiet hours after 2200 hours. Parties are not allowed in tent area or camper sites.

# NORTH CAROLINA

## CAPE HATTERAS
## RECREATIONAL QUARTERS (NC09R1)
Cape Hatteras Coast Guard Group
Buxton, NC 27920-0604

**TELEPHONE NUMBER INFORMATION:** Main installation numbers: C-252-995-3676.

**LOCATION:** On base. From US-158 or US-64, take NC-12 to Buxton (approximately 50 miles south of Nags Head). East on Old Lighthouse Road, .5 miles to base. *USMRA: page 45 (P-3)*. NMC: Elizabeth City, 110 miles northwest.

**DESCRIPTION OF AREA:** No camping or RV parking. On Outer Banks of NC in Cape Hatteras National Seashore. Beautiful bathing beach and ocean fishing. Site of famous Wright brothers' first airplane flight, 50 miles north. Beach is 100 yards from facility. Sick bay with corpsman available for medical care Mon, Wed, Fri 0830-1200 hours. Full range of support facilities available at Norfolk Naval Base VA, 150 miles northwest.

**SEASON OF OPERATION:** Year round.

**ELIGIBILITY:** Active/Reservists/Retired/CG civilians.

**RESERVATIONS:** Required with advance payment: 30-90 days in advance by mail or phone. Address: Cape Hatteras Recreational Quarters, CG Group Cape Hatteras, P.O. Box 604, Buxton, NC 27920-0604. **C-252-995-3676/6435** 0830-1630 hours Mon-Fri summer, 0830-1230 hours Mon-Fri winter. Check in with motel manager. Check in time 1400-1800 hours 1 Apr-1 Nov, 0830-1230 hours other times.

**Motel:** VIP suite (1), O4+, sleeps five, furnished, private bath, kitchen, small refrigerator, microwave, A/C, CATV, housekeeping service; suite (1), sleeps seven, furnished, private bath, kitchen, small refrigerator, microwave, toaster, pots/pans (rooms 2 and 8), dishes, A/C, CATV, housekeeping service; room (6), sleeps five, furnished, rollaway ($5 per night), private bath, small refrigerator, microwave, A/C, CATV, housekeeping service. Rates: $55 daily VIP suite, $37-$52 daily suite (depending on rank), $25-$32 daily room (depending on rank). Off-season rates available.

**SUPPORT FACILITIES:**

| | | |
|---|---|---|
| Beach | Grills | Medical Clinic |
| Picnic Area | Showers/outside | Sports Field |
| Trails | | |

Marinas in Hatteras Inlet area, 11 miles south. Sunfish, surfboards, jet skis, fishing gear, and most items for water sports can be rented in area.

**ACTIVITIES:**

| | |
|---|---|
| Fishing | Water Sports |

**CREDIT CARDS ACCEPTED:** Visa and MasterCard.

**RESTRICTIONS:** No pets allowed. No open fires. No smoking. Seven day limit. This is a seasonal area for shops, stores, etc; many close during winter months.

## CHERRY POINT MWR FAMCAMP (NC04R1)
Cherry Point Marine Corps Air Station
Cherry Point, NC 28533-0022

**TELEPHONE NUMBER INFORMATION:** Main installation numbers: C-252-466-2811, D-312-582-1110.

**LOCATION:** On base. On NC-101, east of US-70, between New Bern and Morehead City. *USMRA: page 45 (M,N-4)*. NMC: Jacksonville, 45 miles southwest.

**DESCRIPTION OF AREA:** Located near Neuse Waterway and Outer Banks area, surrounded by Croatan National Forest. FAMCAMP within walking distance of full range of support facilities available on base.

**SEASON OF OPERATION:** Year round.

**ELIGIBILITY:** Active/Reservists/Retired.

**RESERVATIONS:** No advance reservations. Address: ITT Director, MWR, PSC 8009, Cherry Point MCAS, NC 28533-0009. **C-252-466-2197/2172, D-312-582-2197.**

**Camper Spaces:** 15, E (110/220V/30A)/S/W hookups. Rates: $10 daily.

*Cherry Point MWR FAMCAMP, continued*

**SUPPORT FACILITIES:**

| | | |
|---|---|---|
| Boat Rental | Camper Rental | Camping Equipment |
| Chapel | Gas | Golf |
| Grills | Laundry | Marina |
| Picnic Area | Pig Cooker Rental | Racquetball |
| Sewage Dump | Snack Bar | Sports Fields |
| Tennis Courts | | |

**ACTIVITIES:**

| | | |
|---|---|---|
| Arts/Crafts | Fishing/license | Hunting/license |

**CREDIT CARDS ACCEPTED:** Visa and MasterCard.

**RESTRICTIONS:** Small pets allowed on leash. Boat rental available at Slocum Creek Marina only, permits must be obtained from Recreation Department.

# ELIZABETH CITY LODGING (NC15R1)

Elizabeth City Coast Guard Support Center
Elizabeth City, NC 27909-5000

**TELEPHONE NUMBER INFORMATION:** Main installation numbers: C-252-338-6379. Police for campsites, C-252-335-6398.

**LOCATION:** On base. From US-17 in Elizabeth City take NC-34 (Halstead Blvd/Weeksville Road) south to main gate of Center. *USMRA: page 45 (O-1).* NMC: Norfolk VA, 40 miles north.

**DESCRIPTION OF AREA:** Located off the Albemarle Sound .5 miles from beach. Attractions include the Outer Banks and Kitty Hawk. Wide range of support facilities available on base.

**SEASON OF OPERATION:** Year round.

**ELIGIBILITY:** Active/Reservists/Retired/DoD civilians/DOT and NASA civilians.

**RESERVATIONS:** Accepted up to 90 days in advance (very busy Apr-Sep). Advance payment required. Address: MWR Office, Bldg 5, Coast Guard Support Center, Elizabeth City, NC 27909-5000. **C-252-335-6397.** Fax: C-252-335-6296. Check in at office, check out 1000 hours. After 2100 hours check in at main gate.

**Mobile Homes:** Two-bedroom (6), sleeps four, furnished, TV. Rates: $20-$35 (depending on rank).

**Camper Spaces:** Gravel (4), E (110/220V/50A)/S/W. Rates: $3-$6 (depending on rank).

**SUPPORT FACILITIES:**

| | | |
|---|---|---|
| Beach | Boat Launch | Camping Equipment |
| Chapel | Convenience Store | Exchange |
| Fishing Pier | Fitness Center | Gas |
| Grills | Laundry | Pavilion |
| Picnic Area | Playground | Pool (weekends only) |
| Rec Center | Restrooms | Sewage Dump |
| Snack Bar | Sports Fields | Trails |

**ACTIVITIES:**

| | | |
|---|---|---|
| Boating | Fishing | Swimming |

**CREDIT CARDS ACCEPTED:** None.

**RESTRICTIONS:** No pets allowed in trailers. No firearms allowed.

# FORT FISHER AIR FORCE RECREATION AREA (NC13R1)

Seymour Johnson Air Force Base
Seymour Johnson AFB, NC 27531-2442

**TELEPHONE NUMBER INFORMATION:** Main installation numbers: C-919-736-5400.

**LOCATION:** Off base. On US-421 south of Wilmington NC, go through Carolina and Kure Beaches to Fort Fisher Air Force Recreation Area. *USMRA: page 45 (L-6).* NMI: Camp Lejeune, 70 miles northeast. NMC: Wilmington NC, 20 miles northwest.

**DESCRIPTION OF AREA:** Fort Fisher is located on Pleasure Island between Cape Fear River and Atlantic Ocean. Its history predates Civil War. Beaches within walking distance. Numerous local attractions: NC Aquarium at Fort Fisher, parks, fishing and museums nearby. No support facilities available at recreation area, full range available at Camp Lejeune.

**SEASON OF OPERATION:** Year round.

**ELIGIBILITY:** Active/Reservists/Retired/DoD civilians.

**RESERVATIONS:** Accepted with advance payment or confirmation with major credit card. May be made up to 90 days in advance for active duty Air Force, up to 85 days for all other active duty, up to 75 days for retired military, up to 60 days for all others. Reservations for groups are welcomed during non-peak use periods. Address: Fort Fisher AF Recreation Area, 118 River Front Road, Kure Beach, NC 28449-5000. **C-910-458-6549.** Check in 1600 hours at Reception Center, check out 1100 hours.

**Beach Cottages:** 4, sleeps 12, CATV, washer/dryer. Rates: $70-$135 daily (depending on season and day of week, additional charge for extra person). 18, sleeps six to eight, CATV, washer/dryer. Rates: $50-$125 daily (depending on season and day of week, additional charge for extra person).

**Coastal Cottages:** 4, sleeps six, CATV, washer/dryer. Rates: $70-$135 daily (depending on season and day of week, additional charge for extra person).

**Mobile Home:** 7, sleeps eight. Rates: $60-$125 daily (depending on season and day of week, additional charge for extra person).

**River Marsh Landing:** Suites (2). Rates: $40-$75 daily (depending on season and day of week, additional charge for extra person). Rooms (6). Rates: $30-$60 daily (depending on season and day of week, additional charge for extra person). No children under 12.

**Lodge:** Suites (6), sleeps four, shared bath. Rates: $30-$50 daily (depending on season and day of week, additional charge for extra person). Suites (7), sleeps six, shared bath, (depending on season and day of week, additional charge for extra person). Rates: $35-$60 daily (depending on season and day of week, additional charge for extra person). Rooms (27), sleeps two, shared bath. Rates: $15-$30 daily (depending on season and day of week, additional charge for extra person).

**Camper Spaces:** Hardstand (16), E (110/220V/30A)/S/W hookups. Rates: $12-$20 daily (depending on season and day of week, additional charge for extra person).

**Tent Spaces:** 35, plus overflow. Rates: $8-$10 daily (depending on season and day of week, additional charge for extra person).

**SUPPORT FACILITIES:**

| | | |
|---|---|---|
| Beach | Boat Launch | Camping Equipment |
| Exercise/Weight Room | General Store | Gift/Beach Shop |
| Jacuzzi | Kennel (fee) | Laundry |

*NORTH CAROLINA*
*Fort Fisher Air Force Recreation Area, continued*

| | | |
|---|---|---|
| Pool | Rec Center | Rec Equipment |
| Restaurant | Restrooms | Sauna |
| Sewage Dump | Showers | Sports Fields |
| Tennis Courts | | |

**ACTIVITIES:**

| | | |
|---|---|---|
| Beach | Boating | Canoeing |
| Clamming | Fishing | Sailing |
| Sightseeing | Swimming | |

**CREDIT CARDS ACCEPTED:** Visa, MasterCard, American Express and Seymour Johnson Club Card.

**RESTRICTIONS:** No pets allowed in accommodations, kennel available. Pets allowed on leash in designated areas only, owner must clean up after pet. No children under 12 in executive quarters.

## NEW RIVER MCAS MARINA (NC07R1)
New River Marine Corps Air Station
New River MCAS, NC 28545-1001

**TELEPHONE NUMBER INFORMATION:** Main installation numbers: C-910-451-1113, D-312-484-1113. Police for Marina 910-450-6111.

**LOCATION:** On base. Off US-17, south of Jacksonville. *USMRA: page 45 (L,M-4,5).* NMC: Jacksonville, 5 miles northeast.

**DESCRIPTION OF AREA:** Situated along New River. Offers water sports, recreational and picnic areas. Improvements to facilities at camping area are currently under construction. Full range of support facilities available on base

**SEASON OF OPERATION:** Year round.

**ELIGIBILITY:** Active/Reservists/Retired/DoD civilians/Dependent ID card holders.

**RESERVATIONS:** Accepted. Address: MWR, New River Marine Corps Air Station, Jacksonville, NC 28540-0128. **C-910-451-6578, D-312-484-6578.** Fax: 910-450-6907.

**Tent Spaces:** Primitive (7), no hookups. Rates: $3 daily.

**SUPPORT FACILITIES:**

| | | |
|---|---|---|
| Auto Craft Shop | Bath House | Beach |
| Boat Launch | Boat Rental/Storage | Boat Slip Rental |
| Chapel | Commissary | Convenience Store |
| Exchange | Fire Rings | Fitness Center |
| Gas | Grills | Ice |
| Marina* | Pavilion | Picnic Area |
| Playground | Rec Equipment | Restrooms |
| Showers | Snack Bar | Sports Fields |
| Telephones | Tennis Courts | Trails |
| Water Sports Equipment Rental | | |

* Patio Room at Marina for parties, by reservation.

**ACTIVITIES:**

| | | |
|---|---|---|
| Boating | Fishing/license | Hunting/license |
| Jet Skiing | Softball | Swimming |
| Volleyball | Water Skiing | |

**CREDIT CARDS ACCEPTED:** Visa and MasterCard.

**RESTRICTIONS:** No pets allowed on beach, allowed on leash in camping area. No firearms.

## ONSLOW BEACH CAMPSITES AND RECREATION AREA (NC14R1)
Camp Lejeune Marine Corps Base
Camp Lejeune MCB, NC 28542-0004

**TELEPHONE NUMBER INFORMATION:** Main installation numbers: C-910-451-1113, D-312-484-1113. Police for campsites and recreation area, C-910-451-2555.

**LOCATION:** On base. Main gate is off NC-24 six miles east of junction with US-17. Campsites located approximately ten miles from gate on NC-172. Clearly marked. *USMRA: page 45 (M-4,5).* NMC: Wilmington, 45 miles southwest.

**DESCRIPTION OF AREA:** Located on island between Inner Coastal Waterway and Onslow Bay. Campsites are on beach or in wooded area. Many commercial fishing and beach areas also available. ITT Office on base has information on recreational activities and discount tickets. Full range of support facilities available on base.

**SEASON OF OPERATION:** Normally open year round. This facility was extensively damaged by a hurricane in 1996. Call for information.

**ELIGIBILITY:** Active/Reservists/Retired.

**RESERVATIONS:** Accepted up to 40 days in advance, depending on status. Address: Attn: MWR/MCRC Beach, 1401 West Road, Camp Lejeune, NC 28547-2539. **C-910-450-7473/7502, D-312-484-7473/7502.**

**Mobile Homes:** 18, private bath, furnished, A/C, heat, TV, utensils. Rates: $22-32 (depending on rank).

**Cabanas:** Sleeps four, furnished, full kitchen, A/C, heat. Rates: $8-$28 (depending on rank).

**Camper Spaces:** 44, E/S/W hookups. Rates: $10 daily.

**SUPPORT FACILITIES:**

| | | |
|---|---|---|
| Bait/Tackle | Boat Dock | Boat Launch |
| Boogie/Surfboards | Exchange | Fishing Equipment |
| Fishing Pier | Golf/on base | Grills |
| Equipment Rental | Marinas (2)/on base | Picnic Area |
| Playground (fenced) | Restrooms | Sewage Dump |
| Showers | Snack Bar | |

**ACTIVITIES:**

| | | |
|---|---|---|
| Fishing | Surfing | Swimming |

**CREDIT CARDS ACCEPTED:** Visa, MasterCard and Discover.

**RESTRICTIONS:** Pets allowed on leash in campsites only, must be under positive control. No firearms allowed.

## SEYMOUR JOHNSON FAMCAMP (NC08R1)
Seymour Johnson Air Force Base
Seymour Johnson AFB, NC 27531-2442

**TELEPHONE NUMBER INFORMATION:** Main installation numbers: C-919-736-5400, D-312-488-1110. Police for FAMCAMP, C-919-736-6412/6413.

*Seymour Johnson FAMCAMP, continued*

**LOCATION:** On base. Take US-70 to Seymour Johnson exit in Goldsboro. Take Berkeley Blvd to base. *USMRA: page 45 (L-3)*. NMC: Raleigh, 50 miles northwest.

**DESCRIPTION OF AREA:** FAMCAMP is surrounded by heavily forested areas and within walking distance of many of support facilities available on base.

**SEASON OF OPERATION:** Year round.

**ELIGIBILITY:** Active/Reservists/Retired/DoD civilians.

**RESERVATIONS:** No advance reservations. Address: Outdoor Recreation, 4 SVS/SVRO, 1515 Goodson Street, Seymour Johnson AFB, NC 27531-5000. **C-919-736-5405, D-312-488-5405.** Fax: C-919-731-4035. E-mail: sjoutrec@esn.net. Check in/out at Outdoor Recreation.

**Camper Spaces:** Hardstand (7), handicap accessible, E (110V/30A)/S/W hookups. Rates: $10 daily.

*Note: Seymour Johnson AFB also leases three trailer spaces at Rogers Bay, Topsail Island with E (110V/30A)/S/W hookups. Rates: $50 Mon-Thu; $65 Fri-Sun, holidays. A cleaning deposit on rented trailers of $20, $25 with pet, is required.*

**SUPPORT FACILITIES:**

| | | |
|---|---|---|
| Auto Craft Shop | Bath House | Commissary |
| Exchange | Fitness Center | Gas |
| Golf | Ice | Laundry |
| Pavilion | Picnic Area | Playground |
| Racquetball Court | Rec Center | Rec Equipment |
| Restrooms | Sewage Dump | Shoppette |
| Skeet/Trap Range | Snack Bar | Sports Fields |
| Telephones | Tennis Courts | |

**ACTIVITIES:**

| | |
|---|---|
| Jogging | Nature Trail |

**CREDIT CARDS ACCEPTED:** Visa and MasterCard.

**RESTRICTIONS:** Pets allowed on leash only.

## SMITH LAKE ARMY TRAVEL CAMPGROUND (NC12R1)

Fort Bragg
Fort Bragg, NC 28307-5000

**TELEPHONE NUMBER INFORMATION:** Main installation numbers: C-910-396-0011, D-312-236-0111. Police for campground, C-910-396-5979.

**LOCATION:** On post. Take I-95 to Business Loop I-95/US-301 to Owen Drive (changes to All-American Freeway) to Gruber Road exit. Follow to Highway 210, turn right. Follow to first paved road, .5 miles, turn left to Travel Camp. Also, from US-401 (Fayetteville Bypass) exit to NC-210, north to Smith Lake. *USMRA: page 45 (I,J-4)*. NMC: Fayetteville, 5 miles southeast.

**DESCRIPTION OF AREA:** JFK Special Warfare Museum and 82d Airborne Division Museum on post, Pinehurst Resort is nearby. Full range of support facilities available on post.

**SEASON OF OPERATION:** Year round.

**ELIGIBILITY:** Active/Reservists/Retired/DoD and MWR civilians with letter of authorization.

**RESERVATIONS:** No advance reservations. Address: CASBC, Attn: Smith Lake, Fort Bragg, NC 28307-5000. **C-910-396-5979, D-312-326-5979.** Discounts available to holders of Golden Age and Golden Access Passports. Check in at cabin at gate to picnic area 0730-1900 hours summer, 0730-1700 hours winter, check out 1200 hours.

**Camper Spaces:** Gravel (13), E (110V/30/50A)/S/W hookups. Rates: $12 daily. Gravel (11), E (110V/20A)/W hookups. Rates: $10 daily.

**SUPPORT FACILITIES:**

| | | |
|---|---|---|
| Auto Craft Shop | Bath House | Beach |
| Boat Rental | Camping Equipment | Chapel/on post |
| Commissary | Convenience Store | Exchange |
| Fitness Center | Gas | Golf/on post |
| Grills | Ice | Laundry |
| Pavilion | Picnic Area | Playground |
| Rec Center | Rec Equipment | Restrooms |
| Sewage Dump | Shoppette | Showers |
| Stables | Telephone | Tennis Courts |

**ACTIVITIES:**

| | |
|---|---|
| Fishing/license | Swimming/summer |

**CREDIT CARDS ACCEPTED:** Visa, MasterCard and Esprit.

**RESTRICTIONS:** Pets allowed on leash in campground only, must be kept under control at all times, no pets in picnic area. No fishing 1 May-30 Sep when the water ski lift is in operation.

# NORTH DAKOTA

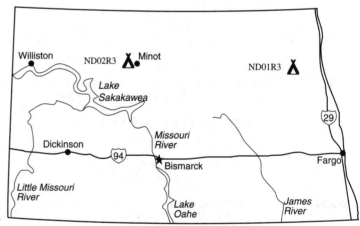

## GRAND FORKS FAMCAMP (ND01R3)

Grand Forks Air Force Base
Grand Forks AFB, ND 58205-6316

**TELEPHONE NUMBER INFORMATION:** Main installation numbers: C-701-747-3000, D-312-362-1110. Police for FAMCAMP, C-701-747-5351.

**LOCATION:** On base. From I-29 take US-2 W for 14 miles to County Road B-3 (Emerado/Air Base), one mile to AFB. *USMRA: page 83 (I-3)*. NMC: Grand Forks, 20 miles southeast.

*NORTH DAKOTA*
*Grand Forks FAMCAMP, continued*

**DESCRIPTION OF AREA:** Located in an open area. Wide variety of recreational activities available. Two hour drive to Canada. Full range of support facilities available on base.

**SEASON OF OPERATION:** 1 May-1 Oct.

**ELIGIBILITY:** Active/Reservists/Retired/DoD civilians and visiting family of all the above.

**RESERVATIONS:** No advance reservations. Address: FAMCAMP, 319 SVS/SVRO, 201 Steen Avenue, Bldg 129, Grand Forks Air Force Base, ND 58205-6316. **C-701-747-3688, D-312-362-3688.** Check in at Outdoor Recreation, Bldg 129, 201 Steen Avenue, 0800-1700 hours Mon, 1000-1700 hours Tue-Thu, 0800-1800 hours Fri, after hours, obtain directions from Security Police at Main Gate, optional check in by filling out registration envelope available at bath house and depositing with money in locked box, check out 1200 hours.

**Camper Spaces:** Gravel (10), E (110/220V/50A)/S/W/CATV hookups. Gravel (10) E (110V/35A)/S/W/CATV hookups. Rates: $12 daily.

**SUPPORT FACILITIES:**

| | | |
|---|---|---|
| Boat Rental | Bowling Alley | Camping Equipment |
| Camper Rental | Chapel | Fishing Equipment |
| Gas | Golf Course | Grills |
| Gun Club | Laundry | Picnic Area |
| Playground | Restrooms | Showers |
| Theatre | | |

**ACTIVITIES:**

| | | |
|---|---|---|
| Boating/nearby | Fishing/license | Hiking |
| Hunting/license | River Rafting/Tubing* | Riding Stables* |

* Nearby

**CREDIT CARDS ACCEPTED:** Visa and MasterCard.

**RESTRICTIONS:** Pets allowed on leash. Firearms are prohibited in the FAMCAMP. For information on hunting and fishing contact the North Dakota Fish and Game Department in Bismarck at C-701-221-6300.

## MINOT AIR FORCE BASE
## FAMCAMP (ND02R3)

Minot Air Force Base
Minot AFB, ND 58075-5003

**TELEPHONE NUMBER INFORMATION:** Main installation numbers: C-701-723-1110, D-312-453-1110, Police for FAMCAMP, C-701-723-3096.

**LOCATION:** On base. Thirteen miles north of Minot on Highway 83. Get directions from Security Police at Visitors Center (main gate). *USMRA: page 83 (D-2)*. NMC: Minot, 13 miles south.

**DESCRIPTION OF AREA:** Located in the north central area of North Dakota. Theodore Roosevelt National Park, North Dakota Badlands, Fort Lincoln State Park nearby. Thirty-five miles to Canada. Full range of support facilities on base.

**SEASON OF OPERATION:** May-Oct.

**ELIGIBILITY:** Active/Reservists/Retired/DoD/NAF civilians and family.

**RESERVATIONS:** No advance reservations. Address: FAMCAMP, SSVS/SVRO, 315 Bomber Blvd, Bldg 510/511, Minot AFB, ND 58705-5000. **C-701-723-3648, D-312-453-3648.** Fax: C-701-723-2175. Check in at Outdoor Recreation.

**Camper Spaces:** 6, E (20A)/W hookups, dump station on site. Rates: $10 daily/$60 weekly.

**SUPPORT FACILITIES:**

| | | |
|---|---|---|
| Grills | Pavilions | Picnic Area |
| Playground | Restrooms | Sports fields |
| Track | | |

**ACTIVITIES:**

| | | |
|---|---|---|
| Boating | Fishing/license | Hiking |
| Horseback riding | Hunting/license | Snow skiing |

**CREDIT CARDS ACCEPTED:** Visa and MasterCard.

**RESTRICTIONS:** Pets allowed on leash. Firearms are prohibited. For information on hunting and fishing contact ND Fish and Game Department at C-701-328-6300.

# OHIO

## WRIGHT-PATTERSON AFB
## FAMCAMP (OH03R2)

Wright-Patterson Air Force Base
Wright-Patterson AFB, OH 45433-5315

**TELEPHONE NUMBER INFORMATION:** Main installation numbers: C-937-257-1110, D-312-787-1110. Police for FAMCAMP, C-937-257-6516.

**LOCATION:** On base. Located on State Route 444, south of Fairborn. From I-70, go south to Highway 444 and proceed to Gate 12A. Also, from I-675 N, take exit 17 and follow signs. Also, from I-75 N, take Highway 4 to Highway 444 and proceed to Gate 12A. Clearly marked. *USMRA: page 67 (B-7)*. NMC: Dayton, 10 miles southwest.

*Wright-Patterson AFB FAMCAMP, continued*

**DESCRIPTION OF AREA:** Home of world's largest and most complete military aviation museum and Wright Brothers Memorial. Summer months are warm to hot and winter months are cold. Full range of support facilities available on base.

**SEASON OF OPERATION:** Year round, no water in winter.

**ELIGIBILITY:** Active/Reservists/Retired.

**RESERVATIONS:** No advance reservations. First come first serve, active duty on PCS are given priority. Address: Outdoor Recreation, 88 SPTG/SVRO, 5215 Thurlow Street, Suite 2, Wright-Patterson AFB, OH 45433-5542. **C-937-257-9889/4374/2579, D-312-787-9889/4374/2579.** Fax: C-937-656-2107, D-312-486-2107. Check out 1200 hours.

**Camper Spaces:** Concrete (19), E (110/220V/20/30A)/W hookups. Rates: $7 daily summer, $5 daily winter (E hookup only).

**Tent Spaces:** Unlimited, no hookups. Rates: $3 daily.

**SUPPORT FACILITIES:**

| | | |
|---|---|---|
| Auto Craft Shop | Boat Rental/Storage | Chapel |
| Commissary | Exchange | Fitness Center |
| Gas | Golf | Grills |
| Pavilion | Picnic Area | Playground |
| Pool | Racquet Sports | Rec Equipment |
| Sewage Dump | Snack Bar | Sports Fields |
| Telephones | Tennis Courts | |

**ACTIVITIES:**

| | | |
|---|---|---|
| Bicycling | Boating | Fishing/stocked |
| Jogging | Swimming | |

**CREDIT CARDS ACCEPTED:** Visa and MasterCard.

**RESTRICTIONS:** Pets allowed on leash. Firearms must be checked with Security. Fishing and hunting in area near campsites are not permitted except according to WPAFBR 126-2. Canopy over gas pumps at Exchange cannot accommodate vehicles over nine feet in height.

# OKLAHOMA

## ALTUS FAMCAMP (OK06R3)

Altus Air Force Base
Altus AFB, OK 73523-5001

**TELEPHONE NUMBER INFORMATION:** Main installation numbers: C-580-481/482-8100, D-312-866-1110. Police for FAMCAMP, C-580-481-7444.

**LOCATION:** On base. Located off US-62 S of I-40 and west of I-44. From US-62 traveling west from Lawton, turn right at first traffic light in Altus and follow road, bear right at fork, to main gate northeast of Falcon Road. *USMRA: page 84 (E-5).* NMC: Lawton, 56 miles east.

**DESCRIPTION OF AREA:** Museum of the Western Prairie (history of southwest Oklahoma) located five minutes from base. Public recreation area at Lake Altus, 17 miles north on US-283. Full range of support facilities available on base.

**SEASON OF OPERATION:** Year round.

**ELIGIBILITY:** Active/Reservists/Retired/DoD civilians.

**RESERVATIONS:** Accepted. Address: Altus AFB FAMCAMP, 97 SVS/SVRO, Bldg 418, Altus AFB, OK 73523-5000. **C-580-481-6420/6704, D-312-866-6704.** Participant in Air Force Frequent Camper program. Check in at Bowling Center, 24 hours daily, check out 1200 hours.

**Camper Spaces:** Gravel (4), E (110V/30A)/S/W hookups. Gravel (3), E (110V/30A) hookup. Rates: $8 daily.

**SUPPORT FACILITIES:**

| | | |
|---|---|---|
| Chapel | Family Bowling | Gas |
| Golf/9 holes | Picnic Area | Port-a-Potties |
| Rec Equipment | Sewage Dump | Showers/gym |
| Sports Fields | Swimming/summer | |

**ACTIVITIES:**

| | |
|---|---|
| Jogging | Tennis |

**CREDIT CARDS ACCEPTED:** Visa, MasterCard and American Express.

**RESTRICTIONS:** Pets allowed on leash. Signature required for action to be taken in event of severe weather.

## BLACKHAWK RECREATIONAL VEHICLE PARK (OK03R3)

Camp Gruber Training Site
Braggs, OK 74423-0029

**TELEPHONE NUMBER INFORMATION:** Main installation number: C-918-487-6001.

**LOCATION:** On post. Highway 62 north from Muskogee, exit Highway 10, 12 miles. Enter at Industrial Gate, report to Bldg 120. *USMRA: page 84 (I-4).* NMC: Muskogee, 12 miles southwest.

**DESCRIPTION OF AREA:** Located in a beautiful wooded area in northeast Oklahoma, close to the lake. Tenkiller Lake is just a few miles away.

**SEASON OF OPERATION:** Year round.

**ELIGIBILITY:** Active/Reservists/Retired/DoD civilians.

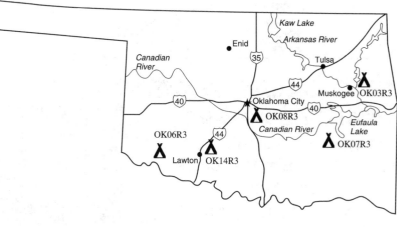

*OKLAHOMA*
*Blackhawk Recreational Vehicle Park, continued*

**RESERVATIONS:** Reserve 15 days in advance. Requests within 15 days will be honored as available. Address: Camp Gruber Training Site, Attn: Billeting Office, P.O. Box 29, Braggs, OK 74423-0029. **C-918-487-6065.** Fax: C-918-487-6135.

**Camper Spaces:** Gravel (12). E (110V/30A)/S/W hookups, picnic tables and BBQ grills at each site and security lights. Rates: $7 daily.

**SUPPORT FACILITIES:**

| | | |
|---|---|---|
| Bath House | Laundry | Pavilion |

**ACTIVITIES:** Boating and fishing nearby.

**CREDIT CARDS ACCEPTED:** None.

**RESTRICTIONS:** No pets allowed. Firearms must be registered with Range Control.

### LAKE ELMER THOMAS RECREATION AREA (OK14R3)
Fort Sill
Fort Sill, OK 73503-5100

**TELEPHONE NUMBER INFORMATION:** Main installation numbers: C-580-442-8111, D-312-639-7090.

**LOCATION:** Off post. Take I-44 to Medicine Park exit (Highway 49) west. Follow signs to LETRA. *USMRA: page 84 (E,F-5)*. NMI: Fort Sill, 12 miles southwest. NMC: Wichita Falls, TX, 64 miles southwest.

**DESCRIPTION OF AREA:** Located in the Wichita Mountains of southwestern Oklahoma, the recreation area offers a 360-acre lake and a wildlife refuge in the Wichita Mountains.

**SEASON OF OPERATION:** Year round.

**ELIGIBILITY:** Active/Reservists/Retired/DoD civilian employees.

**RESERVATIONS:** MWR, Fort Sill, OK 73503-5100. **C-580-442-5858/9.**

**Camper Spaces:** Gravel (62), E (110V/50A)/S/W hookups. Rates: $12 daily, off season rates available.

**Tent Spaces:** Grass (10), no hookups. Rates: $3 daily.

**SUPPORT FACILITIES:**

| | | |
|---|---|---|
| Bath House | Boat Launch | Convenience Store |
| Equipment Rental | Laundry | Marina |
| Multi-Purpose Bldg | Picnic Pavilions | Playgrounds |
| Restaurant | Snack Bar | |

**ACTIVITIES:**

| | | |
|---|---|---|
| Fishing | Hiking | Miniature Golf |
| Swimming | Water Slide | |

**CREDIT CARDS ACCEPTED:** Visa, MasterCard and American Express.

### MURPHY'S MEADOW (OK07R3)
McAlester Army Ammunition Plant
McAlester, OK 74501-5000

**TELEPHONE NUMBER INFORMATION:** Main installation numbers: C-918-420-7490, D-312-956-7490.
**LOCATION:** On post. Off US-69 south of McAlester. *USMRA: page 84 (I-5)*. NMC: Tulsa, 90 miles north.

**DESCRIPTION OF AREA:** Located in southeast Oklahoma on shores of Brown Lake. Mostly rolling pasture land with timber-covered hills and creek bottoms. Great area for vacationing: many lakes offer fishing, boating and water sports. A thirty minute drive to Lake Eufaula, third largest artificial lake in US. Small community of Savanna, approximately two miles away, provides essentials not available on post. Limited support facilities available on post within walking distance of camp, full range of facilities available at Tinker AFB, 116 miles northwest.

**SEASON OF OPERATION:** Year round.

**ELIGIBILITY:** Active/Reservists/Retired/DoD civilians.

**RESERVATIONS:** Call ahead for availability of campsites; very limited availability Oct-Nov. All sites are first come, first serve. A self pay drop box is available for after hours arrivals. Address: Commander, McAlester Army Ammunition Plant, Attn: SIOMC-CAO, McAlester, OK 74501-5000. **C-918-420-7484/6673, D-312-956-7484.** Discounts available to holders of Golden Age and Golden Access Passports.

**Camper Spaces:** Gravel (17), E (110V/30A)/W hookups. Overflow, grass (34), E (110V/30A)/W hookups. Rates: $7 daily.

**Camper/Tent Spaces:** Primitive, no hookups. Rates: $3 daily.

**SUPPORT FACILITIES:**

| | | |
|---|---|---|
| Boat Launch | Boat Rental | Bowling |
| Community Club | Equipment Rental | Exchange |
| Golf Driving Range | Grills | Health Clinic |

*Murphy's Meadow, continued*

| | | |
|---|---|---|
| Pavilions | Picnic Area | Playground |
| Rec Equipment | Restrooms* | Sewage Dump |
| Showers* | Snack Bar | Softball Field |
| Tennis Court | | |

* Handicap accessible.

**ACTIVITIES:**

Boating          Fishing/license

**CREDIT CARDS ACCEPTED:** Visa, MasterCard, American Express and Discover.

**RESTRICTIONS:** Pets must be on a leash. No swimming. No water skiing.

## TINKER FAMCAMP (OK08R3)
Tinker Air Force Base
Tinker AFB, OK 73145-9011

**TELEPHONE NUMBER INFORMATION:** Main installation numbers: C-405-732-7321, D-312-884-1110.

**LOCATION:** On base. Off I-40, five miles east of Oklahoma City. Enter Gate 1 off Air Depot Blvd. Ask for directions to Outdoor Recreation, Bldg 5935. *USMRA: page 84 (G-4).* NMC: Oklahoma City, 5 miles west.

**DESCRIPTION OF AREA:** Located in the midst of Oklahoma City/Midwest City metropolitan area. FAMCAMP is situated in well-developed recreation area offering two fishing ponds. Full range of support facilities available on base.

**SEASON OF OPERATION:** Year round.

**ELIGIBILITY:** Active/Reservists/Retired/DoD civilians.

**RESERVATIONS:** No advance reservations. Address: Outdoor Recreation, 72nd SPTG/SVRO, Bldg 5935, Tinker AFB, OK 73145-8101. **C-405-734-2289, D-312-884-2289.**

**Camper Spaces:** Hardstand (29), E (110/220V/30A)/W hookups. Rates: $10 daily. Overflow, no hookups. Rates: $4 daily.

**Tent Spaces:** 5, no hookups. Rates: $4 daily.

**SUPPORT FACILITIES:**

| | | |
|---|---|---|
| Chapel | Gas | Golf |
| Laundry | Picnic Areas | Playgrounds |
| Restrooms | Sewage Dump | Showers* |

* Handicap accessible.

**ACTIVITIES:**
Fishing

**CREDIT CARDS ACCEPTED:** Visa and MasterCard.

**RESTRICTIONS:** No firearms allowed. No swimming or boating in ponds.

# OREGON

## CAMP RILEA (OR07R4)
Camp Rilea Armed Forces Training Center
Warrenton, OR 97146-9711

**TELEPHONE NUMBER INFORMATION:** Main installation number: 503-861-4018.

**LOCATION:** On post. From Portland, Oregon, take US-26 W to Oregon Coast approximately 65 miles. When you reach US-101, proceed north 12 miles. Located between seaside and Astoria. *USMRA: page 100 (B-1).* NMC: Astoria, five miles north.

**DESCRIPTION OF AREA:** Exchange and Commissary available on Route 101 in Astoria at Coast Guard gas station.

**SEASON OF OPERATION:** Year round.

**ELIGIBILITY:** Active/Reservists/Retired.

**RESERVATIONS:** Accepted up to 90 days in advance. Address: Camp Rilea, Route 2, Box 497E, Warrenton, OR 97146-9711. **C-503-861-4048, D-312-355-3972.** Fax: C-503-861-4049.

**Camper Spaces:** 10, E (110V/50A)/S/W hookups. Rates: $5 daily.

**SUPPORT FACILITIES:**

| | | |
|---|---|---|
| Beach | Exchange | Fitness Center |
| Picnic Area | Restrooms | Sewage Dump |
| Shoppette | Showers | Snack Bar |
| Telephones | | |

**CREDIT CARDS ACCEPTED:** Visa and MasterCard.

**RESTRICTIONS:** No pets allowed. No RVs longer than 30'.

# PENNSYLVANIA

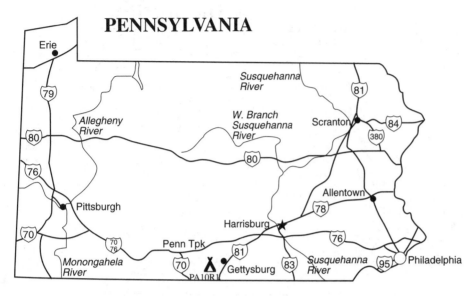

**SUPPORT FACILITIES:**

| | |
|---|---|
| Bath House | Fire Rings |
| Fitness Trail | Golf |
| Grills | Laundry |
| Nature Trail | Picnic Area |
| Playground | Pool |
| Restrooms | Sewage Dump |
| Showers | Telephones |

Limited support facilities available on base.

**ACTIVITIES:**

| | |
|---|---|
| Boating | Fishing/license |
| Hiking | Jogging |
| Swimming | Tennis |

**CREDIT CARDS ACCEPTED:** None.

**RESTRICTIONS:** Pets allowed on leash.

## LETTERKENNY ARMY TRAVEL CAMP (PA10R1)

Letterkenny Army Depot
Chambersburg, PA 17201-4150
***Scheduled to downsize in 1999.***

**TELEPHONE NUMBER INFORMATION:** Main installation numbers: C-717-267-8111, D-312-570-5110.

**LOCATION:** On post. From I-81 take exit 8. West on PA-997 to gate 6. Clearly marked with signs for depot. *USMRA: page 22 (E-7).* NMI: Carlisle Barracks, 30 miles north. NMC: Chambersburg, 5 miles south.

**DESCRIPTION OF AREA:** Beautiful Cumberland Valley of Pennsylvania. Near historic Gettysburg and Antietam Battlefields and Caledonia State Park. Also within driving distance of Hershey, Lancaster, Reading outlet stores, and other places of interest. Sites have large oak trees. Some support facilities available on base within walking distance, full range at Carlisle Barracks.

**SEASON OF OPERATION:** 1 Mar-31 Oct.

**ELIGIBILITY:** Active/Reservists/Retired/DoD civilians.

**RESERVATIONS:** Recommended. A 50% non-refundable deposit, up to a $25 maximum, is required to confirm reservations. Unconfirmed reservations will be held until 1700 hours. Make checks payable to IMWRF. Address: Letterkenny Army Depot, Attn: Travel Camp (SIOLE-RMC), 640 Pennsylvania Avenue, Chambersburg, PA 17201-4150. **C-717-267-9494, D-312-570-9494.** Senior discount available (62 and over). Check in at travel camp, located along Pennsylvania Avenue, 0800-1300 hours, check out 1300 hours.

**Camper Spaces:** Concrete (8), handicap accessible, E (110V/30A)/W hookups. Rates: $12 daily. Gravel (12), handicap accessible, E (110V/15A)/W hookups. Rates: $7.

**Tent Spaces:** Grass (4), no hookups. Rates: $6 daily.

# RHODE ISLAND

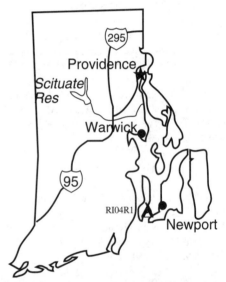

## CARR POINT RECREATION AREA(RI04R1)

Newport Naval Education and Training Center
Newport, RI 02841-5000

**TELEPHONE NUMBER INFORMATION:** Main installation number: C-401-841-3456. Police for recreation area, C-401-841-3241.

**LOCATION:** Off base. From North and East, at the junction of Routes 24 and 114, take Route 114 S for 1.7 miles to Stringham Road. From South and West, take Route 95 to Route 138 E, to Route 114 N. Follow Route 114 for 4.7 miles to Stringham Road. Follow Stringham for 2.3 miles to the turn into the facility. Clearly marked. NMC: Providence, 30 miles northwest.

**DESCRIPTION OF AREA:** Located on Naragansett Bay. Summer resort area. Home of the Newport Jazz Festival, Ben & Jerry's Folk Festival, International boat shows and famous Newport mansions. Great public beaches and seafood restaurants nearby. Limited support facilities available on base.

**SEASON OF OPERATION:** Memorial Day weekend-30 Sep.

*Carr Point Recreation Area, continued*

**ELIGIBILITY:** Active/Reservists/Retired/DoD civilians.

**RESERVATIONS:** Reservations accepted from 15 Apr-30 Sep. Address: MWR Ticket Connection, 656 Whipple Street, Newport, RI 02841-5000. **C-401-841-7917** 0830-1700 hours. Fax: C-401-841-4500.

**Camper Spaces:** Gravel (6), E (120/240V/50A)/W hookups. Rates: $12 daily/$75 weekly.

**Tent Spaces:** Gravel (5), no hookups. Rates: $5 daily.

**SUPPORT FACILITIES:**

Beach            Grills            Picnic Area
Playground

*No restroom facilities at park. Restroom/shower facilities located on base (Gym 109). Private pump station located nearby.

**ACTIVITIES:**
Swimming

**CREDIT CARDS ACCEPTED:** Visa and MasterCard.

**RESTRICTIONS:** Two week maximum visit, campers may return after one week.

# SOUTH CAROLINA

## SHADY OAKS FAMILY CAMPGROUND (SC12R1)
Charleston Air Force Base
Charleston AFB, SC 29404-4924

**TELEPHONE NUMBER INFORMATION:** Main installation numbers: C-843-566-6000, D-312-673-2100.

**LOCATION:** On base. From I-26 exit east to West Aviation Avenue, continue to second traffic light, right on Perimeter Road around runway through gate to Outdoor Recreation Center located behind picnic grounds. *USMRA: page 44 (H-8)*. NMC: Charleston, 5 miles southeast.

**DESCRIPTION OF AREA:** Situated near wooded picnic area in one of the country's most picturesque and historic seaport cities. Full range of support facilities available on base.

**SEASON OF OPERATION:** Year round.

**ELIGIBILITY:** Active/Reservists/Retired/DoD civilians.

**RESERVATIONS:** No advance reservations. Address: Outdoor Recreation Center, 437 SVS/SVRO, Bldg. 647, Charleston AFB, SC 29404-5000. **C-843-566-5271/5270, D-312-673-5271** 0900-1700 hours.

**Camper Spaces:** Hardstand (17), handicap accessible, E (110V/20/30A)/W hookups. Grass (6), handicap accessible, E (110V/20/30A)/W hookups. Rates: $10 daily.

**Tent Spaces:** Grass (6), E (110V/20/30A) hookup. Rates: $6 daily.

**SUPPORT FACILITIES:**

| | | |
|---|---|---|
| Auto Craft Shop | Bath House | Beach |
| Boat Rental/Storage | Chapel | Commissary |
| Equipment Rental | Exchange | Fitness Center |
| Golf | Grills | Laundry |
| Nature Trails | Pavilions | Picnic Area |
| Playground | Rec Equipment | Restrooms* |
| Sewage Dump | Shoppette | Showers |
| Sports Fields | Telephones | Tennis Courts |

* Handicap accessible.

**ACTIVITIES:**

Fishing            Historic Tours            Swimming

**CREDIT CARDS ACCEPTED:** Visa and MasterCard.

**RESTRICTIONS:** Pets allowed on leash. FAMCAMP parking is not authorized for Space-A travelers.

## SHORT STAY NAVY OUTDOOR RECREATION AREA (SC02R1)
Charleston Naval Weapons Station
Goose Creek, SC 29445-5000

**TELEPHONE NUMBER INFORMATION:** Main installation numbers: 1-800-447-2178, C-843-761-8353, 843-743-1366.

**LOCATION:** Off base. On Lake Moultrie five miles north of Moncks Corner. Take US-52 north from Charleston. Follow the signs. *USMRA: page 44 (H-8)*. NMI: Charleston Naval Weapons Station, 25 miles southeast. NMC: Charleston, 40 miles southeast.

**DESCRIPTION OF AREA:** Situated on a 55-acre peninsula at southern tip of Lake Moultrie. Excellent freshwater fishing. Family programs and activities during summer months. Full range of support facilities at Charleston Naval Weapons Station.

**SEASON OF OPERATION:** Year round.

**ELIGIBILITY:** Active/Reservists/Retired/DoD civilians.

**RESERVATIONS:** Accepted. Address: Short Stay, Navy Outdoor Recreation Area, 211 Short Stay Road, Moncks Corner, SC 29461-5000. **C-1-800-447-2178, C-843-761-8353.** Fax: C-843-761-4792. E-mail: jtully@ awod.com. HP: http://www.shortstay.com. Check in 1500 hours, check out 1100 hours.

**SOUTH CAROLINA**
*Short Stay Navy Outdoor Recreation Area, continued*

**Villas:** Three-bedroom (12), sleeps six, furnished, private bath, full kitchen, CATV. Patrons must provide soap and toiletries. Rates: $51-$62 daily (depending on rank and season, weekly and monthly rates). Two-bedroom (24-2 handicap accessible), sleeps four, furnished, private bath, full kitchen, CATV. Patrons must provide soap and toiletries. Rates: $40-$50 daily (depending on rank, weekly and monthly rates).

**Cabins:** Two-bedroom (6-1 handicap accessible), sleeps four, furnished, private bath, full kitchen, CATV. Patrons must provide soap and toiletries. Rates: $55-$66 daily (depending on rank, weekly and monthly rates).

**Log Cabins:** 5, sleeps two, A/C, heated, picnic table, grill. Rates: $18-$22 daily (depending on rank, weekly and monthly rates).

**RV/Camper Spaces:** Waterfront (13), E (110V/30A)/W hookups. Rates: $9-$15 daily (depending on rank, weekly and monthly rates).

**Camper Spaces:** Wooded (70), E (110V/30A)/W hookups. Rates: $5-$12 daily (depending on rank, weekly and monthly rates).

**Camper/Tent Spaces:** Primitive (25), no hookups. Rates: $2.50-$9 daily (depending on rank, weekly and monthly rates).

**SUPPORT FACILITIES:**

| | | |
|---|---|---|
| Bath House | Beach | Boat Launch |
| Boat Rental/Storage | Conference Center* | Convenience Store |
| Fishing License Sales | Fire Rings | Fishing Pier |
| Gas | Golf | Grills |
| Ice | Laundry | Pavilions** |

| | | |
|---|---|---|
| Picnic Areas | Playground | Rec Equipment |
| Restrooms | Sewage Dump | Showers |
| Snack Bar | Trails | |

\* Conference Room (1), seats 200.
\*\* Pavilions (4), seats 200-375.

**ACTIVITIES:**

| | | |
|---|---|---|
| Boating | Fishing/license | Swimming |

**CREDIT CARDS ACCEPTED:** Visa, MasterCard and American Express.

**RESTRICTIONS:** No pets allowed in villas or cabins, allowed on leash in campground. Admission fee for day users.

## WATEREE RECREATION AREA (SC05R1)
Shaw Air Force Base
Shaw AFB, SC 29152-5023

**TELEPHONE NUMBER INFORMATION:** Main installation numbers: C-803-668-8110, D-312-965-1110.

**LOCATION:** Off base. Off Highway 97. *USMRA: page 44 (G-5).* NMI: Shaw AFB, 39 miles east. NMC: Columbia, 35 miles southwest.

**DESCRIPTION OF AREA:** Situated in peaceful, quiet, 24-acre, wooded area bordering Lake Wateree. Full range of support facilities available at Shaw AFB and Fort Jackson.

**SEASON OF OPERATION:** Year round.

*Wateree Recreation Area, continued*

**ELIGIBILITY:** Active/Reservists/Retired/DoD civilians.

**RESERVATIONS:** For cabins, available up to 60 days in advance for active duty stationed at Shaw AFB. Reservation must be made in person. All others, up to 45 days in advance and by phone. Address: Outdoor Recreation, P.O. Box 52696, Shaw AFB, SC 29152-5000. **C-803-895-2204, D-312-965-3245.** Wateree Recreation Area phone number is C-803-432-7976. Check in at Shaw AFB Outdoor Recreation 0800-1800 hours Sun-Thu, 0800-1900 hours Sat-Sun and holidays. *Note: A $0.440 million Cabins and Facilities project has been approved in the Fiscal Year 1998 MWR Major and Minor Construction Program.*

**Cabins:** Three-bedroom (2), handicap accessible, fully equipped, microwave, pots/pans, dishes, TV/VCR, linens. Rates: $85 daily. Two-bedroom (3), handicap accessible, fully equipped, microwave, pots/pans, dishes, TV/VCR, linens. Rates: $65 daily. Two-bedroom (8), handicap accessible, fully equipped, microwave, pots/pans, dishes, TV/VCR, linens. Rates: $60.

**Camper Spaces:** 15, E (110V/30A)/W hookups. Rates: $10 daily.

**Tent Spaces:** Almost unlimited, no hookups. Rates: $5 daily.

**SUPPORT FACILITIES:**

| | | |
|---|---|---|
| Bait/Retail | Bath House | Boat Launch |
| Boat Rental | Boat Storage | Boat Tie-up Docks |
| Check-out Store | Grills | Ice |
| Fishing | Marina | Pavilions |
| Picnic Area | Playground | Pontoon Boat/Rental |
| Rec Room (New) | Restrooms | Sewage Dump |
| Showers | Ski Rental | Water Sports |
| | | Equipment Rental |

**ACTIVITIES:**

| | | |
|---|---|---|
| Fishing/license | Swimming | Water Skiing |

**CREDIT CARDS ACCEPTED:** Visa and MasterCard.

**RESTRICTIONS:** No pets allowed in cabins or on decks. Pets allowed on leash in camping area. Firearms allowed only during hunting season with notification of Site Manager at area. Site office closed 2200-0600 hours. Roped-off swimming area with sandy beach.

# WESTON LAKE RECREATION AREA AND TRAVEL CAMP (SC03R1)
Fort Jackson
Fort Jackson, SC 29207-5000

**TELEPHONE NUMBER INFORMATION:** Main installation numbers: C-803-751-7511, D-312-734-1110. Police for recreation area, C-751-3115.

**LOCATION:** On post. From I-20 north of Fort take exit 80 onto Clemson Road, left on Percival Road (SC-12), then right onto Wilcat Road, drive seven miles across Fort Jackson, then left on Leesburg Road (SC-262) 2.5 miles to Weston Lake Recreation Area on the left. Leesburg Road (SC-262) is also accessible from US-76/378 south of post *AND* from US-601 east of post. Fort Jackson is located 12 miles east of Columbia on SC-262 (Leesburg Road). Travel camp is 4.5 miles east of main post on SC-262. *USMRA: page 44 (G-6).* NMC: Columbia, 12 miles southwest.

**DESCRIPTION OF AREA:** Located adjacent to 240-acre lake with lots of wildlife to watch, from deer to black squirrels. Site offers wide range of outdoor activities. Museum and Ernie Pyle Media Center located on post.

Columbia, the state capital, offers varied sightseeing, including zoo, Capitol and Coliseum. Full range of support facilities available on post.

**SEASON OF OPERATION:** Year round.

**ELIGIBILITY:** Active/Reservists/Retired/DoD civilians.

**RESERVATIONS:** Accepted for cabins and duplex up to one year in advance. Not accepted for travel camp. Address: Weston Lake Recreation Area, Recreation Division, Fort Jackson, SC 29207-5000. **C-803-751-LAKE, D-312-734-LAKE.** Check in at Bldg M-2644, by 1630/1730 hours (depending on season), check out 1200 hours.

**Cabins:** Four-bedroom (1). Rates: $50 daily Mon-Thu/$53 Fri-Sun. Three-bedroom (2), furnished, private bath, kitchen, microwave, stove, pots/pans, dishes, TV, linens (fee). Rates: $45 daily Mon-Thu/$48 Fri-Sun. Two-bedroom (2), furnished, private bath, kitchen, microwave, stove, pots/pans, dishes, TV, linens (fee). Rates: $35 daily Mon-Thu/$38 Fri-Sun. Lakefront cabins come with use of rowboat.

**Log Cabin:** Two-bedroom (1). Rates: $45 daily Mon-Thu/$48 Fri-Sun.

**Duplex:** One-bedroom (2), furnished, private bath, kitchen, microwave, stove, pots/pans, dishes, TV, linens (fee). Rates: $30 daily Mon-Thu/$33 Fri-Sun.

**Kamping Kabins:** 2. Rates: $15 daily Mon-Thu/$18 Fri-Sun.

**Camper Spaces:** Hardstand (13), E (110V/30A)/S/W hookups. Rates: $11 daily. Hardstand (5), E (110V/30A)/W hookups. Rates: $9 daily.

**Tent Spaces:** 10, E (110V/30A)/W hookups. Rates: $5 daily.

**SUPPORT FACILITIES:**

| | | |
|---|---|---|
| Beach | Boat Launch | Boat Rental |
| Golf | Grills | Marina |
| Nature Trail | Picnic Area* | Playground |
| Pontoon Boat | Rec Equipment | Restrooms |
| Sewage Dump | Showers | Sports Fields |
| Swing/wheelchair | Trails | |

Group Meeting Facilities available.

* Handicap accessible.

**ACTIVITIES:**

| | | |
|---|---|---|
| Boating | Fishing | Hunting |
| Jet Ski | Swimming | |

**CREDIT CARDS ACCEPTED:** None.

**RESTRICTIONS:** No pets allowed in cabins or recreation area, allowed on leash in travel camp. No firearms allowed except unloaded hunting weapons. Hunting and fishing require state and post permits. Nominal fee charged for use of recreation area, campers/lodgers exempt when registered in camping/lodging facilities. Call or write for operation hours, maps and information. Staffing is restricted Nov-Mar.

*SOUTH DAKOTA/TENNESSEE*

# SOUTH DAKOTA

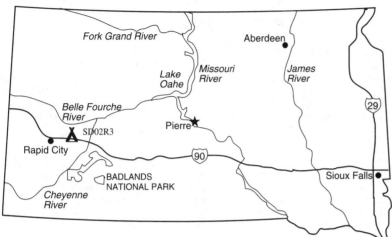

### ELLSWORTH AFB FAMCAMP (SD02R3)

Ellsworth Air Force Base
Ellsworth AFB, SD 57706-4808

**TELEPHONE NUMBER INFORMATION:** Main installation numbers: C-605-385-1000, D-312-675-1110. Police for FAMCAMP, C-605-385-4001.

**LOCATION:** On base. I-90 exit 66, north to Liberty gate (main gate), ten miles east of Rapid City. FAMCAMP first right after gate. *USMRA: page 85 (B-5)*. NMC: Rapid City, 10 miles west.

**DESCRIPTION OF AREA:** Located in the southwest corner of SD. Black Hills National Forest, Mount Rushmore National Memorial, Crazy Horse Memorial and Badlands National Park are a short distance away. Full range of support facilities available on base.

**SEASON OF OPERATION:** 15 May-15 Oct, full hookups available.

**ELIGIBILITY:** Active/Reservists/Retired/DoD and NAF civilians.

**RESERVATIONS:** Reservations accepted for PCS and TDY with copy of orders, others first come first serve. Address: Outdoor Recreation, 2750 George Drive, Ellsworth AFB, SD 57706-4910. **C-605-385-2997, D-312-675-2997.** Fax: C-605-385-4327, D-312-675-4327. HP: http://www.ellsworth.af.mil. Check in at FAMCAMP.

**Camper Spaces:** Hardstand (24), E (110V/30/20A)/S/W hookups. Rates: $19 daily. Hardstand (12), E (110V/30/20A) hookup. Rates: $10 daily.

**Tent Spaces:** Open (12), no hookups. Rates: $8 daily.

**SUPPORT FACILITIES:**

| | |
|---|---|
| Auto Craft Shop | Bath House |
| Bowling Center | Chapel |
| Commissary | Exchange |
| Fitness Center | Gas |
| Golf | Grills |
| Laundry | Pavilion |
| Playgrounds | Pools |
| Rec Equipment | Restrooms |
| Sewage Dump | Shoppette |
| Showers | Sports Fields |
| Telephones | Tennis Courts |

**ACTIVITIES:**

| | |
|---|---|
| Bicycling | Fishing/license |
| Hiking | Hunting/license |
| Sightseeing | Snow Skiing |
| Swimming | |

**CREDIT CARDS ACCEPTED:** Visa and MasterCard.

**RESTRICTIONS:** Pets allowed on leash. Firearms must be checked in with Security Police. No open fires. Fifteen day limit.

# TENNESSEE

*See map below.*

### ARNOLD FAMCAMP (TN03R2)

Arnold Air Force Base
Arnold AFB, TN 37389-5000

**TELEPHONE NUMBER INFORMATION:** Main installation numbers: C-931-454-3000, D-312-340-5011/3000. Security Police for FAMCAMP, C-931-454-5662, D-312-340-5662.

**LOCATION:** On base. From I-24 take exit 117 W toward Tullahoma. Follow signs to recreation areas and FAMCAMP. At Gate 2 turn left onto Pump Station Road. Go to end, turn right, go through three-way stop. FAMCAMP is approximately one mile on left. *USMRA: page 41 (I-9).* NMC: Chattanooga, 60 miles southeast, Nashville, 60 miles northwest.

**DESCRIPTION OF AREA:** Terrain is flat and rolling hills. Area offers a 400-acre lake and a variety of recreational and historical sites within a 70-mile radius of the base including Tim's Ford State Park, Old Stone Fort State Park, Tennessee Aquarium, Jack Daniel's Distillery in Lynchburg and George Dickle Distillery in Tullahoma. Limited support facilities available on base.

**SEASON OF OPERATION:** Year round.

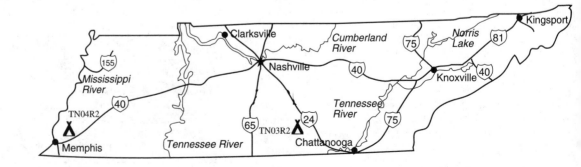

*Arnold FAMCAMP, continued*

**ELIGIBILITY:** Active/Reservists/Retired/DoD Contract personnel/ Arnold AFB civilians.

**RESERVATIONS:** Accepted 45 days in advance for active duty, all others 30 days in advance. Security deposit required within 72 hours of phone reservation. Address: 656 SPTS/SVB (FAMCAMP), Community Center, 100 Kindel Drive, Suite C319, Arnold AFB, TN 37389-5000. **C-931-454-4520/6084, D-312-340-4520/6084.** Fax: C-931-454-4095, D-312-340-4095. E-mail: famcamp@hap.arnold.af.mil.

**Camper Spaces:** Gravel (32), up to 30' (limited sites over 30'), handicap accessible, E (110V/30A)/W hookups. Rates: $12 daily/$270 monthly (Apr-Sep)/$125 monthly (Oct-Mar).

**Tent Spaces:** Primitive, 6, no hookups. Rates: $6 daily.

**SUPPORT FACILITIES:**

| | | |
|---|---|---|
| Auto Craft Shop | Bath House | Beach |
| Boat Launch | Boat Rental | Commissary |
| Convenience Store | Exchange | Fire Rings |
| Fishing Pier | Fitness Center | Gas |
| Golf/9 holes | Grills | Ice |
| Marina | Pavilion | Picnic Areas |
| Playground | Rec Center | Rec Equipment |
| Restrooms | Sewage Dump | Showers |
| Snack Bar | Sports Fields | Tennis Courts |
| Trails | | |

**ACTIVITIES:**

| | | |
|---|---|---|
| Boating | Fishing/license | Hunting/license |
| Softball | Swimming | Water Skiing |

**CREDIT CARDS ACCEPTED:** None.

**RESTRICTIONS:** Pets allowed on leash. No firearms.

# NAVY LAKE RECREATION AREA (TN04R2)

Memphis Naval Support Activity
Millington, TN 38054-5045

**TELEPHONE NUMBER INFORMATION:** Main installation numbers: C-901-874-5111, D-312-882-5111.

**LOCATION:** On base. From US-51 in Millington exit to Navy Road, east approximately five miles to first gate on left. Take a right on Attu (first road inside gate) until you reach the Lakehouse. Also accessible from TN-14, I-40 and I-240. *USMRA: page 40 (B-9,10).* NMC: Memphis, 20 miles southwest.

**DESCRIPTION OF AREA:** Recreation area has two lakes and 14 picnic areas with cabanas and BBQ facilities. Lakes are stocked with bass, bream, catfish and crappie. Full range of support facilities on base.

**SEASON OF OPERATION:** Year round, tent camping best 1 Apr-1 Nov.

**ELIGIBILITY:** Active/Reservists/Retired/DoD civilians.

**RESERVATIONS:** No advance reservations. Address: MWR Department, Memphis NAS, P.O. Box 54278, NSA Mid-South, Millington, TN 38054-0278. **C-1-800-779-4252, C-901-874-5163, D-312-882-5163.** Fax: 901-874-5690, D-312-882-5690. Recreation Area, C-901-872-3660. E-mail: mwrmemphis@bigriver.net. HP: http://www.mwrmemphis.com.

**Camper Spaces:** Paved (12), E (110/220V/30A)/S/W hookups. Rates: $10-$14 daily with full hookup, $5-$10 daily without full hookup.

**Tent Spaces:** Overflow/Gravel, no hookups. Rates: $3-$7 daily.

**SUPPORT FACILITIES:**

| | | |
|---|---|---|
| Boat Rental | Camping Equipment | Ice |
| Golf | Grills | Laundry |
| Picnic Areas | Playgrounds | Rec Equipment |
| Restrooms | Sewage Dump* | Showers |
| Softball Fields | Stables** | Vending Machine |

* At Rec area and at car wash on base.
** NAS riding stables by lake area, horses and stalls to rent. Boarding of privately owned horses available (Current year coggins and health required). Call for fee information.

**ACTIVITIES:**

| | | |
|---|---|---|
| Boating | Canoeing | Fishing |
| Horseback Riding | Softball | Volleyball |

**CREDIT CARDS ACCEPTED:** Visa, MasterCard and American Express.

**RESTRICTIONS:** Pets allowed on leash. Firearms must be checked in at Security, they are not allowed in the recreation area.

# TEXAS

*See map on following page.*

## BELTON LAKE OUTDOOR RECREATION AREA (TX07R3)

Fort Hood
Fort Hood, TX 76544-5056

**TELEPHONE NUMBER INFORMATION:** Main installation numbers: C-254-287/288-1110, D-312-737/738-1110. Police for recreation area, C-254-287-8303.

**LOCATION:** On post. From north, take I-35, bear right after Belton area to Highway 190 W, exit on Loop 121 N. From south on I-35, exit to Loop 121 or take Exit 293A to Highway 190 W and exit to Loop 121. From Fort Hood area, take Martin Drive N and exit to N Nolan Road, turn left at BLORA entrance. *USMRA: page 87 (K-4).* NMC: Austin, 60 miles south.

**DESCRIPTION OF AREA:** Primarily range country, consisting of 2,032 acres bordering Belton Lake. Recreational opportunities include hiking in nearby wooded areas and a wide variety of water sports. Belton Lake is known for black and white bass and crappie. Full range of support facilities available on post.

**SEASON OF OPERATION:** Year round.

**ELIGIBILITY:** Active/Reservists/Retired/DoD civilians currently employed.

**RESERVATIONS:** Required for cottages, accepted 180 days in advance; no advance reservations for RV or camping spaces. Deposit for half of total reservation fee required. Address: Business Operations Division, AFZF-CA-BOD-OR-BLORA, Fort Hood, TX 76544-5056. **C-254-287-2523/8308, D-312-737-2523** 24 hours daily. Fax: C-254-287-3722. Check in after 1500 hours, check out 1200 hours.

**Cottages:** One-bedroom (10), handicap accessible, sleeps four, furnished, A/C, TV. Patrons must provide toiletries. Rates: $35 daily.

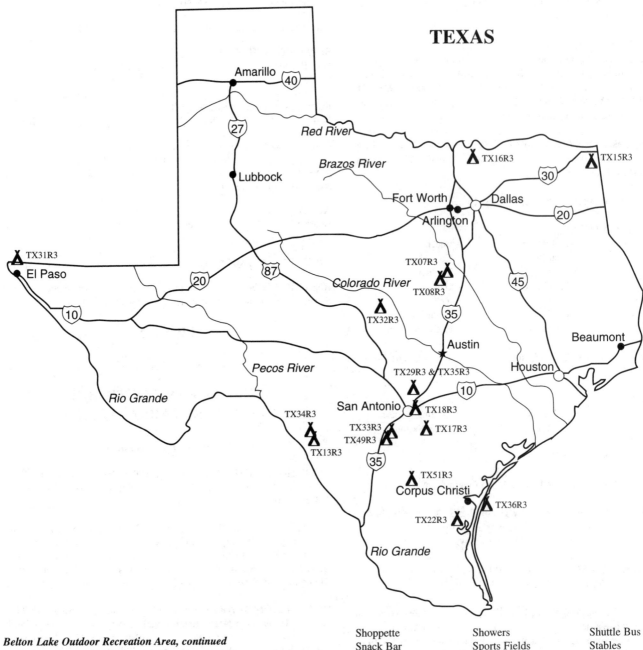

**TEXAS**

*(Map of Texas showing cities including Amarillo, Lubbock, Fort Worth, Dallas, Arlington, El Paso, Austin, Beaumont, Houston, San Antonio, Corpus Christi, and rivers Red River, Brazos River, Colorado River, Pecos River, Rio Grande. Camping facility locations marked: TX16R3, TX15R3, TX31R3, TX07R3, TX08R3, TX32R3, TX29R3 & TX35R3, TX34R3, TX18R3, TX33R3, TX49R3, TX17R3, TX13R3, TX51R3, TX36R3, TX22R3. Highways: 40, 27, 30, 20, 45, 87, 35, 10.)*

---

*Belton Lake Outdoor Recreation Area, continued*

**Camper Spaces:** Asphalt (11), E (110V/30A)/S/W hookups. Rates: $15 daily. Concrete (22), E (110V/30A)/W hookups. Rates: $12 daily. Gravel (31), E (30A)/W hookups. Rates: $12 daily.

**Tent Spaces:** Primitive, unlimited, no hookups. Rates: $3 daily.

**SUPPORT FACILITIES:**

| | | |
|---|---|---|
| Auto Craft Shop | Bait Store | Bath House |
| Beach | Boat Launch | Boat Rental/Storage |
| Chapel | Commissary | Convenience Store |
| Exchange | Fire Rings | Fishing Pier |
| Fitness Center | Gas | Golf |
| Grills | Ice | Laundry |
| Marina | Pavilions | Picnic Areas |
| Playground | Pool | Rec Center |
| Rec Equipment | Restrooms | Sewage Dump |

| | | |
|---|---|---|
| Shoppette | Showers | Shuttle Bus |
| Snack Bar | Sports Fields | Stables |
| Telephones | Tennis Courts | Trails |
| Water Sports Equipment Rental | | |

**ACTIVITIES:**

| | | |
|---|---|---|
| Bicycling | Fishing/license | Horseback Riding |
| Jet Skiing | Jogging | Paddleboat Rides |
| Swimming | Water Skiing | Waterslides |

**CREDIT CARDS ACCEPTED:** Visa, MasterCard, American Express and Esprit.

**RESTRICTIONS:** Pets must be on leash at all times, not allowed in cottages, owner must clean up after pets, owner will be assessed charges for any damage incurred by pets. No firearms. No hunting in park. Swimming only at Sierra Beach while lifeguards are on duty. Nominal user fee for use of park (annual pass available). Fort Hood boating license required to rent boat with motor (tests on Wed-Sun 0600-2030 hours).

## BROOKS FAMCAMP (TX17R3)

Brooks Air Force Base
Brooks AFB, TX 78235-5120

**TELEPHONE NUMBER INFORMATION:** Main installation numbers: C-210-536-1110, D-312-240-1110.

**LOCATION:** On base. From Loop 410 take I 37 N and exit Brooks AFB/S.E. Military Drive. Left at second traffic light to main entrance of base. *USMRA: page 87 (J-6) and 91 (C-4).* NMI: Fort Sam Houston, 10 miles north. NMC: San Antonio, 5 miles northwest.

**DESCRIPTION OF AREA:** Fifteen hard-surface pads have been set up in a peaceful and quiet part of the base. Site of the 1995 S*M*A*R*T National Muster. Full range of support facilities.

**SEASON OF OPERATION:** Year round.

**ELIGIBILITY:** Active/Reservists/Retired/DoD civilians.

**RESERVATIONS:** No advance reservations. Address for space availability: 70 ABG/SVML, Attn: Lodging Office, 2804 5th Street, Brooks AFB, TX 78235-5143. **C-210-536-1844, D-312-240-1844,** 24 hours daily. Check in Bldg 214, Base Lodging Office, for information on pad availability. Address for other information: 70 ABG/SVRO, Attn: Outdoor Recreation, 2804 5th Street, Brooks AFB, TX 78235-5143. C-210-536-2881, D-312-240-2881.

**Camper Spaces:** Hardstand (7), E (110V/20/30A)/S/W hookups. Rates: $10 daily. Hardstand (8), E (110V/20/30A)/W hookups. Rates: $8 daily.

**Tent Spaces:** Open, no hookups. Rates: $3 daily.

**Camper/Tent Spaces:** Overflow, no hookups. Rates: $3 daily.

**SUPPORT FACILITIES:**

| | | |
|---|---|---|
| Grills | Laundry | Picnic Area |
| Playground | Restrooms | Sewage Dump |
| Showers | | |

**ACTIVITIES:**
San Antonio's attractions (i.e., the Alamo, Missions, Riverwalk, Sea World, etc.). Two nearby lakes offer excellent fishing and boating.

**CREDIT CARDS ACCEPTED:** None.

**RESTRICTIONS:** Pets allowed on leash. Firearm owners must inform security police after arriving on base.

## ELLIOTT LAKE
## RECREATION AREA (TX15R3)

Red River Army Depot
Texarkana, TX 75507-5000
*Scheduled for realignment by 1999.*

**TELEPHONE NUMBER INFORMATION:** Main installation numbers: C-903-334-2141, D-312-829-4110. Police for recreation area, C-903-334-2911.

**LOCATION:** On post. Red River is west of Texarkana, south of I-30 on US-82. Take Red River Army Depot exit to main gate. Follow signs from main post to lake area. *USMRA: page 87 (N-2).* NMC: Texarkana, 18 miles east.

**DESCRIPTION OF AREA:** Located in a wooded area on 183-acre Elliott Lake in northeast corner of state. Excellent for overnight camping,

vacationing, sightseeing and trips into scenic Arkansas mountains. Recreation area is a 210-acre reserve. Wide range of support facilities available on post.

**SEASON OF OPERATION:** Year round.

**ELIGIBILITY:** Active/Reservists/Retired/DoD civilians.

**RESERVATIONS:** Required for cabins and shelters. Address: Community Recreation Branch, Bldg 15, Attn: SDSRR-U, Red River Army Depot, Texarkana, TX 75507-5000. **C-903-334-2254, D-312-829-2254.** Fax: C-903-334-3290. Check in at Elliott Lake Country Store, 1300 hours for cabins. Check out 1200 hours.

**Cabins:** Two-bedroom (16), some handicap accessible, furnished, private bath, kitchen, microwave, coffee maker, TV. Patrons must provide cookware and linens. Rates: $30 daily + $25 refundable deposit.

**Camper Spaces:** Asphalt (16), E (110V/30A)/S/W hookups. Rates: $10 daily/$50 weekly. Gravel (16), E (110V/30A)/W hookups. Rates: $7 daily/$35 weekly.

**Shelters:** Gravel (2), E/W hookups. Rates: $10 daily. Gravel (3), E hookup. Rates: $6 daily.

**Tent Spaces:** Gravel (20), no hookups. Rates: $2 daily.

**SUPPORT FACILITIES:**

| | | |
|---|---|---|
| Bait | Beach | Boat Launch |
| Boat Rental | Canoes | Country Store |
| Laundry | Marina | Picnic Areas |
| Playground | Rec Equipment | Restrooms |
| Sewage Dump | Showers* | |

* Handicap accessible.

**ACTIVITIES:**

| | | |
|---|---|---|
| Archery | Boating | Fishing/license |
| Hiking | Hunting/license | Swimming |

**CREDIT CARDS ACCEPTED:** Visa, MasterCard and American Express.

**RESTRICTIONS:** No pets allowed in cabins, can be kept outside on leash. No firearms. Recreation permit required for all patrons. No lifeguards, swim at your own risk. ATVs restricted.

## ESCONDIDO RANCH (TX51R3)

Kingsville Naval Air Station
Kingsville NAS, TX 78363-5110

**TELEPHONE NUMBER INFORMATION:** Main installation numbers: C-512-516-6136, D-312-861-6136.

**LOCATION:** Off base. Located 23 miles northwest of Freer. *USMRA: page 87 (J-8).* NMI: Kingsville NAS, 90 miles southeast. NMC: Corpus Christi, 80 miles east.

**DESCRIPTION OF AREA:** Located on a hunting ranch in a remote desert area. Check supplies before coming into area, as no support facilities are available.

**SEASON OF OPERATION:** Year round.

**ELIGIBILITY:** Active/Reservists/Retired/DoD civilians.

*TEXAS*
*Escondido Ranch, continued*

**RESERVATIONS:** Escondido Ranch, Attn: Reservations, P.O. Box 1810, Freer, TX 78357-1810. **C-830-373-4419.** Fax: C-830-373-4421. Payment

must be received no later than five working days after reservation is made or it will be canceled. Make checks payable to MWR.

**Cottages:** 1, two double beds, three sets of bunk beds, bathroom, kitchen, porch. Rates: $50 daily.

**Lodge:** Room (17), sleeps four, furnished, double bed, sofabed or double bed, bunk beds. Patrons must provide linens. Rates: $25 daily. Bunk bed in a shared room (sleeps six). Rates: $10 daily.

**Camper Spaces:** 12, E (220V/50A)/S/W hookups. Rates: $10 daily.

**Tent Spaces:** Unlimited, no hookups. Near pond on open space. Rates: $4 daily.

**SUPPORT FACILITIES:**
The lodge is adjacent to a cook house with four BBQ pits, electric stove and electric grill. The lodge also has a huge lounge with tables, TV/VCR, sofas, pool table, electronic darts, and microwave.

**ACTIVITIES:**

| | | |
|---|---|---|
| Archery | Bird watching | Fishing |
| Hiking | Snake Hunting | Wildlife Photography |

**CREDIT CARDS ACCEPTED:** Visa, MasterCard and American Express.

## FORT BLISS RV PARK (TX31R3)
Fort Bliss
Fort Bliss, TX 79916-6816

**TELEPHONE NUMBER INFORMATION:** Main installation numbers: C-915-568-2121, D-312-978-0831. Police for campground, C-915-568-2115.

**LOCATION:** On post. From I-10 take US-54 E to exit 5, left on Ellerthorpe to Gerlich, left into campground. *USMRA: page 86 (B,C-5,6).* NMC: El Paso, adjacent.

**DESCRIPTION OF AREA:** In west Texas near Rio Grande River. Carlsbad Caverns National Park, easy drive west. White Sands National Monument, is a two-hour drive north. Ciudad Juarez, Mexico's largest border city, is a short distance across Rio Grande River. Three museums on post. Full range of support facilities available on post.

**SEASON OF OPERATION:** Year round.

**ELIGIBILITY:** Active/Reservists/Retired/DoD civilians at Fort Bliss.

**RESERVATIONS:** No advance reservations. Address: Fort Bliss RV Park, Bldg 4130, Fort Bliss, TX 79916-5000. **C-915-568-4693, D-312-978-4693/0106.** Fax: C-915-568-2028, D-312-978-2028. Discount to holders of Golden Age and Golden Access Passports. Check in at office, check out 1300 hours

**Camper Spaces:** Hardstand (73), pull through, handicap accessible, E (220V/20/30/50A)/S/W hookups. Rates: $13 daily/$78 weekly.

**Tent Spaces:** Grass (8), no hookups. Rates: $5 daily.

## SUPPORT FACILITIES:

| | | |
|---|---|---|
| Auto Craft Shop | Bath House | Bowling |
| Chapel | Clubs | Commissary |
| Convenience Store | Exchange | Fire Rings |
| Fitness Center | Gas | Golf |
| Grills | Ice | Laundry |
| Marina | Miniature Golf | Pavilion |
| Picnic Area | Playground | Pool |
| Rec Center | Rec Equipment | Restrooms |
| RV Storage | Sewage Dump | Showers |
| Snack Bar | Sports Fields | Stables |
| Telephones | Tennis Courts | Theater |
| Trails | | |

## ACTIVITIES:

| | | |
|---|---|---|
| Bowling | Golf | Horseback Riding |
| Swimming | Tennis | |

**CREDIT CARDS ACCEPTED:** Visa and MasterCard.

**RESTRICTIONS:** Pets allowed on leash only, owner must clean up after pets, pets must be walked in designated area. No open fires. Fourteen day limit, may be extended if space is available on scheduled date of departure.

# FORT SAM HOUSTON CAMPGROUND (TX18R3)

Fort Sam Houston
Fort Sam Houston, TX 78234-5020

**TELEPHONE NUMBER INFORMATION:** Main installation numbers: C-201-221-1110, D-312-471-1110.

**LOCATION:** On post. Take the Fort Sam Houston exit from I-35 N or S in San Antonio. *USMRA: page 91 (C,D-2,3).* NMC: San Antonio, northeast section of the city.

**DESCRIPTION OF AREA:** Surrounded by San Antonio, this historic post has seen much colorful military history, from its namesake to the "Rough Riders" and Teddy Roosevelt, and key roles in WWI and WWII. Full range of support facilities available on post.

**SEASON OF OPERATION:** Year round.

**ELIGIBILITY:** Active/Reservists/Retired.

**RESERVATIONS:** Not accepted. Address: Fort Sam Houston Camping, Attn: MWR, Outdoor Equipment Center, P.O. Box 8297, San Antonio, TX 78215-0297. **C-210-221-5224.**

**Camper Spaces:** Hardstand (6), E (110V/20/30A)/W hookups. Rates: $6 daily.

*Note: This facility is scheduled to close upon completion of a new 52-space campground in December 1998. Keep up to date with* **Military Living's R&R Space-Report®.**

# FORT SAM HOUSTON RECREATION AREA AT CANYON LAKE (TX29R3)

Fort Sam Houston
Fort Sam Houston, TX 78234-5020

**TELEPHONE NUMBER INFORMATION:** Main installation numbers: C-210-221-1110/1211, D-312-471-1110/1211. Police for Recreation Area, C-830-964-3318.

**LOCATION:** Off post. Take I-35 to Canyon Lake exit 191. Turn west onto FM 306, and drive approximately 16 miles to Canyon City. Continue another 1.5 miles past the blinking light in Canyon City to Jacob Creek Park Road. Turn left, and the recreation area will be on the right. *USMRA: page 87 (J-6).* NMI: Randolph AFB, 35 miles south. NMC: San Antonio, 48 miles south.

**DESCRIPTION OF AREA:** Nestled in the scenic hill country between San Antonio and Austin, Canyon Lake's 80 miles of shoreline shimmer with a singular beauty found only in central Texas. Mild winter temperatures make this natural haven a year-round attraction for fishing, camping, boating and picnicking. The Fort Sam Houston Recreation Area includes 300 feet of well-maintained sandy beach and .25 acres marina. Full range of support facilities at Fort Sam Houston.

**SEASON OF OPERATION:** Year round. (Closed Christmas and New Year's Day.)

**ELIGIBILITY:** Active/Reservists/Retired/DoD civilians/Foreign Military.

**RESERVATIONS:** Required for mobile homes and cabanas, reservations may be made up to one year in advance with payment. No advance reservations for camping areas and RV spots. Address: 698 Jacobs Creek Park Road, New Braunfels, TX 78133. **C-1-888-882-9878, C-830-964-3318, D-312-471-3318** 0800-1630 hours Mon-Fri, 0800-1600 hours Sat. Snowbirds welcome year round. Discounts available for entrance fee only to holders of Golden Age, Golden Access and Golden Eagle Passports. Check in at office 1600 hours, check out 1200 hours.

**Mobile Homes:** Three-bedroom (31-1 handicap accessible), furnished, refrigerator, microwave, stove, TV/VCR. Patrons must provide towels and toiletries. Rates: $45-$50 daily (depending on seasons/days).

**Cabins:** 10, handicap accessible, bunk beds, E/W hookups. Rates: $25 daily.

**Camper Spaces:** Hardstand (29), E/W (110/30A) hookups. Rates: $10 daily.

**Tent Spaces:** Open (50), no hookups. Rates: $8 daily.

## SUPPORT FACILITIES:

| | | |
|---|---|---|
| Bath House | Beach | Boat Launch |
| Boat Rental | Boat Slip | Cabanas/fee |
| Convenience Store | Fire Rings | Fishing Pier |
| Fishing Tackle | Gas | Grills |
| Ice | Laundry | Marina |
| Party Boat | Pavilion | Picnic Areas*/** |
| Playgrounds | Rec Equipment | Restrooms* |
| Sewage Dump | Shelters/screened | Showers* |
| TV Room | TV/VCR Rental | |

\* Handicap accessible.
\*\* Group picnic area available by reservation.

## ACTIVITIES:

| | | |
|---|---|---|
| Boating | Fishing/license | Hiking |
| Jet Skiing | Volleyball (Sand) | Swimming |
| Water Skiing | | |

**CREDIT CARDS ACCEPTED:** Visa, MasterCard, American Express, Discover and Diners'.

**RESTRICTIONS:** Pets allowed on leash. No firearms are allowed. Open fires in designated areas only. Nominal entrance fee into park ($4 per vehicle/annual permit $30).

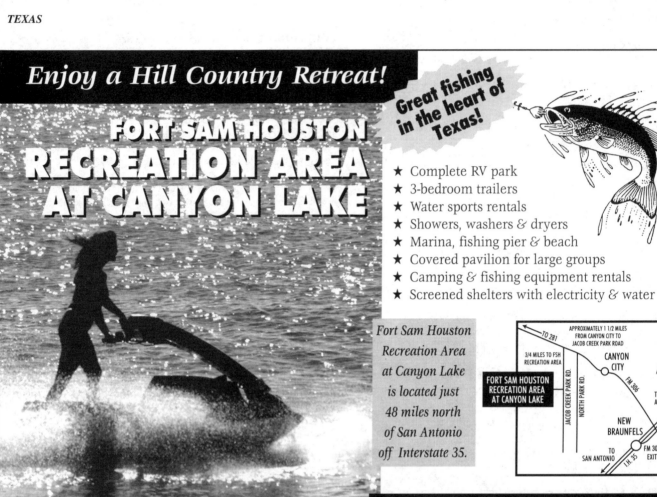

## GOODFELLOW AFB
## RECREATION CAMP (TX32R3)

Goodfellow Air Force Base
Goodfellow AFB, TX 76908-4304

**TELEPHONE NUMBER INFORMATION:** Main installation numbers: C-915-654-3231, D-312-477-3217.

**LOCATION:** Off base. From all directions, take Route 67 (turns into Loop 306) south of the city to Knickerbocker Road (Ranch Road 584). Proceed south three miles. Turn left on South Concho (left turn is shortly after crossing Lake Nasworthy). Campground is on the left and marked by a sign. *USMRA: page 86 (H-7)*. NMI: Goodfellow AFB, 10 miles northeast. NMC: San Angelo, 10 miles north.

**DESCRIPTION OF AREA:** Located on Lake Nasworthy in flat, open terrain with some trees and covered picnic areas. Full range of support facilities available on base.

**SEASON OF OPERATION:** Year round: Thu-Mon.

**ELIGIBILITY:** Active/Reservists/Retired/DoD civilians.

**RESERVATIONS:** No advance reservations. Address: 1950 S. Concho Drive, San Angelo, TX 76504-5000. **C-915-944-1012, D-312-477-3217** (ask operator to ring 944-1012).

**Camper Spaces:** 21, E (110V/30A)/S/W hookups. Rates: $10 daily.

**Tent Spaces:** Unlimited, no hookups. Rates: $3 daily.

**SUPPORT FACILITIES:**

| | | |
|---|---|---|
| Boat Launch | Boat Rental | Fishing Pier |
| Gas | Marina | Pavilion* |
| Picnic Area | Pool | Racquet Courts |
| Rec Equipment | Restrooms | Sewage Dump |
| Showers | Snack Bar | Sports Fields |

* Handicap accessible.

**ACTIVITIES:**

| | | |
|---|---|---|
| Fishing | Sailing | Water Skiing |

**CREDIT CARDS ACCEPTED:** Visa and MasterCard

**RESTRICTIONS:** Pets allowed on leash, owner must clean up after pets. Firearms are prohibited. No open fires. Campers already in the camping area on days when it is closed will not be required to leave.

## KELLY FAMCAMP (TX33R3)

Kelly Air Force Base
Kelly AFB, TX 78241-5828
*Scheduled to close July 2001.*

**TELEPHONE NUMBER INFORMATION:** Main installation numbers: C-210-925-1110, D-312-945-1110. Police for FAMCAMP, C-210-925-6811.

**LOCATION:** On base. From US-90 go south on Cupples Road for two miles (past the Kelly AFB main gate and over the overpass), left at the East Kelly AFB entrance. The FAMCAMP is on the first street to the right past the guard. *USMRA: page 91 (B-3,4).* NMC: San Antonio, 3 miles northeast.

**DESCRIPTION OF AREA:** Located in the San Antonio metropolitan area which offers many sightseeing opportunities, e.g., the Alamo, Riverwalk, Mission Concepcion (the oldest church in Texas), Institute of Texan Cultures, zoological gardens and aquarium, and Fiesta Week in April. FAMCAMP is surrounded by pecan trees. Full range of support facilities available on base. *Note: Kelly FAMCAMP was the first military FAMCAMP built.*

**SEASON OF OPERATION:** Year round.

**ELIGIBILITY:** Active/Reservists/Retired/DoD civilians.

**RESERVATIONS:** Reservations accepted up to 120 days prior to arrival. Address: Kelly AFB FAMCAMP, 76 SPTG/SVRF, 250 Goodrich Drive, San Antonio, TX 78241-5818. FAMCAMP located at Bldg 3503, 299 Offutt Street, East Kelly AFB, TX 78241-6549. **C-210-925-5725, D-312-975-5725.** Check in at Bldg 3503.

**Camper Spaces:** Paved (32), E (110V/30A)/S/W hookups. Rates: $10 daily/$63 weekly/$255 monthly. Guests $14 daily.

**Tent Spaces:** Grass, no hookups. Rates: $3 daily.

**Overflow:** Patrons may use water, restrooms, showers and laundry available at FAMCAMP. Rates: $5 daily.

**SUPPORT FACILITIES:**

| | | |
|---|---|---|
| Laundry* | Picnic Area | Rec Equipment |
| Restrooms* | Sewage Dump** | Showers* |

\* Handicap accessible.
\*\* Dump station available for $3.

**ACTIVITIES:**

| | |
|---|---|
| Horseshoes | Sightseeing |

**CREDIT CARDS ACCEPTED:** Visa and MasterCard.

**RESTRICTIONS:** Pets are allowed. Quiet hours from 2200-0600 hours. Thirty day limit.

## LACKLAND FAMCAMP (TX49R3)
Lackland Air Force Base
Lackland AFB, TX 78236-5113

**TELEPHONE NUMBER INFORMATION:** Main installation numbers: C-210-671-1110, D-312-473-1110. Police for FAMCAMP, C-210-671-2018, Crime Stop, C-210-671-1100.

**LOCATION:** On base. From US-90 west of San Antonio take exit (Lackland) south onto Military Drive. Enter Selfridge Gate West, straight ahead to Carswell on Selfridge, right on Carswell to Equipment Check-out, Bldg 7214. *USMRA: page 87 (J-6,7).* NMC: San Antonio, 16 miles northeast.

**DESCRIPTION OF AREA:** FAMCAMP is located on flat terrain. Pad for RV is 10'x35', for vehicle, 9'x19'. San Antonio offers many and varied opportunities for sightseeing. Conveniently located to a full range of support facilities available on base.

**SEASON OF OPERATION:** Year round.

**ELIGIBILITY:** Active/Reservists/Retired/DoD civilians in some areas/Sponsored visitors.

**RESERVATIONS:** No advance reservations. Address: Outdoor Recreation, 37 SVS/SVROF, 1420 Stewart Street, Lackland AFB, TX 78236-5234. For information, **C-210-671-3106, D-312-473-3106** 0800-1700 hours Mon, Tue, Thu, Fri; 0900-1200 hours Sat; 1400-1700 hours Sun. FAMCAMP, C-210-671-5179. Frequent Camper Coupons accepted. Check out 1200 hours.

**Camper Spaces:** Asphalt (29), E (110V/30/50A)/S/W/CATV hookups. Rates: $12 daily.

**SUPPORT FACILITIES:**

| | | |
|---|---|---|
| Bowling | Commissary | Exchange |
| Gas | Golf | Laundry |
| Parks | Pools | RV Resale lot |
| RV Storage | Showers* | Shuttle/Bus |
| Stables | ITT | |

\* Handicap accessible.

**ACTIVITIES:**

| |
|---|
| Sightseeing |

**CREDIT CARDS ACCEPTED:** Visa and MasterCard.

**RESTRICTIONS:** Pets allowed on leash no longer than ten feet, must have current immunizations, owner must clean up after pet. Firearms to be checked in to the base armory. No open fires. Quiet hours 2200-0600 hours. Fourteen day limit.

## LAUGHLIN FAMCAMP (TX13R3)
Laughlin Air Force Base
Laughlin AFB, TX 78843-5135

**TELEPHONE NUMBER INFORMATION:** Main installation numbers: C-830-298-3511, D-312-732-1110. Police for recreation area, C-911.

**LOCATION:** On base. Off US-90 east of Del Rio. Clearly marked. From main gate, drive straight ahead to the RV area. Camp host will park vehicle.. *USMRA: page 86 (H-9).* NMC: Del Rio, 6 miles west.

**DESCRIPTION OF AREA:** Situated near Texas/Mexico border and near Presa de la Amistad Reservoir and recreation area. Full range of support facilities on base.

**SEASON OF OPERATION:** Year round.

**ELIGIBILITY:** Active/Reservists/Retired/DoD civilians.

**RESERVATIONS:** No advance reservations accepted currently; policy under review. Address: Laughlin AFB FAMCAMP, 47 SPTG/SVRO, 416 Liberty Drive, Laughlin AFB, TX 78843-5134. **C-830-298-5830, D-312-732-5830.** Fax: C-830-298-5554, D-312-732-5554.

**Camper Spaces:** Hardstand (21), handicap accessible, E (110V/50A)/S/W/CATV hookups. Rates: $10 daily/$200 monthly.

**SUPPORT FACILITIES:**

| | | |
|---|---|---|
| Auto Craft Shop | Boat Launch | Boat Rental/Storage |
| Chapel | Commissary | Convenience Store |
| Exchange | Fishing Pier | Fitness Center |
| Gas | Golf | Grills |
| Ice | Laundry | Marina |
| Pavilion | Picnic Area | Playground |

*TEXAS*
*Laughlin FAMCAMP, continued*

| | | |
|---|---|---|
| Pool | Rec Center | Rec Equipment |
| Restrooms* | Sewage Dump | Shoppette |
| Snack Bar | Sports Fields | Stables |
| Telephones | Tennis Courts | Trails |

* Handicap accessible.

**ACTIVITIES:**

| | | |
|---|---|---|
| Fishing/license | Hiking | Hunting/license |
| Swimming | | |

**CREDIT CARDS ACCEPTED:** Visa and MasterCard.

**RESTRICTIONS:** Pets allowed on leash. All firearms must be registered with security police.

## NASKING RECREATION FAMCAMP (TX22R3)

Kingsville Naval Air Station
Kingsville NAS, TX 78363-5110

**TELEPHONE NUMBER INFORMATION:** Main installation numbers: C-512-516-6136, D-312-861-6136. Police for FAMCAMP: C-512-516-6217.

**LOCATION:** On base. Take Highway 77 S into Kingsville, exit to the left on Carlos Truan Blvd or General Cavasoz and proceed approximately 1.5 miles to security gate (have proof of insurance, valid driver's license, and vehicle registration) where directions to the park will be provided. *USMRA: page 87 (K-9).* NMC: Corpus Christi, 50 miles northeast.

**DESCRIPTION OF AREA:** Park is on the South Texas Birding Trail, 20 minutes from Baffin Bay (trophy trout capital of the world), 45 minutes from beautiful Corpus Christi, and near the world famous King Ranch (the largest working cattle ranch in the continental United States). Full logistical support facilities available on base.

**SEASON OF OPERATION:** Year round.

**ELIGIBILITY:** Active/Reservists/Retired/DoD civilians.

**RESERVATIONS:** An $8 deposit is accepted for reservations over the phone with a Visa or MasterCard. Or mail to Nasking Recreation Camp, Outdoor Recreation, 3765 Nimitz Avenue, Kingsville NAS, TX 78363. **C-512-516-6443, D-312-861-6443.** Order of priority follows: active duty 21 days in advance, retirees and reservists 14 days in advance, DoD civilians seven days in advance.

**Camper:** 18' (2), sleeps five, E (110V/20A)/W hookups. Rates: $30 daily. 16' (2), sleeps five, E (110V/20A)/W hookups. Rates: $25 daily.

**Camper Spaces:** 8, E (110V/20A)/W hookups. Rates: $8 daily. 10, W hookup. Rates: $5 daily.

**Camper/Tent Spaces:** Primitive, unlimited, no hookups. Rates: $2 daily.

**SUPPORT FACILITIES:**

| | | |
|---|---|---|
| Bicycles | Boat Rentals | Bowling Center |
| Equipment Rental | Fitness Center | Grills |
| Mini-Mart | Pay Phones | Picnic Areas |
| Pool | Sewage Dump | Showers |
| Sports Fields | Tennis Courts | |

**ACTIVITIES:**

| | | |
|---|---|---|
| Birding | Boating | Deep Sea Fishing |
| Hunting | Swimming | Tours of the |
| | | King Ranch |

**CREDIT CARDS ACCEPTED:** Visa and MasterCard.

**RESTRICTIONS:** Pets allowed on leash, owners must have proof of vaccinations for pets. All firearms must be registered with security upon arrival. Maximum length of stay is 14 days.

## RANDOLPH OUTDOOR RECREATION AREA - CANYON LAKE (TX35R3)

Randolph Air Force Base
Randolph AFB, TX 78150-4537

**TELEPHONE NUMBER INFORMATION:** Main installation numbers: C-210-652-1110, D-312-487-1110. Police for recreation area, C-210-652-5510.

**LOCATION:** Off base. From I-35 north from San Antonio, through New Braunfels to Canyon Lake Exit. Turn left on Farm Road 306, follow for 16 miles to Canyon City. Go another 1.5 miles past the blinking traffic light to Jacobs Creek Park Road, turn left. Clearly marked. *USMRA: page 87 (J,K-6).* NMI: Randolph AFB, 43 miles southeast. NMC: San Antonio, 48 miles south.

**DESCRIPTION OF AREA:** Located on northeast end of Canyon Reservoir. Terrain is characteristically hilly and rocky with scatterings of cedar, live oak and Spanish oak trees. Campground located around cove. There is a majestic view of 8,240-acre lake and its 80-mile shoreline. Temperatures in summer make air conditioning desirable for enclosed trailers and recreational vehicles. Heat is needed only occasionally in winter. Variety of water-oriented activities. Full range of support facilities at Randolph AFB.

**SEASON OF OPERATION:** Year round, marina closed Mon-Tue.

**ELIGIBILITY:** Active/Reservists/Retired/DoD civilians at Randolph AFB.

**RESERVATIONS:** Accepted for all but tent spaces. Address: 781 Jacobs Creek Road, Canyon Lake, TX 78133-5000. **C-1-800-280-3466, C-830-964-4134.** Marina, C-830-964-3804.

**Cabins:** 6, two-bedroom, sleeps six, double bed, two single beds, sofabed, private bath, kitchen, refrigerator, microwave, stove, A/C, heat. Patrons must provide linens. Rates: $50 daily.

**Shelters:** 5, beds, refrigerator, E (110V/15A) hookups, A/C. Rates: $25 daily. 4, open-air shelter, no hookups. Rates: $20 daily.

**Camper Spaces:** 9, concrete, E (110V/15/30A)/S/W hookups. Rates: $15 daily. 8, E (110V/15A)/W hookups. Rates: $10 daily.

**Tent Spaces:** 45, no hookups. Rates: $8 daily, shoreline sites $10 daily. Primitive, unlimited, no hookups. Rates: $8.

**Group Camping Area:** 2, includes six vehicle passes. Rates: $20 unit, $20 personal use.

**SUPPORT FACILITIES:**

| | | |
|---|---|---|
| Boat Launch | Boat Rental | Fishing Pier |
| Gas/boats only | Grills | Marina |
| Nature Trail | Pavilion | Picnic Areas |
| Playground | Recreation Equipment | Restrooms |

| | | |
|---|---|---|
| Sailboat/minifish | Sewage Dump/nearby | Showers |
| Snacks | Volleyball | |

Sailing classes are offered seasonally

**ACTIVITIES:**

| | | |
|---|---|---|
| Fishing | Sailing | Scuba Diving |
| Water Skiing | Windsurfing | |

**CREDIT CARDS ACCEPTED:** Visa and MasterCard.

**RESTRICTIONS:** Pets allowed on leash. No firearms allowed in park. Entry fee ($3) to recreation area. Boat launch fee is $1.

## SHEPPARD AFB
## RECREATION ANNEX (TX16R3)

Sheppard Air Force Base
Sheppard AFB, TX 76311-2540

**TELEPHONE NUMBER INFORMATION:** Main installation numbers: C-940-676-2511, D-312-736-2511. Police for recreation annex, C-903-893-4388.

**LOCATION:** Off base. From US-82 east of Gainesville, take US-377 N approximately 11 miles (pass Gordonville exit) to TX FM-901 and turn left. (Just prior to this exit is a green SAFB Annex sign.) Go two miles, turn right at SAFB Annex sign. Follow signs approximately five miles to recreation annex. Recreation area is located on Texas side of Lake Texoma. *USMRA: page 87 (K-1,2)*. NMI: Dallas NAS, 95 miles south. NMC: Dallas, 95 miles south.

**DESCRIPTION OF AREA:** Located approximately 120 miles east of base at Wichita Falls, near the Texas/Oklahoma line on one of the largest, most popular inland lakes in the area. Some of the best fishing is available as well as a variety of other water sports. Full range of support facilities available at Dallas NAS and Carswell AFB in Fort Worth.

**SEASON OF OPERATION:** Year round.

**ELIGIBILITY:** Active/Reservists/Retired/Dependents/Federal Civilian employees.

**RESERVATIONS:** Accepted. Address: 1030 SAFB Annex Road, Whitesboro, TX 76273-5000. **C-903-523-4613** 0800-1700 hours. Check in at main lodge, 1500 hours, check out 1300 hours.

**Cabins:** Two-bedroom (1), furnished, private bath, microwave, A/C, TV/VCR. Rates: $40-$45 daily (depending on season). 1, sleeps four, furnished, private bath, microwave, A/C, TV/VCR. Rates: $43-$48 daily (depending on season). 42, sleeps four to six, furnished, private bath, microwave, A/C, TV/VCR. Rates: $31-$36 daily (depending on season).

**Mobile Home:** 1, sleeps six, furnished, private bath, microwave, A/C, TV/VCR. Rates: $40-$45 daily (depending on season).

**Camper Spaces:** Gravel (8), E (110V/30A)/S/W hookups. Rates: $11 daily/$55 weekly/$200 monthly. Gravel (16), E (110V/30A)/W hookups. Rates: $9 daily/$45 weekly/$165 monthly.

**Tent Spaces:** Many, no hookups. Rates: no charge.

**Dry Boat Storage:** Many. Rates: $18-$25 monthly (depending on season).

**Day Act Slips:** 30, E hookup. Rates: $3 daily.

**SUPPORT FACILITIES:**

| | | |
|---|---|---|
| Airstrip/grass | Bait | Beach |
| Boat Launch | Boat Slips | Convenience Store |
| Crappie House | Fitness Center | Gas |
| (fishing house) | Grills | Laundry |
| Movies | Multi-Purpose Court | Pavilions |
| Picnic Area | Playgrounds | Rec Equipment |
| Rec Room/TV | Restrooms | Sewage Dump |
| Showers | Snack Bar | Steakhouse/Lounge* |
| Telephone | Trails | Vending Machine |
| Video Rental | | |

* Open Friday and Saturday Nights 1700-2400 hours.

**ACTIVITIES:**

| | | |
|---|---|---|
| Basketball | Driving Range | Fishing |
| Hiking | Horseshoes | Volleyball |
| Water Skiing | Softball | Swimming |

Special seasonal holiday activities.

**CREDIT CARDS ACCEPTED:** Visa, MasterCard and American Express.

**RESTRICTIONS:** Pets are allowed with a $25 fee. No firearms. No fireworks. No hunting permitted on the annex.

## SHIELDS PARK NAS
## RECREATION AREA (TX36R3)

Corpus Christi Naval Air Station
Corpus Christi, TX 78419-5021

**TELEPHONE NUMBER INFORMATION:** Main installation numbers: C-512-939-2811, D-312-861-1110. Police for recreation area, C-512-939-2480.

**LOCATION:** On base. From Corpus Christi take TX-358 E. Follow sign to NAS. Ask gate sentry for directions to marina and RV campground. *USMRA: page 87 (K-8)*. NMC: Corpus Christi, 8 miles west.

**DESCRIPTION OF AREA:** Located on beautiful Corpus Christi Bay. Corpus Christi offers a symphony, USS Lexington museum, historical homes, art museum, the Texas State Aquarium, greyhound race track, Harbor Playhouse and the Columbus ships.

**SEASON OF OPERATION:** Year round, some activities are seasonal.

**ELIGIBILITY:** Active/Reservists/Retired/DoD civilians.

**RESERVATIONS:** Accepted for active duty only. Address: Outdoor Recreation, Bldg 39, Code 22, Corpus Christi Naval Air Station, TX 78419-5000. **C-512-937-5071.**

**Camper Spaces:** Gravel (12), E (110V/30A)/S/W hookups. Rates: $9 daily Active, $10 Retired, $11 Civilian. Gravel (24), E (110V/30A)/W hookups. Rates: $7 daily Active, $8 Retired, $9 Civilian.

**Tent Spaces:** 7, W hookup. Rates: $3 daily A/D, $4 Retired, $5 Civilian.

**SUPPORT FACILITIES:**

| | | |
|---|---|---|
| Beach | Boat Launch/Rental | Bowling Center |
| Ceramic Shop | Chapel | Fishing Piers/lighted |
| Gas/Auto Shop | Golf | Library |
| Marina | Mini Mart | Pavilion/Picnic Area |
| Racquet Sports | Sewage Dump | Skeet Range |
| Sports Fields | | |

*TEXAS*
**Shields Park NAS Recreation Area, *continued***

**ACTIVITIES:**

| | | |
|---|---|---|
| Birding | Boating | Camping Equipment |
| Fishing | Kayaking | Sailing |
| Shelling | Swimming | Water Skiing |
| Windsurfing | | |

**CREDIT CARDS ACCEPTED:** Visa, MasterCard and American Express.

**RESTRICTIONS:** Pets allowed on leash. Firearms must be checked in with Security. Open fires allowed, must obtain fire permit from NAS Fire Chief, C-512-939-3491.

## SOUTHWINDS MARINA ON LAKE AMISTAD (TX34R3)

Laughlin Air Force Base
Laughlin AFB, TX 78843-5135

**TELEPHONE NUMBER INFORMATION:** Main installation numbers: C-830-298-3511, D-312-732-1110. Police for recreation area, C-911.

**LOCATION:** Off base. From US-90 north of Del Rio, take Amistad Dam Road (Spur 349) to Recreation area. *USMRA: page 86 (H-9).* NMI: Laughlin AFB, 22.5 miles southeast. NMC: Del Rio, 12 miles southeast.

**DESCRIPTION OF AREA:** Situated near Amistad Dam which serves as passageway to Mexico. Ideal fresh water recreation area and outstanding fishing. Many deer in the area. Good base for day trips into Mexico. Convenient to Ciudad Acuna, Mexico. Full range of support facilities at Laughlin AFB.

**SEASON OF OPERATION:** Year round. 16 Apr-15 Oct: 0800-2000 hours Thu-Sun, holidays. 16 Oct-15 Apr: 0800-1700 hours Sat-Sun, holidays.

**ELIGIBILITY:** Active/Reservists/Retired/DoD and NAF civilians/Others with Federal ID at discretion of commander.

**RESERVATIONS:** Required with payment in advance. Address: HCR #3, Box 37J, Del Rio, TX 78840-5000. **C-830-775-5971/7800.** Fax: C-830-298-7800. Check in at store 0800-2000 hours 16 Apr-15 Oct, 0800-1600 hours 16 Oct-15 Apr. Check out 1300 hours.

**Cabins:** 2, sleeps six, double bed, two single beds, sofabed, bath, kitchen, microwave, stove, dishes, utensils. Rates: $22.50 daily, plus one time $15 cleaning fee.

**Campers:** 4, 20', sleeps four, E (110V/30A)/W hookups. 2, 16', sleeps two, E (110V/30A)/W hookups. Rates: $18 daily (weekly and monthly winter rates available, TV hookups available).

**Camper/Tent Spaces:** Concrete (5), E (110V/30A)/W hookups. Rates: $8 daily (weekly and monthly winter rates available, TV hookups available).

**SUPPORT FACILITIES:**

| | | |
|---|---|---|
| Boat Rental | Convenience Store | Grills |
| Laundry | Marina | Picnic Areas |
| Restrooms* | Showers* | Sewage Dump |

* Handicap accessible.

**ACTIVITIES:**

| | | |
|---|---|---|
| Boating | Fishing | Natural History |
| Sailing | Sightseeing | Water Skiing |

**CREDIT CARDS ACCEPTED:** Visa and MasterCard.

**RESTRICTIONS:** Pets allowed on leash. No firearms allowed. Campers already registered on Tue will not be asked to leave. Generators are permitted.

## WEST FORT HOOD TRAVEL CAMP (TX08R3)

Fort Hood
Fort Hood, TX 76544-5005

**TELEPHONE NUMBER INFORMATION:** Main installation numbers: C-254-287/288-1110, D-312-737/738-1110. Police for travel camp, C-254-287-2176.

**LOCATION:** On post. Four miles west of main post area. From I-35 take Killeen/Fort Hood exit, west on US-190, left on West Fort Hood turn-off. Travel Camp is on Clarke Road, .25 miles on your right. Area marked. *USMRA: page 87 (K-4).* NMC: Austin, 60 miles south.

**DESCRIPTION OF AREA:** Fort Hood (largest military reservation in the world), is located in ranching and recreation country in central Texas. It's only a 30-minute drive to Lake Belton and Lake Stillhouse, famous for recreation, black and white bass, and catfish. Travel camp boasts resident family of armadillos, summer night fire-fly shows, and visits from the wild deer and rabbits. Full range of support facilities on post.

**SEASON OF OPERATION:** Year round.

**ELIGIBILITY:** Active/Reservists/Retired/DoD civilians.

**RESERVATIONS:** Required for groups with 20 to 60 units, accepted for others. Address: West Fort Hood Travel Camp, AFZF-CA-BOD-WFHTC, Bldg 70004, Clarke Road, P.O. Box K, Fort Hood, TX 76544-5056. **C-254-288-9926, D-312-738-9926.** Discount to holders of Golden Age and Golden Access Passports. Check in at office 0700-1730 hours Mon-Fri, 1000-1730 hours Sat-Sun, closed Federal holidays.

**Camper Spaces:** Hardstand (64), phone service available at 32 sites, E (110V/20/30/50A)/S/W/CATV hookups. Rates: $9.50 daily/$267 monthly.

**Tent Spaces:** Primitive (20), no hookups. Rates: $2 daily.

**RV/ Boat Storage:** Open Stand (116), fenced, lighted. Rates: $15-$20 monthly (fees depend on size of vehicle).

**SUPPORT FACILITIES:**

| | | |
|---|---|---|
| CATV | Chapel | Convenience Store |
| Game Room | Gas | Golf |
| Grills | Laundry | Picnic Area |
| Playground | Rec Equipment | Restrooms |
| Sewage Dump/fee | Showers | Trails |

Equipment Checkout Center offers camping packages for rent from tents and motor homes to sleeping bags. Set-up available at travel camp.

**ACTIVITIES:**

| | | |
|---|---|---|
| Fishing/license | Hunting*/license | Jogging |
| Swimming | Water Skiing | |

* Annual deer harvest: bow and shotgun Oct-Nov, rifle (guided hunt) Nov-Dec. Wild turkey hunt in Apr; dove and quail in Sep.

**CREDIT CARDS ACCEPTED:** Visa, MasterCard, American Express and Esprit.

**RESTRICTIONS:** Pets allowed on leash. Firearms not allowed in compound and must be registered with MPs on post. Twenty-four hour hookup availability, register when office is open. Sixty day limit, exceptions up to 180 days available at office.

# UTAH

# CARTER CREEK CAMP (UT01R4)

Hill Air Force Base
Hill AFB, UT 84056-5720

**TELEPHONE NUMBER INFORMATION:** Main installation numbers: C-801-777-7221, D-312-458-1110. Police for camp, C-801-777-3525.

**LOCATION:** Off base. From I-80 near Evanston WY, take WY/UT-150 S 30 miles to Bear River Service Station, .1 mile to east (left) on Mill Creek RS-7. Approximately four miles to camp on the right side of the road. *USMRA: page 112 (F-3).* NMI: Hill AFB, 105 miles west. NMC: Salt Lake City, 105 miles southwest.

**DESCRIPTION OF AREA:** The surroundings of Carter Creek are typical of the Uintah Mountains with lodgepole pines and quaking aspen, a perfect combination of sight and sound. Rustic campsite in mountains reaching heights of 13,500 feet. Fishing lakes and ponds nearby. Full range of support facilities available at Hill AFB.

**SEASON OF OPERATION:** Weekend prior to 4 Jul-31 Oct.

**ELIGIBILITY:** Active/Reservists/Retired/DoD civilians at Hill AFB.

**RESERVATIONS:** Required. Address: Outdoor Recreation, Bldg 524, Hill Air Force Base, UT 84056-5000. **C-801-777-2225/9666** 0800-1700 hours Mon-Fri. Check in 1400-2000 hours with camp manager, check out 1300 hours.

**Cabins:** One-bedroom (6), sleeps five, double bed, single bed, bunk beds, refrigerator, microwave, stove, sink, heater. Patrons must provide pots/pans, dishes, silverware, bed linens, towels, soap, warm clothing, ice for personal coolers, fishing gear and other recreational equipment. Limit five people. Rates: $35 daily Sun-Thu, $40 daily Fri-Sat and holidays (cabin #3 is two-bedroom, sleeps seven, add $10).

**Trailers:** 3. Rates: $15 daily.

**Camper Spaces:** Gravel (3), E (110/220V/20/30/50A)/W hookups. Rates: $10-$12 daily.

**Tent Spaces:** Wilderness (3), no hookups. Rates: $5 daily.

**SUPPORT FACILITIES:**

| | | |
|---|---|---|
| BBQ Fireplaces | Grills | Picnic Area |
| Playground | Restrooms | Shower |
| Trails | | |

**ACTIVITIES:**

| | | |
|---|---|---|
| Fishing/license | Hiking | Horseshoes |
| Hunting/license | Volleyball | |

**CREDIT CARDS ACCEPTED:** Visa and MasterCard.

**RESTRICTIONS:** Pets allowed on leash, owner must clean up after pet. No shooting in or near camp. Fires permitted in designated areas only. No phone available. No provisions for drop-in patrons. No firearms allowed in camp.

# HILL FAMCAMP (UT07R4)

Hill Air Force Base
Hill AFB, UT 84056-5720

**TELEPHONE NUMBER INFORMATION:** Main installation numbers: C-801-777-7221, D-312-458-1110. Police for recreation facilities: C-911.
**LOCATION:** On base. Between Ogden and Salt Lake City. I-15 to exit 336, east on UT-193 two miles to South Gate of base. *USMRA: page 112 (D-2,3).* NMC: Ogden, 10 miles north.

**DESCRIPTION OF AREA:** Located near mountains at edge of urban area. FAMCAMP convenient to recreation areas and points of interest around Great Salt Lake. Pineview Reservoir for boating and swimming, 25 miles east. Museum and aerospace park on base. Full range of support facilities available on base.

**SEASON OF OPERATION:** Year round.

**ELIGIBILITY:** Active/Reservists/Retired/DoD civilians.

**RESERVATIONS:** Required seven days in advance Address: Outdoor Recreation, 75 Services, Hill AFB, UT 84056-5000. **C-801-777-3250, D-312-458-3250.** Check in at FAMCAMP on 11th Street.

**Camper Spaces:** Paved (28), E (110/220V/20/30/50A)/S/W hookups. Rates: $10 daily. Overflow (14), no hookups. Rates: $8 daily.

**Tent Spaces:** Grass (6), no hookups. Rates: $5 daily.

**SUPPORT FACILITIES:**

| | | |
|---|---|---|
| Boat Rental | Chapel | Gas |
| Golf | Grills | Laundry |
| Picnic Area | Rec Equipment | Restrooms |
| Sewage Dump | Showers | |

*UTAH/VIRGINIA*
*Hill FAMCAMP, continued*

**ACTIVITIES:**

| | | |
|---|---|---|
| Bird Watching | Jogging | Sightseeing |
| Skiing | | |

**CREDIT CARDS ACCEPTED:** Visa and MasterCard.

**RESTRICTIONS:** Pets allowed on leash only, must be walked in designated area, owner must clean up after pet. No firearms allowed. Fourteen day limit.

## OQUIRRH HILLS TRAVEL CAMP (UT06R4)
Tooele Army Depot
Tooele, UT 84074-5000

**TELEPHONE NUMBER INFORMATION:** Main installation numbers: C-435-833-3211, D-312-790-1110. Police for travel camp, C-435-833-2314.

**LOCATION:** On post. From I-80 west of Salt Lake City, take UT-36 S approximately 25 miles to main entrance. *USMRA: page 112 (C-4).* NMC: Salt Lake City, 35 miles northeast.

**DESCRIPTION OF AREA:** View of largest open pit copper mine from top of Settlement Canyon. Enjoy sightseeing of canyons, mountains and desert. Wide range of support facilities on post, full range at Dugway Proving Ground 40 miles southwest.

**SEASON OF OPERATION:** 1 May-30 Oct.

**ELIGIBILITY:** Active/Reservists/Retired/DoD civilians.

**RESERVATIONS:** Accepted five to 30 days in advance. Address: Community and Family Activities, Bldg 1011, Tooele Army Depot, Tooele, UT 84074-5001. **C-435-833-3129, D-312-790-3129.**

**Camper Spaces:** Gravel (14), E (110V/20/30/50A)/W hookups. Rates: $8 daily/$50 weekly.

**Tent Spaces:** Open (8), no hookups. Rates: $2 daily.

**SUPPORT FACILITIES:**

| | | |
|---|---|---|
| Archery | Boat Rental | Bowling Alley |
| Camping Equipment | Camper Rental | Chapel |
| Exchange | Golf Driving Range | Laundry |
| Playground | Pool/summer | Racquetball |
| Rec Equipment | Restrooms | Sewage Dump |
| Showers | Skeet/Trap Range | Sports Equipment |
| Sports Fields | Stables | |

**ACTIVITIES:**

| | |
|---|---|
| Fishing | Snow Skiing (one hour away) |

**CREDIT CARDS ACCEPTED:** Visa.

**RESTRICTIONS:** Pets allowed on leash.

Visit Military Living on the
world-wide web at
**www.militaryliving.com**

# VIRGINIA

*See map on following page.*

## A.P. HILL RECREATION FACILITIES (VA39R1)
Fort A.P. Hill
Bowling Green, VA 22427-5000

**TELEPHONE NUMBER INFORMATION:** Main installation numbers: C-804-633-5041, D-312-934-8710. Police for recreation facilities, C-804-633-8425.

**LOCATION:** On post. From the north, exit I-95 at Bowling Green/Fort A. P. Hill, (exit 126) US-17 E (bypass), to VA-2, south to Bowling Green, take US-301 NE to main gate. From the south, I-95 to exit 104, VA-207, north to US-301 and main gate. Three miles east of Bowling Green. *USMRA: page 47 (L,M-6,7).* NMC: Fredericksburg, 14 miles northwest.

**DESCRIPTION OF AREA:** The post is 77,000 acres of woodlands with lakes and ponds covering more than 300 acres and offers abundant hunting and fishing opportunities in accordance with the laws of the state of Virginia. Some support facilities on post, full range available at Quantico MC Development Command, 45 miles northwest and Naval Surface Warfare Center, VA, 25 miles northeast.

**SEASON OF OPERATION:** Year round.

**ELIGIBILITY:** Active/Reservists/Retired/DoD civilians.

**RESERVATIONS:** Required for lodging, not necessary for camp facilities. Address: Department of the Army Community Recreation Division, 18380 4th Street, Fort A.P. Hill, VA 22427-3113. **C-804-633-8219, D-312-934-8219.** Discounts available to holders of Golden Age and Golden Access Passports. Check in at Community Recreation Division, Bldg 106, 0800-2030 hours Mon-Fri (Sat 1 Sep-31 May).

**Lodge:** One-bedroom (9), maximum of 18 occupants in mixed group (gender), 20 in same group, furnished, dining room, kitchen, utensils, linens, overlooking a lake. Rates: $25 person daily/$150 minimum daily (a two night stay is required during weekends).

**Log Cabins:** Three-bedroom (4), living room, dining room, kitchen, utensils, sleeps six, furnished, linens, on Bullocks Pond. Rates: $25 person daily (family rates available based on rank of sponsor).

**Camper Spaces:** Hardstand (48), E (110V/30/50A)/S/W hookups. Rates: $10 daily ($5 with Golden Age or Golden Access Card).

**SUPPORT FACILITIES:**

| | | |
|---|---|---|
| Boat Rental | Pool | Rec Center |
| Rec Equipment | Skeet Range | |

**ACTIVITIES:**

| | | |
|---|---|---|
| Bicycling | Fishing | Hunting |

**CREDIT CARDS ACCEPTED:** Visa, MasterCard and American Express.

**RESTRICTIONS:** No pets allowed in cabins or lodge, allowed on leash in camping area. No firearms allowed except those carried by bona-fide hunters during state-regulated hunting season.

# VIRGINIA

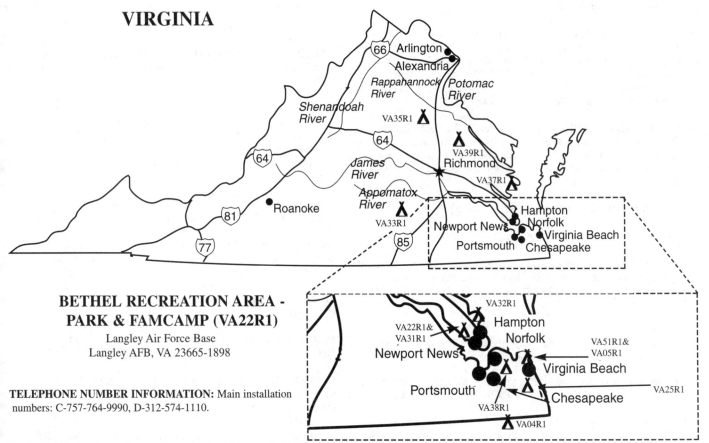

## BETHEL RECREATION AREA - PARK & FAMCAMP (VA22R1)

Langley Air Force Base
Langley AFB, VA 23665-1898

**TELEPHONE NUMBER INFORMATION:** Main installation numbers: C-757-764-9990, D-312-574-1110.

**LOCATION:** Off base. From I-64 take VA-134 N approximately five miles, turn left onto Big Bethel Road to a right on Saunders Road, approximately .25 miles on the right. Also, from I-64 take exit 261A to a right on Big Bethel Road. Follow Big Bethel Road for 2.5 miles and turn left onto Saun

ders Road. Bethel Park is located on Big Bethel Road, near the Saunders Road intersection. *USMRA: page 47 (N-9) and page 52 (D-3).* NMI: Langley AFB, 5 miles southeast. NMC: Hampton, 7 miles south.

**DESCRIPTION OF AREA:** Situated in a beautiful lake setting at the border of York County and Hampton. The Park offers facilities for picnics and sports and the entire area can accommodate approximately 800 people. Historical areas are nearby. Full range of support facilities available on base.

**SEASON OF OPERATION:** FAMCAMP is open year round. The Park is closed Oct-Apr and the fishing area is closed Dec-Jan. The Park and fishing areas are open four days a week in summer and the fishing area is open on weekends only in the fall, winter and early spring.

**ELIGIBILITY:** Active/Reservists/Retired/DoD civilians.

**RESERVATIONS:** Required for covered pavilions (fee), C-757-764-7170. Accepted for RV camping with half payment. Address: Bethel Recreation Area - Park & FAMCAMP, 1 SVS/SVRO, 123 Saunders Road, Hampton, VA 23665-5000. **C-757-766-3017 Park, C-757-766-7627 FAMCAMP.** For information, C-757-764-7170/6510 Outdoor Recreation.

**Camper Spaces:** Blacktop (20), E (110V/30A)/W hookups. Rates: $10 daily.

**Tent Spaces:** Primitive (10). Rates: $5 daily.

**SUPPORT FACILITIES:**

| | | |
|---|---|---|
| Bath House* | Boat Launch | Boat Rental |
| Fishing Pier | Fishing Tackle | Grills |
| Laundry* | Nature Trail | Pavilions |
| Picnic Area | Playground | Rec Equipment |
| Restrooms* | Sewage Dump | Showers* |
| Snack Bar | Sports Fields | |

\* Handicap accessible.

**ACTIVITIES:**

| | | |
|---|---|---|
| Boating | Canoeing | Fishing |
| Horseshoes | Softball | Tennis |
| Volleyball | Paddle Boats | Row Boats |

**CREDIT CARDS ACCEPTED:** Visa and MasterCard.

**RESTRICTIONS:** Pets allowed on leash. Park is off limits when closed. No fishing in the lake while Park is closed. Swimming is not allowed and gas motors cannot be run in any part of the reservoir. Trolling motors may be used.

## CAPE HENRY INN (VA51R1)

Fort Story
Fort Story, VA 23459-5034

**TELEPHONE NUMBER INFORMATION:** Main installation numbers: C-757-422-7305, D-312-438-7305.

**LOCATION:** On post. From North, take I-95 S to I-295 E around Richmond to I-64 E. Exit on13 N-Northampton Blvd. Then exit on Shore Drive (last exit before Bay Bridge-Tunnel). Follow Shore Drive east to Fort

*VIRGINIA*
*Cape Henry Inn, continued*

Story entrance on left. Inn is first left turn after the gate. Also, take 13 S through Delaware, Maryland, and Virginia across the Chesapeake Bay Bridge-Tunnel. Exit east on Shore Drive and proceed to Fort Story. From South, take I-95 N to 58 E to 64 W. Exit 13 E Northampton Blvd. Exit on Shore Drive E and proceed to Fort Story. *USMRA: page 47 (O-9) and page 52 (I-5,6).* NMC: Virginia Beach, 3 miles south.

**DESCRIPTION OF AREA:** Located between Seashore State Park and the Virginia Beach oceanfront on the environmentally protected dunes overlooking the Chesapeake Bay. A variety of wildlife, including red fox, make their home in the dunes, and wildflowers are abundant. Convenient to Williamsburg, Jamestown, Yorktown, Norfolk.

**SEASON OF OPERATION:** Year round.

**ELIGIBILITY:** Active/Reservists/Retired/DoD civilians.

**RESERVATIONS:** Accepted up to a year in advance. One night deposit required, 14 day cancellation policy. Address: Cape Henry Inn, Bldg 1116, Fort Story, VA 23459-5034 **C-757-422-8818.** Fax: C-757-422-6397. Check in 1600-2300 hours.

**CABINS:**
**Tidewater:** Three-bedroom (6), sleeps eight, sofabed, living room, full kitchen. Rates: $75-$80 (depending on season).

**Chesapeake:** Two-bedroom (12-1 handicap accessible), sleeps six, sofabed, living room, full kitchen. Rates: $70-$75 (depending on season).

**Bungalow:** Two-bedroom (8), sleeps six, sofabed, living room, dining room or kitchen, two TVs (in most), ground level, screened-in front/back porches, most are close to the fishing beach, but no water view. Near Fort Story center, built in 1942. Rates: $60-$74 (depending on season).

**Dune:** One-bedroom (30), sleeps six, two full beds, sofabed, kitchenette. Rates: $39-$65 (depending on season).

**Pelican:** One-bedroom (10), handicap accessible, sleeps two, queen size bed, kitchenette. Rates: $35-$60 (depending on season).

**Sandpiper:** One-bedroom (10), sleeps four, two full beds, five cubic foot refrigerator. Rates: $29-$55 (depending on season).

**Log Cabins:** Two-bedroom (9), sleeps eight, two full beds, two twin beds, sofabed, loft, living room, kitchen. Rates: $50-$66 (depending on season). One-bedroom (4), sleeps six, one full bed, two twin beds, sofabed, loft, living room, kitchen. Rates: $45-$61 (depending on season).

**SUPPORT FACILITIES:**

| | | |
|---|---|---|
| Bike Rental | CATV | Chapel |
| Gym | Laundromat | Modems* |
| Refrigerators | Restaurants nearby | Sports Field |
| Telephones with voice mail | Tennis Courts | |

* Limited number of rooms with modems available.

**ACTIVITIES:**

| | | |
|---|---|---|
| Beaches | Dolphin watching | Sightseeing |
| Swimming/summer | Biking | |

**CREDIT CARDS ACCEPTED:** Visa, MasterCard and American Express.

**RESTRICTIONS:** Pets and smoking allowed in bungalows and log cabins only. No grills allowed. Permanent grills provided.

# CAPE HENRY TRAVEL CAMP (VA05R1)
Fort Story
Fort Story, VA 23459-5034

**TELEPHONE NUMBER INFORMATION:** Main installation numbers: C-757-422-7305, D-312-438-7305. Police for travel camp, C-757-422-7601.

**LOCATION:** On post. From the south exit of Chesapeake Bay Bridge-Tunnel (US-13), take US-60 E (Atlantic Avenue) to Fort Story. From I-64 take US-60 E. From VA-44 (Norfolk-VA Beach Expressway) exit US-58, turn left to north on Atlantic Avenue (US-60) to 89th Street, to Fort Story. *USMRA: page 47 (O-9) and page 52 (I-5,6).* NMC: Virginia Beach, 3 miles south.

**DESCRIPTION OF AREA:** Fort Story, a sub-installation of Fort Eustis, is the site of the first stop of English settlers in the U.S. The Cross at Cape Henry is located here. Old Cape Henry Lighthouse is the first lighthouse built by the federal government. The statue of Admiral Francois Joseph Paul de Grasse presented to the Virginia Beach Bicentennial Commission in 1976 is also located here. Full range of support facilities available on post.

**SEASON OF OPERATION:** Campground, year round; Beach, Memorial Day-Labor Day.

**ELIGIBILITY:** Active/Reservists/Retired/DoD civilians at Fort Story and Fort Eustis.

**RESERVATIONS:** Required. Address: Outdoor Recreation, Attn: Travel Camp, Fort Story, VA 23459-5034. **C-757-422-7601, D-312-438-7601.** Discounts to holders of Golden Age and Golden Access Passports.

**Kamping Kabins:** 3, one 12'x12' room, sleeps four, A/C. Rates: $30 daily.

**Camper Spaces:** Gravel (24), E (110V/50A)/W hookups. Rates: $15 daily.

**SUPPORT FACILITIES:**

| | | |
|---|---|---|
| Beach | Chapel | Gas |
| Picnic Area | Rec Equipment | Restrooms |
| Sewage Dump | Showers | Sports Fields |
| Tennis Courts | | |

**ACTIVITIES:**
Swimming

**CREDIT CARDS ACCEPTED:** Visa and MasterCard.

**RESTRICTIONS:** Pets allowed on leash.

# CHEATHAM ANNEX RECREATION CABINS AND RV PARK (VA31R1)
Cheatham Annex Fleet and Industrial Supply Center
Williamsburg, VA 23187-8792

**TELEPHONE NUMBER INFORMATION:** Main installation numbers: C-757-887-4000, D-312-953-4000. Police: C-757-887-7222. After hours: C-757-887-7454.

**LOCATION:** On base. From I-64 near Williamsburg, take exit 242B, east on VA-199 to main gate. *USMRA: page 47 (N-8).* NMC: Newport News, 8 miles south.

**DESCRIPTION OF AREA:** Located in historic triangle of Jamestown, Colonial Williamsburg and Yorktown. Convenient to Busch Gardens, Pottery Factory, and College of William and Mary. Limited support facilities on base; full range at Yorktown Naval Weapons Station, seven miles south.

*Cheatham Annex Recreation Cabins and RV Park, continued*　　　　

**SEASON OF OPERATION:** Year round.

**ELIGIBILITY:** Active/Reservists/Retired.

**RESERVATIONS:** Accepted by phone only, 0800-1530 hours Mon, up to 90 days in advance with non-refundable deposit. Address: MWR, FISC, Cheatham Annex, 108 Sanda Avenue, Williamsburg, VA 23185-8792. **C-757-887-7224, D-312-953-7224.** Fax: C-757-887-7643. Check in MWR, check out 1200 hours. *Note: A $2.058 million Recreation Cabins/RV Park improvement has been approved in the Fiscal Year 1998 MWR Major and Minor Construction Program.*

**Cabins:** One- to three-bedroom (13-1 handicap accessible), sleeps four to ten, furnished, kitchen, refrigerator, dishes, utensils, A/C, central heat, wood burning stove, fireplace, CATV, phone, linens, wood, boat (with motor, battery, battery charger, paddles, cushions). Located along Cheatham Lake. Rates: $50-$70 daily/$300-$420 weekly 1 Apr-31 Oct (one week stay required); $45-$65 daily/$270-$390 weekly 1 Nov-31 Mar (two night stay required).

**Camper Spaces:** 19, E (110V/50A)/S/W/CATV hookups, overlooking York River and Kings Creek. Rates: $12 daily/$72 weekly.

**Pop-up Campers:** 6, overlooking York River and Kings Creek. Rates: $16 daily.

**Tent Spaces:** Primitive (6), central W, fire pit. Rates: $7 daily.

**SUPPORT FACILITIES:**

| | | |
|---|---|---|
| Boat Rental | Bowling Center | Camping Equipment |
| Fishing Pier* | Golf | Grills |
| Grocery/limited | Gymnasium | Laundry |
| Nature Trails | Pavilion | Pay Telephone |
| Picnic Area | Playground | Pool |
| Racquetball Court | Rec Equipment | Restrooms |
| Sewage Dump | Showers | Snack Bar |
| Sports Field | Tennis Courts | Weight Room |
| Youth Pier** | | |

\* Handicap accessible.
\*\* Fishing for children under 15 years old.

**ACTIVITIES:**

| | | |
|---|---|---|
| Bicycling | Boating | Bowling |
| Crabbing | Fishing | Golfing |
| Hiking | Horseshoes | Hunting |
| Swimming | | |

**CREDIT CARDS ACCEPTED:** Visa MasterCard, American Express and Discover.

**RESTRICTIONS:** No pets allowed in cabins. No firearms, bow and arrows, pellet guns or BB guns. No campfires. Guests responsible for cleanliness of facility upon departure. No refunds for early departure.

# THE COLONIES TRAVEL PARK (VA32R1)
Fort Monroe
Fort Monroe, VA 23464-6130

**TELEPHONE NUMBER INFORMATION:** Main installation numbers: C-757-727-2111, D-312-680-2111. Police for travel park, C-757-727-2238.

**LOCATION:** On post. From I-64 at Hampton, take exit 268. Follow historic sign markers to Fortress Monroe. *USMRA: page 47 (N-9) and page 52 (F-4).* NMC: Hampton, adjacent to post.

**DESCRIPTION OF AREA:** Quiet, serene campsite named after the Thirteen Colonies. Post is located at the hub of many historic and recreational areas, e.g., Williamsburg, Jamestown, Yorktown, Busch Gardens, Virginia Beach. Full range of support facilities on post.

**SEASON OF OPERATION:** Year round.

**ELIGIBILITY:** Active/Reservists/Retired/DoD civilians working at Fort Monroe.

**RESERVATIONS:** Accepted with $10 non-refundable deposit. Address: Community Recreation, Attn: MCECC, P.O. Box 51106, Fenwick Road, Fort Monroe, VA 23651-6144. **C-757-727-4305, D-312-680-4305.** Fax: C-757-727-3786, D-312-680-3786. E-mail: pilkintj@monroe.army.mil. Discounts to holders of Golden Age and Golden Access Passports. Check in 1200 hours, check out 1200 hours.

**Camper Spaces:** Hardstand (13), up to 35', E (110/220V/30A)/S/W hookups. Rates: $15 daily. Grass (13), up to 35', E (110/220V/30A)/S/W hookups. Rates: $12.50.

**SUPPORT FACILITIES:**

| | | |
|---|---|---|
| Auto Craft Shop | Bath House | Beach/fee |
| Boat Launch | Boat Rental | Camping Equipment |
| Camper Rental | Chapel | Commissary |
| Equipment Rental | Exchange | Fishing Pier |
| Fitness Center | Gas | Grills |
| Ice | Laundry | Marina |
| Pavilion | Playground | Picnic Area |
| Playground | Pool | Port-a-Potties* |
| Racquetball | Rec Equipment | Rec Center |
| Restrooms | Sewage Dump | Showers |
| Sports Fields | Telephones | Tennis Courts |

\* Handicap accessible.

**ACTIVITIES:**

| | | |
|---|---|---|
| Bicycling | Boat Tours | Crabbing |
| Fishing | Historical Tours | Jogging |
| Swimming | Windsurfing | |

**CREDIT CARDS ACCEPTED:** Visa and MasterCard.

**RESTRICTIONS:** Two pets allowed on leash no longer than six feet, proof of rabies vaccination required, owner must clean up after pet. No firearms allowed. No open fires. No metal detectors or digging permitted.

*VIRGINIA*

# LITTLE CREEK MWR RV PARK (VA38R1)

Little Creek Naval Amphibious Base
Norfolk, VA 23521-2231

**TELEPHONE NUMBER INFORMATION:** Main installation numbers: C-757-444-0000, D-312-680-7000.

**LOCATION:** On base. From I-64 take Northampton Blvd exit (US-13) north to Amphibious Base exit, north on Independence Blvd (VA-225) to Gate 5. Also, from Bay Bridge-Tunnel (US-13), take US-60 W to Gate 5. The RV park is located near Gate 4 on Amphibious Drive. *USMRA: page 47 (N,O-9) and page 52 (H-5,6).* NMC: Norfolk, 6 miles west.

**DESCRIPTION OF AREA:** The Naval Amphibious Base is nestled among many lakes and other bodies of water in a wooded area near the Chesapeake Bay. Full range of support facilities available on base and conveniently located.

**SEASON OF OPERATION:** Year round.

**ELIGIBILITY:** Active/Reservists/Retired.

**RESERVATIONS:** No advance reservations accepted. Address: MWR, 1432 Hewitt Drive, Little Creek Naval Amphibious Base, Norfolk, VA 23521-2522. **C-757-462-7376, D-312-253-7373.**

**RV Spaces:** Gravel (45), E (110V/30/50A)/W hookups. Rates: $10 daily/$60 weekly/$240 monthly.

**Tent Spaces:** Grass (6), no hookups. Rates: $5 daily.

**SUPPORT FACILITIES:**

| | | |
|---|---|---|
| Archery* | Beaches* | Boat Rental* |
| Camper Rental* | Chapel* | Fitness Trail* |
| Gas* | Golf* | Grills |
| Jogging Trail* | Marina | Miniature Golf* |
| Pay Telephones | Picnic Area | Playground |
| Restrooms | Sewage Dump/fee | Showers |

* Nearby

**ACTIVITIES:**

| | | |
|---|---|---|
| Boating | Hiking | Fishing/license |
| Jogging | Swimming | |

**CREDIT CARDS ACCEPTED:** Visa, MasterCard and American Express.

**RESTRICTIONS:** Pets allowed on leash. No fires.

# LUNGA PARK (VA35R1)

Quantico Marine Corps Base
Quantico, VA 22134-5012

**TELEPHONE NUMBER INFORMATION:** Main installation numbers: C-703-784-2121, D-312-278-2121. Police for campground, C-703-784-2251.

**LOCATION:** On base. From the north on I-95 take exit 148 (Quantico USMC Base). West on MCB-4 approximately 7.5 miles to Lunga Reservoir office (.5 miles past FBI Academy). *USMRA: page 47 (L-5,6).* NMC: Washington DC, 30 miles north.

**DESCRIPTION OF AREA:** Campgrounds are situated along a 440-acre stocked reservoir in a wooded park. All improvements to park are blended in with the natural beauty of the area. Area is within driving distance of numerous points of interest in Fredericksburg, Manassas, Mount Vernon and Washington DC. Full range of support facilities available on base, ten miles from campgrounds.

**SEASON OF OPERATION:** Year round.

**ELIGIBILITY:** Active/Reservists/Retired.

**RESERVATIONS:** Reservations accepted for a limited number of full hookup sites. Address: Lunga Park, c/o Recreation Branch, P.O. Box 186, Quantico Marine Corps Base, VA 22134-0186. **C-703-784-5270, D-312-278-5270.**

**Camper Spaces:** Gravel (2), E (110V/20A)/S/W hookups. Rates: $15 daily. Gravel (2), E (110V/20A)/W hookups. Rates: $12 daily.

**Camper/Tent Spaces:** Gravel (9), E (110V/20/30/50A)/S/W hookups. Rates: $18 daily. Gravel (6), E (110V/20/30/50A)/W hookups. Rates: $15 daily. Wilderness (18), no hookups. Rates: $6 daily.

**SUPPORT FACILITIES:**

| | | |
|---|---|---|
| Archery Range | Boat Launch/fee | Boat Rental |
| Chapel/on base* | General Store* | Golf/on base |
| Grills | Marina/Potomac | Nature/Fitness Trail |
| Pavilions/fee* | Picnic Area* | Pit Toilets |
| Playgrounds | Sewage Dump | Stables/on base |

* Handicap accessible.

**ACTIVITIES:**

| | | |
|---|---|---|
| Archery | Bird Watching | Boating Equipment |
| Fishing/license | Picnicking | Hiking |

**CREDIT CARDS ACCEPTED:** Visa and MasterCard.

**RESTRICTIONS:** Pets allowed on leash. Firearms must be registered on base. No swimming in the reservoir. Boat rentals and General Store available 15 Apr-15 Oct.

# PICKETT TRAVEL CAMP (VA33R1)

Virginia Army National Guard
Maneuver Training Center at Fort Pickett
Blackstone, VA 23824-5000

**TELEPHONE NUMBER INFORMATION:** Main installation numbers: C-804-292-8621, D-312-438-8621. Police for travel camp, C-804-292-8444.

**LOCATION:** On post. From US-460 west of Petersburg, take Fort Pickett exit, follow the signs to Fort Pickett. *USMRA: page 47 (K-9).* NMC: Petersburg, 40 miles northeast.

**DESCRIPTION OF AREA:** Nine lakes and ponds available within installation boundaries. Travel camp is in wooded area adjacent to main post. Petersburg and Richmond have many museums, dinner theaters and historic sights. Wide range of support facilities available on post.

**ELIGIBILITY:** Active/Reservists/Retired.

**RESERVATIONS:** Required. Address: ARNG-MTC, Attn: VAFP-LH PRN: 10C, Fort Pickett, Blackstone, VA 23824-9000. **C-804-292-2443, D-312-438-2443** 0730-1600 hours Mon-Fri. Fax: C-804-292-8617. Other hours MP Station Bldg 471. Check in Billeting Office, Bldg T-469

**SEASON OF OPERATION:** Year round.

**Pegram Camper Spaces:** 5, E (110V/30A)/S/W hookups. Rates: $9 daily.

**Tent Spaces:** 6, no hookups. Rates: $5 daily.

**SUPPORT FACILITIES:**

| | | |
|---|---|---|
| Laundry | Restrooms | Sewage Dump |
| Showers | | |

**CREDIT CARDS ACCEPTED:** Visa, MasterCard, American Express, Discover and Diners'.

**RESTRICTIONS:** Pets allowed on leash. Firearms allowed subject to Federal, VA, and county laws.

# SEA MIST RECREATIONAL VEHICLE CAMPGROUND (VA25R1)

Dam Neck Fleet Combat Training Center Atlantic
Virginia Beach, VA 23461-5000

**TELEPHONE NUMBER INFORMATION:** Main installation numbers: C-757-444-0000, D-312-564-0111.

**LOCATION:** On base. From I-64, take I-44 E to Virginia Beach. Exit right on Birdneck Road (Exit 8) to General Booth Blvd. Go right on General Booth Blvd to Dam Neck Road, left on Dam Neck Road and follow to main gate. *USMRA: 47 (O-10) and page 52 (J-8)*. NMC: Virginia Beach, 2 miles northeast.

**DESCRIPTION OF AREA:** Located along the ocean, Sea Mist offers a beach, seasonal tourist attractions, surf fishing, hunting and many other recreational activities.

**SEASON OF OPERATION:** Year round.

**ELIGIBILITY:** Active/Reservists/Retired/Dam Neck DoD personnel. Active duty military personnel have priority if arriving at same time.

**RESERVATIONS:** Address: Attn: Host/Manager, Sea Mist Recreation Vehicle Campground, Dam Neck, VA 23461-2098. **C-757-433-6384 (office), C-757-433-7545 (camp), D-312-757-7545.** Fax: C-757-433-7356. E-mail: jslider55@aol.com. After hours, C-757-433-7545.

**Camper Spaces:** Concrete (24), E (110V/30A)/W hookups. Rates: $12 daily Oct-Feb, $15 daily Mar-Sep (weekly and monthly rates available).

**SUPPORT FACILITIES:**

| | | |
|---|---|---|
| Auto Craft Shop | Clubs | Exchange |
| Fitness Center | ITT | Laundry |
| Pool | Rec Equipment | Restrooms |
| Sewage Dump | Showers | Vending Machines |

**ACTIVITIES:**

| | | |
|---|---|---|
| Beaches | Boat Rental | Fishing |
| Hunting | Swimming | (fresh & saltwater) |
| (deer & duck) | | |

**CREDIT CARDS ACCEPTED:** Visa and MasterCard accepted at office, cash or check accepted at campground.

**RESTRICTIONS:** Firearms must be checked in with security.

# STEWART CAMPGROUND (VA04R1)

Chesapeake Naval Security Group Activity Northwest
Chesapeake, VA 23322-5000

**TELEPHONE NUMBER INFORMATION:** Main installation numbers: C-757-421-8000, D-312-564-1336. Police for campground, C-757-421-8334.

**LOCATION:** On base. At North Carolina/Virginia border, between Hickory VA. and Moyock NC. From I-64 south of Norfolk, take VA-168 S (Battlefield Blvd) approximately 16 miles to traffic light at Ballahack Road, right approximately three miles to Relay Road, left through gate, left on Olympic Avenue. *USMRA: page 47 (N,O-10)*. NMC: Norfolk VA, 35 miles north.

**DESCRIPTION OF AREA:** Located 75 miles north of Outer Banks NC. Region noted as vacationer's and sportsman's paradise. Civil War cemetery on base with graves of both Union and Confederate soldiers. Campground is in a wooded area secluded from installation operations area. Located six miles from Northwest River Park (NWRP), a boating and fishing area. Limited support facilities on base; full range at Norfolk NS, 30 miles north.

**SEASON OF OPERATION:** 1 May-31 Oct.

**ELIGIBILITY:** Active/Reservists/Retired/DoD civilians.

**RESERVATIONS:** Accepted with deposit. Address: Recreation Services, MOU #1 Box 697, NSGA Northwest, Chesapeake, VA 23322-5000. **C-757-421-8262** 0745-1615 hours Mon, 0745-1800 hours Tue-Fri, 0900-1700 hours Sat summer; 0745-1615 hours Mon-Fri winter. Fax: C-757-421-8785, D-312-564-1336 ext 262.

**Pop-up Campers:** 4, E (110V/20A)/S/W hookups. Rates: $15 daily/$30 weekend.

**Camper Spaces:** Dirt (11), E (110V/50A) hookup. Rates: $8 daily. Dirt (7), no hookups. Rates: $8 daily.

**Tent Spaces:** Grass (3), no hookups. Rates: $3 daily.

**SUPPORT FACILITIES:**

| | | |
|---|---|---|
| Auto Craft Shop | Boat Rental | Camper Rental |
| Convenience Store | Fitness Center | Gas |
| Grills | Pavilion/screened | Picnic Area |
| Playground | Pool | Rec Equipment |
| Restrooms* | Shoppette | Showers* |
| Snack Bar | Sports Field | Tennis Courts |
| Trails | | |

* Renovated in 1997.

**ACTIVITIES:**

| | | |
|---|---|---|
| Fishing | Hunting/license | Softball |

**CREDIT CARDS ACCEPTED:** Visa and MasterCard.

**RESTRICTIONS:** Pets allowed on leash. No firearms allowed. No open fires on ground. No ATVs. Water available at comfort station for filling only.

## YORKTOWN CG CAMPGROUND (VA37R1)

Yorktown Coast Guard Reserve Training Center
Yorktown, VA 23602-5000

**TELEPHONE NUMBER INFORMATION:** Main installation numbers: C-757-898-3500. Police for campground, C-757-898-3500.

**LOCATION:** On base. I-64 to Yorktown exit, northeast on US-17 through Yorktown, approximately eight miles. Reserve Training Center is two miles northeast of town. *USMRA: page 47 (N-8)*. NMC: Newport News, 15 miles southeast.

**DESCRIPTION OF AREA:** Situated in a wooded area along the York River. Historic and recreational areas of Yorktown, Jamestown, Colonial Williamsburg, Busch Gardens and Water Country USA are nearby. Fresh-water fishing in the lake behind the campground (bass, crappie, catfish and blue gill), also salt-water fishing (flounder, trout, croaker, spots and more). Limited support facilities on base; full range available at Yorktown Naval Weapons Station, five miles north.

**SEASON OF OPERATION:** Year round, no water Oct-Apr.

**ELIGIBILITY:** Active/Reservists/Retired/DoD, DOT and NAF civilian employees.

**RESERVATIONS:** Required for camper spaces, at least one week in advance, with non-refundable $10 deposit if no-show. Address: Morale, Welfare & Recreation, USCG Reserve Training Center, Yorktown, VA 23690-9761. **C-757-898-2128.** Check in at Gymnasium, Bldg 53, after 1200 hours, check out 1200 hours.

**Camper Spaces:** Gravel (9), E (110V/30A)/W hookups. Rates: $10 daily.

**Tent Spaces:** Gravel (5), no hookups. Rates: $5 daily. Prior to pitching tent, check in with Gym Watch, Bldg 53, for approval of location.

**SUPPORT FACILITIES:**

| | | |
|---|---|---|
| Auto Craft Shop | Bath House | Boat Launch |
| Boat Rental | Chapel | Commissary |
| Equipment Rental | Exchange | Fishing Pier |
| Fitness Center | Gas | Grills |
| Ice | Laundry | Pavilion |
| Picnic Area | Playground | Pool |
| Restrooms | Sewage Dump | Showers |
| Sports Fields | Tennis Courts | |

**ACTIVITIES:**

| | | |
|---|---|---|
| Boating | Fishing/license | Racquetball |
| Softball | Swimming | Tennis |

**CREDIT CARDS ACCEPTED:** None.

**RESTRICTIONS:** Pets allowed on leash, owner must clean up after pets. No open fires. Two week limit. No vehicles permitted in tent areas. Trash cans and bags are provided for daily clean-up, which is the responsibility of campers.

# WASHINGTON

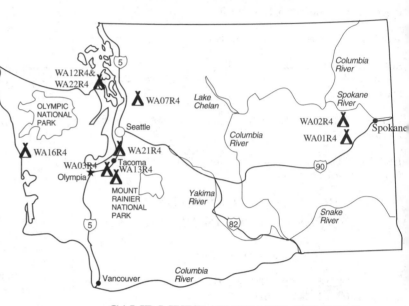

## CAMP MURRAY BEACH (WA21R4)

Camp Murray, WA 98430-5000

**TELEPHONE NUMBER INFORMATION:** Main installation numbers: C-253-584-5411. Police for camp, C-253-512-7900.

**LOCATION:** On post. From I-5 south of Tacoma, take exit 122 W across railroad tracks, left through Camp Murray gate and follow signs to beach. Register at office using forms provided. *USMRA: page 101 (C-5)*. NMC: Tacoma, 10 miles north.

**DESCRIPTION OF AREA:** Camp Murray is located on the southern end of Puget Sound in the Olympia Mountain region. Quiet, wooded site along American Lake. Winter temperature range 35-45º, summer 65-80º. No support facilities on post; full range available at Fort Lewis, two miles south.

**SEASON OF OPERATION:** Year round.

**ELIGIBILITY:** Active/Reservists/Retired.

**RESERVATIONS:** Recommended. Address: Camp Murray Beach, P.O. Box 92055, Tillicum, WA 98492-5004. **C-253-584-5411.** Check out 1200 hours.

**Camper Spaces:** Gravel (24), E (110V/30A)/S/W hookups. Rates: $11 daily/$70 weekly.

**Tent Spaces:** Open, no hookups. Rates: $5 daily/$35 weekly.

**SUPPORT FACILITIES:**

| | | |
|---|---|---|
| Beach | Laundromat | Marina |
| Picnic Area | Playground | Restrooms |
| Showers | | |

**ACTIVITIES:**

| | | |
|---|---|---|
| Basketball | Boating | Fishing/license |
| Horseshoes | Jogging | Laundry |
| Snorkeling | Swimming | Volleyball |
| Water Skiing | | |

**CREDIT CARDS ACCEPTED:** Visa and MasterCard.

**RESTRICTIONS:** Pets allowed on leash, must be walked in designated areas only. No firearms allowed. Quiet hours 2200-0800 hours. No off-road vehicles.

# CLEAR LAKE RECREATION AREA (WA01R4)

Fairchild Air Force Base
Fairchild AFB, WA 99011-8536

**TELEPHONE NUMBER INFORMATION:** Main installation numbers: C-509-247-1212, D-312-657-1110. Police for recreation area, C-911.

**LOCATION:** Off base. From I-90 take exit 264 north on Salnave Road, right on Clear Lake Road .5 miles to area. *USMRA: page 101 (I-4).* NMI: Fairchild AFB, 7.5 miles north. NMC: Spokane, 12 miles northeast.

**DESCRIPTION OF AREA:** Located on Clear Lake in a state where natural wildlife is a challenge and recreation an adventure, this 34-acre area is the perfect place for camping, water skiing, fishing and boating. Full range of support facilities available on base.

**SEASON OF OPERATION:** Mid Apr-mid Jun: 0700-1900 hours Thu-Mon. Mid-Jun to 30 Sep: 0900-2100 hours Thu-Mon, 1100-1900 hours Tue-Wed. Hours subject to change after Labor Day.

**ELIGIBILITY:** Active/Reservists/Retired/DoD civilians.

**RESERVATIONS:** Accepted 30 days in advance with deposit. Address: Clear Lake Recreation Area, S 14824 Clear Lake Road, Cheney, WA 99004-5000. **C-509-299-5129.** Fax: C-509-247-5759. For information off-season, contact: 92 SVS/SVROE, 121 N Doolittle Avenue, Fairchild AFB, WA 99011-5000. C-509-247-5366, D-312-657-5366. Check in at office, check out 1200 hours.

**Cabins:** One-bedroom (3), kitchen. Patrons must provide utensils and linens. Rates: $20 daily/$120 weekly.

**Yurts:** 16'(1). Patrons must provide utensils and linens. Rates: $7 daily, $42 weekly. *Note: A yurt is a cabin/tent structure with wooden floor, deck and door, two windows, and stretched-canvas covering with skylight. It is furnished, but has no bathroom or kitchen.*

**Camper Spaces:** Paved (24), E (110V/30A)/S/W hookups. Rates: $11 daily/$66 weekly. Overflow (3) E hookup. Rates: $7 daily/$42 weekly.

**Tent Spaces:** 10, some with W. Rates: $5 daily/$30 weekly.

**SUPPORT FACILITIES:**

| | | |
|---|---|---|
| Bath House | Beach | Boat Launch* |
| Boat Rental/Storage | Camping Equipment | Fire Rings |
| Fishing Pier | Gas/regular | Grills |
| Ice | Pavilions | Picnic Areas |
| Playgrounds | Rec Equipment | Restrooms |
| Sewage Dump | Showers | Snack Bar |
| Telephone | | |

* Handicap accessible.

**ACTIVITIES:**

| | | |
|---|---|---|
| Boating | Fishing/license | Sailing |
| Swimming | Water Skiing | |

**CREDIT CARDS ACCEPTED:** Visa and MasterCard.

**RESTRICTIONS:** Pets allowed on leash; must not be left unattended outside; owner must clean up after pet. No fireworks. No fires outside of fire rings. Quiet hours are 2200-0700.

# CLIFFSIDE RV PARK (WA12R4)

Whidbey Island Naval Air Station
Oak Harbor, WA 98278-2500

**TELEPHONE NUMBER INFORMATION:** Main installation numbers: C-360-257-2211, D-312-820-0111. Police for RV park, C-360-257-3122.

**LOCATION:** On base. Off WA-20, four miles northwest of Oak Harbor. From WA-20 turn onto Ault Field Road, right at Langley Blvd, through Main Gate of NAS to a four-way stop, left onto Midway Street to stop sign, then right onto Saratoga Street, left onto Intruder Street which is a paved road leading into Cliffside Park. *USMRA: page 101 (C-2,3).* NMC: Seattle, 60 miles southeast.

**DESCRIPTION OF AREA:** Beautiful scenic area with salt-water beach and marina nearby offering many water sports. Full range of support facilities available on base.

**SEASON OF OPERATION:** Year round.

**ELIGIBILITY:** Active/Reservists/Retired/DoD civilians with MWR User Card.

**RESERVATIONS:** Accepted with Deposit: up to 90 days in advance for active duty, up to 60 days for others. Address: Outdoor Recreation Center, 1130 W Storm Lane, Whidbey Island Naval Air Station, Oak Harbor, WA 98278-2100. **C-360-257-2434, D-312-820-2434.** Check out 1100 hours.

**Camper Spaces:** Gravel (18), E (110/220V/20/30A)/W hookups. Gravel (2), up to 40', E (110/220V/20/30A)/W hookups. Rates: $10 daily/$60 weekly for military; $11 daily/$66 weekly for DoD.

**Tent Spaces:** Grass (6), no hookups. Rates: $5 daily/$30 weekly for military; $6 daily/$36 weekly for DoD.

**SUPPORT FACILITIES:**

| | | |
|---|---|---|
| Boat Launch | Boat Rental | Grills |
| Marina | Picnic Area | Rec Equipment |
| Restrooms | Sewage Dump | Showers |

**ACTIVITIES:**

| | | |
|---|---|---|
| Boating | Fishing | Water Sports |

**CREDIT CARDS ACCEPTED:** Visa, MasterCard, America Express and Discover.

**RESTRICTIONS:** House pets allowed on leash, must not be left unattended outside, owner must clean up after pet. No firearms allowed. No open fires on ground or beach. Quiet hours 2300-0800 hours. Two week limit during July and August. Maximum of eight persons and two vehicles per site.

# FAIRCHILD AFB FAMCAMP (WA02R4)

Fairchild Air Force Base
Fairchild AFB, WA 99011-8536

**TELEPHONE NUMBER INFORMATION:** Main installation number: C-509-247-1212, D-312-657-1212. Security Police for base: C-509-247-5493.

**LOCATION:** On base. From I-90 take US Highway 2 W exit through Air Way Heights. Continue to entrance for base on left. Turn right on Fairchild Highway to the end. Turn left on Offutt Parkway for .5 miles, right on O'Malley for .25 miles, road becomes Galveston. FAMCAMP entrance is on left. *USMRA: page 101 (I-4).* NMC: Spokane, 12 miles east.

*WASHINGTON*
*Fairchild AFB FAMCAMP, continued*

**DESCRIPTION OF AREA:** The FAMCAMP is located in a grove of locust trees in a meadow of native grasses. Full range of support facilities on base.

**SEASON OF OPERATION:** Year round.

**ELIGIBILITY:** Active/Reservists/Retired/DoD/NAF civilians and their guests per AFR 215-1.

**RESERVATIONS:** No advance reservations. Address: 92 SVS/SVROE, 120 N Foulois, FAFB, WA 99011-9599. **C-509-247-2511/5366, D-312-657-2511** 1000 hours until dark. Fax: C-509-247-4495. Camp Host, C-509-244-3247. If unattended check in, go to Equipment Check-out (#19) on map, check out time is 1200 hours.

**Camper Spaces:** Gravel (16-1 handicap accessible), E (110V/30A)/S/W hookups. Rates: $11 daily. Scheduled to be paved September 1998.

**SUPPORT FACILITIES:**

| | | |
|---|---|---|
| Auto Craft Shop | Boat Rental/Storage | Chapel |
| Commissary | Convenience Store | Equipment Rental |
| Exchange | Fitness Center | Gas |
| Grills | Ice | Laundry |
| Marina | Picnic Area | Playground |
| Pools | Rec Center | Restrooms |
| Sewage Dump | Showers | Snack Bar |
| Sports Fields | Telephones | Tennis Courts |

**ACTIVITIES:**

| | | |
|---|---|---|
| Archery | Bicycling | Boating |
| Fishing/license | Golf Driving Range | Hiking |
| Parks | Skeet Trap | Swimming |

**CREDIT CARDS ACCEPTED:** Visa and MasterCard are accepted at the Equipment Checkout, Bldg 2249.

**RESTRICTIONS:** Pets allowed on leash, owner must clean up after pets and keep them inside at night and when leaving the area. Open fires prohibited. Quiet hours 2300-0700 hours, no generators operated at night. No tent camping. Each site allowed one camping unit and one towing vehicle. Motorcycles allowed only to leave or enter park. No smoking in restrooms or laundry. Grills provided at site, must be cleaned after use. Stay limited to a 14-day period, occupant may re-register for a waiting list after the 15th day. Use of FAMCAMP will not exceed 90 days. Posted speed limit five miles per hour.

# FORT LEWIS TRAVEL CAMP (WA13R4)

Fort Lewis
Fort Lewis, WA 98433-9500

**TELEPHONE NUMBER INFORMATION:** Main installation numbers: C-253-967-1110, D-312-357-1110. Police for travel camp, C-253-967-3107.

**LOCATION:** On post. From I-5 take exit 122. Follow signs to North Fort Lewis. Take first right after guard shack. *USMRA: page 101 (C-5)*. NMC: Tacoma, 5 miles north.

**DESCRIPTION OF AREA:** Located at southern end of Puget Sound in unique, snow-topped Olympia Mountain region. Tranquil, wooded site along American Lake. Winter temperature range 35°-45°, summer, 65°-80°. Enjoy the beautiful weather in Washington. If you don't, wait five minutes and it will change! Full range of support facilities available on post.

**SEASON OF OPERATION:** Year round.

**ELIGIBILITY:** Active/Reservists/Retired/DoD and NAF civilians.

**RESERVATIONS:** Advised, accepted up to 60 days in advance with first night's payment. Address: Fort Lewis Travel Camp, Northwest Adventure Center, P.O. Box 33156, Fort Lewis, WA 98433-5000. **C-253-967-5415/7744, D-312-357-5415/7744.** Fax: C-253-964-5294. Check out 1100 hours.

**Log Cabins:** One-bedroom (6-1 handicap accessible), sleeps four, furnished, bathroom, kitchenette, utensils, linens. Rates: $55 daily.

**Log Bungalows:** 4-1 handicap accessible, sleeps two, furnished, bathroom, kitchenette, utensils, linens. Rates: $45 daily.

**Camper Spaces:** Hardstand (49), E (110V/20/30/50A)/S/W/CATV hookups. Rates: $13 daily/$85 weekly May-Sep; $11 daily/$70 weekly Oct-Apr.

**Tent Spaces:** 5, no hookups. Rates: $5.50 daily/$30 weekly.

**In addition, there are 30 rustic camper and tent spaces available at Chambers Lake and Lewis Lake.** These sites have no hookups and are free.

**SUPPORT FACILITIES:**

| | | |
|---|---|---|
| Auto Craft Shop | Bath House | Beach |
| Boat Launch | Boat Rental/Storage | Chapel |
| Commissary | Exchange | Fishing Pier |
| Fitness Center | Gas | Golf |
| Grills | Laundry | Marina |
| Pavilion | Picnic Area | Rec Center |
| Rec Equipment | Restrooms* | Sewage Dump |
| Shoppette | Showers* | Sports Fields |
| Telephones | Tennis Courts | Trails |

* Handicap accessible.

Travel trailers may be rented from Outdoor Equipment Resource Center.

**ACTIVITIES:**

| | | |
|---|---|---|
| Fishing/license | Hunting | Kayaking |
| Skiing | Swimming | White Water Rafting |

**CREDIT CARDS ACCEPTED:** Visa, MasterCard and Esprit.

**RESTRICTIONS:** No pets in cabins, but allowed on leash at camp, owner must clean up after pets. No open fires or wood fires. Quiet hours after 2200 hours. Two week limit.

# HOLIDAY PARK FAMCAMP (WA03R4)

McChord Air Force Base
McChord AFB, WA 98438-1304

**TELEPHONE NUMBER INFORMATION:** Main installation numbers: C-253-512-1910, D-312-984-1110. Police for FAMCAMP, C-253-984-5624.

**LOCATION:** On base. From I-5 south of Tacoma, take exit 125 E for McChord AFB. Follow signs to McChord AFB and through main gate, right on Fairview Road, left on Lincoln Blvd, right on Outer Drive, right at Holiday Park sign. *USMRA: page 101 (C-5) and page 103 (B-7)*. NMC: Tacoma, 8 miles northeast.

**DESCRIPTION OF AREA:** Located in western area of state at base of Puget Sound. FAMCAMP offers a base for prime sightseeing and recreational opportunities on numerous waterways and lakes in Puget

Sound area and nearby national parks: Mount Rainier, Olympic and North Cascades. Camp area is quiet, wooded area surrounded by giant firs and pines, populated by wildlife. Full range of support facilities on base.

**SEASON OF OPERATION:** Year round.

**ELIGIBILITY:** Active/Reservists/Retired/DoD civilians.

**RESERVATIONS:** No advance reservations. Address: Holiday Park FAMCAMP, c/o Adventures Unlimited, 62 SVS/SVRO, Bldg 739, McChord AFB, WA 98438-5000. **C-253-984-5488.** Check in at office 1100 hours, check out 1000 hours.

**Camper Spaces:** Asphalt (18-some handicap accessible), E (110V/30A)/S/W hookups. Rates: $11 daily/$70 weekly/$260 monthly winter. Asphalt (18), E (110V/30A)/W hookups. Rates: $10 daily/$65 weekly/$240 monthly winter. Open, many, no hookups. Rates: $5 daily/$32.50 weekly.

**Tent Spaces:** 12, no hookups. Rates: $3 daily/$19.50 weekly.

**SUPPORT FACILITIES:**

| | | |
|---|---|---|
| Auto Craft Shop | Bicycle Rental | Boat Rental/Storage |
| Chapel | Commissary | Exchange |
| Fitness Center | Gas | Golf |
| Grills | Hiking Equipment | Laundry/new |
| Pavilion | Picnic Areas | Playground |
| Pool/summer | Rec Equipment | Restrooms*/new |
| Sewage Dump | Shoppette | Showers/new |
| Shuttle Bus | Sports Fields | Telephones/pay |
| Trails | Vending Machine | |

* Handicap accessible.

**ACTIVITIES:**

| | | |
|---|---|---|
| Bicycling | Boating | Fishing/permit |
| Hiking | Horseshoes | Sightseeing |
| Softball | Swimming/summer | Volleyball |

**CREDIT CARDS ACCEPTED:** None.

**RESTRICTIONS:** Pets allowed on leash, must have certificate and tag for current rabies vaccination. Firearms must be cleared at Security Gate. No open fires. Two week limit May-Sep.

# JIM CREEK REGIONAL OUTDOOR RECREATION AREA (WA07R4)

Jim Creek Naval Radio Station
Arlington, WA 98223-8599

**TELEPHONE NUMBER INFORMATION:** Main installation numbers: C-425-304-5315, D-312-727-5315. Base Police-425-304-5314, D-312-727-5314.

**LOCATION:** On base. From I-5, take exit 208, east on SR-530 for approximately three miles, through Arlington, cross bridge, after approximately four miles take right on Jim Creek Road (266th Street NE) six miles to the end. *USMRA: page 101 (D-3).* NMC: Seattle, 60 miles southwest.

**DESCRIPTION OF AREA:** Jim Creek borders the Mt Baker-Snoqualmie National Forest and the Boulder River Wilderness Area. Located in the foothills of the North Cascades about one hour north of Seattle, Jim Creek

has over 5,000 acres-most of it wilderness, with a wide variety of recreational opportunities. Twin Lakes (famous for great fishing, canoeing, and wildlife viewing) is home to 250 acres of Old Growth forest accessible by hiking. No support facilities on base; full range available at Everett NAS, 30 miles west.

**SEASON OF OPERATION:** Year round.

**ELIGIBILITY:** Active/Reservists/Retired/DoD civilians.

**RESERVATIONS:** Accepted. Address: Outdoor Recreation Area, 21027 Jim Creek Road, Jim Creek NRS, Arlington, WA 98223-8599. **C-425-304-5315/5363, or C-1-888-463-6697** (good in Washington State only), **D-312-727-5315.** Fax: C-425-304-5364. Check out 1200 hours.

**RV Spaces:** Concrete (4), handicap accessible, E (110V/30/50A)/W hookups. Rates: $12 daily.

**Campsites:** Gravel/Dirt (16), no hookups. Rates: $10 daily.

**Log Cabins:** 2. No electricity, no water. Rates: $20 daily.

**Camp:** Day Camp, Group Camping for Scouts, Campfire Girls, etc. Rates: Minimum $25 daily or $1 per person.

**SUPPORT FACILITIES:**

| | | |
|---|---|---|
| Boat Rental | Conference Center | Fire Rings |
| Fishing Pier | Grills | Ice |
| Laundry | Lodge | Pavilion |
| Picnic Area | Playground | Rec Equipment |
| Restrooms* | Sewage Dump | Showers* |
| Telephones | Trails | |

* Handicap accessible.

**ACTIVITIES:**

| | | |
|---|---|---|
| Backpacking | Boating | Fishing/license |
| Hiking | Mountain Biking | River rafting* |
| Rock Climbing* | Snow Skiing/XC* | |

* Activities nearby base.

**CREDIT CARDS ACCEPTED:** Visa, MasterCard, American Express and Discover.

**RESTRICTIONS:** Pets allowed on leash. No firearms or fireworks. Open fires only in designated areas. Smoking only in designated areas. No unlicensed off-road vehicles, no private boats, and no swimming allowed. Cameras allowed in unrestricted areas only. Level of radio frequency is considered a potential hazard to people employing electronic life aid/support systems.

# PACIFIC BEACH RESORT AND CONFERENCE CENTER (WA16R4)

Everett Naval Station
Everett, WA 98207-5001

**TELEPHONE NUMBER INFORMATION:** Main installation numbers: C-425-304-3000, D-312-727-3000. Police for center, C-911.

**LOCATION:** Off base. From I-5 at Olympia, take exit 104 (Aberdeen/Port Angeles), west on US-8 and US-12 through Aberdeen to Hoquiam. Follow US-101 N approximately four miles to sign indicating Ocean Beaches, turn left and continue on Ocean Beach Road through Copalis Crossing, Carlisle and Aloha to Pacific Beach. Follow Main Street to entrance to Pacific Beach Recreation and Conference Center. Watch for signs to office. *USMRA: page 101 (A-4,5).* NMI: Fort Lewis, 115 miles northeast. NMC: Aberdeen, 25 miles southeast.

*WASHINGTON*
*Pacific Beach Resort And Conference Center, continued*

**DESCRIPTION OF AREA:** Situated on Olympic Peninsula, overlooking Pacific Ocean, providing starting point for exploring the Peninsula with its spectacular rain forest, Quinalt Indian Reservation and Ocean Shores area. It also offers steelhead and salmon fishing. Limited support facilities on base, full range available at Fort Lewis.

**SEASON OF OPERATION:** Year round.

**ELIGIBILITY:** Active/Reservists/Retired/DoD civilians/100% DAV.

**RESERVATIONS:** Recommended for RV park, studios and motel units, required for cabins and suites, with deposit: up to 90 days in advance for active duty, up to 60 days in advance for retired and reserve, up to 30 days in advance for all others. Minimum two-night stay. Address: Pacific Beach Center, 108 First Street, P.O. Box O, Pacific Beach, WA 98571-5000. (Make checks payable to Pacific Beach.) **C-1-888-463-6697, C-425-276-4414** 0800-1600 hours Mon-Fri, 0800-1600 hours Sat-Sun. Fax: C-425-276-4615. For information only, C-425-304-3122. Check in 1600-2000 hours.

**Beach Houses:** Four-bedroom (5), sleeps eight, fully equipped, cribs. Rates: $45-$65 daily. Three-bedroom (23), sleeps six, fully equipped, cribs. Rates: $40-$60 daily (depending on rank, days of week, and season). Oceanview with fireplace, $10 additional daily. $5 additional daily for units with wood stoves. Patrons must provide linens, $5 per visit. (Weekly and monthly rates available.)

**Suites:** 6, adults only, sleeps two, fully equipped, cribs. Rates: $35-$55 daily (depending on rank, days of week, and season). Oceanview with fireplace, $10 additional daily. $5 additional daily for units with wood stoves. Patrons must provide linens, $5 per visit. (Weekly and monthly rates available.)

**Studios:** 15, sleeps two, fully equipped, cribs. Rates: $15-$25 daily (depending on rank, days of week, and season). Oceanview with fireplace, $10 additional daily. $5 additional daily for units with wood stoves. Patrons must provide linens, $5 per visit. (Weekly and monthly rates available.)

**Family Units:** 12, sleeps two adults and two children, cribs. Rates: $20-$30 daily (depending on rank, days of week, and season). Oceanview with fireplace, $10 additional daily. $5 additional daily for units with wood stoves. Patrons must provide linens, $5 per visit. (Weekly and monthly rates available.)

**RV Spaces:** Hardstand (43), E (110V/30A)/W hookups. Rates: $7-$11 daily (depending on rank, days of week, and season). $1 additional daily for 33 RV spaces with CATV. (Weekly and monthly rates available.)

**Camper/Tent Spaces:** 100, no hookups. 25, fire pits, private parking, shower facilities, and restrooms. Rates: $5 daily.

**SUPPORT FACILITIES:**

| | | |
|---|---|---|
| Bowling | CATV | Conference Facility |
| Exercise Room | Hot Tubs/Spa | Laundry |
| Lounge | Meeting Rooms | Pay Telephones |
| Restaurant | Restrooms | Sewage Dump |
| Showers | Social Room | Weight Room |

Most restrooms and buildings are handicap accessible.

**ACTIVITIES:**

| | | |
|---|---|---|
| Basketball | Beachcombing | Bingo |
| Card Tournament | Clamming | Crabbing |
| Dancing | Fishing | Group Activities |
| Hiking | Hunting | Kiddie Bingo |
| Weekly Events | | |

Scheduled activities for all ages.

**CREDIT CARDS ACCEPTED:** Visa, MasterCard and American Express.

**RESTRICTIONS:** Pets allowed on leash and must be registered, owner must clean up after pet. No open fires except in covered picnic area, in grills and camp stoves, must not be left unattended at any time. Quiet hours 1000-0700 hours. Two-night minimum, three-night minimum on holiday weekends (Fri-Mon), 14-day limit. No cooking in studios and family units, no children, pets nor smoking in suites. Any excess cleaning/repair will be billed to patron. Sponsor must accompany guest during stay. No RV/camper parking at beach houses. Hunting rifles must be declared, no other firearms are allowed.

# ROCKY POINT RV PARK (WA22R4)

Whidbey Island Naval Air Station
Oak Harbor, WA 98278-2500

**TELEPHONE NUMBER INFORMATION:** Main installation numbers: C-360-257-2211, D-312-820-0111. Police for RV park, C-360-257-3122.

**LOCATION:** Off base. Off WA-20, four miles northwest of Oak Harbor. From WA-20 turn onto Ault Field Road and continue straight on Ault which will take you to Clover Valley Road (do not bear right on Ault). Continue straight on Clover Valley Road, bear left at Golf Course Road where you will see the course. Sign in at the Pro Shop at the Gallery Golf Course. *USMRA: page 101 (D-4).* NMC: Seattle, 60 miles southeast.

**DESCRIPTION OF AREA:** RV park located within walking distance of local Gallery Golf Course. Sites with water view, and salt-water beach and picnic area nearby. Full range of support facilities available on base three miles away.

**SEASON OF OPERATION:** Year round.

**ELIGIBILITY:** Active/Reservists/Retired/DoD civilians with MWR User Card.

**RESERVATIONS:** Not accepted. Address: Gallery Golf Course, 3065 N Cowpens Road, Whidbey Island Naval Air Station, Bldg 130, Oak Harbor, WA 98278-1900. **C-360-257-2178, D-312-820-2178.** Check in at pro shop 0630-1930, check out 1100 hours.

**RV Spaces:** Self-contained (23), no hookups. Rates: $7 daily/$42 weekly for military; $8 daily/$48 weekly for DoD.

**SUPPORT FACILITIES:**

| | | |
|---|---|---|
| Boat Launch | Boat Rental | Grills |
| Marina | Picnic Area | Port-a-Potties |
| Rec Equipment | | |

**ACTIVITIES:**

| | | |
|---|---|---|
| Boating | Fishing | Golf |
| Water Sports | | |

**CREDIT CARDS ACCEPTED:** Visa and MasterCard.

**RESTRICTIONS:** Pets allowed on leash, domestic, must not be left unattended outside, owner must clean up after pet. No firearms allowed. No open fires on ground or beach. Quiet hours 2300-0800 hours. Maximum of eight person and two vehicles per site.

# WEST VIRGINIA

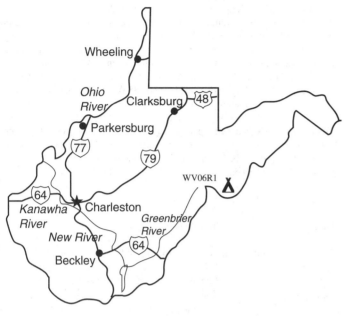

## SUGAR GROVE CABINS (WV06R1)

Sugar Grove Naval Security Group Activity
Sugar Grove, WV 26815-9700

**TELEPHONE NUMBER INFORMATION:** Main installation numbers: C-304-249-6366, D-312-564-7276. Police for cabin area: C-304-249-6312/6310.

**LOCATION:** On base. Take US-33 west from Harrisonburg VA to Brandywine WV (approximately 30 miles). At Brandywine, turn left onto West Virginia State Route 21 and proceed approximately five miles to the Navy base. *USMRA: page 47 (I-6).* NMC: Harrisonburg VA, 34 miles southeast.

**DESCRIPTION OF AREA:** Located in the mountain section of West Virginia, the Station is bisected by US-33. It is an area of quiet beauty with hills and mountains, beautiful valleys, and deep gorges where streams have carved their way through the mountains. Limited support facilities available on base; full range available at Quantico Marine Corps Base, VA approximately a 3.5 hour drive east.

**SEASON OF OPERATION:** Year round.

**ELIGIBILITY:** Active/Reservists/Retired/DoD civilians.

**RESERVATIONS:** Required. Address: MWR Department, Bldg 20, Naval Security Group Activity, Sugar Grove, WV 26815-9700. **C-304-249-6309, D-312-564-7276.** Fax: C-304-249-6385. Check in at MWR Office.

**Rustic Log Cabin:** One-room (1), sleeps up to four, furnished, full bathroom, refrigerator, stove, electricity, A/C, heat, kerosene heat, most linens. Rates: $20 daily. Two-bedroom (4), sleeps seven, furnished, refrigerator, stove, dishwasher, A/C, heat, linens. Rates: $35 daily.

**SUPPORT FACILITIES:**

| | | |
|---|---|---|
| Boat Motors | Boat Rental | Camping Equipment |
| Camper Rental | Community Center | EM Club |
| Picnic Area | Port-a-Potties | Rec Equipment |
| Tent Rental | | |

**ACTIVITIES:**

| | | |
|---|---|---|
| Bowling | Fitness Trail | Fishing |
| Gym | Hiking | Hunting |
| Picnicking | Pool | Volleyball (Sand) |
| Softball Fields | Tennis Courts | |

**CREDIT CARDS ACCEPTED:** Visa and MasterCard.

**RESTRICTIONS:** Pets allowed on leash. Firearms must be checked in with Security Department.

# WISCONSIN
## PINE VIEW RECREATION AREA (WI01R2)

Fort McCoy
Fort McCoy, WI 54656-5141

**TELEPHONE NUMBER INFORMATION:** Main installation numbers: C-608-388-2222, D-312-280-1110.

**LOCATION:** On post. Exit I-90 at Sparta to WI-21, eight miles northeast to main gate. Well marked. Recreation area off west Headquarters Road, one mile west of Post Headquarters. *USMRA: page 68 (C,D-7).* NMC: LaCrosse, 35 miles west.

**DESCRIPTION OF AREA:** Beautiful wooded area bounded by Squaw Lake and LaCrosse River. Eleven ponds and small lakes on post are ideal for fishing activities. Squaw Lake is well stocked with rainbow trout. Wide range of support facilities available on post.

**SEASON OF OPERATION:** 18 Apr-30 Nov.

**ELIGIBILITY:** Active/Reservists/Retired/DoD and NAF civilians.

**RESERVATIONS:** Recommended. Address: DPCA, 1439 South M Street, Attn: Pine View Recreation Area, Fort McCoy, WI 54656-5141. **C-608-388-3517/2619, D-312-280-3517.** Discounts to holders of Golden Age Passports.

*WISCONSIN*
*Pine View Recreation Area, continued*

**Duplex:** One-bedroom (2), private bath, kitchenette, refrigerator, microwave, coffee maker, toaster, A/C. heat, clock radio. Rates: $35 daily.

**Cabins:** One-bedroom (2), sofabed, private bath, loft, living room, kitchen, refrigerator, stove, microwave, coffee maker, toaster, A/C, heat, clock radio. Rates: $35 daily.

**Cabin:** One-room (1), double bed, sofabed, loft, refrigerator, stove, coffee maker. Rates: $25 daily.

**Campers:** 30' (6). Rates: $35 daily.

**Camper Spaces:** Gravel (29), E (110V/30A)/S/W hookups. Rates: $14 daily. Gravel (70), E (110V/20/30A) hookup. Rates: $10 daily.

**Camper/Tent Spaces:** 8, no hookups. Rates: $8 daily.

**Tent Spaces:** 12, no hookups. Rates: $8 daily.

**SUPPORT FACILITIES:**

| | | |
|---|---|---|
| Bicycle Rental | Boat Rental | Camp Store |
| Camper Rental | Grills | Hiking Trail |
| Laundry/nearby | Miniature Golf | Pavilion/fee |
| Picnic Area | Playground | Restrooms |
| RV Storage | Sewage Dump | Showers |

**ACTIVITIES:**

| | | |
|---|---|---|
| Bicycling | Fishing/license | Hiking |
| Horseshoes | Hunting/license | Pedal Boating |
| Swimming | Volleyball | Winter Sports |

**Whitetail Ridge Recreation Area**, catering to all levels of skiers, Dec-Mar, depending on the weather. Facilities include: four lighted ski slopes with snowmaking capability, downhill and five mile cross-country skiing, 185' vertical and 1300' long runs, two ski lifts, tubing slope with handle tow, equipment rental, chalet and snack bar. Groomed snowmobile trail network also passes through the Whitetail Ridge area. For information, C-608-388-4498, D-312-280-4498.

**CREDIT CARDS ACCEPTED:** Visa, MasterCard and American Express.

**RESTRICTIONS:** Pets allowed on leash. Hunting firearms allowed only.

# RAWLEY POINT COTTAGE (WI04R2)
Milwaukee Coast Guard Group
Milwaukee, WI 53207-1997

**TELEPHONE NUMBER INFORMATION:** Main installation numbers: C-414-747-7185. Police for cottages, C-911.

**LOCATION:** Off base. From I-43 near Two Rivers take exit 79, north on WI-42 into the city. Right on 17th Street, cross drawbridge, right on East Street, four blocks to Two Rivers CG Station at 13 East Street. Cottage is located five miles north of CG Station. Directions to cottage will be sent when reservations are made.

**DESCRIPTION OF AREA:** Historical 115-year-old lighthouse overlooking Lake Michigan. Cottage is situated within 2800-acre Point Beach State Park. Twin cities of Two Rivers/Manitowoc are rich in festivals, fishing derbies and maritime events. Charter boats provide offshore fishing for lake trout and salmon. Limited support facilities at Two Rivers CG Station; full range at Fort McCoy, 175 miles west.

**SEASON OF OPERATION:** Year round.

**ELIGIBILITY:** Active/Reservists/Retired/DOT civilians/CG Auxiliary.

**RESERVATIONS:** Required, by phone, up to 90 days in advance for active duty CG, 40 days in advance for all other active duty and retirees, 15 days in advance for reserve and auxiliary. Full payment required seven working days prior to check-in. Cancellations must be made seven working days prior to check-in to avoid having to pay full amount. Address: Commander, Group Milwaukee USCG, 2420 South Lincoln Memorial Drive, Milwaukee, WI 53207-1997. **C-414-747-7185** 0700-1500 hours. Check in at 1300 hours, check out by 1200 hours.

**Townhouse:** Two-bedroom apartment (2), sleeps eight, furnished, private bath, kitchen, microwave, pots/pans, dishes, TV/VCR, washer/dryer. Patrons must provide bed linens (queen, full and twin), blankets, towels and toiletries. Rates: $30 daily.

**SUPPORT FACILITIES:**

| | | |
|---|---|---|
| Beach | Bicycles | Grills |
| Picnic Area | Telephones | |

**Nearby park and commercial facilities offer:**

| | | |
|---|---|---|
| Camping | Chapel | Golf |
| Grocery | Laundry | Marina |
| Rec Center | Tours | Trails |

Free Tour of Nuclear Power Generating Plant (off base).

**ACTIVITIES:**

| | | |
|---|---|---|
| Fishing | Hiking | Hunting |
| Swimming | Snow Skiing/XC | |

**CREDIT CARDS ACCEPTED:** None.

**RESTRICTIONS:** Pets allowed on leash, owner responsible for any damages, must clean up after pet daily. Use and possession of firearms must be in accordance with Federal, State, and local laws. No smoking in townhouse. Must bring own paper products and linens. Two night to one week limit. Military member/spouse must be present during the entire reservation. If unable to use reservation, it is not transferrable but must be cancelled. Townhouse must be fully cleaned prior to departure.

# SHERWOOD POINT COTTAGE (WI03R2)
Milwaukee Coast Guard Group
Milwaukee, WI 53207-1997

**TELEPHONE NUMBER INFORMATION:** Main installation numbers: C-414-747-7185.

**LOCATION:** Off base. From US-41 at Green Bay, take WI-57 N to Sturgeon Bay. To get to cottage take WI-42/57 S to County S, turn right on Duluth Street, left on Elm Street to County M, turn left just before Fishing Hole Tavern. This is the access road to the Coast Guard lighthouse. Approximately nine miles from Elm and County M. *USMRA: page 68 (H-5).* NMI: Fort McCoy, 190 miles southwest. NMC: Green Bay, 45 miles southwest.

**DESCRIPTION OF AREA:** Lighthouse situated on western shores of Lake Michigan. Beautiful cottage overlooking bay and wooded area. Near winter ski area. Wide range of support facilities available at Fort McCoy, 190 miles southwest.

**SEASON OF OPERATION:** Year round.

**ELIGIBILITY:** Active/Reservists/Retired/CG Auxiliary.

**RESERVATIONS:** Required, by telephone only, up to 90 days in advance for active duty CG, up to 40 days in advance for other active duty and Retired, up to 15 days in advance for Reserve and Auxiliary. Full payment required seven working days prior to check-in. Cancellations must be made seven working days prior to check-in to avoid having to pay full amount. Address: Commander, Coast Guard Group Morale Fund, 2420 South Lincoln Memorial Drive, Milwaukee, WI 53207-1997. **C-414-747-7185** 0700-1500 hours. Check in at Coast Guard Station, 2501 Canal Road, 1300-2100 hours to get keys, check out by 1200 hours.

**Cottage:** One-bedroom (1), sleeps eight, furnished, except linens, toiletries, community kitchen, microwave, TV/VCR, washer/dryer, pots/pans, dishes. Blankets provided. Rates: $35 daily.

**SUPPORT FACILITIES:**

| | | |
|---|---|---|
| Bicycles | Grill | Picnic Area |
| Telephone | | |

**ACTIVITIES:**

| | | |
|---|---|---|
| Bicycling | Fishing | Hiking |

**CREDIT CARDS ACCEPTED:** None.

**RESTRICTIONS:** Pets allowed on leash, owners responsible for any damages, must clean up after pets daily. Use and possession of firearms must be in accordance with Federal, State, and local laws. No smoking in townhouse. Must bring own paper products and linens. Two night to one week limit. Military member/spouse must be present during the entire reservation. If unable to use reservation, it is not transferrable, but must be cancelled. Cottage must be fully cleaned prior to departure.

# WYOMING

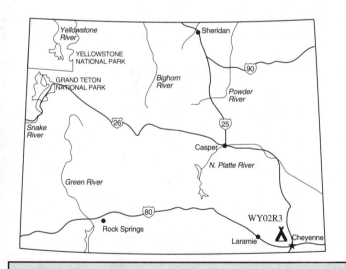

## F.E. WARREN FAMCAMP (WY02R3)
### Francis E. Warren Air Force Base
Francis E. Warren AFB, WY 82005-2573

**TELEPHONE NUMBER INFORMATION:** Main installation numbers: C-307-773-1110, D-312-481-1110. Police for FAMCAMP, C-307-773-3874 in season, C-307-773-2988 year round.

**LOCATION:** On base. Off I-25, two miles north of I-80. Clearly marked. Stop at Main Gate. Go directly to FAMCAMP, enter FAMCAMP through Missile Drive. *USMRA: page 102 (I-8).* NMC: Cheyenne, adjacent.

**DESCRIPTION OF AREA:** Located in open, rolling country in southeast corner of state. Laramie and Medicine Bow National Forest are short driving distance west. Full range of support facilities available on base. Fishing creek located adjacent to FAMCAMP.

**SEASON OF OPERATION:** 15 May-15 Sep, self-contained camping only Oct-Apr.

**ELIGIBILITY:** Active/Reservists/Retired/DoD civilians.

**RESERVATIONS:** No advance reservations accepted. Address: Outdoor Recreation, 7103 Randall Avenue, F.E. Warren AFB, WY 82005-2987. **C-307-773-2988, D-312-481-2988** 0900-1900 hours. E-mail: cox.carol @warren.af.mil. During off season check in at Outdoor Recreation, Bldg 316. Use drop box for overnight camping.

**Camper Spaces:** 40, some pull through sites, E (110V/20/40A) hookup. Rates: $11 daily.

**Camper/Tent Spaces:** 20, no hookups. Rates: $6 daily.

**SUPPORT FACILITIES:**

| | | |
|---|---|---|
| Hot Tub | Laundry | Picnic Area |
| Nature Walk Path | Rec Equipment | Restrooms |
| Sewage Dump | Showers | |

Exchange and Commissary within walking distance.

**ACTIVITIES:**

| | | |
|---|---|---|
| Dinner Theatre | Fishing | Hunting |
| Swimming | | |

Trips through Outdoor Adventure Program

**CREDIT CARDS ACCEPTED:** Visa and MasterCard.

**RESTRICTIONS:** Pets allowed on leash. **CAUTION:** Access off Randall Avenue has low clearance of 11'6" under railroad trestle; use Missile Drive entrance.

# UNITED STATES POSSESSIONS

## GUAM

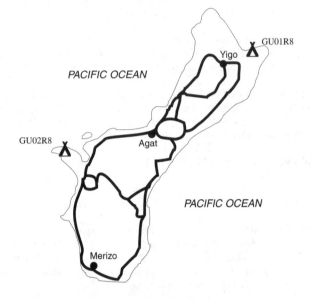

PACIFIC OCEAN

GU01R8

Yigo

GU02R8

Agat

PACIFIC OCEAN

Merizo

## ANDERSEN AFB RECREATION (GU01R8)

Andersen Air Force Base
APO AP 96543-4003

**TELEPHONE NUMBER INFORMATION:** Main installation numbers: C-671-366-1110, D-315-366-1110.

**LOCATION:** On base. On the north end of the island, accessible from Marine Drive (GU-1) which extends as a series of highways around the entire perimeter of the island of Guam. Sites are located on Taradue Beach. *USMRA: page 130 (E,F-1,2)*. NMC: Agana, 15 miles south.

**DESCRIPTION OF AREA:** Lots of sunshine, beaches, coral reefs, exciting WWII shipwrecks to explore for scuba enthusiasts. Hikers enjoy tropical mountains and jungles.

**SEASON OF OPERATION:** Year round.

**ELIGIBILITY:** Active/Reservists/Retired/DoD civilians.

**RESERVATIONS:** Accepted. Addresses: Andersen AFB Outdoor Recreation, 36 SVS/SVRO, Unit 14004, APO AP 96543-4003. **C-671-366-5204** 0900-1800 hours Mon-Fri, 0900-1200 hours Sat-Sun.

**Tent Spaces:** Beach (48), no hookups. Rates: $5 daily.

**SUPPORT FACILITIES:**

| | | |
|---|---|---|
| Beaches | Camping Equipment | Picnic Area |
| Restrooms | | |

**ACTIVITIES:**

| | | |
|---|---|---|
| Bicycling | Fishing | Scuba Diving |
| Swimming | | |

**CREDIT CARDS ACCEPTED:** Visa and MasterCard.

**RESTRICTIONS:** No pets. No firearms allowed. No glass bottles. No entry to water without a lifeguard on duty. Limit ten people per site.

## GUAM NAVAL STATION CABANAS (GU02R8)

Guam Naval Station
FPO AP 96540-1157

**TELEPHONE NUMBER INFORMATION:** Main installation numbers: C-671-351-1110, D-315-322-1110.

**LOCATION:** On base. South on Marine Drive (GU-1) from Agana, through main gate, on west side of island. Clearly marked. Cabanas are located near the marina on San Luis Beach. *USMRA: page 130 (C-3)*. NMC: Agana, 10 miles north.

**DESCRIPTION OF AREA:** Lots of sunshine, beaches, coral reefs, exciting WWII shipwrecks to explore for scuba enthusiasts. Hikers enjoy tropical mountains and jungles.

**SEASON OF OPERATION:** Year round.

**ELIGIBILITY:** Active/Reservists/Retired/DoD civilians.

**RESERVATIONS:** Accepted. Addresses: Guam NS MWR, PSC 455, Box 169, FPO AP 96540-1099. **C-671-564-1826** 0730-1630 hours Mon-Fri.

**Cabanas:** 2, no hookups. Rates: $25 refundable cleaning deposit.

**SUPPORT FACILITIES:**

| | | |
|---|---|---|
| Beaches | Marina | Restrooms |

**ACTIVITIES:**

| | | |
|---|---|---|
| Boating | Scuba Diving | Swimming |

**CREDIT CARDS ACCEPTED:** None.

**RESTRICTIONS:** No pets. No firearms allowed. No fishing. No entry to water without a lifeguard on duty. Bring plastic bags to dispose of trash.

## PUERTO RICO

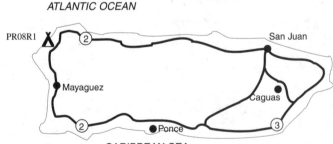

ATLANTIC OCEAN

PR08R1

San Juan

Mayaguez

Caguas

Ponce

CARIBBEAN SEA

## BORINQUEN RECREATION AREA (PR08R1)

Borinquen Coast Guard Air Station
Aguadilla, PR 00604-5000

**TELEPHONE NUMBER INFORMATION:** Main installation numbers: C-787-890-8400, D-312-831-3392/3399.

*Borinquen Recreation Area, continued*

**LOCATION:** On base. At the old Ramey CGAS, north of Aguadilla. From San Juan, take PR-22 W to PR-2 W to Aguadilla. Turn right on PR-110 or PR-7 to Rafel Hernandez Airport. Follow signs to Ramey Plaza and enter CG Housing Main Gate on Wing Road. Also, north from Mayaguez to PR-110 N. Follow above directions to CG Housing. *USMRA: page 130 (B,C-2).* NMC: San Juan, 65 miles east.

**DESCRIPTION OF AREA:** The recreation area is located in western Puerto Rico on a high cliff overlooking the Caribbean-the perfect setting for beautiful sunsets and whale watching. The converted lighthouse has two apartments which reflect the tropical flavor of the area. Additional recreation cottages are located within the CG housing area. Temperatures range from 70-85° and humidity is usually low due to a steady easterly breeze. Limited support facilities available on base approximately two miles from the lighthouse.

**SEASON OF OPERATION:** Year round.

**ELIGIBILITY:** Active/Reservists/Retired/DoD and DOT civilians.

**RESERVATIONS:** Required. Phone for reservations up to 45 days in advance for active duty, up to 30 days for all others. PCS personnel have priority up to 60 days in advance. Ask for information regarding car rentals when making your reservations. Address: Commanding Officer, US Coast Guard Air Station Borinquen, Attn: MWR (for lighthouse reservations add Lighthouse Reservations), Aguadilla, Puerto Rico 00604-5000. **C-787-890-8492.** Fax: C-787-890-8493.

**Apartments:** Two-bedroom (2), furnished, microwave, A/C, CATV, housekeeping service. Rates: $45-$65 daily (depending on rank).

**Houses:** Three-bedroom (16), furnished, microwave, A/C, CATV, housekeeping service. Rates: $40-$65 daily (depending on rank).

**SUPPORT FACILITIES:**

| | | |
|---|---|---|
| Gym/Fitness Center* | Laundry | Pavilion |
| Picnic Area | Pool* | Rec Equipment |

* On base.

**ACTIVITIES:**

| | | |
|---|---|---|
| Fishing | Golf | Scuba Diving |
| Sightseeing | Snorkeling | Surfing |
| Swimming | | |

**CREDIT CARDS ACCEPTED:** Visa, MasterCard, American Express, Discover and Diners'.

**RESTRICTIONS:** No pets allowed.

*CANADA*

# FOREIGN COUNTRIES
## CANADA

**ELIGIBILITY:** Active/Reservists/Retired/DND employees.

**RESERVATIONS:** Accepted. Confirmed upon receipt of payment. Booking starts in April. Address: P.O. Box 964, Greenwood, Nova Scotia B0P 1N0. **C-902-765-8165, D-312-568-5412.** Fax: C-902-765-8165, D-312-568-1745. HP: http://www.14wing.grwd.dnd.ca. Check in 1200 hours, check out 1130 hours.

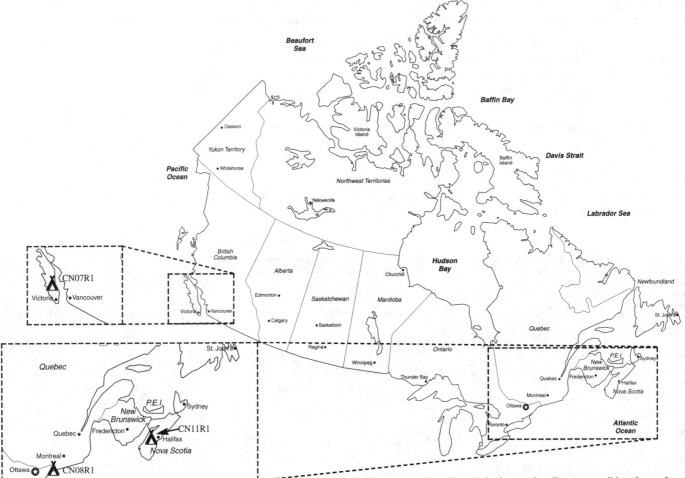

## LAKE PLEASANT RECREATIONAL FACILITY (CN11R1)
### 14 Wing Greenwood
### Greenwood, Nova Scotia B0P 1N0
### *Canada Forces Base*

**TELEPHONE NUMBER INFORMATION:** Main installation numbers: C-902-765-1494, D-312-568-1494. Police for rec area C-902-547-2882.

**LOCATION:** Off base. From Halifax, take 103 to Bridgewater. Turn left on Highway 10 N and go 9 kilometers to Springfield. A large communications tower is the landmark for the point where two lakes are visible. Signs for LPCC lead down a dirt road for .6 kilometers to main gate. NMI: 14 Wing Greenwood, 21 kilometers northeast. NMC: Halifax, 45 kilometers east.

**DESCRIPTION OF AREA:** Located midway between Middleton and Bridgewater, the area is a series of lakes and woodlands.

**SEASON OF OPERATION:** Mid May-mid Oct.

**Cabins:** Bungalow (7), two-bedroom, handicap accessible, sleeps four, kitchen. Rates: $15 daily. Chalet (1), one-bedroom, handicap accessible, sleeps eight, kitchen. Rates: $15 daily.

**Camper Spaces:** Gravel (70), handicap accessible, E/S/W hookups. Rates: $13 daily/$80.50 weekly/$300 monthly.

**Tent Spaces:** 20, no hookups. Rates: $6.50 daily.

**SUPPORT FACILITIES:**

| | | |
|---|---|---|
| Bath House | Beach | Boat Launch |
| Boat Rental/Storage | Canoes | Club House |
| Fire Rings | Games Area | Ice |
| Laundry | Paddle Boats | Picnic Area |
| Playground | Rec Center | Restrooms |
| Showers | Snack Bar | Telephones |
| Trails | | |

**ACTIVITIES:**

| | | |
|---|---|---|
| Bicycling | Fishing | Hiking |
| Horseshoes | | |

*Lake Pleasant Recreational Facility, continued*

**CREDIT CARDS ACCEPTED:** Visa and MasterCard.

**RESTRICTIONS:** Pets allowed on leash. No firearms.

## TEE PEE PARK/ AIR FORCE BEACH (CN07R1)

19th Wing Comox
Lazo, British Columbia V0R 2K0
*Canada Forces Base*

**TELEPHONE NUMBER INFORMATION:** Main installation numbers: C-250-339-8211. Police for park C-250-339-8211 ext 8888.

**LOCATION:** On base. Take Island Highway N. Follow signs to base. Just before main gate, turn left onto Little River Road. Take the next right, follow to end and turn right into the campground. NMC: Victoria, 84 kilometers south.

**DESCRIPTION OF AREA:** Tee Pee Park is a modern facility equivalent to BC Provincial parks. Wooded and ocean view sites overlooking the Straights of Georgia are available. Air Force Beach, adjacent to the campground, is regarded as one of the nicest on Vancouver Island. Full support facilities available on base.

**SEASON OF OPERATION:** Apr-Sep.

**ELIGIBILITY:** Active/Reservists/Retired.

**RESERVATIONS:** Required. Cancellations must be received at least 24 hours in advance of arrival. Address: Canadian Forces Base Comox, Attn: Tee Pee Park, P.O. Box 1000, Station Main, Lazo, British Columbia V0R 2K0. **C-250-339-8211 ext 8483, D-312-252-8211 ext 8483.** Fax: C-250-339-8233, D-312-252-8233. Check out 1100 hours.

**Camper/Tent Spaces:** Gravel/Grass (85), W hookup. Rates: $12 daily/$72 weekly/$245 monthly. *Note: Rates refer to Canadian currency.*

**SUPPORT FACILITIES:**

| | | |
|---|---|---|
| Beach* | Boat Launch | Fire Rings |
| Grills | Ice | Laundry |
| Pavilion* | Playground | Restrooms* |
| Sewage Dump | Showers* | Snack Bar |
| Telephones | | |

* Handicap accessible.

**ACTIVITIES:**

| | | |
|---|---|---|
| Bicycling | Boating | Fishing/license |
| Hiking | Scuba Diving | Swimming |

**CREDIT CARDS ACCEPTED:** None.

**RESTRICTIONS:** No firearms.

## TWIN RIVERS OF PETAWAWA (CN08R1)

Petawawa Canadian Forces Base
Petawawa, Ontario K8H 2X3
*Canada Forces Base*

**TELEPHONE NUMBER INFORMATION:** Main installation numbers: C-613-687-5331. Police for Recreation Area C-613-687-4444.

**LOCATION:** On base. From Ottawa take 417 W past Pembroke, watch for signs for CFB Petawawa. Turn right off exit ramp and follow to Bldg Q103 at the end of the road. NMC: Ottawa, 195 kilometers east.

**DESCRIPTION OF AREA:** Located in a small town twenty minutes from Petawawa. Full range of support facilities available on base.

**SEASON OF OPERATION:** May-Oct.

**ELIGIBILITY:** Active/Reservists/Retired/DND employees.

**RESERVATIONS:** C-613-687-5331. Fax: C-613-687-5511 ext 5275.

*Note: Community Access Card (CAC) membership or $20 access fee per club required for use of any club facilities on base. US military personnel are eligible to purchase a full CAC membership for $120.*

**Trailers:** E/S/W hookups. Rates: $20 daily/$100 weekly/$530 seasonal CAC members; $84 daily/$140 weekly/$575 seasonal non-CAC members. Early bird seasonal rates available if paid before 22 February 1999.

**Tent Spaces:** E/S/W hookups. Rates: $16 daily/$96 weekly/$385 seasonal CAC members; $18 daily/$108 weekly/$440 seasonal non CAC-members. Early bird seasonal rates available if paid before 22 February 1999.

*Note: Rates refer to Canadian currency.*

**SUPPORT FACILITIES:**

| | | |
|---|---|---|
| Beach | Fishing Pier | Golf |
| Laundry | Marina | Picnic Area |
| Playground | Rec Center | Rec Equipment |
| Restrooms | Showers | Snack Bar |
| Telephones | Trails | |

**ACTIVITIES:**

| | | |
|---|---|---|
| Bicycling | Fishing/license | Hunting/license |
| Swimming | | |

**CREDIT CARDS ACCEPTED:** Visa, MasterCard and Shell.

**RESTRICTIONS:** Pets allowed on leash. No alcohol permitted on grounds. Visitors must report to office to get a visitor's pass for $5.00.

# GERMANY

*See map on the following page.*

## BIG MIKE TRAVEL CAMP (GE85R7)

Vilseck Base Support Battalion
APO AE 09112-5000

**TELEPHONE NUMBER INFORMATION:** Main installation numbers: C-(US) 011-49-966-283-2563, C-(GE) 09662-83-2563.

**LOCATION:** On base. From Nurnberg take Autobahn A-6 to Amberg. Take exit 65 (Amberg W) to Route 299 NE for seven kilometers through Amberg. Watch for signs to Vilseck. Continue on Route 299, crossing over Routes 85 and 14, for an additional 16 kilometers to Grosschonbrunn, then turn northwest on Secondary Road for seven kilometers to Vilseck. Signs to 7th Army Rose Barracks clearly marked. NMC: Nurnberg, 55 kilometers northwest.

# GERMANY

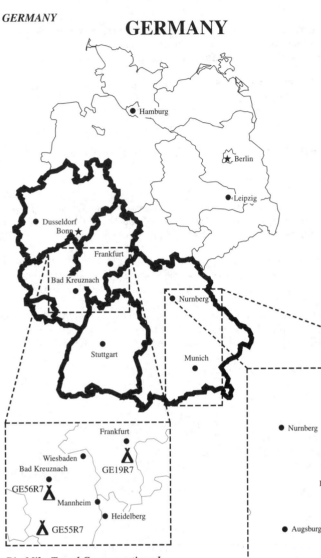

**Big Mike Travel Camp, continued**

**DESCRIPTION OF AREA:** This area is located near Big Mike Lake and has a playground at the park. It is located with plenty of trees around for privacy at the campground. Bathrooms and showers are available for campers.

**SEASON OF OPERATION:** Year round.

**ELIGIBILITY:** Active/Reservists/Retired/DoD civilians and their guests/US civilians with valid passports.

**RESERVATIONS:** Accepted. Address: Outdoor Recreation, 409th BSB, APO AE 09112-5000. **C-011-49-9662-83-2563.** Check in for the travel camp at Bldg 2236.

**Cabins:** Three-bedroom (2), furnished, living room, kitchen, dishes, utensils, linens. Rates: $70 daily. Two-bedroom (2), furnished, living room, kitchen, dishes, utensils, linens. Rates: $60 daily.

**Camper Spaces:** 30, E (220V)/W hookups. Rates: $10 daily.

**Camper/Tent Spaces:** 100, no hookups. Rates: $7 daily.

**ACTIVITIES:**

| | | |
|---|---|---|
| Bicycling | Canoeing | Hiking |
| Paddle boats | Rock Climbing | Scuba Diving |
| Skiing | Whitewater Rafting | |

**CREDIT CARDS ACCEPTED:** Visa and MasterCard.

**RESTRICTIONS:** Pets permitted in cabins. No firearms allowed.

## CHIEMSEE AFRC TRAVEL CAMP (GE57R7)
APO AE 09098-5000

**TELEPHONE NUMBER INFORMATION:** Main installation numbers: C-(USA) 011-49-8051-8030, DSN-E: 440-2575.

**LOCATION:** On post. Located directly off Munich-Salzburg Autobahn A-8 (E-52) toward Salzburg, Austria. Take 107 (Felden) to traffic light, turn right and cross over Autobahn. Follow road keeping right, to lake hotel (on northwest side of Autobahn). At southwest end of the parking lot there is an underpass to Park Hotel and AFRC Campground. NMC: Munich, 81 kilometers northwest.

**DESCRIPTION OF AREA:** Situated on southern shores of Chiemsee Lake, Bavaria's largest lake. Enjoy a variety of water sports or take advantage of the nearby Chiemgauer Alps offering scenic panoramas and opportunities for skiing, hiking and hang gliding. Limited support facilities at AFRC, additional facilities at Bad Aibling Station.

**SEASON OF OPERATION:** Year round.

**ELIGIBILITY:** Active/Reservists/Retired/DoD civilians stationed in USEUCOM.

**RESERVATIONS:** Required: Accepted up to 180 days in advance with deposit. Address: Vacation Planning Center, AFRC Europe, Unit 24501, APO AE 09053-5000. **C-(US) 011-49-8821-72981, DSN-E: 440-2575** 0700-2100 hours Mon-Fri, 0800-1800 hours Sat-Sun, 0900-1700 hours American Holidays. Fax: (US) 011-49-8821-3942. E-mail: vacation@ afrc.garmisch.army.mil.

**Camper Spaces:** Gravel, E (220V)/S/W hookups. Rates:* $15-$19 daily (depending on rank). Gravel, S/W hookups. Rates:* $13-$16 daily (depending on rank).

**Tent Spaces:** S/W hookups. Rates:* $10-$14 daily (depending on rank).

* Rates are for up to four persons, $3.50 daily each additional adult, $1.75 each additional child, aged six to 16 (monthly and seasonal rates available)

**SUPPORT FACILITIES:**

| | | |
|---|---|---|
| Boat Launch | Conference Center | Convenience Store |
| Dishwashing Facility | Equipment Rental | Fitness Center |
| Game Room | Gift Shop | Grills |
| Laundry | Picnic Area | Playground |
| Restaurant | Showers/hot | Snack Bar |
| TV Room | | |

**ACTIVITIES:**

| | | |
|---|---|---|
| Basketball Court | Beach | Bicycle Rental |
| Boat Rental | Children's Program | Hang Gliding |
| Hiking | Miniature Golf | Paddle Boats |
| Paragliding | Sailing | Scuba Diving |
| Snowboarding | Snow Skiing | Swimming |
| Tours | Whitewater Rafting | Windsurfing |

**CREDIT CARDS ACCEPTED:** Visa, MasterCard, American Express, Discover and Diners'.

**RESTRICTIONS:** Pets allowed on leash, must be attended at all times.

# GARMISCH AFRC TRAVEL CAMP (GE58R7)
APO AE 09053-5000

**TELEPHONE NUMBER INFORMATION:** Main installation numbers: C-(USA) 011-49-8821-72981, DSN-E: 440-2575.

**LOCATION:** On post. Take Autobahn A-95 (E-533) S from Munich to Oberau, then Route 2 to Garmisch-Partenkirchen. From Austria take national roads numbered 2 or 187. NMC: Munich, 97 kilometers north.

**DESCRIPTION OF AREA:** Located at the foot of Zugspitze, Germany's tallest mountain. Oberammergau, famous for wood carving and for its Passion Play, is 7.8 kilometers away. A wide variety of sports and tours as well as a full range of support facilities are available.

**SEASON OF OPERATION:** Year round.

**ELIGIBILITY:** Active/Reservists/Retired/DoD civilians stationed in USEUCOM.

**RESERVATIONS:** Accepted up to 180 days in advance with deposit. Address: Vacation Planning Center, AFRC Europe, Unit 24501, APO AE 09053-5000. **C (US)-011-49-8821-72981, DSN-E: 440-2575** 0800-2100 hours Sun-Thu summer, 0800-1900 Fri-Sat winter. Fax: (US) 011-49-8821-3942. E-mail: vacation@ afrc.garmisch.army.mil.

**Rental Trailers:** Four and five berth, E (220V)/W hookups. Rates:* $32-$52 daily.

**Camper Spaces:** Gravel Sites (84-varies with season), E (220V)/W hookups. Rates:* $15-$19 daily for four (depending on rank).

**Tent/Van Spaces:** 12, W hookup. Rates:* $13-$16 daily for four (depending on rank).

**Tent Spaces:** Open/Grass, W hookup. Rates:* $10-$14 daily for four, (depending on rank).

* Rates are for up to four persons, $3.50 daily each additional adult, $1.75 each additional child, aged six to 16 (monthly and seasonal rates available)

*Note: Five cabins under construction are scheduled to be available in Spring 1999. Fees will be determined at a later date. Keep up to date with* **Military Living's R&R Space-Report®.**

**SUPPORT FACILITIES:**

| | | |
|---|---|---|
| Convenience Store | Dishwashing | Equipment Rental |
| Golf/9 holes | Laundry | Playground |
| Restaurant | Restrooms | Sewage Dump |
| Showers/hot | Trailer Rental | |

**ACTIVITIES:**

| | | |
|---|---|---|
| Bicycling | Canoeing | Children's Program |
| Climbing/Rappelling | Hiking | Ice Skating |
| Jogging | Kayaking | Mountain Biking |
| Paragliding | Skiing | Snowboarding |
| Swimming | (Alpine and XC) | Tours |
| Whitewater Rafting | | |

**CREDIT CARDS ACCEPTED:** Visa, MasterCard, American Express, Discover and Diners'.

**RESTRICTIONS:** No pets in rental trailers or cabins. Pets allowed on leash in other areas, must be attended at all times.

# KUHBERG COMMUNITY PARK AND TRAVEL CAMP (GE56R7)
Bad Kreuznach Community
APO AE 09111-5000

**TELEPHONE NUMBER INFORMATION:** Main installation numbers: C-(US) 011-49-671-609-113, D-314-490-1110, C-(GE) 0671-609-113, DSN-E: 490-113. Police for travel camp, DSN-E: 114 or 490-6366/7357/7327. Medical/fire emergencies DSN-E: 490-117.

**LOCATION:** Off post. Approximately 36 kilometers southwest of Frankfurt. Camping area is located approximately 1.8 kilometers southwest of Rose Barracks. From the north, take A-60 to A-61, turn off onto B-41, left at signal to B-428, pass B-K, turn right at Hackenheim, right again at T intersection. Turn left at sign for US Army Recreation and Training Area, Jugendherberge. Drive 2.4 kilometers through vineyards, left at fork, after 400 meters left into parking lot (Rheingrafenstein Community Park and Travel Camp). From the south, take A-61 N, take the exit Bad Kreuznach onto B-41, then follow above directions. NMI: Rose Barracks, BSB Bad Kreuznach, 1.2 kilometers north. NMC: Bad Kreuznach, 1.8 kilometers north.

**DESCRIPTION OF AREA:** Located above the scenic Nahe Valley, the travel camp boasts a variety of outdoor activities and a helpful staff to provide information and directions to numerous local attractions such as Germany's oldest radium spa. Beautiful parks and forest areas. Area along the Rhein River has many castles and vineyards. Full range of support facilities at Rose Barracks, BSB Bad Kreuznach.

**SEASON OF OPERATION:** Year round, minimal operational support in winter.

**ELIGIBILITY:** Active/Reservists/Retired/DoD civilians/NATO Forces.

**RESERVATIONS:** Recommended, one night's fee and personal data required. Checks should be made payable to: BK CMWRF. Address: Bad Kreuznach Outdoor Recreation, 410th BSB, Unit 24308, APO AE 09252-5000. **C-(US) 011-49-671-609-6498/6496, D-314-671-6498/6496.** Fax: C-011-49-671-609-7108, D-314-671-7108. Check in at Bldg 5414.

**Camper/Tent Spaces:** Hardstand (26), E (220V) hookup. Rates: $5 daily; $3 adult, $2 child, $1 infant daily.

**Tent Spaces:** Grass (55), no hookups. Rates: $3 adult, $2 child, $1 infant daily.

**SUPPORT FACILITIES:**

| | | |
|---|---|---|
| Archery Range | Basketball Courts | Camp Supply Resale |
| Dishwashing Area | Fitness Course | Gas |
| Grills | Horseshoe Pits | Ice |
| Laundry | Miniature Golf | Multi-purpose Room |
| Pavilions | Picnic Areas* | Playgrounds |
| Rec Equipment | Recycle Station | Restrooms* |
| Sewage Dump | Showers/hot | Snack Bar |
| Sports Fields | Tennis Courts | Volleyball (sand) |

* Handicapped accessible

Group picnic/party facilities (i.e. pavilions, family picnic shelters, super grills, rotisserie) available.

*GERMANY*
*Kuhberg Community Park and Travel Camp, continued*

**ACTIVITIES:**

| | | |
|---|---|---|
| Badminton | Basketball | Beach Volleyball |
| Castle Hikes | Field Sports | Jogging |
| Kite Flying | Mountain Biking | Ping Pong |
| Rafting Tours | Rock Climbing | Ski Tours |
| Softball | Volksmarching | |

**CREDIT CARDS ACCEPTED:** Visa and MasterCard.

**RESTRICTIONS:** Pets allowed on leash. Only charcoal grill and stove fires permitted. Trash separation/recycling required by law. Check with travel camp management regarding policy on firearms.

# RHEIN-MAIN RECREATION AREA/ CAMPGROUND (GE09R7)

Rhein-Main Air Base
APO AE 09050-5000

**TELEPHONE NUMBER INFORMATION:** Main installation numbers: C-(US) 011-49-69-699-7274, D-314-330-1110, DSN-E: 330-7274. Police for campground, DSN-E: 114.

**LOCATION:** On base. Adjacent to Frankfurt International Airport off Autobahn A-5(E-45) to Darmstadt. NMC: Frankfurt, 16 kilometers north.

**DESCRIPTION OF AREA:** Cosmopolitan Frankfurt has a zoo, fairgrounds and convention center. Wiesbaden, with spas and gambling casinos, is nearby. Many vineyards and castles in the area. Campground is a well-preserved and maintained site. Full range of support facilities on base.

**SEASON OF OPERATION:** Apr-Oct.

**ELIGIBILITY:** Active/Reservists/Retired/DoD and NAF civilians/NATO ID Card holders.

**RESERVATIONS:** Not required. First come, first serve. Address: 469th ABG/SVMO, Attn: Outdoor Recreation, Rhein-Main AB, APO AE 09050-5000. **C-011-49-69-699-7274, D-314-330-7274** 1000-1700 hours Mon-Fri. Check in at campground, self registration, Bldg 705 24 hours daily, check out 1300 hours.

**Camper Spaces:** Grass (10), E (220V) hookup. Rates: $10 daily.

**Camper/Tent Spaces:** Grass (64), no hookups. Rates: $6 daily.

**SUPPORT FACILITIES:**

| | | |
|---|---|---|
| Grills | Playground | Rec Equipment |
| Restrooms | Showers | |

**ACTIVITIES:**

| | | |
|---|---|---|
| Bicycling | Jogging | Swimming |
| Walking | | |

**CREDIT CARDS ACCEPTED:** None.

**RESTRICTIONS:** Pets allowed on leash. No open fires. No hunting.

# ROLLING HILLS TRAVEL CAMP (GE55R7)

Baumholder Community
APO AE 09034-5000

**TELEPHONE NUMBER INFORMATION:** Main installation numbers: C-(US) 011-49-6783-6-7182, D-314-485-7182, DSN-E: 485-113. Police for campground, DSN-E: 114.

**LOCATION:** Off post. Camp is in the Baumholder Community Recreation Area. From Kaiserslautern, take Autobahn A-6 (E-50) W to exit 12. Take Autobahn A-62 NW toward Trier to exit 5 (Friessen). Continue north toward Baumholder on Secondary Road for approximately nine kilometers. Clearly marked. NMI: Ramstein AB, 15 kilometers. NMC: Kaiserslautern, 56 kilometers southeast.

**DESCRIPTION OF AREA:** Gem city of Idar-Oberstein, famous for its precious-stone industry and diamond factory, is nearby. Area has castles, Palatinate Forest, Mosel River, and vineyards. Bosen Lake, 11.4 kilometers from post, offers swimming, fishing and windsurfing. Recreation area has most support facilities. Baumholder Lake is one kilometer away and offers swimming during the summer months.

**SEASON OF OPERATION:** Year round. Regular season is 1 May-31 Sep, winter months are half price.

**ELIGIBILITY:** Active/Reservists/Retired/DoD civilians/Local nationals.

**RESERVATIONS:** Accepted, advisable to make reservations at least two weeks in advance for campsites. Address: CRD, Outdoor Recreation Baumholder, 222 Base Support Battalion, DCA Box 18, Unit 23746, APO AE 09034-5000. **C-(US) 011-49-6783-6-7182, C-(GE) 06783-67-182, D-314-485-7182, DSN-(E) 485-7182.** Fax: C-(US) 011-49-6783-67244, C-(GE) 06783-67-244, D-314-485-7244, DSN-(E) 485-7244. E-mail: hahnko2@yahoo.com. Check out 1200 hours.

**Camper Spaces:** Hardstand (32), handicap accessible, E (220V) hookup. Rates: $10 daily.

**Tent Spaces:** 32, no hookups. Rates: $5 daily.

**Camping/groups of 20+:** Primitive, no hookups. Rates: $30 daily/group.

**SUPPORT FACILITIES:**

| | | |
|---|---|---|
| Bath House | Fire Rings | Fitness Center |
| Golf | Grills | Ice |
| Pavilions | Picnic Areas | Playground |
| Pool/indoor | Rec Equipment | Restrooms |
| Showers | Sports Fields | Tennis Courts |
| Telephones | Tennis Courts | Trails |

**ACTIVITIES:**

| | | |
|---|---|---|
| Fishing/license* | Hiking | Indoor Climbing Wall |
| Kayaking | Rafting | Rock Climbing |
| Sightseeing | Snow Ski/DH&XC | Windsurfing |

* Special permit required from German government for a fishing license. For information, contact C-(US) 011-49-6783-66345, DSN-(E) 485-6345.

**CREDIT CARDS ACCEPTED:** Visa and MasterCard.

**RESTRICTIONS:** Pets allowed on leash. No firearms permitted. No water Nov-Apr.

# ITALY

**SEASON OF OPERATION:** Year round.

**ELIGIBILITY:** Active/Reservists/Retired/DoD civilians assigned overseas.

**RESERVATIONS:** Required. Deposit required for first day, check payable to MWR 10120, include your address and DSN number (if available) for confirmation. Address: Morale, Welfare and Recreation, PSC 817, Box 9, FPO AE 09622-5000. **C-011-39-081-526-1579.** Fax: 011-39-081-526-4813.

**Cabins:** 26, furnished. Rates: $30-$45 daily (weekly rates available).

**Camper Spaces:** Hardstand (2), E (220V)/S/W hookups. Rates: $15 daily.

**Tent Spaces:** Grass/Gravel (30). Rates: $10 daily.

**SUPPORT FACILITIES:**

| | |
|---|---|
| Chapel/NSA | Camping Equipment |
| Convenience Store | Exchange** |
| Golf/9 holes | Grills |
| Laundry | Miniature Golf |
| Picnic Area | Pizzeria** |
| Playground | Pool** |
| Restrooms* | Showers/hot |
| Snack Bar | Sports Fields |
| Ski Equipment | Tennis Courts, |
| | lighted |

\* Handicapped accessible
\*\* Summer only.

Summer day camp program (ages 5-12). Register by day or week.

**ACTIVITIES:**

| | |
|---|---|
| Baseball | Basketball |
| Football | Soccer |
| Softball | Volleyball |

**CREDIT CARDS ACCEPTED:** Visa, MasterCard, American Express and Discover.

**RESTRICTIONS:** No pets allowed. No firearms allowed.

## ADMIRAL CARNEY PARK (IT03R7)

Naples Naval Support Activity
FPO AE 09619-1053

**TELEPHONE NUMBER INFORMATION:** Main installation numbers: C-011-39-081-724-1110, D-314-625-1110. Police for park D-625-4195.

**LOCATION:** Off base. On the west coast of Italy in Admiral Carney Park. From north (B-1) or south (A-3), take Autostrada to Naples. After passing toll booth, take Tangenziale exit, then take exit 12 via Campana; at end of ramp, enter traffic circle, complete 3/4 turn, then right, follow signs. NMI: Naples NSA, 10 kilometers southwest. NMC: Naples, 20 kilometers south.

**DESCRIPTION OF AREA:** Active port city of Naples. The Roman cities of Herculanum and Pompeii and active volcano Vesuvius are nearby. The beautiful island of Capri is 13.2 kilometers away by boat or helicopter. Carney Park, with its large grassy fields and paved roads, is a 96-acre recreation facility located in the crater of an extinct 13th century volcano. It has five festivals annually. Full range of support facilities available at NSA Naples.

## SEA PINES CAMP AND LODGE (IT02R7)

Camp Darby
APO AE 09613-5000

**TELEPHONE NUMBER INFORMATION:** Main installation numbers: C-011-39-050-54-7111, D-314-633-7225, DSN-E: 633-7225. Police DSN-E: 633-7575.

**LOCATION:** On post. Located midway between Livorno and Pisa. From north, follow Autostrada A-12 to Pisa Centro exit. After the toll booth, follow the roads marked for Livorno, bear left at the yield sign, turn right onto Via Aurelia (SS1). After approximately seven kilometers, make a right onto the first paved road after the Agip gas station. The road passes over a canal. Camp Darby is on the left. NMC: Pisa, 9 kilometers north.

**DESCRIPTION OF AREA:** Situated in the midst of a beautiful Umbrella Pine forest halfway between Pisa and Livorno. Famous Leaning Tower of Pisa is 3.6 kilometers away, the walled city of Lucca is 12 kilometers and

*ITALY-JAPAN*
*Sea Pines Camp and Lodge, continued*

Florence is 45 kilometers. The site is just a few kilometers from the American Beach on the Tyrrhenian Sea where safe swimming is available (minimal fee). The many support facilities available on post are within easy walking distance.

**SEASON OF OPERATION:** Year round.

**ELIGIBILITY:** Active/Reservists/Retired/DoD civilians/NATO Forces.

**RESERVATIONS:** Required. May be made up to one year in advance, with deposit for reservations made 30 days or more in advance. Payment of balance is due upon arrival and in US dollars only. Guests arriving between 22 May and 2 Sep can enjoy free entry to the American Beach compliments of the Sea Pines Lodge, parking not included. Address: CDR Livorno AST, Attn: Sea Pines Lodge, Unit 31301 Box 60, APO AE 09613-5000. **C-011-39-050-54-7225, DSN-E: 633-7225** 0700-2100 hours, 24 hours daily in summer. Check in at Sea Pines Lodge, check out 1000 hours.

**Sea Pines Lodge:** Rooms (24), sleeps four, private bath, refrigerator, TV/VCR. Community kitchen, social room with TV/VCR, slot machines. Rates: $61 daily for four, $56 daily for three, $51 daily for two, $41 daily for one, $3.50 daily for pet, $3 additional daily for crib.

**Cabins:** Two-bedroom (20), one queen size bed, one bunk bed, table and chairs, heated. Common shower room. Patrons must provide linens. Occupants must use shower facilities. Rates: $46-$51 daily (depending on rank).

**Camper Spaces:** 125-2 handicap accessible, E (220V)/W hookups. Rates: $10-$14 daily. W hookup. Rates: $8-$12 daily. Group Sites, ten or more. Rates: $2 daily each person.

**SUPPORT FACILITIES:**

| | | |
|---|---|---|
| Beach/summer | Camping Equipment | Chapel |
| Convenience Store | Gas | Grills |
| Laundry | Miniature Golf | Picnic Area |
| Playground | Racquet Courts | Rec Center |
| Rec Equipment | Restrooms* | Showers* |
| Shuttle Bus | Snack Bars | |

\* Handicapped accessible

**ACTIVITIES:**

| | | |
|---|---|---|
| Boating | Scuba Diving | Swimming |
| Tennis | Tours | Windsurfing |

**CREDIT CARDS ACCEPTED:** Visa, American Express and Discover.

**RESTRICTIONS:** Pets allowed on leash, must not be left unattended, must have valid health certificate and vaccination record, allowed in Lodge rooms: $3.50 daily, $50 damage deposit. Pets are not permitted on beaches. No ground fires. Quiet hours 2200-0800 hours. No hunting.

## VICENZA TRAVEL CAMP (IT08R7)
Vicenza Community
APO AE 09630-5000

**TELEPHONE NUMBER INFORMATION:** Main installation numbers: C-011-39-0444-517111, D-634-7111. Police for camp D-634-7626.

**LOCATION:** On post. Take Vicenza (east) exit from Autostrada A-4 which runs from Trieste to Milano. Follow signs to Caserma Carlo Ederle. Main gate is on Viale Della Pace, the road from Vincenza to Padova. The Caserma Ederle is at the intersection of Viale Della Pace and Via Aldo Moro or the northwest side of the intersection. NMC: Vicenza, in city limits.

**DESCRIPTION OF AREA:** Non-wooded, open area. Great sightseeing opportunities: Venice, the canal city, Lido di Jesolo beaches on the Adriatic, and Romeo and Juliet's city, Verona. Full range of support facilities available on post. Convenient to Exchange, Commissary, Burger King, gym, pool.

**SEASON OF OPERATION:** Year round.

**ELIGIBILITY:** Active/Reservists/Retired/DoD civilians assigned overseas.

**RESERVATIONS:** No advanced reservations. Address: HQ 22nd ASG, Outdoor Recreation (CRD), Unit 31401 CMR 427 Box 80, APO AE 09630-5000. **C-011-39-0444-517094, D-634-7094.**

**Camper Spaces:** E (110/220V) hookup. Rates: $15 daily.

**Tent Spaces:** No hookups. Rates: $10 daily.

**SUPPORT FACILITIES:**

| | | |
|---|---|---|
| Bath House | Rec Center | Rec Equipment |

**ACTIVITIES:**

| | | |
|---|---|---|
| Hiking | Mountain Climbing | Scuba Courses |
| Snow Skiing | Swimming/summer | Tennis |

**CREDIT CARDS ACCEPTED:** Visa, American Express and Discover.

**RESTRICTIONS:** Pets allowed on leash. No firearms allowed. No open fires. Noise control after 2300 hours.

# JAPAN

*See map on following page.*

## OKUMA BEACH RESORT-OKINAWA (JA09R8)
Kadena Air Base
APO AP 96368-5134

**TELEPHONE NUMBER INFORMATION:** Main installation numbers: C-011-81-98-041-5164, D-315-634-4601.

**LOCATION:** Off base. On Okinawa, take highway 58 N from Kadena AB approximately 30 kilometers. Turn left just before Hentona. NMI: Kadena AB, 30 kilometers south. NMC: Naha JA, 37.2 kilometers south.

**DESCRIPTION OF AREA:** This 120-acre recreational complex is a beautiful, quiet getaway on a peninsula with snow-white beaches on both the Pacific Ocean and East China Sea. Picturesque drive takes you through pineapple fields and acres of sugar cane. Full range of support and outdoor recreational facilities available.

**SEASON OF OPERATION:** Year round. Closed Mon-Tue: 1 Nov-31 Mar.

**ELIGIBILITY:** Active/Reservists/Retired/DoD civilians assigned overseas.

**RESERVATIONS:** Required up to 90 days in advance. Address: Leisure Resource Center, Schilling Recreation Center, 18 SVS/SVMR, Unit 5135, Box 10, APO AP 96368-5135. **C-011-81-611-734-4322, D-315-634-4322** 0800-1700 hours Mon-Fri summer, Wed-Mon winter. Check in 1500 hours at Okuma main office, check out 1100 hours.

# JAPAN

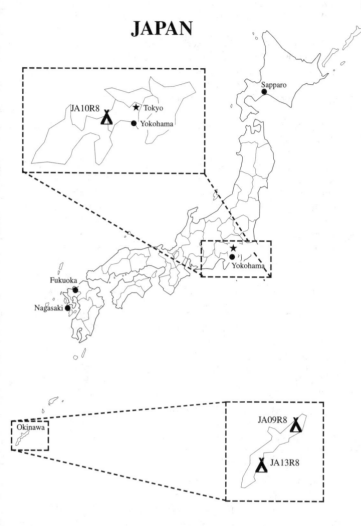

Okuma has improved its facilities quite a bit in the last year-restaurant and lounge has been renovated, new fire pits and BBQ grills have been added as well as picnic tables.

## ACTIVITIES:

| | | |
|---|---|---|
| Bicycling | Boating | Croquet |
| Fishing | Hiking | Horseshoes |
| Sailing | Scuba Diving | Skin Diving |
| Snorkeling | Swimming | Tours |
| Water Skiing | Windsurfing | |

Glass bottom boat tours and water instructional classes are available.

**CREDIT CARDS ACCEPTED:** Visa and MasterCard.

**RESTRICTIONS:** No pets allowed. No glass. In order to rent sailboat and windsurfing equipment, certification by a sanctioned organization (or the passing of a qualification test given by the chief instructor) is required. Certification is also required for use of any diving equipment and/or service.

# TAMA OUTDOOR RECREATION AREA (JA10R8)

Yokota Air base
APO AP 96328-5123

**TELEPHONE NUMBER INFORMATION:** Main installation numbers: C-011-81-423-77-7009, D-315-224-3421/22.

**LOCATION:** Off base. Nine kilometers southeast of Yokota AB. NMC: Tokyo, adjacent.

**DESCRIPTION OF AREA:** A 500-acre retreat west of Tokyo, Tama was originally built by the Japanese Imperial Army in 1938 as a munitions storage area. After extensive repairs and renovations the center was reopened in 1983. The lodge and cabins all have private baths. Hot tubs are available year round. It is a quiet, wooded getaway offering a large range of facilities.

**SEASON OF OPERATION:** Year round.

**ELIGIBILITY:** Active/Reservists/Retired/DoD civilians.

**RESERVATIONS:** Required up to three months in advance. Address: Tama Outdoor Recreation Area, 374 SPTG/SVBL, Unit 5119, APO AP 96328-5119. **C-011-81-423-77-7009, D-315-224-3421/3422.**

**Lodge:** Suite (4). Rates: $35 daily. Rooms (14). Rates: $25 daily.

**Cabins:** Double and single (14). Rates: $25-$50 daily.

**Camp/Tent Spaces:** 21, W hookup. Rates: $1 daily.

## SUPPORT FACILITIES:

| | | |
|---|---|---|
| Archery/fee | Camping Equipment | Exchange |
| Golf/18 holes | Grills/fee | Laundry/fee |
| Miniature Golf | Picnic Area/fee | Playground |
| Pool | Rec Equipment | Restrooms |
| Showers | Stables | Tennis Courts/fee |
| Trails | Trap Range | |

## ACTIVITIES:

| | | |
|---|---|---|
| Bicycling | Camping | Horseback Riding |
| Jogging | Trap Shooting | |

---

*Okuma Beach Resort - Okinawa, continued*

**Cabanas:** Suite (10), four double beds, private bath, refrigerator, microwave, utensils, A/C, TV/VCR. One-bedroom (10), two double beds, private bath, refrigerator, microwave, utensils, A/C, TV/VCR. One-bedroom (12-for couples only), one double bed, private bath, refrigerator, microwave, utensils, dry bar, A/C, TV/VCR. One-bedroom (10), two double beds, shared bath, refrigerator, microwave, utensils, A/C, TV/VCR. Rates: $25-$55.

**Campsite #1:** Families only, south beach. Rates: $6 per tent daily.

**Campsite #2:** Singles and groups, west beach #2. Rates: $6 per tent daily.

## SUPPORT FACILITIES:

| | | |
|---|---|---|
| Beach | Bicycle Rental | Chapel |
| Conference Room | Convenience Store | Dispensary |
| Golf/9 holes | Laundry | Library |
| Lounge | Miniature Golf | Movies |
| Multi-Purpose Court | Nature Trails | Picnic Area |
| Rec Center | Restaurant | Restrooms* |
| Showers* | Tennis Courts | Theater |
| Water Sports Equipment Rental | | |

* Handicap accessible

*Tama Outdoor Recreation Area, continued*

**CREDIT CARDS ACCEPTED:** Visa, MasterCard and American Express.

**RESTRICTIONS:** Pets allowed only in cabins.

## WHITE BEACH RECREATION SERVICES (JA13R8)

FPO AP 96370-1100

**TELEPHONE NUMBER INFORMATION:** Main installation numbers: C-011-81-642-2264/2266, Operator: 098-892-5111. Police for recreation area, C-011-81-642-2200/2300.

**LOCATION:** On base. On the Pacific Island of Okinawa, south of Japan. On east side of the island on Katsuren Peninsula in Buckner Bay. From JA-24, north of Okinawa City, turn east on JA-329 to JA-8 to White Beach. NMC: Naha, 20 kilometers south.

**DESCRIPTION OF AREA:** Beautiful beach, many recreational activities, Ocean Cliff and Port of Call Club at White Beach. The clubs are open to all ranks and provide a full-menu dining room, amusement center, ballroom, and casual bar.

**SEASON OF OPERATION:** Cabins year round, campers Apr 1-Nov 30.

**ELIGIBILITY:** Active/Reservists/Retired/DoD civilians.

**RESERVATIONS:** Required with full payment ten days in advance. You must include the following information: Name, Return Address and telephone number (DSN only), Status/branch of service, cabin or camper, first choice check in and check out date, and second choice check in and check out date. Address: Commander, Fleet Activities Okinawa, PSC 480, MWR Department, FPO AP 96370-0057. **C-011-81-634-6952/6954.**

**Cabins:** One-bedroom (4), queen size bed, private bath, furnished, living room, kitchen, TV/VCR, towels. Rates: $50 daily. Studio (8), queen size bed, private bath, furnished, living room, kitchen, TV/VCR, towels. Rates: $40 daily. Getaway Special (for two) includes cabin or room, dinner and breakfast for two: $60 daily, or duplex cabin for two, $70 daily.

**Campers:** 32, sleeps two adults, three children, E (110V)/W hookups. Rates: $35 daily.

**SUPPORT FACILITIES:**

| | | |
|---|---|---|
| Barber Shop | Beach | Fishing Piers |
| Fitness Center | Grills | Marina |
| Pavilions | Picnic Areas | Post Office |
| Pool | Racquetball Court | Rec Hall |
| Restrooms* | Sauna | Shoppette |
| Showers | Snack Bars | Sports Fields |
| Tennis Courts | Weight Room | |

* Handicap accessible.

**ACTIVITIES:**

| | | |
|---|---|---|
| Bicycling | Canoeing | Croquet |
| Fishing/Charter | Horseshoes | Jet Skis |
| Miniature Golf | Paddle Boats | Sailing |
| Snorkeling | Softball | Swimming |
| Volleyball | | |

**CREDIT CARDS ACCEPTED:** None.

**RESTRICTIONS:** No pets allowed. No firearms allowed.

---

**S*M*A*R*T®**

Special Military Active Retired Travel Club, Inc.
600 University Office Blvd. #1A
Pensacola, FL 32504
(904) 478-1986 • (800) 354-7681
E-mail: 102546.2476@compuserve.com

# What is S•M•A•R•T?

**S•M•A•R•T** is the acronym for Special Military Active Retired Travel Club. The club promotes comradeship among Retired and Active Military persons who are interested in Recreational Vehicle traveling and living. It provides travel and camping information specifically related to persons with a Military background. SMART membership is presently limited to retirees and active duty personnel from the United States and Canada.

In addition to providing social and recreational activities for members on a local level, a SMART National Muster is hosted each spring and Regional musters are held in the fall. Most of the club's activities are held at Military installations across the country. Also, the club assist Military Installations with improving and expanding their Family Camps (FAMCAMP).

The club is presently divided into 8 regions. There are 42 chapters across the United States, including a "Ham" chapter and a Computer Users chapter. **S•M•A•R•T** membership currently exceeds three thousand. **S•M•A•R•T** publishes a quarterly magazine, "*SMART Traveler*," that contains national, regional and chapter news, along with caravan descriptions, schedules, chapter muster schedules and general interest items.

# SECTION II - Military Golf Courses

## UNITED STATES
### ALABAMA

### CANE CREEK GOLF COURSE
Fort McClellan
Fort McClellan, AL 36205-5000

**LOCATION:** On post. From I-20 E or W, take AL-21 N to fort on right. Also located 25 miles southeast of I-59. Take US-431 S to fort.

**SEASON OF OPERATION:** Year round.

**ELIGIBILITY:** Active/Reservists/Retired/DoD civilians/Dependents/ General Public/Guests.

**COURSE INFORMATION:** Address: Cane Creek Golf Course, Bldg 2247, Fort McClellan, AL 36205-5000. **C-256-848-3623/3604/3242, D-312-865-3623/3604/3242** 0700-1900 hours Apr-Sep, 0800-Dusk Oct-Mar. One 18 hole golf course.

|          | Back Tees | Middle Tees | Front Tees |
|----------|-----------|-------------|------------|
| Length   | 7,026     | 6,460       | 5,950      |
| Par      | 72        | 72          | 72         |
| Slope    | 121       | 118         | 120        |
| USGA Rating | 73.0   | 68.0        | 69.0       |

| RATES: | Weekday | Weekend |
|--------|---------|---------|
| E1-E4 | $3 (9), $6 (18) | $4 (9), $8 (18) |
| E5+ | $ 8 (9), $14 (18) | $10 (9), $18 (18) |
| DoD civilians | $10 (9), $18 (18) | $11 (9), $20 (18) |
| General Public | $11 (9), $19 (18) | $13 (9), $24 (18) |

*Note: Number in ( ) indicates number of holes.*

**SUPPORT FACILITIES:**

| | | |
|---|---|---|
| Bar/Lounge | Chipping Area | Driving Range |
| Equipment Rental | Golf Carts/Power | Golf Carts/Pull |
| Lessons | Lockers | Pro at Facility |
| Pro Shop | Putting Area | Restaurants |
| Showers | Soda Vending | |

**RESTRICTIONS:** Must use golf cart during tournament.

**CREDIT CARDS ACCEPTED:** Visa, MasterCard, American Express and Discover.

### CYPRESS TREE GOLF COURSE
Maxwell Air Force Base
Maxwell AFB, AL 36112-5000

**LOCATION:** On base. Take I-85 south to I-65 north. Take Herron Street exit to Bell Street and follow signs to Bell Street Gate.

**SEASON OF OPERATION:** Year round.

**ELIGIBILITY:** Active/Reservists/Retired/DoD civilians/Dependents/ General Public/Guests.

**COURSE INFORMATION:** Address: Cypress Tree Golf Course, 1461 March Street, Maxwell AFB, AL 36112. **C-334-263-7507.** Two 18 hole golf course.

**West Course**

|        | Back Tees | Front Tees |
|--------|-----------|------------|
| Length | 6,917     | 5,325      |
| Par    | 72        | 73         |
| Slope  | 132       | 123        |

**East Course**

|        | Back Tees | Front Tees |
|--------|-----------|------------|
| Length | 6,217     | 5,090      |
| Par    | 71        | 71         |
| Slope  | 122       | 118        |

| RATES: | Weekday | Weekend |
|--------|---------|---------|
| E1-E4 | $5 (9), $7 (18) | $6 (9), $8 (18) |
| E5-O3 | $7 (9), $10 (18) | $8 (9), $12 (18) |
| O4+ | $8 (9), $13 (18) | $9 (9), $15 (18) |
| Guests | $10 (9), $16 (18) | $12 (9), $18 (18) |

**SUPPORT FACILITIES:**

| | | |
|---|---|---|
| Banquet Facilities | Bar/Lounge | Chipping Area |
| Driving Range | Equipment Rental | Golf Carts/Power |
| Golf Carts/Pull | Lessons | Lockers |
| Pro at Facility | Pro Shop | Putting Area |
| Restaurants | Showers | Snack Vending |
| Soda Vending | | |

**RESTRICTIONS:** Soft spike shoes only.

**CREDIT CARDS ACCEPTED:** Visa and MasterCard.

### REDSTONE ARSENAL GOLF COMPLEX
Redstone Arsenal
Redstone Arsenal, AL 35898-5000

**COURSE INFORMATION:** Address: Redstone Golf Complex, Bldg T-107, Redstone Arsenal, AL 35898. **C-205-876-6888, D-312-746-6888.** Three 9 hole golf courses (Whispering Pines, Meadow View and Hillside). Bar/Lounge, Chipping Area, Driving Range, Equipment Rental, Golf Carts/Power, Golf Carts/Pull, Lockers, Pro at Facility, Pro Shop, Showers, Snack Bar.

### SILVER WINGS GOLF COURSE
Fort Rucker
Fort Rucker, AL 36362-5000

**LOCATION:** On post. From US-231, take AL-249 S to Daleville. Go right through Daleville to Fort Rucker. Golf course is on the northern side of post off Andrews across from NCO Club.

**SEASON OF OPERATION:** Year round.

**ELIGIBILITY:** Active/Reservists/Retired/DoD civilians/Dependents/ Guests.

**COURSE INFORMATION:** Address: Silver Wings Golf Course, Bldg 20067 Combat Road, P.O. Box 620189, Fort Rucker, AL 36362-5000. **C-334-255-9539** 0700-2000 hours summer, 0700-1800 hours winter. One 9 hole golf course.

**ALABAMA-ARIZONA**
*Silver Wings Golf Course, continued*

|  | Back Tees | Middle Tees | Front Tees |
|---|---|---|---|
| Length | 3,273 | 3,194 | 2,937 |
| Par | 36 | 36 | 36 |
| Slope* | 116 (B,F) | 117 (M,F) | 113 (B,M) |
| USGA Rating* | 73.0 (B,F) | 68.0 (M,F) | 69.0 (B,M) |

* Information based on 18 hole game from different combination of tees. (B-Back Tees, M-Middle Tees, F-Front Tees).

| RATES: | Weekday | Weekend |
|---|---|---|
| Enlisted | $11 | $13 |
| Officers | $11 | $13 |
| Guests | $13 | $16 |
| Civilians | $13 | $16 |

**SUPPORT FACILITIES:**

| | | |
|---|---|---|
| Chipping Area | Driving Range | Golf Carts/Power |
| Golf Carts/Pull | Lessons | Lockers |
| Parking | Pro at Facility | Pro Shop |
| Putting Area | Showers | Snack Bar |

**RESTRICTIONS:** Tee times required Sat, Sun and holidays.

**CREDIT CARDS ACCEPTED:** Visa and MasterCard.

# ALASKA

## BEAR VALLEY GOLF COURSE
Kodiak Coast Guard Integrated Support Command
Kodiak, AK 99619-5014

**LOCATION:** On base. From the city of Kodiak, take the main road southwest for seven miles. Base is on the left. From main gate, continue two miles to west on Buskin River Road, then continue straight three miles to golf course.

**SEASON OF OPERATION:** May-Oct.

**ELIGIBILITY:** Active/Reservists/Retired/DoD civilians/Dependents/ General Public/Guests.

**COURSE INFORMATION:** Address: Bear Valley Golf Course, USCG ISC, Kodiak, AK 99619-5000. **C-907-486-7561** 0700-Dusk. One 9 hole golf course.

| Length | 2,865 |
|---|---|
| Par | 36 |
| Slope | 121 |
| USGA Rating | 67.8 |

| RATES: | Weekday | Weekend |
|---|---|---|
| Enlisted | $9 | $13 |
| Officers | $12 | $17 |
| DoD civilians | $15 | $21 |

**SUPPORT FACILITIES:**

| | | |
|---|---|---|
| Chipping Area | Driving Range | Equipment Rental |
| Golf Carts/Pull | Pro Shop | Putting Area |
| Snack Bar | | |

**CREDIT CARDS ACCEPTED:** None.

## CHENA BEND GOLF CLUB
Fort Wainwright
Fort Wainwright, AK 99703-6600

**COURSE INFORMATION:** Address: Chena Bend Golf Club, P.O. Box 35365, Fort Wainwright, AK 99703-5000. **C-907-353-6223.** One 18 hole golf course.

## EAGLE GLEN GOLF COURSE
Elmendorf Air Force Base
Elmendorf AFB, AK 99506-2760

**LOCATION:** On base. From Glenn Highway AK-1, take Muldoon Gate, Boniface Gate, Post Road Gate or Government Hill Gate exits. AFB is two miles northeast of Anchorage and next to Fort Richardson. Follow signs.

**SEASON OF OPERATION:** 1 May-10 Oct.

**ELIGIBILITY:** Active/Reservists/Retired/DoD civilians/Dependents/ General Public/Guests.

**COURSE INFORMATION:** Address: Eagle Glen Golf Course, Bldg 23-100, Elmendorf AFB, AK 99506-5000. **C-907-552-3821** 0530-2200 hours. One 18 hole golf course.

|  | Back Tees | Front Tees |
|---|---|---|
| Length | 6,689 | 5,457 |
| Par | 72 | 72 |
| Slope | 126 | 119 |
| USGA Rating | 71.6 | 70.4 |

| RATES: | Weekday | Weekend |
|---|---|---|
| Enlisted | $10 | $10 |
| Officers | $15 | $15 |
| Guests | $32 | $32 |

**SUPPORT FACILITIES:**

| | | |
|---|---|---|
| Chipping Area | Driving Range | Equipment Rental |
| Golf Carts/Power | Golf Carts/Pull | Lessons |
| Lockers | Pro at Facility | Pro Shop |
| Putting Range | Snack Bar | Soda Vending |

**CREDIT CARDS ACCEPTED:** Visa and MasterCard.

## MOOSE RUN GOLF COURSE
Fort Richardson
Fort Richardson, AK 99505-6625

**COURSE INFORMATION:** Address: Moose Run Golf Course, P.O. Box 5310, Fort Richardson, AK 99505. **C-907-428-0056.** One 18 hole golf course.

# ARIZONA

## FALCON DUNES GOLF COURSE
Luke Air Force Base
Luke AFB, AZ 85309-1520

**LOCATION:** Off base. I-10 west to exit 128 to north on Lichfield Road, then right on Northern Avenue. Continue straight for 1.5 miles to golf course.

**SEASON OF OPERATION:** Year round.

*Falcon Dunes Golf Course, continued*

**ELIGIBILITY:** Active/Reservists/Retired/DoD civilians/Federal Employees/Dependents.

**COURSE INFORMATION:** Address: Falcon Dunes Golf Course, 15100 W Northern Avenue, Waddell, AZ 85355-5000. **C-602-535-8355, D-312-896-8864** 0530-1800 hours. One 18 hole golf course.

| | Back Tees | Front Tees |
|---|---|---|
| Length | 6,611 | 5,174 |
| Par | 71 | 71 |
| Slope | 130 | 113 |
| USGA Rating | 71.7 | 71.0 |

| RATES: | Member | Non-Member | Twilite and 9 hole |
|---|---|---|---|
| E1-E4 | $12.75 | $15 | $8 |
| E5+ | $17 | $20 | $12.75 |
| Retired Military | $17 | $20 | $12.75 |
| DoD civilians | $17 | $20 | $12.75 |
| Civilians guests | N/A | $35 | $15 |
| Juniors | $12.75 | $12.75 | $12.75 |

**SUPPORT FACILITIES:**

| | | |
|---|---|---|
| Banquet Facilities | Chipping Area | Driving Range |
| Equipment Rental | Golf Carts/Power | Lessons |
| Lockers | Pro at Facility | Pro Shop |
| Putting Area | Restaurants | Showers |
| Snack Bar | | |

**RESTRICTIONS:** During the first two weeks, golf carts must stay on cart paths after overseeding of grass.

**CREDIT CARDS ACCEPTED:** Visa and MasterCard.

## GENERAL WILLIAM BLANCHARD GOLF COURSE
### Davis-Monthan Air Force Base
### Davis-Monthan AFB, AZ 85707-0001

**COURSE INFORMATION:** Address: General William Blanchard Golf Course, 3945 South Craycroft, Davis-Monthan AFB, CA 85707-4032. **C-520-228-3734.** One 18 hole golf course; Length: 6,611 yards back tees and 5,792 yards front tees; Par: 72; USGA Ratings: 70.5 (M), 71.5 (L). Equipment Rental, Lessons, Golf Carts, Pro at Facility, Pro Shop.

## MOUNTAIN VIEW GOLF COURSE
### Fort Huachuca
### Fort Huachuca, AZ 85613-6000

**LOCATION:** On post. From I-10 E or W, take AZ-90 S to Sierra Vista and main gate of fort. Turn right after main gate, go 500 yards, located on the south side of the street.

**SEASON OF OPERATION:** Year round.

**ELIGIBILITY:** Active/Reservists/Retired/DoD civilians/Dependents/General Public/Guests.

**COURSE INFORMATION:** Address: Mountain View Golf Course, Bldg 15479, Fort Huachuca, AZ 85613-6000 or Mountain View Golf Course, P.O. Box, 12920, Fort Huachuca, AZ 85670-5000. **C-520-533-7092, D-312-821-7092** 0630-1830 hours summer, 0800-1730 hours winter. One 18 hole golf course.

| | Back Tees | Middle Tees | Front Tees |
|---|---|---|---|
| Length | 6,879 | 6,514 | 5,815 |
| Par | 72 | 72 | 72 |
| Slope | 126 | 123 | 125 |
| USGA Rating | 71.9 | 70.3 | 71.5 |

| RATES:* | Weekday | Weekend |
|---|---|---|
| Enlisted | $10-$16 | $10-$16 |
| Officers | $18 | $18 |
| Guests | $20 | $20 |
| Civilians | $25 | $25 |

\* Twilite rates start at 1430 hours

**SUPPORT FACILITIES:**

| | | |
|---|---|---|
| Banquet facilities | Bar/Lounge | Chipping Area |
| Driving Range | Golf Carts/Power | Golf Carts/Pull |
| Lessons | Lockers | Parking |
| Pro at Facility | Pro Shop | Putting Area |
| Restaurants | Showers | Soda Vending |
| Snack Bar | Snack Vending | |

**CREDIT CARDS ACCEPTED:** Visa, MasterCard and American Express.

# ARKANSAS

## DEER RUN GOLF COURSE
### Little Rock Air Force Base
### Little Rock AFB, AR 72099-5288

**COURSE INFORMATION:** Address: Deer Run Golf Course, Bldg 1075, Little Rock AFB, AR, 72099. **C-501-987-6199.** One 18 hole golf course. Driving Range, Golf Carts/Power, Pro Shop, Snack Bar.

## DEER TRAILS GOLF COURSE
### Fort Chaffee Maneuver Training Center
### Fort Chaffee, AR 72905-5000

**LOCATION:** On post. From I-40 E or W, take the I-540 spur south to Fort Smith. From I-540, exit at Fort Chaffee exit 3 sign. Take Highway 59 S across Arkansas River to Highway 22. it goes past Fort Chaffee main gate. From main gate, continue to left at first stop sign, then continue for approximately five miles to golf course.

**SEASON OF OPERATION:** Year round.

**ELIGIBILITY:** Active/Reservists/Retired/DoD civilians/Dependents/General Public (Tue-Fri before 1300)/Guests.

**COURSE INFORMATION:** Address: Deer Trails Golf Course, Bldg 3910, Arkansas Blvd, Barling, AR 72923-5000. **C-501-478-6971** 0700-Dusk summer, 0800-Dusk winter. One 9 hole golf course.

| | |
|---|---|
| Length | 6,070 |
| Par | 71 |
| Slope (M) | 107 |
| Slope (L) | 93 |
| USGA Rating (M) | 67.0 |
| USGA Rating (L) | 60.0 |

\* Information based on 18 hole game.

ARKANSAS-CALIFORNIA
*Deer Trails Golf Course, continued*

| RATES: | Weekday | Weekend |
|---|---|---|
| Enlisted | $5 | $8 |
| Officers | $5 | $8 |
| DoD civilians | $7 | $10 |
| Guests | $10 | $15 |

**SUPPORT FACILITIES:**

| | | |
|---|---|---|
| Chipping Area | Driving Range | Equipment Rental |
| Golf Carts/Power | Golf Carts/Pull | Lessons |
| Pro at Facility | Pro Shop | Putting Area |
| Showers | Snack Bar | |

**CREDIT CARDS ACCEPTED:** None.

## PINE BLUFF ARSENAL GOLF COURSE
Pine Bluff Arsenal, AR 71602-9500

**LOCATION:** On post. From main gate to left on Sibert Road, then continue straight to golf course.

**SEASON OF OPERATION:** Year round.

**ELIGIBILITY:** Active/Reservists/Retired/DoD civilians/Dependents/ Guests.

**COURSE INFORMATION:** Address: CMDR, Pine Bluff Arsenal, Bldg 16-310, Sibert Road, Pine Bluff, AR 71602-9500. **C-870-540-3028, D-312-966-3028** 0930-1800 hours daily. One 9 hole golf course.

| RATES: | Weekday | Weekend |
|---|---|---|
| All | $7.50 | $7.50 |

**SUPPORT FACILITIES:**

| | | |
|---|---|---|
| Driving Range | Golf Carts/Power | Golf Carts/Pull |
| Lockers | Pro Shop | Showers |
| Snack Vending | Soda Vending | |

**CREDIT CARDS ACCEPTED:** Visa and MasterCard.

# CALIFORNIA

## ADMIRAL BAKER GOLF COURSE
San Diego Naval Station
San Diego, CA 92136-5000

**COURSE INFORMATION:** Address: Admiral Baker Golf Course, MWR Department, Code 10 Box 15, San Diego, CA 92136-5015. **C-619-556-5162.** 36 hole golf facility.

## CHINA LAKE GOLF COURSE
China Lake Naval Air Warfare Center Weapons Division/
Naval Air Weapons Station
China Lake, CA 93555-6100

**COURSE INFORMATION:** Address: China Lake Golf Course, MWR Department, P.O. Box 6169, Ridgecrest, CA 93555. **C-760-939-2990, D-312-437-2990.** One 18 hole golf course. *Note: $2.061 million golf course irrigation project has been approved in the Fiscal Year 1998 MWR Major and Minor Construction Program.*

## CYPRESS LAKES GOLF COURSE
Travis Air Force Base
Travis AFB, CA 94535-2045

**LOCATION:** Off base. I-80 to Fairfield. Exit Air Base Parkway to Peabody Road, to Vanden Road, to a right on Cannon Road, to Meridian Road.

**SEASON OF OPERATION:** Year round.

**ELIGIBILITY:** Active/Reservists/Retired/DoD civilians/Dependents/ Guests.

**COURSE INFORMATION:** Address: Cypress Lakes Golf Course, 5601 Meridian Road, Vacaville, CA 95687-5000. **C-707-424-5797** administration, **C-707-448-7186** Pro shop 0630-Dusk. One 18 hole golf course.

| | Back Tees | Front Tees |
|---|---|---|
| Length | 6,798 | 5,669 |
| Par | 72 | 73 |
| Slope | 121 | 120 |
| USGA Rating | 72.7 | 73.0 |

| RATES: | Weekday | Weekend |
|---|---|---|
| E1-E4 | $8 | $10 |
| E5+ | $13 | $15 |
| Officers | $13 | $15 |
| Guests | $20 | $25 |
| Civilians | $20 | $25 |

**SUPPORT FACILITIES:**

| | | |
|---|---|---|
| Chipping Area | Driving Range | Golf Carts/Power |
| Golf Carts/Pull | Lessons | Parking |
| Pro at Facility | Pro Shop | Putting Area |
| Showers | Snack Bar | |

**CREDIT CARDS ACCEPTED:** Visa and MasterCard.

**RESTRICTIONS:** Active Duty seven day advance tee time. Spike free course.

## DESERT WINDS GOLF COURSE
Twentynine Palms Marine Corps Air/Ground Combat Center
Twentynine Palms, CA 92278-8102

**LOCATION:** Off base. From I-10 to Highway 62. Continue on Highway 62 to town of Twentynine Palms. Once in town take Adobe Road north to base, approximately 5 miles.

**SEASON OF OPERATION:** Year round.

**ELIGIBILITY:** Active/Reservists/Retired/DoD civilians/Dependents/ Guests.

**COURSE INFORMATION:** Address: Desert Winds Golf Course, Bldg 3812, MCAGCC, Twentynine Palms, CA 92278. **C-760-830-6132** 0600-1930 hours summer, 0700-1700 hours winter. One 18 hole golf course.

| | Back Tees | Front Tees |
|---|---|---|
| Length | 6,949 | 6,299 |
| Par | 72 | 72 |
| Slope | 121 | 116 |
| USGA Ratings | 72.7 | 70.2 |

*Desert winds golf course, continued*

| RATES: | Weekday | Weekend |
|---|---|---|
| Enlisted | $5-$9 | $6-$10 |
| Officers | $6.5-$10 | $7.5-$11 |
| DoD civilians | $8.5-$11 | $9.5-$12 |
| Guests | $8.5-$11 | $9.5-$12 |

**SUPPORT FACILITIES:**

| | | |
|---|---|---|
| Chipping Area | Driving Range | Equipment Rental |
| Golf Carts/Power | Golf Carts/Pull | Lockers |
| Pro Shop | Putting Area | Showers |
| Snack Bar | | |

**CREDIT CARDS ACCEPTED:** Visa, MasterCard, American Express, Discover and DPP.

# JOHN E. CLARK GOLF COURSE
Point Mugu Naval Air Weapons Center
Point Mugu, CA 93042-5001

**COURSE INFORMATION:** Address: John E. Clark Golf Course, MWR Department Code 836000E, Bldg 162, 521 9th Street.Point Mugu, CA 93042-5001. **C-805-989-7109.** One 9 hole golf course.

# LAWRENCE LINKS GOLF COURSE
McClellan Air Force Base
McClellan AFB, CA 95652-2001

**LOCATION:** Off base. From I-5 exit north onto Watt Avenue, then continue straight for 6 miles to right on Blackfoot Way and continue to golf course.

**SEASON OF OPERATION:** Year round.

**ELIGIBILITY:** Active/Reservists/Retired/DoD civilians/Dependents/ Guests.

**COURSE INFORMATION:** Address: Lawrence Links Golf Course, 3825 Blackfoot Way, Antelope, CA 95843. **C-916-643-3313, D-312-633-3313** Dawn-Dusk daily. One 9 hole golf course.

| | Back Tees | Front Tees |
|---|---|---|
| Length | 3,140 | 2,974 |
| Par | 36 | 36 |
| Slope | | |
| USGA Ratings* | 69.7 | 69.7 |

* Information based on 18 hole game.

| RATES: | Weekday | Weekend |
|---|---|---|
| E1-E4 | $6 | $7 |
| E5+ | $11 | $13 |
| Guests | $18 | $18 |

**SUPPORT FACILITIES:**

| | | |
|---|---|---|
| Chipping Area | Driving Cage | Equipment Rental |
| Golf Carts/Power | Golf Carts/Pull | Lockers |
| Pro at Facility | Pro Shop | Putting Area |
| Snack Bar | | |

**RESTRICTIONS:** At least one power golf cart must be used with foursomes.

**CREDIT CARDS ACCEPTED:** Visa and MasterCard.

# MARINE MEMORIAL GOLF COURSE
Camp Pendleton
Camp Pendleton, CA 92055-5019

**COURSE INFORMATION:** Address: Marine Memorial Golf Course, Bldg 18415, Camp Pendleton, CA 92055. **C-760-725-4756.** One 18 hole golf course. Lessons, Pro at Facility.

# MARINE MEMORIAL GOLF COURSE
El Toro Marine Corps Air Station
Santa Ana, CA 92709-5000
*Scheduled to close June 1999.*

**COURSE INFORMATION:** Address: Marine Memorial Golf Course, Bldg 464, MCAS El Toro, CA 92709. **C-714-726-2577.** One 18 hole golf course.

# MARSHALLIA RANCH GOLF COURSE
Vandenberg Air Force Base
Vandenberg AFB, CA 93437-6223

**LOCATION:** Off base. Take Highway-1 to San Antinio West, follow signs.

**SEASON OF OPERATION:** Year round.

**ELIGIBILITY:** Active/Reservists/Retired/DoD civilians/Dependents/ Guests.

**COURSE INFORMATION:** Address: Marshallia Ranch Golf Course, Bldg 1335, Vandenberg AFB, CA 93437. **C-805-734-1333/4764, D-312-866-6262** 0600-Dusk daily. One 18 hole golf course.

| | Back Tees | Middle Tees | Front Tees |
|---|---|---|---|
| Length | 6,845 | 6,388 | 5,404 |
| Par | 72 | 72 | 72 |
| Slope | 130 | 124 | 111 |
| USGA Rating | 73.4 | 71.1 | 66.1 |

| RATES: | Weekday | Weekend |
|---|---|---|
| Enlisted | $17 | $17 |
| Officers | $17 | $17 |
| Civilians | $44 | $54 |
| Guests | $29 | $34 |

**SUPPORT FACILITIES:**

| | | |
|---|---|---|
| Chipping Area (2) | Driving Range | Equipment Rental |
| Golf Carts/Power | Golf Carts/Pull | Lessons |
| Pro at Facility | Pro Shop | Putting Area (2) |
| Snack Bar | | |

**CREDIT CARDS ACCEPTED:** Visa and MasterCard.

# MIRAMAR MEMORIAL GOLF COURSE
Miramar Marine Corps Air Station
San Diego, CA 92145-2008

**LOCATION:** On base. Fifteen miles north of San Diego, off I-15 N or S. Take Miramar Way exit. From main gate to West Miramar Way to right on Rigel to golf course parking lot.

**SEASON OF OPERATION:** Year round.

**ELIGIBILITY:** Active/Reservists/Retired/DoD civilians/Dependents/ Guests.

*CALIFORNIA*
*Miramar Memorial Golf Course, continued*

**COURSE INFORMATION:** Address: Miramar Memorial Golf Course, Miramar MCAS, San Diego, CA 92145-5000. **C-619-537-4155** Dawn to Dusk daily. One 18 hole golf course.

|  | Back Tees | Front Tees |
|---|---|---|
| Length | 6,719 | 5,349 |
| Par | 72 | 73 |
| Slope | 125 | 120 |
| USGA Rating | 71.7 | 69.8 |

| **RATES:** | Weekday | Weekend |
|---|---|---|
| Enlisted | $6 | $7 |
| Officers | $12-$13 | $14 |
| DoD civilians | $19 | $19 |
| Guests | $21 | $26 |

**SUPPORT FACILITIES:**

| | | |
|---|---|---|
| Bar/Lounge | Chipping Area | Driving Range |
| Equipment Rental | Golf Carts/Power | Golf Carts/Pull |
| Lessons | Pro at Facility | Pro Shop |
| Putting Area | Soda Vending | Snack Bar |
| Snack Vending | | |

**CREDIT CARDS ACCEPTED:** Visa and MasterCard.

# MUROC LAKE GOLF COURSE
Edwards Air Force Base
Edwards AFB, CA 93524-1860

**COURSE INFORMATION:** Address: Muroc Lake Golf Course, P.O. Box 207, Edwards AFB, CA 93524. **C-805-277-7589/3468.** One 18 golf course; Length: 6,920; Par: 72. Chipping Area, Driving Range, Equipment Rental, Golf Carts/Power, Golf Carts/Pull, Lessons, Lockers, Pro Shop, Putting Area, Restaurants, Snack Bar.

# NAVY GOLF COURSE
Monterey Naval Postgraduate School
Monterey, CA 93943-5001

**COURSE INFORMATION:** Address: Navy Golf Course, MWR Department Code 45, Monterey, CA 93943-5027. **C-408-656-2167, C-312-878-2167.** One 18 hole golf course.

# NAVY GOLF COURSE
Seal Beach Naval Weapons Station
Seal Beach, CA 90740-5000

**COURSE INFORMATION:** Address: Navy Golf Course, Quality of Life Department, Bldg 11, 800 Seal Beach Blvd, Seal Beach, CA 90740-5000. **C-562-430-9913, D-312-873-9913.** 27 hole golf facility.

# PRESIDIO GOLF COURSE
Presidio of San Francisco
Presidio of San Francisco, CA 94129-5006

**COURSE INFORMATION:** Address: Presidio Golf Course, P.O. Box 29103, San Francisco, CA 94129. **C-415-751-0562.** One 18 hole golf course. Bar/Lounge, Chipping Area, Driving Range, Equipment Rental, Golf Carts/Power, Golf Carts/Pull, Lessons.

# SEABEE GOLF CLUB
Port Hueneme Naval Construction Battalion Center
Port Hueneme, CA 93043-4301

**LOCATION:** On base. From US-101 exit south on Ventura Road, then right to Pleasant Valley Road.

**SEASON OF OPERATION:** Year round.

**ELIGIBILITY:** Active/Reservists/Retired/DoD civilians/Dependents/Guests.

**COURSE INFORMATION:** Address: Seabee Golf Club, CBC Code 19, 1000, 2300 Avenue, Port Hueneme, CA 93043. **C-805-982-2620** 0700-Dusk Mon-Fri, 0600-Dusk Sat-Sun and Holidays. One 18 hole golf course. *Note: A $1.886 million new club house has been approved in the Fiscal Year 1998 MWR Major and Minor Construction Program.*

|  | Back Tees | Front Tees |
|---|---|---|
| Length | 6,275 | 5,995 |
| Par | 71 | 71 |
| Slope | 112 | 107 |
| USGA Rating | 69.1 | 67.4 |

| **RATES:** | Weekday | Weekend |
|---|---|---|
| Enlisted | $12 | $14 |
| Officers | $12 | $14 |
| DoD civilians | $15 | $20 |
| Guests | $15 | $20 |

**SUPPORT FACILITIES:**

| | | |
|---|---|---|
| Chipping Area | Driving Range | Equipment Rental |
| Golf Carts/Power | Golf Carts/Pull | Lessons |
| Lockers | Pro at Facility | Pro Shop |
| Putting Range | Restaurants | |

**CREDIT CARDS ACCEPTED:** Visa, MasterCard, American Express and Discover.

# RECCE POINT GOLF COURSE
Beale Air Force Base
Beale AFB, CA 95905-1525

**LOCATION:** On base. From main gate to Gavial Mandery to left on A Street. Continue to right on Warren Shingle Blvd and to the golf course.

**SEASON OF OPERATION:** Year round.

**ELIGIBILITY:** Active/Reservists/Retired/DoD civilians/Dependents/Guests.

**COURSE INFORMATION:** Address: Recce Point Golf Course, 24081 Warren Shingle Blvd, Beale AFB, CA 95903. **C-530-788-0192, D-312-368-2124** Dawn-Dusk daily.

|  | Back Tees | Middle Tees | Middle Tees | Front Tees |
|---|---|---|---|---|
| Length | 6,847 | 6,814 | 5,598 | 4,624 |
| Par | 72 | 72 | 72 | 72 |
| Slope* | 124 | 132 | 110 | |
| USGA Rating | 70.3 | 72.4 | 66.9 | |

| **RATES:** | Weekday | Weekend |
|---|---|---|
| Enlisted | $7-$12 | $7-$12 |
| Officers | $12-$14 | $12-$14 |
| Guests | $20 | $20 |

## SUPPORT FACILITIES:

| | | |
|---|---|---|
| Bar/Lounge | Chipping Area | Driving Range |
| Equipment Rental | Golf Carts/Power | Golf Carts/Pull |
| Lessons | Lockers | Pro at Facility |
| Pro Shop | Putting Range | Showers |
| Snack Bar | | |

**CREDIT CARDS ACCEPTED:** Visa and MasterCard.

## SEA N' AIR GOLF CLUB

Coronado Naval Amphibious Base
San Diego, CA 92155-5000

**LOCATION:** On base. From McCain Blvd to Rogers Road, then continue 1 mile to left to golf course.

**SEASON OF OPERATION:** Year round.

**ELIGIBILITY:** Active/Reservists/Retired/DoD civilians/Dependents/Guests.

**COURSE INFORMATION:** Address: Sea N' Air Golf Club, Bldg 800, NASN1, San Diego, CA 92135-7081. **C-619-545-9659** Dawn to Dusk daily. One 18 hole golf course.

| | Back Tees | Middle Tees | Front Tees |
|---|---|---|---|
| Length | 6,275 | 6,066 | 5,462 |
| Par | 72 | 72 | 72 |
| Slope | 117 | 113 | 121 |
| USGA Rating | 70.3 | 69.2 | 72.2 |

| RATES: | Weekday | Weekend |
|---|---|---|
| E1-E4 | $6 | $6 |
| E5+ | $12 | $12 |
| DoD civilians | $15 | $20 |

## SUPPORT FACILITIES:

| | | |
|---|---|---|
| Bar/Lounge | Chipping Area | Driving Range |
| Equipment Rental | Golf Carts/Power | Golf Carts/Pull |
| Lessons | Lockers | Pro at Facility |
| Pro Shop | Putting Putting Area | Showers |
| Snack Bar | Soda Vending | |

**RESTRICTIONS:** Proper golf attire required.

**CREDIT CARDS ACCEPTED:** Visa and MasterCard.

## TEES & TREES GOLF COURSE

Barstow Marine Corps Logistics Base
Barstow, CA 92311-5001

**LOCATION:** Off base. Make a left just before you enter the main gate and cross railroad tracks, then continue through tunnel to right to golf course.

**SEASON OF OPERATION:** Year round.

**ELIGIBILITY:** Active/Reservists/Retired/DoD civilians/Dependents/Guests.

**COURSE INFORMATION:** Address: Tees & Trees Golf Course, Bldg 44, Barstow, CA 92317. **C-760-577-6431** 0700-1900 hours spring and summer, 0700-1700 hours fall and winter.

| | Back Tees | Front Tees |
|---|---|---|
| Length | 3,211 | 3,191 |
| Par | 72 | 72 |
| Slope | 117 | 117 |
| USGA Rating | | |

| RATES: | Weekday | Weekend |
|---|---|---|
| Enlisted | $7 | $7 |
| Officers | $9 | $9 |
| DoD civilians | $11 | $11 |
| Guests | $11 | $11 |

## SUPPORT FACILITIES:

| | | |
|---|---|---|
| Banquet Facilities | Bar/Lounge | Chipping Area |
| Driving Range | Golf Carts/Power | Golf Carts/Pull |
| Lessons | Lockers | Pro at Facility |
| Pro Shop | Putting Area | Showers* |
| Snack Bar | | |

* Male showers only.

**CREDIT CARDS ACCEPTED:** None.

# COLORADO

## CHEYENNE SHADOWS GOLF COURSE

Fort Carson
Fort Carson, CO 80913-4104

**COURSE INFORMATION:** Address: Cheyenne Shadows Golf Course, Bldg 7800, Fort Carson, CO 80913. **C-719-579-4122.** One 18 hole golf course. Banquet Facilities, Bar/Lounge, Chipping Area, Driving Range, Golf Carts/Power, Golf Carts/Pull, Lockers, Pro Shop, Putting Area, Restaurants, Snack Bar.

## EISENHOWER GOLF CLUB

United States Air Force Academy
USAF Academy, CO 80840-9999

**LOCATION:** On base. West of I-25 N from Colorado Springs. Two gates, about five miles apart, provide access from I-25 and are clearly marked. From main gate to Stadium Blvd to Parade Loop then to golf club.

**SEASON OF OPERATION:** Year round.

**ELIGIBILITY:** Active/Reservists/Retired/DoD civilians/Dependents.

**COURSE INFORMATION:** Address: Eisenhower Golf Club, P.O. Box 72, USAFA, 080840-5000. **C-719-333-3456, D-312-333-3456.** Two 18 hole golf courses.

**Blue Course**

| | Back Tees | Middle Tees | Front Tees |
|---|---|---|---|
| Length | 6,516 | 6,051 | 5,559 |
| Par (M) | 72 | 72 | 72 |
| Par (L) | 74 | 74 | 74 |
| Slope (M) | 128 | 120 | 115 |
| Slope (L) | 131 | 132 | 130 |
| USGA Rating (M) | 70.5 | 68.2 | 65.3 |
| USGA Rating (L) | 76.3 | 74.0 | 70.6 |

COLORADO-FLORIDA
*Eisenhower Golf Club, Continued*

**Silver Course**

| | Back Tees | Middle Tees | Front Tees |
|---|---|---|---|
| Length | 6,017 | 5,479 | 5,215 |
| Par (M) | 72 | 72 | 72 |
| Par (L) | 72 | 72 | 72 |
| Slope (M) | 116 | 108 | 105 |
| Slope (L) | 127 | 123 | 119 |
| USGA Rating (M) | 68.0 | 65.4 | 63.5 |
| USGA Rating (L) | 73.8 | 71.2 | 69.0 |

**RATES:** Call for current rates.

**SUPPORT FACILITIES:**

| | | |
|---|---|---|
| Banquet Facilities | Bar/Lounge | Chipping Area |
| Driving Range | Golf Carts/Power | Golf Carts/Pull |
| Lessons | Lockers | Pro at Facility |
| Pro Shop | Putting Area | Showers |
| Snack Bar | Soda Vending | |

**CREDIT CARDS ACCEPTED:** Visa and MasterCard.

## SILVER SPRUCE GOLF COURSE
Peterson Air Force Base
Peterson AFB, CO 80914-1130

**COURSE INFORMATION:** Address: Silver Spruce Golf Course, Bldg 1054, Peterson AFB. **C-719-556-7414, D-312-834-7414** 0630-1930 hours daily summer, 0730-1700 Tue-Sun winter. One 18 hole golf course. Chipping Area, Driving Range, Equipment Rental, Lessons, Lockers, Putting Area, Snack Bar.

# CONNECTICUT

## GOOSE RUN GOLF COURSE
New London Naval Submarine Base
Groton, CT 06349-5000

**COURSE INFORMATION:** Address: Goose Run Golf Course, MWR Department, Box 14, Groton, CT 06349-5014. **C-860-449-3763, D-312-241-3763.** One 9 hole golf course.

# DELAWARE

## EAGLE CREEK GOLF COURSE
Dover Air Force Base
Dover AFB, DE 19902-6447

**COURSE INFORMATION:** Address: Eagle Creek Golf Course, Bldg 827, Dover ARB, DE 19902. **C-302-677-6039.** One 18 hole golf course. Equipment Rental, Golf Carts, Lockers, Pro Shop, Snack Bar.

# DISTRICT OF COLUMBIA

## GREENLEAF POINT GOLF COURSE
Fort Lesley J. McNair
Washington, DC 20319-5058

**COURSE INFORMATION:** Address: Greenleaf Point Golf Course, bldg 262, 3rd Avenue SW, Washington, DC 20319. **C-202-685-3138/3415/3570.** One 9 hole golf course. Equipment Rental, Golf Carts/Power, Golf Carts/Pull, Pro Shop, Putting Area, Snack Bar.

# FLORIDA

## A.C. READ GOLF CLUB
Pensacola Naval Air Station
Pensacola NAS, FL 32508-5217

**LOCATION:** On base. Take Navy Blvd from US-98 or US-29 directly to NAS.

**SEASON OF OPERATION:** Year round.

**ELIGIBILITY:** Active/Reservists/Retired/Guests.

**COURSE INFORMATION:** Address: A.C Read Golf Club, Bldg 3495, NAS Pensacola, FL 32508. **C-850-452-2454** 0700-1800 hours daily. Three 9 hole golf courses (Bayou, Lakeview and Bayview) and one 18 hole golf course (Executive).

**9 hole courses**

| | Back Tees | Front Tees |
|---|---|---|
| Length* | 6,662-6,544 | 5,236-5,170 |
| Par | 72 | 72 |
| Slope | 124 | 117 |
| USGA Rating* | 71.7-71.3 | 69.9-69.4 |

\* For 18 hole game. Information varies by which combination of 9 hole courses played.

**Executive Course**
Information is not yet available.

| **RATES:** | Weekday | Weekend |
|---|---|---|
| Enlisted | $11 | $11 |
| Officers | $11 | $11 |
| Guests | $20 | $20 |

**SUPPORT FACILITIES:**

| | | |
|---|---|---|
| Bar/Lounge | Chipping Area | Driving Range |
| Equipment Rental | Golf Carts/Power | Golf Cart/Pull |
| Lessons | Lockers | Pro at Facility |
| Pro Shop | Putting Area | Restaurants |
| Showers | Snack Bar | |

**CREDIT CARDS ACCEPTED:** Visa, MasterCard, American Express and Discover.

## BAY PALMS GOLF COMPLEX
MacDill Air Force Base
MacDill AFB, FL 33621-5313

**LOCATION:** On base. From I-75 N or S, take FL-618 exit west to FL-573 exit to main gate. From any gate to Bayshore Blvd south to clubhouse.

**SEASON OF OPERATION:** Year round.

**ELIGIBILITY:** Active/Reservists/Retired/DoD civilians/Dependents.

**COURSE INFORMATION:** Address: Bay Palms Golf Complex, 1805 Golf Course Road, MacDill AFB, FL 33621-5000. **C-813-840-6915/6904, D-312-968-4494** 0630-1830 hours summer, 0630-1730 hours winter. Two 18 hole golf courses.

## North Golf Course

|  | Back Tees | Middle Tees | Front Tees |
|---|---|---|---|
| Length | 6,433 |  | 5,204 |
| Par | 72 | 72 | 72 |
| Slope | 120 | 118 | 117 |
| USGA Rating | 70.9 | 69.7 | 70.8 |

## South Golf Course

|  | Back Tees | Middle Tees | Front Tees |
|---|---|---|---|
| Length | 6,763 |  | 5,099 |
| Par | 72 | 72 | 71 |
| Slope | 125 | 119 | 113 |
| USGA Rating | 72.5 | 70.4 | 68.9 |

| RATES: | Weekday | Weekend |
|---|---|---|
| E1-E4 | $6 | $7 |
| E5-E9 | $9 | $10 |
| O1-O3 | $9 | $10 |
| O4+ | $10 | $12 |
| DoD civilians | $15 | $20 |

### SUPPORT FACILITIES:

| | | |
|---|---|---|
| Banquet Facilities | Chipping Area | Driving Range* |
| Equipment Rental | Golf Carts/Power | Golf Carts/Pull |
| Lessons | Lockers | Pro at Facility |
| Pro Shop | Putting Area* | Restaurants |
| Showers | Snack Bar | Soda Vending |

* Lighted facilities.

**RESTRICTIONS:** Must ride motor golf carts prior to 1300 hours daily.

**CREDIT CARDS ACCEPTED:** Visa and MasterCard.

## CASA LINDA OAKS GOLF COURSE
### Jacksonville Naval Air Station
### Jacksonville, FL 32212-5000

**LOCATION:** On base. Access from US-17 (Roosevelt Blvd) south of Jacksonville, near intersection with I-295.

**SEASON OF OPERATION:** Year round.

**ELIGIBILITY:** Active/Reservists/Retired/DoD civilians/Dependents/ Guests.

**COURSE INFORMATION:** Address: Casa Linda Oaks Golf Course, Bldg 808, Jacksonville NAS, FL 32212-5000. **C-904-542-3249, D-312-942-3095** 0630-1900 hours. One 18 hole golf course.

|  | Back Tees | Middle Tees | Front Tees |
|---|---|---|---|
| Length | 6,559 | 6,216 | 5,577 |
| Par | 72 | 72 | 72 |
| Slope (M) | 130 | 127 | 121 |
| Slope (L) |  | 134 | 126 |
| USGA Rating (M) | 71.0 | 69.5 | 66.6 |
| USGA Rating (L) |  | 76.4 | 72.8 |

| RATES: | Weekday | Weekend |
|---|---|---|
| Enlisted | $7 | $8 |
| Officers | $8 | $10 |
| DoD civilians | $9 | $12 |
| Guests | $15 | $18 |

### SUPPORT FACILITIES:

| | | |
|---|---|---|
| Bar/Lounge | Chipping Area | Driving Range |
| Equipment Rental | Golf Carts/Power | Golf Carts/Pull |
| Lessons | Pro at Facility | Pro Shop |
| Putting Area | Restaurants | Soda Vending |

**RESTRICTIONS:** Must ride in carts on weekends and holidays until 1530.

**CREDIT CARDS ACCEPTED:** Visa, MasterCard and American Express.

## EGLIN GOLF COURSE
### Eglin Air Force Base
### Eglin AFB, FL 32542-6823

**LOCATION:** On base. From I-10 Exit #12 to Highway-855. Continue for approximately 16 miles to golf course.

**SEASON OF OPERATION:** Year round.

**ELIGIBILITY:** Active/Reservists/Retired/DoD civilians/Dependents/ Guests.

**COURSE INFORMATION:** Address: Eglin Golf Course, 1527 Fairway Drive, Niceville, FL 32578. **C-850-882-2949/4914, D-312-872-2949/4914.** Two 18 hole golf course.

### Falcon Course

|  | Back Tees | Front Tees |
|---|---|---|
| Length | 6,869 | 5,175 |
| Par | 72 | 72 |
| Slope | 130 | 118 |
| USGA Rating | 73.8 | 69.7 |

### Eagle Course

|  | Back Tees | Front Tees |
|---|---|---|
| Length | 6,567 | 5,158 |
| Par | 72 | 73 |
| Slope | 135 | 119 |
| USGA Rating | 71.5 | 69.5 |

| RATES: | Weekday | Weekend |
|---|---|---|
| E1-E4 | $9 | $9 |
| E5+ | $15 | $15 |
| Guests | $23 | $23 |

### SUPPORT FACILITIES:

| | | |
|---|---|---|
| Banquet Facilities | Chipping Area | Driving Range |
| Equipment Rental | Golf Carts/Power | Golf Carts/Pull |
| Lessons | Lockers | Pro at Facility |
| Pro Shop | Putting Area | Showers |
| Snack Bar | Soda Vending |  |

**CREDIT CARDS ACCEPTED:** Visa and MasterCard.

## FIDDLER'S GREEN GOLF COURSE
### Cecil Field Naval Air Station
### Cecil Field NAS, FL 32215-0184

**COURSE INFORMATION:** Address: Fiddler's Green Golf Course, MWR Dept. Box 109, Cecil Field NAS, FL 32215. **C-904-778-5245.** One 18 hole golf course.

*FLORIDA-GEORGIA*

## FRANK DOLLINGER GOLF COURSE
Whiting Field Naval Air Station
Milton, FL 32570-5000

**COURSE INFORMATION:** Address: Frank Dollinger Golf Course, 8271 USS Intrepid Road, Milton, FL 32570. **C-850-623-7348/7521.** One 18 hole golf course. Chipping Area, Driving Range, Equipment Rental, Golf Carts/Power, Golf Carts/Pull, Putting Area, Snack Bar.

## GATOR LAKES GOLF CLUB
Hurlburt Field
Hurlburt Field, FL 32544-5272

**COURSE INFORMATION:** Address: Gator Lakes Golf Club, Bldg 91300, Hurlburt Field, FL. **C-850-881-2251, D-312-641-2251** 0630-1800 hours daily summer, 0630-1700 hours daily winter. One 18 hole golf course. Driving Range, Equipment Rental, Pro Shop, Putting Area, Snack Bar.

## MAYPORT GOLF CLUB
Mayport Naval Station
Mayport NS, FL 32228-0042

**COURSE INFORMATION:** Address: Mayport Golf Club, MWR Code N9, Bldg 414, P.O. Box 280048, Mayport, FL 32228. **C-904-270-5380, D-312-960-5380.** One 18 hole golf course.

## PELICAN POINT GOLF COURSE
Tyndall Air Force Base
Tyndall AFB, FL 32403-5428

**LOCATION:** On base. Take I-10, exit to US-231 south to US-98 east, then continue to clearly marked base.

**SEASON OF OPERATION:** Year round.

**ELIGIBILITY:** Active/Reservists/Retired/DoD civilians/Dependents/ Guests.

**COURSE INFORMATION:** Address: Pelican Point Golf Course, Bldg 3029, Tyndall AFB 32403. **C-850-283-2565/4389** 0700-Dusk daily. One 18 hole golf course.

|        | Back Tees | Front Tees |
|--------|-----------|------------|
| Length | 7,100     |            |
| Par    | 72        | 67         |
| Slope  | 125       | 116        |

| RATES:   | Weekday | Weekend |
|----------|---------|---------|
| Enlisted | $13     | $14     |
| Officers | $17     | $18     |
| Guests   | $25     | $25     |

**SUPPORT FACILITIES:**

| | | |
|---|---|---|
| Bar/Lounge | Chipping Area | Driving Range |
| Equipment Rental | Golf Carts/Pull | Lessons |
| Lockers | Pro at Facility | Pro Shop |
| Putting Area | Sand Trap | Showers |
| Snack Bar | | |

**CREDIT CARDS ACCEPTED:** Visa, MasterCard and Military Club Cards.

## WHITING FIELD GOLF COURSE
Whiting Field Naval Air Station
Milton, FL 32570-5000

**COURSE INFORMATION:** Address: Whiting Field Golf Course, MWR Department, Bldg 1417, 7180 Langley Street, Milton, FL 32570-5000. **C-850-623-7348, D-312-868-7348.** One 18 hole golf course.

# GEORGIA

## FORT BENNING GOLF COMPLEX
Fort Benning
Fort Benning, GA 31905-5000

**LOCATION:** On post. Located on south side of Columbus. Accessible from US-80, I-185, US-27, US-280 and US-165. Clearly marked.

**SEASON OF OPERATION:** Year round.

**ELIGIBILITY:** Active/Reservists/Retired/DoD civilians/Dependents/ Approved civilians/Guests.

**COURSE INFORMATION:** Address: Fort Benning Golf Complex, Bldg 390, 1st Division. Road, Fort Benning, GA 31905-5000. **C-706-687-1940** Dawn-Dusk. Two 18 hole golf courses.

**Lakeside Golf Course**

|             | Back Tees | Middle Tees | Front Tees |
|-------------|-----------|-------------|------------|
| Length      | 6,145     | 5,887       | 5,122      |
| Par         | 72        | 72          | 72         |
| Slope       | 118       | 116         | 116        |
| USGA Rating | 69.3      | 68.1        | 69.1       |

**Pineside Golf Course**

|             | Back Tees | Middle Tees | Front Tees |
|-------------|-----------|-------------|------------|
| Length      | 6,606     | 6,303       | 5,547      |
| Par         | 72/74     | 72/74       | 72/74      |
| Slope       | 126       | 123         | 115        |
| USGA Rating | 71.6      | 70.2        | 70.6       |

| RATES:        | Weekday | Weekend |
|---------------|---------|---------|
| E1-E5         | $6      | $6      |
| E6+           | $12     | $12     |
| DoD Civilians | $18     | $18     |
| Guests        | $18     | $18     |

**CREDIT CARDS ACCEPTED:** Visa, MasterCard, American Express and Discover.

## FORT STEWART GOLF COURSE
Fort Stewart
Fort Stewart, GA 31314-5132

**LOCATION:** On post. From main gate to Wilson Avenue, then continue straight through traffic light to golf course.

**SEASON OF OPERATION:** Year round.

**ELIGIBILITY:** Active/Reservists/Retired/DoD civilians/Dependents/ Guests.

**COURSE INFORMATION:** Address: Fort Stewart Golf Course, 2150 Gulick Avenue, Fort Stewart, GA 31314. **C-912-767-2370** 0730-2200 hours summer, 0730-2000 hours winter. One 18 hole golf course.

| | Back Tees | Middle Tees | Front Tees |
|---|---|---|---|
| Length | 6,305 | 5,886 | 4,774 |
| Par | 72 | 72 | 72 |
| Slope | | | |
| USGA Rating | 69.9 | 68.1 | 67.3 |

| RATES: | Weekday | Weekend |
|---|---|---|
| Enlisted | $7 | $9 |
| Officers | $11 | $13 |
| Guests | $12 | $15 |

**SUPPORT FACILITIES:**

| | | |
|---|---|---|
| Chipping Area | Driving Range | Equipment Rental |
| Golf Carts/Power | Golf Cart/Pull | Lessons |
| Pro at Facility | Pro Shop | Putting Area |
| Restaurants | Snack Vending | Soda Vending |

**CREDIT CARDS ACCEPTED:** Visa, MasterCard, Discover and Diners'.

## THE GOLFERS' CLUB AT FORT MCPHERSON

Fort McPherson
Fort McPherson, GA 30330-1049

**LOCATION:** On post. Off I-75 N or S take Lakewood Freeway east (GA-166), exit to US-29 (Main Street exit) to main gate.

**SEASON OF OPERATION:** Year round.

**ELIGIBILITY:** Active/Reservists/Retired/DoD civilians/Dependents/Federal Employees/Guests.

**COURSE INFORMATION:** Address: The Golfers' Club at Fort McPherson, 1466 Wetzell Drive, Fort McPherson, GA 30330-5000. **C-404-464-2178, D-312-367-2178** 0700-1900 hours summer, 0800-1700 hours winter. One 18 hole golf course. *Note: A new clubhouse and course layout is scheduled to be completed in spring 1999.*

| | Back Tees | Middle Tees | Front Tees |
|---|---|---|---|
| Length | 6,210 | 5,672 | 4,891 |
| Par | 70 | 70 | 70 |
| Slope | 125 | 119 | 118 |
| USGA Rating | 70.0 | 67.0 | 68.3 |

| RATES: | Weekday | Weekend |
|---|---|---|
| Enlisted | $15-$18 | $21-$24 |
| Officers | $12-$15 | $18-$21 |
| DoD/Fed civilians | $12-$18 | $18-$24 |
| Guests | $21 | $27 |

**SUPPORT FACILITIES:**

| | | |
|---|---|---|
| Banquet Facilities | Bar/Lounge | Chipping Area |
| Driving Range | Golf Carts/Power | Golf Cart/Pull |
| Lessons | Pro at Facility | Pro Shop |
| Putting Area | Restaurants | |

**CREDIT CARDS ACCEPTED:** Visa, MasterCard and American Express.

## GORDON LAKES GOLF COURSE

Fort Gordon
Fort Gordon, GA 30905-5000

**LOCATION:** On post. Between US-78/278 and US-1. Gates are on both Highways.

**SEASON OF OPERATION:** Year round.

**ELIGIBILITY:** Active/Reservists/Retired/DoD civilians/Dependents/Guests.

**COURSE INFORMATION:** Address: Gordon Lakes Golf Course, Bldg 537, Rauge Road, Fort Gordon, GA 30907. **C-706-796-2433.** One 18 hole golf course and one 9 hole golf course. *Note: A $1.025 million new golf maintenance facility has been approved in the Fiscal Year 1998 MWR Major and Minor Construction Program.*

**18 hole course**

| | Back Tees | Middle Tees | Middle Tees | Front Tees |
|---|---|---|---|---|
| Length | 7,077 | 6,644 | 6,292 | 5,888 |
| Par | 72 | 72 | 72 | 72 |
| Slope | 136 | 129 | 123 | 130 |
| USGA Rating | 74.0 | 71.8 | 70.4 | 73.7 |

| RATES: | Weekday | Weekend |
|---|---|---|
| Enlisted | $10 | $11 |
| Officers | $15 | $18 |
| Guests | $18 | $23 |

**SUPPORT FACILITIES:**

| | | |
|---|---|---|
| Chipping Area | Driving Range | Golf Carts/Power |
| Golf Cart/Pull | Lessons | Pro at Facility |
| Pro Shop | Putting Area | Snack Bar |

**CREDIT CARDS ACCEPTED:** Visa, MasterCard and American Express.

## HUNTER GOLF CLUB

Hunter Army Airfield
Hunter AAF, GA 31409-5014

**COURSE INFORMATION:** Address: Hunter Golf Club, Bldg 8215, Hunter AAF, GA 31409-5003. **C-912-352-5622.** One 18 hole golf course. Banquet Facilities, Chipping Area, Driving Range, Equipment Rental, Golf Carts/Power, Golf Carts/Pull, Lessons, Pro Shop, Putting Area, Snack Bar.

## KINGS BAY GOLF CLUB

Kings Bay Naval Submarine Base
Kings Bay, GA 31547-2606

**LOCATION:** On base. From main gate to left at second traffic light, then continue to right at end of road. Golf course is on the right.

**SEASON OF OPERATION:** Year round.

**ELIGIBILITY:** Active/Reservists/Retired/DoD civilians/Dependents/Guests.

**COURSE INFORMATION:** Address: Kings Bay Golf Club, 1063 USS Tennessee Avenue, QL 225, NAVSUBASE, Kings Bay, GA 31547. **C-912-673-2001 ext 8475** 0730-Dusk daily. One 18 golf course.

| | Back Tees | Middle Tees | Front Tees |
|---|---|---|---|
| Length | 6,575 | 5,948 | 5,278 |
| Par | 72 | 72 | 72 |
| Slope | 125 | 119 | 112 |
| USGA Rating | 70.9 | 68.0 | 69.6 |

*GEORGIA*
*Kings Bay Golf Club, continued*

| RATES: | Weekday | Weekend |
|---|---|---|
| E1-E6 | $7 | $9 |
| E7+ | $8 | $10 |
| DoD civilians | $10 | $12 |
| Guests | $14 | $16 |

**SUPPORT FACILITIES:**

| | | |
|---|---|---|
| Banquet Facilities | Bar/Lounge | Chipping Area |
| Driving Range | Golf Carts/Power | Golf Cart/Pull |
| Lessons | Pro at Facility | Pro Shop |
| Putting Area | Snack Bar | |

**RESTRICTIONS:** Golf carts mandatory weekends and holidays until 1300.

**CREDIT CARDS ACCEPTED:** Visa, MasterCard, American Express and Discover.

# MOODY QUIET PINES GOLF COURSE
Moody Air Force Base
Moody AFB, GA 31699-1507

**LOCATION:** On base. On GA-125, 10 miles north of Valdosta. Also, can be reached from I-75 via GA-122. Golf course is across from main gate.

**SEASON OF OPERATION:** Year round.

**ELIGIBILITY:** Active/Reservists/Retired/DoD civilians/Dependents/Guests.

**COURSE INFORMATION:** Address: Moody Quiet Pines Golf Course, 155011 Prewitte Street, Moody AFB, GA 31699. **C-912-257-3297, D-312-460-3297** 0700-Dusk daily. One 9 hole golf course.

| | Back Tees | Middle Tees | Front Tees |
|---|---|---|---|
| Length | 6,715 | 6,541 | 4,991 |
| Par | 72 | 72 | 72 |
| Slope | 127 | 125 | 114 |
| USGA Rating | 72.5 | 71.7 | 78.5 |

| RATES: | Weekday | Weekend |
|---|---|---|
| E1-E4 | $8 | $8 |
| E5+ | $11 | $11 |
| Guests | $14 | $14 |

**SUPPORT FACILITIES:**

| | | |
|---|---|---|
| Driving Range | Equipment Rental | Golf Carts/Power |
| Golf Carts/Pull | Lessons | Pro at Facility |
| Pro Shop | Putting Area | Snack Bar |
| Soda Vending | | |

**CREDIT CARDS ACCEPTED:** Visa and MasterCard.

# PINE OAKS GOLF COURSE
Robins Air Force Base
Robins AFB, 31098-2235

**LOCATION:** On base. From main gate (gate #2) continue straight to right on Robins Parkway, then turn left onto Warner Robins Street. Continue for approximately 1 mile go course on left.

**SEASON OF OPERATION:** Year round.

**ELIGIBILITY:** Active/Reservists/Retired/DoD civilians/Dependents/Guests

**COURSE INFORMATION:** Address: Pine Oaks Golf Course, 755 Warner Robins Street, Robins AFB, GA 31098. **C-912-926-4103** 0700-Dusk daily. One 18 hole golf course.

| | Back Tees | Middle Tees | Front Tees |
|---|---|---|---|
| Length | 6,343 | 6,059 | 5,530 |
| Par | 71 | 71 | 74 |
| Slope | 125 | 121 | 125 |
| USGA Rating | 71.0 | 69.7 | 72.3 |

| RATES: | Weekday | Weekend |
|---|---|---|
| E1-E4 | $5 (9), $8 (18) | $6 (9), $9 (18) |
| E5+ | $7.5 (9), $12 (18) | $9 (9), $14 (18) |
| Guests | $10 (9), $15 (18) | $10 (9), $15 (18) |

**SUPPORT FACILITIES:**

| | | |
|---|---|---|
| Chipping Area | Driving Range | Equipment Rental |
| Golf Carts/Power | Golf Carts/Pull | Lessons |
| Lockers | Pro at Facility | Pro Shop |
| Putting Area | Restaurants | Showers |
| Snack Bar | | |

**CREDIT CARDS ACCEPTED:** Visa and MasterCard.

# TWIN OAKS GOLF COURSE
Albany Marine Corps Logistics Base
Albany, GA 31704-1128

**LOCATION:** On base. From US-82 E or W, take Albany exit to Mock Road south to left on Fleming Road to main gate. Also accessible from US-19 and 300 south, take Mock Road exit and right on Fleming Road to main gate.

**SEASON OF OPERATION:** Year round.

**ELIGIBILITY:** Active/Reservists/Retired/DoD civilians/Dependents/General Public/Guests.

**COURSE INFORMATION:** Address: Twin Oaks Golf Course, Bldg 7800, E Mathews Blvd, Albany MCLB, GA 31704-5000. **C-912-439-5211.** One nine hole golf course.

| | |
|---|---|
| Length | 3,078 |
| Par | 36 |
| Slope | 120 |
| USGA Rating | 69.3 |

| RATES: | Weekday | Weekend |
|---|---|---|
| Enlisted | $7-$8 | $10-$12 |
| Officers | $8-$10 | $10-$12 |
| Civilians | $11 | $13 |

**SUPPORT FACILITIES:**

| | | |
|---|---|---|
| Golf Carts/Power | Golf Carts/Pull | Lessons |
| Snack Bar | Snack Vending | Soda Vending |
| Parking | Pro at Facility | Pro Shop |

**RESTRICTIONS:** Threesomes or foursomes until 1200 hours, on weekends and holidays.

**CREDIT CARDS ACCEPTED:** Visa, MasterCard and Discover.

# HAWAII

## BARBERS POINT GOLF COURSE
Barbers Point Naval Air Station
Barber Point NAS, HI 96862-5050

**COURSE INFORMATION:** Address: Barbers Golf Course, MWR Department, Bldg 929, Barbers Point NAS, HI 96862-5050. **C-808-682-1911.** One 18 hole golf course.

## KANEOHE KLIPPER GOLF COURSE
Kaneohe Marine Corps Base
Kaneohe Bay, HI 96863-3002

**LOCATION:** On base. From Honolulu, take H-1 W to Pali Highway to H3 MCBH. H# ends at front gate. Continue straight through two traffic lights. Left on Manning Street. The club house is located on the right.

**SEASON OF OPERATION:** Year round.

**ELIGIBILITY:** Active/Reservists/Retired/DoD civilians/Dependents/Navy League/Marine Corps League/Guests.

**COURSE INFORMATION:** Address: Kaneohe Klipper Golf Course, MCBH, Bldg 3088, Box 63073, Kaneohe Bay, HI 96863-5000. **C-808-254-2107** 0600-1900 hours. Tee time reservations: **C-808-254-1745/3220.** One 18 hole golf course.

|  | Back Tees | Middle Tees | Front Tees |
|---|---|---|---|
| Length | 6,559 | 6,216 | 5,577 |
| Par | 72 | 72 | 72 |
| Slope (M) | 130 | 127 | 121 |
| Slope (L) |  | 134 | 126 |
| USGA Rating (M) | 71.0 | 69.5 | 66.6 |
| USGA Rating (L) |  | 76.4 | 72.8 |

| RATES: | Weekday | Weekend |
|---|---|---|
| O4+ | $16 | $16 |
| E6-O3 | $14 | $14 |
| E1-E5 | $8 | $8 |
| DoD MCB | $20 | $20 |
| DoD civilians | $22 | $22 |
| Guests | $22 | $22 |
| Civilians | $37 | $37 |

**SUPPORT FACILITIES:**

| | | |
|---|---|---|
| Banquet Facilities | Bar/Lounge | Chipping Area |
| Driving Range | Golf Carts/Power | Golf Carts/Pull |
| Lessons | Lockers | Parking |
| Pro at Facility | Pro Shop | Putting Area |
| Restaurants | Showers | Snack Bar |
| Snack Vending | Soda Vending | |

**CREDIT CARDS ACCEPTED:** Visa, MasterCard, American Express and Discover.

## MAMALA BAY GOLF COURSE
Hickam Air Force Base
Hickam AFB, HI 96853-5385

**LOCATION:** On base. Adjacent to Honolulu IAP. Accessible from H-1 or Nimitz Highway. Clearly marked.

**SEASON OF OPERATION:** Year round.

**ELIGIBILITY:** Active/Reservists/Retired/DoD civilians/Dependents/Guests.

**COURSE INFORMATION:** Address: Mamala Bay Golf Course, 15 SVS/SVBG, 800 Hangar Avenue, Hickam AFB, HI 96853-5246. **C-808-449-2525/2047/6490** 0630-1830 hours daily. One18 hole golf course and one 9 hole par 3 golf course.

|  | Back Tees | Front Tees |
|---|---|---|
| Length | 6,868 | 5,695 |
| Par | 72 | 73 |
| Slope | 129 | 120 |
| USGA Rating | 71.9 | 72.9 |

| RATES: | Weekday | Weekend |
|---|---|---|
| E1-E5 | $8 | $8 |
| E6-O3 | $13 | $13 |
| O4+ | $14 | $14 |
| Guests | $32 | $32 |

**SUPPORT FACILITIES:**

| | | |
|---|---|---|
| Banquet Facilities | Bar/Lounge | Chipping Area |
| Driving Range | Equipment Rental | Golf Carts/Power |
| Golf Carts/Pull | Lessons | Lockers |
| Pro at Facility | Pro Shop | Putting Area |
| Restaurants | Showers | Snack Bar |

**CREDIT CARDS ACCEPTED:** Visa and MasterCard.

## NAVY MARINE GOLF COURSE
Pearl Harbor Naval Base
Honolulu, HI 96818-5020

**LOCATION:** Off base.

**SEASON OF OPERATIONS:** Year round.

**ELIGIBILITY:** Active/Reservists/Retired/Dependents/Guests.

**COURSE INFORMATION:** Address: Navy Marine Golf Course, 943 Valkenburgh Street, Honolulu, HI 96818. **C-808-471-0348** 0630-1830 hours daily. One 18 hole golf course.

|  | Back Tees | Middle Tees | Front Tees |
|---|---|---|---|
| Length | 6,771 | 6,566 | 5,740 |
| Par | 72 | 72 | 73 |
| Slope | 127 | 124 | 129 |
| USGA Rating | 72.2 | 70.7 | 73.4 |

| RATES: | Weekday | Weekend |
|---|---|---|
| E1-E5 | $8 | $8 |
| E6-O3 | $13 | $13 |
| O4+ | $15 | $15 |
| Guests | $30-$40 | $30-$40 |

**SUPPORT FACILITIES:**

| | | |
|---|---|---|
| Banquet Facilities | Bar/Lounge | Driving Range |
| Equipment Rental | Golf Carts/Power | Golf Carts/Pull |
| Lessons | Lockers | Pro at Facility |
| Pro Shop | Putting Area | Restaurants |
| Showers | Snack Bar | |

**CREDIT CARDS ACCEPTED:** Visa and MasterCard (for merchandise only).

## SCHOFIELD BARRACKS GOLF COMPLEX

Schofield Barracks, HI 96857-5000

**COURSE INFORMATION:** Address: Leilehua Golf Course, Wahiawa, HI 96786. **C-808-655-4653/9833.** Two 18 hole golf courses (Leilehua and Kalakaua). Banquet Facilities, Chipping Area, Driving Range, Equipment Rental, Golf Carts/Power, Golf Carts/Pull, Lessons, Lockers, Pro Shop, Putting Area, Showers, Snack Bar. *Note: A $1.612 million new golf maintenance facility has been approved in the Fiscal Year 1998 MWR Major and Minor Construction Program.*

## WALTER J. NAGORSKI GOLF COURSE

Fort Shafter
Fort Shafter, HI 96858-5100

**COURSE INFORMATION:** Address: Nagorski Golf Course, Bldg 716, Fort Shafter, HI 96858. **C-808-438-9587.** One 9 hole golf course. Chipping Area, Lockers, Pro Shop, Putting Area, Snack Bar. *Note: A new clubhouse is scheduled to open November 1998.*

# IDAHO

## SILVER SAGE GOLF COURSE

Mountain Home Air Force Base
Mountain Home AFB, ID 83648-5237

**LOCATION:** On base. From I-84 take ID-67 twelve miles southwest to base through main gate. From main gate, continue straight in left lane. After "Y" in road take third left. Golf course is four blocks down on right.

**SEASON OF OPERATIONS:** Mar-Nov.

**ELIGIBILITY:** Active/Reservists/Retired/DoD civilians/Dependents/Guests.

**COURSE INFORMATION:** Address: Silver Sage Golf Course, 366 SVS/SVRG, 775 Pine Street, Mountain Home AFB, ID 83648-5000. **C-208-828-6559, D-312-728-6559** 0730-Dusk. One 18 hole golf course.

|  | Back Tees | Middle Tees | Front Tees |
|---|---|---|---|
| Length | 6,759 | 6,533 | 5,630 |
| Par | 72 | 72 | 72 |
| Slope |  | 116 | 108 |
| USGA Rating |  | 70.5 | 70.0 |

| RATES: | Weekday | Weekend |
|---|---|---|
| E1-E4 | $10 | $10 |
| E5+ | $13 | $13 |
| DoD civilians | $13 | $13 |
| Guests | $15 | $15 |

**SUPPORT FACILITIES:**

| | | |
|---|---|---|
| Driving Range | Equipment Rental | Golf Carts/Power |
| Golf Carts/Pull | Lessons | Lockers |
| Pro Shop | Putting Area | Showers |
| Snack Bar | | |

**CREDIT CARDS ACCEPTED:** Visa and MasterCard.

# ILLINOIS

## RIVER'S EDGE GOLF CLUB

Charles Melvin Price Support Center
Granite City, IL 62040-1801

**LOCATION:** On post. From I-70 in St. Louis, MO take McKinley Bridge exit, cross Mississippi River, follow signs north to Granite City and Center. From I-270, cross river bridges and take first Granite City exit (IL-3) south five miles to Center.

**SEASON OF OPERATION:** Year round.

**ELIGIBILITY:** Active/Reservists/Retired/DoD civilians/Dependents/General Public/Guests.

**COURSE INFORMATION:** Address: River's Edge Golf Club, CMPSC-MWR, Bldg 141, Granite City, IL 62040-5000. **C-618-452-4444** 0700-Dusk daily. One 9 hole golf course. *Note: Play two consecutive rounds from different tees for complete 18 hole game.*

|  | Back Tees | Front Tees |
|---|---|---|
| Length | 6,407 | 5,461 |
| Par | 72 | 72 |
| Slope | 104 | 113 |
| USGA Rating | 68.9 | 70.7 |

| RATES: | Weekday | Weekend |
|---|---|---|
| Enlisted | $7 (9), $12 (18) | $8 (9), $13 (18) |
| Officers | $7 (9), $12 (18) | $8 (9), $13 (18) |
| DoD civilians | $8 (9), $13 (18) | $9 (9), $14 (18) |
| Guests | $8 (9), $13 (18) | $9 (9), $14 (18) |

**SUPPORT FACILITIES:**

| | | |
|---|---|---|
| Banquet Facilities | Bar/Lounge | Chipping Area |
| Driving Range | Equipment Rental | Golf Carts/Power |
| Golf Carts/Pull | Putting Area | Snack Bar |

**CREDIT CARDS ACCEPTED:** Visa and MasterCard.

## ROCK ISLAND ARSENAL GOLF CLUB

Rock Island U.S Army Armament & Chemical
Acquisition & Logistics Activity
Rock Island, IL 61299-5000

**COURSE INFORMATION:** Address: Rock Island Golf Club, 312 Gillespie Avenue, Rock Island, IL 61201. **C-309-793-1601/2.** One 18 hole golf course. Equipment Rental, Golf Carts, Pro Shop, Restaurants.

## WILLOW GLEN GOLF COURSE

Great Lakes Naval Training Center
Great Lakes, IL 60088-5001

**LOCATION:** On base. From I-94 north or US-41 north of Chicago, exit to IL-137 east to Sheridan Road, then turn right into the gate.

**SEASON OF OPERATION:** Apr-Nov.

**ELIGIBILITY:** Active/Reservists/Retired/DoD civilians/Dependents/Guests.

**COURSE INFORMATION:** Address: Willow Glen Golf Course, Bldg 160, Great Lakes, IL 60088-5100. **C-847-688-4593, D-312-792-4593** 0600-Dusk daily. One 18 golf course.

*Willow Glen Golf Course, continued*

## TRAILS WEST GOLF COURSE
Fort Leavenworth
Fort Leavenworth, KS 66027-2303

|  | Back Tees | Front Tees |
|---|---|---|
| Length | 6,377 | 5,461 |
| Par | 72 | 74 |
| Slope | 118 | 119 |
| USGA Rating | 69.9 | 72.6 |

| RATES: | Weekday | Weekend |
|---|---|---|
| Enlisted | $7-$11 | $8-$12 |
| Officers | $7-$11 | $8-$12 |
| DoD civilians | $10-$14 | $11-$15 |
| Guests | $13-$20 | $15-$25 |

**SUPPORT FACILITIES:**

| | | |
|---|---|---|
| Bar/Lounge | Chipping Area | Driving Range |
| Equipment Rental | Golf Carts/Power | Golf Carts/Pull |
| Lessons | Lockers | Pro at Facility |
| Pro Shop | Putting Area | Restaurants |
| Showers | | |

**CREDIT CARDS ACCEPTED:** Visa, MasterCard, American Express and Discover.

# KANSAS

## CUSTER HILL GOLF COURSE
Fort Riley
Fort Riley, KS 66442-6421

**LOCATION:** On post. From I-70 E or W take exit 301, follow for five miles north on Normandy Drive to golf course.

**SEASON OF OPERATION:** Year round.

**ELIGIBILITY:** Active/Reservists/Retired/DoD civilians/Dependents/ General Public/Guests.

**COURSE INFORMATION:** Address: Custer Hill Golf Course, Bldg 5202, Normandy Drive, P.O. Box 2368, Fort Riley, KS 66442-5000. **C-785-784-6000, D-312-856-5412** 0800-1900 hours Apr-Oct, 0700-1900 hours Nov-Mar. One 18 hole golf course.

|  | Back Tees | Middle Tees | Front Tees |
|---|---|---|---|
| Length | 7,072 | 6,722 | 5,323 |
| Par | 72 | 72 | 72 |
| Slope | 127 | 125 | 119 |
| USGA Rating | 74.2 | 72.5 | 70.0 |

| RATES: | Weekday | Weekend |
|---|---|---|
| Enlisted | $10 | $12.50 |
| Officers | $10 | $12.50 |
| DoD civilians | $10 | $15 |
| Guests | $10 | $15 |

**SUPPORT FACILITIES:**

| | | |
|---|---|---|
| Driving Range | Equipment Rental | Lessons |
| Lockers | Golf Carts/Power | Golf Carts/Pull |
| Pro at Facility | Pro Shop | Putting Area |
| Showers | Snack Bar | Snack Vending |
| Soda Vending | | |

**CREDIT CARDS ACCEPTED:** Visa, MasterCard, American Express, Discover and Diners'.

**LOCATION:** On post. From I-70 E or W take US-73 N to Leavenworth. From I-29 N or S exit 18 to MO-92 west to Leavenworth. Fort is adjacent to and north of the city of Leavenworth. From main gate, continue straight on Grant Avenue to left on Cody Road (2nd light) to golf course on right.

**SEASON OF OPERATION:** Year round.

**ELIGIBILITY:** Active/Reservists/Retired/DoD civilians/Dependents/ Guests.

**COURSE INFORMATION:** Address: Trails West Golf Course, 306 Cody Road, Fort Leavenworth, KS 66027-5000. **C-913-651-7176** Dusk to Dawn. One 18 hole golf course.

|  | Back Tees | Middle Tees | Front Tees |
|---|---|---|---|
| Length | 6,198 | 5,762 | 4,845 |
| Par | 71 | 71 | 71 |
| Slope | 121 | 117 | 113 |
| USGA Rating | 70.8 | 69.1 | 67.6 |

| RATES: | Weekday | Weekend |
|---|---|---|
| Enlisted | $6-$10.75 | $7-$12 |
| O3-O6 | $10.75-$15.50 | $13-$17.75 |
| O7+ | $12-$16.75 | $14.25-$19 |
| DoD civilians | $10.75-$15.50 | $13-$17.75 |
| Guests | $16.50-$23.75 | $16.50-$23.75 |

**SUPPORT FACILITIES:**

| | | |
|---|---|---|
| Chipping Area | Driving Range | Equipment Rental |
| Golf Carts/Power | Golf Carts/Pull | Lessons |
| Lockers | Pro at Facility | Pro Shop |
| Putting Area | Sand Trap | Showers |
| Snack Bar | | |

**RESTRICTIONS:** All players must have their own clubs and bags, golf spikes or flat soled tennis shoes only, carts must remain on designated paths and dress code strictly enforced.

**CREDIT CARDS ACCEPTED:** Visa, MasterCard and American Express.

## TWIN LAKES GOLF COURSE
McConnell Air Force Base
McConnell AFB, KS 67221-3504

**COURSE INFORMATION:** Address: Twin Lakes Golf Course, Bldg 1336, McConnell AFB, KS 67221-4006. **C-316-652-4038** 0630-Dusk summer, 0700-Dusk spring, 0900-Dusk winter. One 18 hole golf course. Equipment Rental, Lessons, Pro at Facility, Pro Shop, Snack Bar.

# KENTUCKY

## COLE PARK GOLF COURSE
Fort Campbell
Fort Campbell, KY 42223-5470

**LOCATION:** On post. In Southwest part of KY, four miles south of intersection of US-41A and I-24. From I-24 N or S, take exit 86 S to 41A toward Fort Campbell.

**SEASON OF OPERATION:** Year round.

*KENTUCKY-LOUISIANA*
*Cole Park Golf Course, continued*

**ELIGIBILITY:** Active/Reservists/Retired/DoD civilians/Dependents/ Guests.

**COURSE INFORMATION:** Address: Cole Park Golf Course, 1601 Club Loop, Fort Campbell, KY 42223-5000. **C-502-798-4906, D-312-835-4906** 0700-2000 hours summer, 0800-1700 hours winter. One 18 hole golf course and one 9 hole par 3 golf course.

|  | Back Tees | Middle Tees | Front Tees |
|---|---|---|---|
| Length | 6,812 | 6,209 | 5,296 |
| Par | 72 | 72 | 72 |
| Slope | 121 | 115 | 116 |
| USGA Rating | 72.01 | 69.2 | 69.6 |

\* Information based on 18 hole game.

| **RATES:** | Weekday | Weekend |
|---|---|---|
| Enlisted | $10 | $10 |
| Officers | $13 | $13 |
| DoD civilians | $13 | $13 |
| Guests | $15 | $17 |

**SUPPORT FACILITIES:**

| | | |
|---|---|---|
| Chipping Area | Driving Range | Equipment Rental |
| Golf Carts/Pull | Lessons | Pro at Facility |
| Pro Shop | Putting Area | Showers |
| Snack Bar | | |

**CREDIT CARDS ACCEPTED:** Visa, MasterCard, American Express, Discover and Diners'.

## FORT KNOX GOLF COURSES
Fort Knox, KY 40121-5000

**LOCATION:** On post. From I-65 in Louisville, exit Gene Snyder Expressway west to US-31 west, go south to Fort Knox. From I-64, exit I-264 (Waterson Expressway) to US-31 west, south to Fort Knox. From I-71, exit I-65 south to Gene Snyder Expressway to US-31 west then south to Fort Knox.

**SEASON OF OPERATION:** Year round.

**ELIGIBILITY:** Active/Reservists/Retired/DoD civilians/Dependents/ General Public/Guests.

**COURSE INFORMATION:** Address: Anderson Golf Course, 7955 Wilson Road, Fort Knox, KY 40121. **C-1-888-548-5728, C-502-943-9929** 0600-Dusk on-season, 0800-Dusk off-season. Two 18 hole golf courses.

**Anderson Golf Course**

|  | Back Tees | Front Tees |
|---|---|---|
| Length | 6,519 | 6,258 |
| Par | 72 | 72 |
| Slope | 116 | 114 |

**Lindsey Golf Course**

|  | Back Tees | Front Tees |
|---|---|---|
| Length | 6,661 | 6,431 |
| Par | 72 | 72 |
| Slope | 116 | 114 |

| **RATES:** | Weekday | Weekend |
|---|---|---|
| E1-E6 | $13 | $15 |
| E7+ | $15 | $17 |
| Guests | $18 | $21 |

**SUPPORT FACILITIES:**

| | | |
|---|---|---|
| Chipping Area | Driving Range | Equipment Rental |
| Golf Carts/Power | Golf Carts/Pull | Lessons |
| Pro at Facility | Pro Shop | Putting Area |
| Restaurants | Showers | Snack Bar |
| Soda Vending | | |

**CREDIT CARDS ACCEPTED:** Visa, MasterCard and American Express.

# LOUISIANA

## BARKSDALE GOLF COURSE
Barksdale Air Force Base
Barksdale AFB, LA 71110-2426

**LOCATION:** On base. Exit I-20 at Airline Drive, go south one quarter mile to left on Old Minden Road, then right on North Gate Drive, then 1 mile to North Gate of base.

**SEASON OF OPERATION:** Year round.

**ELIGIBILITY:** Active/Reservists/Retired/DoD civilians/Dependents/ Guests.

**COURSE INFORMATION:** Address: Barksdale Golf Course, 185 Bossier Road, Barksdale AFB, LA 71110. **C-318-456-2263, D-312-781-2263** Dawn-Dusk daily. One 18 hole golf course.

|  | Back Tees | Front Tees |
|---|---|---|
| Length | 5,904 | 5,075 |
| Par | 70 | 71 |
| Slope | 117 | 112 |
| USGA Ratings | 68.7 | 69.3 |

| **RATES:** | Weekday | Weekend |
|---|---|---|
| E1-E4 | $6 | $6 |
| E5-E7 | $8 | $8 |
| E8+ | $12 | $12 |
| DoD civilians | $12 | $12 |
| Guests | $18 | $18 |

**SUPPORT FACILITIES:**

| | | |
|---|---|---|
| Chipping Area | Driving Range | Equipment Rental |
| Lessons | Lockers | Golf Carts/Power |
| Golf Carts/Pull | Pro at Facility | Pro Shop |
| Putting Area | Snack Bar | Soda Vending |
| Showers | | |

**CREDIT CARDS ACCEPTED:** Visa and MasterCard.

## COLOMBEL MEMORIAL GOLF COURSE
New Orleans Naval Air Station
New Orleans, LA 70143-5012

**COURSE INFORMATION:** Address: Colombel Memorial Golf Course, MWR Department, Bldg 400 Code 100, New Orleans, LA 70143-5000. **C-504-678-3453, D-312-678-3453.** One 18 hole golf course.

## WARRIOR HILLS GOLF COURSE
Fort Polk/Joint Readiness Training Center
Fort Polk, LA 71459-5227

**COURSE INFORMATION:** Address: Warrior Hills Golf Course, Bldg 323, Patterson Drive, Fort Polk, LA 71459. **C-318-531-4661.** One 18 hole golf course. Golf Carts, Lessons, Pro Shop.

# MAINE

## MERE CREEK GOLF COURSE
Brunswick Naval Air Station
Brunswick NAS, ME 04011-5000

**LOCATION:** On base. From I-95 N or S exit US-1 N to Brunswick, Old Bath Road (Route 24) south to main gate of NAS. From main gate continue straight to left at first stop sign, then straight for two miles to golf course.

**SEASON OF OPERATION:** 15 Apr-1 Nov.

**ELIGIBILITY:** Active/Reservists/Retired/DoD civilians/Dependents/General Public.

**COURSE INFORMATION:** Address: Mere Golf Course, Bldg 78, 551 Fitch Avenue, Brunswick, ME 04011-5000. **C-207-921-2155, D-312-476-2155.** One 9 hole golf course.

|  | Back Tees | Front Tees |
|---|---|---|
| Length | 6,284 | 5,594 |
| Par | 72 | 74 |
| Slope | 119 | 119 |
| USGA Ratings | 68.9 | 71.4 |

| RATES: | Weekday | Weekend |
|---|---|---|
| Enlisted | $8-$10 | $9-$11 |
| Officers | $12.50 | $13.50 |
| DoD civilians | $13.50 | $14.50 |
| Guests | $17 | $20 |
| General Public | $17 | $20 |

**SUPPORT FACILITIES:**

| | | |
|---|---|---|
| Driving Range | Equipment Rental | Lessons |
| Lockers | Golf Carts/Power | Golf Carts/Pull |
| Pro at Facility | Pro Shop | Putting Area |
| Snack Bar | Showers | |

**CREDIT CARDS ACCEPTED:** Visa, MasterCard and American Express.

# MARYLAND

## ANDREWS GOLF COMPLEX
Andrews Air Force Base
Andrews AFB 20762-6421

**COURSE INFORMATION:** Address: Andrews Golf Complex, Bldg 4442, 1535 Command Drive, Andrews AFB, MD 20331-7002. **C-301-981-4404** 0700-Dusk daily. Three 18 hole golf courses (East, West and South). Equipment Rental, Golf Carts, Pro at Facility, Pro Shop, Snack Bar.

## CEDAR POINT GOLF COURSE
Patuxent River Naval Air Station
Patuxent River, MD 20670-1132

**LOCATION:** On base. From gate #2, continue straight on Cedar Point Road to golf course.

**SEASON OF OPERATION:** Year round.

**ELIGIBILITY:** Active/Reservists/Retired/DoD civilians/Dependents/Guests.

**COURSE INFORMATION:** Address: Cedar Point Golf Course, 23248 Cedar Point Road, Patuxent River NAS, MD 20670. **C-301-342-3597** call for hours. One 18 hole golf course.

|  | Back Tees | Middle Tees | Front Tees |
|---|---|---|---|
| Length | 6,810 | 6,560 | 5,442 |
| Par | 72 | 71 | 70 |
| Slope | 121 | 117 | 119 |
| USGA Rating | 72.0 | 71.0 | 70.0 |

| RATES: | Weekday | Weekend |
|---|---|---|
| E1-E4 | $5.25 (9), $8,50 (18) | $7.50 (9), $10.50 (18) |
| E5-O3 | $8 (9), $13 (18) | $9 (9), $15 (18) |
| O4+ | $9 (9), $14 (18) | $10 (9), $16 (18) |
| DoD civilians | $11 (9), $16 (18) | $13 (9), $20 (18) |
| Guests | $12 (9), $18 (18) | $13 (9), $20 (18) |

**SUPPORT FACILITIES:**

| | | |
|---|---|---|
| Bar/Lounge | Chipping Area | Driving Range |
| Equipment Rental | Golf Carts/Power | Golf Carts/Pull |
| Lessons | Lockers | Pro at Facility |
| Pro Shop | Putting Area | Showers* |
| Snack Bar | | |

* Male showers only.

**RESTRICTIONS:** Priority given to foursomes and children under 10 must have prior approval from course management to be on course.

**CREDIT CARDS ACCEPTED:** Visa, MasterCard and American Express.

## THE COURSES AT FORT MEADE
Fort George G. Meade
Fort Meade, MD 20755-5078

**LOCATION:** On post. Off Baltimore-Washington Parkway, I-295, exit MD-198 east to Fort Meade Road. Base clearly marked.

**SEASON OF OPERATION:** Year round.

**ELIGIBILITY:** Active/Reservists/Retired/DoD civilians/Dependents/Guests.

**COURSE INFORMATION:** Address: The Courses at Fort Meade, Bldg 6800, Taylor Avenue, Fort Meade,. MD 20755. **C-301-677-4308/5326** seasonal hours. Two 18 hole golf courses. *Note: A $0.904 million new driving range has been approved in the Fiscal Year 1998 MWR Major and Minor Construction Program.*

**Applewood**

|  | Back Tees | Middle Tees | Front Tees |
|---|---|---|---|
| Length | 6,494 | 6,216 | 5,436 |
| Par | 72 | 72 | 74 |
| Slope (M) | 116 | 113 | 105 |
| Slope (L) | | | 113 |
| USGA Rating (M) | 70.8 | 69.4 | 65.6 |
| USGA Rating (L) | | | 70.2 |

**Floyd L. Parks**

|  | Back Tees | Middle Tees | Front Tees |
|---|---|---|---|
| Length | 6,811 | 6,295 | 5,333 |
| Par | 72 | 72 | 73 |
| Slope (M) | 117 | 115 | 106 |
| Slope (L) | | | 110 |
| USGA Rating (M) | 71.6 | 69.2 | 64.8 |
| USGA Rating (L) | | | 69.0 |

**MARYLAND-MASSACHUSETTS**
*The Courses at Fort Meade, continued*

| RATES: | Weekday | Weekend |
|---|---|---|
| E1-E5 | $14 | $14 |
| E7+ | $17 | $17 |
| DoD civilians | $17 | $17 |
| Guests | $26 | $26 |

**SUPPORT FACILITIES:**

| | | |
|---|---|---|
| Banquet Facilities | Bar/Lounge | Chipping Area |
| Driving Range | Golf Carts/Power | Golf Carts/Pull |
| Lessons | Pro at Facility | Pro Shop |
| Putting Area | Restaurants | Showers |
| Snack Bar | | |

**CREDIT CARDS ACCEPTED:** Visa, MasterCard, American Express, Discover and Diners'.

## INDIAN HEAD GOLF COURSE

Indian Head Division, Naval Surface Welfare Center
Indian Head, MD 20640-5000

**LOCATION:** On base. Take I-495 (Capital Beltway) east, exit to MD-210 south for 25 miles to center.

**SEASON OF OPERATION:** Year round.

**ELIGIBILITY:** Active/Reservists/Retired/DoD civilians/Dependents/ General Public/Guests.

**COURSE INFORMATION:** Address: Indian Head Golf Course, Bldg D-61, Indian Head, MD 20640. **C-301-743-4662** 0700-Dusk Apr-Oct, 0800-Dusk Nov-Mar. One 9 hole golf course.

| | |
|---|---|
| Length | 2,656 |
| Par* | 70 |
| Slope* | 114 |
| USGA Rating* | 65.2 |

* Information based on 18 hole game.

| RATES: | Weekday | Weekend |
|---|---|---|
| Enlisted | $8 | $10 |
| Officers | $8 | $10 |
| Guests | $10 | $12 |

**SUPPORT FACILITIES:**

| | | |
|---|---|---|
| Chipping Area | Driving Range | Equipment Rental |
| Golf Carts/Power | Golf Carts/Pull | Lessons |
| Pro at Facility | Pro Shop | Putting Area |
| Snack Bar | | |

**CREDIT CARDS ACCEPTED:** Visa and MasterCard.

## RUGGLES GOLF COURSE

Aberdeen Proving Grounds
Aberdeen Proving Grounds, MD 21005-5001

**LOCATION:** On post. From I-95 N or S, take exit 85 to MD-22 east for two miles to main gate.

**SEASON OF OPERATION:** Year round.

**ELIGIBILITY:** Active/Reservists/Retired/DoD civilians/Dependents/ Harford Company/Guests.

**COURSE INFORMATION:** Address: Ruggles Golf Course, Aberdeen Proving Ground, Bldg 5600, Aberdeen Proving Ground, MD 21005. **C-410-278-4794** 0600-Dusk summer, 0700-1700 winter. One 18 hole golf course (Ruggles) and two 9 hole golf courses (Plumb Point and Exton).

**Ruggles Golf Course (18 hole course)**

| | Back Tees | Front Tees |
|---|---|---|
| Length | 7,100 | 5,546 |
| Par | 72 | 72 |
| Slope | 120 | 125 |
| USGA Rating | 73.2 | 71.2 |

**SUPPORT FACILITIES:**

| | | |
|---|---|---|
| Banquet Facilities | Bar/Lounge | Driving Range |
| Equipment Rental | Golf Carts/Power | Golf Carts/Pull |
| Lessons | Lockers | Pro at Facility |
| Pro Shop | Putting Area | Showers |
| Snack Bar | | |

**CREDIT CARDS ACCEPTED:** Visa and MasterCard..

## UNITED STATES NAVAL ACADEMY GOLF CLUB

United States Naval Academy/Annapolis Naval Station
Annapolis, MD 21402-5073

**LOCATION:** On base. Off US-50/301, clearly marked.

**SEASON OF OPERATION:** Year round.

**ELIGIBILITY:** Active/Retired/Dependents/Guests.

**COURSE INFORMATION:** Address: U.S. Naval Academy Golf Club, Annapolis, MD 21402. **C-410-757-2022** after 1000 daily. One 18 hole golf course.

| | Back Tees | Middle Tees | Middle Tees | Front Tees |
|---|---|---|---|---|
| Length | 6,611 | 6,222 | 5,974 | 5,634 |
| Par | 71 | 71 | 71 | 74 |
| Slope | 132 | 124 | 118 | 124 |
| USGA Rating | 71.7 | 69.9 | 68.8 | 71.4 |

| RATES: | Weekday | Weekend |
|---|---|---|
| Active Enlisted | $7-$11 | $7-$12 |
| Active Officers | $10-$18 | $11-$22 |
| Retired Enlisted | $10-$13 | $11-$18 |
| Retired Officers | $14-$24 | $18-$30 |
| Guests | $18-$30 | $24-$38 |

**SUPPORT FACILITIES:**

| | | |
|---|---|---|
| Driving Range | Equipment Rental | Golf Carts |
| Pro Shop | Putting Area | Snack Bar |

**RESTRICTIONS:** No spike shoes, blue jeans or cutoff shorts. Collared shirts required.

**CREDIT CARDS ACCEPTED:** None.

# MASSACHUSETTS

## OTIS GOLF COURSE

Otis Air National Guard Base/Cape Cod Coast Guard Air Station
Otis ANGB, MA 02542-5024

*Otis Golf Course, continued*

| Pro Shop | Putting Area | Snack Bar |
|---|---|---|
| Soda Vending | | |

**LOCATION:** On post. Off MA-28 at the base of Cape Cod.

**CREDIT CARDS ACCEPTED:** None.

**SEASON OF OPERATION:** Year round.

**ELIGIBILITY:** Active/Reservists/Retired/DoD civilians/Dependents.

**COURSE INFORMATION:** Address: Otis Golf Course, Bldg 3352, Gunther Road, VSCG Air Station, Cape Cod, Otis ANGB, MA 02542. **C-508-968-6453** 0700-2000 hours Apr-Oct, 0900-1600 hours Nov-Mar. One 9 hole golf course.

| | Back Tees | Middle Tees | Front Tees |
|---|---|---|---|
| Length* | 6,706 | 6,012 | 5,300 |
| Par* | 72 | 72 | 72 |
| Slope* | 118 | 113 | 119 |
| USGA Rating* | 72.0 | 68.2 | 70.2 |

* Information based on 18 hole game.

| RATES: | Weekday | Weekend |
|---|---|---|
| Enlisted | $5 | $5 |
| Officers | $5 | $5 |
| Retired | $15 | $15 |
| Guests | $20 | $20 |

**SUPPORT FACILITIES:**

| | | |
|---|---|---|
| Banquet Facilities | Bar/Lounge | Chipping Area |
| Driving Range | Equipment Rental | Golf Carts/Power |
| Golf Carts/Pull | Lessons | Lockers |
| Pro at Facility | Pro Shop | Putting Area |
| Showers | Snack Bar | |

**CREDIT CARDS ACCEPTED:** Visa and MasterCard.

## PATRIOT GOLF COURSE
Hanscom Air Force Base
Hanscom AFB, MA 01731-2012

**LOCATION:** Off base. From Route 128 Exit #31B to Route 62 through Bedford. Continue to Hillside Road, then follow signs to VA Hospital and to Spring Road and golf course.

**SEASON OF OPERATION:** 3 Mar-24 Dec.

**ELIGIBILITY:** Active/Reservists/Retired/DoD civilians/Dependents.

**COURSE INFORMATION:** Address: Patriot Golf Course, 200 Spring Road, Bldg 49, Bedford MA 01730. **C-781-687-2396** 0600-Dusk daily. One 9 hole golf course.

| | Back Tees | Front Tees |
|---|---|---|
| Length: | 5,754 | 5,220 |
| Par | 70 | 68 |
| Slope | 125 | 117 |
| USGA Rating | 67.5 | 65.1 |

| RATES: | Weekday | Weekend |
|---|---|---|
| E1-E4 | $8 (9) $12 (18) | $10 (9) $14 (18) |
| E5+ | $12 (9) $17 (18) | $14 (9) $19 (18) |
| Guests | $10 (9) $15 (18) | $11 (9) $16 (18) |

**SUPPORT FACILITIES:**

| | | |
|---|---|---|
| Chipping Area | Equipment Rental | Golf Carts/Power |
| Golf Carts/Pull | Lessons | Pro at Facility |

# MICHIGAN

## SELFRIDGE GOLF COURSE
Selfridge Air National Guard Base
Selfridge ANGB, MI 48045-5000

**COURSE INFORMATION:** Address: Selfridge Golf Course, Bldg 599, Selfridge ANGB, MI 48045. **C-313-463-7744, D-312-263-4344.** One 18 hole golf course. Banquet Facilities, Chipping Area, Driving Range, Equipment Rental, Golf Carts/ Power, Golf Carts/Pull, Lessons, Pro Shop, Putting Area, Snack Bar. *Note: $5.290 million new club house has been approved in the Fiscal Year 1998 MWR Major and Minor Construction Program.*

# MISSISSIPPI

## BAY BREEZE GOLF COURSE
Keesler Air Force Base
Keesler AFB, MS 39534-2554

**LOCATION:** On base. From I-10 exit 46, follow signs to base. From US-90, north on White Avenue to main gate.

**SEASON OF OPERATION:** Year round.

**ELIGIBILITY:** Active/Reservists/Retired/DoD civilians/Dependents/Guests.

**COURSE INFORMATION:** Address: Bay Breeze Golf Course, 500 Ploesti Drive, Bldg 6727, Keesler AFB, MS 39534. **C-601-377-3832/3827** 0615-Dusk daily. One 18 hole golf course.

| | Back Tees | Front Tees |
|---|---|---|
| Length | 6,047 | 5,052 |
| Par | 70 | 71 |
| Slope | 121 | 117 |
| USGA Rating | 69.5 | 69.5 |

| RATES: | Weekday | Weekend |
|---|---|---|
| E1-E4 | $3.25 (9), $6.25 (18) | $3.75 (9), $7.50 (18) |
| E5-O3 | $4.25 (9), $8.50 (18) | $5 (9), $10 (18) |
| O4+ | $4.75 (9), $9.50 (18) | $5.75 (9), $11.50 (18) |
| Guests | $7 (9), $14 (18) | $8 (9), $16 (18) |

**SUPPORT FACILITIES:**

| | | |
|---|---|---|
| Chipping Area | Driving Range | Equipment Rental |
| Golf Carts/Power | Golf Carts/Pull | Lessons |
| Lockers | Pro at Facility | Pro Shop |
| Putting Area | Sand Trap | Showers |
| Snack Bar | Soda Vending | |

**CREDIT CARDS ACCEPTED:** Visa and MasterCard.

## PINE BAYOU GOLF COURSE
Gulfport Naval Construction Battalion Center
Gulfport, MS 38501-5001

**COURSE INFORMATION:** Address: Pine Bayou Golf Course, MWR Department, 5200 CBC 2nd Street, Gulfport, MS 39501-5001. **C-601-871-2124, D-312-868-2124.** One 9 hole golf course and a second 9 hole golf course under construction.

# PONTA CREEK GOLF COURSE

Meridian Naval Air Station
Meridian, MS 39309-5500

**LOCATION:** On base. From main gate, take first right and continue to golf course.

**SEASON OF OPERATION:** Year round.

**ELIGIBILITY:** Active/Reservists/Retired/DoD civilians/Dependents/Guests.

**COURSE INFORMATION:** Address: Ponta Creek Golf Course, 1155 Rosenbaum Avenue Suite 13, Meridian NAS, MS 39309-5003. **C-601-679-2526/2129, D-312-637-2526/2129** 0700-Dusk daily. One 18 hole golf course.

|  | Back Tees | Front Tees |
|---|---|---|
| Length | 6,595 | 6,219 |
| Par | 72 | 72 |
| Slope | 127 | 120 |
| USGA Rating | 72.3 | 69.9 |

| RATES: | Weekday | Weekend |
|---|---|---|
| Enlisted | $8 | $8 |
| Officers | $8 | $8 |
| DoD civilians | $10 | $10 |
| Guests | $10 | $10 |

**SUPPORT FACILITIES:**

| | | |
|---|---|---|
| Chipping Area | Driving Range | Equipment Rental |
| Golf Carts/Power | Golf Carts/Pull | Lessons |
| Lockers | Pro at Facility | Pro Shop |
| Putting Area | Showers | Snack Bar |

**CREDIT CARDS ACCEPTED:** Visa, MasterCard, American Express and Discover.

# WHISPERING PINES GOLF COURSE

Columbus Air Force Base
Columbus AFB, MS 39701-7901

**LOCATION:** On base. North on Simler Blvd to left on C Street, then continue two blocks to right to golf course.

**SEASON OF OPERATION:** Year round.

**ELIGIBILITY:** Active/Reservists/Retired/DoD civilians/Dependents/Guests.

**COURSE INFORMATION:** Address: Whispering Pines Golf Course, Bldg 570, C Street, Columbus AFB, MS 39710. **C-601-434-7932** 0700-Dusk daily. One 9 hole golf course.

|  | Back Tees | Front Tees |
|---|---|---|
| Length | 2,665 | 2,610 |
| Par | 36 | 36 |
| Slope | 127 | 127 |

| USGA Rating | 66.7 | 66.7 |
|---|---|---|

| RATES*: | Weekday | Weekend |
|---|---|---|
| Enlisted | $12 | $12 |
| Officers | $10 | $10 |
| DoD civilians | $14 | $14 |
| Guests | $14 | $14 |

* Rates based on 18 hole game.

**SUPPORT FACILITIES:**

| | | |
|---|---|---|
| Chipping Area | Driving Range | Equipment Rental |
| Golf Carts/Power | Golf Carts/Pull | Lessons |
| Pro at Facility | Pro Shop | Putting Area |
| Snack Bar | | |

**CREDIT CARDS ACCEPTED:** Visa and MasterCard.

# MISSOURI

## PINEY VALLEY GOLF COURSE

Fort Leonard Wood
Fort Leonard Wood, MO 65473-5000

**LOCATION:** On post. Two miles south of I-44, adjacent to St. Robert and Waynesville, at Fort Leonard exit.

**SEASON OF OPERATION:** Year round.

**ELIGIBILITY:** Active/Reservists/Retired/DoD civilians/Dependents/Guests/General Public.

**COURSE INFORMATION:** Address: Piney Valley Golf Course, Bldg 10221, Fort Leonard Wood, MO 65473-5000. **C-573-329-4770** 0700-Dusk daily. One 18 hole golf course.

|  | Back Tees | Front Tees |
|---|---|---|
| Length | 7,014 | 6,731 |
| Par | 72 | 72 |
| Slope | 121 | 117 |
| USGA Rating | 72.8 | 71.4 |

| RATES: | Weekday | Weekend |
|---|---|---|
| E1-E4 | $9 | $12 |
| E5+ | $15 | $17 |

**SUPPORT FACILITIES:**

| | | |
|---|---|---|
| Banquet Facilities | Chipping Area | Driving Range |
| Equipment Rental | Golf Carts/Power | Golf Carts/Pull |
| Lessons | Pro at Facility | Pro Shop |
| Putting Area | Sand Trap | Showers |
| Snack Bar | | |

**RESTRICTIONS:** Soft spike shoes only and collar on shirt.

**CREDIT CARDS ACCEPTED:** Visa, MasterCard and American Express.

## THE ROYAL OAKS GOLF COURSE

Whiteman Air Force Base
Whiteman AFB, MO 65305-5000

**LOCATION:** Off base. From Highway-50 take Highway-23 south for approximately 2.5 miles to golf course on west side of highway.

**SEASON OF OPERATION:** Year round.

**ELIGIBILITY:** Active/Reservists/Retired/DoD civilians/Dependents/ Guests.

**COURSE INFORMATION:** Address: Royal Oaks Golf Course, Bldg S-3076, Whiteman AFB, MO 65305. **C-660-687-5572, D-312-975-5572** Dawn-Dusk daily. One 18 hole golf course.

|  | Back Tees | Front Tees |
|---|---|---|
| Length | 6,880 | 5,150 |
| Par | 72 | 71 |
| Slope | 118 |  |
| USGA Rating |  |  |

| RATES: | Weekday | Weekend |
|---|---|---|
| E1-E4 | $8 | $10 |
| E5-O3 | $10 | $12 |
| O4+ | $12 | $14 |
| Guests | $10 | $16 |

**SUPPORT FACILITIES:**

| | | |
|---|---|---|
| Chipping Area | Driving Range | Equipment Rental |
| Golf Carts/Power | Golf Carts/Pull | Lessons |
| Pro at Facility | Pro Shop | Putting Area |
| Snack Bar | | |

**RESTRICTIONS:** Must adhere to dress code.

**CREDIT CARDS ACCEPTED:** Visa and MasterCard.

# NEBRASKA

## WILLOW LAKES GOLF COURSE
Offutt Air Force Base
Offutt AFB, NB 68113-5000

**COURSE INFORMATION:** Address: Willow Lakes Golf Course, Bldg 9950, Offutt AFB, NB 68113. **C-402-294-3362** 0600-Dusk summer, 0800-Dusk winter. One 18 hole golf course. Driving Range, Equipment Rental, Golf Carts/Power, Golf Carts/Pull, Pro Shop.

# NEVADA

## SUNRISE VISTA GOLF COURSE
Nellis Air Force Base
Nellis AFB, NV 89191-7073

**LOCATION:** On base. From Nellis Blvd gate to south end of runway. Course on right side of Tyndall Road.

**SEASON OF OPERATION:** Year round.

**ELIGIBILITY:** Active/Reservists/Retired/DoD civilians/Dependents/ Stand-Bys.

**COURSE INFORMATION:** Address: Sunrise Vista Golf Course, 2841 Kinley Drive, Nellis AFB, NV 89191. **C-702-652-2602, D-312-682-2602,** Fax: 702-652-8572. Three 9 hole golf courses (Fanthom, Falcon and Eagle).

| RATES: | Weekday | Weekend |
|---|---|---|
| E1-E4 | $9 | $9 |
| E5-O3 | $13 | $13 |
| O4+ | $16 | $16 |
| DoD civilians | $35 | $35 |
| Guests | $35 | $35 |

**SUPPORT FACILITIES:**

| | | |
|---|---|---|
| Bar/Lounge | Chipping Area | Driving Range |
| Equipment Rental | Golf Carts/Power | Lessons |
| Pro at Facility | Pro Shop | Putting Area |
| Showers | Snack Bar | |

**RESTRICTIONS:** Must be at least 11 years of age to play on courses.

**CREDIT CARDS ACCEPTED:** Visa and MasterCard.

# NEW JERSEY

## FOUNTAIN GREEN GOLF COURSE
Fort Dix Army Garrison
Fort Dix, NJ 08640-5130

**LOCATION:** On post. From New Jersey Turnpike Exit #7 to Route 68 to golf course.

**SEASON OF OPERATION:** Year round.

**ELIGIBILITY:** Active/Reservists/Retired/DoD civilians/Dependents/ Guests.

**COURSE INFORMATION:** Address: Fountain Green Golf Course, Bldg 3152, Fort Dix, NJ 08640. **C-609-562-4043/5443** Dawn-Dusk daily. One 18 hole golf course.

|  | Back Tees | Front Tees |
|---|---|---|
| Length | 6,389 | 5,466 |
| Par | 71 | 72 |
| Slope | 118 | 123 |
| USGA Rating | 70.6 | 71.8 |

| RATES: | Weekday | Weekend |
|---|---|---|
| Enlisted | $10 | $10 |
| Officers | $10 | $10 |
| DoD civilians | $20 | $20 |
| Guests | $20 | $20 |

**SUPPORT FACILITIES:**

| | | |
|---|---|---|
| Bar/Lounge | Driving Range | Equipment Rental |
| Golf Carts/Power | Golf Carts/Pull | Lessons |
| Lockers | Pro at Facility | Pro Shop |
| Putting Area | Showers | Snack Bar |

**CREDIT CARDS ACCEPTED:** Visa, MasterCard and American Express.

## PICATINNY GOLF CLUB
Picatinny Arsenal, NJ 07806-5000

**LOCATION:** On post. From main gate, 1 mile to right at first light then veer left to club on left.

**SEASON OF OPERATION:** Mar-Nov.

**ELIGIBILITY:** Active/Reservists/Retired/DoD civilians/Dependents/Guests.

*NEW JERSEY-NEW MEXICO*
*Picatinny Golf Club, continued*

**COURSE INFORMATION:** Address: Picatinny Golf Club, Bldg 121B, Picatinny Arsenal, NJ 07806. **C-973-989-2466** 0700-1900 hours daily. One 18 hole golf course.

| | Back Tees | Front Tees |
|---|---|---|
| Length | 6,816 | 5,430 |
| Par | 72 | 72 |
| Slope | 125 | 122 |
| USGA Rating | 72.8 | 71.4 |

| RATES: | Weekday | Weekend |
|---|---|---|
| Enlisted | $10 | $14 |
| Officers | $19 | $24 |
| DoD civilians | $25 | $35 |
| Guests | $25 | $35 |

**CREDIT CARDS ACCEPTED:** Visa, MasterCard and American Express.

# PINE RIDGE GOLF COURSE
Lakehurst Naval Air Engineering Station
Lakehurst, NJ 08733-5040

**LOCATION:** On base. From New Jersey Parkway, take Route 37 to Lakehurst.

**SEASON OF OPERATION:** Year round.

**ELIGIBILITY:** Active/Reservists/Retired/DoD civilians/Dependents/ Guests.

**COURSE INFORMATION:** Address: Pine Ridge Golf Course, bldg 33, NAES, Lakehurst, NJ 08733-5040. **C-732-323-7483**, Fax: C-732-323-1373 0700-Dusk Apr-Oct, 0900-1700 Nov-Mar. One 9 hole golf course.

| | Back Tees | Front Tees |
|---|---|---|
| Length: | 6,111 | 6,111 |
| Par | 71 | 71 |
| Slope | 116 | 119 |
| USGA Rating | 34.4 | 35.3 |

| RATES: | Weekday | Weekend |
|---|---|---|
| Enlisted | $7 (9) $9 (18) | $8 (9) $11 (18) |
| Officers | $7 (9) $9 (18) | $8 (9) $11 (18) |
| Guests | $10 (9) $15 (18) | $11 (9) $16 (18) |

**SUPPORT FACILITIES:**

| | | |
|---|---|---|
| Bar/Lounge | Chipping Area | Golf Carts/Power |
| Golf Carts/Pull | Lockers | Pro Shop |
| Putting Area | | |

**CREDIT CARDS ACCEPTED:** None.

# SUNEAGLES GOLF COURSE
Fort Monmouth
Fort Monmouth, NJ 07703-5113

**COURSE INFORMATION:** Address: Suneagles Golf Course, Tinton Avenue, Bldg 2067, Fort Monmouth, NJ 07703. **C-732-532-4307.** One 18 hole golf course. Banquet Facilities, Chipping Area, Driving Range, Equipment Rental, Golf Carts/Power, Golf Carts/Pull, Lessons, Pro Shop, Putting Area, Snack Bar.

# NEW MEXICO

## APACHE MESA GOLF COURSE
Holloman Air Force Base
Holloman AFB, NM 88330-8035

**COURSE INFORMATION:** Address: Apache Mesa Golf Course, 151 West Gate Avenue, Holloman AFB, NM 88330. **C-505-475-3574** 0700-1900 daily. One 9 hole golf course; Par: 36. Equipment Rental, Golf Carts.

## TIJERAS ARROYO GOLF COURSE
Kirtland Air Force Base
Kirtland AFB, NM 87117-5521

**COURSE INFORMATION:** Address: Tijeras Arroyo Golf Course, Bldg 28054, Kirtland AFB, NM 87117. **C-505-846-1169, D-312-246-1169** 0700-2000 daily. One 18 hole golf course. Pro Shop, Snack Bar.

## WHISPERING WINDS GOLF COURSE
Cannon Air Force Base
Cannon AFB, NM 88103-5000

**LOCATION:** On base. From main gate turn right past the airplane display to golf course.

**SEASON OF OPERATION:** Year round.

**ELIGIBILITY:** Active/Reservists/Retired/DoD civilians/Dependents/ Guests.

**COURSE INFORMATION:** Address: Whispering Winds Golf Course, 105 forrest Drive, Cannon AFB, NM 88103. **C-505-784-2800, C-312-681-2800** 0800-Dusk daily. One 18 hole golf course.

| | Back Tees | Front Tees |
|---|---|---|
| Length | 6,032 | 5,536 |
| Par | 70 | 70 |
| Slope | 104 | 100 |
| USGA Rating | 67.6 | 65.5 |

| RATES: | Weekday | Weekend |
|---|---|---|
| E1-E4 | $6 | $7 |
| E5-O3 | $8 | $9 |
| O4+ | $10 | $12 |
| DoD civilians | $10 | $12 |
| Guests | $12 | $12 |

**SUPPORT FACILITIES:**

| | | |
|---|---|---|
| Chipping Area | Driving Range | Equipment Rental |
| Golf Carts/Power | Lessons | Lockers |
| Pro Shop | Putting Area | Showers |
| Snack Bar | | |

**CREDIT CARDS ACCEPTED:** Visa and MasterCard.

## WHITE SANDS MISSILE RANGE GOLF COURSE
White Sands Missile Range
Whites Sands Missile Range, NM 88002-5000

**LOCATION:** On base. From main gate to Martin Luther King Drive to first right to golf course 0.5 mile down on the left.

**SEASON OF OPERATION:** Year round.

**ELIGIBILITY:** Active/Reservists/Retired/DoD civilians/Dependents/ Guests.

**COURSE INFORMATION:** Address: White Sands Missile Range Golf Course, Bldg 1338, White Sands Missile Range, NM 88002. **C-505-678-1759, D-312-258-1759** 0800-1900 hours Tue-Fri, 0700-1900 hours Sat-Sun (summers); 0800-1700 hours Tue-Sun (winter). Closed mondays. One 9 hole golf course.

| | |
|---|---|
| Length | 6,650 |
| Par | 72 |
| Slope | 120 |

* Information based on 18 hole game.

| **RATES:** | Weekday | Weekend |
|---|---|---|
| E1-E6 | $8 | $10 |
| E7+ | $12 | $14 |
| DoD civilians | $13 | $15 |
| Guests | $12 | $14 |

**SUPPORT SERVICES:**

| | | |
|---|---|---|
| Chipping Area | Driving Range | Equipment Rental |
| Golf Carts/Power | Golf Carts/Pull | Lessons |
| Lockers | Pro at Facility | Pro Shop |
| Putting Area | Restaurants | Showers |
| Snack Bar | Snack Vending | Soda Vending |

**CREDIT CARDS ACCEPTED:** Visa and MasterCard.

# NEW YORK

## WEST POINT GOLF COURSE
United States Military Academy, West Point
West Point, NY 10996-5000

**LOCATION:** Off post. Palisades Parkway to Bear Mountain Circle. Take 9W north 5.5 miles. Exit at Route 218 to parking lot on right.

**SEASON OF OPERATION:** 1 April-30 November, weather permitting.

**ELIGIBILITY:** Active/Reservists/Retired/DoD civilians/Dependents/ General Public

**COURSE INFORMATION:** Address: West Point Golf Course, USMA West Point, Bldg 681, West Point, NY 10996. **C-914-938-2435** 0700-Dusk, Mon-Fri; 0630-Dusk, Sat-Sun. One 18 hole golf course.

| | Back Tees | Front Tees |
|---|---|---|
| Length | 6,255 | 4,809 |
| Par | 71 | 72 |
| Slope | 127 | 117 |
| USGA Rating | 70.0 | 67.5 |

| **RATES:** | Weekday | Weekend |
|---|---|---|
| Cadets, E1-E6 | $9 | $11 |
| E7+ | $14 | $16 |
| DoD civilians | $14 | $16 |
| Guests: | $25 | $35 |
| General Public | $30 | $40 |

**SUPPORT FACILITIES:**

| | | |
|---|---|---|
| Chipping Area | Golf Carts/Power | Golf Carts/Pull |
| Lessons | Lockers | Pro at Facility |
| Pro Shop | Putting Area | Showers |

**CREDIT CARDS ACCEPTED:** Visa and MasterCard.

# NORTH CAROLINA

## FORT BRAGG GOLF COMPLEX
Fort Bragg
Fort Bragg, NC 28307-5000

**COURSE INFORMATION:** Address: Fort Bragg Golf Complex, 1 Normandy Drive, Bldg I-5625, Fort Bragg, NC 28307. **C-910-436-3390/3811.** Two 18 hole golf courses (Ryder and Stryker). Banquet Facilities, Chipping Area, Driving Range, Equipment Rental, Golf Carts/Power, Golf Carts/Pull, Lessons, Pro Shop, Putting Area, Snack Bar.

## PARADISE POINT GOLF COURSE
Camp Lejeune Marine Corps Base
CAmp Lejeune MCB, NC 28542-0004

**COURSE INFORMATION:** Address: Paradise Point Golf Course, Bldg 1915,Camp Lejeune MCB, NC 28542. **C-919-451-5445** 0800-Dusk Mon-Fri, 0700-Dusk Sat-Sun. Two 18 hole golf courses (Gold, Scarlet). Driving Range, Equipment Rental, Golf Carts, Lessons, Pro Shop, Pro at Facility, Putting Area, Snack Bar.

## THREE EAGLES GOLF COURSE
Seymour Johnson Air Force Base
Seymour Johnson AFB, NC 27531-2442

**COURSE INFORMATION:** Address: Three Eagles Golf Course, 1385 Andrews Street, Seymour Johnson AFB, 27531. **C-919-736-6249.** One 18 hole golf course; Par: 70. Equipment Rental, Pro Shop, Snack Bar.

## WILLOW LAKES GOLF COURSE
Pope Air Force Base
Pope AFB, NC 28308-2375

**LOCATION:** On base. Just inside Reilly Gate.

**SEASON OF OPERATION:** Year round.

**ELIGIBILITY:** Active/Reservists/Retired/DoD civilians/Dependents/ General Public/Guests.

**COURSE INFORMATION:** Address: Willow Lakes Golf Course, 227 Reilly Street, Bldg 193, Pope AFB, NC 28308. **C-910-394-2325** 0700-1900 hours summer, 0800-1700 hours winter. One 18 hole golf course.

| | Back Tees | Middle Tees | Middle Tees | Front Tees |
|---|---|---|---|---|
| Length | 7,024 | 6,384 | 5,610 | 5,320 |
| Par | 72 | 72 | 72 | 76 |
| Slope | 132 | 126 | 111 | 118 |
| USGA Rating | 73.6 | 70.7 | 67.6 | 70.8 |

| **RATES:** | Weekday | Weekend |
|---|---|---|
| Enlisted | $6.75-$9 | $7.50-$10 |
| Officers | $9-$10 | $10-$11 |
| DoD civilians | $13 | $16 |
| Guests | $13 | $16 |

**SUPPORT FACILITIES:**

| | | |
|---|---|---|
| Driving Range | Equipment Rental | Golf Carts/Power |
| Golf Carts/Pull | Lessons | Lockers |
| Pro at Facility | Pro Shop | Putting Area |
| Showers | Snack Bar | |

**CREDIT CARDS ACCEPTED:** Visa and MasterCard.

# NORTH DAKOTA

## PLAINSVIEW GOLF COURSE

Grand Forks Air Force Base
Grand Forks, ND 58205-6319

**LOCATION:** On base. From I-29 N or S, take US-2 W exit for 14 miles to Grand Forks. County Road B-3 (Emerado/Air Base) north one mile to AFB on right. Golf course on south side of base.

**SEASON OF OPERATION:** Apr-Oct.

**ELIGIBILITY:** Active/Reservists/Retired/DoD civilians/Dependents.

**COURSE INFORMATION:** Address: Plainsview Golf Course, Bldg 811, 641 Alert Avenue, Grand Forks AFB, ND 58205. C-**701-747-4279, D-312-362-4279** 0630-2200 hours. One 9 hole golf course.

| Length | 6,700 |
|---|---|
| Par | 72 (18 holes) |
| Slope | 102 |
| USGA Rating | 69.9 |

| RATES: | Weekday | Weekend |
|---|---|---|
| E1-E4 | $8 | $8 |
| E5-E6 | $9 | $9 |
| E7+ | $10 | $10 |
| DoD civilians | $11 | $11 |
| Guests | $11 | $11 |

**SUPPORT FACILITIES:**

| | | |
|---|---|---|
| Bar/Lounge | Chipping Area | Driving Range |
| Golf Cart/Power | Golf Cart/Pull | Golf Simulator |
| Lessons | Lockers | Pro at Facility |
| Pro Shop | Putting Area | Snack Bar |
| Soda Vending | | |

**CREDIT CARDS ACCEPTED:** Visa and MasterCard.

## ROUGHRIDER GOLF COURSE

Minot Air Force Base
Minot AFB, ND 58705-5003

**LOCATION:** On base. Just outside the main gate.

**SEASON OF OPERATION:** 15 Apr-15 Oct.

**ELIGIBILITY:** Active/Reservists/Retired/DoD civilians/Dependents/Guests.

**COURSE INFORMATION:** Address: Roughrider Golf Course, 220 Golf Drive, Minot AFB, ND 58705. C-**701-723-3164, D-312-453-3164** 0800-2100 hours Mon-Fri, 0700-2100 hours Sat-Sun. One 9 hole golf course.

| | Back Tees | Front Tees |
|---|---|---|
| Length | 6,214 | 5,316 |
| Par | 71 | 70 |
| Slope | 109 | 111 |
| USGA Rating | 68.9 | 69.5 |

| RATES: | Weekday | Weekend |
|---|---|---|
| E1-E4 | $5 | $7 |
| E5+ | $8 | $10 |
| DoD civilians | $8 | $10 |
| Guests | $9 | $12 |

**SUPPORT FACILITIES:**

| | | |
|---|---|---|
| Bar/Lounge | Driving Range | Equipment Rental |
| Golf Carts/Power | Golf Carts/Pull | Lessons |
| Lockers | Pro at Facility | Putting Area |
| Snack Bar | Soda Vending | |

**CREDIT CARDS ACCEPTED:** Visa and MasterCard.

# OHIO

## COLUMBUS DEFENSE SUPPLY CENTER GOLF COURSE

Columbus Defense Supply Center
Columbus, OH 43216-5000

**COURSE INFORMATION:** Address: Columbus Defense Supply Center Golf Course, 3990 E. Broad Street, Bldg 20, Columbus, OH 43216. C-**614-239-6669.** Driving Range, Pro Shop.

## WRIGHT-PATTERSON GOLF CLUB

Wright-Patterson Air Force Base
Wright-Patterson AFB 45433-5315

**COURSE INFORMATION:** Address: Wright-Patterson Golf Club, 645SVS/SVBG, 4690 Skeel Avenue, Wright-Patterson AFB, OH 45433-5218. C-**937-257-7961.** One 18 hole golf course (Prairie Trace Golf Course) and one 9 hole golf course. Driving Range, Equipment Rental, Golf Carts/Power, Golf Carts/Pull, Lessons, Pro Shop, Putting Area, Snack Bar.

# OKLAHOMA

## TINKER GOLF COURSE

Tinker Air Force Base
Tinker AFB, OK 73145-9011

**LOCATION:** On base. Base located off of I-40 southeast of Oklahoma City.

**SEASON OF OPERATION:** Year round.

**ELIGIBILITY:** Active/Reservists/Retired/DoD civilians/Dependents/Guests.

**COURSE INFORMATION:** Address: Tinker Golf Course, 6441 Arnold Street, Tinker AFB, OK 73145. C-**405-734-2909, D-312-884-2909** 0530-2000 hours summer, 0630-Dusk winter. One 18 hole golf course.

*Tinker Golf Course, continued*

|  | Back Tees | Middle Tees | Front Tees |
|---|---|---|---|
| Length | 6,451 | 6,159 | 5,373 |
| Par | 72 | 72 | 73 |
| Slope | 111 | 110 | 125 |
| USGA Rating | 69.3 | 68.1 | 71.9 |

| RATES: | Weekday | Weekend |
|---|---|---|
| E1-E4 | $9 | $9 |
| E5-E9 | $9 | $11 |
| Officers | $11 | $11 |
| DoD civilians | $11 | $11 |
| Guests | $13 | $16 |

**SUPPORT FACILITIES:**

| | | |
|---|---|---|
| Chipping Area | Driving Range | Equipment Rental |
| Golf Carts/Power | Golf Carts/Pull | Lessons |
| Lockers | Pro at Facility | Putting Area |
| Pro Shop | Showers | Snack Bar |

**RESTRICTIONS:** Soft spikes only. Call golf course for dress course.

**CREDIT CARDS ACCEPTED:** Visa and MasterCard.

## WINDY TRAILS GOLF COURSE
Altus Air Force Base
Altus AFB, OK 73523-5000

**LOCATION:** On base. From Highway-62 take Veterans Drive to Base. From the main gate enter the circle, then take first exit which leads to the golf course.

**SEASON OF OPERATION:** Year round.

**ELIGIBILITY:** Active/Reservists/Retired/DoD civilians/Dependents/ Guests.

**COURSE INFORMATION:** Address: Windy Trails Golf Course, Bldg 35, Altus AFB, OK 73523-5000. **C-580-481-7207, D-312-866-7207** 0700-Dusk summer, 0900-1700 hours winter. One 18 hole golf course.

|  | Back Tees | Middle Tees | Front Tees |
|---|---|---|---|
| Length | 6,963 | 6,334 | 5,382 |
| Par | 72 | 72 | 72 |
| Slope | 120 | 118 | 122 |
| USGA Rating | 72.8 | 69.7 | 71.7 |

| RATES: | Weekday | Weekend |
|---|---|---|
| E1-E4 | $7 | $8 |
| E5+ | $10 | $11 |
| DoD civilians | $15 | $16 |
| Guests | $15 | $16 |

**SUPPORT FACILITIES:**

| | | |
|---|---|---|
| Lessons | Pro at Facility | Driving Range |
| Putting Area | Chipping Area | Pro Shop |
| Snack Bar | Golf Carts | Clubs Rental |
| Lockers | Showers | |

**CREDIT CARDS ACCEPTED:** Visa MasterCard.

# PENNSYLVANIA

## NAVICP GOLF COURSE
Mechanicsburg Naval Inventory Control Point
Mechanicsburg, PA 17055-0788

**LOCATION:** On base. From I-83, exit 20 to US-11, four miles. Or, from PA Turnpike I-76, exit 16 Carlisle, eight miles to center. Make a left at main gate, follow to Bldg 214 for info and day fees.

**SEASON OF OPERATION:** Year round.

**ELIGIBILITY:** Active/Reservists/Retired/DoD civilians/Dependents.

**COURSE INFORMATION:** Address: NAVICP Golf Course, 5450 Carlisle Pike, Mechanicsburg, PA 17055. **C-717-605-3948, D-312-430-3948** 0800-Dusk. One 9 hole golf course.

| RATES: | Weekday | Weekend |
|---|---|---|
| Enlisted | $6 | $7 |
| Officers | $6 | $7 |
| DoD civilians | $7 | $8 |
| Guests | $7 | $8 |

**SUPPORT FACILITIES:**

| | | |
|---|---|---|
| Chipping Area | Golf Carts/Pull | Parking |
| Putting Area | Soda Vending | |

**RESTRICTIONS:** No riding carts.

**CREDIT CARDS ACCEPTED:** None.

## RIVERVIEW GOLF CLUB
Defense Distribution Region East
New Cumberland, PA 17070-5000

**LOCATION:** On post. From I-83, exit 18 to PA-114, east for one mile to Old York Road, left three-quarter-of-a-mile to Ross Avenue, right for one mile to main gate.

**SEASON OF OPERATION:** Year round.

**ELIGIBILITY:** Active/Reservists/Retired/DoD civilians/Dependents/ Guests.

**COURSE INFORMATION:** Address: Riverview Golf Club, 300 A Avenue, New Cumberland, PA 17070. **C-717-770-5199** 0630-Dusk Apr-Oct, 0630-1630 Nov-Mar. One 9 hole golf course.

|  | Back Tees | Front Tees |
|---|---|---|
| Length | 5,927 | 5,209 |
| Par | 70 | 70 |
| Slope | 114 | 113 |
| USGA Rating | 67.9 | 68.9 |

| RATES: | Weekday | Weekend |
|---|---|---|
| Enlisted | $10 | $10 |
| Officers | $10 | $10 |
| DoD civilians | $13 | $13 |
| Guests | $16 | $16 |

**SUPPORT FACILITIES:**

| | | |
|---|---|---|
| Chipping Area | Equipment Rental | Golf Carts/Power |
| Golf Carts/Pull | Lessons | Pro at Facility |
| Putting Area | Snack Bar | |

**CREDIT CARDS ACCEPTED**: Visa and MasterCard.

## ROCKY SPRING GOLF COURSE
Letterkenny Army Depot
Chambersburg, PA 17201-4150

**LOCATION:** On post. From gate 6 to Coffey Avenue, then turn right across from fire department. From gate 1, to Coffey Avenue, then turn left at fire department to golf course.

**SEASON OF OPERATION:** Apr-Nov.

**ELIGIBILITY:** Active/Reservists/Retired/DoD civilians/Dependents.

**COURSE INFORMATION:** Address: Rocky Spring Golf Course, Bldg 529, Letterkenny Army Depot, Chambersburg, PA 17201-5000. **C-717-267-9449, D-312-570-9449** 0800-1900 hours daily. One 9 hole golf course.

|  | Back Tees | Front Tees |
|---|---|---|
| Length | 2,969 | 2,933 |
| Par | 36 | 35 |
| Slope | 116 | 113 |
| USGA Rating | 67.8 | 70.1 |

| **RATES:** | Weekday | Weekend |
|---|---|---|
| Depending on Rank | $8-$12 | $9-$14 |

**SUPPORT FACILITIES:**

| | | |
|---|---|---|
| Banquet Facilities | Chipping Area | Driving Range |
| Equipment Rental | Golf Carts/Power | Golf Carts/Pull |
| Lessons | Lockers | Pro at Facility |
| Pro Shop | Putting Area | Showers |
| Snack Bar | Snack Vending | Soda Vending |

**CREDIT CARDS ACCEPTED**: None.

# SOUTH CAROLINA

## CAROLINA LAKES GOLF COURSE
Shaw Air Force Base
Shaw AFB, SC 29152-5023

**LOCATION:** On base. Off Highway 378/76 west of Sumter, ten miles on right. Clearly marked. From main gate, after going through second traffic light, take first left, road goes straight to club house.

**SEASON OF OPERATION:** Year round.

**ELIGIBILITY:** Active/Reservists/Retired/DoD civilians/Guests.

**COURSE INFORMATION:** Address: Carolina Lakes Golf Course, 400 Stewart Street, Shaw AFB, SC 29152-5000. **C-803-895-1399, D-312-965-1399** 0730-2000 hours summer, 0800-1700 hours winter. One 18 hole golf course.

|  | Back Tees | Front Tees |
|---|---|---|
| Length | 6,522 | 4,911 |
| Par | 71 | 71 |
| Slope | 125 | 108 |
| USGA Rating | 71.1 | 66.9 |

| **RATES:*** | Weekday | Weekend |
|---|---|---|
| E1-E4 | $7 | $8 |
| E5-E9 | $10 | $11 |
| O1-O3 | $10 | $11 |
| O4+ | $12 | $13 |
| Guests | $20 | $23 |

* Civilians according to grade.

**SUPPORT FACILITIES:**

| | | |
|---|---|---|
| Banquet Facilities | Driving Range | Golf Carts/Power |
| Golf Carts/Pull | Lessons | Lockers |
| Parking | Pro at Facility | Pro Shop |
| Putting Area | Showers | Snack Bar |

**CREDIT CARDS ACCEPTED:** Visa and MasterCard.

## FORT JACKSON GOLF CLUB
Fort Jackson US Army Training Center
Fort Jackson, SC 29207-5000

**LOCATION:** On post. From I-77, Exit 10 Jackson Blvd. Enter Traffic Circle at main gate, turn right on Marion Drive. At second light, turn right on Semmes Road, 1.5 miles to club on right.

**SEASON OF OPERATION:** Year round.

**ELIGIBILITY:** Active/Reservists/Retired/DoD civilians/Dependents/ Federal Employees/Guests.

**COURSE INFORMATION:** Address: Fort Jackson Golf Club, Bldg #3652, Fort Jackson, SC 29207-5000. **C-803-787-4344/4437** 0700-1900 hours summer, 0800-1730 hours winter. Two 18 holes golf courses.

| **Old Hickory** | Back Tees | Front Tees |
|---|---|---|
| Length | 6,624 | 5,164 |
| Par | 72 | 72 |
| Slope | 137 | 126 |
| USGA Rating | 71.6 | 69.8 |

| **Wildcat** | Back Tees | Front Tees |
|---|---|---|
| Length | 6,721 | 5,426 |
| Par | 72 | 72 |
| Slope | 125 | 120 |
| USGA Rating | 71.2 | 70.0 |

| **RATES:** | Weekday | Weekend |
|---|---|---|
| Enlisted | $10 | $15 |
| Officers | $10 | $15 |
| Guests | $10 | $15 |
| Civilians | $15 | $20 |

**SUPPORT FACILITIES:**

| | | |
|---|---|---|
| Banquet facilities | Bar/Lounge | Chipping Area |
| Driving Range | Golf Carts/Power | Golf Carts/pull |
| Lessons | Lockers | Parking |
| Pro at Facility | Pro Shop | Putting Area |
| Restaurants | Showers | Snack Bar |

**CREDIT CARDS ACCEPTED:** Visa, MasterCard and American Express.

## REDBANK GOLF COURSE
Charleston Naval Weapons Station
Charleston, SC 29445-5000

*Redbank Golf Course, continued*

**LOCATION:** On base. Take I-26 to Highway 78 N and follow signs to NWS.

**SEASON OF OPERATION:** Year round.

**ELIGIBILITY:** Active/Reservists/Retired/DoD civilians/Dependents

**COURSE INFORMATION:** Address: Redbank Golf Course, Bldg 270, Charleston, SC 29408-5000. **C-843-764-7802, D-312-794-7802** 0730-1900 hours summer; 0730-1700 hours winter. One 18 hole golf course.

|  | Back Tees | Front Tees |
|---|---|---|
| Length | 6,325 | 6,114 |
| Par | 71 | 71 |
| Slope | 100 | 100 |
| USGA Rating | 65.6 | 66.8 |

**RATES:**

|  | Weekday | Weekend |
|---|---|---|
| Enlisted | $9 | $9 |
| Officers | $11 | $11 |
| Guests | $14 | $14 |
| Civilians | $14 | $14 |

**SUPPORT FACILITIES:**

| | | |
|---|---|---|
| Bar/Lounge | Chipping Area | Driving Range |
| Golf Carts/Power | Golf Carts/Pull | Lessons |
| Lockers | Parking | Pro at Facility |
| Pro Shop | Putting Area | Showers |
| Snack Bar | Soda Vending | |

**CREDIT CARDS ACCEPTED:** Visa, MasterCard, American Express, Discover and Diners'.

## WRENWOODS GOLF COURSE

Charleston Air Force Base
Charleston, SC 28404-4924

**LOCATION:** On base. From I-26 east, exit to West Aviation Avenue to traffic light, then continue through light to second right, follow road around end of runway to gate 2 (Rivers Gate).

**SEASON OF OPERATION:** Year round.

**ELIGIBILITY:** Active/Reservists/Retired/DoD civilians/Dependents/Guests.

**COURSE INFORMATION:** Address: Wrenwoods Golf Course, 201 Arthur Drive, Bldg 370, Charleston, SC 29404. **C-843-5664174/77, D-312-963-4177** 0700-1800 hours daily. One 18 hole golf course.

|  | Back Tees | Middle Tees | Front Tees |
|---|---|---|---|
| Length | 6,595 | 6,216 | 5,605 |
| Par | 72 | 72 | 72 |
| Slope | 128 | 123 | 113 |
| USGA Rating | 71.6 | 69.6 | 66.2 |

**RATES:**

|  | Weekday | Weekend |
|---|---|---|
| E1-E4 | $8 | $9 |
| E5-E9 | $11 | $13 |
| O1-O3 | $11 | $13 |
| O4+ | $12 | $14 |
| DoD Civilians | $14 | $16 |
| Guests | $14 | $16 |

**SUPPORT FACILITIES:**

| | | |
|---|---|---|
| Chipping Area | Driving Range | Equipment Rental |
| Golf Carts/Power | Golf Carts/Pull | Lessons |
| Parking | Pro at Facility | Pro Shop |
| Putting Area | Snack Bar | Soda Vending |

**CREDIT CARDS ACCEPTED:** Visa and MasterCard.

# SOUTH DAKOTA

## PRAIRIE RIDGE GOLF COURSE

Ellsworth Air Force Base
Ellsworth AFB, SD 57706-4710

**LOCATION:** On base. From I-90 Exit #66 north for .25 mile to golf course on left side of street.

**SEASON OF OPERATION:** Year round.

**ELIGIBILITY:** Active/Reservists/Retired/DoD civilians/Dependents

**COURSE INFORMATION:** Address: Prairie Ridge Golf Course, 239 N. Ellsworth Road, Box Elder, SD 57719. **C-605-923-4999** 0730-Dusk Mon-Fri, 0630-Dusk Sat-Sun and Holidays. One 9 hole golf course.

|  | Back Tees | Front Tees |
|---|---|---|
| Length | 3,228 | 3,228 |
| Par | 36 | 36 |
| Slope | 116 | 1112 |
| USGA Rating | 34.8 | 33.9 |

**RATES:**

|  | Weekday | Weekend |
|---|---|---|
| E1-E4 | $6 (9), $11 (18) | $6 (9), $11 (18) |
| E5-O2 | $8 (9), $14 (18) | $8, (9), $14 (18) |
| O3+ | $9 (9), $15 (18) | $9 (9), $15 (18) |
| Civilians | $8 (9), $14 (18) | $8 (9), $14 (18) |

**SUPPORT FACILITIES:**

| | | |
|---|---|---|
| Chipping Area | Driving Range | Golf Carts/Power |
| Golf Carts/Pull | Lessons | Parking |
| Pro at Facility | Pro Shop | Putting Area |

**CREDIT CARDS ACCEPTED:** Visa and MasterCard.

# TENNESSEE

## ARNOLD GOLF COURSE

Arnold Air Force Base
Arnold AFB, TN 37389-5000

**LOCATION:** On base. Going east from Tullahoma, take Arnold Engineering Development Center (AEDC) access highway. From I-24, take AEDC exit 117 W, four miles south of Manchester. Clearly marked. From I-24, approximately ten miles on Wattendorf Highway. Follow signs to golf course.

**SEASON OF OPERATION:** Year round.

**ELIGIBILITY:** Active/Reservists/Retired/DoD civilians/Dependents/Contractors/City Officials/Guests.

**COURSE INFORMATION:** Address: Arnold Golf Course, 100 Kindel Drive, Suite C-321, Arnold, TN 37389-5000. **C-931-455-5870** 0730-Dusk. One nine hole golf course (played twice).

**TENNESSEE-TEXAS**
*Arnold Golf Course, continued*

|  | Back Tees | Middle Tees | Front Tees |
|---|---|---|---|
| Length | 3,195 | 2,885 | 2,707 |
| Par | 36 |  | 35 |
| Slope | 126 | 119 | 126 |
| USGA Rating | 71.0 | 70.1 | 73.2 |

| RATES:* | Weekday | Weekend |
|---|---|---|
| E1-E4, GS1-GS4, Jrs age 6-14 | $3-$5 | $4-$6 |
| E5-E7, GS5-GS7 | $6-$9 | $7-$11 |
| E8-O3, GS8-GS10 | $7-$10 | $8-$12 |
| O4+, GS11+ | $8-$11 | $9-$13 |
| Contractor/Guest | $9-$12 | $12-$16 |

* Higher rates indicate cost of playing 18 holes.

**SUPPORT FACILITIES:**

| | | |
|---|---|---|
| Chipping Area | Driving Range | Golf Carts/Power |
| Golf Carts/Pull | Lessons | Lockers |
| Parking | Pro at Facility | Pro Shop |
| Putting Area | Showers | Snack Bar |
| Snack Vending | Soda Vending | |

**CREDIT CARDS ACCEPTED:** Visa and MasterCard.

## GLEN EAGLES GOLF COURSE
Memphis Naval Support Activity
Millington, TN 38054-5045

**COURSE INFORMATION:** Address: Glen Eagles Golf Course, MWR Department, P.O. Box 54278, Millington, TN 38054-0278. **C-901-874-5168.** One 18 golf course.

# TEXAS

## BROOKS GOLF COURSE
Brooks Air Force Base
Brooks AFB, TX 78235-5120

**LOCATION:** On base. At intersection of I-37 and Loop 13 (Military Drive). Inside I-410 beltway in southeast San Antonio.

**SEASON OF OPERATION:** Year round.

**ELIGIBILITY:** Active/Reservists/Retired/DoD civilians/Dependents/Guests.

**COURSE INFORMATION:** Address: Brooks Golf Course, Bldg 820, Brooks AFB, TX 78235. **C-210-536-2636** 0730-Dusk daily. One 9 hole golf course.

|  | Back Tees | Front Tees |
|---|---|---|
| Par | 72 | 72 |
| Slope | 118 | 118 |
| USGA Rating | 72.4 | 72.4 |

| RATES: | Weekday | Weekend |
|---|---|---|
| Enlisted | $8 | $10 |
| Officers | $10 | $12 |
| DoD civilians | $6-$10 | $7-$12 |
| Guests | $12 | $14 |

**SUPPORT FACILITIES:**

| | | |
|---|---|---|
| Chipping Area | Driving Range | Golf Carts/Power |
| Golf Carts/Pull | Lessons | Pro at Facility |
| Pro Shop | Putting Area | Snack Bar |
| Soda Vending | | |

**CREDIT CARDS ACCEPTED:** Visa and MasterCard.

## FORT HOOD GOLF FACILITY
Fort Hood, TX 76544-5005

**COURSE INFORMATION:** Address: Clear Creek Golf Course, Bldg 52381, Fort Hood, TX 76544. **C-254-287-3466.** Two 18 hole golf courses (Clear Creek and Anderson). Equipment Rental, Golf Carts, Lessons, Pro Shop, Snack Bar. *Note: A $6.316 million club house renovation has been approved in the Fiscal Year 1998 MWR Major and Minor Construction Program.*

## FORT SAM HOUSTON GOLF COURSES
Fort Sam Houston
Fort Sam Houston, TX 78234-5020

**COURSE INFORMATION:** Address: Fort Sam Houston Golf Courses, Bldg 2901, Harry Wurzbach Road, Fort Sam Houston, TX 78234. **C-210-221-5863/4388** 0715-1800 hours daily. Two 18 hole golf courses (La Loma Grande and Salado El Rio). Equipment Rental, Lockers, Pro Shop, Restaurants.

## GULF WINDS GOLF COURSE
Corpus Christi Naval Air Station
Corpus Christi, TX 78419-5021

**LOCATION:** On base. From South Gate to golf course on Lexington Blvd.

**SEASON OF OPERATION:** Year round.

**ELIGIBILITY:** Active/Reservists/Retired/DoD civilians/Dependents/Guests.

**COURSE INFORMATION:** Address: Gulf Winds Golf Course, Bldg 1272, Corpus Christi NAS, TX 78419-5000. **C-512-961-3250** Dawn to Dusk daily. One 18 hole golf course.

|  | Back Tees | Middle Tees | Front Tees |
|---|---|---|---|
| Length | 6,309 | 5,700 | 4,865 |
| Par | 71 | 71 | 71 |
| Slope | 114 | 107 | 108 |
| USGA Rating | 70.4 | 67.3 | 66.6 |

| RATES: | Weekday | Weekend |
|---|---|---|
| Enlisted | $7 | $8 |
| Officers | $8 | $9 |
| DoD civilians | $9 | $10 |
| Guests | $9 | $10 |

**SUPPORT FACILITIES:**

| | | |
|---|---|---|
| Bar/Lounge | Chipping Area | Driving Range |
| Equipment Rental | Golf Carts/Power | Golf Carts/Pull |
| Lessons | Lockers | Pro at Facility |
| Pro Shop | Putting Area | Snack Bar |
| Showers | | |

**CREDIT CARDS ACCEPTED:** Visa, MasterCard and American Express.

# KELLY GOLF CLUB
Kelly Air Force Base
Kelly AFB, TX 78241-5828

**COURSE INFORMATION:** Address: Kelly Golf Club, 2311 Oak Trace, Kelly AFB, TX 78232. **C-210-977-5079/5100.** One 18 hole golf course.

# LEANING PINE GOLF COURSE
Laughlin Air Force Base
Laughlin AFB, TX 78843-5135

**LOCATION:** On base. From main gate, follow signs to course.

**SEASON OF OPERATION:** Year round.

**ELIGIBILITY:** Active/Reservists/Retired/DoD civilians/Dependents/ Guests.

**COURSE INFORMATION:** Address: Leaning Pine Golf Course, Bldg 494, Laughlin AFB, TX 78843. **C-830-298-5451, D-312-732-5451** 0730-Dusk daily. One 9 hole golf course.

|  | Back Tees | Front Tees |
|---|---|---|
| Length | 6,460 | 5,566 |
| Par | 72 | 72 |
| Slope | 115 | 115 |
| USGA Rating | 71.1 | 71.1 |

| RATES: | Weekday | Weekend |
|---|---|---|
| Enlisted | $7 | $9 |
| Officers | $9 | $11 |
| DoD civilians | $13 | $16 |
| Guest | $13 | $16 |

**SUPPORT FACILITIES:**

| | | |
|---|---|---|
| Chipping Area | Driving Range | Golf Carts/Power |
| Golf Carts/Pull | Lessons | Lockers |
| Pro Shop | Putting Area | Showers |
| Snack Vending | | |

**CREDIT CARDS ACCEPTED:** Visa and MasterCard.

# MESQUITE GROVE GOLF COURSE
Dyess Air Force Base
Dyess AFB, TX 79607-1139

**COURSE INFORMATION:** Address: Mesquite Grove Golf Course, 766 Mesquite Trail, Dyess AFB, TX 79607. **C-915-696-4384** Dawn-Dusk daily. One 18 hole golf course. Snack Bar.

# RANDOLPH OAKS GOLF COURSE
Randolph Air Force Base
Randolph AFB, TX 78150-4537

**COURSE INFORMATION:** Address: Randolph Oaks Golf Course, Bldg 1300, Randolph AFB, TX 78150. **C-210-652-4570/4653** 0630-Dusk summer, 0700-1700 hours winter. One 18 hole golf course.

# UNDERWOOD GOLF COMPLEX
Fort Bliss
Fort Bliss, TX 79916-6816

**LOCATION:** On post. From I-10, take Airway Blvd exit, follow signs left at Airport Road, curve left with Fred Wilson Blvd, turn right on Sheridan Road to golf course.

**SEASON OF OPERATION:** Year Round.

**ELIGIBILITY:** Active/Reservists/Retired/DoD civilians/Dependents/ Guests.

**COURSE INFORMATION:** Address: Underwood Golf Complex, 3200 Coe Avenue, Bldg 3191, Fort Bliss, TX 79904-5000. **C-915-562-1273/2066/7255** 0630-2000 hours. Two 18 hole golf courses.

**Sunrise Course**

|  | Back Tees | Middle Tees | Front Tees |
|---|---|---|---|
| Length | 6,942 | 6,420 | 5,498 |
| Par | 72 | 72 | 72 |
| Slope | 117 | 113 | 124 |
| USGA Rating | 70.4 | 68.1 | 71.1 |

**Sunset Course**

|  | Back Tees | Middle Tees | Front Tees |
|---|---|---|---|
| Length | 6,629 | 6,328 | 5,531 |
| Par | 72 | 72 | 72 |
| Slope | 120 | 117 | 109 |
| USGA Rating | 70.4 | 68.9 | 70.4 |

| RATES: | Weekday | Weekend |
|---|---|---|
| E1-E6 | $6 | $8 |
| E7+ | $10 | $13 |
| Officers | $10 | $13 |
| Guests | $15 | $18 |
| Civilians | $15 | $18 |

**SUPPORT FACILITIES:**

| | | |
|---|---|---|
| Banquet Facilities | Bar/Lounge | Chipping Area |
| Driving Range | Golf Carts/Power | Golf Carts/Pull |
| Lessons | Lockers | Parking |
| Pro at Facility | Pro Shop | Putting Area |
| Restaurants | Showers | |

**CREDIT CARDS ACCEPTED:** Visa, MasterCard, American Express and Discover.

# WIND CREEK GOLF COURSE
Sheppard Air Force Base
Sheppard AFB, TX 76311-2540

**LOCATION:** On base. Take US-281 north fro Wichita Falls, exit to TX-325 which leads to main gate.

**SEASON OF OPERATION:** Year round.

**ELIGIBILITY:** Active/Reservists/Retired/DoD civilians/Dependents/ Guests.

**COURSE INFORMATION:** Address: Wind Creek Golf Course, 82 SVS/SVBG, 900 First Avenue, Sheppard AFB, TX 76311-2727. **C-940-676-6369, D-312-736-6369** 0700-Dusk daily. One 18 hole golf course.

|  | Back Tees | Middle Tees | Front Tees |
|---|---|---|---|
| Length | 7,028 | 6,683 | 5,267 |
| Par | 72 | 72 | 72 |
| Slope | 123 | 120 | 116 |
| USGA Rating | 72.6 | 71.3 | 69.4 |

*TEXAS-VIRGINIA*
*Wind Creek Golf Course, continued*

**RATES:**

| | Weekday | Weekend |
|---|---|---|
| E1-E4 | $4 (9), $7 (18) | $4 (9), $7 (18) |
| E5-O3 | $6 (9), $10 (18) | $7 (9), $11 (18) |
| O4+ | $7 (9), $11 (18) | $8 (9), $12 (18) |
| DoD civilians | Same as Military Equivalent | |
| Guests | $8 (9), $15 (18) | $10 (9), $16 (18) |

**SUPPORT FACILITIES:**

| | | |
|---|---|---|
| Lessons | Pro at Facility | Pro Shop |

**CREDIT CARDS ACCEPTED:** Visa and MasterCard.

# UTAH

## DUGWAY GOLF COURSE

Dugway Proving Ground
Dugway Proving Ground, UT 84022-5000

**COURSE INFORMATION:** Address: Dugway Golf Course, Bldg 5950, Dugway Proving Ground, UT 84022. **C-431-831-2305.** One 9 hole golf course. Driving Range, Putting Area.

## HUBBARD MEMORIAL GOLF COURSE

Hill Air Force Base
Hill AFB, UT 84056-5720

**COURSE INFORMATION:** Address: Hubbard Memorial Golf Course, Bldg 720, Hill AFB, UT 84056. **C-801-777-3272** 0630-Dusk daily. One 18 hole golf course.

# VIRGINIA

## AEROPINES GOLF COURSE

Oceana Naval Air Station
Virginia Beach, VA 23460-5000

**COURSE INFORMATION:** Address: Aeropines Golf Course, MWR Department, Bldg 531, Virginia Beach, VA 23460-5120. **C-757-433-2866, D-312-433-2866.** 27 hole golf facility with 9 more holes under construction.

## THE CARDINAL GOLF CLUB

Fort Lee
Fort Lee, VA 23801-1709

**COURSE INFORMATION:** Address: The Cardinal Golf Club, Bldg 11810, P.O. Box 5010, Fort Lee, VA 23801. **C-804-734-2899/7190.** One 18 hole golf course. Driving Range, Equipment Rental, Golf Carts, Lessons, Lockers, Pro at Facility, Pro Shop, Putting Area, Snack Bar.

## DEER COVE GOLF COURSE

Cheatham Annex Fleet and Industrial Supply Center
Williamsburg, VA 23185-8792

**LOCATION:** On post. From main gate, stay on Sanda Avenue for 2 miles to golf course entrance.

**SEASON OF OPERATION:** Year round.

**ELIGIBILITY:** Active/Reservists/Retired/DoD civilians/Dependents/General Public/Guests.

**COURSE INFORMATION:** Address: Deer Cove Golf Course, 108 Sanda Avenue, Williamsburg, VA 23185-5000. **C-757-887-7101/7159, D-312-953-7159** 0700-Dusk daily. One 18 hole golf course.

| | Back Tees | Front Tees |
|---|---|---|
| Length | 4,398 | 3,773 |
| Par | 65 | 65 |
| Slope | 93 | 90 |
| USGA Rating | 61.1 | 60.1 |

| **RATES:** | Weekday | Weekend |
|---|---|---|
| Enlisted | $6 | $8 |
| Officers | $6 | $8 |
| DoD civilians | $10 | $14 |
| Guests | $10 | $14 |

**SUPPORT FACILITIES:**

| | | |
|---|---|---|
| Putting Area | Practice Net | Pro Shop |
| Snack Bar | Banquet Facilities | Golf Carts/Power |
| Equipment Rental | Showers | |

**CREDIT CARDS ACCEPTED:** Visa, MasterCard, American Express and Discover.

## EAGLE HAVEN GOLF COURSE

Little Creek Naval Amphibious Base
Norfolk, VA 23521-2231

**LOCATION:** On base. From gate 5 (main gate) go to second light and turn left onto Gator Blvd, then continue to right on Hewitt to golf course on the right before the beach.

**SEASON OF OPERATION:** Year round.

**ELIGIBILITY:** Active/Reservists/Retired/DoD civilians/Dependents/Guests.

**COURSE INFORMATION:** Address: Eagle Haven Golf Course, Bldg 3690, Little Creek NAB, Norfolk, VA 23521-5000. **C-757-462-8526** 0630-2030 hours summer, 0630-1730 winter. One 18 hole golf course.

| | Back Tees | Middle Tees | Front Tees |
|---|---|---|---|
| Length | 6,206 | 5,854 | 4,934 |
| Par | 71 | 71 | 71 |
| Slope (M) | 122 | 118 | |
| Slope (L) | | 103 | 118 |
| USGA Rating (M) | 70.4 | 69.0 | |
| USGA Rating (L) | | 67.1 | 72.6 |

| **RATES:** | Weekday | Weekend |
|---|---|---|
| Military | $7.75 (9), $11.50 (18) | $7.75 (9), $11.50 (18) |
| DoD civilians | $12 (9), $22 (18) | $12 (9), $22 (18) |
| Guests | $12 (9), $22 (18) | $12 (9), $22 (18) |

**SUPPORT FACILITIES:**

| | | |
|---|---|---|
| Banquet Facilities | Bar/Lounge | Chipping Area |
| Driving Range | Equipment Rental | Golf Carts/Power |
| Golf Carts/Pull | Lessons | Pro at Facility |
| Pro Shop | Putting Area | Restaurants |
| Showers | Snack Bar | Soda Vending |

**RESTRICTIONS:** Must wear soft spikes.

**CREDIT CARDS ACCEPTED:** Visa, MasterCard, American Express and Discover.

# EAGLEWOOD GOLF COURSE

Langley Air Force Base
Langley AFB, VA 23665-1898

**LOCATION:** On base. From Elm Street to left on Sweeny to right on Perimeter Road to Weyland Clubhouse on the left.

**SEASON OF OPERATION:** Year round.

**ELIGIBILITY:** Active/Reservists/Retired/DoD civilians/Dependents/ Guests.

**COURSE INFORMATION:** Address: Eaglewood Golf Course, 630 Weyland Road, Langley AFB, VA 23665. **C-757-764-3744/4547, D-312-574-4547** Dawn-Dusk daily. Two 18 hole golf courses.

**Blue Course**

|  | Back Tees | Front Tees |
|---|---|---|
| Length | 6,428 | 5,154 |
| Par | 72 | 72 |
| Slope | 120 | 104 |
| USGA Rating | 71.0 | 68.6 |

**Red Course**

|  | Back Tees | Front Tees |
|---|---|---|
| Length | 6,284 | 5,316 |
| Par | 72 | 72 |
| Slope | 117 | 109 |
| USGA Rating | 69.6 | 68.9 |

**RATES:**

|  | Weekday | Weekend |
|---|---|---|
| E1-E4 | $9 | $9 |
| E5-E9 | $12 | $12 |
| O1-O3 | $14 | $14 |
| O4+ | $16 | $16 |
| DoD civilians | Same as Military Equivalent | |
| Guests | $18 | $18 |

**SUPPORT FACILITIES:**

| | | |
|---|---|---|
| Banquet Facilities | Chipping Area | Driving Range |
| Equipment Rental | Golf Carts/Power | Golf Carts/Pull |
| Lessons | Pro at Facility | Pro Shop |
| Putting Area | Showers | Snack Bar |
| Snack Vending | Soda Vending | |

**RESTRICTIONS:** Soft spike shoes only and collared shirts.

**CREDIT CARDS ACCEPTED:** Visa and MasterCard.

# FORT BELVOIR GOLF FACILITY

Fort Belvoir
Fort Belvoir, VA 22060-5908

**LOCATION:** Off post. From US-95 N-S to Newington/Fort Belvoir Exit (166A) to the Fairfax County Parkway. Then continue to a left onto John J. Kingman Road and then a left onto Beulan Street (Route 613). The clubhouse will be on the left.

**SEASON OF OPERATION:** Year round.

**ELIGIBILITY:** Active/Reservists/Retired/DoD civilians/Dependents/ Guests.

**COURSE INFORMATION**: Address: DPCA ATTN: Golf Facility, 5820 21st Street, Suite 112, Fort Belvoir, VA 22060-5937. **C-703-806-5892/5899/6016** for 18 hole courses, **C-703-806-5917** for 9 hole course 0600-2000 hours daily (seasonal hours). Two 18 hole golf courses and one 9 hole golf course.

**Gunston Golf Course**

|  | Back Tees | Middle Tees | Middle Tees | Front Tees |
|---|---|---|---|---|
| Length | 6,908 | 6,608 | 6,152 | 5,250 |
| Par | 72 | 72 | 72 | 71/68 |
| Slope (M) | 132 | 131 | 128 | 111 |
| Slope (L) | | | 127 | 117 |
| USGA Rating(M | 73.0 | 71.8 | 69.4 | 65.5 |
| USGA Rating(L) | | | 73.9 | 70.1 |

**Woodlawn Golf Course**

|  | Back Tees | Middle Tees | Middle Tees | Front Tees |
|---|---|---|---|---|
| Length | 6,832 | 6,434 | 6,005 | 5,291 |
| Par | 72 | 72 | 72 | 72/70 |
| Slope (M) | 127 | 126 | 123 | 113 |
| Slope (L) | | | 127 | 119 |
| USGA Rating(M | 73.4 | 71.3 | 69.7 | 64.0 |
| USGA Rating(L) | | | 74.7 | 71.0 |

**South Nine Golf Course**
Information not available.

**RATES*:**

|  | Weekday | Weekend |
|---|---|---|
| E1-E6 | $13 | $13 |
| E7-E9 | $17 | $17 |
| O1-O5,W1-W3 | $17 | $17 |
| W4+, O6+ | $26 | $26 |
| DoD civilians | $26 | $26 |
| Guests | $26 | $26 |

\* Rates for Gunston and Woodlawn courses.

**RATES*:**

|  | Weekday | Weekend |
|---|---|---|
| E1-E6 | $6 (9), $11 (18) | $6 (9), $11 (18) |
| E7-O5, W1-W5 | $8 (9), $15 (18) | $8 (9), $15 (18) |
| O6+ | $9 (9), $17 (18) | $9 (9), $17 (18) |
| FB DoD civilians | $9 (9), $17 (18) | $9 (9), $17 (18) |
| Visiting DoD civilians | $13 (9), $23 (18) | $13 (9), $23 (18) |
| Guests | $13 (9), $23 (18) | $13 (9), $23 (18) |

\* Rates for South Nine course.

**SUPPORT FACILITIES:**

| | | |
|---|---|---|
| Banquet Facilities | Bar/Lounge | Chipping Area |
| Driving Range | Equipment Rental | Golf Carts/Power |
| Golf Carts/Pull | Lessons | Lockers |
| Pro at facilities | Pro Shop | Putting Area |
| Restaurants | Sand Trap | Showers |
| Soda Vending | | |

**RESTRICTIONS:** Must let faster players play through, keep golf carts 15 feet away from tees and greens, each player must have own set of clubs and players must wear proper attire.

**CREDIT CARDS ACCEPTED:** Visa and MasterCard.

# HOLLY OAKS GOLF COURSE

Yorktown Naval Weapons Station
Yorktown, VA 23691-0160

**COURSE INFORMATION:** Address: Holly Oaks Golf Course, MWR Department, P.O. Box 2 Bldg 2011, Yorktown, VA 23691-5000. **C-757-887-4545 ext 4323.** One 9 hole golf course.

*VIRGINIA*

# MEDAL OF HONOR GOLF COURSE

Quantico Marine Corps Base
Quantico, VA 22134-5012

**LOCATION:** On base. From main gate, 1.5 miles to golf course on left.

**SEASON OF OPERATION:** Year round.

**ELIGIBILITY:** Active/Reservists/Retired/DoD civilians/Dependents/FBI Academy Students/Guests.

**COURSE INFORMATION:** Address: Medal of Honor Golf Course, P.O. Box 183, Quantico, VA 22554. **C-703-784-2463/2424, D-312-278-2463/2424** 0700-1900 hours daily. One 18 hole golf course.

|  | Back Tees | Front Tees |
|---|---|---|
| Length | 6,711 | 4,960 |
| Par | 72 | 72 |
| Slope | 126 | 115 |
| USGA Rating | 72.0 | 68.4 |

| RATES: | Weekday | Weekend |
|---|---|---|
| Enlisted | $12-$16 | $12-$16 |
| Officers | $15-$18 | $15-$18 |
| DoD civilians | $23 | $23 |
| Guests | $27 | $27 |

**SUPPORT FACILITIES:**

| | | |
|---|---|---|
| Banquet Facilities | Bar/Lounge | Chipping Area |
| Driving Range | Equipment Rental | Golf Carts/Power |
| Golf Carts/Pull | Lessons | Lockers |
| Pro at Facility | Pro Shop | Putting Area |
| Restaurants | Showers | Snack Bar |
| Soda Vending | | |

**CREDIT CARDS ACCEPTED:** Visa, MasterCard, American Express and Discover.

# PINES GOLF COURSE

Fort Eustis
Fort Eustis, VA 23604-5114

**LOCATION:** On base. From Washington Blvd to right on Wilson Street then left on Mulberry Island Road. Continue straight to golf course on left side of street.

**SEASON OF OPERATION:** Year round.

**ELIGIBILITY:** Active/Reservists/Retired/DoD civilians/Dependents/General Public/Guests.

**COURSE INFORMATION:** Address: Pines Golf Course, Bldg 3501, Fort Eustis, VA 23604. **C-757-878-2252/2965, D-312-927-2252/2965** 0630-2000 hours summer, 0730-1700 hours winter. Three 9 hole golf courses (Pines 1,2 and 3).

**Pines 1 and 3 (Primary 18 holes)**

|  | Back Tees | Middle Tees | Front Tees |
|---|---|---|---|
| Length | 6,882 | 6,488 | 5,323 |
| Par | 72 | 72 | 70 |
| Slope | 120 | 112 | 113 |
| USGA Rating | 72.2 | 70.0 | 69.4 |

| RATES: | Weekday | Weekend |
|---|---|---|
| E1-E4 | $ 5 (9), $8 (18) | $7 (9), $10 (18) |
| E5+ | $ 8 (9), $12 (18) | $9 (9), $14 (18) |
| Guests | $11 (9), $16 (18) | $12 (9), $18 (18) |

**SUPPORT FACILITIES:**

| | | |
|---|---|---|
| Banquet Facilities | Chipping Area | Driving Range |
| Equipment Rental | Golf Carts/Power | Golf Carts/Pull |
| Lessons | Lockers | Parking |
| Pro at Facility | Pro Shop | Putting Area |
| Showers | Snack Bar | |

**CREDIT CARDS ACCEPTED:** Visa, MasterCard and American Express.

# SWELLS POINT GOLF COURSE

Norfolk Naval Base
Norfolk, VA 23511-1219

**LOCATION:** Off base. From I-64 N or S, take I-564 straight into Naval Station. Take the I-564 split to Naval Base, and get off at Terminal Blvd exit. Look for golf course in the right.

**SEASON OF OPERATION:** Year round.

**ELIGIBILITY:** Active/Reservists/Retired/DoD civilians/Dependents/Guests.

**COURSE INFORMATION:** Address: Sewells Point Golf Course, NAVSTA Bldg C-99, Norfolk, VA 23511-5000. **C-757-444-5572** 0630-Dark. One 18 hole golf course.

|  | Back Tees | Middle Tees | Front Tees |
|---|---|---|---|
| Length | 6,280 | 6,027 | 5,748 |
| Par | 71 | 71 | 71 |
| Slope (M) | 125 | 122 | 120 |
| Slope (L) | | 115 | 113 |
| USGA Rating (M) | 70.1 | 68.9 | 67.6 |
| USGA Rating (L) | | 73.1 | 71.9 |

| RATES:* | Weekday | Weekend |
|---|---|---|
| E1-E6 | $7/$10 | $7/$10 |
| E7-O3 | $8/$12 | $8/$12 |
| O4-O10 | $9/$14 | $9/$14 |
| DoD NB | $12/$19 | $12/$19 |
| Guests | $16/$24 | $16/$24 |

* Lower rate indicates cost of playing nine holes.

**SUPPORT FACILITIES:**

| | | |
|---|---|---|
| Banquet Facilities | Bar/Lounge | Chipping Area |
| Driving Range | Golf Carts/Power | Golf Carts/Pull |
| Lessons | Lockers | Parking |
| Pro at Facility | Pro Shop | Putting Area |
| Showers | Snack Bar | |

**RESTRICTIONS:** First available tee time on weekdays 0730 hours, twosome required. First available tee time on weekends 0700 hours, threesome required. Dependents may be bumped on weekends. Shirts must have sleeves; shorts must have two side pockets.

**CREDIT CARDS ACCEPTED:** Visa and MasterCard.

# WASHINGTON

## FORT LEWIS GOLF COURSE

Fort Lewis
Fort Lewis, WA 98433-9500

**LOCATION:** Off post. From I-5 Exit #116 to golf course.

**SEASON OF OPERATION:** Year round.

**ELIGIBILITY:** Active/Reservists/Retired/DoD civilians/Dependents/ Guests.

**COURSE INFORMATION:** Address: Fort Golf Course, Bldg 1529, P.O. Box 33175, Fort Lewis, WA 98433. **C-253-967-6522, D-312-357-6522** Dawn-Dusk daily. One 18 hole golf course and one 9 hole golf course.

| 18 hole course | Back Tees | Middle Tees | Front Tees |
|---|---|---|---|
| Length | 6,865 | 6,388 | 5,906 |
| Par | 72 | 72 | 74 |
| Slope | 125 | 1121 | 116 |
| USGA Rating | 72.6 | 70.4 | 68.3 |

| 9 hole course | Back Tees | Middle Tees | Front Tees |
|---|---|---|---|
| Length | 3,423 | 3,338 | 3,167 |
| Par | 37 | 37 | 738 |
| Slope | 126 | 124 | 120 |
| USGA Rating | 72.5 | 71.0 | 69.4 |

| RATES*: | Weekday | Weekend |
|---|---|---|
| E1-E5 | $11 | $11 |
| E6-O3 | $17 | $17 |
| O4+ | $18 | $18 |
| DoD civilians | $18 | $18 |
| Civilian Guests | $23 | $23 |

* Twilight rates also available.

**SUPPORT FACILITIES:**

| | | |
|---|---|---|
| Banquet Facilities | Driving Range | Equipment Rental |
| Golf Carts/Power | Golf Carts/Pull | Lessons |
| Lockers | Pro at Facility | Pro Shop |
| Putting Area | Snack Bar | Showers |
| Soda Vending | Snack Vending | |

**CREDIT CARDS ACCEPTED:** Visa, MasterCard and American Express.

## GALLERY GOLF COURSE

Whidbey Naval Air Station
Oak Harbor, WA 98278-2500

**LOCATION:** Off base. North end of town. Take Highway 20 (Alf Field Road) west for approximately 4 km through two lights past the CPO Club and down the hill to golf course.

**SEASON OF OPERATION:** Year round.

**ELIGIBILITY:** Active/Reservists/Retired/DoD civilians/Dependents/ General Public/Guests.

**COURSE INFORMATION:** Address: Gallery Golf Course, Whidbey NAS, Bldg 130, Oak Harbor, WA 98278-5000. **C-360-257-2178** 0600-2030 hours summer, 0730-1630 hours winter. One 18 hole golf course.

| | Back Tees | Front Tees |
|---|---|---|
| Length | 6,351 | 5,454 |
| Par | 72 | 74 |
| Slope (M) | 122 | 113 |
| Slope (L) | 128 | 118 |
| USGA Rating (M) | 70.1 | 66.0 |
| USGA Rating (L) | 76.1 | 71.1 |

| RATES: | Weekday | Weekend |
|---|---|---|
| E1-E5 | $8 | $10 |
| E6-O3 | $12 | $14 |
| O4+ | $13 | $15 |
| DoD civilians/NAF | $14 | $16 |
| Guests | $20 | $22 |

**SUPPORT FACILITIES:**

| | | |
|---|---|---|
| Lessons | Pro at Facility | Driving Range |
| Putting Area | Chipping Area | Pro Shop |
| Restaurants | Snack Bar | Golf Carts/Power |
| Golf Carts/Pull | Equipment Rental | Lockers |

**CREDIT CARDS ACCEPTED:** Visa, MasterCard, American Express and Discover.

## WHISPERING FIRS GOLF COURSE

McChord Air Force Base
McChord AFB, WA 98438-1304

**LOCATION:** On base. From I-5, take exit 125 to clearly marked base.

**SEASON OF OPERATION:** Year round.

**ELIGIBILITY:** Active/Reservists/Retired/DoD civilians/Dependents/ Guests.

**COURSE INFORMATION:** Address: Whispering Firs Golf Course, Bldg 888, McChord AFB, WA **98438. C-253-984-2053/4928/4929/4930** (automated phone numbers), is patron does not have a PIN number call **C-253-984-4927, C-312-984-4927.** One 18 hole golf course.

| | Back Tees | Middle Tees | Front Tees |
|---|---|---|---|
| Length | 6,646 | 6,345 | 5,818 |
| Par (M) | 72 | 72 | 72 |
| Par (L) | 73 | 73 | 73 |
| Slope | 122 | 119 | 120 |
| USGA Rating | 71.8 | 70.5 | 73.3 |

| RATES: | Weekday | Weekend |
|---|---|---|
| E1-E4 | $9 | $9 |
| E5+ | $16 | $16 |
| DoD civilians | $16 | $16 |
| Civilian Guests | $25 | $25 |

**SUPPORT FACILITIES:**

| | | |
|---|---|---|
| Driving Range | Equipment Rental | Golf Carts/Power |
| Golf Carts/Pull | Lessons | Lockers |
| Pro at Facility | Pro Shop | Putting Area |
| Snack Bar | Showers | |

**RESTRICTIONS:** Golf carts must stay on paths, finish round within 4 hours and 15 minutes, no children under 8 years old allowed on course and driving range and proper attire required.

**CREDIT CARDS ACCEPTED:** Visa and MasterCard.

# WYOMING

### F.E. WARREN GOLF COURSE
Francis E. Warren Air Force Base
Francis E. Warren AFB, WY 82005-2573

COURSE INFORMATION: Address: Golf Course, Bldg 2110, Francis E. Warren AFB, WY 82005. **C-307-773-3556.** One 18 hole golf course. Driving Range, Equipment Rental, Golf Carts, Lessons, Lockers, Pro Shop, Putting Area, Snack Bar.

# UNITED STATES POSSESSIONS

## GUAM

### ADMIRAL NIMITZ GOLF COURSE
Guam Naval Computer & Telecommunications Area Master Station
FPO AP 96540-1157

COURSE INFORMATION: Address: Admiral Nimitz Golf Course, MWR Department, PSC 488, P.O. Box 109, FPO AP 96537-1807. **C-671-344-5936.** One 18 golf course.

### PALM TREE GOLF COURSE
Andersen Air Force Base
APO AP 96543-4003

COURSE INFORMATION: Address: Palm Tree Golf Course, 633 SVS/SVBG, Unit 14003 Box 28, APO AP 96543. **C-671-362-4653** 0730-1730 hours Mon-Fri, 0600-1930 hours Sat-Sun. One 18 hole golf course; Par: 70. Pro Shop.

## PUERTO RICO

### FORT BUCHANAN GOLF COURSE
Fort Buchanan
Fort Buchanan, PR 00934-5007

COURSE INFORMATION: Address: Fort Buchanan Golf Course, Bldg 171, Fort Buchanan, PR 00934. **C-787-273-3980.** One 9 hole golf course.

### ROOSEVELT ROADS GOLF COURSE
Roosevelt Roads Naval Station
FPO AA 34051-3591

COURSE INFORMATION: Address: Roosevelt Roads Golf Course, Bldg 1211, Roosevelt Roads, PSC 1008 Box 3015, FPO AA 34051-3015. **C-787-865-4851** 0630-1830 daily. One 9 hole golf course. Driving Range, Equipment Rental, Golf Carts/Power, Golf Carts/Pull, Lockers, Pro at Facility, Pro Shop. *Note: $3.335 million golf course addition has been approved in the Fiscal Year 1998 MWR Major and Minor Construction Program.*

# FOREIGN COUNTRIES

## CANADA

### GLACIER GREENS GOLF CLUB
Comox Canadian Forces Base
Lazo, British Columbia V0R 2K0

LOCATION: On base. Just before main gate turn right then take first left onto Knight Road. Continue straight to golf course.

SEASON OF OPERATION: Year round.

ELIGIBILITY: Active/Reservists/Retired/DoD civilians/Dependents/Guests.

COURSE INFORMATION: Address: Glacier Greens Golf Club, CFB Comox, Lazo, British Columbia V0R 2K0. **C-250-339-6515.** One 18 hole golf course.

| | |
|---|---|
| Length | 6,303 |
| Par | 71 |
| Slope | 128 |
| USGA Rating | 70.5 |

| RATES: | Weekday | Weekend |
|---|---|---|
| Enlisted | $13 (9), $20 (18) | $13 (9), $20 (18) |
| Officers | $13 (9), $20 (18) | $13 (9), $20 (18) |
| DoD civilians | $13 (9), $20 (18) | $13 (9), $20 (18) |
| Civilian Guests | $20 | $30 |

SUPPORT FACILITIES:

| | | |
|---|---|---|
| Driving Range | Golf Carts/Power | Golf Carts/Pull |
| Lessons | Pro at Facility | Pro Shop |
| Putting Area | | |

CREDIT CARDS ACCEPTED: Visa and MasterCard.

### TWIN RIVERS GOLF CLUB
Petawawa Canadian Forces Base
Petawawa, Ontario K8H 2X3

LOCATION: On base. From I-417 E or W, exit at Petawawa. Clearly marked. From main gate, take first right and follow to the marina.

SEASON OF OPERATION: Spring, Summer and Fall.

ELIGIBILITY: Active/Reservists/Retired/DoD civilians/Dependents/Guests.

COURSE INFORMATION: Address: Twin Rivers Golf Club, Bldg Q103, Petawawa CFB, Ontario, Canada K8H 2X3. **C-613-687-5331/8294** 0700-2000 hours daily. One 18 hole golf course.

| | Back Tees | Front Tees |
|---|---|---|
| Length | 6,560 | 5,200 |
| Par | 72 | 72 |
| Slope | 127 | |
| USGA Rating | 71.0 | 70.5 |

*Twin Rivers Golf Club, continued*

| RATES: | Weekday | Weekend |
|---|---|---|
| All | $11 (9), $20 (18) | $15 (9), $25 (18) |

**SUPPORT FACILITIES:**

| | | |
|---|---|---|
| Banquet Facilities | Bar/Lounge | Driving Range |
| Equipment Rental | Golf Carts/Power | Golf Carts/Pull |
| Lessons | Lockers | Pro at Facility |
| Pro Shop | Putting Area | Restaurants |
| Showers | Snack Bar | Soda Vending |

**CREDIT CARDS ACCEPTED:** Visa and MasterCard.

# GERMANY

## BAMBERG GOLF CLUB

Bamberg Community
APO AE 09139-5000

**COURSE INFORMATION:** Address: Bamberg Golf Club, APO AE 09139-0033. **C-011-49-951-400-113, D-314-469-7583.** One 9 hole golf course.

## GARMISCH AFRC GOLF COURSE

Garmisch Armed Forces Recreation Camp
APO AE 09053-5000

**LOCATION:** Off post. Take Autobahn A95/E-6 south from Munich to Garmisch.

**SEASON OF OPERATION:** Apr-Oct.

**ELIGIBILITY:** Active/Reservists/Retired/DoD civilians/Dependents/NATO Forces/Guests.

**COURSE INFORMATION:** Address: AFRC-Garmisch Golf Course, Unit 24501, APO AE 09053. **C-011-49-8821-2473, D-314-440-2626** 0800-1800 daily. One 9 hole golf course.

| | Back Tees | Front Tees |
|---|---|---|
| Length | 6,522 | 5,964 |
| Par | 72 | 72 |
| Slope | | |
| USGA Rating | 72.0 | 72.0 |

| RATES: | Weekday | Weekend |
|---|---|---|
| E1-E5 | $5 | $7 |
| E5+ | $10 | $12 |
| NATO Forces | $10 | $12 |
| Guest (NON-ID holding) | $20 | $30 |

**SUPPORT FACILITIES:**

| | | |
|---|---|---|
| Banquet Facilities | Chipping Area | Driving Range |
| Equipment Rental | Golf Carts/Pull | Lessons |
| Pro at Facility | Pro Shop | Putting Area |
| Restaurants | Snack Bar | |

**CREDIT CARDS ACCEPTED:** Visa, MasterCard, American Express, Discover and Diners'.

## GRAFENWOEHR GOLF COURSE

Grafenwoehr Community
APO AE 09114-5000

**COURSE INFORMATION:** Address: Grafenwoehr Golf Course, APO AE 09114-5000. **C-011-9641-83-6116, D-314-379-6116.** One 9 hole golf course; Par 68*, Slope 11* (information based on 18 hole game). Bar/Lounge, Driving Area, Golf Carts/Pull, Lessons, Lockers, Pro Shop, Putting Area.

## HEIDELBERG GOLF CLUB

Heidelberg Community
APO AE 09102-5000

**LOCATION:** Off post. Autobahn A6 to Exit #6, then continue to right at first stop light. Continue straight to sign for "Golf Club" then turn left to club.

**SEASON OF OPERATION:** Year round.

**ELIGIBILITY:** Active/Reservists/Retired/DoD civilians/Dependents/NATO Forces/Guests.

**COURSE INFORMATION:** Address: Heidelberg Golf Club, CMR 419, Box 1908, APO AE 09102. **C-011-49-6202-53767, D-314-379-6139** 0700-2000 hours Mon-Fri and 0600-2000 hours Sat-Sun summer, 0800-1700 hours daily winter. One 18 hole golf course.

| | Back Tees | Middle Tees | Front Tees |
|---|---|---|---|
| Length | 6,378 | 5,943 | 5,176 |
| Par | 72 | 72 | 72 |
| Slope | 128 | 124 | 117 |
| USGA Rating | 70.6 | 68.7 | 69.0 |

| RATES: | Weekday | Weekend |
|---|---|---|
| E1-E4 | $7 | $11 |
| E5+ | $14 | $22 |
| DoD civilian | $14 | $22 |

**SUPPORT FACILITIES:**

| | | |
|---|---|---|
| Banquet Facilities | Chipping Area | Driving Range |
| Equipment Rental | Golf Carts/Power | Golf Carts/Pull |
| Lessons | Pro at Facility | Pro Shop |
| Putting Area | Restaurants | Soda Vending |

**CREDIT CARDS ACCEPTED:** Visa, MasterCard and American Express.

## KITZINGEN GOLF COURSE

Kitzingen Community
APO AE 09031-5000

**COURSE INFORMATION:** Address: Kitzingen Golf Course, Larson Barracks, APO AE 09031. **C-011-49-9321-702-609.** One 9 hole golf course; Par 72, Slope 113; USGA Rating 72.0.

## RHEINBLICK GOLF COURSE

Wiesbaden Base Support Battalion
APO AE 09096-5000

**LOCATION:** Off post. From Frankfurt, take Autobahn A3 towards Koln to Wiesbaden Exit to Autobahn A66. Continue on A66 to Frauenstein Exit. Continue through Frauenstein to left immediately after city limit to golf course.

*GERMANY-ITALY*
*Rheinblick Golf Course, continued*

**SEASON OF OPERATION:** Apr1-31 Oct.

**ELIGIBILITY:** Active/Retired/DoD civilians/Dependents/Guests.

**COURSE INFORMATION:** Address: Rheinblick Golf Course, ATTN: Business Operations Division, 221st BSB Unit 29646-5000, APO AE 09096. **C-0611-428118/420675, D-314-336-2791/2816.** One 18 hole golf course.

|  | Back Tees | Front Tees |
|---|---|---|
| Length | 6,644 | 5,708 |
| Par | 72 | 72 |
| Slope | 134 | 129 |
| USGA Rating | 72.0 | 72.9 |

| **RATES:** | Weekday | Weekend |
|---|---|---|
| E1-E6 | $10 | $15 |
| E5+ | $15 | $23 |
| DoD civilians | $15 | $23 |
| Guest | $25 | $35 |

**SUPPORT FACILITIES:**

| | | |
|---|---|---|
| Banquet Facilities | Chipping Area | Driving Range |
| Equipment Rental | Golf Carts/Power | Golf Carts/Pull |
| Lessons | Lockers | Pro at Facility |
| Pro Shop | Putting Area | Showers |
| Snack Bar | | |

**CREDIT CARDS ACCEPTED:** Visa, MasterCard and American Express.

# ROLLING HILLS GOLF COURSE
Baumholder Community
APO AE 09034-5000

**COURSE INFORMATION:** Address: Rolling Hills Golf Course, Bldg 8888, 55774 Baumholder, APO AE 09034. **C-011-49-6783-67299.** One 9 hole golf course. Equipment Rental, Pro Shop, Snack Bar.

# STUTTGART GOLF COURSE
Stuttgart Community
APO AE 09131-5000

**LOCATION:** Off post. B-27 north to Ludwigsburg to Pattonville exit then immediate right. Continue straight 2 miles to course on left.

**SEASON OF OPERATION:** Year round.

**ELIGIBILITY:** Active/Reservists/DoD civilians/Dependents/Guests.

**COURSE INFORMATION:** Address: Stuttgart Golf Course, NSAST, CMR 447, APO AE 09154. **C-011-49-7141-879-151.** One 18 hole golf course.

|  | Back Tees | Front Tees |
|---|---|---|
| Length | 6,850 | 6,150 |
| Par | 73 | 73 |
| Slope | 127 | 124 |
| USGA Rating | 71.9 | 71.7 |

| **RATES:** | Weekday | Weekend |
|---|---|---|
| E1-E4 | $9 (9), 12 (18) | $11 (9), $14 (18) |
| E5-O3 | $8 (9), $14 (18) | $10 (9), $18 (18) |
| O4+ | $12 (9), $14 (18) | $16 (9), $18 (18) |

| DoD civilians | Same as Military Equivalent |
|---|---|
| Guests | Same as Sponsor |

**SUPPORT FACILITIES:**

| | | |
|---|---|---|
| Banquet Facilities | Bar/Lounge | Chipping Area |
| Driving Range | Equipment Rental | Golf Carts/Pull |
| Lessons | Lockers | Pro at Facility |
| Pro Shop | Putting Area | Restaurants |
| Showers | | |

**CREDIT CARDS ACCEPTED:** Visa and MasterCard.

# WOODLAWN GOLF COURSE
Ramstein Air Base
APO AE 09094-5000

**LOCATION:** On base. Adjacent to Mannheim-Saarbrucken Autobahn A6/E-12. Take the Flugplatz Ramstein exit. East and west gates are within two miles of exit.

**SEASON OF OPERATION:** Year round.

**ELIGIBILITY:** Active/Reservists/Retired/DoD civilians/Dependents/Guests.

**COURSE INFORMATION:** Address: Woodlawn Golf Course, 86 SVS/SVBG, Unit 3240, Box 535, APO AE 09094. **C-06371-47-5975, D-314-480-5975** 0700-2000 hours Apr-Oct, 0800-1700 hours Nov-Feb. One 18 hole golf course.

|  | Back Tees | Front Tees |
|---|---|---|
| Length | 6,044 | 5,089 |
| Par | 70 | 71 |
| Slope | 122 | 119 |
| USGA Rating | 67.2 | 68.4 |

| **RATES:** | Weekday | Weekend |
|---|---|---|
| E1-E4 | $10 | $12 |
| E5+ | $13 | $16 |
| DoD civilians | $13 | $16 |
| Guest (Non-DoD) | $40 | $50 |

**SUPPORT FACILITIES:**

| | | |
|---|---|---|
| Banquet Facilities | Bar/Lounge | Chipping Area |
| Driving Range | Equipment Rental | Golf Carts/Power |
| Golf Carts/Pull | Lessons | Lockers |
| Pro at Facility | Pro Shop | Putting Area |
| Restaurants | Showers | Snack Bar |
| Snack Vending | Soda Vending | |

**RESTRICTIONS:** Children under six not allowed on course, only two people may ride in powered golf carts, each player must have a set of clubs, drink coolers not allowed on course, no fivesomes and maximum playing time two hours per nine holes.

**CREDIT CARDS ACCEPTED:** Visa and MasterCard.

# ITALY

## ALPINE GOLF COURSE
Aviano Air Base
APO AE 09601-5260

*Alpine Golf Course, continued*

**COURSE INFORMATION:** Address: Golf Course, Bldg 1399, Aviano AB, APO AE 09601. **C-011-39-434-667386** 0700-2030 hours summer, 0800-1700 hours winter. One 9 hole golf course. Pro Shop, Snack Bar. *Note: A $0.358 million golf course irrigation project has been approved in the Fiscal Year 1998 MWR Major and Minor Construction Program.*

## CARNEY PARK GOLF COURSE
Admiral Carney Park
FPO AE 09619-1013

**LOCATION:** On post. On the west coast of Italy, seven miles southwest of Naples.

**SEASON OF OPERATION:** Year round.

**ELIGIBILITY:** Active/Reservists/Retired/DoD civilians/Dependents/Guests.

**COURSE INFORMATION:** Address: Carney Park Golf Course, Bldg 550, FPO AE 09622-0009. **C-011-39-81-526-4296.** One 9 hole golf course.

| RATES: | Weekday | Weekend |
|---|---|---|
| Enlisted | $10 | $12.50 |
| Officers | $10 | $12.50 |
| Guests | $10 | $12.50 |

**SUPPORT FACILITIES:**

| | | |
|---|---|---|
| Driving Range | Pro Shop | Putting Area |
| Snack Bar | | |

**CREDIT CARDS ACCEPTED:** Visa, MasterCard, American Express, Discover and Diners'.

# JAPAN

## ATSUGI GOLF COURSE
Atsugi Naval Air Facility
FPO AP 96306-1232

**COURSE INFORMATION:** Address: Atsugi Golf Course, MWR Department, PSC 477 Box 20, FPO AP 96306-1220. **C-011-81-46-777-6749.** One 18 hole golf course.

## BANYAN TREE GOLF COURSE
Kadena Air Base
APO AP 96368-5134

**COURSE INFORMATION:** Address: Banyan Tree Golf Course, 18 MWRSS/MWBG, Unit 5135, Box 10, APO AP 96368-5135. **C-011-81-6117-34-1528.** One 18 hole golf course. Driving Range, Pro Shop.

## CAMP ZAMA GOLF COURSE
Camp Zama
APO AP 96343-5006

**COURSE INFORMATION:** Camp Zama Golf Course, Honshu, Unit 45001, APO AP 96343. **C-011-814-6256-8474, D-315-263-4966.** One Par 72, 18 hole golf course. Bar/Lounge, Driving Range, Pro Shop, Restaurants. *Note: $2.905 million new golf maintenance facility has been approved in the Fiscal Year 1998 MWR Major and Minor Construction Program.*

## GOSSER MEMORIAL GOLF CLUB
Misawa Air Base
APO AP 96319-5021

**LOCATION:** On base. From main gate to left on Falcon Drive, then continue for approximately 4 miles to golf club.

**SEASON OF OPERATION:** Apr-Dec.

**ELIGIBILITY:** Active/Reservists/Retired/DoD civilians/Dependents/Guests.

**COURSE INFORMATION:** Address: Gosser Memorial Golf Club, 35th SVS/SVBG, APO AP 96319-5000. **D-315-226-9000** 0600-1800 hours daily. One 18 hole golf course.

| | Frontside Tees | Backside Tees |
|---|---|---|
| Length | 6,033 | 5,863 |
| Par | 71 | 71 |
| Slope | 124 | 122 |
| USGA Rating | 69.2 | 68.4 |

| RATES: | Weekday | Weekend |
|---|---|---|
| Enlisted | $6.50-$10 | $6.50-$10 |
| Officers | $10 | $10 |
| Guests | $10 | $10 |

**SUPPORT FACILITIES:**

| | | |
|---|---|---|
| Lessons | Driving Range | Chipping Area |
| Pro Shop | Restaurants | Bar/Lounge |
| Snack Bar | Vending Machines | Soft Drink Machines |
| Golf Carts/Power | Golf Carts/Pull | Equipment Rental |
| Lockers | Showers | |

**CREDIT CARDS ACCEPTED:** Visa and MasterCard.

## TAMA HILLS GOLF CLUB
Yokota Air Base
APO AP 96328-5123

**COURSE INFORMATION:** Address: Tama Hills Golf Club, 374 SPTG/SVBG, Unit 5119, APO AP 96328. **C-011-81-425-52-2511.** One 18 hole golf course. Golf Carts/Power, Lessons, Pro Shop, Restaurants, Snack Bar. *Note: A $1.444 million new club house, a $0.260 million golf maintenance facility and a $0.290 golf equipment storage facility have been approved in the Fiscal Year 1998 MWR Major and Minor Construction Program.*

## TORII PINES GOLF COURSE
Torii Station
APO AP 96376-5115

**LOCATION:** On base. Located on Okinawa. Off Highway 58 north to Highway 6.

**SEASON OF OPERATION:** Year round.

**ELIGIBILITY:** Active/Reservists/Retired/Dependents/Guests.

**COURSE INFORMATION:** Address: Torii Pines Golf Course, MWR Recreation Division, PSC 561, P.O. Box 911 FPO AP 96310. **C-011-81-827-214171 ext 3402, D-315-253-3402** 0800-1900 hours weekdays, 0700-1900 hours weekends and holidays. One 9 hole golf course.

*JAPAN-KOREA*
*Torii Pines Golf Course, continued*

### Summer Greens

|  | Frontside Tees | Backside Tees |
|---|---|---|
| Length | 2,526 | 2,571 |
| Par | 68 | 68 |
| Slope | N/A | N/A |
| USGA Rating | 67.0 | 67.0 |

*Note: Play 9 hole course twice for 18 hole game by using different tees.*

### Winter Greens

|  | Frontside Tees | Backside Tees |
|---|---|---|
| Length | 2,454 | 2,482 |
| Par | 68 | 68 |
| Slope | N/A | N/A |
| USGA Rating | 67.0 | 67.0 |

*Note: Play 9 hole course twice for 18 hole game by using different tees.*

| RATES: | Weekday | Weekend |
|---|---|---|
| E1-E5 | $3 | $4 |
| E6+ | $5 | $6 |
| DoD civilians | $5 | $6 |
| Guests | Same as Sponsor | |

**SUPPORT FACILITIES:**

| | | |
|---|---|---|
| Lessons | Pro at Facility | Driving Range* |
| Putting Area | Chipping Area | Practice Cage |
| Pro Shop | Restaurants | Bar/Lounge |
| Banquet Facilities | Vending Machines | Soft Drink Machines |
| Golf Carts/Pull | Equipment Rental | Lockers |
| Showers** | | |

* Night use only.
** Available starting in summer 1999.

**CREDIT CARDS ACCEPTED:** Visa, MasterCard, American Express, Discover and Diners'.

# KOREA

## EVERGREEN GOLF CLUB
Camp Henry/Walker
APO AP 96219-0562

**LOCATION:** On base. Located in city of Taegu, which is in the valley bounded on the north by the Palgong Mountains and on the south by the Nakdong River. Taegu to adjacent to Highway 1 and is 200 miles south of Seoul.

**SEASON OF OPERATION:** Year round.

**ELIGIBILITY:** Active/DoD civilians/Dependents/Guests.

**COURSE INFORMATION:** Address: Evergreen Golf Club, Bldg S-230, COD, ADCFA DCA, 20th Support Group, Unit 15494, APO AP 96218-0562. **C-011-82-53-470-4628/4601** 0530-1900 hours summer, 0600-1800 hours winter. One 9 hole golf course.

|  | Frontside Tees* | Backside Tees* |
|---|---|---|
| Length | 2,636 | 2,415 |
| Par | 34 | 36 |
| USGA Rating | 66.0 | 66.0 |

* Refers to first 9 holes played (Frontside) and second 9 holes played (Backside) for complete 18 hole game.

| RATES: | Weekday | Weekend |
|---|---|---|
| E1-E4 | $1 | $2 |
| E5-E6 | $2 | $3 |
| E7-E9 | $7 | $8 |
| O1-O3 | $8 | $9 |
| O4+ | $9 | $10 |
| DoD civilians | $7-$9 | $8-$10 |

**SUPPORT FACILITIES:**

| | | |
|---|---|---|
| Chipping Area | Driving Range | Golf Carts/Pull |
| Lessons | Lockers | Pro Shop  Putting |
| Area | Showers | |

**CREDIT CARDS ACCEPTED:** Visa, MasterCard and American Express.

## SUNG NAM GOLF CLUB
Yongsan Army Garrison
APO AP 96205-0177

**LOCATION:** Off post. Take shuttle from Commiskey's on South Post.

**SEASON OF OPERATION:** Year round.

**ELIGIBILITY:** Active/Reservists/Retired/DoD civilians/Guests.

**COURSE INFORMATION:** Address: Sung Nam Golf Club, Bldg 5800, HQ 34th Support Group, PSC 303, Box 48, APO AP 96204-0048. **D-315-736-3483/3490** seasonal hours. One 18 hole golf course.

|  | Frontside Tees | Backside Tees |
|---|---|---|
| Length | 7,012 | 6,478 |
| Par | 72 | 72 |
| Slope | 136 | 130 |
| USGA Rating | 73.2 | 70.7 |

| RATES: | Weekday | Weekend |
|---|---|---|
| Enlisted | $7-$12 | $9-$16 |
| Officers | $12-$20 | $16-$24 |
| Civilians | $75 | $87.50 |
| Guests | $75 | $87.50 |

**SUPPORT FACILITIES:**

| | | |
|---|---|---|
| Lessons | Driving Range | Pro Shop |
| Restaurants | Bar/Lounge | Snack Bar |
| Vending Machines | Soft Drink Machines | Golf Carts/Power |
| Golf Carts/Pull | Equipment Rental | Lockers |
| Showers | | |

**RESTRICTIONS:** Soft spike shoes only.

**CREDIT CARDS ACCEPTED:** Visa, MasterCard and American Express.

## WEST WINDS GOLF COURSE
Kunsan Air Base
APO AP 96264-2102

**LOCATION:** On base. On the west central coast of the Republic of Korea. Exit from Seoul-Pusan Expressway 1, directions to AB clearly marked.

**SEASON OF OPERATION:** Year round.

**ELIGIBILITY:** Active/Reservists/Retired/DoD civilians/Guests.

*West Winds Golf Course, continued*

**COURSE INFORMATION:** Address: Kunsan Air Base, West Winds Golf Course, Bldg 1904, 8SVS/SVBG, Unit 2105, APO, AP 96264-2105. **C-011-82-654-470-5435, D-315-782-5435** 0700-Dusk, Mon and Wed-Sun, closed Tue. One 9 hole golf course.

| Length | 4,169 |
|---|---|
| Par | 66 |
| Slope | 94 |
| USGA Rating | 63.0 |

| RATES: | Weekday | Weekend |
|---|---|---|
| E1-E4 | $5 | $5.50 |
| E6-E9 | $7 | $8 |
| O1-O4 | $8 | $9 |
| O5-O10 | $9 | $10 |
| DoD civilians | Same as Military Equivalent | |
| Guests | $23 | $30 |

**SUPPORT FACILITIES:**

| | | |
|---|---|---|
| Chipping Area | Driving Range | Golf Carts/Pull |
| Lessons | Lockers | Pro Shop |
| Putting Area | Showers | |

**CREDIT CARDS ACCEPTED:** Visa and MasterCard.

# PANAMA

## FORT CLAYTON GOLF COURSE
Fort Clayton
APO AA 34004-5000

**COURSE INFORMATION:** Address: Fort Clayton Golf Course, APO AA 34004. **C-011-507-282-4511, C-011-507-287-5455.** One 18 hole golf course. *Note: Course information taken from Military Living Publications' history files. Information may not be complete or current.*

## HOROKO GOLF COURSE
Howard Air Force Base
APO AA 34001-5000

**COURSE INFORMATION:** Address: Horoko Golf Course, APO AA 34001-5000. **C-011-507-283-6346, D-313-283-6346.** One 18 hole golf course; Length approximately 6,800 yards, Par 72.

# PORTUGAL

## TERCEIRA ISLAND GOLF COURSE
Lajes Field (Azores)
APO AE 09720-5000

**COURSE INFORMATION:** Address: Terceira Island Golf Course, 65 SVS/SVBG, PSC 76, APO AE 09720. **C-011-351-95-92299.** One 18 hole golf course; Length: 5,995 yards; Par: 70. Pro at Facility, Pro Shop. *Note: Course information taken from Military Living Publications' history files. Information may not be complete or current.*

# SPAIN

## CAPTAIN JAKE DENNIS MEMORIAL GOLF COURSE
Rota Naval Station
FPO AE 09645-5500

**COURSE INFORMATION:** Address: Jake Dennis Memorial Golf Course, MWR Department, Box 14, PSC 819, FPO AE 09645-2000. **C-011-34-568-22260.** One 18 hole golf course. Chipping Area, Driving Range, Equipment Rental, Golf Carts/Power, Golf Carts/Pull, Lessons, Pro at Facility, Pro Shop, Putting Area.

# TURKEY

## HODJA LAKES GOLF COURSE
Incirlik Air Base
APO AE 09824-0175

**COURSE INFORMATION:** Address: Hodja Lakes Golf Course, 39 SVS/SVBG, Unit 8915 Box 165, APO AE 09824-5615. **C-011-90-322-316-6249.** One 9 hole golf course. Equipment Rental, Golf Carts/Power, Golf Carts/Pull, Lessons, Lockers, Pro Shop, Snack Bar. *Note: Course information taken from Military Living Publications' history files. Information may not be complete or current.*

# UNITED KINGDOM

## RAF LAKENHEATH GOLF COURSE
RAF Lakenheath
APO AE 09464-0105

**COURSE INFORMATION:** Address: RAF Lakenheath Golf Course, Bldg 1298, APO AE 09464. **C-011-44-1638-522223.** One 9 hole golf course. Equipment Rental, Pro Shop. *Note: Course information taken from Military Living Publications' history files. Information may not be complete or current.*

# SECTION III - Military Marinas

# UNITED STATES

## ALABAMA

### LAKE MARTIN MAXWELL/ GUNTER RECREATION AREA

Maxwell Air Force Base
Maxwell AFB, AL 36112-5000

**LOCATION:** Off base. Located near Dadeville, southeast of Birmingham, northeast of Montgomery. From I-85 north of Montgomery take exit 32, north on AL-49 to Stillwaters Road (County Road 34) and proceed 2.5 miles to recreation area.

**SEASON OF OPERATION:** Year round.

**ELIGIBILITY:** Active/Reservists/Retired/DoD civilians working at Maxwell or Gunter.

**MARINA INFORMATION:** Address: Lake Martin/Maxwell Gunter Rec Area, 350 Air Force Road, Dadeville, AL 36853-5000. **C-256-825-6251** 0700-1900 hours summer, 0800-1700 hours winter. Slips (12: 10 are 20'L, 2 are 25'L), Launching Ramps (1).

| RATES: | SLIPS |
|--------|-------|
| Monthly | $45 |

**MARINA SERVICES:**
| | |
|---|---|
| Boat Rental | Gas |

**MARINA SUPPORT FACILITIES:**
| | | |
|---|---|---|
| Laundry | Mail | Parking |
| Showers | | |

**CREDIT CARDS ACCEPTED:** Visa and MasterCard.

### MAXWELL/GUNTER RECREATION AREA

Maxwell Air Force Base
Maxwell AFB, AL 36112-5000

**LOCATION:** On base. Take I-65 N or S to northern bypass AL-152, six miles east to exit on US-231, continue west one mile to AFB. Also, from I-85, follow signs and take eastern bypass north one mile to US-231, then west one mile to AFB.

**SEASON OF OPERATION:** Year round.

**ELIGIBILITY:** Active/Reservists/Retired/DoD civilians/Dependents.

**MARINA INFORMATION:** Address: Maxwell/Gunter Recreation Area, 350 Air Force Road, Dadeville, AL 36853-5000. **C-256-825-6251** 0700-1900 hours. Slips (15: 10'L, 20'W, 8'D), Transient Slips (5), Launching Ramps. E (20/30/50A)/W hookups.

| RATES: | SLIPS |
|--------|-------|
| Monthly | $45 |
| Transient | Free |

**MARINA SERVICES:**
| | |
|---|---|
| Boat Rental | Gas |

**MARINA SUPPORT FACILITIES:**
| | | |
|---|---|---|
| Laundry | Mail | Parking |
| Sewage Dump | Showers | |

**CREDIT CARDS ACCEPTED:** Visa, MasterCard and Services Club Card.

## ALASKA

### GLASS PARK YACHT CLUB/MARINA

Fort Wainwright
Fort Wainwright, AK 99703-6600

**MARINA INFORMATION:** Address: Glass Park Yacht Club/Marina, 4241 Homer Spit Road, Homer, AK 99703-5000. **C-1-800-478-7847, C-907-353-6349.**

## CALIFORNIA

### DEL MAR MARINA

Camp Pendleton Marine Corps Base
Camp Pendleton MCB, CA 92055-5019

**LOCATION:** On base. From San Diego, I-5 N to Camp Pendleton main gate. From I-15, take Fallbrook exit, follow signs to Fallbrook and go through Fallbrook Naval Weapons Station gate to mainside Camp Pendleton. From I-5, get off at Oceanside Harbor drive. Head west to Del Mar gate.

**SEASON OF OPERATION:** Year round.

**ELIGIBILITY:** Active/Reservists/Retired/DoD civilians/Dependents/MWR Personnel.

**MARINA INFORMATION:** Address: Del Mar Marina, MWR-Recreation Div, BX 555020, Camp Pendleton, CA 92055-5000. **C-760-725-SAIL (7245) or C-760-725-2820** 0900-1730 spring/summer, 0800-1630 hours fall/winter. Slips (53: up to 45'L), Moorings (3).E (30A)/W/S/CATV/Telephone hookups.

| RATES: | SLIPS |
|--------|-------|
| Monthly | $6 per foot |
| Transient | $.50 per foot/per day/min $15 |

**MARINA SERVICES:**
| | | |
|---|---|---|
| Boat Lessons | Boat Rental | Boat Repair* |
| Dry Docks | Gas/Diesel* | Pump Station* |

* Available at Oceanside Harbor.

**MARINA SUPPORT FACILITIES:**
| | | |
|---|---|---|
| Laundry | Parking | Sewage Dump* |
| Showers | Soda Vending | |

* Available at Oceanside Harbor.

**CREDIT CARDS ACCEPTED:** None.

# FIDDLER'S COVE MARINA & RV PARK

Coronado Naval Amphibious Base
San Diego, CA 92155-5000

**LOCATION:** Off base. From the north, on I-5 in San Diego, take Coronado Bridge exit; cross bridge and go south (left) on CA-75 (Orange Avenue). From the south on I-5, exit to Palm Avenue W, which later becomes CA-75.

**SEASON OF OPERATION:** Year round.

**ELIGIBILITY:** Active/Reservists/Retired/DoD civilians/Dependents.

**MARINA INFORMATION:** Address: Fiddler's Cove Marina, c/o NAS NI MWR, Dept Code 92, Box 357081, San Diego, CA 92135-7081. **C-619-435-8788/4700** 24 hours daily. Slips (264: 30'-45'L, 11'-15'W), Transient Slips, Moorings (140), Launching Ramps. E (120V/30A)/W hookups.

| RATES: | SLIPS |
|---|---|
| Monthly | $5 per foot |
| Transients | $10 |

**MARINA SERVICES:**

| | | |
|---|---|---|
| Boating Lessons | Boat Rental | Pump Station |

**MARINA SUPPORT FACILITIES:**

| | | |
|---|---|---|
| Parking | Sewage Dump | Showers |
| Snack Bar | Soda Vending | |

**CREDIT CARDS ACCEPTED:** Visa and MasterCard.

# McCLELLAN MARINA

McClellan Air Force Base
McClellan AFB, CA 95652-1226

**MARINA INFORMATION:** Address: McClellan Marina, 652 ABG/SVRO, 5931 Dudley Blvd, Bldg 684, McClellan AFB, CA 95652-1226. **C-916-643-2738** 1000-2000 hours Mon-Thu, 0700-1800 hours Fri, 0700-1500 hours Sat, Sun and holidays.

# MONTEREY YACHT CLUB/MARINA

Monterey Naval Postgraduate School
Monterey, CA 93943-5027

**MARINA INFORMATION:** Address: Monterey Yacht Club/Marina, NSA Code 45 NSAMB, Monterey NPGS, Monterey, CA 93943-5027. **C-408-656-2159.**

# PRESIDIO YACHT CLUB

Travis Air Force Base
Travis AFB, CA 94535-2045

**LOCATION:** Off base. From Highway 101, Alexande Avenue exit at north end of Golden Gate Bridge to Fort Baker.

**SEASON OF OPERATION:** Year round.

**ELIGIBILITY:** Active/Reservists/Retired/DoD civilians/Dependents/ Federal Employees.

**MARINA INFORMATION:** Address: Presidio Yacht Club, Bldg 679, Fort Baker, Sausalito, CA 94965-5000. **C-415-332-2319** 0930-1700 hours Mon-Fri, 0930-1600 hours Sat-Sun. E-mail: pyc@hooked.net. HP: www.wenet.net/npyc/. Slips (75: 20'-40'L, 8'14'W, 3'-10'D), Transient Slips (5), E (110V/30A)/W hookups.

| RATES: | SLIPS |
|---|---|
| Monthly | $3 per foot |
| Transients | $10 per day |

**MARINA SERVICES:**

| | | |
|---|---|---|
| Boating Lessons | Boat Rental | Boat Repair |
| Gas | | |

**MARINA SUPPORT FACILITIES:**

| | | |
|---|---|---|
| Banquet Facilities | Bar/lounge | Parking |
| Snack Bar | | |

**CREDIT CARDS ACCEPTED:** None.

# SAN DIEGO MCRD BOATHOUSE

San Diego Marine Corps Recruit Depot
San Diego, CA 92140-5023

**LOCATION:** On base. From I-5 S take the Old Town exit. Take a right on Witherby Street to Gate 4. From Gate 4, take a right on Tripoli, a left on Santo Domingo Street, a right on Chosin Avenue, a left on Henderson, a right on Dunlap Road, and a left on Neville Road to marina.

**SEASON OF OPERATION:** Year round.

**ELIGIBILITY:** Active/Reservists/Retired/DoD civilians/Dependents.

**MARINA INFORMATION:** Address: San Diego MCRD Boathouse, 3800 Chosin Avenue, Bldg 131, San Diego, CA 92140-5196. **C-619-524-5269** 0600-1800 hours Sat-Sun, holidays, 0730-1800 hours Mon-Fri summer; 0730-1700 hours Sat-Sun, holidays, 0730-1700 Mon-Fri. Fax: C-619-524-5025. Slips (90: 25'L, 14'W, 10'D), Transient Slip (1), Moorings (2), Launching Ramps. E (120V)/W hookups.

| RATES: | SLIPS |
|---|---|
| Daily | $12 |
| Monthly | $5 per foot/$125 minimum |
| Transients | $12 |

**MARINA SERVICES:**

| | | |
|---|---|---|
| Boating Lessons | Boat Rental | Pump Station (Diesel) |
| Pump Station (Gas) | | |

**MARINA SUPPORT FACILITIES:**

| | | |
|---|---|---|
| Banquet Facilities | Bar/Lounge | Mail |
| Parking | Restaurants | Sewage Dump |
| Showers | Snack Bar | Snack Vending |
| Soda Vending | | |

**CREDIT CARDS ACCEPTED:** None.

# CONNECTICUT

## THAMES VIEW MARINA

New London Naval Submarine Base
Groton, CT 06349-5000

*CONNECTICUT-FLORIDA*

**LOCATION:** On base. From I-95 N or S take exit 86 to CT-12 N. Go left on Crystal Lane, right to main gate. Clearly marked. From main gate, turn right just before light and follow to end. Turn left through parking lot, then right onto Shark Blvd. Take the first left past the golf course and follow one-lane road under railroad overpass into Marina parking lot.

**SEASON OF OPERATION:** 1 May-1 Nov.

**ELIGIBILITY:** Active/Reservists/Retired/DoD civilians/Dependents.

**MARINA INFORMATION:** Address: Thames View Marina, MWR, Box 14, Groton, CT 06349-5000. **C-860-694-3164** 1000-2000 hours summer, 1000-1700 hours spring and fall. Slips (60: up to 45'L), Transient Slips (2), Moorings (10). E/W hookups.

| RATES: | SLIPS |
|---|---|
| Daily | $.55-$.80 per foot |
| Annually | $36 per foot |

**MARINA SERVICES:**

| | |
|---|---|
| Boating Lessons | Boat Rental |

**MARINA SUPPORT FACILITIES:**

| | | |
|---|---|---|
| Laundry | Parking | Showers |

**CREDIT CARDS ACCEPTED:** Visa, MasterCard, American Express and Discover.

# DISTRICT OF COLUMBIA

## BOLLING AFB MARINA
Bolling Air Force Base
Bolling AFB, DC 20332-0503

**LOCATION:** On base. From I-95 (east portion pf Capital Beltway, I-495) N or S, exit to I-295 N, exit to South Capitol Street and main entrance to Bolling AFB. Also, I-395 (Southeast Freeway) N, exit South Capitol Street, cross Anacostia River on South Capitol Street, main gate to AFB on right. Take MacDill Blvd towards the river, turn left on Arnold Avenue and continue along river to marina.

**SEASON OF OPERATION:** Year round, weather permitting.

**ELIGIBILITY:** Active/Reservists/Retired/DoD civilians/Dependents.

**MARINA INFORMATION:** Address: Bolling AFB Marina, 463 Giovannoli Way, Bldg 90, Bolling AFB, DC 20332-5200. **C-202-767-4651, D-312-297-4651** 0800-1700 hours summer, 0800-1700 Mon-Fri winter. Slips (105: 20'-40'L, 4'-6'W), Transient Slips (10), Launching Ramps. E (30A)/W hookups.

| RATES: | SLIPS |
|---|---|
| Daily | $12 |
| Weekly | $80 |
| Monthly | $4.25 per foot |
| Transients | $12 |

**MARINA SERVICES:**

| | | |
|---|---|---|
| Boat Rental | Boat Repair | Dry Docks |
| Pump Station (Gas) | | |

**MARINA SUPPORT FACILITIES:**

| | | |
|---|---|---|
| Bar/Lounge | Laundry | Mail |
| Parking | Sewage Dump | Showers |
| Snack Vending | Soda Vending | |

**CREDIT CARDS ACCEPTED:** Visa and MasterCard.

## WASHINGTON NAVAL STATION MARINA
Washington Naval Station, Anacostia Annex
Washington, DC 20374-5823

**LOCATION:** On base.

**SEASON OF OPERATION:** Apr-Nov.

**ELIGIBILITY:** Active/Reservists/Retired/DoD civilians/Dependents.

**MARINA INFORMATION:** Address: Washington Naval Station Marina, Bldg 72, 2701 South Capitol Street SW, Washington D.C. 20374-5823. **C-202-433-2265/2068, D-312-288-2269/2068** 24 hours daily. Slips (27), Transient Slips (1). E/W/Telephone hookups.

| RATES: | SLIPS |
|---|---|
| Daily | $5 |
| Weekly | $25 |
| Monthly | $4 per foot |

**MARINA SERVICES:**
Gas/Diesel

**MARINA SUPPORT FACILITIES:**

| | |
|---|---|
| Restaurant | Showers |

**CREDIT CARDS ACCEPTED:** Visa, MasterCard and American Express.

# FLORIDA

## COON'S CREEK RECREATION AREA
MacDill Air Force Base
MacDill AFB, FL 33621-5313

**LOCATION:** On base. From I-75 N or S, take FL-618 exit west to FL-573 exit to main gate.

**SEASON OF OPERATION:** Year round.

**ELIGIBILITY:** Active/Reservists/Retired/DoD civilians/Dependents/Guests/Members.

**MARINA INFORMATION:** Address: Coon's Creek Recreation Area, 10303 Marina Bay Drive, MacDill AFB, FL 33621-5000. **C-1-800-821-4982, C-813-840-6919, C-813-828-4982, D-312-968-4985** 0700-1900 hours Mon-Fri, 0700-2000 hours Sat-Sun, holidays summer; 0700-1730 hours winter. Slips (27: 30'L), Transient Slips (6), Launching Ramps. E hookup.

| RATES: | SLIPS |
|---|---|
| Monthly | $3 per foot |
| Transients | $3.50 with storage |
| Transients | $4 without storage |

**MARINA SERVICES:**

| | | |
|---|---|---|
| Boat Rental | Dry Docks | Pump Station (Gas) |

*Coon's Creek Recreation Area, continued*

**MARINA SUPPORT FACILITIES:**

| Laundry | Mail | Parking |
|---|---|---|
| Sewage Dump | Ship Store | Showers |
| Snack Bar | | |

**CREDIT CARDS ACCEPTED:** Visa and MasterCard.

## HIDDEN COVE MARINA

Panama City Coastal Systems Station Naval Surface Warfare Center
Panama City, FL 32407-7001

**LOCATION:** On base. Located on US-98 at the foot of the Hathaway Bridge in Panama City Beach. Clearly marked. The marina is .5 miles from the main gate on the left.

**SEASON OF OPERATION:** Year round.

**ELIGIBILITY:** Active/Reservists/Retired/DoD civilians/Dependents.

**MARINA INFORMATION:** Address: Hidden Cove Marina, 6703 W Highway 98, Panama City, FL 32407-7001. **C-850-234-4402, D-312-436-5900.** Slips (13: 20'L, 10'W, 4'D), Launching Ramps. E (110V/15A)/W hookups.

**RATES:**          SLIPS
Monthly           $70

**MARINA SERVICES:**

| Boat Rental | Dry Docks | Gas |
|---|---|---|

**MARINA SUPPORT FACILITIES:**

| Mail | Parking | Sewage Dump |
|---|---|---|
| Showers | Soda Vending | Snack Vending |

**CREDIT CARDS ACCEPTED:** Visa, MasterCard, American Express and Discover.

## MANATEE COVE MARINA

Patrick Air Force Base
Patrick AFB, FL 32925-3341

**LOCATION:** On base. Take I-95 N or S to exit 73 (Wickam Road) east, three miles to State Road 404 (Pineda Causeway), six miles, left on A-1A, three miles to AFB. Take the first right after main gate to stop sign, turn left. Follow road and turn right at sign for Yacht Club/Golf Course.

**SEASON OF OPERATION:** Year round.

**ELIGIBILITY:** Active/Reservists/Retired.

**MARINA INFORMATION:** Address: Manatee Cove Marina, Bldg 1493, 876 Marina Road, P.O. Box 254065, Patrick AFB, FL 32925-0065. **C-407-494-7455/7456, D-312-854-7456.** Slips (234 wet, 185 dry), Transient Slips, Launching Ramps. E/W hookup.

**MARINA SERVICES:**

| Dry Docks | Pump Station (Gas) |
|---|---|

**MARINA SUPPORT FACILITIES:**

| Bar/Lounge | Parking | Ship Store |
|---|---|---|
| Showers | Snack Bar | |

**CREDIT CARDS ACCEPTED:** Visa, MasterCard and American Express.

## MULBERRY COVE MARINA

Jacksonville Naval Air Station
Jacksonville, FL 32212-5000

**LOCATION:** On base. Access from US-17 (Roosevelt Blvd) south of Jacksonville, near intersection with I-295. Enter main gate on Yorktown Avenue. Turn right on Ranger Street and continue to end of street and marina.

**SEASON OF OPERATION:** Year round.

**ELIGIBILITY:** Active/Reservists/Retired/DoD and NAF civilians/Dependents.

**MARINA INFORMATION:** Address: Mulberry Cove Marina, Bldg 1072, Box 14, Jacksonville NAS, FL 32212-5000. **C-904-542-3260, D-312-942-3260** 0730-1830 hours Mon-Fri, 0730-1930 hours Sat-Sun summer; 0800-1730 hours Mon-Fri, 0730-1730 hours Sat-Sun winter. Slips (57: any L, 7'D), Transient Slips (15), Moorings (55), Launching Ramps. E (15A)/W hookups. *Note: 30 amp electric power upgrade project scheduled for completion by 2000.*

| RATES: | SLIPS | BUOY |
|---|---|---|
| Daily | $6-$7 | $4-$5 |
| Weekly | $42-$49 | $28-$35 |
| Monthly | $3.50 per foot | $35-$37 |
| Annually | $3 per foot | $350-370 |
| Transients | $6-$7 | $4-$5 |

**MARINA SERVICES:**

| Boating Lessons | Boat Rental | Dry Docks |
|---|---|---|
| Pump Station (Gas) | | |

**MARINA SUPPORT FACILITIES:**

| Bar/Lounge | Restaurant | Parking |
|---|---|---|
| Sewage Dump | Showers | Ship Store |

**CREDIT CARDS ACCEPTED:** Visa, MasterCard and American Express.

## PENSACOLA MARINAS

Pensacola Naval Air Station
Pensacola, FL 32508-5217

**LOCATION:** On base. I-10 to exit 2. South on Pine Forest Road. Turn right on highway 173 (Blue Angel Parkway) which will lead south 12 miles and enter back entrance to NASP. From main gate (Warrington), proceed left at fork. Continue to credit union building, turn left and follow road to end.

**SEASON OF OPERATION:** Year round.

**ELIGIBILITY:** Active/Reservists/Retired/DoD civilians/Dependents.

**MARINA INFORMATION:** Address: Pensacola Marinas, Co Code 22000, 190 Radford Blvd, Pensacola, FL 32508-5217. **C-850-452-4152** (Bayou Grande) 0800-1800 hours Thu-Mon summer, 0800-1700 hours Thu-Mon winter, **C-850-452-3369** (Sherman Cove) 0700-1800 hours Mon, Thu, Fri. Marinas (2), Wet Slips (216), Transient Slips, Moorings (15), Launching Ramps. E (30/50A)/W hookups.

**Sherman Cove Marina**
A smaller marina offering boat rentals, dry-wet storage, launching ramps, fishing gear, boating lessons, snacks and soft drinks. Off the Intracoastal Waterway, five minutes to the Gulf of Mexico.

*FLORIDA-GEORGIA*
*Pensacola Marinas, continued*

**Bayou Grande Marina**

| RATES: | SLIPS | MOORINGS |
|---|---|---|
| Monthly | $3.25 per foot | $43 |
| Transient | $10 daily | |

**MARINA SERVICES:**

| | | |
|---|---|---|
| Boating Lessons | Boat Rental | Pump Station |

**MARINA SUPPORT FACILITIES:**

| | | |
|---|---|---|
| Banquet Facilities | Laundry | Showers |
| Soda Vending | | |

**CREDIT CARDS ACCEPTED:** Visa, MasterCard and American Express.

## SIGSBEE MARINA
Key West Naval Air Station
Key West NAS, FL 33040-9037

**LOCATION:** On base. From US-1, exit at mile marker 8, Boca Chica Key. Sigsbee Park is off Kennedy Avenue. Clearly marked.

**SEASON OF OPERATION:** Year round.

**ELIGIBILITY:** Active/Reservists/Retired/DoD civilians/Dependents.

**MARINA INFORMATION:** Address: Sigsbee Marina, Bldg V-3000, Key West, FL 33040-5000. **C-305-293-4434, D-312-483-4434** 0700-1800 hours. Slips (1 wet, 22 dry: 28'L, 10'W, 2'D), Transient Slips (1 wet, 2 dry), Moorings (1 wet), Launching Ramps. *Note: A $1.948 million marina expansion has been approved in the Fiscal Year 1998 MWR Major and Minor Construction Program.*

| RATES: | SLIPS |
|---|---|
| Daily | $5 wet, 2 week minimum; $1 dry |
| Monthly | $25 dry |

**MARINA SERVICES:**

| | | |
|---|---|---|
| Boat Rental | Dry Docks | Pump Station (Gas) |

**MARINA SUPPORT FACILITIES:**

| | | |
|---|---|---|
| Parking | Ship Store | Snack Bar |

**CREDIT CARDS ACCEPTED:** Visa, MasterCard and Discover.

## TYNDALL MARINA
Tyndall Air Force Base
Tyndall AFB, FL 32403-5717

**MARINA INFORMATION:** Address: Tyndall Marina, 325 SVS/SVRO 31, Bldg 2699, Tyndall AFB, FL 32403-5717. **C-850-283-4473, C-850-283-3059** 1000-2200 Mon-Tue, 1000-2400 hours Wed-Thu, 1000-0200 hours Fri, 0800-2200 hours Sat, 0800-2200 hours Sun and holidays. Slips (wet and dry).

**MARINA SERVICES:**
Boat Rental

**MARINA SUPPORT FACILITIES:**
Snack Bar

# GEORGIA

## FORT GORDON MARINA
Fort Gordon
Ford Gordon, GA 30905-5000

**LOCATION:** Off post. From I-20 west of Augusta, take exit 61 Appling to GA-47 N to end (Washington Road). Left on Washington Road to recreation area.

**SEASON OF OPERATION:** Year round.

**ELIGIBILITY:** Active/Reservists/Retired/DoD civilians.

**MARINA INFORMATION:** Address: Fort Gordon Recreation Area, P.O. Box 67, Appling, GA 30802-5000. **C-706-541-1057** 0800-1830 hours summer, by reservation winter. Slips (96: 12'L, 18'W or 10'L, 24'W), Transient Slips (8), Launching Ramps (2). E/W hookups.

| RATES: | SLIPS |
|---|---|
| Monthly | $50 uncovered |
| | $75 covered |
| Transient | $5 daily |

**MARINA SERVICES:**

| | |
|---|---|
| Boat Rental | Gas |

**MARINA SUPPORT FACILITIES:**

| | | |
|---|---|---|
| Laundry | Mail | Parking |
| Showers | Snack Bar | |

**CREDIT CARDS ACCEPTED:** Visa, MasterCard and American Express.

## LAKE ALLATOONA ARMY RECREATION AREA
Fort McPherson
Fort McPherson, GA 30330-1049

**LOCATION:** Off post. From Atlanta, take I-75 N to exit 121. Take a left on Highway 92, go right on top of the bridge, road ends into Highway 293, turn left. Follow Highway 293, turn right immediately after crossing the lake onto Sandtown. Clearly marked.

**SEASON OF OPERATION:** Year round.

**ELIGIBILITY:** Active/Reservists/Retired/DoD civilians/Dependents.

**MARINA INFORMATION:** Address: Lake Allatoona Army Recreation Area, 40 Old Sandtown Road, Cartersville, GA 30121-5000. **C-770-974-3413/9420** 0800-1900 hours Fri, Sat, 0800-1700 hours Sun-Thu summer; 0800-1600 hours winter. Fax: C-770-974-1278. Slips (16: 20'L, 10'W'; 18-24'L, 10'W), Transient Slips, Launching Ramps. E hookup.

| RATES: | SLIPS |
|---|---|
| Daily | $3 |
| Monthly | $65-$90 based on length and season |

**MARINA SERVICES:**

| | |
|---|---|
| Boat Rental | Pump Station (Gas) |

**MARINA SUPPORT FACILITIES:**

| | | |
|---|---|---|
| Laundry | Parking | Showers |

**CREDIT CARDS ACCEPTED:** Visa, MasterCard and American Express.

## LOTTS ISLAND MARINA
Hunter Army Airfield
Savannah, GA 31409-5000

**MARINA INFORMATION:** Address: Lotts Island Marina, Outdoor Rec, Bldg 8454 Shooting Star Road, Hunter Army Airfield, Savannah, GA 31409-5000. **C-912-352-5916/5772, D-312-870-5722.**

## UCHEE CREEK ARMY CAMPGROUND/MARINA
Fort Benning
Fort Benning, GA 31905-5000

**LOCATION:** On post. Located on south side of Columbus. Accessible from US-80, I-185, US-27, US-280 and US-165. Clearly marked.

**SEASON OF OPERATION:** Year round.

**ELIGIBILITY:** Active/Reservists/Retired/DoD civilians/Dependents.

**MARINA INFORMATION:** Address: Uchee Creek Army Campground/Marina, Bldg 1707, Gillespie Street, P.O. Box 53323, Fort Benning, GA 31905-5000. **C-706-545-7238/4053** 0900-1800 Mon-Thu, 0700-1900 Fri-Sun. Slips (16: 10'L, 20'W covered; 10'L 28'W uncovered), Transient Slips (20), Launching Ramps (2). E (120V/20A)/W hookups.

**RATES:** SLIPS
| | |
|---|---|
| Daily | $6-$10 |
| Weekly | $35-$50 |
| Monthly | $70-$120 |
| Annually | $180-$315 |

**MARINA SERVICES:**
| | |
|---|---|
| Boat Rental | Gas |

**MARINA SUPPORT FACILITIES:**
| | | |
|---|---|---|
| Banquet Facilities | Laundry | Parking |
| Ship Store | Showers | Soda Vending |
| Snack Bar | Snack Vending | |

**CREDIT CARDS ACCEPTED:** Visa, MasterCard and American Express.

## WORLD FAMOUS NAVY LAKE SITE
Atlanta Naval Air Station
Marietta, GA 30060-5099

**LOCATION:** Off base. From I-75, take exit 122 (Emerson), go south for 3.5 miles. Clearly marked.

**SEASON OF OPERATION:** Year round.

**ELIGIBILITY:** Active/Reservists/Retired/DoD civilians/Dependents.

**MARINA INFORMATION:** Address: World Famous Navy Lake Site, 166 Sandtown Road, Cartersville, GA-30121-5000. **C-770-974-6309** 0900-1900 hours summer, 0900-1700 hours winter. Slips (78: 68 are 10'L, 24'W and 10 are 12'L, 24'W), Transient Slips (6), Launching Ramps (2).

**RATES:** SLIPS
| | |
|---|---|
| Quarterly | $251 |
| Annually | $921 |
| Transients | $2.50 daily |

**MARINA SERVICES:**
| | | |
|---|---|---|
| Boat Rental | Dry Docks | Gas |

**MARINA SUPPORT FACILITIES:**
| | | |
|---|---|---|
| Parking | Showers | Soda Vending |
| Snack Vending | | |

**CREDIT CARDS ACCEPTED:** Visa, MasterCard, American Express and Discover.

# HAWAII

## HICKAM HARBOR RECREATION AREA
Hickam Air Force Base
Hickam AFB, HI 96853-5385

**LOCATION:** On base. On the south coast of Oahu, next to Pearl Harbor. Follow H-1 signs to Pearl Harbor/Hickam AFB, take Hickam exit through main gate (vehicles without military pass must check in). Follow signs to Hickam Harbor/Beach.

**SEASON OF OPERATION:** Year round.

**ELIGIBILITY:** Active/Reservists/Retired/DoD civilians/Dependents.

**MARINA INFORMATION:** Reservations required for sailing lessons and some rentals. Address: Recreation Services, 15 SVS/SVRO, 900 Hangar Avenue, Hickam AFB, HI 96853-5246. **C-808-449-6980/5215, D-315-430-5215** 0900-1800. Slips (20: 26'L, 5'D), Moorings (10: 36'L), Launching Ramps (1). E hookup.

**RATES:** SLIPS
| | |
|---|---|
| Daily | $5 |
| Weekly | $20 |
| Monthly | $65 |
| Transients | $5 |

**MARINA SERVICES:**
| | | |
|---|---|---|
| Boating Lessons | Boat Rental | Dry Docks |
| Gas | | |

**MARINA SUPPORT FACILITIES:**
| | | |
|---|---|---|
| Banquet Facilities | Bar/Lounge | Parking |
| Restaurants | Snack Bar | Snack Vending |
| Soda Vending | | |

**CREDIT CARDS ACCEPTED:** Visa and MasterCard.

## KANEOHE BAY MARINA
Kaneohe Marine Corps Base
Kaneohe Bay, HI 96863-3002

**LOCATION:** On base. From Honolulu, take H-3 N to the front gate of base. At first stop light after main gate, make a left. Go to stop sign and turn left. At D Street turn left, Bldg 1698.

**SEASON OF OPERATION:** Year round.

**ELIGIBILITY:** Active/Reservists/Retired/DoD civilians/Dependents/MWR Personnel.

**MARINA INFORMATION:** Address: MWR Marina, P.O. Box 63073, Kaneohe Bay, HI 96863-3073. **C-808-254-7667** 0800-1800 hours Thu-Mon. Slips (40: 20'-30'L, 10'-12'W, 15'D), Transient Slips, Moorings (20), Launching Ramp. E (125V/30A)/W hookups.

**RATES:** SLIPS
| | |
|---|---|
| Monthly (20') | $65 |
| Monthly (30') | $75 |
| Transients | $5 daily |

*HAWAII-INDIANA*
*Kaneohe Bay Marina, continued*

**MARINA SERVICES:**

| | | |
|---|---|---|
| Boating Lessons | Boat Rental | Dry Docks |
| Gas/Diesel | Pump Station | |

**MARINA SUPPORT FACILITIES:**

| | | |
|---|---|---|
| Parking | Sewage Dump/nearby | Showers |
| Snack Vending | Soda Vending | |

**CREDIT CARDS ACCEPTED:** Visa, MasterCard and American Express.

## RAINBOW BAY MARINA

Pearl Harbor Naval Station
Pearl Harbor, HI 96860-6000

**LOCATION:** Off base. Off H-1 adjacent to Honolulu International Airport. Take the Pearl Harbor exit, enter Nimitz Gate. Follow signs to Arizona Memorial and marina is nearby.

**SEASON OF OPERATION:** Year round.

**ELIGIBILITY:** Active/Reservists/Retired/DoD civilians/Dependents.

**MARINA INFORMATION:** Address: Rainbow Bay Marina, 57 Arizona Memorial Drive, Slip 101, Honolulu, HI 96818-5000. **C-808-471-9680** 0930-1800 hours. Slips (80: up to 55'L, 16' beam, 10' draft), Transient Slips (8), Moorings (30), Launching Ramps. E (20/30A)/W/CATV/ Telephone hookups.

| RATES: | SLIPS |
|---|---|
| Monthly | $3 per foot |
| Transients | $8 daily, up to 3 days |

**MARINA SERVICES:**

| | | |
|---|---|---|
| Boating Lessons | Boat Rental | Dry Docks |
| Pump Station (Diesel) | Pump Station (Gas) | |

**MARINA SUPPORT FACILITIES:**

| | | |
|---|---|---|
| Bar/Lounge | Laundry | Mail |
| Parking | Restaurants | Showers |

**CREDIT CARDS ACCEPTED:** None.

# IDAHO

## STRIKE DAM MARINA

Mountain Home Air Force Base
Mountain Home AFB, ID 83648-5237

**LOCATION:** Off base. From I-84 east of Boise, follow signs to Mountain Home AFB (on ID-67) and on to C.J. Strike Reservoir.

**SEASON OF OPERATION:** Apr-Sep.

**ELIGIBILITY:** Active/Reservists/Retired/DoD civilians/Dependents.

**MARINA INFORMATION:** Address: Strike Dam Marina, 775 Pine Street, Mountain Home AFB, ID 83648-5000. **C-208-828-2723/6288, D-312-728-6333** 1200-2000 hours Fri, 0800-2000 hours Sat-Sun. Launching Ramps.

**MARINA SERVICES:**

| | |
|---|---|
| Boat Rental | Pump Station (Gas) |

**MARINA SUPPORT FACILITIES:**

| | |
|---|---|
| Parking | Snack Bar |

**CREDIT CARDS ACCEPTED:** Visa and MasterCard.

# ILLINOIS

## GREAT LAKES MARINA

Great Lakes Naval Training Center
Great Lakes, IL 60088-5000

**LOCATION:** On base. From I-94 N or US-41 N to IL-137 (Buckley Road) to NTC. Clearly marked. After passing though the main gate, turn right. At the next intersection, turn left and look for signs.

**SEASON OF OPERATION:** Mid Apr-mid Oct.

**ELIGIBILITY:** Active/Reservists/Retired/DoD civilians/Dependents/ Civilians.

**MARINA INFORMATION:** Address: Great Lakes Marina, 2701 Sheridan Road, Bldg 13, Great Lakes, IL 60088-5021. **C-847-688-5417** 0800-1900 hours. Fax: C-847-688-5421. Slips (125), Transient Slips (129), Launching Ramps. E (30A)/W hookups.

| RATES: | SLIPS |
|---|---|
| Daily | $.50 per foot |
| Annually | $42 per foot |
| Transient | $.50 per foot |

**MARINA SERVICES:**

| | | |
|---|---|---|
| Boating Lessons | Boat Rental | Dry Docks |
| Pump Station (Gas) | Travel Lift | |

**MARINA SUPPORT FACILITIES:**

| | | |
|---|---|---|
| Parking | Sewage Dump | Ship Store |
| Showers | Soda Vending | Snack Bar |
| Snack Vending | | |

**CREDIT CARDS ACCEPTED:** Visa, MasterCard, American Express and Discover.

# INDIANA

## CRANE MWR CAMPGROUND MARINA

Crane Division, Naval Surface Warfare Center
Crane, IN 47522-5001

**MARINA INFORMATION:** Address: MWR Campgrounds, Bldg 1909, 300 Highway 361, Crane, IN 47522-5001. **C-812-854-1368, D-312-482-1368** 0600-1800 hours.

**CREDIT CARDS ACCEPTED:** Visa and MasterCard.

# LOUISIANA

## TOLEDO BEND MARINA

Fort Polk
Fort Polk, LA 71459-5227

**MARINA INFORMATION:** Address: 1310 Army Rec Road, Florien, LA 71429-4830. **C-1-888-718-9088.** No slips, no moorings.

**MARINA SERVICES:**
Boating Lessons　　　Boat Rental

**MARINA SUPPORT FACILITIES:**
Snack Bar

**CREDIT CARDS ACCEPTED:** Visa, MasterCard and American Express.

# MARYLAND

## ANNAPOLIS NAVAL STATION MARINA

United States Naval Academy/Annapolis Naval Station
Annapolis, MD 21402-5073

**LOCATION:** On base. Thirty-five miles northeast of Washington DC. US-50 to MD-450. Clearly marked.

**SEASON OF OPERATION:** May-Sep.

**ELIGIBILITY:** Active/Reservists/Retired/DoD civilians/Dependents/ Guests.

**MARINA INFORMATION:** Address: Annapolis NS Marina, MWR Department, 89 Bennion Road, Annapolis, MD 21402-5000. **C-410-293-2058/3731, D-312-281-2058/3731** 0800-1700 hours Mon-Thu, 0800-2000 Fri-Sun. Slips (16: 32'L, 14'W, 15'D), Transient Slips, Moorings (38), Launching Ramps (1). E (115V/30A)/W hookups.

| RATES: | SLIPS |
| --- | --- |
| Daily | $15 |
| Weekly | $70 |
| Monthly | $104 |
| Annually | $730 |

**MARINA SERVICES:**
Boating Lessons　　　Boat Rental　　　Dry Docks
Travel Lift

**MARINA SUPPORT FACILITIES:**
Parking　　　　　　Showers　　　　　Soda Vending

**CREDIT CARDS ACCEPTED:** None.

## GOOSE CREEK/WEST BASIN MARINA

Patuxent River Naval Air Station
Patuxent River NAS, MD 20670-1132

**MARINA INFORMATION:** Address: Goose Creek/West Basin Marina, P.O. Box 724, Patuxent River NAS, MD 20670-5000. **C-301-342-3573.**

# MISSISSIPPI

## KEESLER OUTDOOR RECREATION/MARINA

Keesler Air Force Base
Keesler AFB, MS 39534-2554

**LOCATION:** On base. From I-10, take I-110 toward Biloxi. Take Highway 90 W for three miles to a right on White Avenue. Clearly marked.

**SEASON OF OPERATION:** Year round.

**ELIGIBILITY:** Active/Reservists/Retired/DoD civilians/Dependents.

**MARINA INFORMATION:** Address: Bldg 6726, 625 Marina Drive, Keesler AFB, MS 35534-2623. **C-228-377-3186/3160, D-312-597-3186/3160** 0700-1800 hours. Slips (86 wet, 25 dry: 24'-32'L), Transient Slips, Launching Ramps (2). E (110/115V)/W hookups.

| RATES: | SLIPS |
| --- | --- |
| Daily | $3 |
| Monthly | $35-$40 |
| Annually | $190-$225 |

**MARINA SERVICES:**
Boating Lessons　　　Boat Rental　　　Dry Docks
Gas　　　　　　　　Travel Lift

**MARINA SUPPORT FACILITIES:**
Parking　　　　　　Restaurants　　　Ship Store
Soda Vending　　　Snack Vending

**CREDIT CARDS ACCEPTED:** Visa and MasterCard.

# MISSOURI

## LAKE OF THE OZARKS RECREATION AREA

Fort Leonard Wood
Fort Leonard Wood, MO 65473-5000

**LOCATION:** Off post. From I-70, take Highway 63 to Jefferson City, then take US-54 to Linn Creek area, left at State Road A for six miles to Freedom, left on Lake Road A-33 for approximately five miles to recreation area. From I-44 northeast of Springfield, MO-7 northwest to Richland, right on State Road A and travel approximately 20 miles to Freedom, right on Lake Road A-33 approximately five miles to recreation area.

**SEASON OF OPERATION:** Apr-Oct.

**ELIGIBILITY:** Active/Reservists/Retired/DoD civilians/Dependents.

**MARINA INFORMATION:** Address: Fort Leonard Wood LORA, Route 1, Box 380, Linn Creek, MO 65052-5000. **C-573-346-5640** 0800-1830 hours. Slips (20: 10 are 10'L, 18'W and 10 are 10'L, 24'W), Launching Ramps.

| RATES: | SLIPS |
| --- | --- |
| Daily | $5 |
| Monthly | $65-$80 (depends on slip) |

**MARINA SERVICES:**
Boat Rental　　　　　Gas

*MISSOURI-NORTH CAROLINA*
*Lake of the Ozarks Recreation Area, continued*

**MARINA SUPPORT FACILITIES:**
Parking                    Soda Vending

**CREDIT CARDS ACCEPTED:** Visa, MasterCard and American Express.

# NEW HAMPSHIRE

## PORTSMOUTH NAVAL SHIPYARD MARINAS
Portsmouth Naval Shipyard
Portsmouth NSY, NH 03804-5000

**LOCATION:** On base. from I-95, cross Piscataqua River Bridge into Maine. Take exit 2 to US-236, to US-1 S, to US-203, left on Walker Street to gate 1. From I-95 S, take exit 2 a,d follow above directions. located on an island between Portsmouth and Kittery, ME.

**SEASON OF OPERATION:** 15 May-31 Oct.

**ELIGIBILITY:** Active/Reservists/Retired/DoD civilians/Dependents/Federal Employees.

**MARINA INFORMATION:** Reservations accepted 1 Apr-30 Apr. Address: Portsmouth Naval Shipyard, 40 Bldg H-10, Portsmouth, NH 03804-5000. **C-207-438-1583/1280** 0800-1600 hours. Marinas (2), Slips (52: 20', 24', 30'L), Transient Slips (2), Moorings (83), Launching Ramps (2-1 small). E (120V/15A)/W hookups. *Note: Electric hookups on transient pier only.*

**Back Channel Marina**

| RATES: | SLIPS | MOORINGS |
|---|---|---|
| Seasonal (20') | $800-$1200* | $525-$685 (35') |
| Seasonal (24') | $880-$1280* | $585-$710 (36'-39') |
| | | $625-$785 (40') |
| Transient | $15-$20 daily | $10 daily |

* Depends on rank.

**Sound Basin Marina**

| RATES: | SLIPS | MOORINGS |
|---|---|---|
| Seasonal (20') | $800-$1200* | $525-$685 (35') |
| Seasonal (30') | $1000-$1400* | $585-$710 (36'-39') |
| Seasonal (40') | $1200-$1600* | $625-$785 (40') |
| Transient | $15-$20 daily | $10 daily |

* Depends on rank. Camel available for $800.

**MARINA SERVICES:**
Boating Lessons            Boat Rental

**MARINA SUPPORT FACILITIES:**
Banquet Facilities         Bar/Lounge           Parking
Snack Bar                  Soda Vending

**CREDIT CARDS ACCEPTED:** None.

*Note: Visa may be accepted in the future.*

# NORTH CAROLINA

## CAMP LEJEUNE MARINAS
Camp Lejeune Marine Corps Base
Camp Lejeune MCB, NC 28542-0004

**LOCATION:** Gottschalk Marina is located off Julian C. Smith Drive, near the entrance to the second marine divisions headquarters. Courthouse Bay Marina is located at the Marine Corps Engineering School.

**MARINA INFORMATION:** Address: MWR Attn: Gottschalk, 1401 West Road, Camp Lejeune, NC 28542-5000. **C-910-451-8307, C-910-451-7386, D-312-484-8307.** Slips.

**Gottschalk Marina**
**MARINA SERVICES:**
Boating Lessons            Boat Rental          Boat Repair
Gas/Diesel

**Courthouse Bay Marina**
**MARINE SERVICES**
Boating Lessons            Boat Rental          Gas/Diesel

## NEW RIVER MARINA
New River Marine Corps Air Station
New River MCAS, NC 228540-0128

**MARINA INFORMATION:** Address: MWR, Bldg AS2800, P.O.Box 4128, New River MCAS, NC 28540-0128. **C-910-451-6578.** Slips.

**MARINA SERVICES:**
Boat Rental

**MARINA SUPPORT FACILITIES:**
Banquet Facilities         Soda Vending

## PELICAN POINT MARINA
Cherry Point Marine Corps Air Station
Cherry Point, NC 28533-0022

**LOCATION:** On base. On NC-101, east of US-70, between New Bern and Morehead City.

**SEASON OF OPERATION:** Year round.

**ELIGIBILITY:** Active/Reservists/Retired/DoD civilians/Dependents.

**MARINA INFORMATION:** Address: Pelican Point Marina, Monroe Drive, PSC Box 8009, MCAS Cherry Point, NC 28533-0009. **C-252-466-2762/4874** 1000-1930 hours summer, 1000-1700 hours winter. Slips (89), Transient Slips (2), Launching Ramps (4). E (30A)/W/Telephone hookups.

| RATES: | SLIPS |
|---|---|
| Monthly | $2 per foot |
| Transients | $5 per day |

**MARINA SERVICES:**
Boating Lessons            Boat Rental          Dry Docks
Pump Station

**MARINA SUPPORT FACILITIES:**
Banquet Facilities         Bar/Lounge           Laundry
Parking                    Restaurants          Sewage Dump
Showers                    Snack Bar            Snack Vending
Soda Vending

**CREDIT CARDS ACCEPTED:** Visa and MasterCard.

# RHODE ISLAND

## NAVY SAILING CENTER

Newport Naval Education and Training Center
Newport, RI 02841-5000

**LOCATION:** On base. From north and east, take Route 24 or Route 114 from I-195. Clearly marked. From south and west, take Route 95 to Route 138 E. Clearly marked. Enter at Gate 1 and Sailing Center is on the left.

**SEASON OF OPERATION:** 1 May-31 Oct.

**ELIGIBILITY:** Active/Reservists/Retired/DoD civilians/Dependents.

**MARINA INFORMATION:** Address: Navy Sailing Center, MWR, 1121 Meyercord Avenue, Bldg 17, Newport, RI 02841-1620. **C-401-841-3283** 0800-dusk Sat-Sun, holidays; 1200-dusk Mon-Fri. Slips (120: 25', 30' and 40'L, 10'D), Transient Slips (5), Moorings (30), Launching Ramps. E (120V/30A)/W hookups.

| RATES: | SLIPS | MOORINGS |
|---|---|---|
| Daily | $1.50 per foot | |
| Weekly | $7 per foot | |
| Monthly | $8 per foot | |
| Annually | $44 per foot | |
| Transient | $1.50 per foot | $25 |

**MARINA SERVICES:**

| Boating Lessons | Boat Rental | Pump Station |
|---|---|---|

**MARINA SUPPORT FACILITIES:**

| Banquet Facilities | Bar/Lounge | Laundry |
|---|---|---|
| Parking | Restaurants | Sewage Dump |
| Showers | Soda Vending | |

**CREDIT CARDS ACCEPTED:** None.

# SOUTH CAROLINA

## PARRIS ISLAND MARINA

Parris Island Marine Corps Recruit Depot
Parris Island MCRD, SC 29905-9001

**MARINA INFORMATION:** Address: MWR Marina, Bldg 204, P.O.Box 5100, Parris Island MCRD, SC 29905-5000. **C-803-525-3301/2.**

## SHORT STAY NAVY MARINA

Charleston Naval Weapons Station
Goose Creek, SC 29445-5000

**MARINA INFORMATION:** Address: Short Stay Navy Outdoor Rec Area Marina, 211 Short Stay Road, Moncks Corner, SC 29461-5000. **C-803-761-8353, C-803-764-7601, D-312-794-7601.** Launching Ramp.

**MARINA SERVICES:**
Boat Rental

**MARINA SUPPORT FACILITIES:**

| Laundry | Ship Store | Snack Bar |
|---|---|---|

## WATEREE MARINA

Shaw Air Force Base
Shaw AFB, SC 29152-5023

**MARINA INFORMATION:** Address: Outdoor Rec, P.O. Box 52696, Shaw AFB, SC 29152-5000. **C-803-668-3245/2204.**

**MARINA SERVICES:**
Boat Rental

# TENNESSEE

## ARNOLD AFB MARINA

Arnold Air Force Base
Arnold AFB, TN 37389-5000

**LOCATION:** Off base. From I-24 take exit 117 W toward Tullahoma. Follow signs for recreation areas. Turn left on Pumpins Station Road, turn right at dead end, turn left at stop sign and marina is on the right.

**SEASON OF OPERATION:** Year round.

**ELIGIBILITY:** Active/Reservists/Retired/DoD civilians/Dependents/ DoD contractors.

**MARINA INFORMATION:** Address: Arnold AFB Marina, 4174 Westover Road, Bldg 3058, Tullahoma, TN 37388-5000. **C-931-454-3838, D-312-340-3838** 0800-dusk Fri-Sun and holidays summer, other times by reservation. No slips, drop anchor.

**MARINA SERVICES:**

| Boat Rental | Dry Docks | Pump Station (Gas) |
|---|---|---|

**MARINA SUPPORT FACILITIES:**

| Bar/Lounge | Parking | Restaurants |
|---|---|---|
| Sewage Dump | Soda Vending | Snack Vending |

**CREDIT CARDS ACCEPTED:** Visa and MasterCard.

# TEXAS

## BELTON LAKE OUTDOOR RECREATION BOAT DOCK

Fort Hood
Fort Hood, TX 76544-5005

**LOCATION:** On post. From north, take I-35, bear right after Belton area to Highway 190 W, exit on Loop 121 N. From south on I-35, exit to Loop 121 or take Exit 293A to Highway 190 W and exit to Loop 121. From Fort Hood area, take Martin Drive N and exit to N Nolan Road, turn left at BLORA entrance. Follow main road for approximately 2.5 miles through the park to boat dock.

**SEASON OF OPERATION:** Year round.

**ELIGIBILITY:** Active/Reservists/Retired/DoD civilians/Dependents.

**MARINA INFORMATION:** Address: Belton Lake Outdoor Recreation Boat Dock, Bldg 20120, Fort Hood, TX 76544-5000. **C-254-287-6073/5526, D-312-737-6073/5526** 0600-2030 hours Apr-Oct, 0700-1630 hours Nov-Mar. Slips (58: 20'L, 8'W, 17'D), Transient Slips (4), Moorings (106), Launching Ramps (2). E (110V/30A)/W hookups.

*TEXAS*
*Belton Lake Outdoor Recreation Boat Dock, continued*

| RATES: | SLIPS |
|---|---|
| Daily | $6 |
| Monthly | $60 |
| Annually | $600 |
| Transient | $6 |

**MARINA SERVICES:**

| | | |
|---|---|---|
| Boat Rental | Dry Docks | Pump Station |

**MARINA SUPPORT FACILITIES:**

| | | |
|---|---|---|
| Laundry | Parking | Sewage Dump |
| Showers | Soda Vending | Snack Bar |
| Snack Vending | | |

**CREDIT CARDS ACCEPTED:** Visa, MasterCard, American Express, Diners' and Esprit.

## CORPUS CHRISTI NAS MARINA
Corpus Christi Naval Air Station
Corpus Christi, TX 78419-5000

**LOCATION:** On post. From south gate turn right on E Street, then continue straight to water then left to marina on left side of street.

**SEASON OF OPERATION:** Year round.

**ELIGIBILITY:** Active/Reservists/Retired/DoD civilians/Dependents.

**MARINA INFORMATION:** Address: MWR, Bldg 39, Code 22, Corpus Christi NAS, TX 78419-5000. **C-512-937-5071, 512-939-9054, D-312-861-2267.** Slips (20: 20'L, 12'W, 4'D), No Transient Slips, No Moorings, Launching Ramps (1). E (110V/20A)/W hookups.

| RATES: | SLIPS |
|---|---|
| Daily | $3 |
| Monthly | $40 |
| Annually | $300 |

**MARINA SERVICES:**

| | |
|---|---|
| Boating Lessons | Boat Rental |

**MARINA SUPPORT FACILITIES:**

| | |
|---|---|
| Snack Vending | Soda Vending |

**CREDIT CARDS ACCEPTED:** Visa, MasterCard and American Express.

## FORT SAM HOUSTON REC AREA MARINA
Fort Sam Houston
Canyon Lake, TX 78133-5000

**LOCATION:** On post.Take I-35 to Canyon Lake exit 191. Turn west onto FM 306, and drive approximately 16 miles to Canyon City. Continue another 1.5 miles past the blinking light in Canyon City to Jacob Creek Park Road. Turn left, and the recreation area will be on the right.

**SEASON OF OPERATION:** Year round.

**ELIGIBILITY:** Active/Reservists/Retired/DoD civilians/Dependents.

**MARINA INFORMATION:** Address:Fort Sam Houston Rec Area Marina, 698 Jacobs Creek Park Road, Canyon Lake, TX 78133-5000. **C-1-888-882-9878, C-830-964-4404/3318,** 0700-2000 hours summer, 0800-1800 hours winter. Slips (80: 24'L, 16'W, 6'D), Launching Ramps (2). E (115V/30A)/W hookups. No slips, drop anchor.

| RATES: | SLIPS |
|---|---|
| Daily | $10 |
| Monthly | $60 single/$120 double |

**MARINA SERVICES:**

| | | |
|---|---|---|
| Boat Rental | Dry Docks | Gas/Diesel |
| Pump Station | Sewage Dump | |

**MARINA SUPPORT FACILITIES:**

| | | |
|---|---|---|
| Laundry | Parking | Showers |
| Snack Bar | | |

**RESTRICTIONS:** Park entry fee $4 per car, per day; $30 season permit.

## GOODFELLOW REC CAMP MARINA
Goodfellow Air Force Base
Goodfellow AFB, TX 76908-4304

**LOCATION:** Off base. From all directions, take Route 67 (turns into Loop 306) south of the city to Knickerbocker Road (Ranch Road 584). Proceed south three miles. Turn left on South Concho (left turn is shortly after crossing Lake Nasworthy).

**SEASON OF OPERATION:** Year round.

**ELIGIBILITY:** Active/Reservists/Retired/DoD civilians/Dependents.

**MARINA INFORMATION:** Address: Goodfellow Rec Camp Marina, 1950 South Cancho Drive, San Angelo, TX 76904-5000. **C-912-944-1012** 1000-2100 hours Mon-Thu summer, 1000-1700 Mon-Thu winter. Slips (20: 20'L, 20'W, 6'D), Launching Ramps (1).

**MARINA SERVICES:**

| | | |
|---|---|---|
| Boating Lessons | Boat Rental | Pump Station (Gas) |
| Travel Lift | | |

**MARINA SUPPORT FACILITIES:**

| | | |
|---|---|---|
| Banquet Facilities | Laundry | Parking |
| Sewage Dump | Showers | Snack Bar |

**CREDIT CARDS ACCEPTED:** Visa and MasterCard.

## RANDOLPH OUTDOOR RECREATION AREA - CANYON LAKE
Randolph Air Force Base
Randolph AFB, TX 78150-4537

**LOCATION:** Off base. From I-35 north from San Antonio, through New Braunfels to Canyon Lake Exit. Turn left on Farm Road 306, follow for 16 miles to Canyon City. Go another 1.5 miles past the blinking traffic light to Jacobs Creek Park Road, turn left. Clearly marked.

**SEASON OF OPERATION:** Year round.

**ELIGIBILITY:** Active/Reservists/Retired/DoD civilians/Dependents.

**MARINA INFORMATION:** Address: Randolph Outdoor Recreation Area Canyon Lake, 781 Jacobs Creek Park Road, Canyon Lake, TX 78133-5000. **C-1-800-280-3466, C-830-964-4134/3804.** Slips (42: 20'L, 8' or 10'W, 12'-20'D), Transient Slips (1), Moorings (30), Launching Ramps. E (15/30A)/S/W hookups.

| RATES: | SLIPS | MOORINGS |
|---|---|---|
| Daily | $5 | |
| Monthly | $65.50 | $45 |
| Annually | $725 | $450 |
| Transients | $5 daily | |

*Randolph Outdoor Recreation Area - Canyon Lake*

**MARINA SERVICES:**

| | | |
|---|---|---|
| Boat Rental | Dry Docks | Gas |

**MARINA SUPPORT FACILITIES:**

| | | |
|---|---|---|
| Parking | Sewage Dump | Ship Store |
| Showers | Snack Bar | Snack Vending |
| Soda Vending | | |

**CREDIT CARDS ACCEPTED:** Visa and MasterCard.

## SHIELDS PARK MARINA
Corpus Christi Naval Air Station
Corpus Christi, TX 78419-5021

**MARINA INFORMATION:** Address: Outdoor Recreation, Bldg 1757, Code 22, Corpus Christi NAS, TX 78419-5000. **C-512-937-5071.** Slips, Launching Ramp.

**MARINA SERVICES:**

| | |
|---|---|
| Boat Rental | Gas |

**MARINA SUPPORT FACILITIES:**

Snack Bar

## SOUTHWINDS MARINA ON LAKE AMISTAD
Laughlin Air Force Base
Laughlin AFB, TX 78843-5135

**LOCATION:** Off base. From US-90 north of Del Rio, take Amistad Dam Road (Spur 349) to Recreation area.

**SEASON OF OPERATION:** Year round.

**ELIGIBILITY:** Active/Reservists/Retired/DoD civilians/Dependents.

**MARINA INFORMATION:** Address: Southwinds Marina on Lake Amistad, HCR #3, Box 37J, Del Rio, TX 78840-5000. **C-830-775-5971/7800** 0800-2000 hours summer, 0800-1700 hours winter. Slips (32: 18'L), Transient Slips, Moorings (3), Launching Ramps. E (50A)/W hookups.

**RATES:**

| | SLIPS |
|---|---|
| Daily | $2 |
| Monthly | $35 |
| Annually | $420 |
| Transients | $2 |

**MARINA SERVICES:**

| | | |
|---|---|---|
| Boating Lessons | Boat Rental | Pump Station (Gas) |

**MARINA SUPPORT FACILITIES:**

| | | |
|---|---|---|
| Laundry | Parking | Sewage Dump |
| Showers | Snack Bar | |

**CREDIT CARDS ACCEPTED:** Visa and MasterCard.

# VIRGINIA

## FORT BELVOIR MARINA
Fort Belvoir
Fort Belvoir, VA 22060-5908

**LOCATION:** On post. From I-95 N or S, take exit 163 (Route 1), follow signs to post. Go through Fort Belvoir on Route 1 and take a right onto Route 235 (Mount Vernon Memorial Highway), then turn right at Walker Gate. Inside the gate, turn left on Hudson Road then right to marina.

**SEASON OF OPERATION:** Year round.

**ELIGIBILITY:** Active/Reservists/Retired/DoD civilians.

**MARINA INFORMATION:** Address: Fort Belvoir Marina, 5820 21st Street, Suite 109, Fort Belvoir, VA 22060-5937. **C-703-781-8282, D-312-655-3745** 0900-1800 hours Wed-Sun. Slips (105: 36'L, 14'W), Transient Slips (4), Launching Ramps. E (30A)/W hookups.

**MARINA SERVICES:**

| | | |
|---|---|---|
| Boat Rental | Boat Repair | Dry Docks |
| Pump Station | Travel Lift | |

**MARINA SUPPORT FACILITIES:**

| | | |
|---|---|---|
| Parking | Sewage Dump | Ship Store |
| Soda Vending | | |

**CREDIT CARDS ACCEPTED:** Visa and MasterCard.

## LANGLEY YACHT CLUB/MARINA
Langley Air Force Base
Langley AFB, VA 23665-5000

**MARINA INFORMATION:** Address: 1 SVS/SVRY, 202 Thornell, Langley AFB, VA 23665-5000. **C-757-764-7170/7220** 1000-1730 hours Mon-Fri.

**MARINA SERVICES:**

Boating Lessons

## LITTLE CREEK COVE MARINA
Little Creek Naval Amphibious Base
Norfolk, VA 23521-2231

**LOCATION:** On base. From I-64 take Northampton Blvd exit (US-13) north to Amphibious Base exit, north on Independence Blvd (VA-225) to Gate 5. Also, from Bay Bridge-Tunnel (US-13), take US-60 W to Gate 5.

**SEASON OF OPERATION:** Year round.

**ELIGIBILITY:** Active/Reservists/Retired/DoD civilians/Dependents.

**MARINA INFORMATION:** Address: Little Creek Cove Marina, MWR, Bldg 3624, Norfolk, VA 23521-5007. **C-757-462-7140** 0700-1800 hours summer, 0800-1600 winter. Slips (151), Transient Slips (6), Launching Ramps (6). E (30A)/W hookups.

**RATES:**

| | SLIPS |
|---|---|
| Daily | $3 per foot |
| Weekly | $5 per day |
| Monthly | $3 per foot |
| Annually | $3 per foot |
| Transients | $5 daily |

*VIRGINIA-WASHINGTON*
*Little Creek Cove Marina, continued*

**MARINA SERVICES:**
Pump Station/Diesel       Pump Station/Gas

**MARINA SUPPORT FACILITIES:**
Laundry          Parking          Sewage Dump
Showers          Snack Bar

**CREDIT CARDS ACCEPTED:** Visa, MasterCard, American Express and Discover.

## LUNGA MARINA
Quantico Marine Corps Base
Quantico, VA 22134-5012

**LOCATION:** On base. From the north on I-95 take exit 148 (Quantico USMC Base). West on MCB-4 approximately 7.5 miles to Lunga Reservoir office (.5 miles past FBI Academy).

**MARINA INFORMATION:** Address: Lunga Reservoir, P.O. Box 186, Quantico, VA 22134-5000. **C-703-784-2359/5270.**

**MARINA SERVICES:**
Boat Rental

## NORFOLK NAVAL BASE MARINA
Norfolk Naval Base
Norfolk NAS, VA 23511-2893

**MARINA INFORMATION:** Address: Naval Sailing Center, Rec Department, 9474 Bacon Avenue, Bldg SP-314, Norfolk NAS, VA 23511-2893. **C-757-444-9342, C-757-444-4388.**

## OLD POINT COMFORT MARINA
Fort Monroe
Fort Monroe, VA 23464-6130

**LOCATION:** On post. From I-64 at Hampton, take exit 268. Follow historic sign markers to Fortress Monroe. Right lane at main gate, straight for .5 miles, located on right.

**SEASON OF OPERATION:** Year round.

**ELIGIBILITY:** Active/Reservists/Retired/DoD civilians/Dependents.

**MARINA INFORMATION:** Address: Old Point Comfort Marina, Bldg 207, P.O. Box 51106, Fort Monroe, VA 23651-5000. **C-757-727-4308/54** 0600-1700 hours 15 Apr-8 Sep, 0800-1700 hours 9 Sep-14 Apr. Slip (208: 50'L, 16' Beam), Transient Slips (10), Launching Ramps (1). E (30/50A)/W hookups. No slips, drop anchor.

**RATES:**           SLIPS
Monthly              $4.25 per foot
Annual               $3.68 per foot/per month
Transients           $.80 per foot daily

**MARINA SERVICES:**
Boat Rental          Boat Repair          Pump Station (Diesel)
Pump Station (Gas)   Travel Lift

**MARINA SUPPORT FACILITIES:**
Banquet Facilities   Bar/Lounge           Laundry
Parking              Restaurants          Ship Store
Showers              Sewage Dump

**CREDIT CARDS ACCEPTED:** Visa and MasterCard.

# WASHINGTON

## CRESCENT HARBOR MARINA
Whidbey Island Naval Air Station
Oak Harbor, WA 98278-2500

**LOCATION:** On base. From I-5 N or S, take WA-20 west to Oak Harbor exit, take a right on Clover Valley Road and then right on Langley Blvd to NAS main gate. Marina is located behind Commissary and Exchange.

**SEASON OF OPERATION:** Year round.

**ELIGIBILITY:** Active/Reservists/Retired.

**MARINA INFORMATION:** Address: Crescent Harbor Marina, 1130 W. Storm Lane, NAS Whidbey Island, Oak Harbor, WA 98277-5000. **C-360-257-3355, D-312-820-3355** 0800-1800 hours. Fax: C-360-257-6545. E-mail: marina@whidbey.net. Slips (40: 24'-50'L), Transient Slips (200), Moorings (20), Launching Ramps. W hookup.

**RATES:**           SLIPS
Daily                $.50 per foot
Monthly              $3 per foot
Transients           $.50 per foot

**MARINA SERVICES:**
Boating Lessons      Boat Rental          Boat Repair
Dry Docks            Gas/nearby

**MARINA SUPPORT FACILITIES:**
Parking              Sewage Dump          Snack Bar/nearby

**CREDIT CARDS ACCEPTED:** Visa, MasterCard and Discover.

## EVERETT NAVAL STATION MARINA
Everett Naval Station
Everett, WA 98207-5001

**LOCATION:** On base. From the south, take I-5 N to Broadway, exit 192. Follow Broadway, turn left onto Pacific Avenue, turn right onto West Marine View Drive. Clearly marked. From the north, take I-5 S to exit 198, West Marine View Drive. Clearly marked. After passing through gate, follow Perry Avenue, turn right on Fletcher Way, turn left on Spruance Blvd and the marina is on the right.

**SEASON OF OPERATION:** Year round.

**ELIGIBILITY:** Active/Retired/Reserve.

**MARINA INFORMATION:** Address: Everett NS Marina, 2000 West Marine View Drive, Everett WA 98207-5000. **C-425-304-3918** 0730-1600 hours. Slips (90: 26', 30' and 36'W), Transient Slips (5), Moorings (85), Launching Ramps. E/W hookups.

**RATES:**           SLIPS
Daily                $10
Monthly              $104 (26'), $120 (30'), $144 (36')
Transients           $10

**MARINA SERVICES:**
Boating Lessons      Boat Rental          Pump Station

*Everett NS Marina, continued*

**MARINA SUPPORT FACILITIES:**

| | | |
|---|---|---|
| Banquet Facilities | Bar/Lounge | Parking |
| Restaurants | Sewage Dump | Snack Bar |

**CREDIT CARDS ACCEPTED:** Visa.

## FAIRCHILD AFB MARINA

Fairchild Air Force Base
Fairchild AFB, WA 99011-8536

**MARINA INFORMATION:** Address: Outdoor Rec, 120 N Foulois Avenue, Bldg 2248D, Fairchild AFB, WA 99011-5000. **C-509-247-5104** , **C-509-299-5129** 0800-1700 hours.

## RUSSELL LANDING MARINA

Fort Lewis
Fort Lewis, WA 98433-9500

**LOCATION:** On post. From I-5 take exit 122, take fork toward North Fort Lewis. Go past main gate and at light go right. At stop sign, turn right to marina.

**SEASON OF OPERATION:** Year round.

**ELIGIBILITY:** Active/Reservists/Retired.

**MARINA INFORMATION:** Address: Russell Landing Marina, Bldg 8981, North Fort Lewis, WA 98433-5000. **C-253-967-2510** 0800-1930 summer; 1100-1700 hours Mon-Fri, 0900-1800 Sat, 1230-1800 Sun winter. Slips (115: 18' and 20'L), Transient Slips, Moorings (107), Launching Ramps (2).

**RATES:**

| | SLIPS |
|---|---|
| Daily | $3 |
| Monthly | $1.75 per foot |

**MARINA SERVICES:**

| | | |
|---|---|---|
| Boat Rental | Boat Repair | Dry Docks |
| Pump Station (Gas) | Travel Lift | |

**MARINA SUPPORT FACILITIES:**

| | | |
|---|---|---|
| Parking | Restaurants | Sewage Dump |
| Showers | Ship Store | Snack Bar |

**CREDIT CARDS ACCEPTED:** Visa, MasterCard and Esprit.

# UNITED STATES POSSESSIONS

## GUAM

### SUMAY COVE MARINA/CLIPPER LANDING

Guam Naval Station
FPO AP 96540-1099

**LOCATION:** On base. From Marine Drive, go south through Naval Station gate to marina on right side of street.

**SEASON OF OPERATION:** Year round.

**ELIGIBILITY:** Active/Reservists/Retired/DoD civilians/Dependents.

**MARINA INFORMATION:** Address: Sumay Cove Marina/Clipper Landing, PSC 455 Box 169 FPO, AP 96540-1099. **C-671-564-1846** 0900-1800 hours Wed-Sun unless weather is bad. Fax: C-671-564-1053. Slips (30: 25'-48'L), Moorings (32), Launching Ramps. E (110/220V)/W hookups.

**MARINA SERVICES:**

| | | |
|---|---|---|
| Boating Lessons | Boat Rental | Boat Repair |
| Dry Docks | | |

**MARINA SUPPORT FACILITIES:**

| | | |
|---|---|---|
| Bar/Lounge | Laundry | Parking |
| Restaurants | Showers | |

**CREDIT CARDS ACCEPTED:** None.

## PUERTO RICO

### PELICAN'S ROOST MARINA/YACHT CLUB

Roosevelt Roads Naval Station
FPO AA 34051-3591

**MARINA INFORMATION:** Address: PSC 1008, Bldg 2334, Box 3015, FPO AA 34051-5000. **C-787-865-3297, C-787-865-3297** 0800-1615 hours Mon, Wed and Thu, 0800-1615 hours Fri, 0700-1830 hours Sat-Sun. Slips (75), Moorings (30), Launching Ramp. E/W hookups.

**MARINA SERVICES:**

| | |
|---|---|
| Boat Rental | Gas/Diesel |

**MARINA SUPPORT FACILITIES:**

| | | |
|---|---|---|
| Laundry | Ship Store | Showers |

# FOREIGN COUNTRIES

## CANADA

### TWIN RIVERS MARINA
Petawawa Canadian Forces Base
Petawawa, Ontario K8H 2X3

**LOCATION:** On base. From I-417 E or W, exit at Petawawa. Clearly marked. From main gate, take first right and follow to the marina.

**SEASON OF OPERATION:** May-Oct.

**ELIGIBILITY:** Active/Reservists/Retired/DoD civilians/Dependents.

**MARINA INFORMATION:** Address: Twin Rivers Marina, Bldg CC58, CFB Petawawa, Ontario K8H 2X3. **C-613-687-5511 ext 5180** 0800-2200 hours. Slips (135). E/W hookups.

**RATES:**     SLIPS
Annually     $200-$425 (depends on boat length)

**MARINA SERVICES:**
Boating Lessons     Boat Rental     Pump Station (Gas)

**MARINA SUPPORT FACILITIES:**
Banquet Facilities     Bar/Lounge     Parking
Snack Bar     Snack Vending     Soda Vending

**CREDIT CARDS ACCEPTED:** Visa, MasterCard and Esprit.

## CUBA

### GUANTANAMO BAY NAVAL STATION MARINA
Guantanamo Bay Naval Station
FPO AE 09593-5000

**MARINA INFORMATION:** Address: Guantanamo Bay NS Marina, Bldg 1082, FPO AE 09593-5000. **C-011-53-99-2955-4360, C-011-53-99-2345** 1000-1800 hours Wed-Thu, 1000-2000 hours Fri, 0700-1800 hours Sat-Sun.

**MARINA SERVICES:**
Boat Rental

**MARINA SUPPORT FACILITIES:**
Soda Vending

## ITALY

### MWR SAILING CENTER
Gaeta Naval Support Activity
FPO AE 09609-1001

**LOCATION:** On base. Located approximately midway between Rome and Naples on IT-7D, in Porto Pozzo. From NATO Fleet Landing gate, go straight, take a left at the water.

**SEASON OF OPERATION:** Year round.

**ELIGIBILITY:** Active/Reservists/Retired/DoD civilians/Dependents.

**MARINA INFORMATION:** Address: MWR Sailing Center, PSC 811, Box MWR, FPO, AE 09609-1001. **C-011-39-0771-709-665, C-011-39-789-798-282, D-314-623-8282.**

**MARINA SERVICES:**
Boating Lessons     Boat Rental

**MARINA SUPPORT FACILITIES:**
Parking

**CREDIT CARDS ACCEPTED:** None.

## JAPAN

### KADENA MARINA
Kadena Air Base
FPO AP 96370-0057

**LOCATION:** On base. Off Highway 58, between gates 1 and 4.

**MARINA INFORMATION:** Address: Kadena Marina, PSC 480, Bldg 3500, FPO AP 96370-0057. **C-011-81-98-892-5111, C-011-81-6117-34-6036/6344, D-315-634-6036/6344.**

**MARINA SERVICES:**
Boating Lessons     Boat Rental

## PANAMA

### RODMAN YACHT CLUB/MARINA
Rodman Naval Station
FPO AA 34061-1000

**MARINA INFORMATION:** Address: Rodman Yacht Club/Marina, Unit 6266, Bldg 655, FPO AA 34061-1000. **C-011-50-72-83-5103/3147/3150** 1000-1800 hours Mon-Fri, 0730-1800 hours Sat-Sun. Moorings.

**MARINA SERVICES:**
Boat Rental

# SPAIN

## MWR MARINA AND REC CENTER

Rota Naval Station
FPO AE 09645-5500

**LOCATION:** On base. From Sevilla take E-25/A-4 southwest to exit at Puerto Real (105 kilometers from Sevilla) to northwest to El Puerto de St Maria and on to Rota and NAS. Clearly marked. From main gate, right at first light, right at second light to marina on left.

**SEASON OF OPERATION:** Year round.

**ELIGIBILITY:** Active/Reservists/Retired/DoD civilians.

**MARINA INFORMATION:** Address: MWR Marina and Rec Center, PSC 819, Box 14, FPO AE 09645-2000. **C-011-34-956-82-2497** 0800-2100 hours summer, 0900-1800 winter. Moorings (5), Launching Ramps (1).

| RATES: | SLIPS |
|---|---|
| Monthly | $30 |

**MARINA SERVICES:**

| | |
|---|---|
| Boating Lessons | Boat Rental |

**MARINA SUPPORT FACILITIES:**

| | |
|---|---|
| Parking | Showers |

**CREDIT CARDS ACCEPTED:** Visa and MasterCard.

# UNITED KINGDOM

## DIEGO GARCIA MARINA

Diego Garcia Atoll Navy Support Facility
FPO AP 96464-0002

**MARINA INFORMATION:** Address: Diego Garcia Marina, British Indian Ocean Territory (BIOT), Diego Garcia Naval Support Facility, PSC 466 Box 2, FPO AP 96464-0002. **D-315-370-2785.**

**MARINA SERVICES:**
Boat Rental

# SECTION IV - Military Outdoor Recreation

Outdoor Recreation varies from base to base, post to post, and service to service. Some Outdoor Recreation offices manage limited activities such as hiking, biking, and fishing. Others offer equipment rental for skiing, canoeing, camping, and sports playing and also sponsor special events and trips. Population, demand, and budgeting generally govern what kind of activities and/or equipment that can be found at the different bases and posts. A list of Outdoor Recreation offices and phone numbers is provided for readers who are in, or will be in, the areas listed.

## UNITED STATES

### ALABAMA
| | |
|---|---|
| Anniston AD | C-256-253-7155 |
| Fort McClellan | C-256-848-4323 |
| Fort Rucker | C-334-255-4305 |
| Gunter Annex | C-334-953-5675 |
| Maxwell AFB | C-334-953-5118 |
| Mobile CGATC | C-334-639-6136 |
| Redstone Arsenal | C-256-876-4868 |

### ALASKA
| | |
|---|---|
| Clear AS | C-907-585-6276 |
| Eielson AFB | C-907-377-1839 |
| Elmendorf AFB | C-907-552-2023 |
| Fort Greely | C-907-873-3183 |
| Fort Richardson | C-907-384-1303 |
| Fort Wainwright | C-907-353-1998 |
| Ketchikan CGISC | C-907-228-0250 |
| Kodiak CGISC | C-907-487-5272 |

### ARIZONA
| | |
|---|---|
| Davis-Monthan AFB | C-520-228-3736 |
| Fort Huachuca | C-520-533-6706 |
| Luke AFB | C-602-856-6267 |
| Yuma APG | C-520-328-2023 |

### ARKANSAS
| | |
|---|---|
| Little Rock AFB | C-501-987-3365 |

### CALIFORNIA
| | |
|---|---|
| Beale AFB | C-530-634-2054 |
| Camp Pendleton | C-760-725-6722 |
| Concord NWS | C-925-246-5354 |
| Coronado NAB | C-619-437-3028 |
| DDRW | C-209-982-2201 |
| Edwards AFB | C-805-277-3546 |
| El Centro NAF | C-619-339-2486 |
| Fort Hunter Liggett | C-831-386-2677 |
| Fort Irwin | C-760-380-3434 |
| Lemoore NAS | C-209-998-4897 |
| March ARB | C-909-655-2816 |
| McClellan AFB | C-916-643-2738 |
| Monterey NPGS | C-831-656-3223 |
| North Island NAS | C-619-545-7235 |
| Oakland Army Base | C-510-466-3470 |
| Port Hueneme CBC | C-805-982-4281 |
| Presidio of Monterey | C-831-242-5506 |
| San Diego MCRD | C-619-524-6769 |
| San Diego NMC | C-619-532-7245 |
| San Diego NS | C-619-556-5570 |
| San Diego NSB | C-619-553-7029 |
| Santa Clara NARS | C-650-691-1216 |

| | |
|---|---|
| Seal Beach NWS | C-562-626-7026 |
| Sierra AD | C-530-827-4354 |
| 29 Palms MCA/GCC | C-760-830-7235 |
| Travis AFB | C-707-424-5240 |
| Vandenberg AFB | C-805-734-0960 |

### COLORADO
| | |
|---|---|
| Fort Carson | C-719-526-8346 |
| Peterson AFB | C-719-556-4867 |
| USAF Academy | C-719-333-4753 |

### CONNECTICUT
| | |
|---|---|
| New London NSB | C-860-694-3380 |

### DELAWARE
| | |
|---|---|
| Dover AFB | C-302-677-5553 |

### DISTRICT OF COLUMBIA
| | |
|---|---|
| Bolling AFB | C-202-404-8895 |
| Walter Reed AMC | C-202-295-8010 |
| Washington NY/NS | C-202-433-2269 |

### FLORIDA
| | |
|---|---|
| Blue Angel Rec Area | C-850-453-9435 |
| Corry Station NTTC | C-850-453-2129 |
| Eglin AFB | C-850-678-6581 |
| Hurlburt Field | C-850-884-6939 |
| Jacksonville NAS | C-904-542-3260 |
| Key West NAS | C-904-293-2682 |
| MacDill AFB | C-800-821-4982 |
| Mayport NS | C-904-270-5221 |
| Panama City CSSNSWC | C-850-234-4402 |
| Pensacola NAS | C-850-452-2535 |
| Patrick AFB | C-407-494-2042 |
| Tyndall AFB | C-850-282-3199 |
| Whiting Field NAS | C-850-623-2383 |

### GEORGIA
| | |
|---|---|
| Athens NSCS | C-706-354-7374 |
| Atlanta NAS | C-770-919-6510 |
| Dobbins ARB | C-770-421-4870 |
| Fort Gordon | C-706-791-2390 |
| Fort Stewart | C-912-767-2717 |
| Hunter AAF | C-912-352-5722 |
| Kings Bay NSB | C-912-673-2001 |
| | ext 8103 |
| Moody AFB | C-912-333-3430 |
| Robins AFB | C-912-926-4001 |

### HAWAII
| | |
|---|---|
| Barbers Point NAS | C-808-682-2019 |
| Barking Sands PMRF | C-808-335-4379 |
| Bellows AFS | C-808-259-5447 |

| | |
|---|---|
| Hickam AFB | C-808-449-5215 |
| Kaneohe Bay MCB | C-808-254-7695 |
| Lualualei Naval Magazine | C-808-474-7933 |
| Pearl Harbor | C-808-474-1198 |
| Schofield Barracks | C-808-655-0143 |
| Wheeler AAF | C-808-655-0143 |

### IDAHO
| | |
|---|---|
| Gowen Field | C-208-422-5381 |
| Mountain Home AFB | C-208-828-6333 |

### ILLINOIS
| | |
|---|---|
| Charles Melvin PSC | C-618-452-4632 |
| Great Lakes NTC | C-847-688-6978 |
| Rock Island AACALA | C-309-782-8630 |
| Scott AFB | C-618-256-3204 |

### INDIANA
| | |
|---|---|
| Crane NSWC | C-812-854-3947 |

### KANSAS
| | |
|---|---|
| Fort Riley | C-785-239-2363 |
| McConnell AFB | C-316-652-4432 |

### KENTUCKY
| | |
|---|---|
| Blue Grass AD | C-606-625-6403 |
| Fort Campbell | C-502-798-2487 |
| Fort Knox | C-502-624-7754 |

### LOUISIANA
| | |
|---|---|
| Barksdale AFB | C-318-456-2679 |
| Fort Polk | C-318-531-6956 |
| New Orleans NAS/JRB | C-504-678-3448 |
| New Orleans NSA | C-504-678-9017 |

### MAINE
| | |
|---|---|
| Brunswick NAS | C-207-921-2488 |
| Cutler NCTSC | C-207-259-8306 |
| Winter Harbor NSGA | C-207-963-5534 |
| | ext 293 |

### MARYLAND
| | |
|---|---|
| Aberdeen PG | C-410-278-5789 |
| Andrews AFB | C-301-981-4109 |
| Fort Detrick | C-301-619-2711 |
| Fort Meade | C-301-677-3810 |
| Indian Head NSWC | C-301-743-4850 |
| Patuxent River NAS | C-301-342-3508 |
| Solomons Rec Center | C-410-326-5103 |
| USNA/Annapolis NS | C-410-293-9200 |

*Military Outdoor Recreation, continued*

## MASSACHUSETTS
| | |
|---|---|
| Hanscom AFB | C-781-377-5316 |
| Westover ARB | C-413-557-3081 |

## MICHIGAN
| | |
|---|---|
| Selfridge ANGB | C-810-307-4344 |

## MINNESOTA
| | |
|---|---|
| MN-St Paul IAP/ARS | C-651-725-5316 |

## MISSISSIPPI
| | |
|---|---|
| Columbus AFB | C-601-434-2507 |
| Gulfport NCBC | C-228-871-2804 |
| Keesler AFB | C-228-377-0002 |
| Meridian NAS | C-601-679-2731 |
| Pascagoula NS | C-228-761-2106 |

## MISSOURI
| | |
|---|---|
| Fort Leonard Wood | C-573-596-4223 |
| Whiteman AFB | C-660-687-5567 |

## MONTANA
| | |
|---|---|
| Malmstrom AFB | C-406-731-3263 |

## NEBRASKA
| | |
|---|---|
| Offutt AFB | C-402-294-2108 |

## NEVADA
| | |
|---|---|
| Fallon NAS | C-702-426-2279 |
| Nellis AFB | C-702-652-8967 |

## NEW HAMPSHIRE
| | |
|---|---|
| New Boston AS | C-603-471-2452 |
| Portsmouth N Shipyard | C-207-438-1514 |

## NEW JERSEY
| | |
|---|---|
| Bayonne MOT | C-201-823-5661 |
| Cape May CGTC | C-609-898-6922 |
| Earle NWS | C-732-866-2351 |
| Fort Dix | C-609-562-6667 |
| Fort Monmouth | C-732-532-2374 |
| McGuire AFB | C-609-724-4271 |
| Picatinny Arsenal | C-973-724-4186 |

## NEW MEXICO
| | |
|---|---|
| Cannon AFB | C-505-784-4190 |
| Holloman AFB | C-505-475-5369 |
| Kirtland AFB | C-505-846-1275 |
| White Sands MR | C-505-678-4134 |

## NEW YORK
| | |
|---|---|
| Brooklyn CGAS | C-718-615-2535 |
| Fort Drum | C-315-772-7902 |
| Scotia NAU | C-518-393-4399 |
| USMA, West Point | C-914-938-2503 |

## NORTH CAROLINA
| | |
|---|---|
| Camp Lejeune MCB | C-910-451-2108 |
| Cherry Point MCAS | C-252-466-4232 |
| Fort Bragg | C-910-396-2303 |
| New River MCAS | C-910-451-6410 |
| Pope AFB | C-910-394-2360 |
| Seymour Johnson AFB | C-919-736-5405 |

## NORTH DAKOTA
| | |
|---|---|
| Cavalier AS | C-701-993-3201 |
| Grand Forks AFB | C-701-747-3688 |
| Minot AFB | C-701-723-3648 |

## OHIO
| | |
|---|---|
| Wright-Patterson AFB | C-937-656-9889 |

## OKLAHOMA
| | |
|---|---|
| Altus AFB | C-580-481-7416 |
| Fort Sill | C-580-355-8270 |
| McAlester AAP | C-918-421-3484 |
| Tinker AFB | C-405-734-5875 |
| Vance AFB | C-580-249-7058 |

## OREGON
| | |
|---|---|
| Portland IAP | C-503-335-4748 |

## PENNSYLVANIA
| | |
|---|---|
| Carlisle Barracks | C-717-245-4935 |
| Charles E. Kelly SF | C-412-693-1858 |
| Fort Indiantown Gap | C-717-861-2622 |
| New Cumberland DDRE | C-717-770-7718 |
| Philadelphia NICP | C-215-697-5217 |
| Tobyhanna AD | C-717-895-7584 |

## RHODE ISLAND
| | |
|---|---|
| Newport NETC | C-401-841-2568 |

## SOUTH CAROLINA
| | |
|---|---|
| Charleston AFB | C-843-963-5271 |
| Fort Jackson | C-803-751-4948 |
| Shaw AFB | C-803-895-2204 |

## SOUTH DAKOTA
| | |
|---|---|
| Ellsworth AFB | C-605-385-2997 |

## TENNESSEE
| | |
|---|---|
| Arnold AFB | C-931-454-6084 |
| Memphis NSA | C-901-872-3660 |

## TEXAS
| | |
|---|---|
| Brooks AFB | C-210-536-2881 |
| Corpus Christi NAS | C-512-939-9054 |
| Dyess AFB | C-915-696-3891 |
| Fort Hood | C-254-287-3722 |
| Fort Sam Houston | C-210-224-7162 |
| Goodfellow AFB | C-915-944-1012 |
| Ingleside NS | C-512-776-4601 |
| Kelly AFB | C-210-925-8346 |
| Kingsville NAS | C-512-516-6191 |
| Lackland AFB | C-210-671-3106 |
| Laughlin AFB | C-830-298-5830 |
| Randolph AFB | C-210-652-3698 |
| Red River AD | C-903-334-2254 |
| Sheppard AFB | C-940-676-4141 |

## UTAH
| | |
|---|---|
| Dugway PG | C-431-831-2318 |
| Hill AFB | C-801-777-9666 |
| Tooele AD | C-435-833-3100 |

## VIRGINIA
| | |
|---|---|
| Dahlgren NSWC | C-540-663-3002 |
| Dam Neck FCTCLANT | C-757-433-6384 |
| Fort A.P. Hill | C-804-633-8219 |
| Fort Belvoir | C-703-805-3714 |
| Fort Eustis | C-757-878-3594 |
| Fort Lee | C-804-765-2212 |
| Fort Monroe | C-757-727-4305 |
| Fort Myer | C-703-696-8849 |
| Fort Pickett | C-804-292-2618 |
| Fort Story | C-757-422-7601 |
| Langley AFB | C-757-764-7170 |
| Little Creek NAB | C-757-464-7516 |
| Oceana NAS | C-757-433-3215 |
| Norfolk NB | C-757-444-4388 |
| Norfolk N Shipyard | C-757-396-3871 |
| Pentagon | C-703-604-4927 |
| Portsmouth CGISC | C-757-483-8671 |
| Quantico MCB | C-703-784-2014 |
| Yorktown NWS | C-757-887-4233 |

## WASHINGTON
| | |
|---|---|
| Bangor NSB | C-360-779-3125 |
| Everett NS | C-425-304-5967 |
| Fairchild AFB | C-509-247-5104 |
| Fort Lewis | C-253-967-6263 |
| Jim Creek NRS | C-425-304-5315 |
| McChord AFB | C-253-984-2206 |
| Puget Sound NS | C-360-476-5872 |
| Whidbey Island NAS | C-360-257-4491 |

## WEST VIRGINIA
| | |
|---|---|
| Sugar Grove NSGA | C-304-249-6363 |

## WISCONSIN
| | |
|---|---|
| Fort McCoy | C-608-388-3360 |

## WYOMING
| | |
|---|---|
| F.E. Warren AFB | C-307-773-2988 |

# US POSSESSIONS

## GUAM
| | |
|---|---|
| Andersen AFB | C-671-366-5197 |
| Guam NAVCOMTELSTA | C-671-355-5273 |
| Marianas COMNAVFOR | C-671-564-1826 |

## PUERTO RICO
| | |
|---|---|
| Fort Buchanan | C-787-273-3436 |
| Roosevelt Roads NS | C-787-865-4757 |

# FOREIGN COUNTRIES

## AUSTRALIA (all are C-011-61-)
| | |
|---|---|
| Woomera AS | 86739-440 |

*Military Outdoor Recreation, continued*

**BAHRAIN** (all are C-011-973-)
Bahrain NSU     724-422

**BELGIUM** (all are C-011-32-)
SHAPE/Chievres AB     65-44-5380

**DENMARK** (all are C-011-299-)
Thule AB     506-36 ext 2445

**GERMANY** (all are C-011-49-)
Aschaffenburg Community   6021-96865
Augsburg Community     821-540-7518
Bad Kreuznach     671-609-6496
Bamberg Community     951-300-8837
Baumholder Community   6783-6-7182
Darmstadt Community    6151-69-6277
Friedberg Community    6031-81-8203
Giebelstadt Community    9321-305-629
Grafenwoehr Community   9641-83-7402
Hanau Community     6181-88-8891
Heidelberg Community    6221-57-8737
Hohenfels Community    9472-83-2060
Illesheim Community    981-183-600
Kaiserslautern Community   631-471-7751
Kirch-Goens Community   6033-82-8203
Kitzingen Community    9321-305-629
Mannheim Community    621-739-251
Ramstein AB     6371-47-5705
Rhein-Main AB     69-699-7274

Spangdahlem AB     6565-61-7176
Stuttgart Community    703-115-774
Vilseck Community     9662-2563
Wiesbaden Community    611-705-5760
Wurzburg Community    932-130-5629

**GREECE** (all are C-011-30-)
GAFB Araxos     693-51189 ext 59

**ICELAND** (all are C-011-354-)
Keflavik NS     425-6498

**ITALY** (all are C-011-39-)
Aviano AB     0434-66-7633
Camp Darby     586-94-7491
Naples NSA     081-724-4835
Sigonella NAS     095-56-4271
Vicenza Community    044-451-7094

**JAPAN** (all are C-011-81-)
Atsugi NAF     3117-64-3784
Camp Butler     6117-734-4322
Camp Zama     462-3117-63-3311
Kadena AB     6117-34-2841
Misawa AB     3117-66-3480
Okinawa     98-634-6957
Sasebo COMFLEACT    956-24-6111
      ext3500
Torii Station     6117-44-4795
Yokosuka     311-743-7250

**KOREA** (all are C-011-82-)
Camp Humphreys     733-690-8811
Osan AB     333-661-4007
Yongsan Community    2-791-3565

**NETHERLANDS** (all are C-011-31-)
Schinnen Community    4493-2406

**PANAMA** (all are C-011-507-)
Fort Clayton     287-5613
Howard AFB     284-6107

**PORTUGAL** (all are C-011-351-)
Lajes Field AB     95-540100
      ext 24140

**SPAIN** (all are C-011-34-95)
Rota NAS     6-82-3101

**TURKEY** (all are C-011-90-)
Incirlik AB     322-316-6044
Izmir AS     232-489-3553

**UNITED KINGDOM** (all are C-011-44-1-)
London COMNAVACT   895-616560
RAF Alconbury     480-3734
RAF Croughton     28-070-8419
Diego Garcia Atoll NSF   C-011-246-370-
   *(not as above)*     2791
RAF Lakenheath     638-52-2146
RAF Mildenhall     638-51-4283
St Mawgan JMF     637-853514

# SECTION V - Military ITRs and ITTs

Army ITR (Information, Tickets and Registration) and Navy, Marine Corps and Air Force ITT (Information, Tickets and Tours) are part of the military MWR (Morale, Welfare and Recreation) System and Air Force Services. They offer military personnel discount tickets to many different events, including sports and recreation. Discount tickets for local attractions, tours, movies and the theater, may be found only at a neighboring military installation, while tickets to larger attractions such as Disneyland and Disney World may be found at many military locations around the world. *Note: All military ID card holders, active or retired; guard and reserve, may utilize these services. Some restrictions may apply. Some hard to get tickets may be limited to active duty personnel.*

## UNITED STATES

### ALABAMA
| | |
|---|---|
| Fort McClellan | C-256-820-6372 |
| Fort Rucker | C-334-255-9517 |
| Gunter Annex | C-334-953-7370 |
| Maxwell AFB | C-334-953-6351 |
| Redstone Arsenal | C-256-876-4531 |

### ALASKA
| | |
|---|---|
| Eielson AFB | C-907-377-2722 |
| Elmendorf AFB | C-907-552-5191 |
| Fort Richardson | C-907-384-1649 |
| Fort Wainwright | C-907-353-2652 |

### ARIZONA
| | |
|---|---|
| Fort Huachuca | C-520-533-2404 |
| Luke AFB | C-602-856-6000 |
| Yuma APG | C-520-329-6374 |

### ARKANSAS
| | |
|---|---|
| Little Rock AFB | C-501-987-3216 |

### CALIFORNIA
| | |
|---|---|
| Barstow MCLB | C-760-577-6541 |
| Beale AFB | C-530-634-3942 |
| Camp Pendleton MCB | C-760-725-5864 |
| | C-760-725-7447 |
| China Lake NAWS | C-760-939-8660 |
| Concord NWS | C-925-246-5795 |
| Coronado NAB | C-619-437-3018 |
| Edwards AFB | C-805-275-7488 |
| El Toro MCAS | C-714-726-2626 |
| Fort Hunter Liggett | C-831-386-2406 |
| Fort Irwin NTC | C-760-380-4767 |
| Lemoore NAS | C-209-998-8905 |
| McClellan AFB | C-916-643-2259 |
| North Island NAS | C-619-545-9576 |
| Oakland Army Base | C-510-466-2141 |
| Onizuka AS | C-831-752-4556 |
| Point Mugu NAWC | C-805-989-7628 |
| | C-805-959-8349 |
| Port Hueneme NCBC | C-805-982-4284 |
| Presidio of Monterey | C-831-242-5377 |
| San Diego MCRD | C-619-524-6772 |
| San Diego NS | C-619-556-7498 |
| San Diego NSB | C-619-553-7162 |
| Santa Clara NARS | C-650-604-1686 |
| Sierra AD | C-530-827-4602 |
| Twentynine Palms MCA/GCC | C-760-830-6163 ext 264 |
| Vandenberg AFB | C-805-736-3824 |

### COLORADO
| | |
|---|---|
| Buckley ANGB | C-303-677-6853 |
| Fitzsimons USAG | C-303-361-8622 |
| Fort Carson | C-719-526-5366 |
| Peterson AFB | C-719-556-7671 |
| USAF Academy | C-719-333-3241 |

### CONNECTICUT
| | |
|---|---|
| New London NSB | C-860-694-3238 |

### DELAWARE
| | |
|---|---|
| Dover AFB | C-302-677-3955 |

### DISTRICT OF COLUMBIA
| | |
|---|---|
| Walter Reed AMC | C-202-782-0600 |
| Washington NS-Anacostia Annex | C-703-433-6666 |

### FLORIDA
| | |
|---|---|
| Cecil Field NAS | C-904-778-6112 |
| Corry Station | C-850-452-6143 |
| Eglin AFB | C-850-882-5930 |
| Jacksonville NAS | C-904-542-3318 |
| MacDill AFB | C-813-828-2478 |
| Mayport NS | C-904-270-5145 |
| Patrick AFB | C-407-494-5158 |
| Pensacola NAS | C-850-452-4229 |
| Tyndall AFB | C-850-283-2230 |

### GEORGIA
| | |
|---|---|
| Atlanta NAS | C-770-919-6499 |
| | C-770-919-6502 |
| Fort Gordon | C-706-798-0990 |
| | C-706-798-7956 |
| Fort Stewart | C-912-767-4363 |
| Hunter AAF | C-912-353-9295 |
| Kings Bay NSB | C-912-673-2001 ext 2289 |
| Robins AFB | C-912-936-2945 |

### HAWAII
| | |
|---|---|
| Camp H.M. Smith MCB | C-808-477-5143 |
| Fort Shafter | C-808-438-1985 |
| Kaneohe MCB | C-808-254-7562 |
| Pearl Harbor NB | C-808-474-1190 |
| Pearl Harbor NS | C-808-474-6156 |
| Schofield Barracks | C-808-655-9971 |
| Tripler Medical Center | C-808-438-1985 |
| Wahiawa NCTAMS EASTPAC | C-808-621-0733 |
| Waianae ARC | C-808-655-9971 |
| Wheeler AAF | C-808-655-9971 |

### ILLINOIS
| | |
|---|---|
| Great Lakes NTC | C-847-688-3537 |
| Crane Division NSWC | C-812-854-6059 |

### IOWA
| | |
|---|---|
| Camp Dodge/Iowa NGB | C-515-270-2445 |

### KANSAS
| | |
|---|---|
| Fort Leavenworth | C-913-684-2580 |

### KENTUCKY
| | |
|---|---|
| Fort Campbell | C-502-798-7436 |
| Fort Knox | C-502-624-5030 |
| | C-502-624-8254 |

### LOUISIANA
| | |
|---|---|
| Fort Polk | C-318-531-1794 |
| New Orleans NAS JRB | C-504-678-3695 |
| New Orleans NSA | C-504-678-2208 |

### MAINE
| | |
|---|---|
| Cutler NCTSC | C-207-259-8201 |

### MARYLAND
| | |
|---|---|
| Aberdeen PG | C-410-278-4011 |
| Andrews AFB | C-301-981-4413 |
| | C-301-981-4401 |
| Fort George G. Meade | C-301-677-7354 |
| Indian Head Division NSWC | C-301-743-4875 |
| Patuxent River NAS | C-301-342-3508 |
| US Naval Academy/Annapolis NS | C-410-293-9200 |

### MASSACHUSETTS
| | |
|---|---|
| Hanscom AFB | C-781-377-3262 |

### MISSISSIPPI
| | |
|---|---|
| Gulfport NCBC | C-228-871-2231 |
| Meridian NAS | C-601-679-2636 |

### MONTANA
| | |
|---|---|
| Malmstrom AFB | C-406-731-4634 |

### NEBRASKA
| | |
|---|---|
| Fallon NAS | C-702-426-2865 |

### NEW HAMPSHIRE
| | |
|---|---|
| Portsmouth Naval Shipyard | C-207-438-2351 |

### NEW JERSEY
| | |
|---|---|
| Bayonne MOT | C-201-823-5319 |

*Military ITRs and ITTs, continued*

| | |
|---|---|
| Cape May CG TC | C-609-898-6989 |
| Earle NWS | C-732-866-2167 |
| Fort Dix AG | C-609-562-4848 |
| Fort Monmouth | C-732-532-3892 |
| McGuire AFB | C-609-723-3111 |
| Picatinny Arsenal | C-973-724-4186 |

**NEW MEXICO**

| | |
|---|---|
| Cannon AFB | C-505-784-2536 |
| Kirtland AFB | C-505-846-2924 |
| White Sands MR | C-505-678-1111 |
| | C-505-678-4134 |

**NEW YORK**

| | |
|---|---|
| Fort Drum | C-315-772-8222 |
| | C-315-772-8223 |
| Fort Hamilton | C-718-630-4911 |
| USMA West Point | C-914-938-2070 |

**NORTH CAROLINA**

| | |
|---|---|
| Camp Lejeune MCB | C-910-451-5380 |
| Cherry Point MCAS | C-252-466-2197 |
| Fort Bragg | C-910-396-1278 |

**NORTH DAKOTA**

| | |
|---|---|
| Minot AFB | C-701-727-6171 |

**OHIO**

| | |
|---|---|
| Columbus DSC | C-614-692-1111 |

**OKLAHOMA**

| | |
|---|---|
| Fort Sill | C-580-442-6211 |
| McAlester AAP | C-918-421-2418 |

**PENNSYLVANIA**

| | |
|---|---|
| Carlisle Barracks | C-717-245-3309 |
| Defense Distribution Region East | C-717-770-7670 |
| Fort Indiantown Gap | C-717-861-2622 |
| Tobyhanna AD | C-717-895-7584 |
| Willow Grove NAS/JRB | C-215-443-6082 |

**RHODE ISLAND**

| | |
|---|---|
| Newport NETC | C-401-841-3116 |

**SOUTH CAROLINA**

| | |
|---|---|
| Beaufort MCAS | C-843-522-6375 |
| | C-843-522-6377 |
| | C-843-522-7340 |
| Fort Jackson | C-803-751-6219 |
| Parris Island MCRD | C-843-525-3302 |
| | ext 7341 |

**TENNESSEE**

| | |
|---|---|
| Arnold AFB | C-931-454-3128 |
| Memphis NSA | C-901-874-5303 |

**TEXAS**

| | |
|---|---|
| Corpus Christi NAS | C-512-939-3637 |
| Fort Bliss | C-915-568-7506 |
| Fort Hood | C-254-287-7310 |
| Fort Sam Houston | C-210-221-2333 |
| | C-210-221-0703 |
| Ingleside NS | C-512-776-4227 |
| Kelly AFB | C-210-925-4584 |
| Kingsville NAS | C-512-516-6449 |
| Lackland AFB | C-210-671-3133 |
| Randolph AFB | C-210-652-2301 |
| Sheppard AFB | C-940-676-2302 |

**UTAH**

| | |
|---|---|
| Tooele AD | C-435-833-3129 |

**VIRGINIA**

| | |
|---|---|
| Cheatham Annex FISC | C-757-887-7107 |
| Dahlgren NSWC | C-540-653-8785 |
| Fort Belvoir | C-703-806-5532 |
| Fort Eustis | C-757-878-3694 |
| Fort Lee | C-804-734-6622 |
| Fort Story | C-757-422-7712 |
| | C-757-422-7472 |
| Henderson Hall USMC | C-703-979-8420 |
| | ext 116 |
| Langley AFB | C-757-764-2983 |
| Little Creek NAB | C-757-464-7665 |
| Norfolk NB | C-757-445-6663 |
| Norfolk Naval Shipyard | C-757-396-7639 |
| Pentagon | C-703-697-9866 |
| | C-703-697-3816 |
| Quantico MCB | C-703-784-2002 |
| | C-703-784-2789 |
| Yorktown NWS | C-757-887-4609 |

**WASHINGTON**

| | |
|---|---|
| Bangor NSB | C-360-396-4026 |
| Everett NS | C-425-304-3167 |
| Fort Lewis | C-253-967-3085 |
| Puget Sound Naval Shipyard | C-360-476-7576 |

**WEST VIRGINIA**

| | |
|---|---|
| Sugar Grove NSGA | C-304-249-6360 |

**WISCONSIN**

| | |
|---|---|
| Fort McCoy | C-608-388-3505 |

**WYOMING**

| | |
|---|---|
| Francis E. Warren AFB | C-307-773-2988 |

# US POSSESSIONS

**GUAM**

| | |
|---|---|
| Guam NCS | C-671-355-5630 |
| Marianas Naval Forces | C-671-564-1847 |

**PUERTO RICO**

| | |
|---|---|
| Roosevelt Roads NS | C-787-865-4757 |
| Sabana Seca NSGA | C-787-261-8406 |

# FOREIGN COUNTRIES

**BAHRAIN** (all are C-011-973-)

| | |
|---|---|
| Bahrain ADMINSUPU | 724-423 |

**BELGIUM** (all are C-011-32-)

| | |
|---|---|
| Shape/Chievres AB | 65-44-5380 |

**GERMANY** (all are C-011-49-)

| | |
|---|---|
| Ansbach Community | 981-85540 |
| Garmisch AFRC | 8821-750-546 |
| Ramstein AB | 6371-47-6330 |
| Spangdahlem AB | 6565-61-6207 |

**ICELAND** (all are C-011-354-)

| | |
|---|---|
| Keflavik NAS | 425-2445 |

**ITALY** (all are C-011-39-)

| | |
|---|---|
| Aviano AB | 0434-66-7385 |
| Camp Darby | 050-54-7589 |
| Gaeta NSA | 0771-70-9682 |
| La Maddalena NSA | 0789-79-8296 |
| Naples NSA | 081-724-4934 |
| Sigonella NAS | 095-56-4215 |
| Vincenza Community/ Caserma Ederle | 044-51-7453 |

**JAPAN** (all are C-011-81-)

| | |
|---|---|
| Atsugi NAF | 4677-2334 |
| Kadena AB | 98-937-9049 |
| Sasebo Fleet Activities | 956-24-6111 |
| | ext 3472 |
| Torii Station | 6117-44-4422 |
| Yokosuka Fleet Activities | 468-26-2710 |

**KOREA** (all are C-011-82-)

| | |
|---|---|
| Camp Henry | 53-470-4135 |
| Chinhae Fleet Activities | 55-342-6638 |
| Seoul Naval Forces | 27-915-6830 |

**PANAMA** (all are C-011-507-)

| | |
|---|---|
| Howard AFB | 284-6161 |
| Rodman NS | 283-5307 |

**SINGAPORE** (all are C-011-65-)

| | |
|---|---|
| Singapore Community | 750-2410 |

**SPAIN** (all are C-011-34-95-)

| | |
|---|---|
| Rota NAS | 6-82-3101 |

**UNITED KINGDOM** (all are C-011-44-1-)

| | |
|---|---|
| Brawdy Wales NF | 437-720654 |
| RAF Croughton | 280-708-874 |
| Diego Garcia Atoll NSF | C-011-246-370- |
| *(not as above)* | 4404 |
| RAF Fairford | 285-71-4279 |
| RAF Lakenheath | 638-52-279 |
| London Naval Activities | 71-514-4368 |
| St Mawgan JMF | 63-787-3867 |

# APPENDIX A

# General Abbreviations

**The general abbreviations used in this book are listed below. Commonly understood abbreviations (e.g., Mon-Fri for Monday through Friday) and standard abbreviations find in addresses have not been included in order to save space.**

**A**
A - Amps
AAF - Army Air Field
AAFES - Army/Air Force Exchange Systems
A/C - Air Conditioning
AE - Army Europe
AF - Air Force
AFAF - Air Force Auxiliary Field
AFB - Air Force Base
AFRC - Armed Forces Recreation Center
AFS - Air Force Station
ANGB - Air National Guard Base
AP - Army Pacific
APO - Army Post Office
ARB - Air Reserve Base
ATTN - Attention
ATV - All Terrain Vehicle

**B**
BBQ - Barbecue
BRAC - Base Realignment and Closure
BSB - Base Support Battalion

**C**
C - Commercial Telephone
CATV - Cable TV
CFB - Canadian Forces Base
CG - Coast Guard
CGAS - Coast Guard Air Station
CGTC - Coast Guard Training Center
CIV - Civilian
COMM - Commercial
CSS - Coastal Systems Station
CW - Chief Warrant Officer

**D**
D - Defense Switched Network Telephone
DAV - Disabled American Veteran
DH - Downhill
DoD - Department of Defense
DoT - Department of Transportation
DSN-E - Defense Switched Network-Europe
DST - Daylight Savings Time
DV - Distinguished Visitor

**E**
E - Electric
ext - Extension

**F**
FAMCAMP - Family Campground
FPO - Fleet Post Office

**G**
GM - General Management
GS - General Schedule

**H**
HP - Homepage
HQ - Headquarters

**I**
I - Interstate
ISC - Integrated Support Command
ITR - Information, Ticketing
        and Reservation Office
ITT - Information, Tour and Travel

**J**
JRB - Joint Reserve Base

**L**
LP - Liquid Propane

**M**
MCAS - Marine Corps Air Station
MCB - Marine Corps Base
MCLB - Marine Corps Logistics Base
MP - Military Police
MWR - Morale, Welfare and Recreation

**N**
NAF - Non-Appropriated Funds
NAS - Naval Air Station
NAWS - Naval Air Weapons Station
NG - National Guard
NMC - Nearest Major City
NMI - Nearest Major Installation
NS - Naval Station
NSA - Naval Support Activity
NSWC - Naval Surface Weapons Center
NTC - Naval Training Center

**O**
OOD - Officer of the Day/on Deck/on Duty

**P**
PCS - Permanent Change of Station

**R**
Rec - Recreation
RR - Rural Route
RV - Recreational Vehicle

**S**
S - Sewer
SES - Senior Executive Service

**T**
TAD - Temporary Attached Duty
TDY - Temporary Duty
TEL - Telephone
TLA - Temporary Lodging Allowance
TLF - Temporary Living Facility

**U**
USA - United States Army
USAF - United States Air Force
USCG - United States Coast Guard
USEUCOM - United States
                European Command
USMC - United States Marine Corps
USMRA - United States Military Road Atlas
USN - United States Navy
USS - United States Ship

**V**
V - Volts
VCR - Video Cassette Recorder

**W**
W - Water
WO - Warrant Officer

**X**
XC - Cross Country

# APPENDIX B

## Camping on Other Federal Property

Thousands of campsites are available to the public on various types of federal reserves around the country. These sites are located in national parks, national forests, game and wildlife refuges, federal water reservoir reserves, Tennessee Valley Authority dam sites, U.S. Army Corps of Engineers Recreation Facilities, and other federal areas.

Many of these sites are near or on routes to military installations to which you may be traveling. A wealth of information is available from a variety of sources concerning these campsites and adjacent recreation areas.

If a military installation is not conveniently located along your route, maybe one of the public areas will be. Or, if you cannot get space at a military area, perhaps you can get space at a nearby public recreation area.

Listed below are addresses of federal agencies from which information about camping on federal lands other than military installations can be obtained. Also listed are titles and descriptions of some of the available material.

Superintendent of Documents, P.O Box 371954, Pittsburgh, PA 15250-7954. Tel: (202) 512-1800. (Orders and inquiries). HP: http://www.nps.gov/hfc/salepubs. You may write for these materials or you may order them by telephone or through the internet using your credit card.

**The National Parks: Index 1997-1998,** 024-005-01182-0, $6.50
**National Trails System Map & Guide,** 024-005-0111-1, $1.25.
**National Park System Map & Guide,** 024-005-01186-2, $1.25.
**The National Parks: Lesser-Known Areas,** 024-005-01152-8, $2.50.

U.S Fish and Wildlife Service. Tel: (301) 876-7203. (Orders and inquiries).

**National Wildlife Refuges: A Visitor's Guide,** 1997, $1.25.

Department of Interior, Bureau of Land Management (BLM), 1849 C Street NW, Room 1013, Washington, DC 20240. Tel: 202-208-4747.

**National Recreation Guide, (Map of the Western portion of the US), Free.**
**Recreational Opportunities on Public Lands, Outdoors America, Free. For other free camping information, including a video, call BLM at 1-888-467-8464.**

US Department of Agriculture, Forest Service, Auditors Bldg, Washington D.C 20250, Attn: PAO, Publications. Tel: (202) 205-0957. HP: http://www.fs.fed.us/links/pubs.shtml.

**A Guide To Your National Forests, 1996, Free.**
**Fishing Your National Forests, Free.**

US Army Corps of Engineers, Publications Depot, 2803 52nd Avenue, Hyattsville, MD 20781-1102.

**Lakeside Recreation Series, EP 1130-2-419 thru 428, 1992, Free.**

Tennessee Valley Authority, Recreation Program, Land Resources, 17 Ridgeway Road, Norris TN 37828-5000, Tel: 423-632-1805/1539, Fax:

423-632-1795, 1-800-MAPS-TVA for maps of TVA administered areas or (502) 924-2000 for information on Land Between The Lakes.
**A Guide to TVA Reservoir Recreation Areas, 1995, Free.**
**Hunting on TVA Lands, 1996, Free.**
**Recreation on TVA Lakes, Great Lakes of the South, 1995, Free.**
**Scenic and Recreational Streams in the Tennessee Valley, 1983, Free.**
**TVA Land Between The Lakes, 1996 Free.**
**TVA Trails, A Trail Guide to the Great Lakes of the South, 1983, Free.**

## Federal Recreation Passport Program

**Federal Recreation Fees:** Under provisions of the **Land and Water Conservation Fund Act (LWCFA),** entering or using facilities or services in some national parks, forests, wildlife refuges or outdoor recreation areas requires payment of entrance fees, use fees, special recreation permit fees, or some combination of these. Where this symbol ![symbol] is displayed, a LWCFA fee is being charged.

There are five congressionally authorized entrance fee passes. The annual **(1) Golden Eagle Passport** and the two lifetime passes, **(2)** the **Golden Age Passport** and **(3)** the **Golden Access Passport,** may be used at all federally operated areas that charge LWCFA entrance fees. Annual **(4) Park-Specific Passes** can be used only at the specific national park areas for which they are purchased. The annual **(5) Federal Duck Stamp** may be used as a pass only at national wildlife refuges that charge entrance fees.

**Golden Eagle Passport:** Admits pass holder, spouse, children and parents, **good for a 12 month period, cost $50** and may be purchased at any federal area where a LWCFA entrance fee is charged (a list of fee locations is available from PAO, National Park Service, P. O. Box 37127, Washington, DC 20013-7127).

**Golden Age Passport:** Admits pass holder, spouse and children and other passengers if entering via a private vehicle, **must be 62 years of age, onetime $10 processing fee, good for life,** and provides 50% discount on LWCFA user fees.

**Golden Access Passport:** Admits pass holder, spouse and children and other passengers if entering via a private vehicle, **must be blind or permanently disabled.** Obtain from locations charging a LWCFA fee, **passport is free** and applicant must show proof of disability.

**Federal Duck Stamp:** Admits stamp holder, spouse, children, parents and accompanying passengers by private vehicle, valid from 1 Jul-30 Jun, unlimited entry to all national wildlife refuges that charge a LWCFA entrance fee. **May be purchased by mail for $15 plus $3.20 postage and handling from: U. S. Postal Service, Philatelic Sales Division, P.O, Box 419636, Kansas City, MO 64179, or call 1-800-782-6724 to order by credit card.**

Visit Military Living on the world-wide web at
# www.militaryliving.com

**MILITARY** PUBLICATIONS *Living*™   *Where the fun begins*™

## HAVING A RETIREE DAY OR PRE-RETIREMENT BRIEFING?
Let Military Living™ help make your big day a success!

Retirees are anxious to know more about flying Space-A on U.S. military aircraft. Military Living Publications is well-known as being a leading authority on military recreation and Space-A travel.

**Military Living™ will send your Retiree Activity Office complimentary sample of copies of Military Living's R&R Space-A Report® and door prizes to give away at the Retiree Day. We can also provide materials for your Pre-Retirement Briefings.**

To participate in Military Living's™ **Retiree Day Program**, simply have your Retiree Activity Office write or fax us on the office letterhead giving the date and time of the next retiree day. A name of the Retiree Office contact and phone number are also necessary. We must have a street address of the Retiree Activity office in order to send the publications by United Parcel Service. We also need to know how many people attended last year and the expected number for this year.

It would be greatly appreciated if you would include the participation of Military Living's **R&R Space-A Report®**, we ask that if there are any leftovers of the newsletter, that you return them to your Retiree Activity Office to give to visitors to your office. Please honor our copyright by not making copies of the **R&R Space-A Report®**. We would appreciate your sending us a copy of your retiree newsletter if there is one being published.

Thanks to all of you who help military retirees so much!

Ann, Roy, and RJ Crawford
Publishers, Military Living Publications
P.O. Box 2347, Falls Church, VA 22042-0347
**Phone (703) 237-0203; FAX (703) 237-2233**

# MILITARY PUBLICATIONS Living™

## CENTRAL ORDER COUPON
P.O. Box 2347, Falls Church, VA 22042-0347
TEL: (703) 237-0203  FAX: (703) 237-2233

Visit us on the web at:
http://www.militaryliving.com
E-mail : milliving@aol.com

| Publications | ISBN / ISSN | Item # | Price | QTY |
|---|---|---|---|---|
| **R&R Space-A Report®.** *The worldwide travel newsletter.* 6 issues/year<br>1 yr/$17.00 - 2 yrs/$27.00 - 3 yrs/$37.00 - 5 yrs/$55.00 | 0740-5073 | | ❑ new<br>❑ renewal | |
| **Military Space-A Air Basic Training.** | 0-914862-66-9 | 23 | $14.95 | |
| **Military Space-A Air Opportunities Around the World.** | 0-914862-69-3 | 1 | $19.95 | |
| **Temporary Military Lodging Around the World.** | 0-914862-72-3 | 12 | $18.45 | |
| **Military RV, Camping & Outdoor Recreation Around the World Including Golf Courses and Marinas.** | 0-914862-74-X | 24 | $16.45 | |
| **U.S. Forces Travel Guide to U.S. Military Installations.** | 0-914862-63-4 | 8 | $14.95 | |
| **U.S. Forces Travel Guide to Overseas U.S. Military Installations.** | 0-914862-43-X | 25 | $17.95 | |
| **U.S. Military Museums, Historic Sites & Exhibits.** (Soft Cover) | 0-914862-34-0 | 10 | $17.95 | |
| **United States Military Road Atlas.** | 0-914862-70-7 | 21 | $19.95 | |
| **U.S. Military Installation Road Map.** (Folded)<br>(1 unfolded wall map in a hard tube)<br>(2 unfolded wall maps in a hard tube) | 0-914862-71-5<br>0-914862-71-5<br>0-914862-71-5 | 14<br>14A<br>14B | $8.45<br>$11.00<br>$19.00 | |
| **COLLECTOR'S ITEM! Desert Shield Commemorative Maps.**<br>(Folded)<br>(2 unfolded wall maps in a hard tube) | <br>0-914862-27-8<br>0-914862-27-8 | <br>15<br>15A | <br>$8.00<br>$18.00 | |
| **Assignment Washington Military Road Atlas.** | 0-914862-68-5 | 6 | $11.95 | |
| **California State Military Road Map -** (Folded)<br>**Florida State Military Road Map -** (Folded)<br>**Mid-Atlantic States Military Road Map -** (Folded)<br>**Texas State Military Road Map -** (Folded) | 0-914862-45-6<br>0-914862-46-4<br>0-914862-47-2<br>0-914862-48-0 | 22A<br>22B<br>22C<br>22D | $5.95<br>$5.95<br>$5.95<br>$5.95 | |
| **Military Living Magazine, Camaraderie Washington.**<br>*Local Area magazine.* 4 seasonal issues. | 0740-5065 | | $8.00/year | |
| **Virginia Addresses add 4.5% sales tax (Books, Maps, & Atlases only)** | | | | |
| **ALL ORDERS SHIPPED BY 1ST CLASS MAIL** | | | **TOTAL $** | |

*If you are an R&R Space-A Report® subscriber, you may deduct $1.00 per book. (No discount on the R&R Report itself or on the maps or atlas.) Mail order prices are for non- APO/FPO addresses within the U.S. APO/FPO addresses which are outside CONUS must add $4.00 per order for insurance and return receipt. Shipments to Canadian addresses must add an additional $2.50 **per item ordered** for additional postage, shipping, insurance and processing. Please consult publisher for International Mail Price. Sorry, no billing. We're as close as your telephone...by using our Telephone Ordering Service. We honor American Express, MasterCard, Visa, and Discover. Call us at **703-237-0203** (Voice Mail after hours); FAX: 703-237-2233 or E-mail: milliving@aol.com and order today! Sorry, no collect calls. Or...fill out and mail the order coupon below.

NAME:_____

STREET:_____

CITY/STATE/ZIP:_____

PHONE:_____ SIGNATURE:_____

RANK (or rank of sponsor):_____Branch Of Service:_____

Active Duty:_____Retired:_____Widow/er:_____100% Disabled Veteran:_____Guard:_____Reservist:_____Other:_____

Credit Card #_____Card Expiration Date:_____

Mail check/money order to Military Living Publications, P.O. Box 2347, Falls Church, VA 22042-0347
Save $$$s by purchasing any of our Books, Maps, and Atlases at your military Exchange.
Prices are subject to change. Please check here if we may ship and bill the difference................................ ☐

THIS FORM MAY BE DUPLICATED

revised 9/98